Insights to Performance Excellence 2021–2022

Insights to Performance Excellence 2021–2022

Using the Baldrige Framework and Other Integrated Management Systems

Mark L. Blazey
and
Paul L. Grizzell

ASQ Quality Press
Milwaukee, Wisconsin

American Society for Quality, Quality Press, Milwaukee 53203

Printed in the United States of America

25 24 23 LS 5 4 3 2 1

ISBN-13 (softcover): 978-1-63694-002-1
ISBN-13 (epub): 978-1-63694-003-8
ISBN-13 (PDF): 978-1-63694-004-5

ASQ advances individual, organizational, and community excellence worldwide through learning, quality improvement, and knowledge exchange.

Bookstores, wholesalers, schools, libraries, and organizations: Quality Press books are available at quantity discounts with bulk purchases for business, trade, or educational uses. For more information, please contact Quality Press at 800-248-1946 or books@asq.org.

To place orders or browse the full selection of Quality Press titles, visit our website at: http://www.asq.org/quality-press.

Quality Press
600 N. Plankinton Ave.
Milwaukee, WI 53203-2914
Email: books@asq.org
Excellence Through Quality™

Mark would like to dedicate this book to the memory of his parents, Everett and Ann, who taught him the value of continuous improvement, and to his family members, who provide support for the continuous search for excellence: brothers Scott, Brian, and Brent; daughter Elizabeth, her husband Josh, granddaughter Madeline Alice and grandson Theodor Marshall; and son Mark, his wife Meghan, and grandsons Miles Everett and Eli Archer. Most of all, Mark would like to dedicate this book to his lifelong partner and loving wife Karen.

Paul would like to dedicate this book to his family, all of whom exhibit performance excellence in all they do: son Nicholas and his wife Sara; and daughter Ashleigh and her husband Jeff. They make him more proud than they can imagine. But no one has been a bigger source of encouragement and support than his wife, Janice. She has exhibited nothing but patience as he tries to bring performance excellence concepts into the home.

Contents

Online Resources

Insights to Performance Excellence 2021–2022 includes online resources available for download from *https://asqassets.widencollective.com/portals/4gpf8u5l/(H1587)InsightstoPerformanceExcellence2021-2022.* These resources include:

2021–2022 Business/Nonprofit Scoring Calibration Guide

2021–2022 Education Scoring Calibration Guide

2021–2022 Health Care Scoring Calibration Guide

Baldrige, Six Sigma, Lean, and Balanced Scorecard Alignment

Baldrige, EFQM, and ISO Crosswalk

Performance Excellence Program Best Practices

Self-Assessments of Organizations and Management Systems

Stakeholder Index

This edition of *Insights to Performance Excellence* contains information that may prove useful for many stakeholders in the Baldrige process, including senior leaders, performance excellence initiative leaders, application writers, and examiners. While reading the entire book would be informative and useful for all stakeholders, certain portions of the book may apply more to one group than another.

The following table indicates sections that certain stakeholders may find more immediately useful.

<table>
<tr><th>Section</th><th>Senior Leaders</th><th>Examiners</th><th>Performance Excellence Initiative Leaders</th><th>Application Writers</th><th>Award Program Administrators</th></tr>
<tr><td>Insights to Performance Excellence</td><td>1–30</td><td>69–74</td><td>1–74</td><td>70–74</td><td></td></tr>
<tr><td>Organizational Profile</td><td></td><td></td><td>75–82</td><td>75–82</td><td></td></tr>
<tr><td>Leadership</td><td>83–106</td><td></td><td>83–106</td><td>83–106</td><td></td></tr>
<tr><td>Strategy</td><td rowspan="7">Take time to study these Categories as a senior leadership team</td><td></td><td>107–131</td><td>107–131</td><td></td></tr>
<tr><td>Customers</td><td></td><td>133–154</td><td>133–154</td><td></td></tr>
<tr><td>Measurement, Analysis, and Knowledge Management</td><td></td><td>155–176</td><td>155–176</td><td></td></tr>
<tr><td>Workforce</td><td></td><td>177–202</td><td>177–202</td><td></td></tr>
<tr><td>Operations</td><td></td><td>203–226</td><td>203–226</td><td></td></tr>
<tr><td>Results</td><td></td><td>227–256</td><td>227–256</td><td></td></tr>
<tr><td>Tips on Preparing a Baldrige Award Application</td><td></td><td></td><td>257–269</td><td></td></tr>
<tr><td>Scoring System</td><td></td><td>271–283</td><td></td><td>271–283</td><td>271–283</td></tr>
</table>

Continued

Continued

Section	Senior Leaders	Examiners	Performance Excellence Initiative Leaders	Application Writers	Award Program Administrators
Clarifying the Baldrige Scoring Requirements		285–293		285–293	285–293
From a Culture of Compliance to a Culture of Excellence—Worldwide	295–302		295–302		
Baldrige-Based Self-Assessment of Organization and Management Systems			303		303
The Site Visit		305–336	305–336		305–336
Best Practices					343–344
Global Excellence Around the World	337–342		337–342		
Clarifying Confusing Terms		345–350	345–350	345–350	
Glossary		351–367	351–367	351–367	

Foreword

LEADERSHIP CHALLENGES

This year the Baldrige National Quality Award celebrates its 32nd year answering the question, "What drives success in high-performing organizations?" Some specific drivers have changed over time but the fundamental drivers are the same. These fundamental drivers of excellence have proven to be the same for all types of organizations, whether in the private sector, education, health care, or government. Dr. Mark Blazey is a leading expert in the application of the Baldrige Criteria to help organizations improve and achieve outstanding levels of performance. He provided extremely valuable insight—through his writings and personal consulting—to help Xerox develop world-class management systems that led to Xerox Business Services being recognized as a 1997 recipient of the Baldrige Award. Mark Blazey and Paul Grizzell have helped organizations of all types and in all sectors develop practical approaches for continuous improvement that serve as the cornerstone for leadership and organizational success. Their personal insight and clear explanations help make complex concepts of this Baldrige Excellence Framework much simpler. That is what makes this book a best seller. *Insights to Performance Excellence 2021–2022* is a book for beginners as well as experts in the field of organizational development and operational excellence. The book delivers the lessons, provides the insights, and sets the framework for a successful journey to performance excellence.

John Lawrence
Retired Vice President of Quality
Xerox Business Services
1997 Baldrige Recipient

Preface

To be successful, organizations must engage their customers—although they may choose to call them many names, such as clients, students, patients, families, residents, constituents, communities, voters, rate-payers, or passengers, to name a few. The nomenclature changes depending upon the language of the organization, but it is these customers who make decisions about whether they will continue to be loyal or go elsewhere. Organizations that can keep customers loyal and attract new ones will thrive. Strange as it may seem, there are organizations that have not put delighting customers at the top of their priority list (or anywhere on the list). Engaged customers are five times more likely to continue to use an organization or recommend that organization to others, than those who are simply satisfied. On the other hand, 80% of dissatisfied customers are likely to walk away without a word to the offending organization.

With the large number of internet-based consumer websites in place today, dissatisfied customers can easily tell thousands about their bad experiences. The twenty-first century has evolved a more demanding, customer-driven economy. If organizations intend to thrive, the workforce and leaders must understand the requirements and expectations of their customers.

Being customer-focused and understanding their requirements are necessary for success, but not sufficient. Organizations must also consistently deliver value to the customers they want to serve. This requires that key work processes produce desired results every time. That is why a process orientation is important.

Unfortunately, even when organizations begin to execute processes consistently, their leaders may find that excellence and optimum performance continue to elude them. Organizations can fail to satisfy and engage customers even when key work processes function as designed—if the design was not based on customer requirements. Internally focused processes are too often driven by designers—without regard for customer concerns. The resulting organizational arrogance—the belief that we know better than the customer—is almost certain to bring about customer dissatisfaction and ultimately revolt, causing customers to demand change or leave.

Successful organizations must consistently understand and precisely execute those processes that deliver the key characteristics that are critical to customer delight. The winners in a highly competitive environment are the organizations that listen to the voice of the customer to understand their expectations, preferences, and requirements and then design and execute work processes aimed at delighting them better than anyone else.

Many leaders find it difficult to determine what customers want, fend off the competition, satisfy and engage workers, and operate within a constrained budget. That is one reason why the development and execution of strategy is essential. Strategy development demands:

- Understanding the direction in which customers are moving, the direction in which the competition is moving, and the direction in which the market is moving
- Coupling that information with the capabilities and desired direction of the organization to promote innovation
- Identifying the few things that are critical to the future success of the organization, such as threats, challenges, advantages, opportunities, current and future core competencies, and the work processes that must be designed and executed to succeed
- Defining, in measurable, outcome-oriented terms, what the organization must actually achieve to be successful in the future
- Converting those strategies into action to align and focus the work of the organization at all levels

Managing the implementation of strategy and related actions requires clear directions and effective monitoring at all levels, which is facilitated by a dashboard showing key performance and process measures throughout the organization.

A good dashboard provides measures of leading indicators to help leaders understand what is important to customers, how well it is delivering on those things that are important, the reaction of its customers, and the capacity of its work processes and delivery systems. With this advance knowledge, leaders can make better decisions about the actions needed to be successful, bring more value to the marketplace, and respond effectively to changing circumstances and strategic opportunities.

While customer focus, strategy, and data to support effective decision-making are critical components of the successful organization, these factors combined are still not sufficient to ensure success. Every high-performing organization must acquire good people, train them, motivate them, and retain them. To be successful today, organizations must develop an engaged workforce that contributes its utmost to the success of the organization and its customers. Workers must have the competencies to use facts and information to make good decisions, and to continue learning and contribute to their own growth and development. In a world where product and service superiority lasts only a short time, it is the capabilities and commitment of the workforce that drive ongoing excellence and differentiation. No longer are top-performing organizations simply looking for workers with the right skills. Today, successful organizations need workers who are data-driven, customer-focused, and process-oriented—engaged people who promote improvement and innovation.

It is the responsibility of leadership to make this system come together and work harmoniously. To do this, leaders must first set the direction very clearly, based on a strategy that brings value to customers and the marketplace; and then establish the environment in which that direction is carried out consistently.

Some leaders find it difficult to establish and articulate a clear vision and serve as a role model for a set of values that lead to success. Without a clear direction, the people in an organization are forced to substitute their own ideas about the right direction. When many do this, the organization finds itself lacking focus—pulled in different directions. Leaders cannot expect people to know what to do if they have not established and continuously reinforced the norms of desired behavior. Great leaders lead by example—role modeling the desired behaviors that are expected of all.

The best organizations in every sector have demonstrated that all parts of the system must be effectively integrated to optimize performance. It is not possible to achieve excellence by only doing the things that are easy and ignoring the rest.

A substantial portion of Mark Blazey and Paul Grizzell's careers has been spent helping people understand the power and benefits of this Integrated Management System and become examiners for many performance excellence awards. These people come from all types of organizations and from all levels within those organizations. Participants include CEOs, generals, admirals, corporate quality directors, planners, state organization chiefs, small-business owners, heads of hospitals, teachers, professors, medical doctors, nurses, and school administrators, to name a few.

This book was originally developed for them. For more than two decades it has been used as a teaching and reference text to guide their decisions and deliberations as they provided feedback to organizations that documented their continuous improvement efforts using Baldrige Award-type management systems. Many examiners who used this text, especially Tom Kubiak, asked Mark Blazey to publish it in a stand-alone format. They wanted to use it to help their own organizations, customers, and suppliers guide and assess their continuous improvement efforts.

These two groups of readers—examiners of quality systems and leaders of organizations seeking high levels of performance—can benefit by understanding not only the parts of the Integrated Management System, but also how these parts connect and align. Our goal for this book is that readers will understand more fully what each area of the system means for organizations and find the synergy within the six major process-oriented parts of the system—leadership; strategy; customers; measurement, analysis, and knowledge management; workforce; and operations—that lead to excellent performance results.

Leaders report that this book provides a valuable, step-by-step approach to help them identify and put in place properly focused continuous improvement systems. As organizations and their leaders evolve, improvement efforts in one area will lead to improvements in other areas. This process is similar to experiences we have all encountered as we carry out home improvement: improve one area, and many other areas needing improvement become apparent. This book will help identify areas that need immediate improvement as well as areas that are less urgent but, nevertheless, vitally linked to organizational and operational excellence.

This book is, in essence, an encyclopedia of knowledge regarding Baldrige and other integrated management systems. In an effort to make it easier for readers to find essential information for their role, we have developed a matrix table of contents—or stakeholder index—to direct various groups to the most relevant information for their needs. We hope you find it valuable, whether you are a senior leader, a performance excellence initiative champion, an examiner or evaluator, or an application writer.

We are continually looking for feedback about this book and suggestions about how it can be improved. Please contact Mark Blazey via email at *authors@asq.org* or *markblazey@gmail.com*, or Paul Grizzell at *paul.grizzell@corevaluespartners.com.*

Acknowledgments

Bob Fangmeyer, Harry Hertz, Curt Reimann, and the dedicated staff of the Baldrige Performance Excellence Program have provided long-standing support and guidance in promoting performance excellence. Karen Davison, Cathy Bergland, and John Lawrence provided substantial editorial and analytical assistance. They have all contributed to analyses that are a part of this book. We greatly appreciate Scott Blazey of Enterprise Design & Publishing for preparing this book for publication. We want to thank the ASQ's (American Society for Quality) Quality Press team for publication guidance.

Many others have helped shape our thinking about performance excellence and refining this book, including Gary Floss, Cath Bergland, Mickey Mayland, Reed Mick, Wanda Thurman, Jim Foote, Joe Sener, Olga E. Soroka, Rosye Cloud, John Barnette, Larry Wyche, Jeff Calhoun, Brian Lassiter, Jean Bronk, Julie Furst-Bowe, Chad Cloud, Mary Gamble, Ken Thompson, Alana Moore Wolfe, Jeri Reinhardt, Angie Germain, Tom Kubiak, Linda Vincent, Jim Percy, Elizabeth Hale, Joan Wills, Steve Hoisington, Liz Menzer, Brett Remington, Jack Evans, Arnie Weimerskirch, Marty Mariner, Carol Ganster Fisher, Bob Ewy, Norm Ridder, Steve Uebbing, Robert Frisina, Ellie Fralick, Charlie Blass, Kelly Gilhooly, Rob Marchelonis, Harry Zechman, Sylvia Rolfs, Patrick O'Boyle, Kevin Deats, Roberto Saco, Maryruth Butler, Raina Knox, Katie Rawls, Ann Warner, Jo-Ann Kratz, Sandra Cokeley, Peggy Siegel, Lynn Erdle, James Miller, Fred Smith, Kathy Malcolm, Linda Farchione Hawks, Mike Stapleton, Jim Barr, Judith Cherrington, Patricia Stevens, Bob Barnett, Laura Kinney, and Dia'lah Hutabalian.

The American Health Care Association/National Center for Assisted Living (AHCA/NCAL) Quality Award Program is making a difference for their members in the long-term care industry. With over 1,200 applicants a year at various levels, this program demonstrates the value of an industry-specific performance excellence program. Dr. David Gifford, Courtney Bishnoi, Urvi Patel, Tim Case, Erin Prendergast, Meghan Karstetter, and KeShawn Franklin are leading and managing this role-model program.

Performance excellence programs around the world are making a difference in the areas they serve, including Russell Longmuir, Gianluca Mulé, and retired Léon Tossaint of the European Foundation for Quality Management (EFQM); Jia Fuxing, Dr. Duan Yonggang, Lv Qing, and Hou Jinfeng of the China Association for

Quality (CAQ); Fred Zhang of ASQ China; Ravi Fernando of Business Excellence Australia; and Dr. Ayed Al-Amri of the Saudi Quality Council.

The chapter on site visits, including the Expected Results Matrix, the Criteria model and Integrated Management Systems analysis, the management and performance excellence surveys, the performance standard for leadership, the sections concerning the potential adverse consequences of not doing what the Criteria require, the chart explaining unduplicated approach elements, the application preparation files, the Item flow diagrams, the engagement questions, and the Scoring Calibration Guides are used with permission of Mark Blazey. He would also like to recognize and thank Cathy Bergland for helping to edit the Scoring Calibration Guides.

The analysis of Six Sigma, Lean, and Balanced Scorecard is used with permission of Paul Grizzell and Mark Blazey.

The following are used with permission of Paul Grizzell and Core Values Partners:

- The description of Global Excellence Models
- *Moving from a Culture of Compliance to a Culture of Excellence* and the related assessments
- *The Site Visit is Not an Audit*
- *The Seven Extra Values of the Baldrige and EFQM Process*
- *Baldrige or EFQM: The Journey is the Reward*

Materials describing the EFQM Model are used with permission of the EFQM. EFQM is making a difference in spreading performance excellence concepts around the world.

The Core Values and Concepts, Excellence Builder, Baldrige Excellence Framework and Criteria for Performance Excellence, selected glossary terms, award recipients, and background information in this book are drawn from information in the public domain supplied by the Malcolm Baldrige National Quality Award program.

Kevin Hendricks and Vinod Singhal provided research results that were used in this book from their study of financial performance. Data from the Economic Evaluation of the Baldrige National Quality Program by Albert Link and John Scott were prepared for the National Institute of Standards and Technology (NIST) in 2001 and 2011. *The Excellence equals Managing Change at an Accelerated Rate* formula is used with permission of Mark Blazey.

Introduction

The Malcolm Baldrige National Quality Award (MBNQA) 2021–2022 Criteria for Performance Excellence and scoring guidelines are powerful assessment instruments that help leaders identify organizational strengths and key opportunities for improvement. The primary task of leaders is then to use the information to improve work processes and achieve higher levels of performance.

Building an effective management system capable of driving performance improvement is an ongoing challenge because of the intricate web of complex relationships among management, workers, customers, stakeholders, partners, and suppliers. The best organizations have put in place a truly integrated management system that improves its work processes continually. They measure every key facet of business activity and closely monitor organizational performance. Leaders of these organizations set high expectations, value workers and their input, communicate clear directions, and align the work of everyone to optimize performance and achieve organizational goals.

The Baldrige Criteria for Performance Excellence (CPE) were first launched over 30 years ago, in 1987–1988. Since then, organizations of all types and sizes have learned that the disciplined approach to continuous improvement required by the Criteria has helped them keep up with the competition and succeed.

In the 1980s, continuous improvement was rare. With even modest efforts, an organization committed to improvement could beat its competitors. Today, however, with more and more organizations working to improve their key processes, programmatic improvement has become common. No longer is occasional improvement sufficient to create or maintain a competitive advantage. The best competitors now know that long-term success and market superiority require that they get better at getting better. The best organizations not only make improvements, but they improve their rate of improvement. They get better faster than their competition.

Einstein explained the relationship of mass and energy with the formula $E=mc^2$. We can borrow the formula and adapt it to describe what top leaders do to thrive in today's economic and competitive climate. Energy becomes Excellence, Mass becomes the ability to Manage organizational change, and the speed of light becomes the accelerated rate of Change, or Change squared. Therefore, *Excellence equals Managing Change at an accelerated rate* or $E=mc^2$. Not a scientific formula for physics, but a practical formula for success.

Excellence equals Managing Change at an accelerated rate: $E=mc^2$

Unfortunately, because of the complexity of modern management systems, the criteria used to examine them are also complex and sometimes difficult to understand. *Insights to Performance Excellence 2021–2022* helps performance excellence examiners, organization-improvement practitioners, and application writers to understand the 2021–2022 Baldrige Framework and the linkages and relationships among the seven Categories and 17 Items.

Seven types of information are provided in this book for each of the Items in Categories 1 through 6:

1. The actual language of each Item, including Notes, presented in the shadow box. [Author's note: The information in these shadow boxes includes the official Baldrige Criteria and serves as the basis for the Award examination.]

2. A plain-English explanation of the elements of each Item with some suggestions about the rationale for the Item and ways to meet key requirements.

3. A table showing the similar elements of the Criteria presented only once at the scoring level where the element first appears.

4. A summary of the requirements of each Item in flowchart form. The flowcharts capture the essence, and isolate the requirements of each Item to help organizations focus on the key points the Item is assessing. Note that most boxes in the flowcharts contain an Item reference in brackets [ ]. This indicates that the Criteria require the action. If there is no Item reference in brackets, it means the action is suggested but not required. Occasionally a reference to *[scoring guidelines]* is included in a box. This means that the authority for the requirement comes from the scoring guidelines.

5. The key linkages between each Item and the other Items. The major or primary linkages are designated using a solid arrow (⟶). The secondary linkages are designated using a dashed arrow (--➤).

6. An explanation of some potential adverse consequences that an organization might face if it fails to implement processes required by each Item. (Examiners may find this analysis useful as they prepare relevant feedback concerning opportunities for improvement. However, these generic statements should be customized—based on key factors, core values, or specific circumstances facing the organization being reviewed—before using them to develop relevant feedback comments supporting opportunities for improvements in Categories 1 through 6.)

7. Examples of effective and ineffective practices that some organizations have developed and followed consistent with the elements of the Item. These samples present some ideas about how to meet elements. (Remember, examiners should not convert these sample effective practices into new requirements for organizations they are examining.)

Features of this 2021–2022 edition include:

- New information from the Baldrige 2021–2022 CPE to help leaders focus on priority opportunities for improvement and better understand the role they must play in refining their management systems and processes.
- Updated tables for each Criteria Item showing the similar elements of the Criteria presented only once at the scoring level where the requirement first appears. This is intended to help examiners determine at what level an element belongs when it appears at the *basic,* and/or *overall,* and *multiple* levels.
- Online resources available with this book that have been modified to bring them up to date with the changes in the Criteria.
- Updated information on other award programs throughout the world such as the European Foundation for Quality Management and the China Association for Quality.
- Additional online resources to help understand the value of using an integrated management system are available from a secure website that allows downloads of resources and the refinement and addition of those resources. These include updated Scoring Calibration Guidelines for Education, Health Care, and Business/Nonprofit/Government organizations.

Reading *Insights to Performance Excellence 2021–2022: Using the Baldrige Excellence Framework and Other Integrated Management Systems* will strengthen your understanding of the Criteria and provide insight on analyzing your organization, improving performance, and applying for the award.

The 2021–2022 Baldrige Excellence Framework booklet is published by the Baldrige Performance Excellence Program, National Institute of Standards and Technology (NIST), U.S. Department of Commerce. It is the official publication of the Baldrige Criteria from which select portions were extracted for this book. The full Criteria and related information is in the Framework booklet, which is available directly from the Baldrige Performance Excellence Program and may be obtained by visiting its website at *https://www.nist.gov/baldrige/products-services/baldrige-excellence-framework.*

Insights to Performance Excellence:
Understanding the Integrated Management System

This book provides information for leaders who seek to transform their organizations to achieve performance excellence. This section:

- Presents a business case for using the Baldrige Framework and Performance Excellence Criteria to improve organizational performance
- Describes the core values and concepts that drive organizational change to high levels of performance and underlie the Baldrige Criteria
- Provides practical insights and lessons learned —ideas on transition strategies to put high-performance systems in place and promote organizational excellence

This section emphasizes themes driven by the 2021–2022 Criteria and Core Values. It also includes suggestions about how to start down the path to systematic organizational improvement, as well as lessons learned from those who chose paths that led nowhere or proved futile despite their best intentions.

BALDRIGE BEGINNINGS AND ONGOING REFINEMENT

During the 1980s, many U.S. businesses suffered losses in the marketplace due to stronger international competition. For nearly 30 years, Japanese business leaders were able to improve the performance of their organizations by following the teachings of W. Edwards Deming and striving to meet the requirements of the Deming Prize criteria. The story of the Japanese recovery from the devastation of World War II to become a dominant global economic power was documented in the CBS white paper *If Japan Can Why Can't We?*

The white paper explained the strong, positive impact the prize had on the desire and ability of Japanese business leaders to improve organizational performance. It served as a catalyst for the creation of a U.S. national quality award. It was hoped that a similar award would help U.S. business leaders focus on the systems and processes that would lead them to recovery much as the Deming Prize helped the Japanese.

After nearly five years of work, in 1987, the U.S. Congress created the national quality award named in honor of the secretary of the Department of Commerce, Malcolm Baldrige, who had died a short time earlier in a rodeo accident. The Baldrige award had one key purpose: to help U.S. businesses improve their competitiveness in the global marketplace.

After much debate and discussion, the creators of the award Criteria—led by Dr. Curt Reimann of the U.S. Department of Commerce—agreed that the award Criteria should not be based on theories of how organizations ought to conduct business in order to win. They had seen too many instances where organizations followed the many piecemeal theories of management consultants that lead nowhere. Furthermore, they realized that what it takes to win in a competitive environment changes over time; therefore, the Criteria should not be static or allowed to become obsolete

Accordingly, the principle was adopted that the Criteria must be periodically refreshed and based on the verified management practices of the world's best-performing organizations that enabled them to achieve such high levels of performance, productivity, customer satisfaction, and market dominance.

To ensure that the Baldrige Criteria for Performance Excellence continue to be relevant, the U.S. Department of Commerce, National Institute of

> ***The Criteria for Performance Excellence is an outcome-focused, evidence-based management model based on the characteristics of high-performing organizations.***

Standards and Technology (NIST) reviews the drivers of high performance each year. Based on these analyses, the CPE are validated and refined on a two-year cycle.

In spite of this ongoing renewal, some critics of the Criteria argue that the Baldrige standards are *outdated* and *passé*. These critics ask, "If the Criteria are updated every two years, why don't they reflect the newest management techniques?"

The main reason why the CPE do not reflect the latest management fads is because fads are unproven. A promising management practice must be recognized as a proven driver of high performance before the practice becomes an element in the Criteria. Such *proofs* require strong evidence of widespread practice and related performance outcomes.

A new management practice might work well for one organization but not for another. Fact-based evidence must demonstrate that the practice leads to high performance in many types of organizations, across multiple sectors including small and large, manufacturing and service, union and nonunion, and public and private.

Because it usually takes two or more years for a *promising practice* to prove its value, the Criteria will lag behind the newest, albeit unproven fads. However, the rigor of the review is part of the value the Criteria add to business excellence. The Criteria help leaders sort out the fads from the proven techniques and protect leaders from authors and consultants who seek to promote their "flavor of the month."

It is important to mention that the Criteria were never intended to limit improvement, innovation, and creativity. In fact, the Criteria require those traits in all process areas. Specifically, the Criteria require leaders to cultivate organizational agility and resilience, accountability, organizational and individual learning, innovation, and intelligent risk-taking [Item 1.1c(1)] and improve their own effectiveness [1.2a(2)].

The best leaders use the principles described by the Criteria as the fundamental way they manage the organization, and then search for methods to refine and enhance their work systems to provide even more competitive advantage. They experiment with new techniques and are not content to simply follow a management cookbook. They install an effective, integrated management system first, then experiment and improve—not the other way around.

Many of these top leaders use the principles of the Integrated Management System without any public announcements or fanfare. They have never applied for the award and do not intend to do so. They are content to achieve excellence and steadily win customers and market share. These leaders have the fortitude ("leadership guts") to do the hard work and make the difficult decisions required to become a high-performing organization.

Nearly all leaders and managers who reject the value of the Criteria out of hand do not understand the principles they contain, even those who claim to have "tried Baldrige." The system that effectively drives top performance in organizations is complex. After all, if it was easy to achieve excellence, everyone would do it. The landscape is littered with organizations that never understood or failed to continue using the validated, leading-edge management practices defined by the Integrated Management System Criteria. *This book is for those leaders who are willing and able to commit to becoming great leaders, optimizing performance, and sustaining the excellence they have helped to achieve.*

THE CASE FOR USING THE PERFORMANCE EXCELLENCE CRITERIA

All leaders know that change is not easy. They will be asked and perhaps be tempted to turn back many times. They may not even be aware of these temptations or of the backsliding that occurs when their peers and subordinates sense their commitment is wavering. Leaders who are dedicated to achieving high performance appreciate examples of success from organizations that are ahead of them on the journey. These excellent leaders have held the course despite nagging doubts, organizational turbulence, and even attempts at sabotage by their subordinates.

Summarizing key research studies conducted over the past decade, the following section of the book:

- Reports research on financial performance of approximately 400 firms that were recognized by local, state, or national awards for quality management practices. (Research results are reported with permission of Dr. Vinod R.

Singhal. Research was conducted by Kevin B. Hendricks and Vinod R. Singhal.)

- Describes public- and private-sector organizations that have gained ground and made rapid strides forward on their journeys, having achieved recognition as recipients of the MBNQA. It then identifies the core values that have guided these organizations to achieve high levels of performance excellence.

VALUE OF THE CRITERIA

In a report titled *The Nation's CEOs Look to the Future,* 308 CEOs from large, small, and several noncorporate organizations described what they believe lies ahead for business in the United States, and the value of the CPE. These trends relate in many ways to the 2021–2022 Criteria and are considered as the Criteria are revised to reflect the current business environment and the most effective management practices for that environment.

The vast majority (67%–79%) of the CEOs believe that the Criteria and Baldrige Awards are very or extremely valuable in stimulating improvements in quality and competitiveness in U.S. businesses. More than 51% of the CEOs reported the following trends as major directions that will be likely to affect business in the years ahead. These include (from most cited, 69%, to least cited, 52%):

- Developing new workforce relationships based on performance
- Improving human resources management
- Improving the execution of strategic plans
- Developing more appropriate strategic plans
- Measuring and analyzing organizational processes
- Developing a consistent global corporate culture
- Outsourcing of manufacturing
- Creating a learning organization

As part of the survey, CEOs were asked to reflect on their own skills and their peer group's skills and to report on which skills were most in need of improvement. The skills cited in the following list were thought by more than 50% to need "a great deal" of improvement. They are key to addressing the major business trends reported earlier in this section. The skills include:

- The ability to think globally and execute strategies successfully
- Flexibility in a changing world
- The ability to develop appropriate strategies and rapidly redefine their business
- The understanding of new technologies

Another 40%–50% of CEOs believe that these skills also need to improve "a great deal." Skills needing improvement include the ability to:

- Work well with different stakeholders
- Create a learning organization
- Make the right bets about the future
- Be a visible, articulate, charismatic leader
- Be a strong enough leader to overcome opposition

When asked which required more improvement—the development or execution of appropriate strategies—CEOs selected *execution* by about a three-to-one margin. This means that alignment of work and realistic action plans needs to be improved along with accountability. If the organization is pulling in different directions, it is more difficult to accomplish individual unit or division priorities—resources and energies are being drained, execution is flawed, and results are suboptimized.

Research Supports the Business Case

Two researchers, interested in quality award recipients, wanted to determine the extent (if any) quality management impacted business performance. The research of Dr. Kevin B. Hendricks from the College of William and Mary, School of Business, and Vinod R. Singhal from the Georgia Institute of Technology, Dupree College of Management, is the basis for the following evidence that supports use of the Baldrige Criteria. Their research looked beyond hype and the popular press to the real impact of quality management and examined the facts surrounding performance excellence. The research was based on about 600 recipients of various quality or performance awards and similar recognition. The recognition provided to these organizations was based upon similar core values and concepts. Companies were mostly manufacturing firms (75%). All were publicly traded companies. Although Hendricks and Singhal did not find that quality management turned "straw into gold," their research added significantly to the business case for using the Criteria as a tool to enhance performance.

Hendricks and Singhal examined the following efficiency or growth measures:

- Percent change in sales
- Stock price performance
- Percent change in total assets
- Percent change in number of employees
- Percent change in return on sales
- Percent change in return on assets

Implementation Costs Do Not Negatively Impact the Bottom Line

The research examined two five-year periods during the quality management implementation cycle. The first period can be called beginning implementation. This period started six years before and ended one year before the receipt of a first award. During this period, organizations were implementing quality management and incurring associated costs of implementation, such as training, communications, and production and design changes. The researchers found no significant differences in financial measures between these companies (winners) and the control group of companies (nonwinners but similar in other respects) for this period. This is important because of the costs (both direct and indirect) associated with implementing quality management systems. The research suggests that the significant cost savings identified during this period of intensified focus on cycle time, time to market, and other factors pay for the implementation costs.

Improved Financial Results Can Be Expected with Successful Implementation

The study then examined results of companies from one year before winning the award to four years after the award was given. This period can be called mature implementation and it is in this period that one would expect the improved management to bear fruit. This was the case with this research. There were significant differences in financial performance between award recipients and controls (nonwinners that are in the Standard and Poor's index). For example, the growth in operating income averaged 91% for winners contrasted to 43% for non-award winners. Award-winning companies reported 69% growth in sales compared with 32% for the control group. The total assets of the winning companies increased 79% compared to 37% for the controls. Winners had significantly better results than the control group. The graphs in Figures 1 and 2 represent the study findings. Researchers found that award-winning companies outperformed control firms (non-award-winning companies) at least two-to-one, as Figure 1 indicates.

Hendricks and Singhal also found that there was no significant difference between the companies prior to the period of implementation of these quality principles. Performance of the award-winning firms was significantly better after implementation, suggesting the difference was due to the performance excellence systems that they installed.

In addition, Hendricks and Singhal found that small companies did significantly better than large companies in implementing the quality principles.

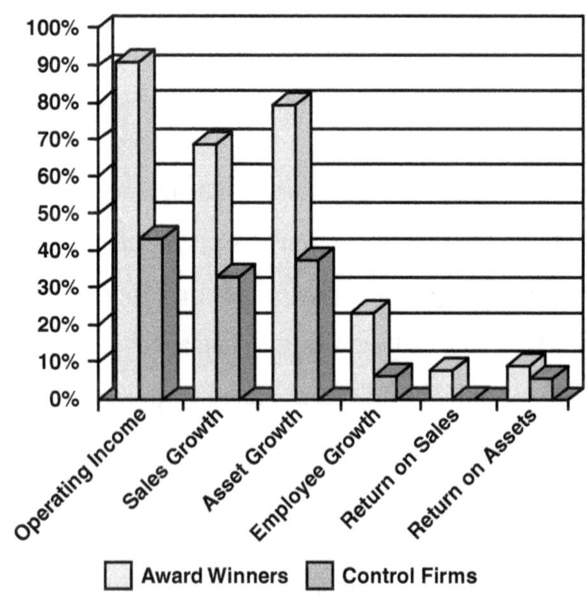

Figure 1 Comparison of award-winning and control firms.

This is depicted in Figure 2. Although large companies may have more resources with which to implement these systems, small companies may have an easier time deploying these systems fully throughout the organization and achieving maximum benefit.

Although both small (less than $600 million) and large firms benefited, small firms did even better. Small winners outperformed the control counterparts by 63%, whereas large firms outperformed their controls by 22%. A similar profile existed for low-capital- versus high-capital-intensive award winners.

Integrated Management System Processes Drive Improved Performance Outcomes

A key management practice that has been part of the CPE for many years is the use of business results to analyze and subsequently improve organizational performance. James R. Evans and Eric P. Jack conducted an extensive correlational study to examine 20 hypothesized linkages between various Baldrige-required management practices and organizational results [Evans, James R. and Eric P. Jack, "Validating Key Results Linkages in the Baldrige Performance Excellence Model." *Quality Management Journal*, 10.2 (April 2003): 7–24]. The study's first 10 hypotheses represent linkages among the endogenous (internal system) variables as follows [Note: The strikethrough hypotheses (H3, H4, and H10) were not supported by the data. All other hypotheses were supported.]:

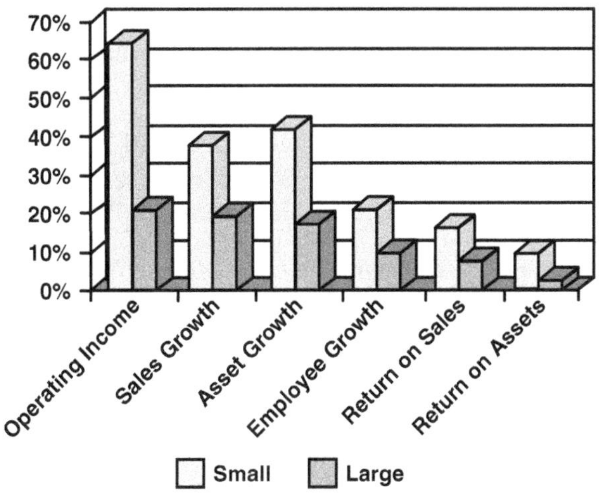

Figure 2 Comparison of large and small award-winning companies.

H1: Employee satisfaction has a positive impact on process performance

H2: Work system improvement has a significant impact on productivity

~~H3: Work system improvement has a significant impact on employee satisfaction~~

~~H4: Work system improvement has a significant impact on process performance~~

H5: Process performance has a significant impact on productivity

H6: Employee satisfaction has a significant impact on service quality

H7: Employee satisfaction has a significant impact on product quality

H8: Process performance has a significant impact on service quality

H9: Process performance has a significant impact on product quality

~~H10: Supplier performance has a significant impact on product quality~~

The next 10 hypotheses evaluate the direct linkages between the exogenous (external) variables and the exogenous results as follows:

H11: Employee satisfaction has a significant impact on market performance

H12: Service quality has a significant impact on customer satisfaction

H13: Product quality has a significant impact on customer satisfaction

H14: Product quality has a significant impact on financial performance

H15: Supplier performance has a significant impact on financial performance

H16: Process performance has a significant impact on financial performance

H17: Productivity has a significant impact on financial performance

H18: Customer satisfaction has a significant impact on market performance

H19: Market performance has a significant impact on financial performance

H20: Customer satisfaction has a significant impact on financial performance

The study's empirical results support the overall hypothesis that improving internal management practices leads to improvements in external results (Evans and Jack, p. 18):

> "Consider the relationships among endogenous variables in the Baldrige Results Category, such as between employee satisfaction and process performance, and between work system improvement and productivity. Strong correlation among these latent variables suggests the importance of many fundamental management practices that are embedded in the Baldrige requirements, such as a focus on employee well-being and motivation, and attention to the design of work systems and their linkage to other Categories, such as operations. By strengthening the practices that lead to improved levels of internal performance, the analysis indicates that improved performance of production/delivery processes will likewise occur. Second, high levels of the endogenous variables are correlated with exogenous performance results as measured by market share, customer satisfaction, and financial performance. This provides evidence that improving the performance of endogenous variables will positively impact the most important external business performance measures. Thus, this research provides new evidence of the validity of the Baldrige integrated management system and its examination/self-assessment process that seeks to validate strong business results as an outcome of high-performance management practices."

The following is a summary of the study findings:

- Employee satisfaction is driven by process performance and product quality. (This is consistent with observations from many Baldrige Award recipients that increased employee satisfaction leads to higher performance.)
- Process performance is correlated significantly with employee satisfaction as a dependent variate, and with product quality and market performance as an independent variate.
- Customer satisfaction is driven by product quality, service quality, and work-system improvement. Customers may indeed be satisfied but still switch allegiance based on other factors. Thus, customer retention is not necessarily a reliable indicator of satisfaction.
- Product quality is driven by employee satisfaction, work-system improvement, and process performance. Product quality drives customer satisfaction and financial performance.
- Service quality is correlated significantly only with customer satisfaction. On-time delivery dominates the relationship.
- Work-system improvement drives product quality, customer satisfaction, and financial performance.
- Financial performance is driven by productivity, market performance, work-system improvement, and product quality. From a practical perspective, this suggests that quality-related initiatives do have a significant impact on financial performance, as many studies have shown (for example, Hendricks and Singhal (1997) and the National Institute of Standards and Technology's continuing study of Baldrige recipients). Cost of quality, prevention cost, and warranty cost are the major contributors to productivity and product quality. Return on assets (ROA) and growth in ROA are the major contributors to market performance.
- Productivity is correlated significantly with financial performance. Rework and scrap contribute strongly to the relationship.
- Market performance is correlated significantly with process performance and financial performance.

Economic Impact of the Baldrige National Quality Program

In October 2001, Albert N. Link, Department of Economics, University of North Carolina at Greensboro, and John T. Scott, Department of Economics at Dartmouth College, reported on a study they completed that examined the economic impact of the Baldrige National Quality Program. Specifically, their study examined the net private benefits associated with the Baldrige National Quality Program to the U.S. private and public sector and the relationship between economy-wide net benefits and the social costs associated with operating the program. (Note: Social costs represent the public funding used to operate the Baldrige Award program.)

Based on information collected from a mail survey of the U.S. organizational members of the American Society for Quality (ASQ), the conservative estimate of the value (in constant 2000 dollars) of the net private benefits associated with the Baldrige National Quality Program was $2.17 billion. Link and Scott estimated the value (in constant 2000 dollars) of social benefits (broad-based economic benefits to consumers as a result of better quality) associated with the Baldrige National Quality Program to be $24.65 billion. Based on information provided by the Baldrige National Quality Program, the value (in constant 2000 dollars) of social costs associated with the program to date was $119 million. Therefore, from an evaluative perspective for the economy as a whole, the benefit-to-cost ratio characterizing the Baldrige National Quality Program was conservatively 207-to-1.

Economic Impact Part 2—What Would Happen if No Baldrige Program or Criteria Existed?

If the U.S. Department of Commerce, National Institute of Standards and Technology did not define the drivers of performance excellence, individual organizations would have had to incur costs to do so on their own. These costs would have been repeated as each separate business, school, government agency, or health care organization struggled to define the drivers of excellence and keep these standards current as the practices needed to achieve excellence changed over time.

In a 2011 study sponsored by the National Institute of Standards and Technology (Source: Albert N. Link and John T. Scott, Economic Evaluation of the Baldrige Performance Excellence Program, December 2011, *https://www.nist.gov/system/files/documents/2017/05/09/report11-2.pdf.*) researchers calculated benefits provided to U.S. organizations by the Baldrige Program and its *Criteria for Performance Excellence.*

To summarize, Link and Scott used two sets of data to calculate costs and benefits that covered the 273 applicants for the Malcolm Baldrige National Quality Award since 2006. The first set of data related to the costs to operate the Baldrige Performance Excellence Program, and the second set related to three categories of benefits directly related to the availability and use of the Baldrige Criteria:

(a) Implementation Costs: Costs that organizations avoided because they did not have to invent/reinvent the Performance Excellence Criteria (Note: Economists refer to this cost as a counterfactual alternative.);

(b) Better Quality Products: Gains to consumers from higher quality products; and

(c) More Effective and Efficient Processes: Gains to the economy from using more effective and efficient operations to produce higher-quality products.

Figure 3 on the next page shows the estimates of the benefit-to-cost ratios in 2010 dollars that Link and Scott produced:

- $3-to-1 ratio based on the benefit (a) Implementation Cost savings (since it was not necessary for applicants to incur the costs to develop their own performance excellence strategies because of the availability of the publicly funded Baldrige Criteria)
- $107-to-1 ratio due to the benefits (a) avoided Implementation Costs and (b) Better Quality Products (the gains to consumers from greater satisfaction due to higher-quality products because the Baldrige Criteria were available and used)
- $820-to-1 ratio due to all three benefits: (a) avoided Implementation Costs, (b) Better Quality Products, and (c) More Effective and Efficient Processes (the gains to the economy from saving scarce resources because successful

performance excellence strategies not only enable higher-quality products or services but also lower the costs of providing them)

The benefit-to-cost ratio for the education sector was estimated to be 119-to-1, for the health care sector 456-to-1, and for the manufacturing sector 357-to-1.

Baldrige and Top 100 Hospitals

According to an October 2011 Thomson Reuters study by David Foster and Jean Chenoweth (Source: Foster, D. A., and Chenoweth, J. 2011, October. Comparison of Baldrige Award Applicants and Recipients with Peer Hospitals on a National Balanced Scorecard. Thomson Reuters. *http://www.nist.gov/baldrige/upload/baldrige-hospital-research-paper.pdf.*) hospitals that implement the Baldrige Criteria outperform the industry:

- Baldrige hospitals displayed faster five-year performance improvement than their peers.
- Baldrige hospitals were about 83% more likely than non-Baldrige hospitals to be awarded a 100 Top Hospitals national award for excellence.
- Baldrige hospitals outperformed non-Baldrige hospitals on nearly all (six out of seven) of the individual measures of performance used in the 100 Top Hospitals composite score.

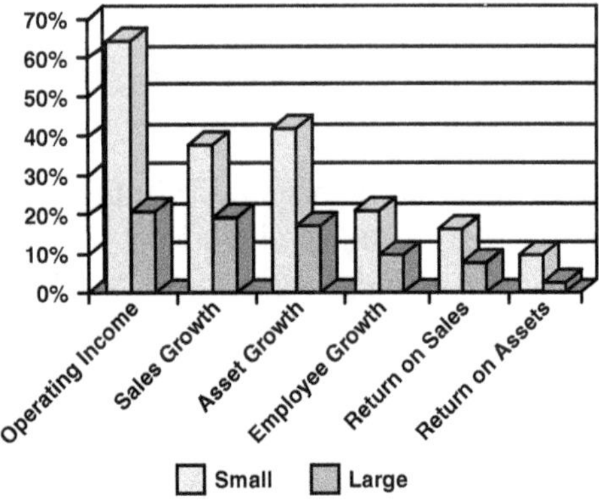

Figure 3 Ratio of benefits to costs of using the Baldrige Criteria.

The results demonstrated that hospitals using the Baldrige process exhibited significantly higher rates of improvement than non-Baldrige hospitals. Also, hospitals using the Baldrige process were significantly more likely than peers to become 100 Top Hospitals award winners, achieving performance equal to or better than the top 3% of all hospitals.

A more recent report showed similar findings. The December 2012 report by Truven Health Analytics found that hospitals that received the Baldrige National Quality Award or received a Baldrige Award site visit outperformed other hospitals in nearly every metric used to determine the 100 Top Hospitals nationwide. (Source: Shook, J., and Chenoweth, J. 2012, October. 100 Top Hospitals CEO Insights: Adoption Rates of Select Baldrige Award Practices and Processes. Truven Health Analytics. *http://www.nist.gov/baldrige/upload/100-Top-Hosp-CEO-Insights-RB-final.pdf.*)

The Truven 100 Top Hospitals winners have extensively adopted the prescribed Baldrige practices although many were not intentionally using the Baldrige Criteria to develop organizational goals or process improvement initiatives.

Teaching hospitals reported the highest formal use of the Baldrige Criteria. Nearly 70% of these hospitals noted that their teams had used the Award Criteria to develop goals and process improvement initiatives.

One of the major challenges facing the majority of CEOs surveyed is organization-wide alignment (for example, the extent to which all parts of an organization work together to support key goals, address key challenges, and respond to sudden changes) as they prepare their hospitals for health care reform. More than 80% of the respondents agreed or strongly agreed that they have implemented the Baldrige-based practices listed on the survey (although the practices were not specifically identified as such).

Baldrige in a Membership Organization

An opportunity for organizations to use an integrated management system such as Baldrige is demonstrated by the American Health Care Association/

National Center for Assisted Living (AHCA/NCAL). During the 2019 ACHA/NCAL Quality Award cycle, more than 1200 applications will be submitted for three levels of recognition.

The AHCA/NCAL Quality Award Program has modeled many of their processes on the Baldrige Quality Award Program but has also improved the Baldrige Award process through the use of the Scoring Calibration Guides and other methods to ensure consistency of evaluation through the various stages of assessment, including Examiner Training, Independent Review, Consensus, Site Visit, and Judging processes.

Membership organizations would do well to benchmark the very effective AHCA/NCAL Quality Award Program as they consider how to provide additional value to their award applicants.

AHCA/NCAL National Quality Award Program

Dr. David Gifford, Senior Vice President, Quality & Regulatory Affairs at AHCA/NCAL, describes the overall approach—and value—of this program.

Today, there are more than 15,000 skilled nursing centers in the United States, serving millions of individuals for short-stay and post-acute rehabilitation and long-term care. The profession represents a sizable portion of the U.S. economy with an estimated $62 billion of all U.S. salaries. The numbers speak for themselves. So, at a time when long-term care is so critical to the lives of millions and to our national economy, the American Health Care Association and the National Center for Assisted Living (AHCA/NCAL) has made it its mission to deliver better solutions for quality care.

AHCA is a nonprofit federation of affiliate state health organizations, together representing more than 13,500 nonprofit and for-profit skilled nursing, assisted living, developmentally disabled, and subacute care providers that care for approximately 1,000,000 elderly and disabled individuals each day. NCAL is the assisted living voice of AHCA. Together, AHCA/NCAL provide national advocacy, education, and tools to members for quality improvement efforts, and one such tool is the AHCA/NCAL National Quality Award Program.

The AHCA/NCAL National Quality Award Program, established in 1996, uses the Baldrige Performance Excellence Framework to recognize and encourage quality improvement in member organizations. The program has three progressive levels of awards: Bronze—Commitment to Quality, Silver—Achievement in Quality, and Gold—Excellence in Quality. Using the Baldrige Criteria, each progressive step requires a more detailed and comprehensive demonstration of systematic and continuous quality improvement. Bronze applicants focus their efforts on completing the Organizational Profile; Silver applicants complete the Organizational Profile and a modified set of the Overall elements of the Criteria; and Gold applicants respond to the full Baldrige Criteria. To be eligible to apply for Gold-level recognition, an applicant must earn Silver-level recognition; participation at the Silver level requires Bronze recognition; Bronze is the entry level.

Over the course of its history, the AHCA/NCAL National Quality Award Program has recognized 5,754 Bronze, 961 Silver, and 38 Gold recipients from across the nation. This makes the program the largest Baldrige-based program in the country.

Members participate in the program due to the effectiveness of the Criteria and cite quality improvement and organizational excellence as a key reason why they apply to the program. This is best demonstrated through publicly reported data, which shows that Silver and Gold award recipients have superior performance compared to the national average in key quality measures (for example, 30-day hospital readmissions, off-label use of antipsychotics), regulatory measures (five-star ratings), and business measures (occupancy rate, operating margin). Receiving a Quality Award is also an opportunity for long-term and post-acute care organizations to engage their staff, show residents, family members, and the community at-large their commitment to continuous quality improvement, and achieve national recognition.

For more information on the AHCA/NCAL National Quality Award Program, visit *https://www.ahcancal.org/qualityaward.*

Performance Excellence is a Long-Term Solution

Organizations that expect immediate gains from performance-enhancing systems are likely to be disappointed. It took years to create the culture that exists today; it can take years to change it. Nevertheless, this research, combined with other results, makes a solid business case for using the Integrated Management System—with the *Criteria for Performance Excellence* as its foundation—as the way to create a thriving organization.

High-Performing Organizations

High-performing organizations outrun their competition (or potential competition) by delivering value to stakeholders through an unwavering focus on customers and improved organizational capabilities. Examples of improved capabilities have occurred in all sectors of the economy, not just the private sector. These results range from time and cost savings to customer retention and loyalty.

Many examples exist of significant improvements from using the Integrated Management System and CPE. Through 2020, 134 Award recipients have been selected across six categories: 31 manufacturing companies, 16 service companies, 30 small businesses, 14 education organizations, 29 health care organizations, and 14 nonprofit organizations. Consider the findings of the Baldrige Board of Examiners from the eleven 2019 and 2020 Baldrige Award recipients:

MESA, a 2020 small business category recipient, provides products and services to control or prevent corrosion and to maintain the structural integrity of steel pipelines, storage, and processing facilities that support the nation's energy infrastructure. Products and services are mostly related to an electrochemical form of corrosion control called cathodic protection (CP). Headquartered in Tulsa, OK, MESA's 260 employees generated a 2019 revenue of $90 million.

This is MESA's third Baldrige Award having previously been recognized in 2006 and 2012.

MESA's overall revenue per employee has improved from about $320,000 in 2014 to $370,000 in 2019, nearly $100,000 more than a competitive benchmark. It has also retained 100% of key customers in its Services segment since 2018 and 97% of key customers in its Materials segment from 2017 to 2019. Since 2017, average customer satisfaction for services has trended at more than 4.5 out of 5.

GBMC HealthCare (GBMC), a 2020 health care recipient, provides inpatient and outpatient care through the Greater Baltimore Medical Center, an acute care community hospital, and GBMC Health Partners, which includes 43 primary and specialty care medical practices; and Gilchrist which provides advanced care, elder care, post-acute care, and in-home and facility hospice, as well as inpatient hospice in three locations. GBMC's 4,388 employees and 1,140 volunteers serve at a main hospital campus in Towson, MD, plus 11 practices in Baltimore city and county, and three inpatient hospices. GBMC generates a net patient revenue of $581 million.

The Centers for Medicare and Medicaid Services (BCMW), have awarded GBMC a five-star rating. Its benchmark performance includes 100% of stroke patients receiving antithrombotic therapy at discharge, 100% of high-risk mothers receiving antenatal steroids, and 100% of patients receiving combination chemotherapy for breast cancer.

Wellstar Paulding Hospital (WPH), a 2020 health care recipient, is a community hospital based in Hiram, GA providing inpatient and outpatient care and emergency services through an acute care hospital and two connected medical office buildings. It is part of Wellstar Health System, one of the largest and most integrated health systems in Georgia. WPH had a net patient revenue of $160 million and a workforce of 997 employees (742 clinical, 255 non-clinical/support), 400 physicians, and 105 volunteers.

WPH achieved top 10% performance on several key measures of inpatient and outpatient engagement, including the top 10% mortality index in the national IBM Watson Health Top 100 Hospitals index. Its overall score of 91% on the Great Place To Work Trust Index Survey from team members in FY19 put it in the Fortune 100 Best Companies To Work For benchmark in all participating industries.

AARP, a 2020 nonprofit category recipient, is the nation's largest nonprofit, nonpartisan organization representing people 50 and older to choose how they live as they age. With nearly 38 million members, AARP advocates for health security, financial stability, and personal fulfillment.

In 2018, AARP established the AARP Brain Health Fund to accelerate research into cures for all types of dementia, including Alzheimer's. To spur breakthrough products and services in the marketplace, AARP created the $40 million AARP Innovation Fund to provide capital to innovative companies focused on improving the lives of the 50-plus and their families. In response to the COVID-19 pandemic, the organization launched AARP Community Connections, an online platform that served more than 470,000 users and helped create nearly 800 mutual aid groups in communities nationwide in its first five months of operation in 2020.

Elevations Credit Union, a 2020 nonprofit category recipient, provides Colorado's Front Range with financial solutions and education. In addition to offering a broad portfolio of consumer and business banking services, Elevations is the No. 1 credit union mortgage lender in Colorado. With assets of over $2.7 billion and more than 560 employees, Elevations serves more than 147,000 members from its 14 branches.

This is Elevation's second Baldrige Award, having been recognized in 2014 in the nonprofit category.

In 2018 and 2019, Elevations produced more mortgages annually than any credit union in the state. The American Credit Union Mortgage Association ranked Elevations #11 out of the top 300 credit unions in the nation. For business and commercial loans, production increased from less than $50 million in 2015 to about $175 million in 2019,

Howard Community College (HCC), a 2019 recipient in the education category, is an open-access, public community college offering associate degrees and certificates, as well as workforce development training and continuing education classes. With 2,724 employees, the college educates about 30,000 students annually through a main campus in Columbia, MD, the Laurel College Center in Laurel, MD, and the Ecker Business Training Center in Columbia, MD.

HCC has consistently outperformed its local and national comparators for attainment of associate degrees and certificates by more than 200%. HCC tripled its graduation rates for Black/African American and Hispanic/Latino first-time-to-college students within two years of entry. The graduate placement rate for health sciences students is 100% for seven out of eight of HCC's health sciences programs. HCC's full-time-equivalent enrollment growth, which impacts state funding of the college, is the best in the state over the last 10 years.

Adventist Health White Memorial (AHWM), a 2019 recipient in the health care category, is a private, faith-based, nonprofit, teaching hospital that provides a full range of inpatient, outpatient, emergency, and diagnostic services. Six service lines include general medicine, cardiovascular, surgical, orthopedic, women's services, and emergency services. AHWM, the only "safety-net" hospital in the East Los Angeles community, serves more than 2 million people, most of whom live below the Federal poverty level. The payor mix is 97% Medicaid and Medicare.

AHWM has had zero emergency department returns after outpatient surgery from 2014 to 2018, putting it in the top 10% nationally. AHWM sustained near or perfect performance since 2013—matching the best performance of the American College of Cardiology—for the delivery of evidence-based care for heart-attack patients.

Mary Greeley Medical Center (MGMC), a 2019 recipient in the health care category, opened in 1916 and is now the largest independent medical center in its primary and secondary markets, a 14-county area of central Iowa. It is a public, nonprofit, 220-bed hospital offering inpatient, outpatient, emergency department, home health care, and hospice services.

MGMC's health care results are in the CMS top decile, including 30-day readmissions, 30-day mortality for heart attack patients, incidence of preventable blood clots, compliance with sepsis practices, influenza vaccinations, stroke bundle compliance, and outpatient imaging measures. Inpatient satisfaction, as measured by the Hospital Consumer Assessment of Healthcare Providers and Systems (HCAHPS), has been at or above top-decile performance since 2016. MGMC has been the market share leader in its primary market overall and for inpatient (43%) and outpatient (48%) care since 2015, in spite of being only one-quarter to one-third the size of two of its closest competitors.

Center for Organ Recovery and Education (CORE), a 2019 recipient in the nonprofit category, is located in Pittsburgh, PA. CORE is a nonprofit organ procurement organization (OPO) with a mission to save and heal lives through donation. With a federally designated service area encompassing 5.5 million people in western Pennsylvania, West Virginia, and one county in New York, CORE is one of 58 independent, nonprofit organ procurement organizations designated by CMS,

CORE has maintained performance among the top 10% of the nation's OPOs from 2014 through 2019. For all four of CORE's key customer groups—donor families, transplant centers, corneal transplant surgeons, and tissue processors—results show satisfaction levels above 90%. The satisfaction rate for donor families has been between 95% and 100%. Managing the costs, efficiency, and effectiveness of its operations, led to two on-site operating rooms and research laboratories CORE achieved cost-savings of over $300,000 in 2014, over $600,000 in 2018, and over $2.6 million to date.

City of Germantown, Tennessee, a 2019 recipient in the nonprofit category, is located near the Mississippi River close to Memphis. The City of Germantown has a population of 40,123 and one defining mission: Excellence, every day. The City comprises 19.8 square miles and its key product offerings include education, economic development, public safety, sanitation, and utilities (water and sewer).

Since 1994, the City of Germantown has received the highest possible credit rating from Standard & Poor's and Moody's. Its unemployment rate improved from 6% in 2014 to just about 2.6% in 2018, better than the current U.S. unemployment rate at the time of 3.7%. Earning a net promotor score of 71 in customer engagement in 2018, Germantown consistently exceeded the benchmark of 50, which is considered excellent; over 70 is considered world-class. The community rating for satisfaction with employee ethical behavior was above 93% since 2014 and approached 100% in 2018.

Illinois Municipal Retirement Fund (IMRF), a 2019 recipient in the nonprofit category, is a public-defined benefit pension plan providing services to the employees of units of local government and school districts throughout the state of Illinois (except for the City of Chicago and Cook County). IMRF's main product is money payments to members in response to an event, such as separation from employment, disability, death, or retirement. With $42.7 billion in assets and about 210 employees, IMRF serves 3,010 employers, 176,517 active members, 119,939 inactive members, and 133,261 benefit recipients. The main office is in Oak Brook, IL, with a satellite office in Springfield and eight regional home offices.

IMRF has received a Standard & Poor's "strong" rating since 2017 and is 90% funded; only 16 of the 100 largest U.S. public pension plans are funded at this level. IMRF contributes to societal well-being and the Illinois economy through benefits paid to retired members. The $1.8 billion in benefits paid in 2018 added $2.7 billion in total economic activity in Illinois, and supported the creation of 18,329 jobs.

Recipients prior to 2019 include:

Integrated Project Management Company, 2018 small business

The Alamo Colleges District, 2018 education

Tri County Tech, 2018 education

Memorial Hospital and Health Care Center, 2018 health care

Donor Alliance, 2018 nonprofit

Bristol Tennessee Essential Services, 2017 small business

Stellar Solutions, 2017 small business

Adventist Health Castle, 2017 health care

Southcentral Foundation, 2017 health care

City of Fort Collins, Colorado, 2017 nonprofit

Don Chalmers Ford, 2016 small business

Momentum Group, 2016 small business

Kindred Nursing and Rehabilitation – Mountain Valley (now Mountain Valley of Cascadia), 2016 health care

Memorial Hermann Sugar Land Hospital, 2016 health care

MidwayUSA, 2015 small business

Charter School of San Diego, 2015 education

Charleston Area Medical Center Health System, 2015 health care

Mid-America Transplant, 2015 nonprofit

PricewaterhouseCoopers Public Sector Practice, 2014 service

Hill Country Memorial, 2014 health care

St. David's HealthCare, 2014 health care

Elevations Credit Union, 2014 nonprofit

Pewaukee School District, 2013 education

Sutter Davis Hospital, 2013 health care

Lockheed Martin Missiles and Fire Control, 2012 manufacturing

MESA Products, 2012 and 2006 small business

North Mississippi Health Services, 2012 health care

City of Irving, Irving, Texas, 2012 nonprofit

Concordia Publishing House, 2011 nonprofit

Schneck Medical Center, 2011 health care

Henry Ford Health System, 2011 health care

Southcentral Foundation, 2011 health care

MEDRAD, 2010 and 2003 manufacturing

Nestlé Purina PetCare, 2010 manufacturing

Freese and Nichols, 2010 small business

K&N Management, 2010 small business

Studer Group, 2010 small business

Advocate Good Samaritan Hospital, 2010 health care

Montgomery County Public Schools, 2010 education

Honeywell Federal Manufacturing & Technologies, 2009 manufacturing

MidwayUSA, 2015 and 2009 small business

AtlantiCare, 2009 health care

Heartland Health, 2009 health care

Veterans Affairs Cooperative Studies Program Clinical Research Pharmacy Coordinating Center, 2009 nonprofit

Cargill Corn Milling North America, 2008 manufacturing

Poudre Valley Health System, 2008 health care

Iredell-Statesville Schools, 2008 education

PRO-TEC Coating Company, 2007 small business

Mercy Health System, 2007 health care

Sharp HealthCare, 2007 health care

City of Coral Springs, 2007 nonprofit

U.S. Army Armament Research, Development and Engineering Center, 2007 nonprofit

Premier, 2006 service

North Mississippi Medical Center, 2006 health care

Sunny Fresh Foods (now Cargill Kitchen Solutions), 2005 manufacturing and 1999 small business

DynMcDermott Petroleum Operations, 2005 service

Park Place Lexus, 2005 small business

Richland College, 2005 education

Jenks Public Schools, 2005 education

The Bama Companies, 2004 manufacturing

Bronson Methodist Hospital, 2005 health care

Texas Nameplate Company, 2004 and 1998 small business

Kenneth W. Monfort College of Business, 2004 education

Robert Wood Johnson University Hospital Hamilton, 2004 health care

Boeing Aerospace Support, 2003 service

Caterpillar Financial Services Corporation U.S., 2003 service

Stoner Solutions, 2003 small business

Community Consolidated School District 15, 2003 education

Baptist Hospital, 2003 health care

Saint Luke's Hospital of Kansas City, 2003 health care

Motorola Commercial, Government, and Industrial Solutions Sector, 2002 manufacturing

Branch-Smith Printing Division, 2002 small business

Sisters of Saint Mary Health Care, 2002 health care

Clarke American Checks, 2001 manufacturing

Chugach School District, 2001 education

The Pearl River School District, 2001 education

The University of Wisconsin-Stout Campus, 2001 education

Pal's Sudden Service, 2001 small business

Dana Corporation, Spicer Driveshaft Division, 2000 manufacturing

KARLEE Company, 2000 manufacturing

Los Alamos National Bank, 2000 small business

Operations Management International, 2000 service

BI, 1999 service (a training organization)

STMicroelectronics, 1999 manufacturing

The Ritz-Carlton Hotel Company (now part of Marriott International), service 1999 and 1992

Boeing Airlift and Tanker, 1998 manufacturing

Solar Turbines, 1998 manufacturing

3M Dental Products Division, 1997 manufacturing

Merrill Lynch Credit Corporation, 1997 service

Solectron Corporation, 1997 and 1991 manufacturing

Xerox Business Services, 1997 service

Custom Research, 1996 small business

ADAC Laboratories of California, 1996 manufacturing

Dana Commercial Credit Corporation, 1996 service

Trident Precision Manufacturing, 1996 small business

Armstrong World Industries, Building Products Operations, 1995 manufacturing

Corning, Telecommunications Products Division, 1995 manufacturing

AT&T Consumer Communications Services (now Consumer Markets Division), 1994 service

Verizon Information Services (formerly GTE Directories Corporation), 1994 service

Wainwright Industries, 1994 manufacturing

Ames Rubber, 1993 small business

Eastman Chemical Company, 1993 manufacturing

AT&T Network Systems Group, Transmissions System Business Unit, 1992 manufacturing

AT&T Universal Card Services (now part of Citigroup), 1992 service

Granite Rock Company, 1992 small business

Texas Instruments, Defense Systems and Electronics Group, 1992 manufacturing

Marlow Industries, 1991 small business

Zytec Corporation (now part of Artesyn Technologies), 1991 manufacturing

Cadillac Motor Car Company, 1990 manufacturing

Federal Express Corporation, 1990 service

IBM Rochester, 1990 manufacturing

Wallace Company, 1990 small business

Milliken and Company, 1989 manufacturing

Xerox Corporation, Business Products and Systems, 1989 manufacturing

Globe Metallurgical, 1988 small business

Motorola, 1988 manufacturing

Westinghouse Electric Corporation, Commercial Nuclear Fuel Division, 1988 manufacturing

THE INTEGRATED COMPONENTS OF OPTIMUM PERFORMANCE

Clearly, in today's highly competitive economy, past success means nothing. Desire, without disciplined and appropriate action, also means nothing. However, it is just as clear that implementing a disciplined approach to performance excellence based on the Baldrige Criteria produces winning levels of performance. The key to the success of the Baldrige Criteria has been the identification of the key drivers of high performance. The Baldrige Performance Excellence Program within NIST ensures that *each element of the Baldrige Criteria is necessary, and that together they are sufficient to achieve the highest levels of performance.* Many management practices of the past have proven to be valuable ingredients of high performance, such as Six Sigma techniques. However, taken piecemeal, these practices *by themselves* have not been sufficient to achieve optimum performance. *See Online Resources: Baldrige, Six Sigma, Lean, and Balanced Scorecard Alignment.*

Achieving top levels of performance requires that each component of the organization's management system be integrated and optimized. In many ways, optimizing the performance of an organization's management system is like making an award-winning cake. Too much or too little of any key ingredient suboptimizes the system. For example, a cake may require eggs, flour, sugar, butter, and cocoa. A cake also requires a specific level of heat for a certain time to bake properly. Too little or too much of any ingredient, including oven temperature, and the system (in this case the cake) fails to achieve desired results. One could argue that to be successful, the cake must contain all of the necessary elements (ingredients) and those elements must be complete and properly assembled (sufficient work processes) to achieve the desired taste (level of excellence). Optimum Outcomes = Necessary and Sufficient.

The same principle applies in an organization. A successful organization requires a strong customer focus, engaged workers, efficient work processes, fact-based decision-making, clear direction, and continuous improvement and innovation. Organizations that do not focus on all of these elements find that their performance suffers. Focusing on only a few of the required ingredients, such as work process improvements or training to improve worker skills, may be necessary but not sufficient to drive high levels of performance.

The following figures depict the elements that are both necessary and sufficient to achieve high levels of performance in any organization or part of an organization—an Integrated Management System. The elements apply to any managed enterprise, regardless of size, sector, product, or service.

Get Results, Produce Value. (Figure 4) In the first place, for organizations, teams, or individuals to stay in business (or keep a job) for any length of time, they must produce desired results. The work results must be valued. History has demonstrated that people, organizations, or even governments that failed to deliver value eventually went away or were overturned. Value can be measured in a variety of ways, including fitness for use, return on assets, profitability, reliability, and durability, to name a few.

Engaged Customers. (Figure 5) Understand and meet their requirements—engage them as advocates. We have learned that it makes no difference if the producer of the goods or services believes they are valuable if the customer or user of the goods or services

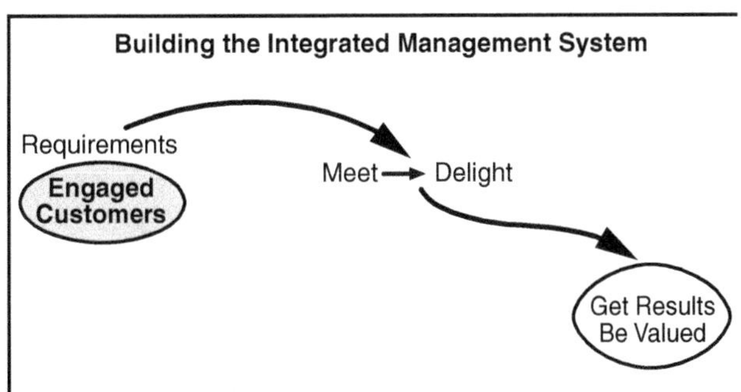

Figure 4 Get results, produce value.

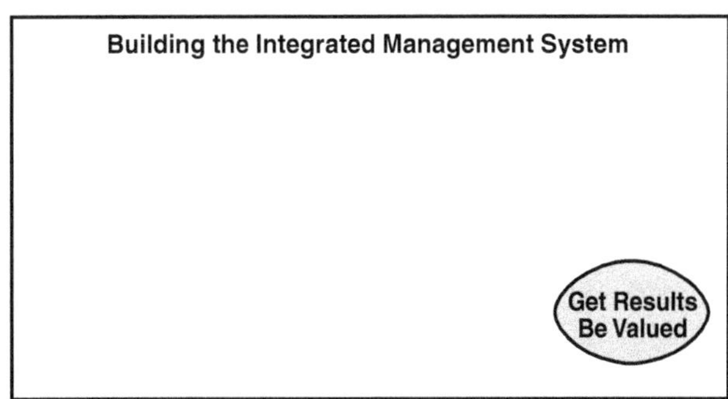

Figure 5 Customer requirements.

believes they are not. The customer is the best entity to legitimately judge the value of the goods or services that suppliers produce. It is the customers who finally decide whether the organization, team, or government organization continues to stay in business.

Imagine that you go to a restaurant, order seafood, and find that it tastes awful. Upon complaining about the bad-tasting meal, you are not impressed with the chef's claim that "only the finest ingredients were used." It also does not help if the chef claims that he likes the taste of the fish. It still tastes bad to you. At this juncture the restaurant has an opportunity to recover customer confidence and build loyalty to better engage the customer. Unless the chef is willing to make an adjustment, you are not going to be satisfied and are unlikely to return. If enough customers find the food or service offensive and do not return, the restaurant goes out of business. On the other hand, by properly managing the complaint and taking steps to promptly resolve the problem *to the satisfaction of the customer,* the restaurant can not only recover but enhance loyalty and better engage its customers so they become active supporters.

Accordingly, it is very important for the organization to obtain feedback from the customers after they have had an opportunity to experience its products or services. The failure to understand the requirements of the customers may cause the organization to deliver the wrong thing, creating customer dissatisfaction, delay, or lower value. Every time our organizations fail to meet customer requirements, value suffers. To consistently produce value, organizations must accurately determine the requirements of their customers and consistently meet those requirements and, if possible, exceed expectations. This creates the initial value chain that provides the competitive advantage for any organization or part of an organization.

To ensure that the customer is satisfied and likely to return (or recommend a service or product to others), it is important to determine if the customer received appropriate value. If the customer is dissatisfied, you have an opportunity to correct the problem and still maintain customer loyalty. In any case, it is important to remember that it is the customer and not the marketing, engineering, or manufacturing departments or the service provider that ultimately judges value received and determines satisfaction.

Engaged Workers. (Figure 6) Engaged workers are key to the next part of the Integrated Management System to ensure optimum performance and value. In any organization or part of an organization, people do the work that produces customer value. As described previously, if the work is not focused on customer requirements, customers may be dissatisfied. To satisfy customers, work may have to be redone, adding cost and suboptimizing value. To optimize output and value, people doing the work must have the willingness and desire to work. The best workers contribute their *utmost* for the success of the organization and its customers. Disgruntled, disaffected, unwilling workers hurt productivity.

However, *motivated workers* means more than simply possessing the willingness to work. Workers must also possess the knowledge and skills to carry out their jobs effectively. The pace of change is accelerating, and with it, knowledge demands are increasing. As new knowledge is created at an accelerating rate, it is more critical than ever to have effective training systems in place to ensure workers stay current and can effectively apply the new knowledge.

In addition, to optimize output, people must be free from bureaucratic barriers and arbitrary restrictions that inhibit work. Every minute that work is delayed while waiting for an unnecessary approval adds cost but not value. Every minute that work has to be redone because of sloppy performance of a coworker adds cost but not value. Every minute that work has to be redone because of inadequate knowledge or ability adds cost but not value.

Remember that one person cannot produce optimum levels of performance. However, one person can prevent optimum levels of performance, and may not

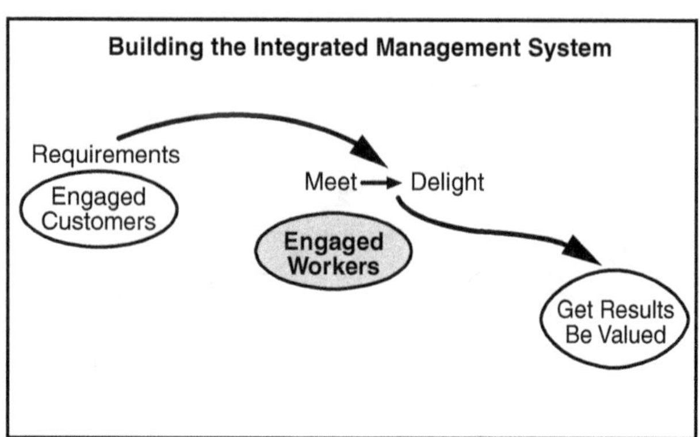

Figure 6 Engaged, motivated people.

be aware that he or she is doing so. The question that should concern management is, "In your organization, how many people are disgruntled, discouraged, underskilled, or prevented from working effectively so that they suboptimize the organization's performance?"

Efficient Processes. (Figure 7) Even the most highly skilled, knowledgeable, and willing workers will fail to optimize value if asked to do stupid things. Over time, even the most efficient processes can become suboptimal and inefficient. Business process Lean and Six Sigma improvement techniques have been seen by some as panaceas for organizational optimization. Certainly these tools allow organizations to redesign and quickly eliminate much of the bureaucratic silliness and inefficiency that grow up over time. However, how long does it take for the newly improved process to lose efficiency relative to newer, more innovative approaches? Even new processes must be evaluated periodically and improved or they eventually become suboptimal and obsolete. Ensuring that processes are optimal requires ongoing, fact-based evaluation and meaningful improvement.

Every process in the organization has the potential for increasing or decreasing the value provided to customers. Obviously, key work processes are perhaps the most important. However, the core processes of an organization frequently are disrupted because of failed support processes or supplier failure. For example, production can come to a halt if key components from the procurement office are not available on time. Production can also be disrupted if key workers who were supposed to be provided by the human resources office are not available. Performance suffers if the transportation provider is always late.

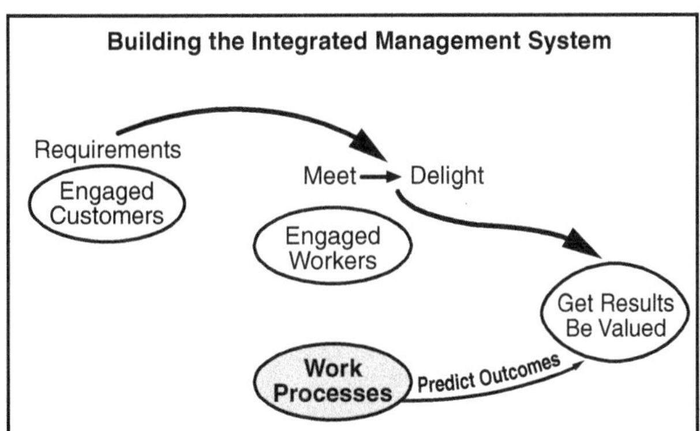

Figure 7 Efficient, effective processes.

As previously discussed, failures must be addressed promptly to satisfy customers. Fixing a problem constitutes rework. Any time an organization engages in rework, value for the customer is suboptimized. To make matters worse, if the need to engage in rework is not discovered until the product or service is complete, the cost of correction is higher, driving value lower. It is important, therefore, to uncover potential problems as early as possible, rather than wait for the end result to determine if the product or service is satisfactory. To uncover potential problems early we must be able to predict the outcomes of our work processes. This requires *in-process* measures. Through the use of these measures, organizations can determine if the product or service is likely to meet expectations. Consider the two examples that follow:

- Example one: A customer comes to the *Wait-And-See* coffee shop and orders a cup of coffee. The coffee is poured and delivered to the customer. The customer promptly takes a sip and informs the server that the coffee is too cold, too bitter, too weak, and has a harsh aroma. Furthermore, the customer complains that it took too long for the coffee to be served. The server, in an effort to satisfy the customer, discards the original coffee, brews a fresh pot, and delivers a new cup of coffee to the customer at no additional charge. This problem happens frequently. As a result, the *Wait-And-See* coffee shop has been forced to raise the price of coffee in order to stay in business and has noticed that fewer customers are willing to pay the higher price. Many customers have stopped coming to this coffee shop entirely. The customers that continue to buy coffee from this shop are subsidizing the sloppy performance and poor quality.
- Example two: To increase the likelihood that its customers will like the coffee it serves, the *In-Process-Measure* coffee shop has asked its customers key questions about the quality of coffee and service that they expect. The *In-Process-Measure* coffee shop has determined through testing and surveys that its customers like coffee served hot (between 170° and 180° Farenheit); not too bitter or acidic (pH > 7.4); strong, but

not too strong (75 grams of super-fine grind per liter of filtered water); and fresh (served within five minutes of brewing). By checking these measures, this coffee shop can predict that nearly all customers will be satisfied with the quality and service it delivers. Since the *In-Process-Measure* coffee shop can consistently deliver coffee within these customer-defined specifications, its customers like the coffee. No rework is required, no coffee is discarded, the price is lower, the value is higher, the store is profitable, and it is taking customers from the *Wait-And-See* coffee shop down the street.

Data and Dashboard to Monitor Progress. (Figure 8) Data and information help the organization and its workers make better decisions about their work. This enables them to spot problems more quickly and take prompt actions to improve performance and correct or minimize non-value-added costs. Without appropriate measures, organizations and their workers must rely on intuition to determine whether customers are likely to be satisfied and willing to return.

One of the problems in basing decisions on intuition or best guesses is that it produces highly variable decisions. The guess of one worker is unlikely to be consistent with the guess of another. Appropriate data, therefore, are critical to increase decision-making consistency and accuracy. For data to be used correctly to support decision-making, organizations must develop a system to manage, collect, analyze, and display the results.

If the data that drive decision-making are not accurate or reliable, effective decision-making suffers. More mistakes are made, costs increase, and value is suboptimized again. Furthermore, in the absence of relevant data and supporting analyses, leaders are generally unwilling to allow subordinates to substitute their intuition for that of the leader. As a result, decisions tend to get pulled to higher and higher levels in an organization, further suboptimizing the contribution of workers who are generally closest to and know the most about the work they do. Failure to fully utilize the talents of workers, as discussed previously, further reduces efficiency and morale, hurts engagement, and suboptimizes value production.

The system described in Figure 8, which includes engaged customers, engaged workers, efficient processes, and a dashboard to monitor progress leading to desired results and value, applies to any managed enterprise. It applies to whole corporations as well as departments, divisions, teams, and individual work.

The system applies to schools, classrooms, government agencies, and health care organizations. In each case, to produce optimal value, the requirements of customers must be understood and met. Workers must be motivated, possess the skill and knowledge needed to do their work, and be free from distractions in order to contribute their utmost. The organization must develop efficient work processes and monitor effectiveness of work to make adjustments in an effort to maximize value.

Leadership. (Figure 9) What makes an organization unique is the direction that top leaders set for it. Leaders must understand the requirements and expectations of customers and the marketplace to decide what direction is necessary to achieve success.

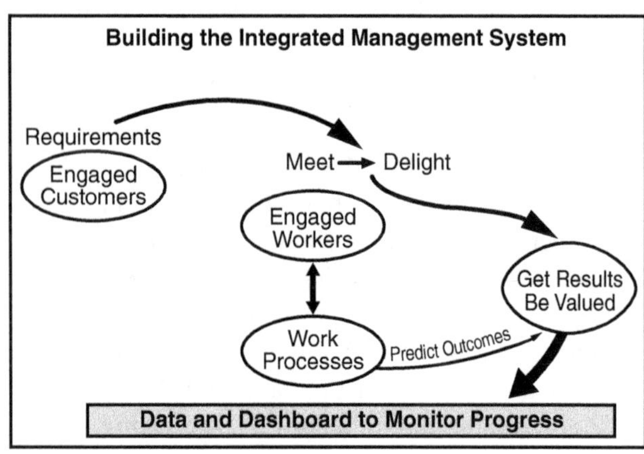

Figure 8 Information and data dashboard.

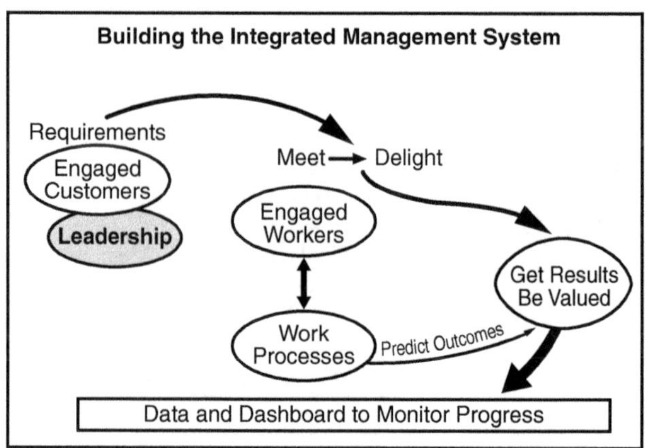

Figure 9 Leadership.

However, it is not enough simply to understand customer requirements and expectations. Leaders must also understand organizational capabilities and the capacity and capabilities of the workforce, partners, and suppliers of critical goods and services. Leaders should reinforce an organizational culture that fosters workforce engagement, equity and inclusion, and produces organizational agility and resilience.

Leaders should be the driving force for organizational excellence, and for leading the transformation that may be required to change the culture and the structure of the organization. They should serve as role models of excellence, communicate effectively, and instill a spirit for innovation and continuous improvement throughout the organization.

Strategy. (Figure 10) Effective leaders use the process of strategy development to determine the most appropriate direction for the organization and identify the levels of performance in key areas that are critical for success (goals and objectives). Strategic objectives must define, in outcome-oriented terms, what the organization must actually achieve to be successful in the future. Once strategic direction and strategic objectives are defined, leaders identify the people and the processes that must be in place to produce desired results and be valued by customers. Leaders must then communicate with the workforce, suppliers, partners, and customers to make certain everyone understands and supports the desired direction and actions.

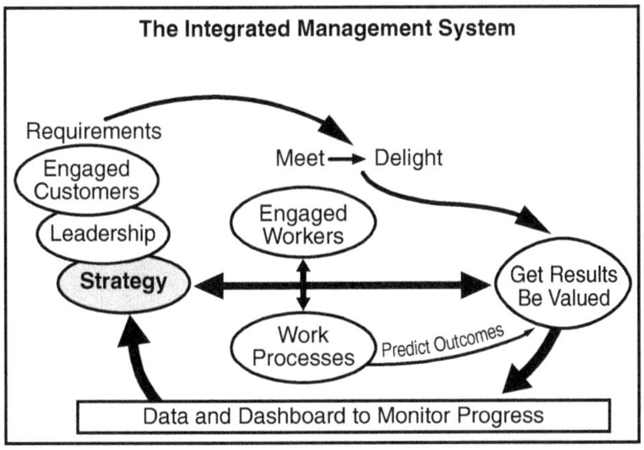

If leaders are not clear about the strategy and actions that must be taken to be successful, they force subordinates to substitute their own ideas about the proper direction and actions. This creates inefficiency within an organization. People come to work and want to be successful. Without direction from the top, they will still work hard but often at cross-purposes. Unless everyone is pulling in the same direction, processes, products, and services will not be optimized and value to customers will be reduced.

The Importance of the Integrated Management System. An effective and powerful Integrated Management System is holistic. We cannot eliminate a single part of this management system and still expect to produce optimum value. Each part is *necessary*. Furthermore, studies repeatedly demonstrate that when these processes are integrated and used to manage work, they are *sufficient* to achieve high levels of performance. Imagine what might happen if one or more of the pieces of the Integrated Management System described previously were missing. Table 1 on the next page provides some suggestions.

Figure 10 Strategy development and execution.

Table 1 Consequences of missing integrated management system elements.

MISSING ELEMENT	ADVERSE CONSEQUENCE LEADING TO MISSING ELEMENT
Systems to understand customer requirements and expectations	Designing, building, and delivering an unsatisfactory product or service. Adds delay. Increases cost due to rework. Wastes resources on low-priority work that does not optimize customer value.
Poor worker skills, minimal initiative or self-direction, a lack of fairness, equity, and inclusion in the workforce	Limited expansion opportunities. Unable to keep up with changing technology. Requires close monitoring. Difficulty in finding better ways to carry out work. Some workforce members feel they do not have the same opportunities as others. Ultimately reduces morale, motivation, and performance.
Data about customer engagement, satisfaction, key-process performance, and overall organizational performance do not exist or are incomplete	Makes it difficult to engage workers in decision-making about their work. Forces decisions to be made at higher levels, usually on the basis of intuition or guesswork. Reduces decision accuracy and increases incorrect decisions. Makes it difficult to allocate resources appropriately or determine the best use of limited resources. Makes accountability difficult to manage.
Leaders do not clearly set direction, performance expectations, vision, or values	Causes subordinates to invent their own ideas and substitute them for a common set of performance expectations, vision, and values. Creates significant inefficiencies as people throughout the organization begin to work at cross-purposes, suboptimizing organizational performance. Makes it difficult to establish accountability for achieving results.
Plans do not contain measurable outcome-oriented objectives and a timeline for accomplishing each objective	Leaders, managers, and employees do not know what level of performance is expected at any given time, making it difficult or impossible to effectively monitor progress.
Leaders do not make it clear that customers are the key to success—they do not create a focus on customers or a customer culture	If managers and employees do not focus on customers, they become internally focused. Managers, engineers, or marketers drive the business, not customers. Customers and their requirements lose importance.
Top leaders do not encourage employees to develop and use their full potential	Employee engagement and satisfaction become optional. Some managers encourage employee participation, innovation, and creativity; most do not. The organization risks losing its best employees to competitors, and gets suboptimal performance from those who stay.
Customer comments and complaints are not encouraged. If a complaint is received it is not resolved promptly. The root cause of complaints is not identified.	Failure to capture customer comments and complaints, identify the root causes of the complaints, and work to prevent the problems from happening again makes it difficult to learn about problems quickly and dooms the organization to repeat its failures. Failure to resolve complaints promptly increases customer dissatisfaction and reduces loyalty.
Poor two-way communication exists between leaders and employees	Unclear top-down communication makes it difficult to ensure alignment and focus throughout the organization, reducing teamwork and increasing bureaucratic stagnation. Poor upward communication maintains organizational fragmentation and prevents problems and barriers to effective work from being discussed and resolved.

THE CORE VALUES TO ACHIEVE PERFORMANCE EXCELLENCE

The Criteria are built upon a set of interrelated core values and concepts, which are embedded beliefs and behaviors found in high-performing organizations. They are the foundation for integrating performance excellence elements that create a basis for action and feedback within a results-oriented framework. *If an organization aspires to be represented by the core values and concepts, then the Baldrige Criteria are the "road map" to help them get there.*

The 2021–2022 Core Values and Concepts follow. The text in the box presents the text of the Baldrige core values and concepts as presented in the Baldrige Framework.

Systems Perspective

Taken together, the Baldrige Criteria promote a systems perspective and define the processes required to achieve optimal organizational performance. As with any viable system, we cannot ignore part of the system and still expect it to perform at peak levels. When part of a well-functioning system begins to underperform or work in a manner that is inconsistent with system requirements, the performance of the whole system suffers.

The same is true of a management system. If leaders are ambiguous, if plans are not clear, if work processes are not consistent, if people are not able to do the work they are asked to do, and if it is difficult to keep track of progress and make appropriate adjustments, it will be impossible for the organization to achieve optimum levels of performance. For most of the twentieth century, a long list of management gurus suggested a variety of quick and simple remedies to enhance organizational performance. By itself, each quick fix ultimately failed. From that, we learned that no single solution is sufficient to optimize performance in a complex system. Leaders who approach management from a systems perspective are more likely to optimize organizational performance than leaders who continue to take a piecemeal approach to organizational management. There is no simple solution to achieve high performance.

There are always better ways to do things. The challenge is to find them, but we are not likely to find them alone. We must create an environment—a work climate where better ways will be sought out, recognized, and put in place by everyone.

Systems Perspective

A systems perspective means managing all the components of your organization as a unified whole to achieve your mission, ongoing success, and performance excellence. A systems perspective also means managing your organization within the context of an interconnected ecosystem of organizations that presents opportunities for new and possibly innovative relationships.

Successfully managing overall organizational performance requires realization of your organization as a system with interdependent operations. Organization-specific synthesis, alignment, and integration make the internal system successful. Synthesis means understanding your organization as a whole. It incorporates key business attributes, including your core competencies, strategic objectives, action plans, work systems, and workforce needs. Alignment means using key organizational linkages to ensure consistency of plans, processes, measures, and actions. Integration builds on alignment, so that the individual components of your performance management system operate in a fully interconnected, unified, and mutually beneficial manner to deliver anticipated results.

In addition, your organization exists within a business ecosystem—a network of organizations, including your partners, suppliers, collaborators, competitors, customers, communities, and other relevant organizations inside and outside your sector or industry. Within this larger system, roles between organizations may be fluid as opportunities arise and needs change. For your business ecosystem, synthesis means understanding your organization as part of a larger whole. It incorporates the key attributes that you contribute to and need from your partners, collaborators, competitors, customers, communities, and other relevant organizations, including those not traditionally considered as collaborators.

These concepts are depicted in the Baldrige Criteria overview. When your organization takes a systems perspective, your senior leaders focus on strategic directions and customers.

Continued

Continued

Your senior leaders monitor, respond to, and manage performance based on your results. With a systems perspective, you use your measures, indicators, core competencies, and organizational knowledge to build your key strategies, link these strategies with your work systems and key processes, manage risk, and align your resources to improve your overall performance and your focus on customers and stakeholders. The core values and concepts, the seven Criteria Categories, and the scoring guidelines are the system's building blocks and integrating mechanism.

Visionary Leadership

Every system, strategy, and method for achieving excellence must be guided by visionary leadership:

- *Effective leaders convey a strong sense of urgency to counter the natural resistance to change that can prevent the organization from taking the steps that these core values for success demand.*
- Leaders make it clear that following these values is not optional.
- Such leaders serve as enthusiastic role models, reinforcing and communicating the core values by their words and actions.
- The actions of great leaders match their words.

Visionary Leadership

Your organization's senior leaders should set a vision for the organization, create a customer focus, demonstrate clear and visible organizational values and ethics, and set high expectations for the workforce. The vision, values, and expectations should balance the needs of all your stakeholders. Your leaders should also ensure the creation of strategies, systems, and methods for building knowledge and capabilities, empowering the workforce, capitalizing on diversity, stimulating innovation, managing risk, ensuring resilience, requiring accountability, achieving performance excellence, and thereby ensuring ongoing organizational success.

The values and strategies leaders define should help guide all of your organization's activities and decisions. Senior leaders should inspire and encourage your entire workforce to contribute, to develop and learn, to be innovative, and to embrace meaningful change. Senior leaders should be responsible to your organization's governance body for their actions and performance, and the governance body should be responsible ultimately to all your stakeholders for your organization's and its senior leaders' ethics, actions, and performance.

Senior leaders should serve as role models through their ethical behavior and their personal involvement in planning, providing a supportive environment for innovation, communicating, coaching and motivating the workforce, developing future leaders, recognizing workforce members, promoting equity and inclusion, and reviewing organizational performance. Senior leaders should demonstrate authenticity and admit to their missteps and opportunities for improvement. As role models, they can reinforce ethics, values, and expectations while building leadership, commitment, and initiative throughout your organization.

Customer-Focused Excellence

This value demonstrates a passion for making the organization customer-driven. Without loyal customers, little else matters. Customers are the final judges of how well the organization did its job, and what they say matters. It is their perception of services and products that will determine whether they remain loyal or constantly seek better providers:

- The organization must focus on systematically listening to customers and acting quickly on what they say.
- The organization must build positive relationships with its customers through focusing on accessibility and management of complaints.
- Dissatisfied customers must be heeded most closely, for they often deliver the most insightful information.
- If only satisfied and loyal customers (those who continue to do business with us no matter what) receive attention, the organization will be led

astray. The most successful organizations keep an eye on customers who are not satisfied and work to understand their preferences and meet their demands.

Customer-Focused Excellence

Your customers are the ultimate judges of your performance and the quality of your products and services. Thus, your organization must consider all product and service features and characteristics, all modes of customer access and support, and all organizational values and behaviors that contribute value to your customers. Such behavior leads to customer acquisition, satisfaction, preference, trust, and loyalty; positive referrals; and, ultimately, the ongoing success of your business. Customer-focused excellence has both current and future components: understanding today's customer desires and anticipating future customer desires and marketplace potential.

Many factors may influence value and satisfaction over the course of your customers' experience with your organization. These factors include your organization's customer relationship management, which helps build trust, confidence, and loyalty.

Customer-focused excellence means much more than reducing defects and errors, merely meeting specifications, or reducing complaints. Nevertheless, these factors contribute to your customers' view of your organization and thus are also important parts of customer-focused excellence. In addition, your success in recovering from defects, service errors, and mistakes; fostering equity and inclusion; adapting to disruptions; and safeguarding customer information is crucial for retaining customers and engaging them for the long term.

A customer-focused organization addresses not only the product and service characteristics that meet basic customer requirements but also those unique features and characteristics that differentiate the organization from competitors. This differentiation may be based on accelerated product development, innovative or customized offerings or customer experience, combinations of product and service offerings, price, societal contributions, or special relationships. These might include participation in alliances or collaborative, multilateral networks (ecosystems) of organizations that drive efficiency, effectiveness, and innovation.

Customer-focused excellence is thus a strategic concept. It is directed toward customer acquisition, retention and loyalty, stronger brand recognition, market share gain, and growth. It demands constant sensitivity to changing and emerging customer and market requirements and to the factors that drive customer engagement. It demands close attention to the voice of the customer. It demands anticipating changes in the marketplace. Therefore, customer-focused excellence demands a customer-focused culture and organizational agility.

Valuing People

Organizations must invest in their people to ensure they have the skills for today and the ability to do what is necessary to succeed in the future. *Learning must be a part of every worker's performance plan and daily work. Improving work processes should be expected of all workers.* This core value has broadened from employee participation and development to valuing workers, partners, collaborators, volunteers, and interns. In high-performing organizations, the people who do the work of the organization should make most of the decisions about how their work is done. A significant barrier exists, however, that limits worker decision-making—lack of access to data and poor data-based decision-making skills.

Organizations cannot effectively push decision-making down to the level where most of the work is done unless those doing the work have access to the necessary data and are skilled at analyzing the data and making fact-based decisions. As mentioned previously, leaders are unwilling to let subordinates make decisions based on intuition—they generally reserve that type of decision for themselves. Access to data and developing skills to manage by fact are prerequisites for optimizing workforce contributions to the organization's success.

Valuing People

An organization's success depends on an engaged workforce that benefits from meaningful work, clear organizational direction, the opportunity to

Continued

Continued

learn, and accountability for performance. That workforce must also have a safe, trusting, and cooperative environment. The successful organization has a culture of equity and inclusion that capitalizes on the diverse backgrounds and characteristics, knowledge, skills, creativity, and motivation of its workforce, partners, and collaborators. Promoting equity means ensuring that all customers and workforce members are treated fairly and that all workforce members can reach their full potential. Inclusion refers to empowering participation and promoting a sense of belonging. The successful organization also values all people who have a stake in the organization, including customers, community members, stockholders, and other people affected by the organization's actions.

Valuing the people in your workforce means committing to their engagement, development, and well-being. Major challenges in valuing your workforce members include (1) demonstrating your leaders' commitment to their success; (2) providing motivation and recognition that go beyond the regular compensation system; (3) supporting work-life balance through flexible work practices tailored to varying workplace and life needs; (4) creating an inclusive, equitable environment for a diverse workforce; (5) offering development and progression within your organization; (6) providing support during disruptions and transitions; (7) sharing your organization's knowledge so that your workforce can better serve your customers and contribute to achieving your strategic objectives; (8) creating an environment that encourages intelligent risk taking to achieve innovation; and (9) developing a system of workforce and organizational accountability for performance. With increased remote work, an additional challenge is ensuring that a geographically dispersed workforce benefits from meaningful work, clear organizational direction, the opportunity to learn, and accountability for performance.

The success of your workforce members—including your leaders—depends on their having opportunities to learn. This learning includes preparing people for future organizational core competencies. On-the-job training offers a cost-effective way to cross-train and to link training more closely to your organization's capacity needs and priorities. If your organization relies on volunteers, their personal development and learning are also important to consider.

To accomplish their overall goals, successful organizations build and value ecosystems of internal and external partnerships and collaborative, multilateral alliances. Internal partnerships might include collaboration between labor and management. Forming internal partnerships might also involve creating network relationships among people across work units and locations, or between employees and volunteers to improve flexibility, responsiveness, learning, and knowledge sharing. As products and services become more and more multidisciplinary, organizations may need new business models and ecosystems, including nontraditional partnerships with competitors or organizations outside the sector, alliances, consortia, and value networks.

Agility and Resilience

Agility is a value usually driven by customer requirements and the desire to improve operating efficiency and lower costs:

- Organizations that develop the capacity to improve faster by eliminating activities and tasks that do not add value find that productivity increases, costs go down, and customers are more satisfied, engaged, and loyal.
- To improve work processes, organizations must focus on improving design quality and preventing problems. The cost of preventing problems and building quality into products and services is significantly less than the cost of taking corrective action later.
- Use information concerning customer preference, competitors' products, cost and pricing, marketplace profiles, and research and development (R&D) to optimize the process from the start and avoid delay and rework.
- Organizational resilience is more apt to be evident in an organization that demonstrates agility. The ability to respond quickly to business disruptions is usually supported by plans to be implemented in the event of emergencies, disasters, or pandemics.
- Plans take into account the workforce, customers, supply network, and other stakeholders impacted by and needing to be a part of a coordinated response to disruptions.

Agility and Resilience

Success in today's ever-changing, globally competitive environment demands agility and organizational resilience. Agility requires a capacity for rapid change and for flexibility in operations. Organizational resilience is the ability to anticipate, prepare for, and recover from disasters, emergencies, and other disruptions, and—when disruptions occur—to protect and enhance workforce and customer engagement, supply-network and financial performance, organizational productivity, and community well-being. Resilience includes the agility to modify plans, processes, and relationships whenever circumstances warrant.

Organizations face ever-shorter cycles for introducing new or improved products and services and for responding rapidly to new or emerging issues. Organizations must be capable of managing risk and making changes on an ever-shorter cycle time. Major improvements in response times often require new work systems; rapid decision-making; reduced bureaucracy; the simplification of work processes; agile, efficient supplier and partner networks; effective, efficient communication with the workforce, partners, and suppliers; and the ability for rapid changeover from one process or one location to another.

All aspects of time performance are now more critical, and cycle time is a key process measure. Other important benefits can be derived from this focus on time; time improvements often drive simultaneous improvements or changes in your work systems, organization, quality, cost, supply-network integration, productivity, and ongoing success in a challenging economy. A major success factor in meeting competitive challenges is design-to-introduction time (the time it takes to initiate a product or service feature) or innovation cycle time. To meet the demands of rapidly changing markets, your organization needs to carry out stage-to-stage integration of activities from research or concept to commercialization or implementation.

Disruptive events are occurring more frequently, triggered by economic upheaval or stress, major weather or health events, social or societal demands, or innovative technologies or product introductions. For an organization to be resilient, leaders must cultivate the agility to anticipate opportunities and threats, adapt strategy to changing circumstances, and have robust governance with a culture of trust. Organizations must embrace data-rich thought processes and equip their employees with ongoing learning of new skills.

Agility and resilience can also be achieved through your business ecosystem, in which collaborations, strategic partnerships, or alliances might offer complementary core competencies that allow rapid response to disruptions, entry into new markets, or a rethinking of customer offerings in a larger context. Your ecosystem might also permit you to address common issues quickly by blending your organization's core competencies or leadership capabilities with other organizations' complementary strengths and capabilities, creating a new source of strategic advantage. The result may be broad, interdependent, agile ecosystems that include traditional partners and collaborators, as well as competitors, customers, communities, and organizations outside your sector or industry.

Organizational Learning

A potent value to promote long-term success is organizational learning. High-performing organizations are learning organizations—their culture embeds evaluation and improvement in everything they do. As more organizations make improvements in more aspects of operations, speed and agility of improvements and innovation will set the best ahead of the rest. The best will continue to get better at getting better:

- A culture of continuous improvement and the related value of innovation is essential to maintaining and sustaining true competitive advantage.
- With systematic and continuous organizational improvement, time becomes a powerful ally. As time passes, the organization grows stronger and smarter.
- Without systematic improvement and ongoing learning, time is an enemy; organizations will ultimately decline and face extinction.
- *Leaders embed this value by linking rewards, recognition, and incentives for workers, supervisors, and managers at all levels to evaluation, improvement, and innovation. Otherwise, people will not think continuous meaningful improvement is important.*

- Personal learning through training, education, and experience that is shared widely becomes organizational learning. Individuals can improve processes they own, but maximum organizational benefit does not occur unless these learnings (improvements) are shared and adopted throughout the organization. It is critical to have processes to capture learning (both continuous and breakthrough improvements) from within the organization and share this new knowledge throughout the organization.

Organizational Learning

Achieving the highest levels of organizational performance requires a well-executed approach to organizational learning that includes sharing knowledge via systematic processes. In today's demanding environment, a cross-trained and empowered workforce and effective management of up-to-date organizational knowledge are vital assets. Organizational learning includes continuous improvement of existing approaches; the adoption of best practices and innovations; and significant, discontinuous change or innovation, leading to new goals, approaches, products, and markets.

Ensuring Learning needs to be embedded in the way your organization operates. This means that learning (1) is a regular part of daily work; (2) results in solving problems at their source (root cause); (3) is focused on building and sharing knowledge throughout your organization; and (4) is driven by opportunities to effect significant, meaningful change and to innovate. Sources for learning include employees' and volunteers' ideas, research and development, customers' input, best-practice sharing, competitors' performance, and benchmarking. Your business ecosystem is another source of learning.

Organizational learning can result in (1) enhanced value to customers through new and improved products and customer services; (2) the development of new business opportunities; (3) the development of new and improved processes or business models; (4) reduced errors, defects, waste, and related costs; (5) increased productivity and effectiveness in the use of all your resources; (6) enhanced performance in making societal contributions; and (7) greater agility in managing change and disruption.

Focus on Success and Innovation

To remain competitive, every organization must be guided by components of success: strategic objectives, measurable outcome-oriented goals, and a well-defined focus on the future:

- Outcome-oriented goals, which emerge from the strategic planning process, help to align the work of everyone in the organization and serve as a basis for factual monitoring of progress.
- Measurable goals allow everyone to know where they are going and when they deviate from the desired path.
- *Without measurable goals, everyone still works hard, but they tend to focus on the things they believe are important, not the direction set by top leaders. As a result, workers, managers, and organization units can easily go in different directions—suboptimizing the success of the organization.*
- Focusing on the future requires the organization's leaders to consider new, even revolutionary and innovative ideas. Strategic objectives should reflect this future focus.

The accelerating rate of change today demands ever-increasing innovation. Such innovation should not be random. It should be focused on factors that are essential to organizational success.

- To be focused, innovation must be managed and concentrated on improving products, services, and processes to create more value for the organization's stakeholders, including the workforce and customers.
- The winners in the highly competitive race to innovate will be the organizations that uncover new paradigms of breakthrough performance. To begin to optimize this breakthrough capacity,

everyone in the organization needs to be involved. The more brain power, the better. *Requirements for innovation should be a part of every worker and managerial performance plan and appraisal.*

- Just like continuous improvement, innovation must be embedded in the culture and fabric of daily work. The best organizations are not satisfied to just improve or innovate. *The best organizations work hard at increasing the speed at which they improve and innovate.* Anything less lets competitors overtake them and allows customer expectations to exceed the speed of change, causing the customers to look elsewhere.
- Combining the previously separate core values of Focus on Success and Managing for Innovation emphasizes the importance of innovation in driving success—now and in the future. *High-performing organizations are innovative organizations.*

Focus on Success and Innovation

Ensuring your organization's success now and in the future requires an understanding of the short- and long-term factors that affect your organization and its environment. It also requires the ability to drive organizational innovation.

Sustained success requires managing uncertainty in the environment, as well as balancing some stakeholders' short-term demands with the need to invest in long-term success. The pursuit of sustained growth and performance leadership requires a strong future orientation and a willingness to make long-term commitments to key stakeholders—your customers, workforce, suppliers, partners, and stockholders; the public; and the community. It also requires the agility to modify plans, processes, and relationships whenever circumstances warrant.

Your organization's planning and resource allocation should anticipate many factors, such as customers' short- and long-term expectations; new business models and collaboration or partnering opportunities; potential crises, including events that disrupt economic and social conditions; technological developments; workforce capacity and capability needs; community and societal expectations and needs; your competitive marketplace; security and cybersecurity risks; evolving regulatory requirements; and strategic moves by competitors. Your strategic objectives and resource allocations need to accommodate these influences. A focus on success includes ensuring resilience; developing your leaders, workforce, and suppliers; accomplishing effective succession planning; and anticipating areas for societal contributions and concerns.

A focus on success also includes a focus on innovation—making meaningful change to improve products, services, programs, processes, operations, business models, or societal well-being, with the purpose of creating new value for stakeholders. Innovation should lead your organization to new dimensions of performance and success. Innovation may be present in organizations of all sizes, sectors, and maturity levels; in some cases, an organization's genesis is an innovation, with work systems and work processes developing as the organization matures.

Innovation is important for all aspects of your operations and all work systems and work processes. Innovation benefits from a supportive environment, a process for identifying strategic opportunities, and the pursuit of intelligent risks. Innovation and continuous incremental improvement are different, but complementary, concepts. Successful organizations use both approaches to improve performance. Your organization should be led and managed so that identifying strategic opportunities and taking intelligent risks become part of the learning culture. Innovation should be integrated into daily work and be supported by your performance improvement system. Systematic processes for identifying strategic opportunities should reach across your entire organization and should explore strategic alliances with complementary organizations and with organizations that have historically been outside your ecosystem.

Innovation may arise from adapting innovations in other industries to achieve a breakthrough in your industry. It builds on the accumulated knowledge of your organization and its people and the innovations of partners, collaborators,

Continued

Continued

competitors, customers, and other relevant organizations, including those outside your sector. It may involve collaboration among people who do not normally work together and are in different parts of the organization. This can lead to the maximizing of learning through shared information and the willingness to use concepts from outside the organization as idea generators. Therefore, the ability to rapidly disseminate and capitalize on new and accumulated knowledge is critical to driving organizational innovation and success.

Management by Fact

Management by fact is the cornerstone value for effective planning, operational decision-making at all levels, employee involvement and empowerment, and leadership:

- People make decisions every day. However, without data, the basis for decision-making is usually intuition—gut feel. Although intuition can be valuable at times, it introduces too much variation into the decision-making process. Intuition is not consistent person-to-person or time-to-time. It is also difficult to explain the rationale for decisions based on intuition. That makes communication more difficult within the organization. Finally, if the decision must be made on the basis of intuition, it is usually the boss's intuition that drives the decision. Because of this phenomenon, issues are pulled to ever-higher levels for resolution. As a result, excessive reliance on intuition minimizes employee empowerment.
- Most car drivers decide when to fill their fuel tanks based on data from the fuel gauge and get very uncomfortable if the gage is broken. Yet people routinely make decisions of enormous consequence about customers, strategies, goals, and workers with little or no data. This is a recipe for disaster, not one designed to ensure optimization.

Management by Fact

Management by fact requires you to measure and analyze your organization's performance, both inside the organization and in your competitive environment. Measurements should derive from business needs and strategy, and they should provide critical data and information about key processes, outputs, results, outcomes, and competitor and industry performance. Organizations need many types of data and information to effectively manage their performance. Data and information may come in many forms, such as numerical, graphical, or qualitative, and from many sources, including internal processes, surveys, and the internet (including social media). Performance measurement should include measurement of customer, product, and process performance; comparisons of operational, market, and competitive performance; supplier, workforce, partner, cost, and financial performance; governance and compliance results; and accomplishment of strategic objectives.

A major consideration in performance improvement and change management is the selection and use of performance measures or indicators. The measures or indicators you select should best represent the factors that lead to improved customer, operational, financial, and societal performance. A comprehensive yet carefully culled set of measures or indicators tied to customer and organizational performance requirements provides a clear basis for aligning all processes with your organization's goals. Measures and indicators support you in making decisions in a rapidly changing environment. By analyzing data from your tracking processes, you can evaluate the measures or indicators themselves and change them to better support your goals.

Analysis means extracting larger meaning from data and information to support evaluation, decision-making, improvement, and innovation. It entails using data to deter-mine trends, projections, and cause-and-effect relationships that might not otherwise be evident. Analysis supports a variety of purposes, such as planning, reviewing your overall performance, improving operations, comparing your performance with competitors' or with best-practice benchmarks, and managing change. To facilitate analysis, data may need to be aggregated from various sources. Data may also need to be segmented by, for example, markets, product lines, and workforce groups to gain deeper understanding.

Societal Contributions

Every high-performing organization practices good public responsibility and citizenship:

- *Organizations must determine and anticipate any adverse effects to the public of their products, services, and operations. Failure to do so can undermine public trust and distract workers, and also adversely affect the bottom line. This is true of both private and public organizations.*
- In past years, we have seen several examples of companies that have been seriously hurt by failing to practice good citizenship or protect the interests of the public from risks they created. Even when unintended, failure to protect stakeholder interests can cripple companies. Consider the examples of Dow-Corning and the litigation over health consequences of leaky silicone breast implants; banks that were sued because they failed to provide adequate security for automatic teller machines (cash machines); or BP for the drilling platform disaster and massive oil spill in the Gulf of Mexico.
- Safety and legal requirements need to be met beyond mere compliance. The best organizations stay ahead of minimum requirements and actually lead efforts to raise the bar. In this manner, when regulatory agencies increase requirements, the best organizations are not caught off guard and may even be able to place their competitors at a disadvantage.

Societal Contributions

Your organization's leaders should stress contributions to the public and the consideration of societal well-being and benefit. Leaders should be role models for your organization and its workforce in the protection of public health, safety, and the environment. This protection applies to any impact of your organization's operations, as well as the life cycles of your products. Also, your organization should emphasize resource conservation, recycling, and waste reduction at the source. Planning should anticipate adverse impacts from the production, distribution, transportation, use, and disposal of your products. Effective planning should reduce or prevent problems; provide for a forthright response if problems occur; and make available the information and support needed to maintain public awareness, safety, and confidence.

Your organization should meet all local, state, and federal laws and regulatory requirements and should also treat these and related requirements as opportunities to excel beyond minimal compliance.

Considering societal well-being and benefit means leading and supporting—within the limits of your resources—the environmental, social, and economic systems in your organization's sphere of influence. Such leadership and support might include improving education, health care, and other services in your community; pursuing environmental excellence; being a role model for addressing socially important issues, such as diversity, equity, and inclusion; practicing resource conservation; reducing your carbon footprint; performing community service and charity; improving industry and business practices; and sharing nonproprietary information. Increasingly, such societal contributions are a customer or stakeholder requirement.

For a role-model organization, leadership also entails influencing other organizations, private and public, to partner for these purposes. Managing societal contributions requires your organization to use appropriate measures and your leaders to assume responsibility for those measures.

Ethics and Transparency

Enron and Arthur Andersen are well-known examples of organizations that went out of business almost overnight because they failed to follow sound, well-established principles of ethics and transparency in operations. Organizations that violate the trust of their customers, workforce, suppliers, and other stakeholders (including the general public) usually face similar consequences. Senior leaders and the governing body set the tone for these core values. And these core values govern the behavior of everyone associated with the organization.

Anything less than full compliance and zero tolerance for breaches in ethical behavior can create major problems for the organization and its ability to maintain current and ongoing success.

Ethics and Transparency

Your organization should stress ethical behavior in all stakeholder transactions and interactions. Your organization's governance body should require highly ethical conduct and monitor all conduct accordingly. Your senior leaders should be role models of ethical behavior and make their expectations of the workforce very clear.

Your organization's ethical principles are the foundation for your culture and values. They distinguish right from wrong. Clearly articulated ethical principles, along with your organizational values, empower your people to make effective decisions and may serve as boundary conditions for determining organizational norms and prohibitions.

Transparency is characterized by consistently candid and open communication, accountability, and the sharing of clear and accurate information by leadership and management. The benefits of transparency are manifold. Transparency is a key factor in workforce engagement and allows people to see why actions are being taken and how they can contribute. Transparency and accountability are also important in interactions with customers and other stakeholders, giving them a sense of involvement, engagement, and confidence in your organization.

Ethical behavior and transparency build trust in the organization and its leaders and engender a belief in the organization's fairness and integrity that is valued by all key stakeholders.

Delivering Value and Results

A results focus and an emphasis on creating value help organizations communicate requirements, monitor actual performance, make appropriate adjustments in priorities, and reallocate resources effectively. Without a results focus, organizations can become fixated on internal, self-directed processes and lose sight of the important factors for success, such as customers and their requirements.

Strategic objectives should be results- or outcome-oriented, not activity-oriented. When the focus shifts from achieving outcomes to completing activities, accountability erodes. Many times managers and workers carry out assigned tasks, but the required outcome or benefit has not occurred.

Delivering Value and Results

By delivering and balancing value for key stakeholders, your organization builds loyalty, contributes to growing the economy, and contributes to society. To meet the sometimes conflicting and changing aims that balancing value requires, your organizational strategy should explicitly include key stakeholder requirements. This will help ensure that plans and actions meet differing stakeholder needs and avoid adverse impacts on any stakeholders. A balanced composite of leading and lagging performance measures is an effective means to communicate short- and long-term priorities, monitor actual performance, and provide a clear basis for improving results.

Your organization's performance measurements need to focus on key results. Results should be used to deliver and balance value for your key stakeholders—your customers, workforce, stockholders, suppliers, partners, and collaborators; the public; and the community. Thus, results need to be a composite of measures that include not just financial results but also product and process results; customer and workforce satisfaction and engagement results; and leadership, strategy, and societal performance.

PRACTICAL INSIGHTS

Connections and Linkages

A popular children's activity, connect the dots, helps them understand that, when properly joined, apparently random dots create a meaningful picture. In many ways, the seven Categories, 17 Items, 40 Areas to Address, and 78 Sub-areas to Address in the Baldrige Business/Nonprofit/Government Framework are like the dots that must be connected to reveal a meaningful picture. With no tools to connect the dots, workforce activities are not aligned to strategic planning; measurement, analysis, and knowledge management are isolated from process management; and improvement efforts are disjointed, fragmented, and do not yield robust results. This book describes the linkages among and between each Item. The exciting part about having them identified is that you can look for these linkages in your own organization and, if they don't exist, start building them.

Transition Strategies

Putting a high-performance, integrated management system in place involves a major commitment. Achieving excellence is an outcome that will not happen quickly or easily. At the beginning, you will need a transition strategy to get you across the bridge from management by opinion or intuition to more data-driven management. Often a major transformation is required to realign culture within the organization to implement the Integrated Management System to achieve performance excellence. The next part of this section describes one approach that has worked for many organizations in various sectors: creating a *performance improvement council.*

Performance Improvement Council

Identify a top-level executive leadership group of six to eight members. Each additional member beyond this number will seem to double the complexity of issues and render decision-making much more cumbersome. The executive leadership group could send a message to the entire organization by naming the group *the performance improvement council*—reinforcing the importance of continuous performance improvement to the future success of the organization.

The performance improvement council should be the primary policy-making body for the organization. It should spawn other performance improvement councils at lower levels to share practices and policies with every employee in the organization as well as to involve customers and suppliers. The structure permeates the organization as members of the performance improvement council become area leaders for major improvement efforts and sponsors for several process or continuous improvement task teams throughout the organization. The council structure, networked and cascaded fully, can effectively align the work and optimize performance at all levels and across all functions.

The performance improvement council should not be formed for the purpose of seeking the Baldrige or other performance excellence awards. The council should be formed with the purpose of implementing and improving processes that will lead to improved results. Receiving a Baldrige Award or similar recognition is an outcome of successfully improving processes and their related results.

Council Membership

Selecting members for the performance improvement council should be done carefully. Each member should be essential for the success of the operation, and together they must generate a synergy sufficient for success. The most important member is the senior leader of the organization or unit. *This person must participate actively, demonstrating the kind of leadership that the Baldrige Criteria require and all should emulate.* Of particular importance is a commitment to consensus building as the *modus operandi* for the council. This tool, a core of performance improvement programs, is often overlooked by leadership. Other council members selected should have leadership responsibility for broad areas of the organization, such as human resources, operations, planning, customers, and data systems. All persons on the council should hold a commitment to the core values described earlier in this chapter.

Council Expertise

The performance improvement council should be extremely knowledgeable about the Integrated

Management System. *If not, as is often the case, performance improvement council members should be among the first in the organization to learn about the system and its continuous improvement tools and processes.*

To be effective, every member of the council (and ultimately every member in the organization) must understand the Baldrige Core Values and Criteria, because they describe the behaviors and components of the Integrated Management System that govern all activities. Participation in examiner training has proved to be a great way to understand the complexities of the system needed to achieve performance excellence. Any additional training beyond this should be carried out in the context of planning and implementing strategy; that is, learn tools and use them to plan the performance improvement implementation, practices, and policies.

The performance improvement council should:

- Develop a business plan that integrates continuous improvement and strategic performance improvement.
- Create the communication plan and infrastructure to transmit performance-improvement policies, practices, and priorities throughout the organization.
- Define the roles of workers, including new recognition and reward structures, to cause needed behavioral changes that are aligned with strategic objectives and action plans.
- Create or strengthen the workforce and leadership development system. Assess skills needed and compare with skills that are in place. Involve team representatives in planning so they can learn skills close to when they are needed. Provide training and development and close the skill gaps.
- Launch improvement projects that will produce both short- and long-term successes. Improvement projects should be clearly defined by the performance improvement council and aligned with strategic priorities. Typical improvement projects include important human resource processes, such as career development, performance measurement, and diversity, as well as improving operational products and services in the line areas. Become a leader in the use of tools such as lean, Six Sigma, or other proven improvement tools, *but be sure to focus those tools on areas of importance to strategic plans, business plans, and human resource and workforce plans.*
- Develop a plan to communicate the progress and successes throughout the organization. Through this approach, the need for—and successes of—performance improvement processes are consistently communicated to workers, partners, suppliers, collaborators, and customers. Barriers to optimum performance are weakened and eliminated.
- Use the performance improvement council to remove barriers to performance excellence through the Categories of the Baldrige Criteria and Integrated Management System.
- *Most important—make continuous improvement and performance excellence a requirement and not an option.*

Category Champions

This section describes the responsibilities of Category champions. The people in the administrative or leadership cabinet should each be the champion of a Category and have appropriate staff support.

Leadership Champion (Category 1)

The *leadership champion* is a senior executive—often the highest ranking official of the organization, such as the CEO—who, in addition to other executive duties, works to coordinate and enhance leadership effectiveness and alignment throughout the organization. It is both a strategic and an operational activity.

From the strategic side, the champion should focus on ensuring that all senior leaders:

- Understand what is expected of them as leaders of organizational change and make sure their actions and words support this change.
- Ensure that effective governance systems are in place to protect the interests of all stakeholder groups and maintain organizational integrity and ethical behavior.

- Consistently speak with one voice as a senior leadership team.
- Serve as positive role models of performance excellence for managers and workers at all levels of the organization. (Remember, like it or not, all leaders serve as role models and lead by example; but only some are good.)
- Develop future leaders (succession planning) throughout the organization.
- Create measurable, outcome-oriented performance expectations and monitor performance to achieve the key improvements and strategic objectives of the organization. This means that necessary data and analyses must be coordinated to ensure appropriate information is available for the champion and the entire senior leadership team.

From the operational side, ensure the organization implements the processes required by Category 1 of the CPE. The champion should work to identify and eliminate both individual and system deficiencies, territorial conflicts, and knowledge shortfalls that limit leaders' ability to meet expectations and goals consistently.

The champion should be the focal point in the organization to ensure all parts of the organization have systematic processes in place, so they fully understand leadership and management requirements. A process should exist to monitor ongoing initiatives to ensure leaders effectively set and communicate organizational values to employees:

- Create a culture that focuses on delivering value to customers and other stakeholders, engages them, and creates a consistently positive customer experience.
- Aggressively reinforce an environment that promotes engagement (empowerment and innovation) throughout the workforce.
- Review policies, systems, work processes, and the use of resources to ensure sufficient data are available to assist in workforce decision-making.
- Review (conduct independent audits) ethical and legal behavior of all leaders and managers and hold them accountable for their actions.
- Evaluate, develop, and enhance their personal leadership skills.

The leadership champion should coordinate the activities involving the review of organizational performance and capabilities:

- Define key performance outcome and in-process measures.
- Install systems to review organizational success, performance, and progress relative to outcome-oriented goals and strategic objectives.
- Use performance review findings to identify priorities for improvement. Communicate those priorities to all units that have responsibilities for making the improvements, including suppliers and partners.
- Systematically use performance review findings, together with employee feedback, to assess and improve senior leadership (including the chief executive) effectiveness and the effectiveness of managers throughout the leadership system.

The champion must work as part of the senior leadership team to help coordinate all facets of the management system to drive high performance. This involves teaching the team about the elements of effective and consistent leadership at all levels and its impact on organizational performance. The senior leader of the organization usually serves as the leadership champion and leads this council.

To be successful, implementing the system to achieve performance excellence cannot be seen as optional.

Finally, the leadership champion must ensure that everyone in a leadership position supports the values and activities critical to achieving performance excellence. Implement policies of zero tolerance for senior leaders who do not support these efforts fully. To be successful, implementing the system to achieve performance excellence cannot be seen as optional. This is essential to ensure the systems and processes required to achieve optimum performance are launched and sustained.

Strategy Champion (Category 2)

The *strategy champion* is a senior executive who, in addition to other executive duties, works to coordinate and enhance strategic planning and action-plan alignment throughout the organization. It is both a strategic and an operational activity.

From the strategic side, the champion should ensure that the focus of strategy development is on sustained competitive leadership, which usually depends on achieving revenue growth, as well as consistently improving operational effectiveness. The *strategy* champion should help the senior leadership team acquire a view of the future and provide clear strategic guidance to the organization through goals, objectives, action plans, and measures.

From the operational side, the champion should work to ensure sufficient data are available regarding:

- The organization's operational and workforce strengths, including core competencies
- Strategic challenges, advantages, and opportunities that may arise from customers, competitors, supplier weaknesses, regulatory changes, economic conditions, the competitive environment, and financial, technological, ethical, and societal risks
- The identification of strategic opportunities and the determination of which strategic opportunities are intelligent risks worth pursuing
- Internal core competencies and the expertise of suppliers and partners to evaluate which work systems should be internal and which should be outsourced

The strategy champion should be the focal point in the organization to ensure all parts of the organization have systematic processes in place, so they fully understand the implications of strategy on their daily work. The champion should ensure that:

- All strategic objectives or goals define, in measurable terms, the *outcomes* the organization must actually achieve to be successful in the future. *Activities are not strategic objectives. Enablers are not strategic objectives.*
- A process exists at each level of the organization to convert measurable, outcome-oriented strategic objectives into actions, which are aligned and used to achieve goals necessary for business success. These actions may define the activities believed to be critical to achieving desired outcomes, but may not substitute for the outcomes.
- Every employee understands his or her role in carrying out actions to achieve the organization's goals.
- Rewards, recognition, incentives, and compensation are aligned to support strategic objectives, action plans, and customer and business success.

The strategy champion should coordinate the work of strategy development and deployment to:

- Acquire and use various types of forecasts, projections, scenarios, or other techniques to understand the plausible range of future options.
- Determine how the projected performance of competitors is likely to compare with the projected performance of the organization in the same time frame in order to set goals to ensure a competitive advantage.
- Define the expected path that growth and performance are likely to take for each strategic objective. Timelines (the schedule) of projected future performance should match the frequency of organizational performance reviews.
- Determine what changes in services or products might be needed as a part of strategic positioning and direction. Strategy should define what the organization must achieve to be successful in the future, not simply justify a continuation of current activities.
- Determine what capabilities or core competencies must be developed within the organization to achieve strategic goals and coordinate with other members of the senior leadership team and Category champions to ensure those capabilities are in place.
- Ensure a system is in place to identify the human resource elements necessary to achieve strategic goals and objectives. This may include training, support services for employees, reorganization, and new recruitment, to name a few.
- Ensure a system is in place to allocate resources throughout the organization sufficient to accomplish the action plans and monitor those resources.

- Coordinate with the leadership system during performance reviews to help ensure that priorities for improvement and innovation at different levels throughout the organization are aligned with strategic objectives and action plans.
- Ensure the processes for strategic planning, determining work systems and core competencies, plan deployment, development of action plans, and alignment of resources to support actions are systematically evaluated and improved each cycle. Also evaluate and improve the accuracy of determining the projected performance of competitors, for use in goal setting.

The strategy champion, together with the leadership champion, should work to promote an organization-wide environment for innovation. Finally, the strategy champion must work as a contributing member of the senior leadership team to help coordinate all facets of the management system to drive high performance. This involves teaching the team about the requirements of strategic planning and its impact on organizational performance.

Customers Champion (Category 3)

The *customers champion* is a senior executive who, in addition to other executive duties, coordinates and enhances customer engagement, satisfaction, relations, and loyalty throughout the organization. It is both a strategic and an operational activity.

From the strategic side, the champion should focus on ensuring that the drivers of customer satisfaction, customer engagement, and related market share (which are key factors in competitiveness, profitability, and organizational sustainability) are considered fully in the strategic planning process. This means that necessary data and analyses must be coordinated to ensure appropriate information is available for the executive planning councils.

From the operational side, the champion should work to identify and eliminate system deficiencies, territorial conflicts, and knowledge shortfalls that limit the organization's ability to engage customers consistently.

The champion should be the focal point in the organization to ensure all parts of the organization have systematic processes in place, so they fully understand key customer, market, and operational requirements are inputs to customer satisfaction, market goals, and customer engagement.

A process should exist to monitor ongoing initiatives to ensure they are aligned with the customer aspects of the strategic direction. This may involve:

- Reviewing policies, systems, work processes, the use of resources, and the availability of workers who are knowledgeable and focus on customer engagement and building relationships
- Ensuring sufficient data are available to assist in decision-making about customer issues
- Ensuring that strategies and actions relating to customer issues are aligned at all levels of the organization from the executives to the work unit or individual job level

The champion should coordinate the activities involving understanding customer requirements for products and support, as well as managing the interaction with customers, including how the organization determines customer satisfaction, engagement, and dissatisfaction; and satisfaction relative to competitors. (Satisfaction relative to competitors and the factors that lead to customer preference are increasingly important to managing in a competitive environment.) For example:

- The champion should also examine the means by which customers have access to seek information or assistance, to comment, or complain.
- The champion should coordinate the customer support requirements (sometimes called customer-service standards) and the deployment of those requirements to all points and people in the organization that interact with customers.
- The champion should ensure that systems exist to respond quickly and resolve complaints promptly to recover customer confidence that otherwise might be lost.
- The champion should ensure that workers responsible for the design and delivery of products and customer support services receive information about customer complaints, so they may eliminate the causes of these complaints.
- The champion should work with appropriate managers to help set priorities for improvement projects based on the potential impact of the cost of complaints and the impact of customer dissatisfaction and attrition on the organization.

- The champion should be charged with coordinating activities to build engagement (loyalty and positive referral), as well as evaluating and improving customer relationship-building processes throughout the organization.

Finally, the champion must work as a contributing member of the senior leadership team to help coordinate all facets of the management system to drive high performance. This involves teaching the team about the requirements of customer and market focus and its impact on organizational performance.

Measurement, Analysis, and Knowledge-Management Champion (Category 4)

The *measurement, analysis, and knowledge-management champion* is an executive-level person who, in addition to other duties, coordinates and enhances information, analysis, and knowledge-management systems throughout the organization to ensure they meet the decision-making needs of managers, workers, customers, partners, collaborators, and suppliers. It is both a strategic and an operational activity.

From the strategic side, information and analyses and the resulting knowledge can provide a competitive advantage. The champion should focus on ensuring, to the extent possible, that timely and accurate information and analyses are available to enhance knowledge acquisition and the development and delivery of new and existing products and customer support services to meet ongoing and emerging customer needs and expectations.

From the operational side, the champion should work to ensure that information and analyses are available throughout the organization and externally for suppliers, partners, collaborators, and customers to aid in decision-making at all levels. This means coordinating with all other champions to ensure data are available for day-to-day review and decision-making at all levels for their areas of responsibility.

The measurement, analysis, and knowledge-management champion has responsibility for the information infrastructure as well as ensuring the appropriate use of data for decision-making. The champion should coordinate activities throughout the organization involving data collection, accuracy, analysis, retrieval, and use for decision-making and improvements. The champion should ensure:

- Complete data are available and aligned to strategic goals, objectives, and action plans to ensure performance against these goals, objectives, and action plans can be effectively monitored.
- Systems are in place to collect and use comparative data and information to support strategy development, goal setting, and performance improvement.
- Data and information are complete, accurate, reliable, and current to enhance fact-based decision-making throughout the organization.
- Data and information are used to support a better understanding of the cost and financial impacts of various improvement options as well as serve as a basis for decisions regarding intelligent risks.
- Appropriate analyses and performance projections are available to support strategic planning and operational decision-making.
- The performance-measurement system is evaluated and improved to ensure it continues to meet organizational needs—especially as those needs change as data volume and complexity expand.
- Data analysis supports the senior executives' organizational performance review and organizational planning, and helps leaders set priorities for meaningful change and innovation.
- Data analysis addresses the overall health of the organization and supports the identification of best practices, promotes the organization-wide sharing of those practices, and identifies opportunities for continuous improvement and innovation.
- Information, data, and supporting analyses are available to work group, functional-level operations, partners, and suppliers to support decision-making at those levels.
- Data analysis supports daily decisions regarding operations throughout the organization to ensure actions align with plans.
- Information management systems, including hardware and software, are easy to use, reliable, and regularly updated to keep them current

with changing decision-making needs. Data in these systems are correct (accurate), consistent (reliable), complete (integrity), free from tampering, cyber attack, or inappropriate disclosure (secure and confidential), and available when needed (timely).

- Knowledge management systems are in place to ensure that important information—whether paper, electronic, or "head knowledge"—is available to those who need it to manage processes or make other decisions.

Finally, the champion must work as a member of an organization-wide council to help coordinate all facets of the management system to drive high performance.

Workforce Champion (Category 5)

The *workforce champion* is an executive-level person who, in addition to other executive duties, coordinates and enhances systems to enable workers (including managers and supervisors at all levels, permanent, temporary, and part-time personnel, and contract employees and volunteers supervised by the organization) to develop and utilize their full potential, consistent with the organization's strategic objectives and values. This includes building and maintaining a work environment conducive to full employee participation and growth. It is both a strategic and an operational activity.

From the strategic side, the workforce constraints of the organization must be considered in the development of strategy, and subsequently mitigated to ensure the workforce is capable of achieving the outcomes necessary for business success.

From the operational side, the champion should ensure that the work climate enhances workforce satisfaction and engagement, and that work is organized and jobs are designed to enable workers to contribute their utmost to achieve optimum levels of performance.

The workforce champion has responsibility for ensuring that workers' developmental and support needs are met to enable them to contribute fully to the organization's goals and objectives. The champion should ensure:

- A culture of workforce cooperation, collaboration, individual initiative, innovation, and flexibility.
- An environment in which workers are motivated to do their utmost for the benefit of the organization and its customers.
- An effective system to provide compensation, reward, recognition, and incentives to support performance and achieve strategic objectives. This includes systems to identify skill gaps.
- Support for business objectives and actions to build workforce knowledge, skills, capacity, and capabilities to enhance career progression and performance. This includes ensuring workers understand tools and techniques of performance measurement, performance improvement, quality control methods, and benchmarking. This also includes ensuring that managers and supervisors reinforce knowledge and skills on the job.
- A healthy and secure work environment with performance measures and targets for each key factor affecting the workplace climate.
- The assessment of workforce engagement and satisfaction, and prompt actions to improve conditions that adversely affect morale, motivation, productivity, and other related performance results.

Finally, the champion must work as part of an organization-wide council to help coordinate all facets of the management system to drive high performance.

Operations Champion (Category 6)

The *operations champion* is an executive-level person who, in addition to other executive duties, coordinates and enhances all aspects of the organization's core competencies and related systems to manage and improve work processes to meet the organization's strategic objectives and action plans. This includes activities and processes to create value for customers and other stakeholders. It is both a strategic and operational activity.

From the strategic side, rapid and accurate design, development, and delivery of products and services create a competitive advantage in the marketplace. From the operational side, the champion should work to ensure all key work processes are examined and optimized to achieve higher levels of performance, reduce cycle time and costs, and subsequently contribute to organizational success and sustainability.

The operations champion has responsibility for creating a fact-based, process-management orientation within the organization. Since all work is a process, the operations champion must ensure that the process owners (including other champions) systematically design, examine, improve, and execute their processes consistently error-free. The champion should ensure:

- Systematic continuous improvement activities are embedded in all processes, which lead to ongoing refinements, breakthrough improvement, innovations, and higher performance and productivity.
- Initial and ongoing customer requirements are incorporated into all product and service designs, production and delivery systems, and processes.
- Design, production, and delivery processes are structured and analyzed to reduce cycle time, increase the use of learning from past projects or other parts of the organization, reduce costs, increase the use of new technology and other effectiveness or efficiency factors, and ensure all products and services meet or exceed performance requirements.
- The supply network is managed to ensure that external procurements fully support the organization's core competencies, work processes, and support processes.
- A safe work environment is provided that prevents accidents and ensures prompt recovery in case of accident.
- The organization is prepared for disasters and emergency situations to maintain business continuity. Potential problems are prevented or managed to ensure work continues, customers are not harmed, and rapid recovery occurs.

Finally, the champion must work as part of an organization-wide council to help coordinate all facets of the management system to drive improvement and innovation throughout the organization.

Results Champion

The *results champion* is an executive-level person who, in addition to other executive duties, coordinates the *display* of the organization's performance results. This champion has substantially different work than the champions for Categories 1 through 6. No actions leading to or resulting from the performance-outcome data are championed by the results champion. Those actions are driven by operations champions because they have responsibility for taking action to implement and deploy procedures necessary to produce the desired results. For example, the measurement, analysis, and knowledge management champion (Category 4) is responsible, in part, for collecting data that reflect all areas of importance that should be reported. The measurement, analysis, and knowledge management champion is also responsible for ensuring data accuracy, reliability, integrity, accessibility, and availability—not the results champion.

The results champion is responsible, however, for ensuring that the organization reports results required by Category 7 to provide evidence of the organization's performance outcomes in key areas and facilitate monitoring by leaders and others in the workforce. These include customer-focused product and service performance; work process effectiveness results; supply-network results; customer satisfaction, dissatisfaction, and engagement results; financial, marketplace, and strategy performance; workforce performance; and leadership results.

When appropriate, results must be broken out by segment and group, such as different customer groups, market segments, or workforce groups. Appropriate comparison data must be included in the results display to judge the relative *goodness* or *strength* of the results achieved. Members of the performance excellence council and other workers use these results to monitor organizational performance and competitiveness.

Finally, the results champion must work as part of an organization-wide council to help coordinate all facets of the management system to drive high performance. For example, if the organization is not collecting data necessary for inclusion in the business results report card, the results champion coordinates work with the other champions on the council to ensure those data are available, used for decision-making, and included in appropriate reports.

LESSONS LEARNED

General Lessons

More than 35 years ago the fierce global competition that inspired the quality improvement movement in the United States was felt primarily by major manufacturers. Today, all sectors are under intense pressure to "be the best or be history." *The demand for performance excellence reaches all corners of the economy, from manufacturing and service industries to professional services, education, health care, public utilities, and even government.* All of these segments have contributed valuable lessons to the performance excellence discipline and have played an important part in our recovery from economic slumps caused by poor service and products. Some insights and lessons learned from leaders of high-performing organizations are worth highlighting.

Desire and History Are Not Enough

> ***While using the Integrated Management System can help an organization reach high levels of performance, leaders cannot expect to sustain those levels of performance without continuing to use the system as the way they run the business.***

It is important to point out a fact that may be obvious to most: *To optimize organizational performance, organizations must actually use the principles contained in the Baldrige Criteria and the Integrated Management System.* It is not enough to think about them. It is not enough to have used them in the past and no longer continue to do so. It is not enough to use a part but not all of the system. To leave out any part suboptimizes the organization's performance.

A Tale of Two Leaders

It was a time of turmoil; it was a time of calm. It was a time of success and failure. It was the happiest of times; it was also the most painful of times. Most of all it was a time that demanded change—although many were comfortable maintaining the status quo.

The following tales are of two leaders. One is consistent and persistent in communicating the direction and message that will bring about excellent results and high performance. Another is uncertain and vague. He does not wish to push his people into anything, let alone the significant commitment to change required to use the Baldrige Criteria and Integrated Management System as the way to run the business. After all, the business is still healthy. Why rock the boat? You may know these people or someone who reminds you of them. If so, you will understand the reason for this section.

There is no lonelier, more challenging, yet critical and rewarding job than that of the senior leader. We work with many, many leaders who listen to advice carefully. They really want to know the best approaches to optimize their organizations and promote long-term sustainability for their customers and workforce. Yet what they do with the advice and counsel is always interesting and unpredictable. This section is intended to help those leaders be more resolute about traveling the right path.

Neither leader exists in real life, but both leader profiles are based on actual events and observations of various people in leadership positions.

Tale One

John was the CEO of a *Fortune 500* manufacturing company that was slowly but surely losing market share. Shareholders and employees were happy because profits and growth, although slower, were still hearty. However, their business that once enjoyed a near monopoly position was rapidly facing more and more competition. Customers who had to beg and plead for limited products and service over the years were happily turning to competitors that were trying in earnest to meet their needs and even delight them. In such an environment, aggressive, customer-focused companies were winning the hearts, minds, and pocketbooks of John's customers. After working with a consulting firm or two and studying the work of W. Edwards Deming, John decided that performance excellence was urgently needed to keep the company in business more than five years.

The First Message to the Leadership Team. John called an urgent meeting of his senior team. Many members of this team had been there since the company began its 20-year growth spurt and had been good soldiers in times of runaway growth and profit.

John was wondering how many members of the senior staff would welcome the message he was about to send. The meeting was scheduled the next week for five days at the corporate headquarters. Short of an emergency illness, attendance was required.

During the next few days, John received 20 phone calls from secretaries who informed John their bosses could not attend because of other priority commitments. Priorities were quickly realigned when they were informed that attendance was not optional.

The week-long meeting began with training—the kind of training in which the group was required to participate, listen, and discuss the content. The training was presented by an outside firm with frequent discussions of company-wide application and emphasis presented by John. At the end of three days, John took over the meeting and asked for input on how best to apply these principles to the organization at all levels. The leadership group voiced resistance to change, some more than others. They basically voiced concern that "this performance excellence stuff with all of its requirements for empowerment and data" would get in the way of their doing business and was not needed.

John clarified the objectives of the group by walking to the white board and writing: "This new program, performance excellence, is in the way of doing business effectively." The senior staff pretty much agreed.

John responded by placing a large *X* through the word *in*. The statement now read, "Performance excellence is the way of doing business effectively." John notified the attendees, "I will negotiate an exit package with anyone who does not understand the implications of this message, and who does not want to be part of this new way of doing business." John learned that day that to institute meaningful change, it may be necessary to fire someone he liked. He also realized that to ignore the challenges and lack of commitment would be seen by everyone as tacit approval and send the message that the new way of doing business was *optional*.

The Next Steps. John focused on two next steps: (1) making sure his top team role-modeled behavior that would facilitate the needed changes; and (2) planning and implementing a company-wide training requirement to communicate the new skills and performance expectations. John started to change his behavior and the behavior of his top staff, feeling that *walking the talk* would signal the importance of new behaviors more than any speech or videotaped presentation. The next top staff meeting was called within a week to plan the design and rollout of training corporate-wide, including all foreign and domestic sites. The top staff had very little interest in training, feeling largely that this was a human resource function and should be delegated to that department. Based on the advice of external advisors, John informed the staff that it was now their job to plan, design, and execute this training. A *core design team* was formed with senior leaders and expert content and course-design specialists to design the training within one month and present it to the senior corporate leaders.

In spite of prior agreements to manage their meetings effectively, to be on time, not interrupt, and follow the agenda, most continued to ignore the rules. Behaviors of the top leadership group at this meeting included the usual set of interruptions, "I told you so's," and everyone talking at the same time. John, whose goal was to create a listening and learning environment, challenged the group to "ante up." He asked that all top leaders bring fifty $20 bills to the next meeting. John introduced new meeting ground rules. They were simple. Interruptions, put downs, blocking behaviors, and talking over someone else were violations of meeting ground rules. On the other hand, building on ideas, clarifying ideas, supporting, and disagreeing respectfully were good meeting behaviors. Every violation was worth a $20 bill. Good meeting behaviors were rewarded, although they did not materialize until several meetings had been completed.

At first, it seemed that the pot would win big time—no one took John seriously. After about the third meeting, with penalties piling up, the unacceptable behavior of the leadership group actually changed. Other meeting-management skills were slowly introduced, such as time-frame limits and action planning. Then John was confident his team could role-model this behavior to others. He required that, "This is the way we treat each other at all meetings, including staff meetings, communication forums, and all company business meetings." A core value and new behavior of courtesy and professionalism became deployed company-wide through the senior management team.

Training and the Change Process. Each five-day, high-performance management course was consistent, ensuring that a uniform message and set of skills were communicated. Each course was eventually taught by two instructors, a shop supervisor and a manager, so that management and the workforce would both be visibly involved in leading the transformation. John personally taught the top leadership team the entire five-day course, assisted by a member of the design team, and this tale spread across the organization like wildfire. It became a good thing to be invited to take part in this instruction because their leader had done it. The core skills became part of the fabric of the organization—the way to conduct business. New behaviors included fact-based decisions, a focus on customers, and using and improving processes. Also included was a way to solve problems continually with a well-defined process at the level the problem was occurring.

The focus had shifted from the status quo to a thirst for improvement. Improvement began to bring rewards whereas the status quo was disdained. A comprehensive business evaluation was conducted and improvement targets were identified. Clear assignments with reasonable but aggressive goals were cascaded to all levels of the organization. Performance planning, goals, compensation, and recognition were aligned to support the organization's strategy, especially the need to focus better on satisfying internal and external customers. Managers who did not work to meet these new goals, who did not role-model the behaviors necessary to achieve high performance, were reassigned to jobs that did not require their management skills. New role models emerged to lead the organization at all levels. Within three years the company regained market share, improved profitability, expanded its workforce, and became, once again, one of the world's most admired companies.

Tale Two

Victor was the CEO of a West Coast manufacturing company that also was a proud member of the *Fortune 500.* Company performance had been uneven over the past few years. Profits were low this year relative to previous years, but the company still met financial targets. Product demands were high and the outlook was fairly good for the next quarter. The industry as a whole was fairly evenly matched as far as management problems. Trends for return on investment were also uneven, and other indicators, such as sales volume and net profit, were up and down. Investors were not happy, especially when other companies consistently outperformed theirs. Victor thought it was time to do something different. Victor consulted several valuable and trusted advisors and then decided that high-performance excellence might be worth considering.

The First Message to the Leadership Team. Victor scheduled a series of weekly dinner meetings over the next month (January) and engaged several top consultants to talk to the group about the business case for using high-performance management. He invited 50 top-level managers from across the country to attend. Most top leaders attended the meetings and enjoyed the dinners, and Victor attended most but not all of them, letting his new consultants do their job. The sessions were interesting—the top leaders found the meetings were a great forum for politicking, posturing, wining and dining, and trying to sharpshoot the consultant. Victor asked his top leaders to come together for a half day in the spring to discuss the content and direction of the high-performance initiative, being convinced intellectually by the dinner discussions that this was the right direction for the company. At the half-day meeting, it was obvious that about half of the group agreed with the CEO and about half were uncertain or downright resistant, particularly one very senior vice president. Victor left the team with this message, "Let me take your comments under advisement and think about them as we go forward." Later, at the consultant's suggestion, he conducted an organizational assessment to identify problems that might be contributory to the uneven, up-and-down performance. The assessment uncovered several serious problems that required change, yet the senior leaders continued to resist.

The Next Steps. Victor finally hired one of the external advisors who had withstood the test of several dinner meetings and the challenges of his threatened senior management team. Victor asked the advisor to speak to the top leaders of the entire company about what a great group they were and how important the performance excellence initiative was going to be for the company. The advisor closed by telling them that only the best go after high performance; if they did not, their competitors would. During the following discussion sessions, Victor's chief operating officer (COO) announced to the group that he was far from convinced and stated he was not going to change the way he did business. That comment went unchallenged by Victor or anyone else in the company. Frustration continued to build.

In an effort to regain momentum, Victor wanted to create a change team. He asked each division to send a person to *facilitate* the initiative and receive appropriate training in managing change. The people selected were far from the best each division could offer, since no selection criteria had been provided and many thought this was a waste of time and talent. The division leaders supplied people who were expendable. The people who formed the facilitator group, for their part, were very enthusiastic but not particularly respected or credible. Because they were given absolutely no relief from any regular duties, they were stretched very thin. Also, the division heads were not supportive in any way of their participation, so they were punished in subtle ways for participating on this team. As the facilitators attempted to please the CEO, there was no clear charter or mission as to what they were actually supposed to accomplish—no way to assess their performance or keep track of progress.

The power struggle intensified between the COO (who thought this was not the way to go and would have none of it) and the CEO. The CEO and the top management team arranged to travel to a leadership conference where they could hear presentations from high-performance organizations that had used the performance excellence techniques successfully. The CEO made it a priority to plan only morning presentations so everyone could play tennis or golf together each afternoon. Tennis and golf, not the need for better management systems, was the main topic of discussion at the evening dinners. A good time was had by all, but no consensus around change developed or was even discussed.

Training and the Change Process. Still, Victor wanted the facilitators to continue their work to assist change. The internal facilitators were placed in charge of conducting training for the entire organization. After the initial training was designed, a date was set to present a half-day version to the senior staff. Although the training designed for employees and lower-level managers was a four-day course, the senior staff did not feel they needed the same intense training or skills as the workforce. However, Victor made it a high priority for his direct reports to attend. At the last minute, Victor had to attend a function related to the board of directors and did not attend the training.

The training was, to put it mildly, a disaster. The executives, prompted by the snide comments of the COO, never gave it a chance. They concluded that the training was not effective and should not be rolled out to the employees. In the face of compelling opposition, Victor quietly diverted his attention elsewhere.

Leadership Style Summary

The current state of John's high-performance *way to run the business* versus the high-performance *initiative* at Victor's company is probably obvious. Perhaps you could spot some of the problems each type of leader addressed and solutions they supported.

Using symbols and language to manage the transition to high performance is tricky and usually demands that some external person be involved who can provide good sound advice to the CEO, based on experience and expertise. Using power constructively is absolutely critical, since failure of the top leader to use all forms of influence available will intensify conflict and act as a *de facto* barrier to change.

Motivating people to act constructively, and not feel threatened, is another challenge. Providing a clear focus on the future state, while rewarding behavior that facilitates the transition, will work to ensure the change actually happens. Victor's vision was unclear. He did not act as a leader. He ensured his facilitators would never succeed by never championing their work in any way. The next time Victor gets a new idea, these people (if they are still working for the organization) will duck and run for cover rather than be at the forefront of the initiative.

John never strayed from his vision or lost persuasive influence as CEO. He ensured his management team was supportive by first defining and clarifying organizational values, direction, and expectations; encouraging them to climb on board; and ensuring they acquired the skills and support to spread the approaches throughout the company.

Leadership Lessons

Based on the organizational performance research cited earlier, coupled with the relentless pace of change in all sectors and increasingly global competition, there are several strong messages leaders need to understand. Then they must be willing to take the necessary steps to change. Focus on the marketplace for cues to change. Ask, for example:

- Is your competition growing weaker?
- Is the economy more stable and secure?
- Are the demands of your customers declining?
- Do you have all of the resources you need to meet your current and future goals?
- Do you believe your workforce will be willing or able to continue working at the pace you have set for them? Will they do more?

If the answer is no to any of these questions, action is needed. Efficiently identifying the necessary steps going forward requires a Baldrige-based assessment of current management systems, the identification of strengths and opportunities for improvement, and a willingness to drive the necessary changes to transform the organization over several years. Once the assessment is complete and priorities are agreed upon, line up plans and resources and support the change wholeheartedly.

Great Leaders Are Great Communicators Who Lead by Positive Example

One characteristic of a high-performance organization is outstanding performance results. How does an organization achieve such results? How does it become world-class? We have found unanimous agreement on the critical and fundamental role of leadership. There is not one example of an organization or unit within an organization that achieves superior levels of performance without the personal and active involvement of its top leadership. Similarly, in all cases where an organization has not been able to achieve or sustain high performance, the cause can be traced to leadership failures.

Top leaders in high-performing organizations create a powerful vision that focuses and energizes the workforce. They engage workers to drive change and innovation. Everyone is pulling together toward the same clearly defined goals and objectives. An inspired vision, combined with appropriately aligned recognition and reward, is the catalyst that builds trust and launches initiatives to overcome the organizational *status quo*.

Great leaders also communicate clear objectives. They assign accountability, ensure that the workforce has the tools and skills required, and create a work climate where individual initiative and the transfer of learning thrive. They reward teamwork and data-driven improvement. Practicing what they preach, they serve as role models for continuous improvement, consensus building, and fact-based decision-making. Their actions match their words. They push authority and accountability to the lowest possible levels.

One lesson from great leaders is to refrain from the use of the word *quality*. Unfortunately, using the word can create an unintended barrier of mistrust and negativism that leaders must overcome before even starting on the road to performance excellence. Too often, when skilled, hard-working, dedicated employees are told by leaders, "We must improve quality," they conclude that their leaders believe their work is poor. They frequently retort with, "We already do quality work!" Registered professionals (engineers, chemists, psychologists, physicians, teachers, to name a few) often exacerbate the communication problem by arguing that they, not customers, are the best ones in a position to know and define quality. These messages confuse the workforce and antagonize customers.

Instead, we advise leaders to create a work climate that enables employees to develop and use their full potential, to improve continually the way they work—to seek higher performance levels and reduce activities that do not add value or optimize performance. Most employees readily agree that there is always room for improvement—all have seen work that does not add value. The use of a phrase like "performance excellence" or "high-performing organization" ensures that the concept is the responsibility of the entire organization—not just the quality department.

The use of the word *quality* can also open leadership to challenges as to what definition of quality the organization should use. This leads to our second lesson learned. Leaders will have to overcome two organizational tendencies—to reject any management model or approach *not invented here* and to think that there are many equally valid models. Quality differs from a decision tree or problem-solving model where there are many acceptable alternatives. The Integrated Management System model—and the many national, state, and organization assessment systems based on it—is accepted as *the* foundation for defining performance excellence in organizations worldwide. The Integrated Management System and the Baldrige Criteria define validated, leading-edge practices for managing an organization to achieve peak performance.

Over 30 years of extraordinary business results shown by Baldrige, EQFM, China Association for Quality, and other excellence award recipients in all sectors of the economy, and numerous state-level, and other national award recipients, have helped convince those willing to learn and listen.

To be effective, leaders must understand the Integrated Management System and communicate to the workforce and leadership their decision to use that approach for assessment and improvement. Without clear, unwavering leadership commitment to achieving the elements of the comprehensive Integrated Management System, resources may be wasted chasing fads, special projects, and isolated, ineffective strategies.

Although programs, such as activity-based costing, management by objective, reengineering, project management, balanced scorecards, Six Sigma, lean enterprise, and ISO 9000 certification, to name a few, have produced some good results, unless leaders focus on the entire Integrated Management System, performance is not optimized.

These are valuable tools within the Integrated Management System where their value is integrated within the overall improvement strategy.

See the article in the online resources titled: "Baldrige, Six Sigma, Lean and Balanced Scorecard Alignment."

Without clear leadership there will be many hikers walking around but no marked trails for them to follow. Unless leaders understand the entire system and take responsibility for transforming the workplace, performance optimization is not attainable. This brings us to our third leadership lesson learned.

A significant portion of senior leaders' time—as much as 60%–80%—should be spent in visible Integrated Management System-related leadership activities, such as goal setting, planning, reviewing performance, recognizing and rewarding high performance, improving their personal leadership skills, and spending time understanding and communicating with customers and suppliers, not micromanaging subordinates' work. In setting goals, planning, and reviewing performance, senior leaders must look at the inside from the outside. Looking at the organization through the critical eyes of external customers, suppliers, and other stakeholders provides a vital perspective.

A key role of the effective senior leader is to focus the organization on engaging customers. Leaders must champion change and ensure actions focus on creating customer value and exceeding their expectations. Leaders must role-model the tools of performance excellence and ensure the organization focuses on its vision, mission, and strategic direction to keep customers loyal.

Listen

Successful leaders know the power in listening to their people—those they rely on to achieve their goals. One vital link to the pulse of the organization is employee feedback. It is important to check with workers to determine whether what you have said has been understood, to ask for feedback, and then to listen carefully. To know whether what you have outlined as a plan makes sense or has gaping faults, ask for feedback and then listen. Your leadership system cannot improve without evaluating and acting on employee feedback.

Manage and Drive Change

Leaders of all types of organizations can count on relentless, rapid change being part of their world. The rate of change confronting organizations today is far greater than ever before. Skills born out of the Industrial Revolution carried our parents through a 40-year work life. Human knowledge now doubles every two to three years, instead of the 40 years it took in the mid- to late-twentieth century. Our children are told to expect *at least* five career (not job) changes during their work life.

Several lessons for leaders arise from this condition today. Change may not occur on the schedule set for it. It is often too fast or too uneven to predict. Also, change driven by leaders is often resisted by their most successful followers—they have difficulty seeing the need to change. Take, for example, a school district that scheduled a Baldrige-based improvement workshop for its middle school faculty. The day before the training, the district leadership received a letter protesting the workshop on the grounds it was not needed. The letter was signed by the 20 *best* teachers in the school. To the credit of the school district leadership, they held the workshop anyway, and the truly outstanding teachers saw the value in continuous improvement once they began to listen and make changes that helped their students.

Leaders who share the values of performance excellence embedded in the Integrated Management System will need to drive change to make the necessary improvements. Meaningful change will not happen naturally or easily. It is rarely driven by those at the bottom (except for revolutionaries and terrorists). Embracing the concepts of organizational (not just individual) learning will facilitate desired cultural and organizational change needed to achieve excellence. Leaders will need to develop a system that drives new knowledge throughout the organization.

Strategy Lessons

Deploy through People, Not Paper

Strategic planning helps leaders examine the factors that will affect an organization's future. The resulting strategic objectives define the things the organization must accomplish or achieve to be successful in the future. The planning process should begin by ensuring that all contributors agree on terminology; otherwise, the strategic plan may turn out to be just a marketing plan, a budget plan, or a financial business plan, depending on who is leading the team.

> ***Strategic objectives must be defined in measurable, outcome-oriented terms. Strategic objectives describe desired outcomes, not enablers or activities that are necessary to achieve outcomes.***

Developing separate, bottom-up plans for each aspect of business success is counterproductive. This approach almost guarantees a nonintegrated, short-lived, fragmented performance-improvement effort. Therefore, leaders should concentrate on the few critical improvement goals necessary for organizational success, such as improving customer loyalty or becoming a performance leader. The well-developed strategic plan also:

- Documents the financial and market impact of achieving these objectives as well as the impact on customers and long-term sustainability.
- Details actions to support the objectives as well as performance timelines and milestones.
- Considers the competitive environment, internal core competencies, and the performance of external suppliers in deciding what work to outsource and what to keep in house.
- Specifies, in measurable terms, the expected performance milestones that must be met to achieve the goals. The milestones (or timelines) match the leaders' cycle for reviewing progress (that is, if leaders review progress quarterly, then the plan predicts quarterly outcome-oriented milestones).

Do not release the plan without established, clear metrics to communicate expectations and monitor progress. *A critical lesson learned when it comes to strategic plans is that there can be no rest until everyone in the organization understands their role in the plan and how their contribution will be measured and rewarded.* The goals, actions, measures, and milestones need not be complex. For every unit, they can be presented on a one-page electronic scorecard to which senior leaders refer during performance reviews. Everyone at all levels should be able to use a personal one-page scorecard to display the plan, define actions needed, and monitor actual progress against expected progress.

Customers Lessons

Customers Expect Solutions to Problems They Don't Know They Have

The high-performing organization systematically determines its customers' short- and long-term service and product requirements. It does this based on information from former as well as current and potential customers. It builds relationships with customers and continuously obtains information, using the data to improve its service and products and better understand customer preferences.

The Criteria require organizations to listen to the customers to prevent misunderstanding or inadvertently changing their requirements. When customer service representatives, sales personnel, engineers, and others fail to listen to the customer, it is easy to misrepresent the customer and fail to design and deliver the right products, programs, and services.

The smart organization prioritizes the drivers of satisfaction and loyalty of its customers, compares itself to its competitors (or organizations providing similar products or services), and continuously improves customer satisfaction and loyalty.

As the organization becomes more systematic and effective in determining customer needs and expectations, it learns that there is high variation among customer groups and segments. The more sophisticated the measurement system, the more variation will be revealed. It is particularly important that organizations focus on this vital process and make it a top priority that their customers have access to people to make known their requirements and their preferences. The effective use of social media such as websites, Twitter, Facebook, LinkedIn, blogs, and consumer chat rooms helps modern organizations ensure they are building solid and positive relationships with their customers.

One specific lesson learned comes from voice mail—a big step forward in convenience and efficiency that, if used poorly, can be a big step backward in customer relationship building. For example, a major international financial institution put its highest priority customers on a new voice-mail system. Customers were never informed about the system and one day called their special line to find rock music and a multitiered voice-menu system instead of their personal financial account manager. Even though the phone was answered on the first ring, these preferred customers were furious. This is a good example of a step in the wrong direction—customers were never asked about their requirements and preferences, and the organization created many frustrated customers and lost accounts.

Another important lesson is to segment customers according to their needs and preferences and do what is necessary to build strong, positive relationships with them. More and more customers are looking for service providers to help define their unique needs and respond to those unique needs. In short, customers are expecting solutions to problems that they, the customers, have not yet realized they have.

Organizations that make it easy for customers to complain are in a good position to hear about problems early so they can fix them and plan ahead to prevent them from recurring. If organizations handle customer complaints effectively at the first point of contact, customer loyalty, satisfaction, and engagement will increase. When organizations do not make it easy for customers to complain, then customers, when finally given the chance to provide feedback, may not bother to complain. They may simply take their business elsewhere.

The next lesson has to do with educating the organization's leadership in the fundamentals of customer engagement and customer-satisfaction research before beginning to collect customer-satisfaction data. Failure to do this may affect the questions asked and the usefulness of the data as a strategic tool. At the very least, it will make the development of data-collection instruments a long, misunderstood effort, creating rework and unnecessary cost.

Do not expect everyone in your organization to welcome customer feedback—many fear accountability that such feedback can force. Time and time again, the organizations most resistant to surveying customers, conducting focus groups, and making it easy for customers to complain are the same organizations that do not have everyday contact-handling systems, customer support standards, or trained and empowered front-line employees to serve customers and resolve their concerns promptly. Front-line employees who do not have sufficient decision-making authority and are not ready to acknowledge customer concerns are not capable of assuming responsibility to solve customer problems.

No single customer-feedback tool is sufficient by itself. Social media and web-based technologies such as Twitter, consumer chat rooms, and blogs provide a variety of information to consider, but not to the exclusion of traditional methods. A mail-based survey does not take the place of personal interviews. Focus groups or Twitter do not replace surveys. High-performance organizations use multiple listening posts and train front-line employees to collect customer feedback and improve those listening posts. In the high-performance organization, for example, even an accounts-receivable system is viewed as a listening post.

Do not lose sight of the fact that the best customer-feedback method, whether it is a survey, focus group, web-based, or one-on-one interview, is only a tool:

- Make sure the data gathered are actionable.
- Aggregate the data from all sources to permit complete analyses to get the whole story.
- Use the data to improve work processes and strategic planning.

Finally, be aware that customers are not interested in your problems. They merely want products or services delivered as promised. They become loyal when consistent value is provided that sets you above all others. Merely meeting their basic expectations brands you as marginal. To be valued you must consistently delight and exceed the customers' expectations.

Measurement, Analysis, and Knowledge Management Lessons

Data-Driven Management

The high-performance organization collects, manages, and analyzes data and information to drive excellence and improve its overall performance. Said another way, information and data are used to drive actions and build accountability. Using data and information as strategic weapons, effective leaders constantly compare their organization to competitors, similar service providers, and world-class organizations. They identify shortfalls in their own organization as a result, and take action to close the gaps.

While people tend to think of data and measurement as objective and hard, there is often a softer by-product of measurement. That by-product is the basic human emotion of fear. This perspective on data and measurement leads to the first lesson learned about measurement, analysis, and knowledge management. Human fear must be recognized and managed to practice data-driven management.

This fear can be found in two types of people. The first are those who have a simple fear of numbers—those who hated mathematics in school and probably stretch their quantitative capabilities to balance their checkbook. These individuals are lost in numerical-data discussions. When asked to measure or when presented with data, they can become fearful, resistant, or even angry. These reactions can undermine improvement efforts.

The second type of individual, who may be comfortable with numbers, realizes that numbers can impose higher levels of accountability.

The fear of accountability is based on the fear of real performance failure that numbers might reveal or, more often, an overall fear of the unknown that will drive important decisions. Power structures can and do shift when decisions are data driven.

Fearful individuals can undermine effective data-driven management systems. In managing this fear, leaders must demonstrate that system and process improvement is the goal, not punishing individuals.

A mature, high-performance organization will collect data on competitors and similar providers and compare itself against world-class leaders. Some individuals may not be capable of seeing the benefit of using this type of process-performance information. The process of collecting these types of data is known as benchmarking. The focus is on identifying, learning from, and adopting best practices or methods from similar processes, regardless of industry or product similarity. Adopting the best practices of other organizations has driven breakthrough improvements and provided great opportunities for gaining a competitive advantage.

Lesson number two, therefore, is that an organization that has difficulty comparing itself with dissimilar organizations is not ready to benchmark and is not likely to be able to optimize or even improve its own performance as a result.

The third lesson in this area relates to not being a DRIP. This refers to a tendency to collect so much data that the organization becomes Data Rich and Information Poor. Avoid wasting capital resources by asking this question: "Will these data help us make better decisions?" If the answer is no, do not waste time collecting, analyzing, or trying to use the data.

Ideally, data should not be collected unless it supports decision-making.

Workforce Lessons

Workforce Engagement: Getting Workers to Contribute Their Utmost

Personnel departments have been renamed in many organizations to *human resources.* This name change is intended to draw attention to the fact that workers are valuable resources of the organization, not just dispensable commodities to be hired, commanded, and fired. Now, however, the leap made by successful organizations is that the capability and capacity of the workforce need to be part of every strategic and operational decision of the organization. This focus goes far beyond the purview of the former departments of human resources. In high-performing organizations, workers are treated as valuable assets—where investment and development are critical to optimize the asset.

One of the valuable lessons learned in this regard is not to let an out-of-date, territorial personnel or human resources director use archaic rules to stop your performance-improvement program. Although many human resources professionals are among the brave pioneers in high-performance organizations, others have tried to keep compensation and promotions tied to length of service, seniority, or tenure, rather than aligned with performance outcomes. The failure to align compensation, rewards, and recognition with actual performance can stop progress in its tracks or slow it significantly.

The Big Challenge Is Engagement

The most powerful drivers of workforce engagement relate to workers feeling valued by their supervisors and organization, and workers feeling involved. The high-performing organization values its workers and demonstrates this by enabling them to develop and realize their full potential while providing them with a clear progression path and appropriate rewards and incentives to do so. The organization that is focused on workforce excellence builds and maintains a climate of work trust. Trust is essential for employee engagement, personal and professional growth, and high organizational performance.

The first workforce lesson is perhaps the most critical one. If leaders personally demonstrate all the correct leadership behaviors, yet continue to recognize and reward *fire-fighting* performance, offer pay and bonuses tied to length of service, and promote individuals who do not represent customer-focused, high-performance role models—workforce engagement will suffer and their organization-wide improvement effort will be short lived.

Strategic objectives must be defined in measurable, outcome-oriented terms. Strategic objectives describe desired outcomes, not enablers or activities that are necessary to achieve outcomes.

Compensation, incentives, recognition, and rewards must be tied to the achievement of key high-performance outcomes, such as customer satisfaction, innovation, performance improvement, and other business results. The compensation/recognition tool is a powerful lever to assist in aligning, or misaligning, the work of the organization.

Developing and Maintaining Skills

A second human resource lesson learned relates to building capacity and capabilities. Training is not a panacea or a goal in itself. The organization must identify the skill, competency, and staffing gaps that relate to performance gaps. Then the organization must take steps to close the gaps. Training, as a tool to close capability and capacity gaps, must be part of an overall business strategy. If not, money and resources are probably better spent on a memorable holiday party.

Timing is critical. Broad-based workforce skill training should not come first. Many organizations rush out and train their entire workforce only to find themselves having to retrain months or years later when the skill is needed. Workers should be involved in developing training plans and schedules to ensure they develop important skills just in time to use them in their assignments, not just in case they need them.

Effective skill development requires management support to reinforce the use of new skills on the job. Training must be offered when an application exists to use and reinforce the skill. Otherwise, most of what is learned will be forgotten. The effectiveness of training must be assessed based on the extent of learning and impact on the job, not merely the likability of the instructor or the clarity of course materials.

Leadership development at all levels of the organization is an indispensable component to high performance. New technology has increased training flexibility so that all knowledge does not have to be transferred in a classroom setting. Consider many options when planning how best to update skills.

Assessing Engagement and Satisfaction

Questions used to assess engagement should examine the following topics: personal contribution; personal capabilities development and career progression; reward, recognition, and compensation; manager attributes; improvement, initiative, innovation; and workplace climate. Sample issues are provided on page 189 in Table 4, as part of the analysis of Item 5.2.

Engaged, satisfied workers enhance organizational productivity, customer engagement and satisfaction, and financial success. Workplace surveys, together with data on grievances, absenteeism, and turnover, are often used to measure and identify weaknesses in workforce engagement and satisfaction that disrupt productivity.

> ***Organizations have success in improving workforce engagement and satisfaction by conducting routine work-climate surveys, promptly meeting with employees to plan improvements, and tying improvements in ratings to managers' compensation and recognition.***

Empowerment to Make Work-related Decisions

Two final workforce excellence lessons have to do with engaging workers in decisions about their work. Engaging workers in decision-making without the right skills or a sense of direction produces chaos, not high performance.

First, leaders who empower workers before communicating and testing that a sense of direction has been fully understood and that the necessary skills are in place will find that they are managing chaos—workers moving in different directions, working at cross-purposes.

Second, not everyone wants to be empowered to make decisions about their work, and to do so may represent a barrier to high performance. While there may be individuals who truly seek to avoid responsibility for making improvements, claiming "that's management's job," these individuals do not last long in a high-performing organization. They begin to stick out like a lone bird during a cold and snowy winter. Team members who want the organization to thrive do not tolerate such people on their team for long.

The bigger reason for individuals failing to *take empowerment and run with it* is management's mixed messages. In short, management must convince workers that they (managers) really believe that workers know their own processes and, with proper training and support, are best suited to make decisions about their work. Consistent leadership is required to help workers overcome legitimate, long-standing fear of traditional management practices used so often in the past to control and punish.

Aligning compensation, incentives, and reward systems to reinforce performance plans and core values is one of the most effective means to enhance organizational performance; however, getting workers to believe their leaders really trust them to contribute their utmost and make decisions to improve their own processes is difficult.

Operations Lessons

Listen to Process Owners and Keep Them Engaged

Operations involves the design, implementation, management, and continuous improvement of processes needed to meet customer requirements and deliver quality products and services including health care services and education services. Every high-performance organization identifies its key work processes and manages them to ensure that customer requirements are met consistently and performance is improved continuously.

The first lesson learned has to do with the visibility of processes. When processes are hard to observe, as so many are in the service, education, and health care sectors, they are hard to improve. The simple exercise of drawing a process-flow diagram with people engaged in a process can be a struggle, but also a valuable source of information that can help identify process shortfalls and improvement opportunities. With no vantage point from which to see work as a process, many people never think of themselves as engaged in a process. Some even deny it. The fact that all work—visible and invisible—is part of a process should be understood before employees can begin to execute and improve key processes effectively or consistently.

Once this is understood, a second process management lesson comes to light. Process owners are the best ones, but not the only ones, to improve their processes. They should be part of process-improvement teams, but outsiders could be involved as well. Effective process-improvement teams often comprise carefully selected cross-discipline, cross-functional, multilevel people who bring detailed knowledge and fresh insight to the examination of a process. Consultants, such as Six Sigma Black Belts, can provide important insights to process owners. However, do not lose sight of the process owners—the people with expert knowledge of the process who should be accountable for long-term improvement. In a misguided effort to ensure that all of its process-improvement teams were cross-functional and multilevel, one organization enlisted volunteers to join process-improvement teams. Using this democratic process, one marketing process-improvement team ended up with no credible marketing expertise among its members. Instead, a group of frustrated support and technical staff members, who knew nothing about marketing, wasted time and money redesigning a process that was doomed to fail from the outset.

The third process management lesson learned involves an issue mentioned earlier. When focusing too closely on internal process data, there is a tendency to lose sight of external requirements. Organizations often succeed at making their processes better, faster, and (maybe) cheaper for them, but not necessarily for the betterment of their customers. When analyzing work processes, someone must stubbornly play the role of advocate for the customers' perspective, ensuring the voice of the customer is heard. Ensure that process changes will help make improvements for customers, key financials, employees, or top result areas. Avoid wasting resources on process improvements that do not appropriately benefit customers, employees, or the key performance objectives of the organization.

A fourth lesson involves design processes, an important but often neglected part of process management. The best organizations have learned that improvements made early in the process, beginning with design, save more time and resources than those made farther *downstream.* To identify how design processes can be improved, it is necessary to include ongoing evaluation and improvement cycles. Create a series of in-process measures to help spot and fix process failures early. Remember the lesson taught by one of the founding fathers of the United States, Benjamin Franklin, "A stitch in time saves nine." To save resources, find the hole and fix it quickly.

Results Lessons

The Right Activities Lead to Desired Results

Results fall into five important categories:

1. Customer-focused product and process results, including product and service outcomes, health care outcomes or student achievement; process effectiveness and efficiency; safety and emergency preparedness; and supply-network performance
2. Customer-focused results, including customer engagement, satisfaction, and dissatisfaction
3. Workforce performance results, including capacity and capability, climate, engagement, and workforce development results
4. Leadership and governance results, such as the extent to which the following were achieved: effective leadership communication, fiscal accountability and other governance results, regulatory and legal compliance, ethics, societal contributions and community support, and strategy implementation
5. Financial, marketplace, and strategy performance results, including achievement of organizational strategy and action plans

Product performance outcomes provide critical information on key measures of the product or service itself. This information allows an organization to predict whether customers are *likely* to be satisfied—without asking them. One important lesson in this area is to select measures that correlate with, and predict, customer preference, satisfaction, and engagement.

Process effectiveness and efficiency results pertain to measures of internal effectiveness that may not be of immediate interest to customers, such as cycle time (how long it takes to brew a pot of coffee), waste (how many pots you have to pour out because the coffee sat too long), and error (serving decaf when regular coffee was requested). Ultimately, improving internal work-process efficiency can result in reduced cost, rework, waste, scrap, and other factors that affect the bottom line, whether profit-driven or budget-driven. In either case, customers are indirectly affected. To stay in business, to remain competitive, or to meet increased performance demands with fewer resources, the organization will be required to improve processes that enhance operational and support service results.

Some organizations have found it beneficial to have their customers help analyze some of their business results with the idea of learning from them as well as building and strengthening relationships. This may or may not be appropriate for your organization, but many successful enterprises have shared results with key customer groups at a level appropriate for their specific organization.

Systems must exist to make sure that results data are used at all levels to plan, monitor progress, identify gaps, and make improvements. Customer-satisfaction data are particularly important. Remember that when customers are asked their opinion, an expectation is created in their minds that the information will be used to make improvements that benefit them. Do not ask for customer feedback without committing to improve.

Workforce performance results provide earlier alerts to problems that may threaten success. Absenteeism, turnover, accidents, low morale and engagement, grievances, poor skills, or ineffective training suboptimize organizational effectiveness. By monitoring performance in these areas, leaders can adjust more quickly and prevent minor problems from overwhelming the organization.

Regulatory and legal compliance, and citizenship, including behaving ethically as an organization and as individuals, have proven critical to long-term organizational survival. Just think of Enron and the problems that poor ethics and inadequate governance caused the entire U.S. economy.

Financial and market performance are keys to survival. Organizations that make changes that do not ultimately improve financial performance are wasting resources and growing weaker financially. This applies to for-profit as well as not-for-profit, education, health care, and government organizations. It is important, however, to avoid overreliance on financial results. Financial results are the lagging indicators of organization performance. Leaders who focus primarily on lagging financial indicators often overlook the root causes of problems or are not alerted in time to be able to respond to changing business needs. Focusing on finances to run the business—to the exclusion of leading indicators such as operational performance and employee satisfaction—is like driving your car by looking only in the rear-view mirror. You cannot avoid potholes and turns in the road.

No single process required by the Integrated Management System leads to winning levels of performance. No single result can alert you to areas that need attention. *The most important lesson is that every element of the entire Baldrige Framework is required to achieve and sustain peak performance.*

LEADERSHIP SUMMARY: SEVEN MUST-DO PRACTICES

Keys to Optimizing Performance

There is no evidence of an organization optimizing performance and achieving Baldrige or top state-level recognition without enhancing the entire management system, from leadership and planning to customers, people, and processes. Although all of these factors are critical in the long term, top leaders have the responsibility to set the direction, values, and expectations that drive change and create a sense of urgency. If leaders fail to take the following actions, the transformation to a high-performing organization will be seriously delayed and most likely not take place at all.

> ***Leader actions absolutely determine the speed and success of the effort to optimize organizational performance.***

1. ***Role-model effective leadership practices.*** Like it or not, leader example drives the actions of others far better than words. Rhetoric without appropriate action is virtually worthless and may be counterproductive. Do not expect anyone else to do the things you will not. The concept of *do as I say, not as I do* has never worked to guide or change behavior. A leader who displays contempt for subordinates and acts as a demigod who is superior to all others never produces a loyal, high-performing workforce or creates an organization capable of excellence:

- If you do not expect performance excellence through your words and actions, others in your organization will think it is optional.

> ***When change is perceived as optional, it is not likely to occur.***

- If you do not have time to innovate, no one else will think innovation is important, and it is not likely to occur.
- If you do not value and engage the employees with whom you work, other managers will follow your lead and fail to value and engage their employees.
- If you do not seek improvement ideas from your subordinates, they will not seek them in turn, and people will not think of ways to improve.
- If you do not hold managers accountable for empowering their subordinates, they will believe empowerment is optional (see the first bullet).
- If you do not learn new things, you may not keep up with important changes affecting your business, and others will not see the value in learning.

Develop a list of attributes you want to role-model in addition to those listed. Check how you are perceived on these leadership attributes from peer, subordinate, and employee feedback. Change where you are role-modeling the wrong things..

2. ***Favor decisions based on fact rather than intuition.*** The lack of facts and data forces leaders to default to intuition as the basis for decision-making. Many great leaders have relied on intuition when facts were unavailable. However, no great leader relied only, or even mostly, on intuition in the face of valid facts. The best leaders make consistently good decisions, which require reliable, accurate, valid, and timely facts and data.

We rarely have access to all of the information we want prior to making decisions. However, we will surely not have enough fact-based information unless we prepare in advance. To make consistently better decisions, the best leaders drive fact-based diagnoses of organizational performance that focus on closing the gaps in areas critical to success. This information must be available when needed and easy to understand.

High-performing leaders ask "How do you know?" when they are given opinion-based information, typically from someone who prefaces their statement with "I think ..."

3. ***Learn constantly.*** Great leaders recognize that current knowledge limits their capabilities and success. You may think you have all of the knowledge and skills you need, but how do you know what you don't know? Do not expect your subordinates to learn for you because they suffer from the same limits. Considering the pace of change and the speed with which human knowledge is doubling, unless you aggressively pursue new knowledge, you will most certainly become obsolete or less effective faster.

Identify and list the things you must learn and the behaviors you must change to become a better leader. Ask your subordinates to give you feedback to help you complete the list. Set learning goals and timelines to monitor the pace of new learning. Make adjustments to stay on track.

4. ***Share knowledge***. Enhance the impact of your new knowledge by sharing it with others. By teaching others and answering their questions, your understanding becomes stronger and you can apply new knowledge faster and better. It is also a good way to role-model the value of learning. Set a schedule to teach others about performance excellence systems and processes at least two to four times each year, and stick to it. When others share their knowledge, actively participate in their session to demonstrate that you are ready to learn constantly (see #3).

5. ***Require other leaders in the organization to do the same.*** The performance of individuals drives the

performance of the organization. If your performance is suboptimal because you lack certain knowledge, skills, and abilities, the same is certainly true for your subordinates and their employees. After they see the value you place in role-modeling effective practices, learning, and coaching, make it clear you expect them to do the same. It is critical to clearly set this expectation for learning, as well as set clear, measurable expectations for work after they complete the training.

Discuss your concerns and expectations, and answer their questions. You will have to do this very often at first. Be consistent. Those who resist change look for loopholes and ways to avoid change. Do not create loopholes for them. Permit no excuses for those who refuse to learn. Champion the requirements leading to optimum organizational performance. Be prepared to remove leaders who do not support continuous improvement and performance excellence systems.

6. ***Align expectations, measures, rewards, and recognition***. The system you have in place is perfectly suited to produce the results you are currently getting. If you want to change the outcomes, you must change the people and processes that produce them. Training is only a part of the change process:

- Express new expectations for both individual and group performance in measurable, outcome-oriented terms.
- Measure progress regularly and give prompt feedback.
- Visibly reward and recognize the desired behavior.
- Find other work for those who cannot or will not do the things needed for driving high performance. By rewarding those who achieve desired results and removing those who do not, you make it clear that performance excellence is crucial to success—it will not be perceived as optional. If you keep a manager in place who has not taken the necessary steps to improve, you must realize that the subordinates of that manager will conclude that such performance must be acceptable in your eyes. Your failure to act sends the wrong message.

To enhance desired performance outcomes, ensure that goals, strategic objectives, actions, measures, analysis, training, compensation, incentives, reward, and recognition are completely aligned. If achieving strategic objectives is truly critical to your future success, be sure to assign actions, make sure your people have the skills they need to do the work, measure and monitor progress, and reward desired behavior and outcomes.

> ***What gets measured gets done. What gets rewarded gets done first.***

7. ***Use training and development as a tool to enhance skills and inform—not as a substitute for personal leadership direction.*** Employees desire and expect important information to come from their leaders. Do not simply tell employees to do something new and different and expect it will be done. You must check understanding, measure and monitor progress, and provide appropriate incentives to actually get the desired behavior:

- Sending subordinate managers and employees to training and expecting the trainer to give the new management directions will rarely produce the desired results. It usually produces high skepticism and hostility, and reinforces the idea that leaders are not serious and committed to the new program or change—otherwise they would introduce it themselves. It also makes the trainer and the curriculum the target of criticism and blame:
  - "This class is a waste of time."
  - "The trainer should tell us what to do when we get back to the office."
  - "I do not know why I am here."
  - "What resources is management going to commit to this effort?"
  - "Just how serious is management about these changes/programs? Have they taken this training?"

Before anyone is sent to training, participants need to understand and *be able to describe* why they are there and what they are expected to get out of the training. These expectations should be set by the leaders who send the participants, not the trainers. Leaders could ask trainers to pretest the class to determine the extent to which participants understand why they are there. Those who are not prepared should be sent back. It should be the job of the sending managers to provide the proper foundation and preparation for their subordinate employees prior to training.

If you do not do the seven listed activities, your actions are telling your workers and subordinate managers that performance excellence is optional—something to do if they feel like it. In that event, you and your organization will most certainly fail to achieve the desired change and improvement.

Taking Action

All leaders have a responsibility for communicating the mission, vision, strategic objectives, and enabling activities to all workers. It is very important that leaders and workers understand and agree fully with the planned objectives. It is even more important that they carry out the actions needed to actually achieve the objectives. Effective leaders do not micromanage the process to deploy and implement strategy throughout the organization. Ineffective leaders want to control every aspect of the plan-deployment process, and effective implementation is rarely achieved. The effective plan-deployment process cascades from top management to all locations and levels of the organization. This means that the top leaders determine the overall objective or target and a lower-level leader determines the more specific target and means. This then sets the target for the next level to determine appropriate means. Figure 11 provides one example of this effect.

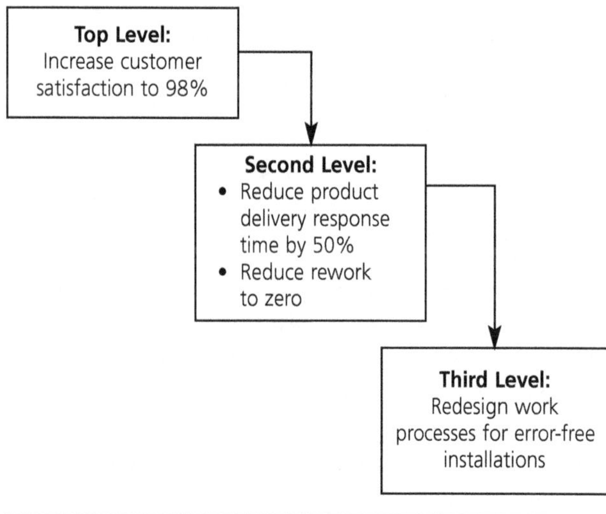

Figure 11 Deploying strategic objectives.

Personal Management Effectiveness —The Use of Upward Evaluations

Before managers and leaders take action to change the way they manage, they should gather facts about their current style. They need to know what aspects of their style are considered strong and should not be changed. The starting point for improving management style, therefore, is an honest assessment of each manager's current behavior by subordinates, peers, and supervisors. This is also called a 360-degree evaluation.

Formal upward evaluations have been used for decades to help assess job performance of leaders. As organizations have become committed to improving workforce relations and manager effectiveness, upward and 360-degree evaluation have become widely used tools that more and more leaders value.

Three reasons why upward evaluation and the resulting feedback are beneficial include:

1. ***Validity***. Subordinates interact regularly with their managers and have a unique vantage from which to assess manager style.
2. ***Reliability***. Confidential feedback from numerous subordinates provides the best chance for accurate data. Workers who are hurt by poor management hope their feedback brings change.
3. ***Involvement and morale.*** Asking people to comment on the effectiveness and style of their managers boosts morale and sends a clear message that the organization is serious about increasing workers involvement—but only if the manager takes action to improve; otherwise, morale and motivation can get worse.

The Feedback Process

1. Leaders solicit feedback on how they perform against specific behaviors that are characteristic of an effective manager. The Baldrige Criteria provide examples.
2. They use this information to plan personal improvement strategies.
3. They share the results of the survey with their workers and discuss possible improvement actions, then refine their plan.

4. They make improvements as planned and start the process again no more than one year later.

Figure 12 maps the process. This process enables workers to help their manager understand how he or she is perceived, as well as identify areas of strength on which the manager can build. However, some important procedures should be in place to prevent improper use of the tool:

- Feedback should always be used and interpreted in the spirit of continuous personal improvement. Personally identifiable results should go only to the manager who was rated and should not be used as a basis for performance ratings, promotion, assignments, or pay adjustments (unless, of course, the manager refuses to work to improve).
- Anonymity for those completing questionnaires should be carefully protected. No one other than the worker should see his or her personal ratings.
- Personally identifiable results should be provided only to the manager named on the questionnaire. When the managers receive the results, they review their own ratings to determine their strengths and opportunities for improvement. Then they take steps to improve.

Aggregate data should be reported to top leadership to monitor as part of an organization-wide improvement priority. If the average scores do not improve appropriately, then the leaders may elect to see personally identifiable data of low-performing managers to encourage them to do more.

The Management Effectiveness Survey in Figure 13 and Supervisor Management Survey in Figure 14 (©Mark Blazey) on the next two pages can provide information that might help leaders and managers at all levels determine areas to address to strengthen their personal effectiveness. It represents one set of questions to examine leadership communication, openness, and effectiveness. Certainly other questions may be asked as circumstances change. In fact, to determine if any survey is asking the correct questions, the survey itself should be evaluated. This can be done by using open-ended questions and asking workers to identify other issues that are of concern to them and should be included in the survey. Also, ask if some of the questions are not relevant or important and should be eliminated; then adjust the survey accordingly.

In addition to aggregating scores from workers, it is also useful to compare the perceptions of workers with the perception of the leader or manager who is the subject of the assessment. Many times, workers identify a specific weakness that the leader believes is much stronger. These differences, together with key

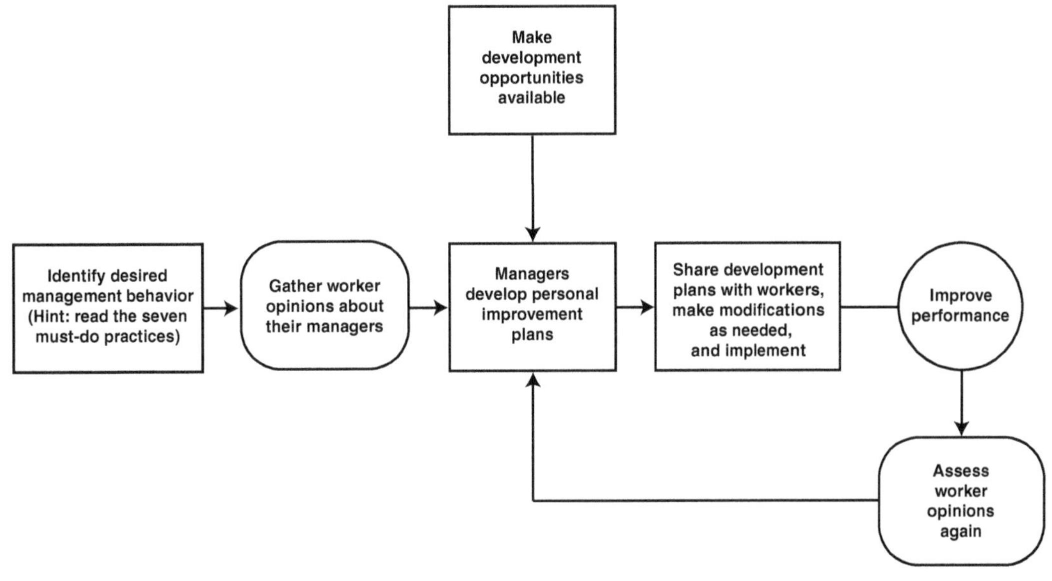

Figure 12 Improving leadership effectiveness.

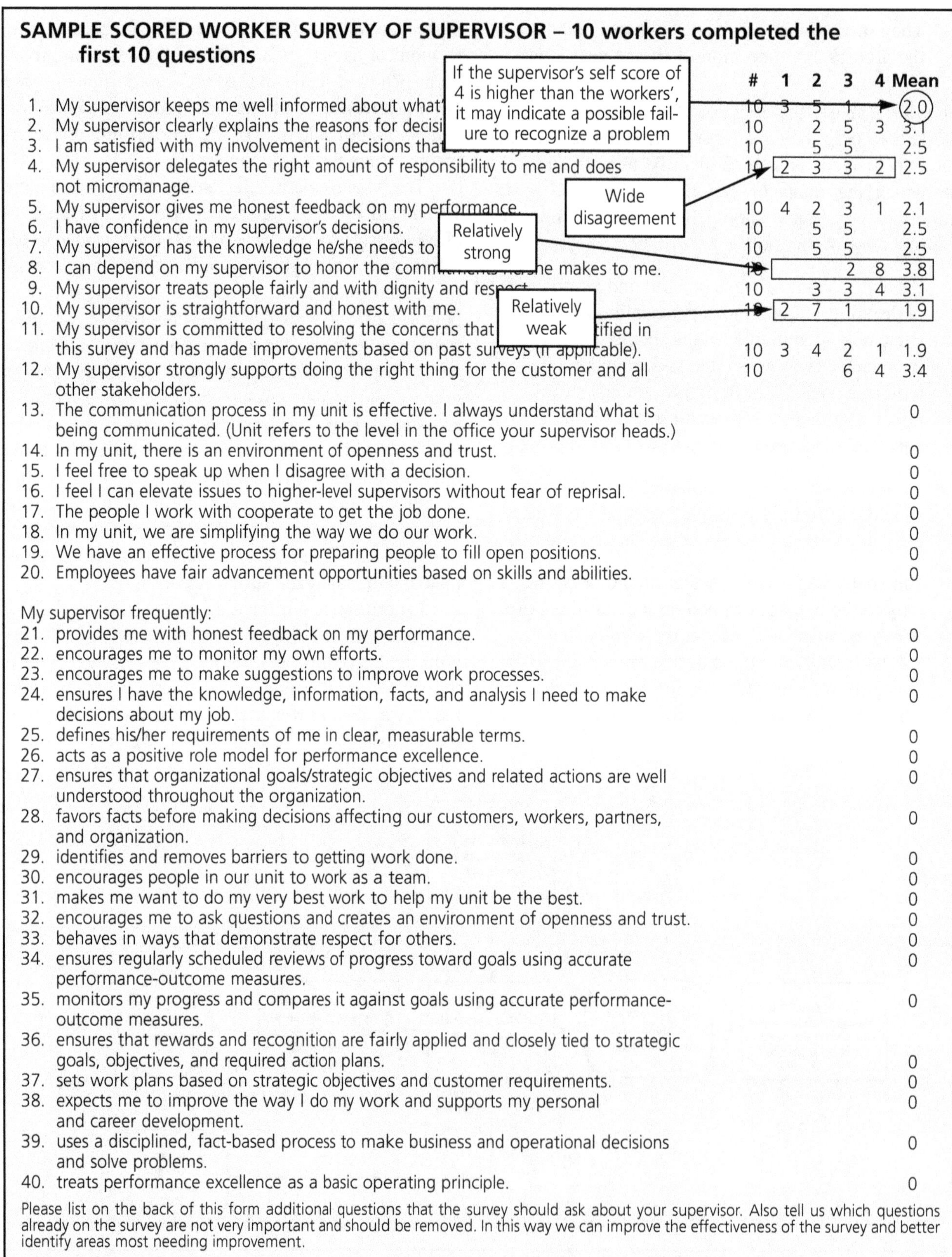

SAMPLE SCORED WORKER SURVEY OF SUPERVISOR – 10 workers completed the first 10 questions

If the supervisor's self score of 4 is higher than the workers', it may indicate a possible failure to recognize a problem
Wide disagreement
Relatively strong
Relatively weak

Question	#	1	2	3	4	Mean
1. My supervisor keeps me well informed about what	10	3	5	1	1	2.0
2. My supervisor clearly explains the reasons for decisi	10		2	5	3	3.1
3. I am satisfied with my involvement in decisions tha	10		5	5		2.5
4. My supervisor delegates the right amount of responsibility to me and does not micromanage.	10	2	3	3	2	2.5
5. My supervisor gives me honest feedback on my performance.	10	4	2	3	1	2.1
6. I have confidence in my supervisor's decisions.	10		5	5		2.5
7. My supervisor has the knowledge he/she needs to	10		5	5		2.5
8. I can depend on my supervisor to honor the comm… he makes to me.	10			2	8	3.8
9. My supervisor treats people fairly and with dignity and resp	10		3	3	4	3.1
10. My supervisor is straightforward and honest with me.	10	2	7	1		1.9
11. My supervisor is committed to resolving the concerns that … tified in this survey and has made improvements based on past su… able).	10	3	4	2	1	1.9
12. My supervisor strongly supports doing the right thing for the customer and all other stakeholders.	10			6	4	3.4
13. The communication process in my unit is effective. I always understand what is being communicated. (Unit refers to the level in the office your supervisor heads.)						0
14. In my unit, there is an environment of openness and trust.						0
15. I feel free to speak up when I disagree with a decision.						0
16. I feel I can elevate issues to higher-level supervisors without fear of reprisal.						0
17. The people I work with cooperate to get the job done.						0
18. In my unit, we are simplifying the way we do our work.						0
19. We have an effective process for preparing people to fill open positions.						0
20. Employees have fair advancement opportunities based on skills and abilities.						0
My supervisor frequently:						
21. provides me with honest feedback on my performance.						0
22. encourages me to monitor my own efforts.						0
23. encourages me to make suggestions to improve work processes.						0
24. ensures I have the knowledge, information, facts, and analysis I need to make decisions about my job.						0
25. defines his/her requirements of me in clear, measurable terms.						0
26. acts as a positive role model for performance excellence.						0
27. ensures that organizational goals/strategic objectives and related actions are well understood throughout the organization.						0
28. favors facts before making decisions affecting our customers, workers, partners, and organization.						0
29. identifies and removes barriers to getting work done.						0
30. encourages people in our unit to work as a team.						0
31. makes me want to do my very best work to help my unit be the best.						0
32. encourages me to ask questions and creates an environment of openness and trust.						0
33. behaves in ways that demonstrate respect for others.						0
34. ensures regularly scheduled reviews of progress toward goals using accurate performance-outcome measures.						0
35. monitors my progress and compares it against goals using accurate performance-outcome measures.						0
36. ensures that rewards and recognition are fairly applied and closely tied to strategic goals, objectives, and required action plans.						0
37. sets work plans based on strategic objectives and customer requirements.						0
38. expects me to improve the way I do my work and supports my personal and career development.						0
39. uses a disciplined, fact-based process to make business and operational decisions and solve problems.						0
40. treats performance excellence as a basic operating principle.						0

Please list on the back of this form additional questions that the survey should ask about your supervisor. Also tell us which questions already on the survey are not very important and should be removed. In this way we can improve the effectiveness of the survey and better identify areas most needing improvement.

Figure 13 Sample Manager Effectiveness Survey of Workers, partially scored.

SUPERVISOR MANAGEMENT SELF-SURVEY

The following questionnaire lists some key indicators to help you **self-assess** your effectiveness in several key areas. Enter 1 for strongly disagree, 2 for disagree, 3 for agree, and 4 for strongly agree. If you cannot answer a question leave it blank.

General

1.	I keep my staff well informed about what's going on in the office.	1 2 3 4
2.	I clearly explain to my staff the reasons for decisions that affect their work.	1 2 3 4
3.	My staff are satisfied with their involvement in decisions that affect their work.	1 2 3 4
4.	I delegate the right amount of responsibility to my staff and I do not micromanage.	1 2 3 4
5.	I give my staff honest feedback on their performance.	1 2 3 4
6.	My staff has confidence in my decisions.	1 2 3 4
7.	My staff believe that I have the knowledge I need to be effective.	1 2 3 4
8.	My staff can depend on me to honor the commitments I make to them.	1 2 3 4
9.	I treat my staff and others fairly and with dignity and respect.	1 2 3 4
10.	I am straightforward and honest with my staff.	1 2 3 4
11.	My staff believe that I am committed to resolving the concerns that may be identified in this survey and that I have made improvements based on past surveys or feedback (if applicable).	1 2 3 4
12.	My staff believe that I strongly support doing the right thing for the customer and all other stakeholders.	1 2 3 4
13.	My staff believe that the communication process in my unit is effective. My staff believe that I always understand what is being communicated. (Unit refers to the level in the office you head.)	1 2 3 4
14.	In my unit, my staff believe that there is an environment of openness and trust.	1 2 3 4
15.	My staff feel that they are free to speak up when they disagree with my decisions.	1 2 3 4
16.	My staff believe that they can elevate issues to higher-level supervisors without fear of reprisal.	1 2 3 4
17.	My staff believe that they cooperate and work well together to get the job done.	1 2 3 4
18.	In my unit, my staff believe that we are simplifying the way we do our work.	1 2 3 4
19.	My staff believe that we have an effective process for preparing people to fill open positions.	1 2 3 4
20.	My staff believe that employees have fair advancement opportunities based on skills and abilities.	1 2 3 4
21.	My staff believe that I provide them with honest feedback on my performance.	1 2 3 4
22.	My staff believe that I encourage them to monitor my own efforts.	1 2 3 4
23.	My staff believe that I encourage them to make suggestions to improve work processes.	1 2 3 4
24.	My staff believe that I ensure they have the knowledge, information, facts, and analysis support they need to make decisions about their job.	1 2 3 4
25.	My staff believe that I understand their requirements of me in clear, measurable terms.	1 2 3 4
26.	My staff believe that I act as a positive role model for performance excellence.	1 2 3 4
27.	My staff believe that I ensure that organizational goals/strategic objectives and related actions are well understood throughout the organization.	1 2 3 4
28.	My staff believe that I favor facts before making decisions affecting our customers, workers, partners, and organization.	1 2 3 4
29.	My staff believe that I identify and remove barriers to getting work done.	1 2 3 4
30.	My staff believe that I encourage people in our unit to work as a team.	1 2 3 4
31.	My staff believe that I make them want to do their very best work to help the unit be the best.	1 2 3 4
32.	My staff believe that I encourage them to ask questions and create an environment of openness and trust.	1 2 3 4
33.	My staff believe that I demonstrate respect for others.	1 2 3 4
34.	My staff believe that I ensure regularly scheduled reviews of progress toward goals using accurate performance-outcome measures.	1 2 3 4
35.	My staff believe that I monitor our organization's progress, compare it against goals using accurate performance-outcome measures, and take steps to close gaps to be successful.	1 2 3 4
36.	My staff believe that I ensure that rewards and recognition are fairly applied and closely tied to strategic objectives and action plans.	1 2 3 4
37.	My staff believe that I set work plans based on strategic objectives and customer requirements.	1 2 3 4
38.	My staff believe that I expect them to improve the way they do their work and develop personally and professionally.	1 2 3 4
39.	My staff believe that I use a disciplined, fact-based process to make business and operational decisions and solve problems.	1 2 3 4
40.	My staff believe that I treat performance excellence as a basic operating principle.	1 2 3 4

Please list on the back of this form additional questions that the survey should ask about you. Also tell us which questions already on the survey are not very important and should be removed. In this way we can improve the effectiveness of the survey and better identify areas most needing improvement.

Figure 14 Sample Supervisor Management Survey—Self.

areas where both parties agree that a weakness exists, could be targeted for specific improvement. By aggregating the assessment data for all managers and making the overall results available to individuals, managers can determine how their stage of development compares with other managers in the office.

Create Performance Excellence Standards for Managers—A Key Job Element

Virtually every organization has the ability to determine what performance elements are critical for the success of employees and managers. These critical performance requirements are usually included as a key component of performance plans and appraisals. If performance excellence is critical to the success of the organization, a specific key performance element should be included in the performance plan (sometimes these are called personal commitment plans, personal improvement plans, personal management objectives, or individual development plans, to name a few) and evaluation of managers and leaders. Using this approach, every manager and supervisor begins to take performance excellence more seriously.

- Using the following performance standards as an example, for a manager to receive a rating at a particular level, that manager must have accomplished all of the activities described for that rating level. If all are not met, the rating goes to the lowest level at which all are met.
- The writer of the performance appraisal should cite measurable examples in the performance appraisal for actions listed under the rating level.
- Supervising reviewers must verify that these actions have indeed been taken. Under this system, managers are strongly encouraged to keep accurate records of activities that might exemplify compliance with these standards.

Overall Performance Standard for Leadership

The individual visibly demonstrates adherence to the high personal standards and characteristics of leaders in a high-performing organization. The individual:

- Understands the business processes of the unit
- Focuses on customers and is customer-driven
- Demonstrates a firm commitment to the principles of customer satisfaction; understands customer requirements and consistently works to meet and exceed them
- Understands and personally uses performance excellence principles and tools for decision-making and planning:
  - Favors the use of data and facts to drive decisions and ensures that employees and subordinate managers do the same
  - Ensures that organizational goals/strategic objectives are converted to appropriate actions to align work within the organizational unit
  - Measures and monitors progress toward achieving the goals/strategic objectives within the organizational unit
- Demonstrates a firm commitment to the principles of workforce engagement and satisfaction:
  - Promotes flexibility, individual initiative, and innovation
  - Encourages and supports the personal and professional development of self and workers
  - Supports effective training aligned to support action plans and reinforces the use of new skills on the job
  - Ensures compensation is aligned to support high-performance business objectives and a customer focus
  - Rewards and recognizes workers who achieve objectives and incorporate the principles of performance excellence in their day-to-day work
  - Fosters an atmosphere of open, honest communication and knowledge sharing among workers and business units throughout the organization
- Rigorously drives the systematic, continuous improvement of key work processes to promote innovation, including personal self-improvement as an effective leader

- Achieves consistently improving performance outcomes in customer satisfaction; worker engagement, motivation, and satisfaction; operational excellence; and financial performance

Rating No. 1: Performance is unsatisfactory. The individual frequently fails to meet the performance standard for leadership.

Rating No. 2: Performance is minimally acceptable. Individual occasionally fails to meet performance standard for leadership. Performs higher than level one but does not meet all level-three requirements.

Rating No. 3: Performance is acceptable. Individual basically meets the performance standard for leadership.

Rating No. 4: Performance is very good. Individual occasionally exceeds the performance standard for leadership. Performs higher than indicated by level three but does not meet all requirements of level five.

Rating No. 5: Performance is superior. Individual consistently exceeds the performance standard for leadership. *Is considered a role model for leadership.*

The Performance Excellence Standards in Table 2 provide behavioral descriptions for each standard at Levels 1, 3, and 5. Levels 2 and 4 should be interpolated; for example, meeting all of Level 1 but not all of Level 3 should earn a Level 2 rating for that standard.

Lessons Learned Conclusions

Successful leaders will create a customer focus and a context for action at all levels of the organization. Effective leaders will distribute authority and decision-making to all organizational levels. Nearly instantaneous, two-way communication will permit clear strategies, measurable outcome-oriented objectives, and priorities to be identified and deployed organization-wide. Problems will be identified and resolved with similar speed. Success in this environment will demand different skills of employees and managers. Unless all managers and employees understand where the organization is going and what must be done to beat the competition, it will be hard to make effective decisions consistent with overall direction and strategy. If employees at all levels are not involved in decision-making, organizational effectiveness is reduced—making it more difficult to win in a highly competitive arena.

In closing this section, we would like to suggest that the scenario previously described is already happening today among the world's best-performing organizations:

- These organizations have effective leadership at all levels, with a clear strategy focused on maximizing customer value. Middle-level managers support, rather than block, the values and direction of the top leaders.
- They have developed ways to challenge themselves and improve their own processes when doing so promotes customer value and improves operating effectiveness.
- They engage workers fully and promote continuous improvement, innovation, and organizational and personal learning at all levels. They ensure that best practices and other relevant knowledge is shared within the organization to avoid duplication of effort.
- They have created effective, easy-to-understand data systems to enhance decision-making at all levels.
- They have developed and aligned reward, recognition, compensation, and incentives to support the desired customer-focused behavior, strategic action plans, and high-performance objectives among all leaders, managers, and employees.
- They have found ways to design effective work processes that meet or exceed all requirements and ensure that those processes are executed consistently and improved continuously. They have outsourced work to the advantage of their organization.
- They closely monitor their performance and the performance of their principal competitors. They use this information to adjust their goals and objectives and their work, and they continue to improve faster than ever.

These organizations are among the best in the world at what they do and they will continue to win, as long as they continue to apply the current principles of performance excellence and the Integrated Management System.

Table 2 Performance excellence standards.

Performance Excellence Standards Table				
Level 1	**Level 2**	**Level 3**	**Level 4**	**Level 5**
Performance is unsatisfactory: Individual frequently fails to meet the performance standard for leadership. Is considered a poor leader.	**Better than level 1 and some of level 3.**	**Performance is acceptable: Individual basically meets the performance standard for leadership. Is considered to be a capable leader.**	**All of level 3 and some of level 5.**	**Performance is superior: Individual consistently exceeds the performance standard for leadership. Is considered a role model for leadership.**
• Does not fully understand the key business processes of the unit		• Understands the key business processes of the unit		• Understands the business processes of the unit in great detail
• Does not tolerate or care for customers well; consistently disregards the needs of customers		• Is customer-driven and promotes customer-focused values throughout the unit – Demonstrates a commitment to the principles of customer satisfaction – Develops systems to understand customer requirements, strengthen customer relationships, resolve customer problems and prevent them from happening again, and obtain information about customer satisfaction and dissatisfaction – Communicates well with customers		• Is customer-driven and actively promotes customer-focused values throughout the unit – Demonstrates a firm commitment to the principles of customer satisfaction – Develops effective systems to understand customer requirements, strengthen loyalty and customer relationships, resolve customer problems immediately and prevent them from happening again, and obtain timely information about customer satisfaction and dissatisfaction – Advocates the needs of customers through the collection and use of information on customer satisfaction, dissatisfaction, and product performance

Continued

Continued

Performance Excellence Standards Table

Level 1	Level 2	Level 3	Level 4	Level 5
Performance is unsatisfactory: Individual frequently fails to meet the performance standard for leadership. Is considered a poor leader.	**Better than level 1 and some of level 3.**	**Performance is acceptable: Individual basically meets the performance standard for leadership. Is considered to be a capable leader.**	**All of level 3 and some of level 5.**	**Performance is superior: Individual consistently exceeds the performance standard for leadership. Is considered a role model for leadership.**
• Does not understand and has not taken steps to implement performance excellence (may even work against the changes needed) – Intuition, not data or facts, tends to dominate decision-making – Organizational goals and actions are not aligned to actions within the unit – May measure and monitor some performance outcomes (such as budget tracking), but most measures are not aligned to organizational goals		• Personally uses many performance excellence principles and tools for decision-making and planning – Visibly supports performance excellence within the organization – Usually uses data and facts to drive decisions and ensures that many workers and subordinate managers do the same – Ensures that key organizational goals are converted to appropriate action to align most work within the organizational unit – Most goals and actions have defined measures of progress and timelines for achieving desired results		• Personally uses performance excellence principles and tools for decision-making and planning – Serves as a performance excellence champion within the organization and as a resource within the work unit, providing guidance, counsel, and instruction in performance excellence tools, processes, and principles – Is a positive role model for using data and facts to drive decisions and ensures that workers and subordinate managers do the same – Ensures that all organizational goals are converted to appropriate actions to align nearly all work within the organizational unit – Defines measures of progress and timelines for achieving desired results for each goal and action

Continued

Continued

Performance Excellence Standards Table

Level 1	Level 2	Level 3	Level 4	Level 5
Performance is unsatisfactory: Individual frequently fails to meet the performance standard for leadership. Is considered a poor leader.	**Better than level 1 and some of level 3.**	**Performance is acceptable: Individual basically meets the performance standard for leadership. Is considered to be a capable leader.**	**All of level 3 and some of level 5.**	**Performance is superior: Individual consistently exceeds the performance standard for leadership. Is considered a role model for leadership.**
• Does not effectively promote workforce engagement, motivation, and morale – Tends to micromanage; does not delegate decision-making authority to the lower levels except as directly instructed to do so – Rarely listens to workers or cares what they think – Does not consistently promote flexibility and individual initiative – Does not consistently encourage and support the personal and professional development of self and employees – May send workers to training but does not consistently reinforce the use of new skills on the job – Has not taken effective steps to ensure compensation and other rewards or recognition are aligned to support business strategies and actions – Reward and recognition are not aligned to support organizational goals or the principles of performance excellence or customer satisfaction		• Demonstrates some commitment to the principles of employee empowerment and satisfaction. Is well-regarded by employees for: – Involving the workforce in identifying improvement opportunities and developing improvement plans – Valuing worker input on work-related matters – Promoting flexibility and individual initiative and ensuring that many subordinate managers do the same – Encouraging and supporting the personal and professional development of self and workers – Supporting effective training and reinforcing the use of new skills on the job – Ensuring compensation is aligned to support business strategies and actions – Rewarding and recognizing workers who incorporate the principles of performance excellence in their day-to-day work		• Demonstrates a firm commitment to the principles of workforce engagement and satisfaction. Is highly regarded by employees for: – Involving the workforce in setting standards of performance, identifying improvement opportunities, and developing improvement plans – Seeking and valuing worker input on work-related matters – Promoting flexibility and individual initiative and ensuring that subordinate managers do the same – Encouraging and supporting the personal and professional development of self and workers – Supporting effective training and reinforcing the use of new skills on the job – Ensuring compensation is aligned to support business strategies and actions – Rewarding and recognizing workers who incorporate the principles of performance excellence in their day-to-day work

Continued

Continued

Performance Excellence Standards Table

Level 1	Level 2	Level 3	Level 4	Level 5
Performance is unsatisfactory: Individual frequently fails to meet the performance standard for leadership. Is considered a poor leader.	**Better than level 1 and some of level 3.**	**Performance is acceptable: Individual basically meets the performance standard for leadership. Is considered to be a capable leader.**	**All of level 3 and some of level 5.**	**Performance is superior: Individual consistently exceeds the performance standard for leadership. Is considered a role model for leadership.**
• Does not communicate effectively or foster an atmosphere of knowledge-sharing among workers and business units		• Fosters an atmosphere of open, honest communication and knowledge sharing among workers and business units throughout the organization • Encourages some two-way communication with workers		• Fosters an atmosphere of open, honest communication and knowledge sharing among workers and business units throughout the organization. Promotes extensive two-way communication with workers. – Checks the effectiveness of nearly all communication and makes changes to improve
• Does not regularly assess or improve work processes, including his or her personal effectiveness as a leader		• Visibly drives continuous improvement of many work processes, including personal effectiveness as a leader • Encourages some innovation		• Rigorously drives the systematic, continuous improvement of all work processes, including personal effectiveness as a leader – Develops personal action plan and always incorporates results of 360-degree feedback to continuously improve personal leadership effectiveness and ensures subordinate managers do the same – Requires continuous improvement and innovation throughout the organization
• Does not achieve consistently improving performance outcomes in customer satisfaction; workforce engagement, motivation, and satisfaction; operational excellence; and financial (cost/budget) performance		• Achieves consistently improving performance outcomes in customer satisfaction; workforce engagement, motivation, and satisfaction; operational excellence; and financial (cost/budget) performance – The levels of performance outcomes are better than average when compared with organizations providing similar programs, products, or services		• Achieves consistently improving performance outcomes in customer satisfaction; workforce engagement, development, motivation, and satisfaction; operational excellence; and financial (cost/budget) performance – The levels of performance outcomes are among the highest in the organization/nation/state and are also high when compared with organizations providing similar programs, products, or services

INTEGRATED MANAGEMENT SYSTEM AND AWARD CRITERIA FRAMEWORK

Organizations must position themselves to respond well to the environment within which they compete. They must understand the key factors that influence their success, which should be described in the Organizational Profile. Successful organizations manage threats and vulnerabilities as well as capitalize on their strengths and opportunities, including the vulnerabilities of competitors. These factors guide strategy development, support operational decisions, and align measures and actions—all of which must be done well for the organization to succeed. Consistent with this overarching purpose, the Award Criteria contain the following basic elements: Driver Triad, Work Core, Brain Center, and Results/Outcomes (Figure 15).

The Driver Triad

The Driver Triad (Figure 16) consists of the Categories of Leadership, Strategy, and Customers. Leaders use these processes to set direction and goals, monitor progress, make resource decisions, and take corrective action when progress is not achieved according to plan. The processes that make up the Driver Triad require leaders to set direction and expectations for the organization to meet customer requirements and fully empower the workforce (Category 1), provide the vehicle for determining the short- and long-term strategies for success as well as communicating and aligning the organization's work (Category 2), and produce information about critical customer requirements and levels of satisfaction and strengthen customer relations and loyalty (Category 3).

The Work Core

The Work Core (Figure 17) describes the processes through which the primary work of the organization takes place and consists of Workforce (Category 5) and Operations (Category 6). These Categories recognize that the people doing processes is the way work is done. To achieve peak performance, these people must possess the right skills and must be allowed to work in an environment that promotes initiative and self-direction to be motivated to contribute their utmost for the success of the organization and its customers. The work processes provide the structure for continuous learning and improvement to optimize performance.

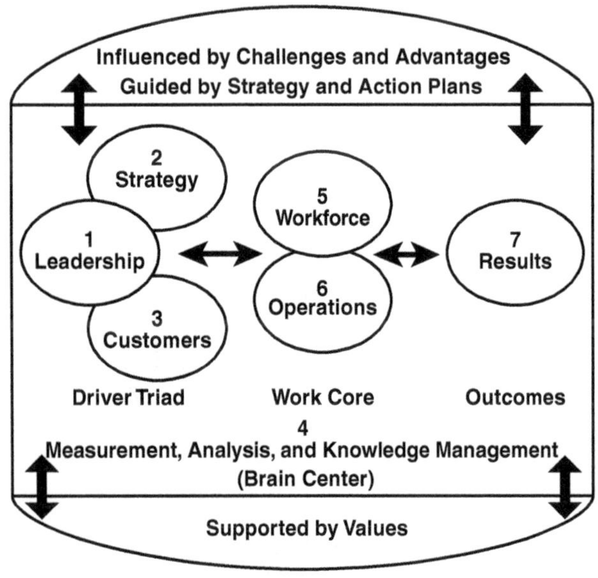

Figure 15 Performance excellence framework.

Figure 16 Driver Triad.

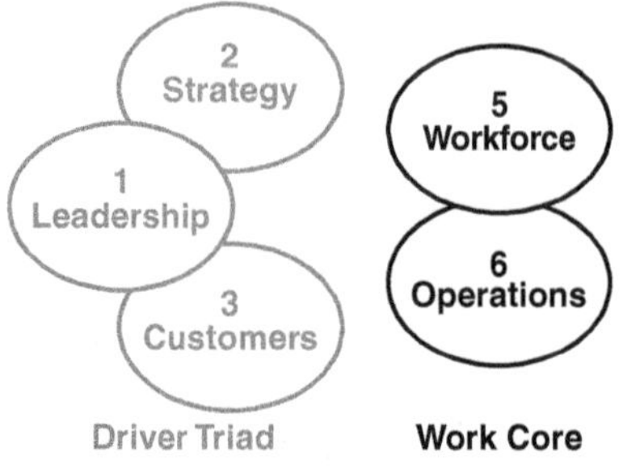

Figure 17 Work Core.

Results/Outcomes

The processes defined by the Driver Triad, Work Core, and Brain Center produce the Results (Category 7). Results (Figure 18) reflect the organization's actual performance and serve as the basis for leaders to monitor progress against goals and make adjustments to increase performance. These results include internal operating effectiveness, customer focus, workforce performance, leadership, governance effectiveness, financial and market performance, and achievement of strategic objectives and action plans.

Brain Center

Measurement, Analysis, and Knowledge Management (Category 4) provides data and analyses to support decision-making at all levels. These processes (Figure 19) capture, store, analyze, and retrieve information and data critical to the effective management of the organization and to a fact-based system for improving organization performance and competitiveness. Rapid access to reliable data and information systems is especially critical to enhance effective decision-making in an increasingly complex, fast-paced, global competitive environment. Measurement, Analysis, and Knowledge Management is also called the Brain Center of an effective management system.

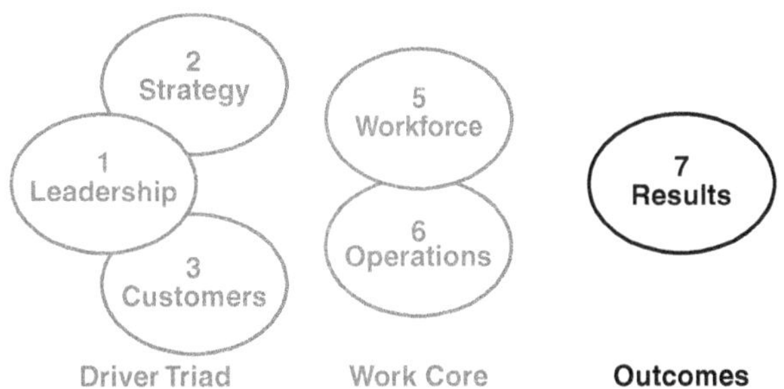

Figure 18 Outcomes.

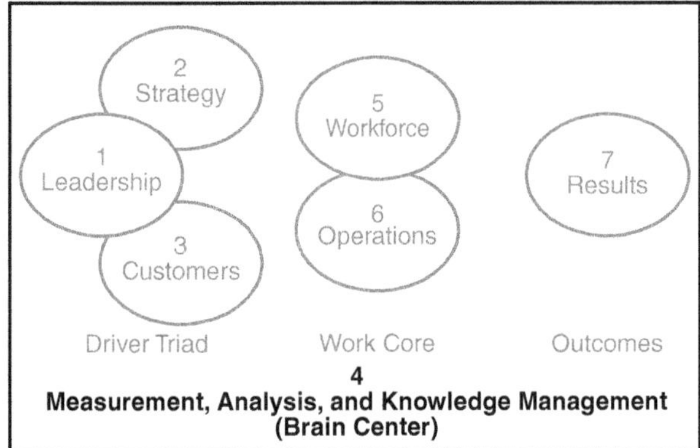

Figure 19 Measurement, Analysis, and Knowledge Management (the Brain Center).

Core Values and Concepts

The Core Values and Concepts describe the characteristics of high-performing organizations. (Figure 20). *If an organization aspires to be represented by the Core Values, then the Criteria are the road map to get there.* These values provide the foundation for integrating and aligning work processes in high-performing organizations.

Guided by Strategy and Action Plans

Organizations develop effective strategic plans that are influenced by strategic challenges, strategy advantages, and core competencies. This information helps set the direction necessary to achieve future success. Unfortunately, these plans are not always communicated and used to drive actions and the direction is not always focused. The planning process and the resulting strategy are virtually worthless if the organization does not use the plan and strategy to guide decision-making at all levels of the organization (Figure 21).

When decisions are not guided by strategy, managers and other members of the workforce tend to substitute their own ideas for the correct direction. This

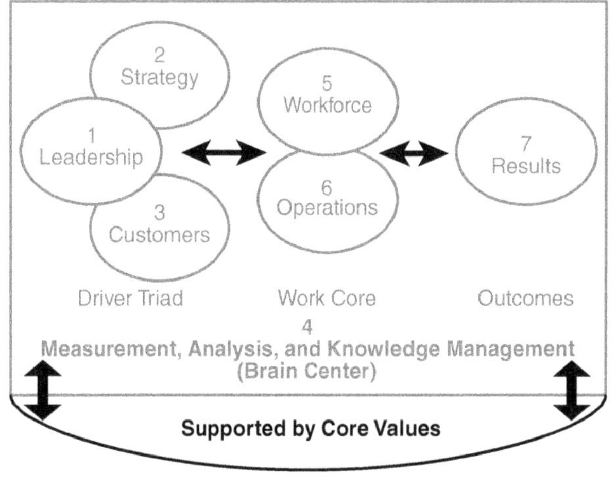

Figure 20 Core Values and Concepts.

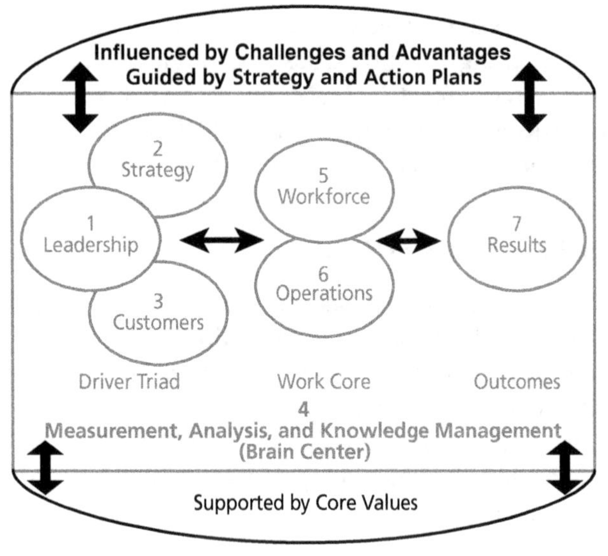

Figure 21 Guide decision-making.

frequently causes teams, individuals, and entire business units to work at cross-purposes, suboptimizing performance and making it more difficult for the organization to achieve desired results.

Taken together, these processes define the essential ingredients of a complex, integrated management system designed to promote and deliver performance excellence. If any part of the system is missing, the performance results suffer. If fully implemented, these processes are sufficient to enable organizations to achieve winning performance.

Award Criteria Structure

Categories

The seven Criteria Categories are subdivided into Items and Areas to Address. Figure 22 demonstrates the organization of Category 1, Leadership.

Items

There are 17 Items, each focusing on a major Criteria element.

Areas to Address

Items consist of one or more Areas to Address (Areas). Applicants submit information in response to the specific elements of these Areas. There are 40

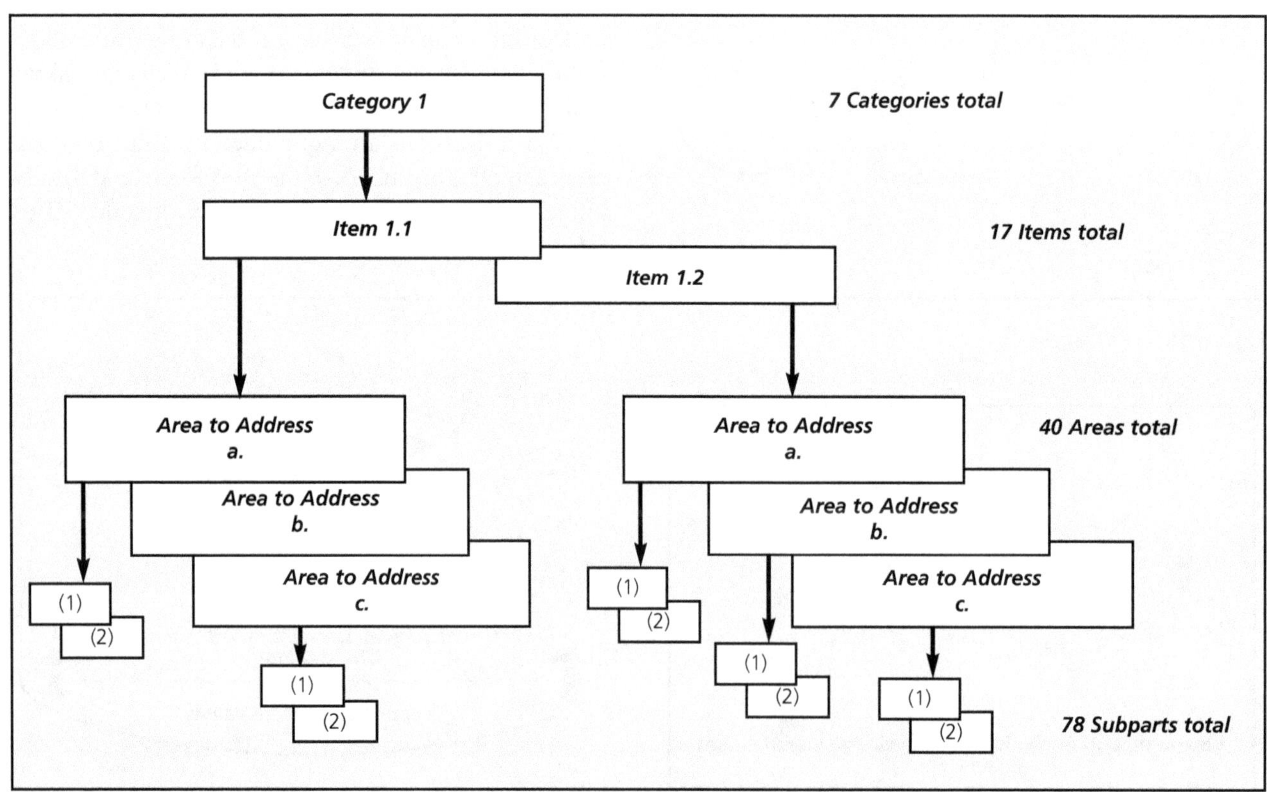

Figure 22 Organization of Category 1 in the business/nonprofit/government framework.

Areas to Address in the Business, Education, and Health Care Criteria.

Subparts

There are 78 subparts in the 2021–2022 Business Criteria, 76 in Education, and 80 in Health Care, not counting the Organizational Profile. Subparts begin with numbers in parentheses. A response should be made to each subpart and Area to Address.

Notes

If a Note indicates the process *should* include something, examiners will interpret it as a requirement. If a Note indicates that the process *might* include something, examiners shall not treat the list as a requirement—only as an example. Some Items have Notes that provide additional guidance specifically for nonprofit organizations. Nonprofit-specific Notes appear at the end of the Item in *italics*. There are 86 notes in the Business Criteria and 84 in Education and Health Care.

KEY CHARACTERISTICS OF THE 2021–2022 PERFORMANCE EXCELLENCE CRITERIA

The Criteria focus on organizational performance results and the processes required to achieve them. Results are a composite of the following organizational performance areas:

- Product and process results
- Customer results
- Workforce results
- Leadership and governance results, including societal contributions results, and processes to achieve strategic objectives
- Financial, market, and strategy results

The use of a composite set of indicators is intended to ensure that strategies are balanced—that they do not inappropriately trade off among important stakeholders, objectives, or short- and long-term goals.

These results areas cover overall organization performance, including financial performance and progress in implementing and achieving strategy and action plans. The results areas also recognize the importance of suppliers and of community and societal well-being.

The Criteria are considered non-prescriptive. They *do not* prescribe that the organization should or should not have any particular functions, such as departments for quality, planning, or personnel. The Criteria do not prescribe how the organization should be structured or how different units in the organization should be managed. Such factors differ among organizations, and they are likely to change within an organization over time as needs and strategies evolve. In summary, the Criteria are nonprescriptive for the following reasons:

- The focus is on results, not on the use of specific procedures, tools, or organizational structure. Organizations are encouraged to develop and demonstrate creative, adaptive, and flexible approaches for addressing the elements contained in the Criteria questions. Nonprescriptive elements are intended to foster incremental and major (*breakthrough*) improvements, which may lead to innovation.
- The selection of tools, techniques, systems, and organizational structure usually depends on factors such as business type and size, organizational relationships, the organization's stage of development, and workforce capabilities and responsibilities.
- A focus on common elements, rather than on specific procedures, fosters better understanding, communication, sharing, alignment, and integration, while supporting diversity and innovation in approaches.

The Criteria support a systems approach to maintaining organization-wide goal alignment. The systems approach to goal alignment is embedded in the integrated structure of the Core Values and Concepts, the Organizational Profile, the Criteria, the Scoring Guidelines, and the results-oriented, cause-effect linkages among the Criteria parts.

Alignment in the Criteria is built around connecting and reinforcing measures derived from the organization's processes and strategy. The measures in the Criteria tie directly to customer and stakeholder value and to overall performance that relates to key internal and external requirements of the organization. Measures serve both as a communications tool

AWARD CATEGORIES AND POINT VALUES

Examination Categories/Items	Maximum Points
Preface Organizational Profile	**(0 points)**
P.1 Organizational Description	0
P.2 Organizational Situation	0
1 Leadership	**(120 points)**
1.1 Senior Leadership	70
1.2 Governance and Societal Contributions	50
2 Strategy	**(85 points)**
2.1 Strategy Development	45
2.2 Strategy Implementation	40
3 Customers	**(85 points)**
3.1 Customer Expectations	40
3.2 Customer Engagement	45
4 Measurement, Analysis, and Knowledge Management	**(90 points)**
4.1 Measurement, Analysis, and Improvement of Organizational Performance	45
4.2 Information and Knowledge Management	45
5 Workforce	**(85 points)**
5.1 Workforce Environment	40
5.2 Workforce Engagement	45
6 Operations	**(85 points)**
6.1 Work Processes	45
6.2 Operational Effectiveness	40
7 Results	**(450 points)**
7.1 Product and Process Results	120
7.2 Customer Results	80
7.3 Workforce Results	80
7.4 Leadership and Governance Results	80
7.5 Financial, Market, and Strategy Results	90
Total Points	**1000**

and a basis for deploying consistent performance requirements. Such alignment ensures consistency of purpose while at the same time supports speed, innovation, and decentralized decision-making.

Learning Cycles and Continuous Improvement

In high-performing organizations, action-oriented learning takes place through feedback between processes and results facilitated by learning or continuous improvement cycles. Learning cycles typically are based on models with clearly defined and well-established stages similar to Plan-Do-Check-Act (PDCA) or Plan-Do-Study-Act (PDSA) (Figure 23):

1. Plan—plan, including design of processes, selection of measures, and deployment of requirements.
2. Do—execute plans.
3. Check/Study—assess progress, taking into account internal and external results.
4. Act—revise plans based on assessment findings, learning, new inputs, new requirements, and opportunities for innovation.

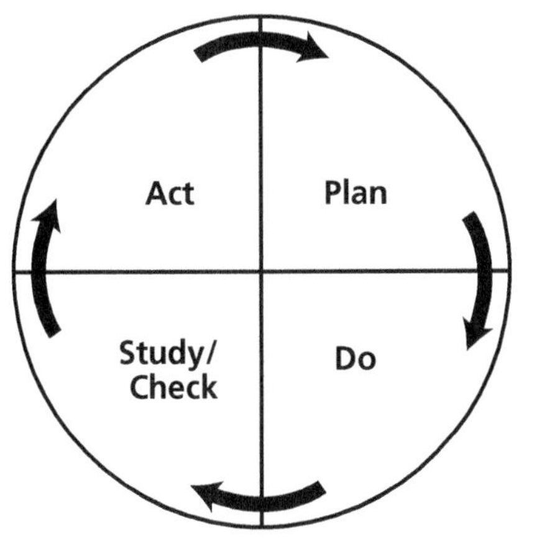

Figure 23 Continuous improvement cycle.

Comparison of Baldrige to other National Quality Awards

The chapters beginning on pages 295 and 337 respectively, compare the core values and elements of the Baldrige criteria with those of the EFQM and the China Quality Award.

Comparison of Baldrige, Lean, Six Sigma, and the Balanced Scorecard

Introduction

"Baldrige? Six Sigma? Lean? Balanced Scorecard? We don't have time for all of these initiatives! Just pick one and go with it!" How many times have you heard (or perhaps even said) something similar to this? The statement suggests the approaches are equivalent. They are not. As has been discussed earlier in this book, the Baldrige Criteria for Performance Excellence represent a comprehensive set of processes that organizations should have in place in order to optimize performance. Six Sigma, Lean, Balanced Scorecard, and other approaches represent some tools, albeit powerful tools, which organizations can use to enhance performance. These tools do not represent a comprehensive, integrated management system.

It is clear that the use of these tools in isolation, without regard to the needs of the entire management system, will not produce optimum benefits or optimum performance for the organization.

Tools like Six Sigma can help an organization take steps toward performance excellence; but, each tool can become more useful if it is used within the context of a Baldrige-based integrated culture of performance excellence. The use of these tools as part of an integrated approach to maximizing performance, which Baldrige represents, is the best way to drive toward better results. Such integration is more likely to lead to breakthrough, rather than incremental improvement.

See the document in the online resources prepared by Paul Grizzell of Core Value Partners that compares the Baldrige Core Values and Criteria with the tools of Lean Thinking, Six Sigma, and the Balanced Scorecard. He can be reached at paul.grizzell@corevaluepartners.com.

Developmental versus Compliance Assessments

The Criteria and the Scoring Guidelines are the two components that combine to create the diagnostic tool, which is part of a developmental assessment. A developmental assessment, unlike a compliance review, seeks to determine how advanced an organization is and then identify the vital few processes that need to be developed to move to the next higher level. The basic systems must be in place before they can be refined and enhanced. In a compliance review, on the other hand, all conditions or requirements must be met or the organization is out of compliance and may not be certified or registered. By design, compliance reviews audit against a set of minimum standards. A developmental review, such as that provided through the Baldrige process, identifies the vital few opportunities to help the organization improve without inundating it with trivial issues. *Meeting minimum compliance standards provides no competitive advantage. Assessing and improving using an integrated management system drives competitive advantage and progress toward high performance.*

Comparing the Baldrige Criteria and the ISO Management System

The Baldrige Framework and the International Organization for Standardization (ISO) Management System Standards provide an important set of Criteria (Baldrige) and Requirements (ISO) for an organization. They are complementary in that both are focused on the use of systems and processes within an organization. There are, however, differences in the purposes of the programs:

- The Baldrige Framework, as discussed in this book, is a developmental program focused on accelerating performance excellence efforts and going "beyond mere compliance." The focus of the Baldrige Framework is providing a model of performance excellence.
- The ISO Management System Standards help provide assurance to customers and others that an organization has processes in place and that those processes are actually in use to ensure consistency of products and services and the way in which they are delivered. The focus of ISO is compliance to a set of requirements.

The use of ISO Standards to ensure process consistency is valuable in helping an organization "systematize" their processes to ensure they meet—or exceed—customer and other stakeholder requirements. However, meeting ISO Standards is not sufficient to meet the high standards of a Baldrige Award or similar award recognition.

The use of ISO is usually driven by two purposes:

1. Customer and other requirements—compliance to ISO standards helps ensure customer confidence in consistency of supplier product and service quality.
2. Process management—compliance to an ISO standard.

See the online resources accompanying this book for the Baldrige–ISO–EFQM Crosswalk prepared by Graham Hull of Ley Hill Solutions and Paul Grizzell of Core Values Partners. Graham is the Managing Partner of Ley Hill Solutions in Chesham, England. Graham has Lead Auditor status for ISO Standards 9001 (Quality), 27001 (Information Security) and 22000 (Food Safety) and has qualifications in the application of ISO 22301 (Business Continuity), ISO 45001 (Health and Safety), ISO 14001 (Environment) and ISO 44001 (Collaborative Business Relationships). He is also an EFQM Certified Advisor and Certified Trainer, and is a highly experienced EFQM Assessment Team Leader. Graham can be reached at info@leyhill.com. Ley Hill Solutions and Core Values Partners partner to provide ISO solutions in the context of Baldrige and EFQM management system models.

CHANGES FROM THE 2019–2020 BALDRIGE EXCELLENCE FRAMEWORK

Revisions have one overarching purpose: for the Framework and the Criteria to reflect the leading edge of validated leadership and performance practice while ensuring that they are as concise and user-friendly as possible.

As the drivers of competitiveness and long-term success have evolved, so, too, have the Baldrige Excellence Framework and the Baldrige Criteria. The CPE initially helped the nation address the quality crisis of the 1980s by enabling and encouraging businesses to adopt a robust, leadership-driven, customer-focused quality management system.

Over the more than 30 years since their creation, the CPE have evolved along with the drivers of organizational competitiveness and long-term success. Originally seen as more of a manufacturing-focused quality system, the Criteria have evolved into the current integrated management system that is relevant to all sectors: business, non-profit, government, health care, and education. Through this gradual evolution, today the Baldrige Excellence Framework offers organizations of all kinds a nonprescriptive leadership and management guide that facilitates a systems approach to achieving organization-wide excellence.

As the Baldrige framework and the Criteria evolve, they continue to balance two important considerations. On the one hand, the Criteria need to reflect a national standard for performance excellence, educating organizations in all aspects of establishing an integrated performance management system. On the other hand, the Criteria need to be accessible and user-friendly for a variety of organizations at varying levels of maturity.

To strike this balance, changes reflected in the 2021–2022 Baldrige Excellence Framework focus on raising or strengthening organizations' awareness of the need for organizational resilience; the benefits of diversity, equity, and inclusion; and the ongoing digitization of nearly all aspects of organizational operations and management. Other changes clarify the role of innovation in organizational competitiveness and success and expand the framework's focus on societal responsibility. Other changes throughout the Criteria clarify the intent of questions.

Resilience. Agility (a capacity for rapid change and for flexibility in operations) has long been a part of the Core Values and Concepts. The accelerating pace of change and the more frequent occurrence of disruptions—from economic upheaval or stress, major weather or health events, social or societal demands, or innovative technologies or product introductions—means that organizations must now focus on resilience. Resilience is the ability to anticipate, prepare for, and recover from disasters, emergencies, and other disruptions, and—when disruptions occur—to protect and enhance workforce and customer engagement, supply-network and financial performance, organizational productivity, and community well-being. Resilience includes the agility to modify plans, processes, and relationships whenever circumstances warrant. The core value titled Agility has been broadened to Agility and Resilience, and the term "resilience" is defined in the Glossary of Key Terms. In the Criteria, organizational resilience is a focus of business continuity planning. It is also a consideration for leaders, in strategic planning, for work accomplishment, and in supply-network management.

Equity and inclusion. Expanding on the concept that the successful organization capitalizes on the diverse backgrounds and characteristics, knowledge, skills, creativity, and motivation of people, this revision of the Baldrige framework includes a stronger focus on equity and inclusion. The core values titled Customer-Focused Excellence, Valuing People, and Societal Contributions now include this stronger focus, and equity and inclusion are now considerations for organizational culture and for customer and workforce engagement, as well as in notes throughout the Criteria.

Digitization and the fourth industrial revolution. In today's digitally and data-enhanced economy, the use of data analytics, the Internet of Things, artificial intelligence, the adoption of cloud operations, large dataset-enabled business and process modeling, enhanced automation, and other "smart" technologies is accelerating rapidly. Although these tools may not affect all organizations, they will most likely affect the competitive environment and new competitors. Notes on digitization and "big data" have been augmented throughout the Criteria. Questions on strategic planning and workforce change, as well as notes throughout the Criteria now include these concepts, complementing the existing focus on incorporating new technology into product and process design.

Societal contributions. This concept has been present in the Baldrige framework since its inception in

1988 (as Public Responsibility), and changes since then have reflected the evolution of the role of societal contributions for successful organizations of all types. High-performing organizations see contributing to society as more than something they must do. Going above and beyond responsibilities in contributing to society can be a driver of customer and workforce engagement and a market differentiator. Employees, customers, and communities increasingly exhibit an interest in organizational social purpose and in how organizations contribute to society. Questions on societal contributions and strategy development, as well as notes throughout the Criteria, now include this strengthened focus.

The most significant changes to the Criteria Items are summarized as follows.

Category 1: Leadership

Item 1.1, Senior Leadership, now includes questions about creating an organizational culture that fosters customer and workforce equity and inclusion, and about cultivating organizational resilience.

Item 1.2 questions now ask how you incorporate, rather than merely consider, societal well-being and benefit as part of your strategy and daily operations.

Category 2: Strategy

In Item 2.1, Strategy Development, questions now ask how your strategic planning process addresses resilience and how you consider relevant technological changes and innovations in your planning.

Category 3: Customers

Item 3.2, Customer Engagement, now asks how your customer experience processes ensure fair treatment for all customers.

Category 5: Workforce

In Item 5.1, questions now ask how you prepare your workforce for changes in workplaces and technology, and how you organize and manage your workforce to reinforce organizational resilience and agility.

In Item 5.2, Workforce Engagement, a new Area to Address asks how you ensure that your performance management, performance development, and career development approaches promote equity and inclusion, and an existing question has been expanded to ask how you ensure that your organizational culture promotes equity and inclusion.

Category 6: Operations

In Item 6.1, Work Processes, the fourth Area to Address is now called Management of Opportunities for Innovation. A note explains that your process for pursuing opportunities for innovation should capitalize on strategic opportunities identified as intelligent risks, as well as intelligent risks arising from performance reviews, knowledge management, and other sources of potential innovations.

In Item 6.2, the third Area to Address is now titled Safety, Business Continuity, and Resilience. It includes questions on how you ensure that your organization can anticipate, prepare for, and recover from disasters, emergencies, and other disruptions.

Category 7: Results

Item 7.4, Leadership and Governance Results, now asks for your results for leaders' communication and engagement to cultivate innovation and intelligent risk taking.

Scoring System

The explanation of the learning evaluation factor clarifies that learning comprises (1) the refinement of approaches through cycles of evaluation and improvement, (2) the adoption of best practices and innovations, and (3) the sharing of refinements and innovations. The Process Scoring Guidelines now specifically refer to these components.

Core Values

The concept of Agility, formerly paired with Organizational Learning, now forms part of the Core Value titled Agility and Resilience. Organizational Learning is a separate Core Value. The Core Value titled Focus on Success and Innovation pairs two formerly separate, but complementary, Core Values: Focus on Success and Managing for Innovation.

Glossary of Key Terms

The Glossary of Key Terms now includes a definition of the term "resilience." The definition of innovation now reflects the clarifications described above. One term, cycle time, has been deleted, as the definition used in the Criteria reflects the definition that is in common use.

Crosswalk Summary of Numbering Changes

Table 3 summarizes the numbering changes between the 2019–2020 Criteria and the 2021–2022 Criteria.

Each Criteria Category has a chapter in this book that explains the elements of each Item in more detail, including a comprehensive table that describes 2021–2022 Criteria Elements Listed Individually Without Duplication. These tables summarize each Item's elements at the *basic*, *overall*, and *multiple* levels. A more complete explanation of these tables is on page 279.

Table 3 Changes from 2019–2020 Criteria.

Paragraph	2019–2020 Reference	2021–2022 Reference
1.1a(1)	Setting Vision and Values	**Establishing** Vision and Values
1.1a(1)	Senior leaders set vision and values	Senior leaders set **and deploy** vision and values
1.1c(1)	create a culture that fosters customer and workforce engagement	create a culture that fosters customer and workforce engagement, **equity, and inclusion**
1.1c(1)	cultivate organizational agility	**cultivate organizational agility and resilience**
1.2c(1)	Consider societal well-being and benefit as a part of your strategy and daily operations	**incorporate** societal well-being and benefit as a part of your strategy and daily operations
2.1a(1)	...and organizational agility?	...and organizational agility **and resilience**?
2.1a(3)	Potential changes in your regulatory and external environment	Potential changes **and disruptions** in your regulatory and external environment
2.1a(3)		**Technological changes and innovations affecting your products, services, and operations**
3.2	Customer Relationships and Support	Customer **Experience**
3.2a(4)		**Fair Treatment How do your customer experience processes ensure fair treatment for different customers, customer groups, and market segments?**
4.1a(1)	~~How frequently do you track these measures?~~	
5.1a(1)	How do you assess the skills, competencies, certifications, and staffing levels you need?	How do you assess the skills, competencies, certifications, and staffing levels you need **in the short and long term**?
5.1a(3)	...prepare your workforce for changes in organizational structure and work systems, when needed	...prepare your workforce for changes in organizational structure, **workplaces, work systems, and technology** when needed
5.1a(3)	...prepare your workforce for changes in organizational structure and work systems, when needed	...prepare your workforce for changes in organizational structure, workplaces, work systems, and technology when needed
5.1a(4)	~~• accomplish the organization's work~~	

Continued

Word changes in the 2021–2022 Criteria are shown in **bold** type.

Continued

Table 3 Changes from 2019–2020 Criteria

Paragraph	2019–2020 Reference	2021–2022 Reference
5.1a(4)	...reinforce a customer business focus	...reinforce **organizational resilience, agility, and** a customer and business focus
5.1b	Workforce Climate	**Workplace** Climate
5.2b	How do you ensure that your organizational culture supports your vision and values, and benefits from the diverse ideas...	How do you ensure that your organizational culture supports your vision and values; **promotes equity and inclusion**, and benefits from the **diversity of** ideas?
5.2c(5)		**Equity and Inclusion – How do you ensure that your performance management, performance development, and career development processes promote equity and inclusion for a diverse workforce and different workforce groups and segments?**
6.1c	Ensure supply network agility	Ensure supply network agility **and resilience**)
6.1d	Innovation Management	**Management of Opportunities for Innovation**
6.1d	How do you pursue your opportunities for innovation?	How do you pursue your **identified** opportunities for innovation
6.2c	Safety and Emergency Preparedness	Safety, **Business Continuity, and Resilience**
6.2c	How do you provide a safe operating environment?	How do you provide a safe operating environment **for your workforce, and other people in your workplace**?
6.2c(2)	How do you ensure that your organization is prepared for disasters or emergencies	How do you ensure that your organization **can anticipate, prepare for, and recover from disasters, emergencies, and other disruptions**?
6.2c(2)	How does your disaster and emergency preparedness system consider prevention, continuity of operations, and recovery?	**How do you consider risk,** prevention**, protection,** continuity of operations, and recovery **in the event of disruptions?**
6.2c(2)	How does your disaster and emergency preparedness system take into account your reliance on your workforce, supply network, and partners?	**How do you take into account customer and business needs** and your reliance on the workforce, supply network, partners**, and information technology systems?**
7.1b(2)	...preparedness for disasters or emergencies?	...preparedness for disasters, emergencies, **and other disruptions**
7.3a(2)	Workforce Climate	**Workplace** Climate
7.4a(1)	...encourage two-way communication, and create a focus on action?	...encourage two-way communication, **cultivate innovation and intelligent risk taking**, and create a focus on action?

Word changes in the 2021–2022 Criteria are shown in **bold** type.

Organizational Profile

*The **Organizational Profile** is a snapshot of your organization and its strategic environment.*

IMPORTANCE OF THE ORGANIZATIONAL PROFILE

The Organizational Profile sets the context for the examination process by providing key background information to help examiners evaluate the appropriateness of systems and processes required by the Criteria. For example, the Organizational Profile asks for details about the nature of competition, customer requirements and groupings, key suppliers and partners, workforce characteristics, key strategic challenges and advantages, and performance improvement processes.

The Organizational Profile is the most appropriate starting point for self-assessment in preparation for strategic planning and for writing an application. The Organizational Profile is used by examiners and judges in all stages of application review, including the site visit, to understand the organization and what it considers important. It sets the context for the assessment.

Compiling this information not only helps examiners and judges conduct a more relevant assessment, it may be used by itself for an initial self-assessment by helping the organization and its leaders understand the dynamic factors that affect its success and sustainability.

In today's highly competitive marketplace it is critical to leverage strategic advantages and mitigate strategic challenges. These advantages or challenges might include:

- Operational costs (such as materials, labor, or geographic location)
- Expanding or decreasing markets
- Mergers or acquisitions (of the applicant organization or of competitors)
- Economic and political conditions, including fluctuating demand for products and services, taxation volatility, and economic downturns
- The availability of new or substitute products, such as generic medications
- Rapid technological changes
- New competitors entering the market
- Availability of skilled labor, including the aging workforce, loss of institutional knowledge from retirements, and time needed to prepare replacement workers

A potentially significant challenge relates to being prepared for game-changing technology that threatens to radically disrupt the marketplace. In the past, such technologies have included quartz watch movements replacing the mechanical movements and nearly killing the Swiss watch industry; personal computers replacing typewriters (and many typists); cell phones replacing land lines and pay phones; overnight delivery services and email reducing the demand for postal package delivery and letters; and email, social media, and virtual meeting technology such as Zoom usurping other means of communication.

However, do not list a challenge or advantage unless it has been validated and deemed critical since each one should be addressed in the strategy development process.

P.1 ORGANIZATIONAL DESCRIPTION: What are your key organizational characteristics?

a. Organizational Environment

(1) **Product Offerings** What are your main product offerings (see the Note on the next page)? What is the relative importance of each to your success? What mechanisms do you use to deliver your products?

(2) **Mission, Vision, Values, and Culture** What are your mission, vision, and values? Other than values, what are the characteristics of your organizational culture? What are your organization's core competencies, and what is their relationship to your mission?

(3) **Workforce Profile** What is your workforce profile? What recent changes have you experienced in workforce composition or in your needs with regard to your workforce? What are

- your workforce or employee groups and segments;
- the educational requirements for different employee groups and segments;
- the key drivers that engage them;
- your organized bargaining units (union representation), if any; and
- your special health and safety requirements, if any?

(4) **Assets** What are your major facilities, equipment, technologies, and intellectual property?

(5) **Regulatory Environment** What are your key applicable occupational health and safety regulations; accreditation, certification, or registration requirements; industry standards; and environmental, financial, and product regulations?

b. Organizational Relationships

(1) **Organizational Structure** What are your organizational leadership structure and governance structure? What structures and mechanisms make up your organization's leadership system? What are the reporting relationships among your governance board, senior leaders, and parent organization, as appropriate?

(2) **Customers and Stakeholders** What are your key market segments, customer groups, and stakeholder groups, as appropriate? What are their key requirements and expectations for your products, customer support services, and operations, including any differences among the groups?

(3) **Suppliers, Partners, and Collaborators** What are your key types of suppliers, partners, and collaborators? What role do they play in producing and delivering your key products and customer support services, and in enhancing your competitiveness? What role do they play in contributing and implementing innovations in your organization? What are your key supply-network requirements?

Notes:

P.1a(1). Product offerings are the goods and services you offer in the marketplace. Mechanisms for delivering products to your customers might be direct or might be indirect, through dealers, distributors, collaborators, or channel partners. *Nonprofit (including government) organizations might refer to their product offerings as programs, projects, or services.*

Continued

Continued

P.1a(2). If your organization has a stated purpose as well as a mission, you should include it in your response. Some organizations define a mission and a purpose, and some use the terms interchangeably. Purpose refers to the fundamental reason that the organization exists. Its role is to inspire the organization and guide its setting of values.

P.1a(2). Your values are part of your organization's culture. Other characteristics of your culture might include shared beliefs and norms that contribute to the uniqueness of the environment within your organization.

P.1a(3). Workforce or employee groups and segments (including organized bargaining units) might be based on type of employment or contract-reporting relationship, location (including remote work), tour of duty, work environment, use of flexible work policies, or other factors. Organizations that also rely on volunteers and interns to accomplish their work should include these groups as part of their workforce.

P.1a(5). In the Criteria, industry refers to the sector in which you operate. Industry standards might include industrywide codes of conduct and policy guidance. *For nonprofit (including government) organizations, this sector might be charitable organizations, professional associations and societies, religious organizations, or government entities—or a subsector of one of these.* Depending on the regions in which you operate, environmental regulations might cover greenhouse gas emissions, carbon regulations and trading, and energy efficiency.

P.1b(1). The governance or oversight structure for privately held businesses, nonprofit organizations, and government agencies may comprise an advisory board, a family council, or local/regional leaders who are assembled to provide guidance. *For some nonprofit (including government) organizations, governance and reporting relationships might include relationships with major funding sources, such as granting agencies, legislatures, or foundations.*

P.1b(1). The Organizational Profile asks for the "what" of your leadership system (its structures and mechanisms). Questions in Categories 1 and 5 ask how the system is used.

P.1b(2). *For some nonprofit (including government) organizations, customers might include members, taxpayers, citizens, recipients, clients, and beneficiaries, and market segments might be referred to as constituencies. For government agencies, the legislature (as a source of funds) may be a key stakeholder.*

P.1b(2). Customer groups might be based on common expectations, behaviors, preferences, or profiles. Within a group, there may be customer segments based on differences, commonalities, or both. You might subdivide your market into segments based on product lines or features, distribution channels, business volume, geography, or other defining factors.

P.1b(2). Customer, stakeholder, and operational requirements and expectations will drive your organization's sensitivity to the risk of product, service, support, and supply-network interruptions, including those due to natural disasters and other emergencies.

P.1b(3). Your supply network consists of the entities involved in producing your products and services and delivering them to your customers. For some organizations, these entities form a chain, in which one entity directly supplies another. Increasingly, however, these entities are interlinked and exist in interdependent rather than linear relationships. The Criteria use the term supply network to emphasize the interdependencies among organizations and their suppliers.

The first part of the Organizational Profile describes the key characteristics and relationships that shape the organization. Compiling this information helps ensure senior leaders clearly understand and are aligned among themselves what is required for organization success now and in the future. P.1 asks the applicant to describe "who are we?" For example, P.1a(1) asks for a list of the organization's product offerings (including health care services and educational programs and services for health care and educational organizations respectively). Do not submit a long list of every product or service the organization provides. Instead, focus on the critical ones that constitute the bulk of the organization's effort. All leaders should agree on the organization's key products and services, the importance of each to its success, and the methods used to deliver them. Listing less-important products and services make it more difficult to focus on the key elements needed for success over time.

Mission describes the essence of the organization—the reason it exists—which should align with the key products and services it delivers. Vision describes where senior leaders want to take the organization in the future, consistent with strategic objectives, goals, and action plans.

Core competencies define the organization's areas of greatest expertise; those strategically important capabilities that are central to fulfilling its mission, achieving its vision, or providing an advantage in the marketplace. The absence of a needed core competency may result in a significant strategic challenge or disadvantage for the organization that should be addressed as a part of strategy development or action planning.

The workforce profile provides insight into the capabilities and needs of the people who do the organization's work, whether unionized or not, highly skilled or not, or paid or volunteer. Also identify recent changes in your workforce composition or needs. A critical point to include in P.1a(3) is an explanation of the key drivers of workforce engagement—what motivates workers to do their best to help the organization succeed. This list of key drivers should be aligned with the processes in Item 5.2a(1) and 5.2a(2) that are used to assess workforce engagement. In other words, if one of the key drivers listed in the Organizational Profile is workers feeling valued by the organization, then that factor should be determined and assessed using the procedures described in 5.2a(1) and 5.2a(2).

The applicable regulatory requirements to which the organization is subject should be clearly listed, as required by P.1a(5). This list creates expectations for examiners in several parts of the Criteria including 1.2b(1), which requires the organization to meet and surpass applicable regulatory and legal requirements, 2.1a(3), which requires that potential changes and disruptions in the regulatory and external environment be considered in strategy development, and 7.4a(3), which requires results for key measures or indicators of meeting and surpassing regulatory and legal requirements.

For P.1b(1), clearly describe the organization's governance systems and reporting relationships to make it easy to identify which functions are performed by senior leaders and, as applicable, by the governance board and/or parent organization. This information should align with and help examiners understand the processes used by the organization to ensure effective governance and accountability described in 1.2a(1) and 1.2a(2).

The list of key customers, market segments, customer groups, and stakeholder groups in P.1b(2) creates several expectations in the Baldrige review. Customer requirements and needs are typically considered in strategy development [2.1]. Processes to listen to customers [3.1a]; determine levels of satisfaction, dissatisfaction, and engagement [3.2b(1)]; provide customer access and support [3.2a(2)]; segment customers [3.2b(1)]; and build relationships to engage customers [3.2a(1)] should address all of the customers and customer groups identified in P.1b(2). In addition, the customer satisfaction and engagement results required in 7.2a should reflect the groups and segments described in P.1b(2) or elsewhere in the application.

The list of key suppliers, partners, and collaborators and the roles they play in the organization's work systems, especially in producing and delivering key products and customer support services [P.1a(3)] should align with the processes the organization uses to manage its supply network and help ensure its agility and resilience [6.1c] including selecting qualified suppliers, measuring and evaluating supplier performance, providing feedback to suppliers to help them improve, and dealing with poor-performing suppliers.

P.1 Key Organizational Description Item Linkages

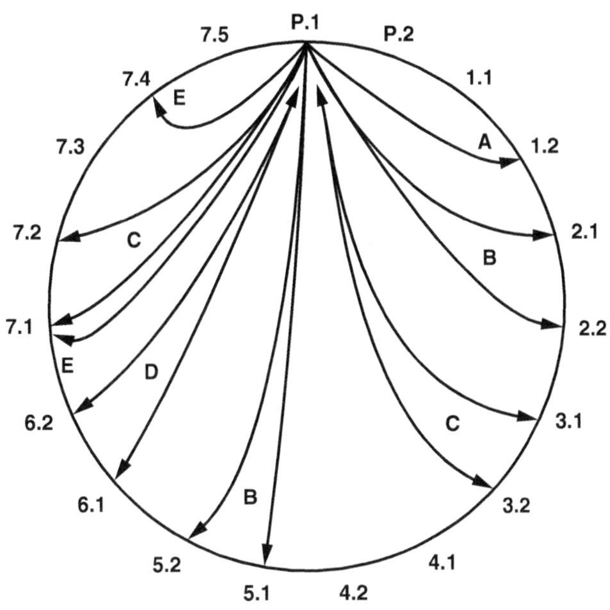

NATURE OF RELATIONSHIP	
A	The organizational structure and governance system described in P.1b(1) sets the context for the review of the management systems for proper governance [1.2a(1)] and ethical behavior [1.2b(2)]. The regulatory environment described in P.1a(5) sets the context for the review of the management systems for public responsibility and should help define compliance processes and help define measures and goals [1.2b(1)].
B	Workforce educational requirements, diversity, and other characteristics [P.1a(3)] may affect the determination of workforce challenges and advantages (if any) as a part of the strategic planning process [2.1a(3)] and the development of key workforce plans [2.2a(4)]. Employee characteristics, such as educational requirements, workforce and job diversity, the existence of bargaining units, the use of contract employees, and other special requirements help set the context for organizational culture, equity, and inclusion [5.2b]; determining appropriate needs by workforce segment for assessing capacity and capability [5.1a(1)]; capitalizing on core competencies to accomplish the organization's work [5.1a(3)]; preparing for and managing changing capability and capacity needs and reinforcing organizational resilience and agility [5.1a(4)]; assuring workplace accessibility, health, and security [5.1b(1)]; workforce development [5.2c(2)]; and tailoring benefits, services, policies [5.1b(2)], and satisfaction assessment methods [5.2a(2)] for the workforce according to various types of categories.
C	The customer and market groups and their product and support requirements reported in P.1b(2) should be consistent with those determined in 3.1b(2) and 3.2a(2). The information in P.1b(2) helps examiners identify the kind of results, broken out by customer and market segment and product, which should be reported in Items 7.1 and 7.2. The product offerings that form the basis for customer support in 3.2a(2) are described in P.1a(1). Product offerings also help determine the focus of customer listening [3.1a], fair treatment [3.2a(4)], and customer satisfaction, engagement, and dissatisfaction [3.2b(1)].

Continued

	NATURE OF RELATIONSHIP *Continued*
D	The product offering information in P.1a(1) aligns with the core competencies, work systems, and key work processes described in 2.1a(4), 6.1, and 6.2. This information helps set the context for the examiner review of those processes.
E	The regulatory and related requirements described in P.1a(5), and the key suppliers listed in P.1b(3) create an expectation that related performance results will be reported in 7.4a(3, 4), 7.1a, and 7.1c respectively [which should be consistent with the measures and goals in 1.2b(1)].

P.2 ORGANIZATIONAL SITUATION: What is your organization's strategic situation?

a. Competitive Environment

(1) **Competitive Position** What are your relative size and growth in your industry or the markets you serve? How many and what types of competitors do you have?

(2) **Competitiveness Changes** What key changes, if any, are affecting your competitive situation, including changes that create opportunities for innovation and collaboration, as appropriate?

(3) **Comparative Data** What key sources of comparative and competitive data are available from within your industry? What key sources of comparative data are available from outside your industry? What limitations, if any, affect your ability to obtain or use these data?

b. Strategic Context

What are your key strategic challenges and advantages?

c. Performance Improvement System

What is your performance improvement system, including your processes for evaluation and improvement of key organizational projects and processes?

Notes:

P.2a. *Nonprofit organizations must often compete with other organizations and alternative sources of similar services to secure financial and volunteer resources, membership, visibility in appropriate communities, and media attention.*

P.2b. Strategic challenges and advantages might be in the areas of business, operations, societal contributions, and workforce. They might relate to products, finances, organizational structure and culture, emerging technology, digital integration, security and cybersecurity, emerging competitors, changing stakeholder requirements, workforce capability or capacity, brand recognition and reputation, your supply network, globalization, and the environment and climate. *Throughout the Criteria, "business" refers to a nonprofit (or government) organization's main mission area or enterprise activity.*

P.2c. The Baldrige Scoring System uses performance improvement through learning and integration as a factor in assessing the maturity of organizational approaches and their deployment. This question is intended to set an overall context for your approach to performance improvement. The approach you use should be related to your organization's needs. Approaches that are compatible with the overarching systems approach provided by the Baldrige framework might include implementing a lean enterprise system, applying Six Sigma methodology, using PDCA methodology, using standards from ISO (for example., the 9000 or 14000 series, or sector-specific standards), using decision science, or employing other improvement tools.

The second part of the Organizational Profile [P.2] seeks information about the competitive environment in which the organization operates, including [P.2b] key strategic challenges and advantages and key changes, if any, which may affect the competitive situation or create opportunities for innovation [P.2a(2)]. P.2 asks the applicant to describe "what is important to us?"

Strategic challenges might include operational costs (for example, materials, labor, or retirements), geographic location, changing markets, mergers or acquisitions, fluctuating demand for products and services, economic downturns, competition from new or substitute products, and rapid technological changes, including data and information security.

Another strategic challenge may face organizations that are not prepared for a technology that disrupts its competitive position or your market. In the past, such technologies have caused several businesses to fail rapidly. Consider digital technology in watches and cellular phones replacing analog technology; personal computers replacing typewriters; cell phones replacing land lines and virtually eliminating pay phones; email replacing fax machines, which had previously captured business from overnight delivery services; and social media challenging all other means of communication. Today, organizations need to detect and recognize such challenges early.

Disruptive technologies or other strategic challenges that hurt one organization may benefit others. However, creating strategic advantages out of challenges may require innovation and rapid process improvement, flexibility and operational agility, resilience, strong supply-network integration, and highly efficient operations.

Lastly, in P.2c the Organization Profile asks how the organization approaches performance improvement and learning. Do not skimp on this explanation because continuous improvement and learning not only provide a significant competitive advantage, but distinguish mature, high-performing organizations from all others [4.1c(2) and 6.1b(3)]. Approaches to process evaluation, improvement, and organizational learning that are compatible with the questions of the Baldrige Framework and CPE may include implementing a lean enterprise system, applying Six Sigma methodology, using PDCA (or PDSA) methodology, using standards from ISO (for example, 9000 or 14000), using decision science, using After Action Reviews (AARs), or employing other improvement tools. Explain the techniques the organization uses for continuous improvement, learning, and innovation here in the Organizational Profile and refer to their use in the application narrative for each Item.

P.2 Key Organizational Situation Item Linkages

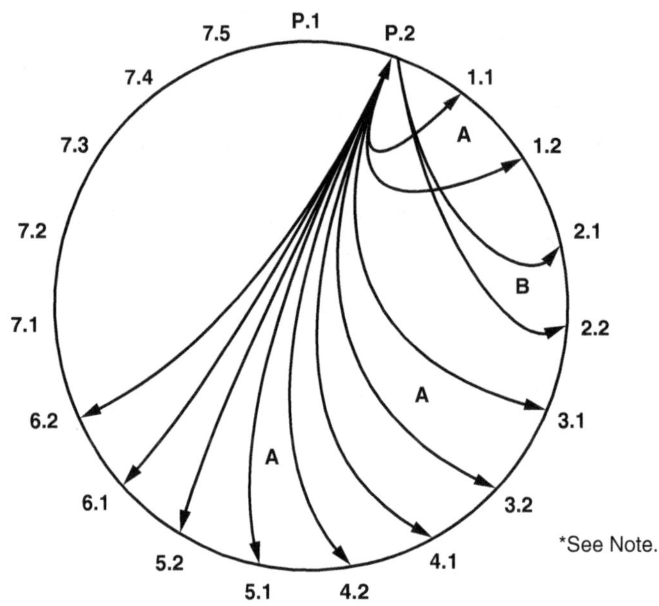

	NATURE OF RELATIONSHIP
A	Leaders [1.1c] are responsible for creating an environment that drives organizational and individual learning, success now and in the future (formerly called sustainability), a culture of equity and inclusion, innovation and intelligent risk taking, and improved organizational performance, which support the overall focus on performance improvement [P.2c]. Leaders [1.1c(1) and 1.1c(2)] are also responsible for creating an environment for success and a focus on action that will promote equity and inclusion, cultivate resilience, improve the organization's performance, set expectations for performance, and demonstrate personal accountability for the organization's actions. The organization should also evaluate and improve the performance of senior leaders, including the chief executive and governance board [1.2a(2)]. The overall approaches to systematic evaluation and improvement identified in P.2c should be consistent with overall requirements for learning (evaluation, improvement, and innovation), specifically required as a part of "Learning' in the Scoring Guidelines for all Process Items in Categories 1–6.
B	The competitive environment defined in P.2a(1, 2, 3) and the strategic context (strategic challenges and advantages) defined in P.2b should be examined as part of the strategy considerations process [2.1a(3) and 2.1b(2)] and should help focus the projection of competitors' future performance in 2.2b. In addition, the strategic challenges and advantages identified in P.2b should be addressed by the strategic objectives in 2.1b(1).

*Note: To make the circle diagrams less cluttered, all of the links described in paragraph *A* will not be repeated on the other diagrams.

1 Leadership—120 Points

*The **Leadership** Category asks how senior leaders' personal actions guide and sustain your organization. It also asks about your organization's governance system; how your organization fulfills its legal and ethical responsibilities; and how it makes societal contributions.*

Senior leaders must set and deploy organizational vision and values, set high performance expectations, and promote an organization-wide focus on engaging customers and workers, and workforce empowerment, learning, and innovation. The Leadership Category looks at how senior leaders' personal actions create an organization that is successful now and in the future; demonstrate their committment to legal and ethical behavior; create a focus on action; set and deploy directions and organizational vision, values, and high-performance expectations; enhance their personal leadership skills; participate in succession planning and develop future leaders; measure organizational performance; and develop an environment that fosters equity and inclusion and high performance. Senior leaders must communicate clear values and performance expectations that address the needs of all stakeholders. The Category also looks at how the organization practices responsible governance; meets its legal, ethical, and societal responsibilities; and supports its key communities.

The Category contains two Items:

Senior Leadership

- Communicating and reinforcing clear vision and values, performance expectations, commitment to legal and ethical behavior, and a focus on creating value for customers and other stakeholders.
- Creating an environment for workforce and customer engagement, organizational evaluation, improvement, and innovation; and workforce and personal learning.
- Creating an environment to achieve innovation and intelligent risk taking including supporting change when needed.
- Developing and enhancing the personal leadership skills of senior leaders.
- Creating a focus on action and a focus on creating a value for customers and a culture that delivers a consistently positive customer experience. (As a part of this focus, leaders drive customer engagement and a customer-focused culture—linked with 3.1 and 3.2.)
- Reviewing organizational performance and capabilities, competitiveness, and progress relative to goals to identify needed actions—linked with 2.1 and 4.1.

Governance and Societal Contributions

- Providing responsible governance that holds senior leaders accountable for their actions, for achieving strategic plans, for fiscal accountability, for transparency in operations, for effective and independent internal and external audits, for protecting stockholder and stakeholder interests, and for succession planning.
- Evaluating and improving the performance of senior leaders, the CEO, and the Board. Using performance evaluations to determine executive compensation.
- Addressing any adverse impacts on society caused by the organization's products, services, and operations.
- Ensuring ethical business practices in all transactions. Meeting legal, ethical, and regulatory responsibilities.
- Considering societal well-being as part of strategy and daily operations.
- Supporting and strengthening key communities *as identified by the organization.*

1.1 SENIOR LEADERSHIP: How do your senior leaders lead the organization? (70 Pts.) PROCESS

a. Vision and Values

(1) **Establishing Vision and Values How do senior leaders set and deploy your organization's vision and values?** How do senior leaders deploy the vision and values through your leadership system, to the workforce, to key suppliers and partners, and to customers and other stakeholders, as appropriate? How do senior leaders' personal actions reflect a commitment to those values?

(2) **Promoting Legal and Ethical Behavior How do senior leaders' personal actions demonstrate their commitment to legal and ethical behavior?** How do senior leaders promote an organizational environment that requires it?

b. Communication

How do senior leaders communicate with and engage the entire workforce, key partners, and key customers? How do they

- encourage frank, two-way communication;
- communicate key decisions and needs for organizational change; and
- take a direct role in motivating the workforce toward high performance and a customer and business focus?

c. Mission and Organizational Performance

(1) **Creating an Environment for Success How do senior leaders create an environment for success now and in the future?** How do they

- create an environment for the achievement of your mission;
- create and reinforce your organizational culture, and a culture that fosters customer and workforce engagement, equity, and inclusion;
- cultivate organizational agility and resilience, accountability, organizational and individual learning, innovation, and intelligent risk taking; and
- participate in succession planning and the development of future organizational leaders?

(2) **Creating a Focus on Action How do senior leaders create a focus on action that will achieve the organization's mission?** How do senior leaders

- create a focus on action that will improve the organization's performance;
- identify needed actions;
- in setting expectations for organizational performance, include a focus on creating and balancing value for customers and other stakeholders; and
- demonstrate personal accountability for the organization's actions?

Notes:

1.1. Your organizational performance results should be reported in Items 7.1–7.5. Results related to the effectiveness of leadership and the leadership system should be reported in Item 7.4.

1.1a(1). Your organization's vision should set the context for the strategic objectives and action plans you describe in Items 2.1 and 2.2.

Continued

Continued

1.1b. Two-way communication may include use of social media, such as delivering periodic messages through internal and external websites, tweets, blogging, and customer and workforce digital forums, as well as monitoring external social media outlets and responding, when appropriate.

1.1b. Senior leaders' direct role in motivating the workforce may include participating in reward and recognition programs.

1.1b. Organizations that rely heavily on volunteers to accomplish their work should also discuss efforts to communicate with and engage the volunteer workforce.

1.1c(1). A successful organization is capable of addressing current business needs and, by addressing risk, agility, resilience, and strategic opportunities, of preparing for its future business, market, and operating environment. In creating an environment for success, leaders should consider both external and internal factors. Factors might include risk appetite and tolerance; the need for technological and organizational innovation, including risks and opportunities arising from emerging technology, data integration, and digitization; readiness for disruptions; organizational culture; work systems; the potential need for changes in structure and culture; workforce capability and capacity; resource availability; societal benefits and social equity; and core competencies.

1.1c(1). Promoting equity means ensuring that all customers and workforce members are treated fairly and that all workforce members can reach their full potential. Inclusion refers to promoting the full participation of all workforce members and ensuring a sense of belonging for them.

1.1c(2). Senior leaders' focus on action considers your strategy, workforce, work systems, and assets. It includes taking intelligent risks, implementing innovations and ongoing improvements in performance and productivity, taking the actions needed to achieve your strategic objectives (see 2.2a[1]), and possibly establishing plans for managing organizational change or responding rapidly to significant new information.

Comparison with the Health Care Criteria

Item 1.1c(1) in the Health Care Criteria adds this phrase to the existing language of the Business Criteria: "Create and reinforce a culture of patient safety."

Item 1.1 examines the key aspects of senior leaders' personal actions to create an organization that is successful now and in the future. Item 1.1 is specifically focused on senior leaders, which typically include the organization's senior management team or the head of the applicant organization and his or her direct reports.

To be successful, senior leaders must understand and champion the Criteria for Performance Excellence, but understanding is not enough. Effective senior leaders *mandate,* through many different techniques, the use of performance excellence criteria as the way to optimize organization performance. These leaders consistently promote high performance, create and balance value for all stakeholders, set clear values and directions, and communicate them effectively to motivate the workforce and make sure all stakeholders understand their responsibilities and align work to achieve desired results.

The most successful leaders possess a strong future orientation; a personal bias for action and intelligent risk taking; a commitment to both personal and organizational improvement and innovation; and a disciplined, uncompromising approach to drive the necessary changes. This requires creating an environment for workforce and customer engagement, equity, inclusion, learning, innovation, and organizational agility, as well as the means for organizational resilience. This

An organization's failure to achieve high levels of performance can almost always be traced to a failure in leadership.

environment cannot be seen by the workforce as optional. Senior leaders should have zero tolerance for subordinates and workers who are not working diligently to achieve these principles.

To be successful and sustain that success now and in the future, senior leaders must improve their personal leadership skills, develop the organization's future leaders, and reward and recognize the performance of those whose behavior is consistent with the stated principles. They personally participate in organizational learning and future leader development, and integrate that development into the organization's succession planning. Role-model leaders recognize the need for and support change when warranted and then lead the effort to fruition.

Senior leaders should personally mentor and teach development courses for other leaders, managers, and workforce members. Senior leaders in high-performing organizations are personally involved to demonstrate their own unwavering commitment to excellence.

Effective communication is a key theme of Item 1.1. Through their outward focus, senior leaders push values, create expectations, and align the organization's work. In promoting high performance, senior leaders set and deploy values, short- and longer-term directions and performance expectations of customer engagement and a consistently positive customer experience, and balance expectations of customers and other stakeholders. Leaders develop and implement systems to ensure vision and values are understood and consistently followed.

Leaders must ensure that organizational values and their own actions actually guide the behavior of the workforce (including supervisors, managers, and workers throughout the organization), or the values are meaningless. To enhance performance excellence, values must be adopted that include a focus on customer engagement and other stakeholders to create a culture of customer engagement. Since various customer and stakeholder groups often have conflicting interests, leaders must strike a balance that optimizes the interests of all groups. Failure to ensure a customer focus usually causes the organization and its workforce to focus internally. Lack of a leader-led customer focus forces workers to default to their own ideas of what customers really need. This increases the risk of being perceived by customers as arrogant and not caring about the requirements of customers. It also increases the potential for creating and delivering products and services that customers do not want or value. That, in turn, increases rework, scrap, waste, and added cost and lower value.

Senior leaders must ensure two-way communication with subordinate leaders and other workers; key suppliers and partners regarding organizational values, directions, and expectations; and key customers regarding their needs and expectations. This communication provides an opportunity for senior leaders to receive feedback about their effectiveness as leaders. Using social media can make two-way communication easier and more pervasive. Social media tools like websites, blogs, tweets, and other digital forums can be valuable additions to traditional means of communication such as print and face-to-face methods. Two-way communication should also foster feedback from workers about leadership effectiveness. Accordingly, part of the communication with workers should involve formal and informal employee and peer feedback of leader effectiveness, such as using a 360-degree feedback survey or an upward evaluation. This information could be structured to help evaluate the leader effectiveness at all levels, including the board of directors, as required in Item 1.2a(2).

Leaders must create an environment for workforce engagement, equity, inclusion, accountability, and agility, as well as the means for rapid and effective application of knowledge. Empowerment means giving workers more authority over decisions about their work. To make consistently good decisions, workers need adequate data and the skills to interpret the data correctly. Agility relates to eliminating barriers and unnecessary control gates that bureaucracies and insecure leaders put in place. Unnecessary levels of review and approval make agility impossible.

Finally, a risk-averse environment reduces opportunities for improvement and innovation, opens the door for competitors, and erodes high performance. Senior leaders are responsible for creating an environment that welcomes—even demands—intelligent risk taking to ensure long-term sustainability and growth.

To demonstrate maturity, the Scoring Guidelines require the organization to have a system in place to improve and innovate the methods its senior leaders use to set organizational vision and values, demonstrate their commitment to legal and ethical behavior, communicate with and engage the entire workforce and key customers, create a successful organization now and in the future, and ensure a focus on action to achieve the organization's mission. Senior leaders should regularly evaluate these processes and demonstrate that they have made meaningful, value-added improvements in their techniques for providing effective leadership.

2021–2022 Criteria Elements Listed Individually Without Duplication

See page 279 for explanation of this table

	Basic Approach Elements [A-B] for Scoring Between 10% and 45%	Additional Approach Elements at the Overall [A-O] Level for Scoring Between 50% and 65%	Additional Approach Elements at the Multiple Level [A-M] for Scoring Between 70% and 100%
1.1 Senior Leadership			
1.1a(1)	Senior leaders "lead" the organization	Senior leaders set and deploy the organization's vision and values	Senior leaders • Deploy the vision and values through the leadership system— – To the workforce, – To key suppliers and partners, and – To customers and other stakeholders, as appropriate • Personal actions reflect a commitment to the organization's values
1.1a(2)		Senior leaders' actions demonstrate their commitment to legal and ethical behavior	Senior leaders promote an organizational environment that requires legal and ethical behavior
1.1b		Senior leaders • Communicate with the entire workforce • Engage the entire workforce • Communicate with key partners • Engage the key partners • Communicate with key customers • Engage key customers	Senior leaders: • Encourage frank, two-way communication • Communicate key decisions and needs for organizational change • Take a direct role in motivating the workforce toward high performance and a customer and business focus
1.1c(1)		Senior leaders create an environment for success now and in the future	Senior leaders: • Create an environment for the achievement of mission • Create and reinforce an organizational culture that fosters customer and workforce engagement, equity, and inclusion • Cultivate organizational agility and resilience, accountability, organizational and individual learning, innovation, and intelligent risk taking • Participate in succession planning and the development of future organizational leaders
1.1c(2)		Senior leaders create a focus on action that will achieve the organization's mission	Senior leaders: • Identify needed actions • In setting expectations for organizational performance, include a focus on creating and balancing value for customers and other stakeholders • Demonstrate personal accountability for the organization's actions

1.1 Senior Leadership

Basic Approach Element: Senior leaders lead the organization

Overall Approach Elements:
- *Senior leaders set the organization's vision and values [1.1a(1)]*
- *Senior leaders' actions demonstrate their commitment to legal and ethical behavior [1.1a(2)]*
- *Senior leaders communicate with and engage the entire workforce, key partners, and key customers [1.1b]*
- *Senior leaders create an environment for success now and in the future [1.1c(1)]*
- *Senior leaders create a focus on action that will achieve the organization's mission [1.1c(2)]*

The following diagram describes key approach elements:

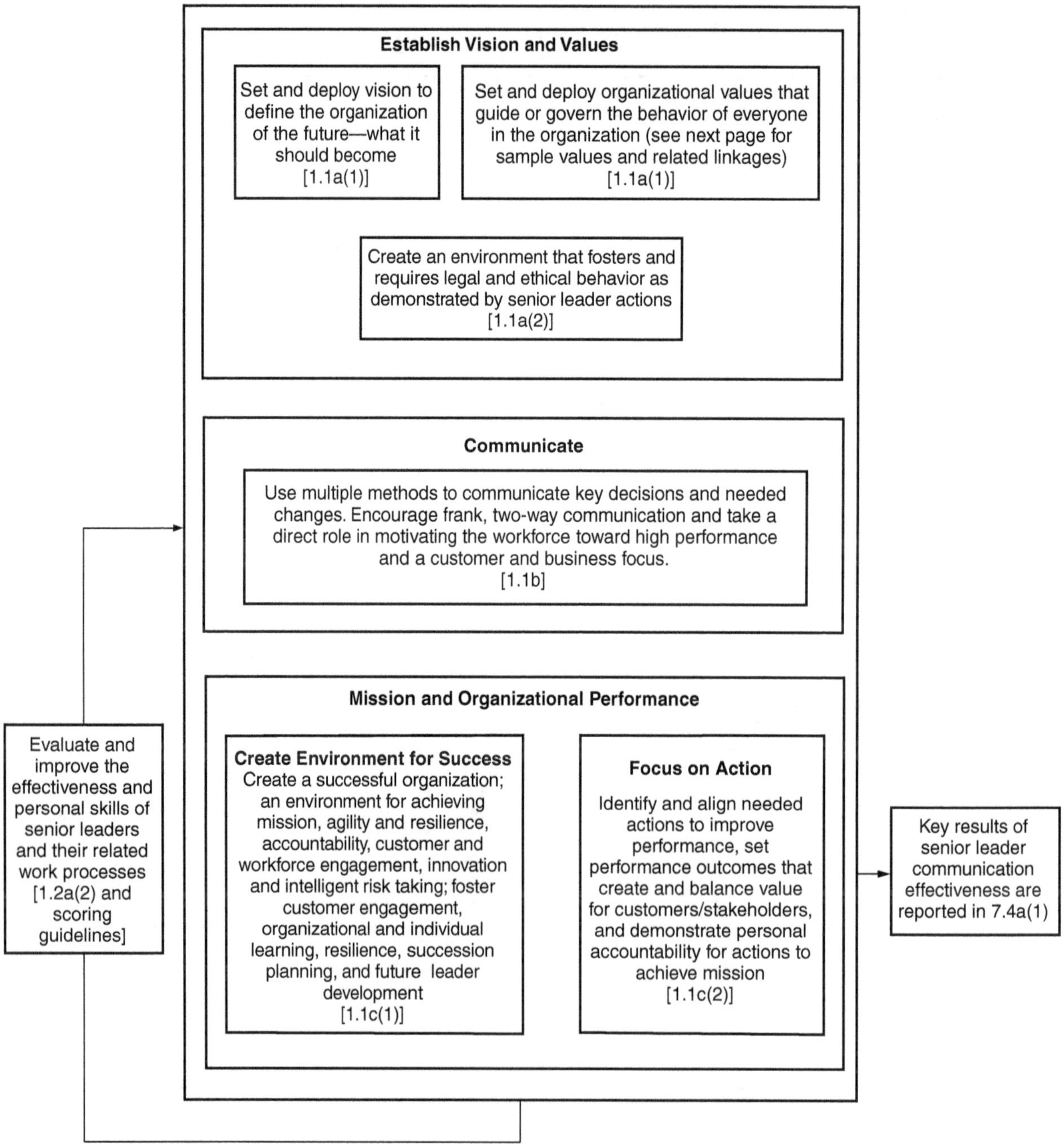

Establish Vision and Values

Set and deploy vision to define the organization of the future—what it should become [1.1a(1)]

Set and deploy organizational values that guide or govern the behavior of everyone in the organization (see next page for sample values and related linkages) [1.1a(1)]

Create an environment that fosters and requires legal and ethical behavior as demonstrated by senior leader actions [1.1a(2)]

Communicate

Use multiple methods to communicate key decisions and needed changes. Encourage frank, two-way communication and take a direct role in motivating the workforce toward high performance and a customer and business focus. [1.1b]

Mission and Organizational Performance

Create Environment for Success
Create a successful organization; an environment for achieving mission, agility and resilience, accountability, customer and workforce engagement, innovation and intelligent risk taking; foster customer engagement, organizational and individual learning, resilience, succession planning, and future leader development [1.1c(1)]

Focus on Action

Identify and align needed actions to improve performance, set performance outcomes that create and balance value for customers/stakeholders, and demonstrate personal accountability for actions to achieve mission [1.1c(2)]

Evaluate and improve the effectiveness and personal skills of senior leaders and their related work processes [1.2a(2) and scoring guidelines]

Key results of senior leader communication effectiveness are reported in 7.4a(1)

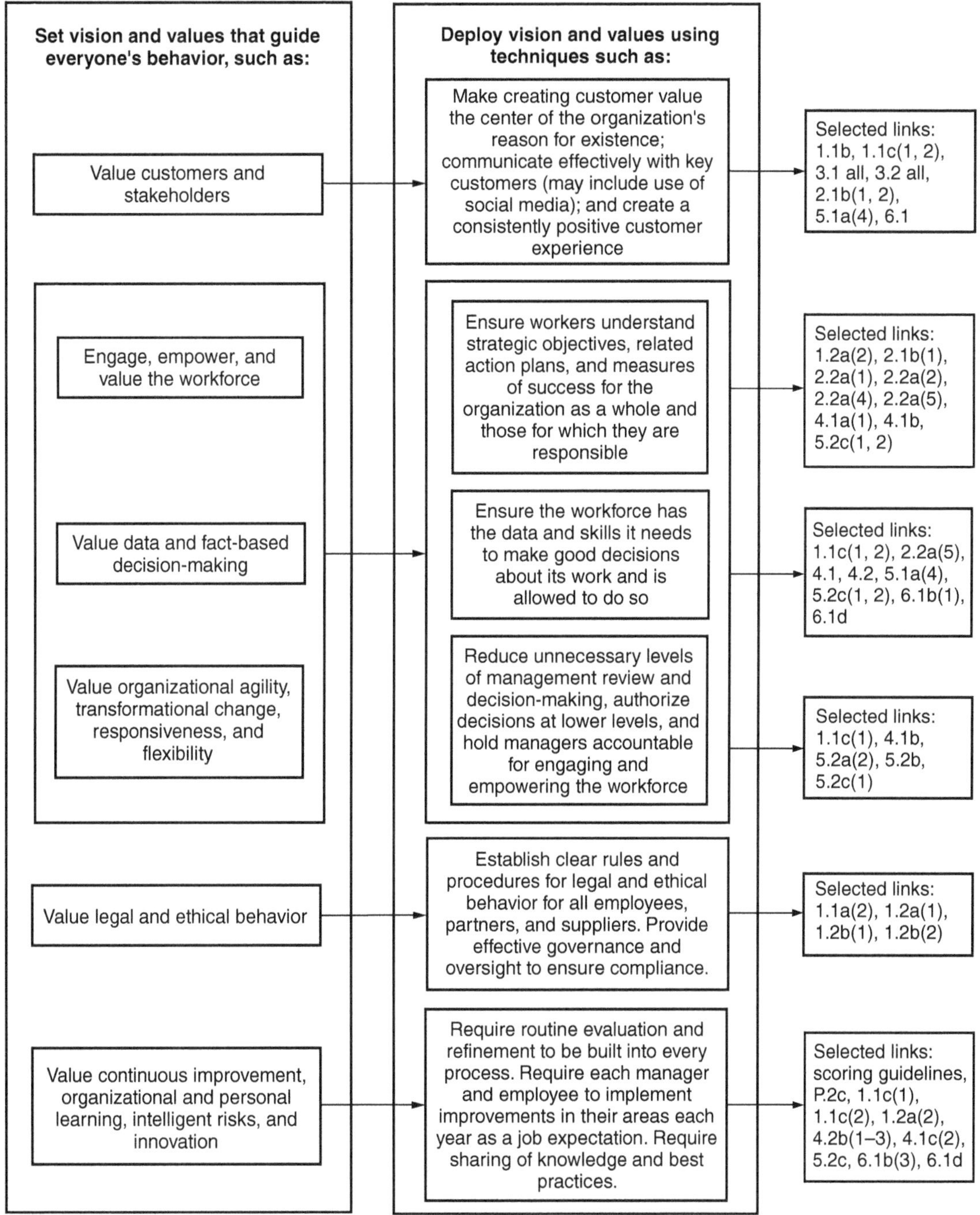
Vision, Values, and Mission Linkages with Process Items
Set vision and values that guide everyone's behavior, such as:
Value customers and stakeholders
Engage, empower, and value the workforce
Value data and fact-based decision-making
Value organizational agility, transformational change, responsiveness, and flexibility
Value legal and ethical behavior
Value continuous improvement, organizational and personal learning, intelligent risks, and innovation
Deploy vision and values using techniques such as:
Make creating customer value the center of the organization's reason for existence; communicate effectively with key customers (may include use of social media); and create a consistently positive customer experience
Ensure workers understand strategic objectives, related action plans, and measures of success for the organization as a whole and those for which they are responsible
Ensure the workforce has the data and skills it needs to make good decisions about its work and is allowed to do so
Reduce unnecessary levels of management review and decision-making, authorize decisions at lower levels, and hold managers accountable for engaging and empowering the workforce
Establish clear rules and procedures for legal and ethical behavior for all employees, partners, and suppliers. Provide effective governance and oversight to ensure compliance.
Require routine evaluation and refinement to be built into every process. Require each manager and employee to implement improvements in their areas each year as a job expectation. Require sharing of knowledge and best practices.
Selected links: 1.1b, 1.1c(1, 2), 3.1 all, 3.2 all, 2.1b(1, 2), 5.1a(4), 6.1
Selected links: 1.2a(2), 2.1b(1), 2.2a(1), 2.2a(2), 2.2a(4), 2.2a(5), 4.1a(1), 4.1b, 5.2c(1, 2)
Selected links: 1.1c(1, 2), 2.2a(5), 4.1, 4.2, 5.1a(4), 5.2c(1, 2), 6.1b(1), 6.1d
Selected links: 1.1c(1), 4.1b, 5.2a(2), 5.2b, 5.2c(1)
Selected links: 1.1a(2), 1.2a(1), 1.2b(1), 1.2b(2)
Selected links: scoring guidelines, P.2c, 1.1c(1), 1.1c(2), 1.2a(2), 4.2b(1–3), 4.1c(2), 5.2c, 6.1b(3), 6.1d

1.1 Key Senior Leadership Item Linkages

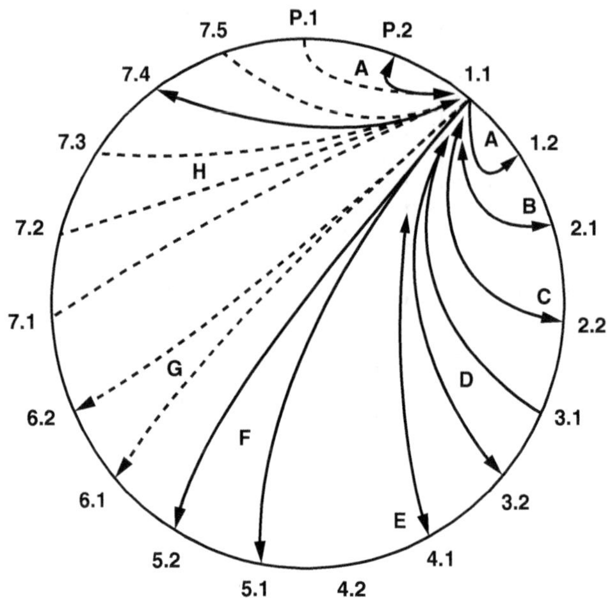

	NATURE OF RELATIONSHIP
A	Leaders in support of organizational values [1.1a(1)] exhibit actions that foster and require ethical behavior [1.1a(2)]; establish programs and processes to ensure ethical and legal behavior [1.2b(1, 2)] and organization responsibility [1.2b(1)]; and practice good citizenship [1.2c]. The organizational structure and governance system described in P.1b(1) set the context for the review of the management systems for proper governance [1.2a] and ethical behavior [1.1a(2) and 1.2b(2)]. Leaders [1.1c(1, 2)] are responsible for creating an environment that drives organizational and personal learning, resilience, and innovation, consistent with the overall focus on performance improvement [P.2c].
B	The vision set and deployed by senior leaders [1.1a(1)] should set the context for the strategic objectives [2.1b] and action plans [2.2.]. To effectively establish organizational direction and expectations, leaders [1.1a(1)] participate in the strategic planning process [2.1a]. As part of this effort, leaders focus on action [1.1c(2)] to identify strategic opportunities and support innovation [2.1a(2)] and, considering core competencies, decide which work will be done externally and which will be internal [2.1a(4)], and ensure that strategic objectives [2.1b(1)] create value and balance the needs of customers and stakeholders.
C	Leaders [1.1b] motivate and communicate clearly with the workforce at all levels throughout the organization in part to align and implement action plans (work) [2.2a(1, 2)]. Leaders [1.1a] also approve the overall strategic action plans and ensure they are consistent with mission, vision, and values based, in part, on information about expected levels of competitor performance [2.2a(6)]. They are also responsible for using comparative data of future projections [from 2.2a(6)] to set meaningful goals to achieve organizational success, resilience, and improve performance [1.1c(1, 2)].
D	Leaders [1.1b] use information learned from current and potential customers about requirements and support preferences [3.1 and 3.2a(2)] and customer engagement, satisfaction, and dissatisfaction [3.2b(1)] to set direction and create opportunity for the organization. Leaders [1.1c(2)] also use this information to help create and drive customer-focused value and new or expanded programs, products,

Continued

	NATURE OF RELATIONSHIP *Continued*
	and services to enhance customer engagement, build better customer relationships [3.2a(1)], and meet customer requirements and expectations for products and support [3.2a(2)] throughout the organization while delivering a consistently positive customer experience and engagement [1.1c(1)].
E	Leaders [1.1c(2)] use analyses of data [4.1b, 4.1c(2)] to monitor organizational performance and understand relationships between performance and the need to respond rapidly to changing organizational needs and challenges in the operating environment, including the need for change in work systems, workforce engagement and satisfaction, customer engagement and satisfaction, market growth, and financial health. These analyses are also used for decision-making and improvement at all levels and to set priorities for action and allocate resources for best practice sharing, performance projection, and continuous improvement and innovation [4.1c(2), 4.2b(2)]. Leaders also develop a timetable for achieving strategic objectives [2.1b(1)] as a basis for defining and monitoring expected progress closely [4.1b]. The timetable in 2.1b(1) should define the expected levels of future performance that the leaders use during the performance reviews [4.1b] to determine if the organization is making appropriate progress against desired goals. Accordingly, if senior leaders review progress quarterly, then timelines to accomplish strategic objectives should define expected performance quarterly.
F	Leaders [1.1c(1)] create an environment for current and future organizational success (sustainability), achievement of mission, strategic objectives, intelligent risk taking, resilience, innovation, accountability, learning, performance leadership, and agility throughout the entire organization by engaging the workforce to achieve organizational and personal success [5.2]. They ensure that the compensation and recognition system [5.2c(1)] encourages workers at all levels to achieve performance excellence in areas most critical to the organization and its customers. Leaders personally reinforce the importance of high performance and a customer focus [1.1b]. Leaders [1.1c(1)] are also responsible for creating an environment that supports workforce learning through workforce and career development [5.2c], and assesses skills and competencies [5.1a(1)], prepares for new skills required [5.2c(3)], and creates effective systems, policies, and benefits to enhance the work climate [5.1b(1, 2)] and equity and inclusion [5.2c)5)].
G	Leaders [1.1c(1) and 1.1c(2)] are responsible for creating an environment that supports success now and into the future, accountability, high performance, innovation, intelligent risk taking, and continuous improvement, including leading change, monitoring processes for the design, management, and improvement of key work processes, supply networks, support services, emergency preparedness, and innovation (including taking intelligent risks to support strategic opportunities) [6.1 and 6.2].
H	To reinforce values and vision and sustain business success, senior leaders [1.1] use performance results data [from Category 7] for many activities, including monitoring organizational performance [4.1b]; deploying priority improvement areas to focus work and ensure alignment; strategic planning [2.1a]; setting goals, strategic objectives [2.1b(1)], and action plans [2.2a(1, 2)]; reinforcing or rewarding workforce performance [5.2c(1)]; and for executive compensation and improving their effectiveness and the effectiveness of leaders at all levels [1.2a(2)]. In addition, key results of leadership performance [1.1], such as results related to the senior leader's focus on action, communication and engagement with customers and workers to deploy vision and values, and two-way communication [7.4a(1)], and meeting strategic objectives [7.5b] are reported.

IF YOU DON'T DO WHAT THE CRITERIA REQUIRE . . .	
Item Reference	**Possible Adverse Consequences**
1.1a(1)	**Setting and Deploying Vision and Values** – If senior leaders fail to make vision, values, and performance expectations clear (especially defining them in measurable terms and ensuring their personal actions reflect a commitment to those values), uncertainty may be created among managers and workers throughout the organization about what they must accomplish, and the direction they must follow. This may cause subordinates to substitute their own ideas, objectives, and directions, which may not be in alignment with those of top leadership or other supervisors and units. The lack of alignment may also contribute to redundancy. As a consequence, some parts of the organization may waste resources working at cross-purposes with other parts of the organization.
1.1a(2)	**Promoting Legal and Ethical Behavior** – If senior leaders do not demonstrate their commitment through their actions to require legal and ethical behavior in all interactions, people will not take it seriously. Those who operate without regard to law and ethics will create problems for the organization that could threaten its existence and adversely affect many other organizations (consider Enron, Volkswagen, and numerous financial institutions).
1.1b	**Communication** – If senior leaders do not effectively communicate with and engage the entire workforce, key partners, and key customers, they risk not fully leveraging the high power of key assets—their people and stakeholders. As a consequence, leaders may be effectively sending a message that customers are unimportant or workers do not have the skills or ability to make decisions on their own, and that micromanagement is the preferred approach within the organization. This kind of environment tends to force decision-making to higher and higher levels in the organization, creating excessive delay and working against organizational agility. Unnecessary levels of review and approval may also tend to minimize innovation, risk taking, and creativity throughout the organization. Taken together, these problems are likely to add cost but not value—making it increasingly difficult to be successful in a highly competitive industry.
1.1c(1)	**Creating an Environment for Success** – Failing to put and keep systems in place to achieve mission, innovate and take intelligent risks, create workforce engagement (equity and inclusion), or sustain high performance has caused some organizations to decline and fail—even past Baldrige Award recipients. Creating a sustainable, successful organization may require top leaders to drive radical, intense (transformational) changes in the organization's structure and culture. This typically requires leaders to embed values of engaging the workforce, breakthrough and continuous improvement (including making improvements in their personal leadership skills), fact-based decision-making, and a passion for satisfying and engaging customers.
1.1c(1)	**Creating an Environment for Success** – Taking intelligent risks strikes a balance between taking no risks (and failing to make progress in the face of challenges) or taking foolish risks (and causing harm or loss to the organization). Organizations with a risk-averse culture seek to minimize change and try to lock in the status quo. In a volatile climate this lack of effective change opens the door for other organizations to compete more successfully, threatening the organization's sustainability. Foolish risk contributes to wasted resources because success is unlikely—similar to betting your paycheck on a 100-to-1 long shot in the Kentucky Derby. Intelligent risk demands a tolerance for failure and an expectation that some actions will not achieve the desired outcomes. However, using data to analyze the potential for gain compared to the potential for loss helps make the risk taking more *intelligent*.

Continued

IF YOU DON'T DO WHAT THE CRITERIA REQUIRE . . . *Continued*	
Item Reference	**Possible Adverse Consequences**
1.1c(2)	**Focus on Action** – If senior leaders do not create an environment that focuses on action to accomplish organizational objectives, improve performance, achieve innovation, and accomplish the mission, workers will focus on their own priorities. Without a focus on creating value for and engaging customers and other stakeholders, workers and managers within the organization may become internally focused and risk averse, negatively impacting the customer value on which every successful organization is built. An internal focus may contribute to a climate within which the workforce is not primarily interested in listening to customer requirements or concerns. This may produce a high level of organizational arrogance where workers believe they know what the customers want better than the customer. This type of behavior can antagonize customers and produce high levels of customer dissatisfaction—working against the creation of a consistently positive customer experience.
1.1c(2)	**Focus on Action** – If senior leaders do not create an environment that focuses on balancing value for customers and other stakeholders—especially when different customer groups have competing interests—customer confidence in one group may be eroded and eventually customers may be lost. For example, end users of a product want inexpensive, reliable products, while stockholders want profits and the stock price to increase. Excessive focus on one group over others makes it difficult to maximize value and keep all end users and stockholders satisfied and loyal.

1.1 SENIOR LEADERSHIP—SAMPLE EFFECTIVE PRACTICES

Perhaps most critical is that senior leaders demonstrate absolute, unwavering commitment to performance excellence—including aligning reward and recognition to provide incentives and disincentives. The best senior leaders do not tolerate a lack of aggressive commitment and urgent action from subordinates throughout the organization in support of performance excellence. They send a clear message to the workforce that the effort is serious.

a. Vision and Values

- Leaders serve as role models (walk the talk) in leading systematic performance improvement and innovation throughout the organization.
- Leader behavior (not merely words) clearly defines what is expected of the organization and its workforce.
- All senior leaders are knowledgeable about and personally involved in performance improvement.
- Senior leaders spend a significant portion of their time on performance improvement activities and promoting effective efforts to achieve innovation.
- Senior leaders carry out many visible activities (for example, setting goals, planning, and recognizing and rewarding performance and process improvement that leads to meaningful, value-added change).
- Senior leaders regularly communicate performance excellence values to subordinates and ensure that those subordinates demonstrate those values in their work.
- Senior leaders clearly and consistently articulate values, mentor managers, and ensure that promotion criteria reflect organizational values, especially customer satisfaction, workforce

engagement, continuous improvement, and breakthrough innovation.

- Senior leaders ensure that organizational values are used to provide direction to the entire workforce to help achieve the mission, vision, and performance goals.

b. Communication

- Senior leaders participate on performance-improvement teams.
- Senior leaders study (benchmark) and learn about the effective practices of other organizations.
- Senior leaders use effective approaches, such as skip-a-level meetings and personally responding to email questions from workers, to reach out to all workers to spread the organization's values and align worker priorities to support organizational goals and action plans.
- Many different techniques are used to reinforce quality values. Leaders at all levels make two-way communication easy through personal methods such as voice mail, email, town hall meetings, and face-to-face meetings (which can include often-used open-door access practices).
- Senior leaders are transparent as they adopt changes to improve their effectiveness as leaders.
- Senior leaders require that all key processes identify internal and external customers and other stakeholders that might have competing interests; define customer and other stakeholders' specific requirements in measurable terms; and develop or assign processes to monitor customer and other stakeholders' satisfaction and correct problems quickly.

c. Mission and Organizational Performance

- Senior leaders effectively surface problems and encourage—even demand—intelligent risk taking to improve processes at all levels in the organization.
- Roles and responsibilities of subordinates are clearly defined, understood by them, and used to evaluate and improve their performance.
- Job definitions with performance targets are clearly delineated for each level of the organization, objectively measured, and presented in a logical and organized structure.
- Systems and procedures are deployed that encourage cooperation and a cross-functional approach to management, team activities, and problem solving.
- Leaders monitor workforce acceptance and adoption of vision and values using annual surveys, employee focus groups, and email questions.
- A systematic process is in place for evaluating and improving the integration or alignment of quality values throughout the organization. For example, after every all-hands meeting, leaders and senior staff randomly ask workers to explain the key points discussed in the meeting.
- Senior leaders take increasingly aggressive actions to assist units that are not meeting goals or performing to plan.
- Leaders at all levels determine how well they carried out their activities using After Action Reviews or *Plus-Delta* (What went well? What didn't go well? What should we do differently?).

Ineffective Practices

Having listed some practices that characterize effective leaders, it should be noted that poor leaders often exercise ineffective practices.

- Poor leaders also serve as role models—but not in a good way.
- Poor leaders care about their own perquisites (such as lavish offices, limousines, personal air transport, housing, and so on), rather than attend to customers, workers, and other stakeholders.
- Poor leaders fail to motivate workers fully—they command and dictate instead.
- Poor leaders do not care—and rarely or never ask workers—what workers think of their leadership.

- Poor leaders micromanage subordinates and inhibit change or innovation unless it comes from them. They are risk averse.
- Poor leaders seek power for its own sake, not to promote organizational success.
- Poor leaders don't actively participate in succession planning and developing future leaders. If the organization falters, they take pride that "they couldn't succeed without me."

Note: We welcome your input and suggestions about effective and ineffective practices. Please feel free to share them with us to add to the book. We can be reached at *markblazey@gmail.com* or *paul.grizzell@corevaluespartners.com*.

1.2 GOVERNANCE AND SOCIETAL CONTRIBUTIONS: How do you govern your organization and make societal contributions? (50 Pts.) **PROCESS**

a. Organizational Governance

(1) **Governance System How does your organization ensure responsible governance?** How does your governance system review and achieve the following?

- Accountability for senior leaders' actions
- Accountability for strategy
- Fiscal accountability
- Transparency in operations
- Selection of governance board members and disclosure policies for them, as appropriate
- Independence and effectiveness of internal and external audits
- Protection of stakeholder and stockholder interests, as appropriate
- Succession planning for senior leaders

(2) **Performance Evaluation How do you evaluate the performance of your senior leaders and your governance board?** How do you use performance evaluations in determining executive compensation? How do your senior leaders and governance board use these performance evaluations to advance their development and improve the effectiveness of leaders, the board, and the leadership system, as appropriate?

b. Legal and Ethical Behavior

(1) **Legal and Regulatory Compliance How do you address current and anticipate future legal, regulatory, and community concerns with your products and operations?** How do you

- address any adverse societal impacts of your products and operations;
- anticipate public concerns with your future products and operations; and
- prepare for these impacts and concerns proactively?

What are your key processes and measures or indicators for promoting and ensuring ethical behavior in your governance structure; throughout your organization; and in interactions with your workforce, customers, partners, suppliers, and other stakeholders? How do you monitor and respond to breaches of ethical behavior?

(2) **Ethical Behavior How do you promote and ensure ethical behavior in all interactions?** What are your key processes and measures or indicators for promoting and ensuring ethical behavior in your governance structure; throughout your organization; and in interactions with your workforce, customers, partners, suppliers, and other stakeholders? How do you monitor and respond to breaches of ethical behavior?

c. Societal Contributions

(1) **Societal Well-Being How do you incorporate societal well-being and benefit into your strategy and daily operations?** How do you contribute to the well-being of your environmental, social, and economic systems?

(2) **Community Support How do you actively support and strengthen your key communities?** What are your key communities? How do you identify them and determine areas for organizational

Continued

Continued

involvement? How do your senior leaders, in concert with your workforce, contribute to improving these communities?

Notes:

1.2. Societal contributions in areas critical to your ongoing success should also be addressed in Strategy Development (Item 2.1) and Operations (Category 6). Key societal results should be reported in Item 7.4.

1.2a(1). In protecting stakeholder interests, the governance system should consider and approve appropriate levels of risk for the organization, recognizing the need to accept risk as part of running a successful organization.

1.2a(1). The governance board's review of organizational performance and progress, if appropriate, is addressed in 4.1(b).

1.2a(1). Transparency in the operations of your governance system should include your internal controls on governance processes. For some privately held businesses and nonprofit (including government) organizations, an external advisory board may provide some or all governance board functions. *For nonprofit (including government) organizations that serve as stewards of public funds, areas of emphasis are stewardship of those funds and transparency in operations.*

1.2a(2). The evaluation of leaders' performance might be supported by peer reviews, formal performance management reviews, and formal or informal feedback from and surveys of the workforce and other stakeholders. *For some privately held businesses and nonprofit and government organizations, external advisory boards might evaluate the performance of senior leaders and the governance board.*

1.2b(1). Proactively preparing for adverse societal impacts and concerns may include conserving natural resources, reducing carbon emissions, and using effective supply-network management processes, as appropriate. *Nonprofit organizations should report, as appropriate, how they meet and surpass regulatory and legal requirements and standards for fundraising and lobbying.*

1.2b(2). Measures or indicators of ethical behavior might include the percentage of independent board members, measures of relationships with stockholder and non-stockholder constituencies, instances of ethical conduct or compliance breaches and responses to them, survey results showing workforce perceptions of organizational ethics, ethics hotline use, and results of ethics reviews and audits. Such measures or indicators might also include evidence that policies, workforce training, and monitoring systems are in place for conflicts of interest; protection and use of sensitive data, information, and knowledge generated through synthesizing and correlating these data; and proper use of funds.

1.2c. *Some charitable organizations may contribute to society and support their key communities totally through the mission-related activities described in response to other Criteria questions. In such cases, it is appropriate to respond here with any "extra efforts" through which you support these communities.*

1.2c(1). Areas of societal well-being and benefit to report are those that go beyond the compliance processes you describe in 1.2b(1). They might include organizational or collaborative efforts to improve the environment; strengthen local community services, education, health, and emergency preparedness; address social inequities; and improve the practices of trade, business, or professional associations.

1.2c(2). Areas for organizational involvement in supporting your key communities might include areas that leverage your core competencies.

Comparison with the Education and Health Care Criteria

Item 1.2a in the Health Care Criteria adds, the governance system must also ensure accountability for patient safety and health care quality.

Item 1.2c(2) in the Health Care Criteria adds to the Community Support paragraph of the Business Criteria a requirement for "building community health."

Item 1.2b(1) in the Education and Health Care Criteria requires these organizations to have compliance processes, measures, and goals for meeting and surpassing accreditation requirements in addition to regulatory and legal requirements.

Item 1.2 looks at the organization's governance system, how it improves its leaders, how it enables the organization to fulfill its public responsibilities, how it ensures ethical and legal behavior, and how it encourages and supports senior leaders and the entire workforce to practice good citizenship.

The first part of this Item [1.2a] looks at how the organization addresses the need for responsible, informed, transparent, and accountable governance. The governing or advisory body should provide sound policy guidance and protect the interests of key stakeholders, such as stockholders in publicly traded companies, as well as stakeholders in private and nonprofit organizations. It should have independent and effective oversight of review and audit functions, and ensure succession planning for all senior leaders.

The organization must evaluate the performance and effectiveness of senior leaders, board members, and the entire leadership system. To ensure the evaluation is accurate, workers should provide feedback to the leaders and managers at all levels, which may be accomplished, in part, by the two-way communication required in Item 1.1b and using tools, such as 360-degree reviews and upward evaluations.

Leaders and managers at all levels should take action, based on the feedback, to improve their effectiveness. It is critical that leaders, managers, and supervisors at all levels and in all parts of the organization effectively drive and reinforce the principles of performance excellence through their words *and* actions.

The second part of this Item [1.2b] looks at how the organization addresses its current and future impact on society in a proactive manner, and how the organization, its senior leaders, and its employees ensure legal and ethical business practices are followed in all stakeholder transactions and interactions.

An integral part of performance management and excellence is proactively addressing the need for ethical behavior, meeting and exceeding legal and regulatory requirements, and addressing risk factors. This requires establishing appropriate measures and indicators that senior leaders track in their overall performance review. The organization should be sensitive to issues of public concern, whether or not these issues are currently embodied in law or regulations. Role-model organizations find opportunities to exceed requirements and to excel in legal and ethical behavior. The failure to address these areas can expose the organization to future problems when it least expects them. Problems can range from a sudden decline in consumer confidence to extensive and costly litigation. In this regard, it is important to anticipate potential problems the public may have with both current and future products. Sometimes a well-intended product or service could create adverse public consequences.

Standards of ethical behavior should be defined (preferably in measurable terms) and everyone in the organization should understand and follow the standards. The organization must systematically monitor ethical behavior throughout the organization, with key suppliers, partners, and collaborators; and within the governance structure. Failing to follow the standards of ethical behavior should have prompt and serious consequences for every governing board member, leader, manager, employee, supplier, partner, and collaborator.

Ensuring ethical business practices are followed by all members of the workforce lessens the organization's risk of adverse public reaction as well as criminal prosecution or civil litigation. Programs to ensure ethical business practices typically seek to prevent activities that might be perceived as criminal or near criminal. Examples of unethical—or unlawful—business practices might include falsifying expense reports or quality-control data, accepting lavish gifts from a contractor, or seeking kickbacks.

Government and nonprofit organizations should anticipate public concerns, including products, programs, and services costs; timely and equitable access to products, programs, and services; and perceptions about the organization's stewardship of its resources.

The organization must also address conservation of natural resources. These processes might include *green* technologies, using benign water-based chemicals instead of hazardous chemicals, reducing its carbon footprint, practicing energy conservation, using cleaner energy sources, and recycling waste and by-products.

Good societal contributions imply going beyond minimum compliance with laws and regulations. Top-performing organizations frequently serve as role models of responsibility and provide leadership in areas key to business success. For example, a manufacturing company might go beyond the requirements of the environmental protection regulations and develop innovative and cost-saving systems to protect the environment and reduce pollution. This has a double benefit. Not only do high-performing organizations develop good relations with regulators (and occasionally receive the benefit of the doubt), but when regulators increase requirements, they may already be in compliance, and way ahead of competitors who only met minimum requirements.

Standards of ethical behavior should be defined (preferably in measurable terms) and everyone in the organization should understand and follow the standards. The organization must systematically monitor ethical behavior throughout the organization, with key suppliers, partners, and collaborators; and within the governance structure. Failing to follow the standards of ethical behavior should have prompt and serious consequences for every governing board member, leader, manager, employee, supplier, partner, and collaborator.

Ensuring ethical business practices are followed by all members of the workforce lessens the organization's risk of adverse public reaction as well as criminal prosecution or civil litigation. Programs to ensure ethical business practices typically seek to prevent activities that might be perceived as criminal or near criminal. Examples of unethical—or unlawful—business practices might include falsifying expense reports or quality-control data, accepting lavish gifts from a contractor, or seeking kickbacks.

This area also looks at how the organization, its senior leaders, and its workforce identify, support, and strengthen key communities as part of good citizenship practices, and consider societal well-being and benefit a routine part of strategy and operations. Social systems, the environment, and economic systems are all affected by the presence of any organization, its processes, and its workforce. To ensure sustainability, the well-being of those systems must be considered and addressed.

Societal contributions typically vary according to the size, complexity, and location of the organization. Larger organizations are generally expected to have a more comprehensive approach to societal contributions than small ones. However, organizations of all sizes should practice good societal contributions, including encouraging and supporting community service by leaders and workforce members.

Examples of good community support may include: influencing the adoption of higher standards in education by communicating employability requirements to schools and school boards; partnering with other businesses and health care providers to improve health in the local community by providing education and volunteer services to address public-health issues; and partnering to influence trade and business associations to engage in beneficial, cooperative activities, such as sharing best practices to improve overall U.S. global competitiveness and the environment. Examples for nonprofit organizations include partnering with other nonprofit organizations or businesses to improve overall performance and stewardship of public and charitable resources.

In addition to activities directly carried out by the organization, opportunities to practice good community support include workforce community service that is encouraged and sponsored by the organization.

Frequently, the organization's leaders actively participate on community boards and support their work. Usually, organizations—like people—support causes and issues they value. Top-performing organizations are not content to simply donate money, people, and products or services to these causes without examining the impact of this support. Just as senior leaders examine the other parts of their business, they also evaluate and refine the effectiveness of community support, consistent with business strategies and objectives to gain the greatest benefit from their support.

To demonstrate maturity, the Scoring Guidelines require that the organization has a system in place to improve and innovate the methods it uses to provide responsible governance, evaluate the performance of its senior leaders and governance board, anticipate and address public concerns with products and operations, ensure ethical behavior in all interactions, consider societal well-being and benefit as part of organizational strategy and daily operations, and actively support and strengthen the organization's key communities. The organization should evaluate these processes on a regular basis and demonstrate that they have made meaningful, value-added improvements in their techniques for providing effective governance and fulfilling its societal contributions.

2021–2022 Criteria Elements Listed Individually Without Duplication See page 279 for explanation of this table			
	Basic Approach Elements [A-B] for Scoring Between 10% and 45%	**Additional Approach Elements at the Overall [A-O] Level for Scoring Between 50% and 65%**	**Additional Approach Elements at the Multiple Level [A-M] for Scoring Between 70% and 100%**
1.2 Governance and Societal Contributions			
1.2a(1)	Govern the organization	Ensure responsible governance	Review and achieve the following key aspects of the governance system • Accountability for senior leaders' actions • Accountability for strategy • Fiscal accountability • Transparency in operations • Selection of governance board members and disclosure policies for them, as appropriate • Independence and effectiveness of internal and external audits • Protection of stakeholder and stockholder interests, as appropriate • Succession planning for senior leaders
1.2a(2)		Evaluate the performance of senior leaders and governance board	Senior leaders and the governance board use performance evaluations • In determining executive compensation • To advance their development and improve the effectiveness of leaders, the board, and leadership system, as appropriate
1.2b(1)		Address current and anticipate future legal, regulatory, and community concerns with products and operations	• Address any adverse societal impacts of the organization's products and operations • Anticipate public concerns with the organization's future products and operations • Prepare for these impacts and concerns proactively • List the organization's key compliance processes, measures, and goals for meeting and surpassing regulatory and legal requirements, as appropriate • List the organization's key processes, measures, and goals for addressing risks associated with the organization's products
1.2b(2)		Promote and ensure ethical behavior in all interactions	• List the key processes and measures or indicators for noting and ensuring ethical behavior in the governance structure; throughout the organization; and in interactions with the workforce, customers, partners, suppliers, and other stakeholders • Monitor and respond to breaches of ethical behavior
1.2c(1)	Make societal contributions	Incorporate societal well-being and benefit as part of strategy and daily operations	Contribute to societal well-being of the organization's environmental, social, and economic systems
1.2c(2)		Actively support and strengthen your key communities	• List the organization's key communities and the methods used to identify them and determine areas for organizational involvement • Senior leaders, in concert with the workforce, contribute to improving these key communities

1.2 Governance and Societal Contributions

Basic Approach Element: Provide governance and make societal contributions

Overall Approach Elements:
- *Ensure responsible governance [1.2a(1)]*
- *Evaluate the performance of senior leaders, including the chief executive and governance board [1.2a(2)]*
- *Anticipate and address current and anticipated future legal, regulatory, and community concerns with the organization's products and operations [1.2b(1)]*
- *Promote and ensure ethical behavior in all interactions [1.2b(2)]*
- *Incorporate societal well-being and benefit as part of the organization's strategy and daily operations [1.2c(1)]*
- *Actively support and strengthen the organization's key communities [1.2c(2)]*

The following diagram describes key approach elements:

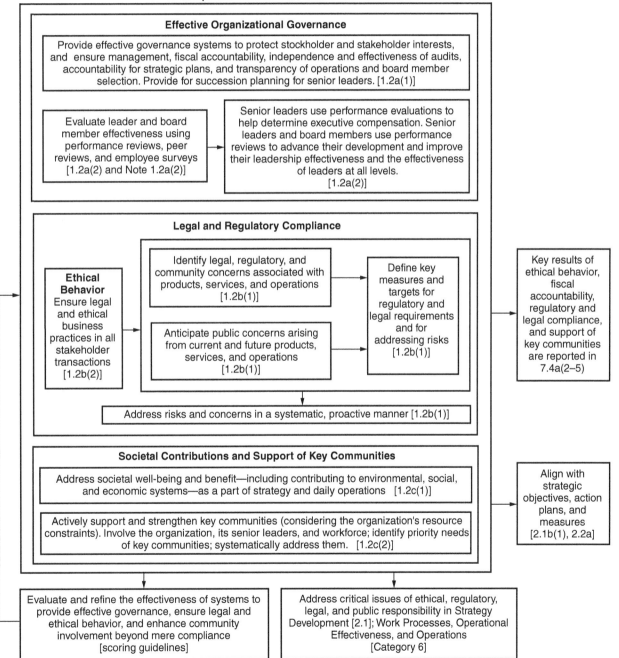

Effective Organizational Governance

Provide effective governance systems to protect stockholder and stakeholder interests, and ensure management, fiscal accountability, independence and effectiveness of audits, accountability for strategic plans, and transparency of operations and board member selection. Provide for succession planning for senior leaders. [1.2a(1)]

Evaluate leader and board member effectiveness using performance reviews, peer reviews, and employee surveys [1.2a(2) and Note 1.2a(2)]

→ Senior leaders use performance evaluations to help determine executive compensation. Senior leaders and board members use performance reviews to advance their development and improve their leadership effectiveness and the effectiveness of leaders at all levels. [1.2a(2)]

Legal and Regulatory Compliance

Ethical Behavior Ensure legal and ethical business practices in all stakeholder transactions [1.2b(2)]

→ Identify legal, regulatory, and community concerns associated with products, services, and operations [1.2b(1)]

→ Anticipate public concerns arising from current and future products, services, and operations [1.2b(1)]

→ Define key measures and targets for regulatory and legal requirements and for addressing risks [1.2b(1)]

→ Address risks and concerns in a systematic, proactive manner [1.2b(1)]

→ Key results of ethical behavior, fiscal accountability, regulatory and legal compliance, and support of key communities are reported in 7.4a(2–5)

Societal Contributions and Support of Key Communities

Address societal well-being and benefit—including contributing to environmental, social, and economic systems—as a part of strategy and daily operations [1.2c(1)]

Actively support and strengthen key communities (considering the organization's resource constraints). Involve the organization, its senior leaders, and workforce; identify priority needs of key communities; systematically address them. [1.2c(2)]

→ Align with strategic objectives, action plans, and measures [2.1b(1), 2.2a]

Evaluate and refine the effectiveness of systems to provide effective governance, ensure legal and ethical behavior, and enhance community involvement beyond mere compliance [scoring guidelines]

Address critical issues of ethical, regulatory, legal, and public responsibility in Strategy Development [2.1]; Work Processes, Operational Effectiveness, and Operations [Category 6]

1.2 Key Governance and Societal Contributions Item Linkages

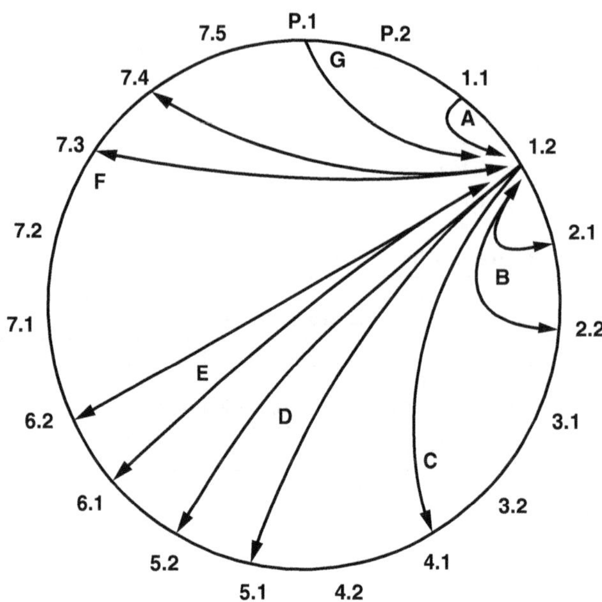

	NATURE OF RELATIONSHIP
A	Leaders [1.1a(2)] have a responsibility for setting values and ensuring that practices and products of the organization and its workers do not adversely impact society or violate legal or ethical standards, regulations, or law [1.2b]. They are also responsible for ensuring societal well-being and benefit are part of daily operations [1.2c(1)] and to be personally involved and to ensure that the organization and its workers support key communities in areas such as local community services, education, health, the environment, and business, professional, and trade associations [1.2c(2)].
B	The regulatory environment, which affects areas such as public health and safety, environmental protection, and waste management issues [1.2b(1)] is important to consider in strategy development [2.1a(3)] and action planning [2.2a].
C	The governance board's review of organizational performance and progress [1.2a(1)] is addressed by the processes in 4.1b.
D	Development opportunities [5.2c] are provided to ensure all leaders and workers understand the organization's ethical business practices [1.2b] as well as the importance of ensuring effective societal contributions [1.2c(1)] and strengthening key communities [1.2c(2)]. In addition, recruitment and hiring [5.1a(2)] should capitalize on the ideas, culture, and thinking of key hiring and customer communities.
E	Governance, ethical, and legal rules [1.2a–b] guide the design [6.1a(3)] and implementation of key work processes [6.1b(1)]. Managers at all levels have responsibility for ensuring that operations of the organization [6.1 and 6.2] are consistent with the organization's standards of law and regulations [1.2b(1)], ethics [1.2b(2)], societal contributions [1.2c(1)], and community support [1.2c(2)].
F	Key results related to processes of fiscal accountability [1.2a], regulatory and legal compliance [1.2b], anticipating public concerns [1.2b(1)], legal and ethical behavior [1.2b(1, 2)], societal contributions and support to key communities [1.2c(1, 2)], are reported in Leadership results [7.4a(2–5)]. In addition, these

Continued

NATURE OF RELATIONSHIP	*Continued*
	results are monitored to determine if process changes are needed. (Results in areas of worker satisfaction with workplace health and security are reported in 7.3a(2), based on processes described in Item 5.1b. Workforce health and safety are not a part of the requirements in 1.2.)
G	The regulatory environment described in P.1a(5), including applicable occupational health and safety regulations; accreditation, certification, or registration requirements; industry standards; and environmental, financial, and product regulations sets the context for the review of the management systems for governance [1.2a] and legal and ethical behavior [1.2b].

IF YOU DON'T DO WHAT THE CRITERIA REQUIRE . . .

Item Reference	Possible Adverse Consequences
1.2a(1)	**Governance System** – The adverse consequences of corrupt or incompetent organizational governance can be sudden and spectacular. One need only consider the impact of poor governance on Enron and similar companies whose businesses failed suddenly, hurting thousands of stakeholders, and tearing the economic fabric of the national economy. With increased stakeholder scrutiny and decreased trust, organizations that do not have visible and effective processes in place to ensure fiscal and management accountability and protect stockholder and stakeholder interests may find it difficult to overcome the climate of distrust that permeates organizations today. Their stock prices, consumer confidence, and public support may remain flat. Intrusive government oversight may increase, which diverts leadership attention and organization resources away from producing products and other value-adding outcomes needed to beat competitors and satisfy customers and other stakeholders.
1.2a(2)	**Performance Evaluation** – Even a new employee can tell the difference between an effective leader and an incompetent one. Unfortunately, an incompetent leader is too often blind to this fact (or ignores it). The combination of organizational performance outcomes and employee (subordinate) feedback can provide critical information to help leaders throughout the leadership system identify personal strengths and opportunities for improvement. Without this information, leaders may not be able to focus effectively on areas in which improvement would be essential not only to personal growth and development but also to better organizational results. Leaders who do not receive accurate feedback about their strengths and weaknesses may not be able to keep pace with changing business needs and directions, as they are challenged to work smarter by customers, competitors, and the demands of stockholders and other stakeholders. They are not likely to lead their organization to winning levels of performance excellence. Failure to link executive performance evaluation to executive compensation ultimately reduces leadership accountability.
1.2b(1)	**Legal and Regulatory Compliance** – Organizations that fail to consider the impact on the public of their products, services, and operations may be seriously impaired in the future if it is determined that these products or services cause harm. In the short term, organizations that fail to comply with regulatory and legal requirements may find themselves facing costly sanctions or be prevented from conducting business. The failure to consider and address risks associated with products, services, and operations may contribute to costly corrective action or litigation.

Continued

IF YOU DON'T DO WHAT THE CRITERIA REQUIRE . . . *Continued*	
Item Reference	**Possible Adverse Consequences**
	Organizations that fail to anticipate and consider potential concerns that society may have with current and future products, services, and operations may be faced with costly redesign or rework. When an organization appears to treat society and the community within which it works with impunity and disregards their concerns, it becomes extremely difficult to recover trust and confidence. When the organization finds it needs public support to carry out its work or expand its operations, it may find it difficult to secure that support.
1.2b(2)	**Ethical Behavior** – Organizations that do not ensure ethical business practices in all transactions and interactions with stakeholders (public, customers, stockholders, workers, suppliers, and so on) run the risk of violating the public trust. Accordingly, these organizations may face serious adverse consequences when their misdeeds are discovered. (One only need consider the difference between Enron and Tylenol. Both companies faced disasters that threatened their existence. Tylenol responded ethically and is still thriving.) Moreover, if the unethical practices of leaders are considered an acceptable business standard in the organization and repeated by others, they can contribute to numerous unpredictable problems that waste human and financial resources to correct.
1.2c	**Societal Contributions** – Organizations that fail to incorporate societal well-being, act as good corporate citizens, contribute to the well-being of environmental, social, and economic systems, and support its hiring and customer community may find it difficult to get support in return, especially for projects or initiatives that require local approval. For example, local communities typically provide the bulk of support for services as well as new workers. Organizations that fail to support local education or trade and professional associations may find themselves faced with a shortage of skilled workers in key areas and important services they need to conduct business.

1.2 GOVERNANCE AND SOCIETAL CONTRIBUTIONS EFFECTIVE PRACTICES

a. Organizational Governance

- Independence of the board of directors is ensured by requiring that a substantial percentage of directors come from outside the organization and are free from financial or other conflicts of interest.
- Fiscal accountability is assured by a variety of industry-accepted processes including independent audits following standard audit protocols, and separation of consultants from auditing functions. Audit and consulting services are not provided by the same or affiliated companies.
- Stockholders approve the election slates for the board of directors and even place names on the slate.
- Board term limits enable rotating membership to ensure fresh and objective voices are present on the board.
- Board audit committees contain financial and quality system experts who are independent of the organization.
- The full board of directors reviews financial statements quarterly after accuracy is certified.
- Small businesses that don't require a board use advisory panels to gain expertise from outside experts.

- Directors with competing interests, such as key suppliers or interlocking directors, are eliminated from the board or their influence is minimized (such as becoming nonvoting members).
- Dissent, debate, and open criticism are encouraged among board members.
- CEOs promote candor and meaningful discussion at board meetings by sharing relevant information with directors prior to meetings to permit careful analysis before deliberations begin.
- Board members formally assess their peers in writing and ask poor-performing members to improve or resign.
- A climate of trust and candor exists among board members. No subgroup wields power to make backroom decisions.
- Demonstrated proficiency in the use of the Integrated Management System and the Baldrige Criteria is a prerequisite for promotion to board or leadership positions.
- A clearly defined portion of executive compensation is at risk each year based on customer satisfaction and workforce engagement scores.

b. Legal and Ethical Behavior

- The organization's principal work activities include systems to analyze, anticipate, and minimize public hazards or risk.
- Indicators for risk areas are identified, monitored, and openly displayed in the organization.
- Improvement strategies are used consistently, target performance levels are set, and progress is reviewed regularly and tied to recognition and reward.
- The organization formally evaluates the impact that its operations, products, and services might have on society and natural resources and considers those impacts in planning and daily operations.
- The effectiveness of systems to meet or exceed regulatory, legal, and ethical requirements is systematically evaluated and improved.
- A formal system is in place to train the workforce about ethical business requirements. Senior leaders help provide the training to emphasize the importance of ethical behavior.
- A process is in place to permit workers to file complaints about unethical or illegal behavior in the workplace or among suppliers or customers without fear of discovery or retaliation (for example, a whistleblower protection program).
- A process is in place to test the understanding of ethical principles for all people who must follow the principles, including the workforce, governing board members, suppliers, and partners.
- An audit process is in place to communicate and ensure ethical requirements and practices are deployed to all levels of the organization and to key partners, suppliers, and members of the board of directors (governance group).
- Senior leaders systematically and routinely check the effectiveness of their leadership activities (for example, seeking feedback at least annually from workers and peers using an upward or 360-degree evaluation). Leaders take steps to improve and this is considered part of their development and appraisal process.

c. Societal Contributions

- As part of strategic planning and strengths, weaknesses, opportunities, threats analysis, issues related to environment, conservation, social systems, and economic systems are considered. Strategic plans, goals, and actions are designed to mitigate societal issues to engender maximum support from the organization's key communities.
- Senior leaders and workers at various levels in the organization are involved in professional organizations, committees, task forces, or other community activities.
- Organizational resources are allocated to support involvement in community activities outside the organization. The effectiveness of these allocations is examined to determine if expectations are met and resources are used wisely.

- Workers participate in local, state, or national quality award programs and receive recognition from the organization for doing so.
- Workers participate in professional quality-and business-improvement associations (such as ASQ).
- The effectiveness of processes to support and strengthen key communities is systematically measured, evaluated, and improved.

Ineffective Practices

Ineffective governing boards not only fail to provide important strategic and policy guidance, they waste the organization's resources as well, forcing organization staff to engage in meaningless, non-value-added activities.

Ineffective governing boards typically contain members who exhibit the following behaviors:

- Seek to interfere with the administration or operational management of the organization, rather than focus on oversight and policy matters
- Seek to disrupt board meetings to serve a personal agenda rather than advance the success of the organization
- Come to meetings unprepared
- Use their position on the board for personal or political gain or aggrandizement
- Violate ethical procedures such as confidentiality in an attempt to undermine the effectiveness of the board or senior leaders

Many examples of failed governance and poor societal contributions appear in news stories each year. Obviously, unethical and illegal behavior usually creates serious problems for organizations, customers, and other stakeholders. The corruption or incompetence does not have to be as massive as Madoff, Enron, BP, Volkswagen, or Goldman Sachs to present major problems for an organization.

2 Strategy—85 Points

*The **Strategy** Category asks how your organization develops strategic objectives and action plans, implements them, changes them if circumstances require, and measures progress.*

The Strategy Category looks at the organization's process for strategic and action planning, and implementation of plans to make sure everyone is working to achieve those plans. This Category examines how plans are changed if change is required, and how accomplishments are measured and sustained. Achieving long-term success in an environment of increasing competition is a key strategic issue that is addressed in overall strategic and action planning. Making the right decisions about core competencies and work systems is an important factor in achieving success now and in the future, and, as a result, these decisions are strategic.

Although many organizations are good at strategic planning, plan execution is still a big challenge. This is especially true when facing volatile economic conditions or disruptive technologies, which can upset an otherwise fast-paced but more predictable marketplace. That is why this Category focuses not only on developing plans, but also on the ability to execute them.

Customer-focused excellence, increasing operational capability, innovation and work process improvement, and worker and organizational learning are key strategic issues that are important to planning and strategic decision-making.

- The Baldrige Core Value of customer-focused excellence is a strategic view of excellence. The focus is on the drivers of customer engagement (customer retention, loyalty, and advocacy), new markets, and increasing market share—key factors in competitiveness, profitability, and organizational success and sustainability.
- Increasing operational capability through ongoing performance improvement and innovation contributes to productivity growth and cost or price competitiveness. Increasing operational speed, responsiveness, and flexibility strengthens an organization's competitive position now and into the future.
- Organizational and workforce learning, linked with improvement and innovation, are strategic considerations. Improvement and learning must be embedded in work processes and throughout the Integrated Management System. Strategy should be used to establish priorities and align work processes and learning initiatives.

Strategic objectives define in outcome-oriented, measurable terms the things an organization must actually achieve to be successful in the future.

Once the organization has determined what must actually be achieved to be successful in the future (the strategic objectives and related goals), it must take steps to execute that plan (develop and carry out actions).

Over the years, much debate and discussion have taken place around planning. Professors in our colleges and universities spend a great deal of time trying to differentiate strategic planning, long-term planning, short-term planning, tactical planning, operational planning, quality planning, business planning, and human resource planning, to name a few. A much simpler view, however, might serve us better.

Strategy helps provide a basis for aligning the organization's work processes with its strategic directions, thereby ensuring people and processes in different parts of the organization are not working at cross-purposes. To the extent that alignment does not occur, the organization's effectiveness and competitiveness are reduced.

The Strategy Category looks at how the organization:

- Understands the key customer, market, and operational requirements that are essential to setting strategic directions. This helps to ensure that ongoing process improvements are aligned with the organization's strategic directions.
- Considers the potential need for change in organizational structure or culture.
- Determines its strengths, weaknesses, opportunities, and threats; builds on its core competencies; and identifies and addresses its strategic opportunities, challenges, and advantages.
- Optimizes the use of resources, ensures the availability of a trained workforce, and bridges short- and long-term requirements that may involve capital expenditures, supplier development, and new workforce recruitment strategies. Evaluates and improves key processes, technology development or acquisition, new partnerships or collaborations, and other factors affecting organizational success.
- Ensures that implementation will be effective—that there are mechanisms to cascade requirements and achieve alignment at all organizational levels including: (1) the executive level; (2) the work-system and work-process level; and (3) the work-unit and individual-job level.

The requirements for the Strategy Category are intended to develop a basis for achieving and maintaining a competitive position. The Criteria do not demand formalized planning departments or specific planning cycles. They do, however, require outcome-oriented plans and the alignment of actions to achieve those plans at all levels.

According to the Baldrige Program Office, an effective system to improve performance and competitive advantage requires clear strategic guidance, particularly when improvement alternatives, including major change or innovation, compete for limited resources. In most cases, priority setting depends heavily upon a cost, opportunity, and threat rationale. However, an organization might also have to deal with critical issues, such as societal responsibilities, which are not driven by cost alone.

A good strategic plan, with clear objectives and defined actions, helps make agility and alignment possible. This Category highlights the need to place a focus not only on developing strategy and action plans, but also on the capability to execute them in order to achieve success, now and in the future.

Strategy Development

Sample elements considered during strategic planning include the following:

- Customers: market requirements and evolving expectations and opportunities
- External threats and opportunities such as the competitive environment and capabilities relative to competitors: industry and market
- Technologies and other innovations that might affect products and services and future business operations such as automation, cloud operations, the use of data analytics, the Internet of Things, artificial intelligence, and large data modeling
- Internal strengths and weaknesses, including core competencies, workforce diversity, equity, inclusion, capability and capacity, resource availability, and operational capabilities and needs
- Financial, societal, ethical, regulatory, technological, security, cybersecurity, and other potential risks that may affect short- and long-term success
- Opportunities to redirect resources to higher-priority products, services, or business areas
- Rapid response to changing organizational needs and challenges including the need for resilience in organizational structure and work systems and key work processes
- Changes in local, national, or global political or economic conditions
- Supplier and supply-network capabilities and needs
- Clear, measurable strategic objectives with timetables that help leaders determine where the organization should be at given points in time so they can effectively monitor progress and make

appropriate changes in processes or the allocation of resources

Strategy Implementation

Factors considered during strategy implementation include the following:

- Develop action plans and related workforce plans
- Deploy action plans to the workforce and to key suppliers and partners to ensure the achievement of key strategic objectives
- Ensure that the key outcomes of action plans are sustained
- Define measures for tracking progress on action plans to ensure actions are monitored and aligned throughout the organization
- Project expected performance results, including assumptions of competitor performance increases, and identify gaps in actual versus projected performance

2.1 STRATEGY DEVELOPMENT: How do you develop your strategy? (45 Pts.) PROCESS

a. Strategy Development Process

(1) **Strategic Planning Process How do you conduct your strategic planning?** What are the key process steps? Who are the key participants? What are your short- and longer-term planning horizons? How does your strategic planning process address the potential need for change, prioritization of change initiatives, and organizational agility and resilience?

(2) **Innovation How does your strategy development process stimulate and incorporate innovation?** How do you identify strategic opportunities? How do you decide which strategic opportunities are intelligent risks to pursue? What are your key strategic opportunities?

(3) **Strategy Considerations How do you collect and analyze relevant data and develop information for use in your strategic planning process?** In this collection and analysis, how do you include these key elements of risk?

- Your strategic challenges and strategic advantages
- Potential changes and disruptions in your regulatory and external environment
- Technological changes and innovations affecting your products, services, and operations
- Potential blind spots in your strategic planning process and information
- Your ability to execute the strategic plan

(4) **Work Systems and Core Competencies How do you decide which key processes will be accomplished by your workforce and which by external suppliers, partners, and collaborators?** How do those decisions consider your strategic objectives; your core competencies; and the core competencies of potential suppliers, partners, and collaborators? How do you determine what future organizational core competencies and work systems you will need?

b. Strategic Objectives

(1) **Key Strategic Objectives What are your organization's key strategic objectives and their most important related goals?** What is your timetable for achieving them? What key changes, if any, are planned in your products, customers and markets, suppliers and partners, and operations?

Continued

Continued

(2) **Strategic Objective Considerations How do your strategic objectives achieve appropriate balance among varying and potentially competing organizational needs?** How do your strategic objectives

- address your strategic challenges and leverage your core competencies, strategic advantages, and strategic opportunities;
- balance short- and longer-term planning horizons; and
- consider and balance the needs of all key stakeholders?

Notes:

2.1. This Item deals with your overall organizational strategy, which might include changes in customer engagement processes and product offerings. However, you should describe the customer engagement and product design strategies, respectively, in Items 3.2 and 6.1, as appropriate.

2.1. Strategy development refers to your organization's approach to preparing for the future. In developing your strategy, you should consider your level of acceptable enterprise risk. To make decisions and allocate resources, you might use various types of forecasts, projections, options, scenarios, knowledge (see 4.2b), analyses, or other approaches to envisioning the future. Strategy development might involve key suppliers, collaborators, distributors, partners, and customers. *For some nonprofit organizations, strategy development might involve organizations providing similar services or drawing from the same donor population or volunteer workforce.*

2.1. The term "strategy" should be interpreted broadly. Strategy might be built around or lead to any or all of the following: new products; redefinition of key customer groups or market segments; definition or redefinition of your role in your business ecosystem (your network of partners, suppliers, collaborators, competitors, customers, communities, and other relevant organizations inside and outside your sector or industry that serve as potential resources); differentiation of your brand; new core competencies; revenue growth; divestitures; mergers and acquisitions; new partnerships, alliances, or roles within them; and new employee or volunteer relationships. It might also be directed toward meeting a community or public need.

2.1a(1). Organizational agility refers to the capacity for rapid change in strategy and the ability to adjust your operations as opportunities or needs arise.

2.1a(3). Integration of data from all sources to generate strategically relevant information is a key consideration. Data and information might relate to customer and market requirements, expectations, opportunities, and risks; financial, societal, ethical, regulatory, technological, security and cybersecurity, and other potential opportunities and risks; your core competencies; the competitive environment and your performance now and in the future relative to competitors and comparable organizations; your product life cycle; workforce and other resource needs; your ability to capitalize on diversity and promote equity and inclusion; your ability to prevent and respond to disasters and emergencies; opportunities to redirect resources to higher-priority products, services, or areas; changes in the local, national, or global economy; requirements for and strengths and weaknesses of your partners and supply network; changes in your parent organization; and other factors unique to your organization.

2.1a(3). Your strategic planning should address your ability to mobilize the necessary resources and knowledge to execute the strategic plan. It should also address your ability to execute contingency plans or, if circumstances require, to shift strategy and rapidly execute new or changed plans.

2.1a(3). Technologies that continue to drive change in many industries include enhanced automation, the adoption of cloud operations, the use of data analytics, the Internet of Things, artificial intelligence, and large dataset-enabled business and process modeling.

2.1a(4). Your work systems are the coordinated combination of internal work processes and external resources you need to develop and produce products, deliver them to your customers, and succeed in your marketplace. External resources might include partners, suppliers, collaborators, competitors, customers, and other entities or organizations that are part of your business ecosystem. Decisions about work systems involve protecting intellectual property, capitalizing on core competencies, and mitigating risk.

2.1b(1). Strategic objectives should focus on your specific challenges, advantages, and opportunities—those most important to your ongoing success and to strengthening your overall performance and your success now and in the future.

Comparison with the Health Care and Education Criteria

Except for semantic differences, such as using terms like health care services and educational programs and services instead of products, no substantive differences exist.

Item 2.1 looks at how the organization determines core competencies, strategic challenges, and advantages, and develops measurable, outcome-oriented strategic objectives to strengthen overall performance, competitiveness, and future success.

The first part of this Item [2.1a(1)] asks the organization to describe its strategic planning process and identify the key participants, key steps, and short- and longer-term planning-time horizons. This helps examiners understand the steps and data used in the planning process. It is a good idea to provide a flowchart of the planning process. This helps examiners understand how the planning process works without wasting valuable space in the application.

The planning process should examine all the key factors, risks, challenges, and core competencies and other advantages or disadvantages that might affect the organization's future opportunities and directions—taking as long-term a view as possible but requiring no specific time horizon. This approach is intended to provide a useful context for the development of a customer- and market-focused strategy to guide ongoing decision-making, resource allocation, and effective management.

The key factors that affect future success include external and internal influences on the organization. Each key factor must be addressed and should show how relevant data and information are gathered and analyzed. Although the organization is not limited to the number of factors it considers important in planning, it must address the factors identified in Item 2.1a unless a valid rationale can be offered as to why the factor is not appropriate. Together, these factors typically cover the most important variables for any organization's future success.

Note to applicants: If a strategic challenge or advantage listed in P.2b is not a true challenge or advantage that must be addressed as a part of strategic planning, delete it from the P.2b list to prevent confusion within the examiner team.

This planning process should cover all types of competitive situations, strategic issues, planning approaches, and plans. The strategic plan produces a future- and results-oriented basis for action.

Achieving and sustaining a leadership position in a competitive market require a view of the future that includes not only the markets or segments in which the organization competes but also how it competes. Competitive leadership may also depend on the organization's ability and willingness to take intelligent risks.

Effective strategy development finds ways to create and ensure sustained competitive leadership.

To maintain competitive leadership, an increasingly important part of strategic planning requires processes to project the future collaborative and competitive environment accurately [see Items 2.2a(6) and 4.1c(1)]. Such projections help detect competitive threats, provide more reaction time, and identify hidden opportunities. Depending on the size and type of organization, the potential need for new core competencies, maturity of markets, pace of change, and competitive parameters (such as price, costs, or innovation rate), organizations might use a variety of modeling scenarios or other techniques to project the competitive and collaborative environment accurately.

The need for agility, resilience, and effective innovation has become more readily apparent among high-performing organizations to help achieve and sustain leadership positions. The requirements that strategic planning processes stimulate and incorporate innovation align with the senior leadership requirement to create an environment of innovation and intelligent risk taking [1.1c(1)]. From a strategy development perspective, future success may depend on the creation of innovations that leverage strategic opportunities. Good decisions about which strategic opportunities are worth pursuing demand intelligent risk taking and balancing the benefits of success with the costs of failure. This new requirement for strategy development helps clarify why strategic planning is both critical and complicated. The factors needed to make intelligent choices about future direction are complex—their impact is critical to the success of the organization, its leaders, stakeholders, customers, partners, suppliers, and workers.

Whether critical work is carried out externally or internally, that work is considered part of the organization's work systems. Key work processes typically involve the majority of an organization's workforce and relate to core competencies—areas in which the organization excels. (See Clarifying Confusing Terms: Work Systems versus Work Processes, page 347.)

It is becoming increasingly evident that decisions about which work systems are to be internal (work processes performed by the workforce) or external (performed by partners or suppliers) have a strategic impact. Accordingly, the Criteria require these decisions to be made as part of the strategy development process [2.1a(4)] and not as a part of operational decision-making [Category 6].

Decisions about whether to outsource certain work or keep it internal are increasingly strategic. The desire to build or sustain core competencies or protect intellectual property may favor keeping work internal. On the other hand, especially when the organization lacks a core competency, the situation may favor a decision to outsource work to a more competent partner or supplier.

The second part of this Item [2.1b] asks for a summary of the organization's key strategic objectives and the timetable for accomplishing them. It also asks for key changes that may be planned for products, customers and markets, suppliers and partners, and operations, and how strategic objectives address the core competencies, challenges, and advantages outlined in the Organizational Profile, as well as strategic opportunities.

Strategic objectives define the outcome or desired end state that the organization must achieve to be successful in the future. Strategic objectives do not define activities or projects or other actions that are needed to *enable* the organization to achieve its outcomes. Many times, organizations confuse outcomes with enablers since both can be measured.

Consider the following parable. A state legislature wants to make better use of the funds it appropriates for its libraries. The legislature learned that the per capita readership in its state is among the lowest in the nation. It wants the state to be in the top ten nationally by the year 2030.

After conducting a survey of library users, the library commission determined that readership had declined because existing libraries were dusty, dark, and inconvenient and because of the internet, fewer people visited the libraries. The strategic objective they developed was "by 2030, build in a dense population center a new library with plenty of open space, light, and free parking." The design and construction of the new library had clear, measurable milestones. The planners were happy with the new objective until the planning consultant asked, "How do you know the new library will bring in sufficient numbers of new readers? Have you ever built a new library and found that most of the users were not new, but simply decided to go to the new library instead of the old one?" The planners frowned a little and said, "Yes, it has happened before."

As it turns out, the building of a new library—best case—is only an enabler. The planners confused the action of building a new library with the legislature's desire to improve per capita readership in the state. In addition, focusing on *building* made other ways to increase readership, such as expanding internet access, easy to overlook. A better strategic objective might have been "increase readership in the state from 3 per thousand to 8 per thousand by 2030." Then, the desired outcomes became clear and a more complete range of actions might be considered.

Building a library may be an appropriate action (enabler) but not an outcome (unless your organization is a construction company). Clearly it is possible to build the library on time and under budget, declare victory for having met the objective, and *still* fail to increase readership to the top ten nationally.

The danger in confusing actions or projects or enablers with outcomes is that leaders and managers can mistakenly believe they are making appropriate progress (completing actions) and yet completely fail to achieve the desired end state (achieving outcomes). Actions are critical to help workers understand their duties, but leaders must be sure to define the true desired outcome needed for future success. Monitoring actions is an important part of deploying and executing the strategic plan (required in Item

2.2), but completing tasks should never be confused with achieving desired results (outcomes). *Success is built on achievement, not just activity.*

The purpose of the timetable required by Item 2.1b(1) is to provide a basis for projecting the path that improvement should take. This enables the leaders who monitor progress to determine when performance is deviating from plan and when to make adjustments to get back on track. Consider Figure 24. The performance goal four years into the future is to achieve a level of performance of 100. The organization's starting level is 20. At the end of year one, the organization achieved a performance level of 40, represented by the circle symbol. It appears that level of performance is on track toward the goal of 100, assuming the desired track is linear. However, the path from the current state to the future state is rarely a straight line. Unless the expected trajectory is known (or at least estimated), it is not possible to evaluate the progress accurately to ensure strategic objectives are integrated with other requirements of senior leader review [4.1b] and improvement [4.1c(2)]. Without meaningful timetables or trajectories, leaders are forced to default to best guess or intuition as a basis for comparing actual, measurable progress against expected progress. Based on intuition, the progress depicted in Figure 24 at the end of year one looks good.

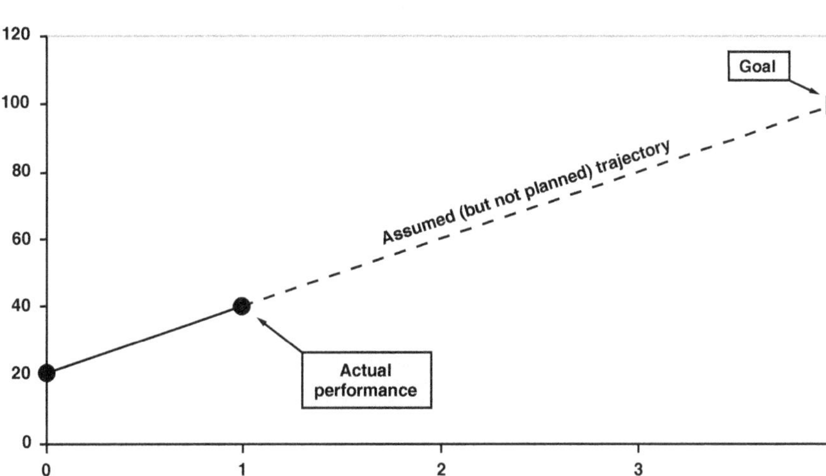

Figure 24 Assumed trajectory.

In Figure 25, the planned trajectory is represented by the triangle symbols. When compared with the current level of performance (circle symbol), it is clear that there is a performance shortfall of approximately 30.

In Figure 26 on the next page, a different planned trajectory is represented by the square symbols. When compared with the current level of performance (the circle symbol), it is clear that the performance is ahead of schedule. There are several possible decisions that leaders could make based on the information in Figure 26. It might mean that the original estimates or goals were low and should be reset. It might also mean that the process did not need all of the resources it had available. These resources may be better used in areas where performance is not ahead of schedule. *In any case, without knowing the expected path toward a goal, leaders are forced to guess whether the level of progress is appropriate.*

The last part of this Item requires the organization to evaluate the options it considered in the strategic planning process to ensure it responded fully to the factors identified in Item 2.1a(3) that were most important to business success

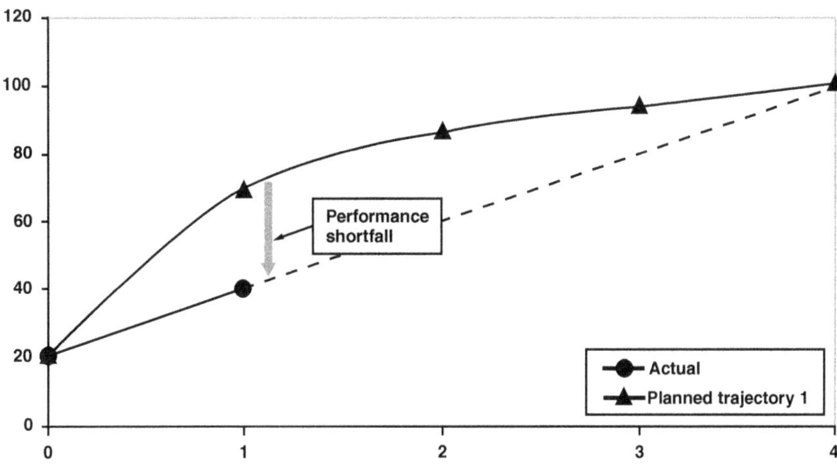

Figure 25 Planned trajectory 1—performance shortfall.

(including strategic challenges, advantages, and opportunities for innovation). This last step helps the organization *close the loop* to make sure the factors influencing organization success are adequately analyzed and support key strategic objectives.

Strategic plan execution is a significant challenge, especially given market demands for agility and preparation for unexpected change, such as disruptive technologies or new regulatory requirements that may upset an otherwise fast-paced but more predictable marketplace. Therefore, this Item and Item 2.2 highlight the need to focus not only on developing plans but also on the capability to execute them.

To demonstrate maturity, the Scoring Guidelines require that the organization has a system in place to improve and innovate the methods it uses to develop its strategy and strategic objectives, stimulate and incorporate innovation, collect and analyze relevant data for the strategic planning process, determine its key work systems critical to organization success, and ensure its strategic objectives achieve balance among varying and potentially competing organizational interests. The organization should evaluate these processes regularly and demonstrate they have made meaningful, value-added improvements in their techniques for strategic plan development.

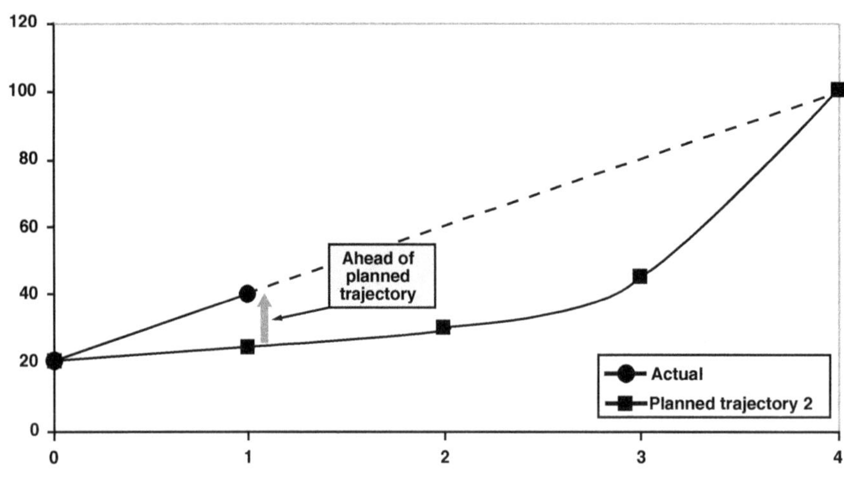

Figure 26 Planned trajectory 2—ahead of plan.

2021–2022 Criteria Elements Listed Individually Without Duplication See page 279 for explanation of this table			
	Basic Approach Elements [A-B] for Scoring Between 10% and 45%	**Additional Approach Elements at the Overall [A-O] Level for Scoring Between 50% and 65%**	**Additional Approach Elements at the Multiple Level [A-M] for Scoring Between 70% and 100%**
2.1 Strategy Development			
2.1a(1)	Develop organizational strategy (to prepare for future success)	Conduct the organization's strategic planning	• Describe the key process steps used to conduct strategic planning • List the key participants in strategic planning • Define the short- and longer-term planning horizons and describe how they are addressed in the planning process • Ensure the strategic planning process addresses the potential need for – Change – Prioritization of change initiatives – Organizational agility and resilience
2.1a(2)		Ensure the strategy development process stimulates and incorporates innovation	• Describe steps to identify strategic opportunities • Decide which strategic opportunities are intelligent risks to pursue • List the organization's key strategic opportunities
2.1a(3)		Collect and analyze relevant data and develop information to use in the strategic planning process	As part of the strategic planning process, collect and analyze relevant data and develop information on the following key elements of risk— • Strategic challenges and strategic advantages • Potential changes and disruptions in the regulatory and external business environment • Technological changes and innovations affecting products, services, and operations • Potential blind spots in the strategic planning process and information • The ability to execute the strategic plan
2.1a(4)		Decide which key processes will be accomplished by the workforce and which by external suppliers, partners, and collaborators	• Ensure these decisions consider the organization's strategic objectives, core competencies, and the core competencies of potential suppliers, partners, and collaborators • Determine future organizational core competencies that may be needed
2.1b(1)		Summarize the organization's • Key strategic objectives • Timetable for achieving them	Summarize— • The organization's most important goals for its strategic objectives • Key changes, if any, that are planned in the organization's products, customers and markets, suppliers and partners, and operations
2.1b(2)		Ensure strategic objectives achieve appropriate balance among varying and potentially competing organizational needs	Ensure strategic objectives— • Address strategic challenges and leverage core competencies, strategic advantages, and strategic opportunities • Balance the short- and longer-term planning horizons • Consider and balance the needs of all key stakeholders

2.1 Strategy Development

Basic Approach Element: *Develop the organization's strategy*

Overall Approach Elements:
- ***Conduct strategic planning [2.1a(1)]***
- ***Stimulate and incorporate innovation [2.1a(2)]***
- ***Collect and analyze relevant data and develop information for use in planning [2.1a(3)]***
- ***Determine which work processes accomplished by workforce or by suppliers, partners, or collaborators [2.1a(4)]***
- ***Summarize the organization's key strategic objectives and timetable for achieving them [2.1b(1)]***
- ***Ensure the objectives balance competing organization needs [2.1b(2)]***

The following diagram describes key approach elements:

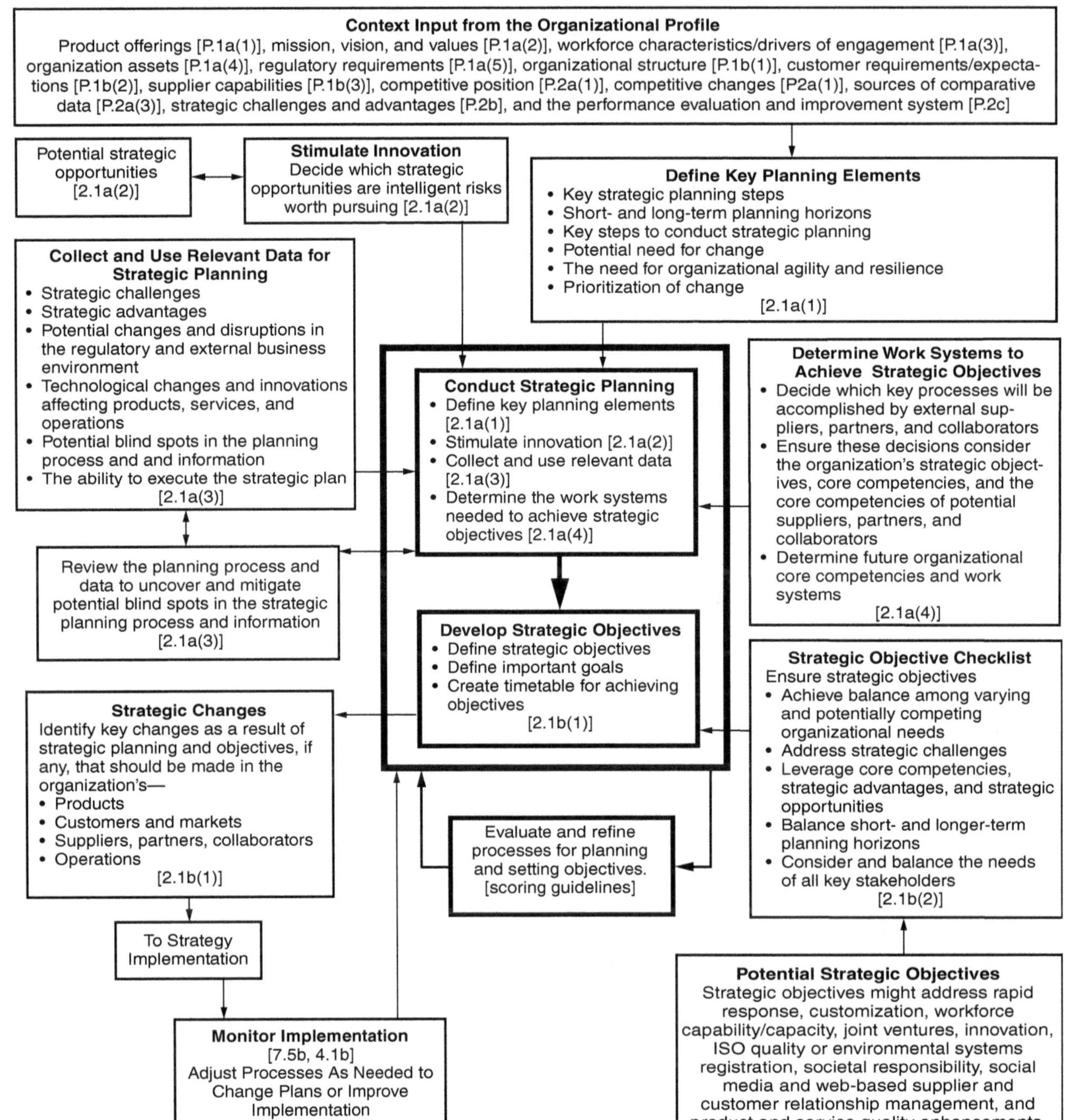

2.1 Key Strategy Development Item Linkages

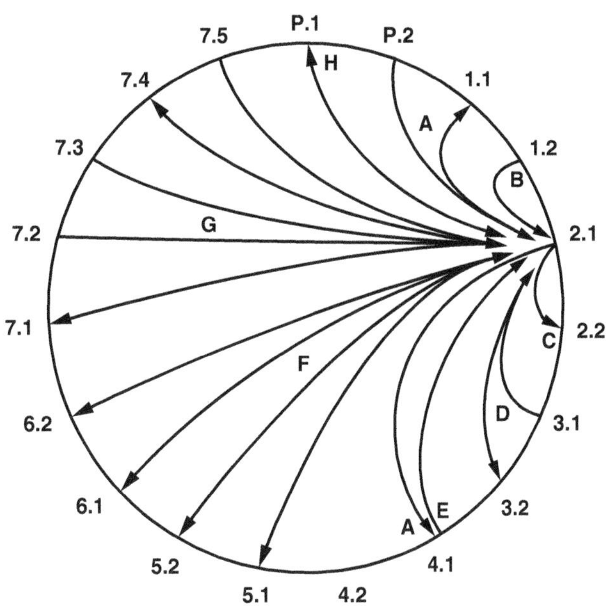

	NATURE OF RELATIONSHIP
A	The strategic planning process [2.1] includes senior leaders—as part of their responsibilities for creating an organizational vision that sets the context for strategic objectives and for creating a successfully sustainable organization [1.1]. In addition, the timetables or expected performance trajectories [2.1b(1)] provide a basis for leaders to determine if progress is on track when they monitor progress [4.1b]. To ensure integration or alignment, timetables [2.1b(1)] should match the performance review cycles [4.1b]. The competitive environment [partly defined in P.2a] may also be examined as part of the strategy development process [2.1a]. In addition, before the planning cycle is complete, leaders must ensure that the strategic objectives [2.1b(2)] address the challenges and advantages identified in the Organizational Profile [P.2b].
B	Public health, environmental, waste management, and related concerns [1.2b(1)] as well as the need to promote legal and ethical behavior in all transactions [1.2b, 1.2c(1)], may be considered, as appropriate, in the strategy development process [2.1a(3)].
C	The planning process [2.1a] produces a set of strategic objectives [2.1b(1)] that must be converted into action plans that are deployed to the workforce and implemented [2.2a].
D	The planning process [2.1] includes information gathered by listening to current and potential customers [3.1a(1, 2)]. The planning process [2.1a(1)] also may consider the projected competitive environment [2.2a(6)], as well as intelligence obtained from customer-contact people (complaints and comments) [3.2a(2, 3)] and customer satisfaction, engagement, and dissatisfaction data [3.2b(1)], and satisfaction relative to customers of competitors [3.2b(2)].
E	Key organizational and competitive comparison data [4.1a(2)] and analytical data, including various reviews, forecasts, and projections [4.1b and 4.1c(1)], are used for planning [Note 2.1], setting objectives [2.1b(1)], and improving the planning process as needed [scoring guidelines].

Continued

NATURE OF RELATIONSHIP	*Continued*
F	Information on workforce capability and capacity [5.1a(1)], changing needs [5.1a(3)], and work process capabilities [Category 6] may be considered in the strategic planning process [2.1a(3)] and to help decide which systems will be internal or external [2.1a(4)]. *To avoid cluttering diagrams in Categories 5 and 6, these linkage arrows will not be repeated in other diagrams.*
G	Product and process [7.1], customer [7.2], workforce [7.3], leadership [7.4], and financial, market, and strategy [7.5] results are considered in the planning process [2.1a] to set strategic objectives [2.1b(1)]. In addition, results in 7.5b must specifically report on progress toward achieving the strategic objectives and action plans and are used in subsequent planning.
H	Workforce development needs, diversity, equity, inclusion, and other characteristics [P.1a(3)] related to workforce strengths and weaknesses are considered during the strategic planning process [2.1a(3)]. Plans consider the requirements of customers [P.1b(2)], and may contribute to the redefinition of key customer groups, market segments, or core competencies [P.1a(2)].

IF YOU DON'T DO WHAT THE CRITERIA REQUIRE . . .

Item Reference	Possible Adverse Consequences
2.1a(1)	**Strategic Planning Process** – Without clearly defined short- and longer-term planning horizons, it may be difficult to properly align the analysis and collection of market and industry forecast data to support effective planning. The shorter the planning horizon, the easier it is to be accurate in forecasting. However, the planning horizon should be at least as long as the time it takes the organization to design, develop, and deliver new products and services required by customers and markets. Increased agility and resilience can shorten organizational response time. For example, if the design-delivery cycle is seven years (as it was in the U.S. automobile industry in the 1970s and 1980s), then to be effective an organization must be able to forecast or anticipate customer and market requirements seven years out—which is difficult to do accurately. Alternatively, if the organization is more agile and reduces its design-delivery cycle time to less than 24 months (as did the Japanese automobile industry), it will be able to reduce the required planning horizon, and more accurately anticipate customer and market requirements and plan strategically.
2.1a(1)	**Strategic Planning Process** – Leaders who rely on incremental change to implement strategy may not be successful if aggressive change is needed. For example, significant change may be needed to shift the culture of an organization to address significant strategic challenges, leverage strategic advantages, and implement strategic opportunities to achieve and sustain success now and in the future. In the face of today's new technological and other challenges, more aggressive changes may be needed.
2.1a(2)	**Innovation** – Strategy development—creating a new future—should stimulate and incorporate innovation. Failure to create an environment that stimulates and supports innovation tends to perpetuate the status quo, both strategically and operationally. This, in turn, causes organizations to fall behind comparable organizations or competitors that use continuous improvement and innovation as a means to achieve excellence and market leadership. Maintaining the status quo when others are improving and innovating contributes to organizational failure. The inability to assess and take intelligent risks increases the likelihood of failure and avoidable loss.

Continued

IF YOU DON'T DO WHAT THE CRITERIA REQUIRE . . . *Continued*	
Item Reference	**Possible Adverse Consequences**
2.1a(3)	**Strategy Considerations** – The failure to address key factors in the planning process (the organization's strategic challenges and advantages), changes or disruptions in the regulatory or business environment, potential blind spots, and the ability to execute the plan usually result in a flawed strategic plan—a plan that has overlooked an element critical to future success. For example, an organization may fail to achieve strategic objectives if it assumed (incorrectly) that a key supplier would be able to deliver critical components at a certain time. Likewise, a strategic plan that does not adequately account for the arrival of competitive offerings or new technologies in the marketplace can be faced with major hurdles (consider the impact of texting, email, Zoom, and other technologies on the postal industry). Planning involves making assumptions about the future that are not always correct. Incorrect assumptions can be considered potential *blind spots* in the planning process. To prevent blind spots, different points of view or information may be needed. Blind spots contribute to flawed plans. Failing to consider or correctly forecast the impact of these elements may result in a strategic plan that cannot be achieved.
2.1a(4)	**Work Systems and Core Competencies** – Focusing organizational resources on the most critical, value-added activities and processes is usually essential in a climate of limited resources and significant competition. Few organizations are able to make the most of limited resources by wasting them on work where others are more competent and effective. Top organizations focus resources to support the internal work processes in which they excel—in which they are the most competent—and outsource work that aligns with the core competencies of suppliers, collaborators, or partners. In most cases, if an organization continues to use its internal resources to carry out work processes that are inferior to external suppliers, it is wasting resources.
2.1b(1)	**Key Strategic Objectives** – Knowing whether the strategy is unfolding as expected is critical to the successful performance of the organization and its leaders. The failure to develop measurable, outcome-oriented strategic objectives makes it difficult to communicate expectations to those responsible for implementing them—the workforce, key suppliers, and other stakeholders. In addition, the failure to develop a timetable with clearly defined targets for accomplishing strategic objectives that are integrated (consistent) with the performance review frequency makes it extremely difficult for leaders to monitor organizational performance effectively. Without defined milestones, leaders may be forced to guess whether the rate of progress is appropriate. Without clear timelines or trajectories for growth, leaders frequently assume the path between current state and desired state (goals) is linear. Data indicate that the actual path is almost never linear, so the assumptions of linearity that leaders make in the absence of clear timelines and trajectories are usually incorrect.
2.1b(2)	**Strategic Objective Considerations** – Strategy development is an ongoing, dynamic process. It is often a difficult process that takes a considerable amount of time to complete initially and then requires continual attention to address rapidly changing threats and opportunities. However, if leaders fail to ensure that strategic objectives consider the strategic challenges, advantages, and opportunities it faces and balance short- and longer-term time horizons and the needs of all key stakeholders, the plan may be ineffective and the time it took to develop the plan may be wasted.

2.1 STRATEGY DEVELOPMENT—SAMPLE EFFECTIVE PRACTICES

a. Strategy Development Process

- Business goals, strategies, and issues are addressed and reported in measurable terms. Strategic objectives consider future requirements needed to achieve organizational leadership after considering the performance levels that other organizations are likely to achieve in the same planning time frame.
- Web-based or e-commerce initiatives are considered as part of developing new business or new markets.
- The planning and objective-setting process encourages input (but not necessarily decision-making) from a variety of people at all levels throughout the organization.
- Data on customer requirements, key markets, benchmarks, suppliers and partners, workforce dynamics, and organizational capabilities (internal and external factors) are used to develop strategy.
- Plans and the processes used to develop plans are evaluated each cycle for accuracy and completeness—more often if needed to keep pace with changing business requirements.
- Opportunities for improvement in the planning process are identified systematically and carried out in each planning cycle.
- Every core competency is the subject of periodic review to make sure potential weaknesses are addressed in the strategic objectives.
- Refinements have been made in the process of planning, plan deployment, and receiving input from work units. Improvements in planning cycle time, resources, and accuracy are documented.
- Risk analysis is built into the strategic planning process, with every strategic objective and strategic opportunity assessed against risk factors.

b. Strategic Objectives

- Strategic objectives define measurable, outcome-oriented results the organization must achieve to be successful in the future. Strategic objectives are then converted into actions that enable the organization to focus the workforce to achieve its objectives—which may be expressed as a series of activities. Strategic objectives clearly address current and future core competencies and one or more strategic opportunities.
- Strategic objectives are identified and a timetable (or planned growth trajectory) for accomplishing the objectives is set. The timelines match the senior leaders' review cycle. For example, if leaders review progress against goals quarterly, the timelines identify the expected level of performance for each quarter.
- Options to obtain best performance for the strategic objectives are systematically evaluated against the internal and external factors used in the strategy development process.
- The processes of setting timelines or trajectories and the accuracy of the projections are analyzed and refined to make sure they align with senior leader review cycles.
- Best practices from other providers, competitors, or outside benchmarks are identified and used to provide better estimates of trajectories.
- Strategic objectives define the desired end state, not *enablers,* projects, or a list of activities such as "design a new service center," or "communicate expectations to all staff." When a project is identified, leaders ask, "Why are we doing this?" to develop strategic objectives.
- Before a new strategic planning cycle is started, the old (existing) process is evaluated for opportunities for improvement. Steps are taken to improve the accuracy of planning assumptions (eliminating potential blind spots) and improve planning efficiency and effectiveness (such as reducing cycle time and costs).

Ineffective Practices

- Leaders keep changing their minds—issuing three or four new "strategic plans" in one year.
- Leaders ask for input on strategy from customers, workers, and other stakeholders and then ignore the input entirely.
- The planning process is used to justify "business as usual" instead of refocusing on drivers of future success.
- Mediocre work processes are kept internal instead of outsourcing to significantly more capable organizations.
- Success is defined by activity measures or resources spent, such as attendance at conferences and hits on websites (inputs), instead of actual achievements (outcomes).
- External assessment and risk evaluation is not completed. Strategy is based on what the organization hopes to accomplish. *Hope is not a method—or a strategy.*
- Employees are discouraged from considering best practices of other organizations. Bringing up the subject of other companies' strengths is seen as disloyal or irrelevant.
- Timelines and performance targets—if set—are viewed as guidelines only, not deadlines that would require accountability.
- Strategy is used to report intentions to bosses, not align the work of everyone in the organization to achieve high performance.

2.2 STRATEGY IMPLEMENTATION: How do you implement your strategy? PROCESS (40 Pts.)

a. Action Plan Development and Deployment

(1) **Action Plans What are your key short- and longer-term action plans?** What is their relationship to your strategic objectives? How do you develop your action plans?

(2) **Action Plan Implementation How do you deploy your action plans?** How do you deploy your action plans to your workforce and to key suppliers, partners, and collaborators, as appropriate, to ensure that you achieve your key strategic objectives? How do you ensure that you can sustain the key outcomes of your action plans?

(3) **Resource Allocation How do you ensure that financial and other resources are available to support the achievement of your action plans while you meet current obligations?** How do you allocate these resources to support the plans? How do you manage the risks associated with the plans to ensure your financial viability?

(4) **Workforce Plans What are your key workforce plans to support your short- and longer-term strategic objectives and action plans?** How do the plans address potential impacts on your workforce members and any potential changes in workforce capability and capacity needs?

(5) **Performance Measures What key performance measures or indicators do you use to track the achievement and effectiveness of your action plans?** How does your overall action plan measurement system reinforce organizational alignment?

(6) **Performance Projections For these key performance measures or indicators, what are your performance projections for your short- and longer-term planning horizons?** If there are gaps between your projected performance and that of your competitors or comparable organizations, how do you address them in your action plans?

b. Action Plan Modification

How do you recognize and respond when circumstances require a shift in action plans and rapid execution of new plans

Notes:

2.2. The development and deployment of your strategy and action plans are closely linked to other Criteria Items. The following are examples of key linkages:

- Item 1.1: how your senior leaders set and communicate organizational direction
- Category 3: how you gather customer and market knowledge as input to your strategy and action plans and to use in deploying action plans
- Category 4: how you measure and analyze data and manage knowledge to support key information needs, support strategy development, provide an effective basis for performance measurements, and track progress on achieving strategic objectives and action plans
- Category 5: how you meet workforce capability and capacity needs, determine needs and design your workforce learning and development system, and implement workforce-related changes resulting from action plans
- Category 6: how you address changes to your work processes resulting from action plans

2.2a(6). Projected performance might consider new ventures; organizational acquisitions or mergers; new value creation; market entry and shifts; new legislative mandates, legal requirements, or industry standards; and significant anticipated innovations in services and technology. Your process for projecting future performance should be reported in 4.1c(1).

Continued

Continued

2.2b. Circumstances that might require shifts in action plans and rapid execution of new plans include disruptive internal or external events, changes in your competitive environment, changing economic conditions, the emergence of disruptive technologies, and sudden changes in customer requirements and expectations.

Comparison with the Health Care and Education Criteria

Except for semantic differences, such as using terms like health care services and educational programs and services instead of products, no substantive differences exist.

Item 2.2 looks at how the organization translates its measurable, outcome-oriented strategic objectives [which were identified in Item 2.1b(1)] into action plans to accomplish the objectives and to enable assessment of progress relative to action plans. Overall, the intent of this Item is to ensure that strategies are implemented or executed at all levels throughout the organization to align work for goal achievement. *Remember, it is usually more difficult to implement a plan than to create one.*

It is important for the organization to achieve alignment and consistency—for example, via the alignment and integration of mission, vision, strategic objectives, work systems, work processes, key measurements, and reward and recognition. Leaders, managers, and other members of the workforce must develop action plans that address all strategic objectives (which were developed using the processes in Item 2.1). Organizations must summarize key short- and longer-term action plans. Particular attention is given to products and services, customers and markets, how the organization operates, and key workforce plans that will enable accomplishment of strategic objectives and action plans.

The organization should identify the key measures and indicators it uses to track progress relative to the action plans. The organization should also use these measures and indicators to ensure organizational alignment of all key work units and stakeholders and explain expectations. Alignment and consistency help provide a basis for setting and communicating priorities for ongoing improvement activities—part of the daily work of all work units.

Without effective alignment, routine work and acts of improvement can be random and serve to suboptimize organizational performance. In Figure 27, the arrows represent the well-intended work carried out by the workers in organizations that lack a clear set of expectations and direction. Workers, managers, and work units strive diligently to achieve goals they believe are important. Each is pulling hard—but not necessarily in ways that ensure performance excellence. The lack of clear, overarching strategic objectives and action plans reinforce *fiefdoms* or *silos* within organizations. The lack of clear direction from leaders forces workers to invent their own priorities.

With a clear, well-communicated strategic objective and related actions, it is easier to know when daily work is out of alignment and not integrated throughout the organization. The large arrow in

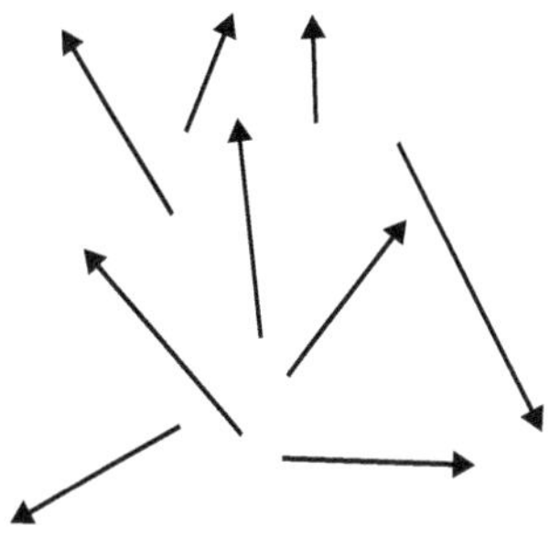

Figure 27 Nonaligned work.

Figure 28 represents the strategic plan pointing the direction the organization must take to be successful and achieve its mission and vision. The strategic plan and accompanying measures make it possible to analyze work and business practices (represented by the smaller arrows) to know when they are not aligned and to help workers, including leaders, know when adjustments are required.

A well-deployed and understood strategy and action plan helps everyone in the organization distinguish between random acts of improvement and aligned improvement. Random acts of improvement give a false sense of accomplishment and rarely produce optimum benefits for the organization. For example, a decision to improve a business process that is not aligned with the strategic plan (as the small bold arrow in Figure 29 represents) usually results in a wasteful expenditure of time, money, and human resources—improvement without benefiting customers or enhancing operating effectiveness.

On the other hand, by working systematically to realign or strengthen processes that are aligned with the strategic plan, the organization moves closer to achieving success, as Figure 30 indicates.

Ultimately, all processes and procedures of an organization should be aligned to maximize the achievement of strategic plans, as Figure 31 depicts. An alignment failure produces suboptimal performance, wastes resources, and hurts worker motivation and morale (undermining engagement).

Adequate resources are also critical to success. The organization can perform many types of analyses to ensure that adequate financial resources are available to support accomplishment of action plans. For ongoing operations, these might include analysis of cash flow, net income statements, and current liabilities versus current assets. For investments to accomplish action plans, the organization may analyze discounted cash flow or return on investment (ROI). Specific types of analyses will vary depending on the organization. These analyses should help assess the financial viability of current operations and the potential viability of and risks associated with action plan initiatives. Whether the organization is for-profit

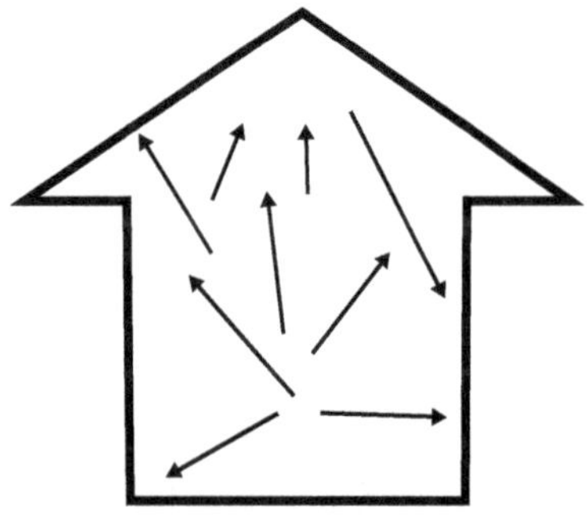

Figure 28 Strategic direction (big arrow).

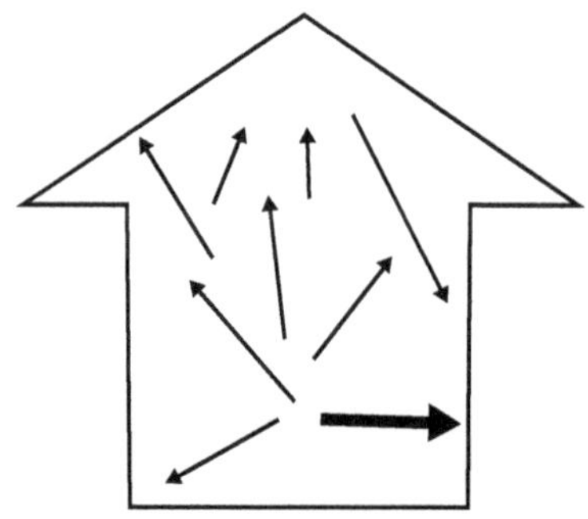

Figure 29 Random, nonaligned improvement.

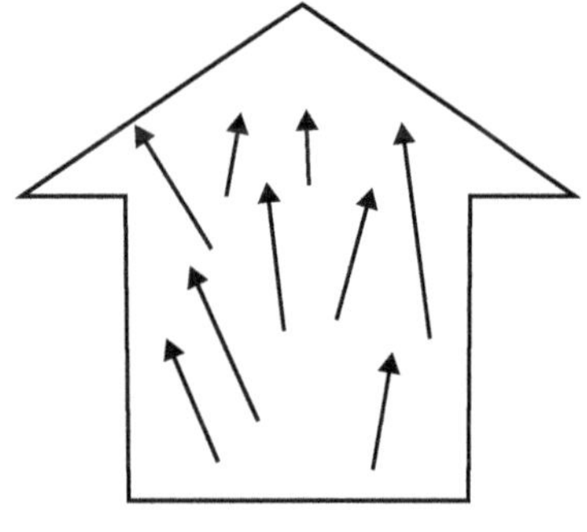

Figure 30 Moving toward alignment.

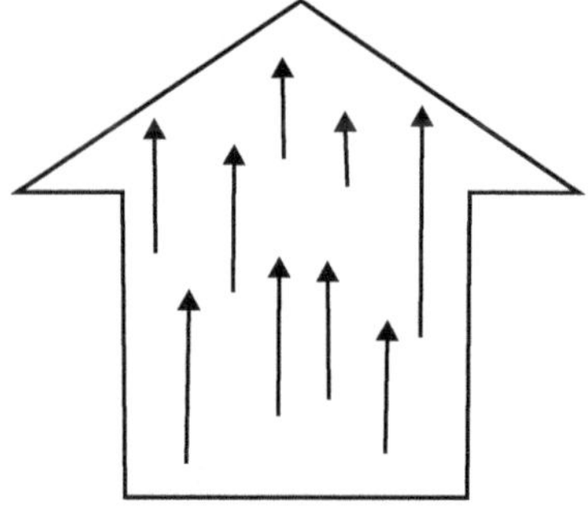

Figure 31 Systematic alignment.

or not-for-profit, an analysis of resources and the ability to execute the plan are essential to success.

Action plans should include workforce plans that support the overall strategy. Workforce plans typically include initiatives needed for successful strategy implementation, such as:

- Redesign work or jobs to increase workforce empowerment (decision-making about their work)
- Promote greater labor-management cooperation
- Prepare for future workforce capability and capacity needs
- Enhance knowledge sharing and organizational learning (links to empowerment)
- Modify compensation and recognition systems (and individual performance plans) to be consistent with strategic objectives and action plans, including stimulating, rewarding, or recognizing improvement and innovation
- Offer new education and training opportunities, such as developmental programs for future leaders and training programs on new technologies important to the future success of the workforce and organization.

The organization should provide a projection of key performance measures and/or indicators, including key performance targets or goals for both short- and long-term planning horizons. This projected performance is the basis for comparing the organization's past performance with the projected performance of appropriate competitors and benchmarks.

Projections and comparisons are intended to help the organization's leaders understand and track dynamic, competitive performance factors. Through this tracking process, they should be better prepared to take into account rate of improvement and change relative to competitors or comparable organizations and relative to their own targets or stretch goals. Such tracking can be a key diagnostic management tool.

In addition to improvement relative to past performance and to competitors, projected performance also might include changes resulting from new business ventures, entry into new markets, e-commerce initiatives, introduction of new technologies, product or service innovations, or other strategic thrusts that may involve some degree of risk.

Without this comparison information, it is possible to set goals that, even if attained, may not result in a competitive advantage. More than one high-performing company has been surprised by a competitor that set and achieved more aggressive goals. Consider the example represented by Figure 32. Imagine that you are ahead of your competition and committed to a 10% increase in profit over your base year. After eight years you are twice as profitable. To your surprise, you find that your competitor has increased 20% each year. You have achieved your goal, but your competitor has beaten you. After 12 years, the competitor has a significant lead. In a competitive market, it is not good enough to achieve your goals unless your goals place you in a winning position.

To demonstrate maturity, the Scoring Guidelines require that the organization has a system in place to improve and innovate the methods it uses to implement its strategy, deploy its action plans, ensure resources are available to support

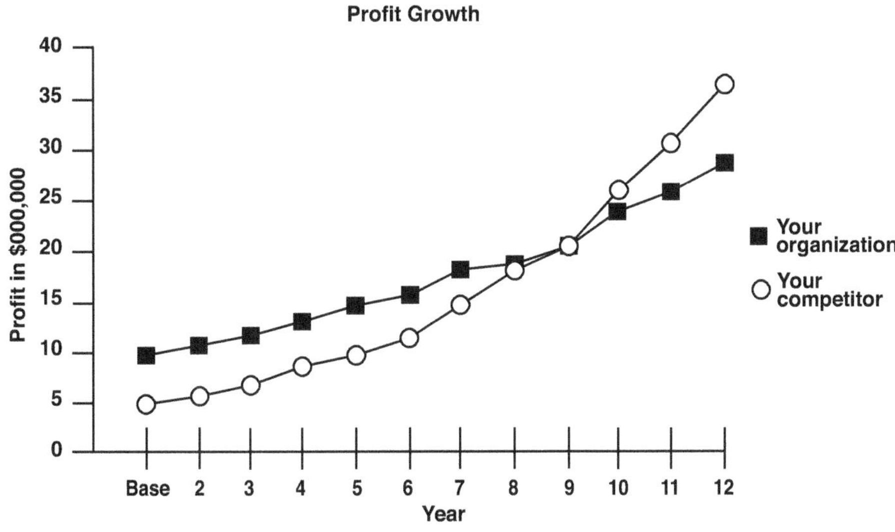

Figure 32 Projecting competitor's future performance.

the achievement of action plans, develop workforce plans to support the strategic actions, develop performance measures to track the achievement of action plans, project the organization's performance compared with performance of other providers or benchmarks, and be able to establish and implement modified action plans if circumstances require rapid execution of new plans. The organization should evaluate these processes on a regular basis and demonstrate that they have made meaningful, value-added improvements in its techniques for strategy implementation.

2021–2022 Criteria Elements Listed Individually Without Duplication

See page 279 for explanation of this table

	Basic Approach Elements [A-B] for Scoring Between 10% and 45%	Additional Approach Elements at the Overall [A-O] Level for Scoring Between 50% and 65%	Additional Approach Elements at the Multiple Level [A-M] for Scoring Between 70% and 100%
2.2 Strategy Implementation			
2.2a(1)		List the organization's key short- and longer-term action plans	• Develop action plans • Describe the relationship of action plans to strategic objectives
2.2a(2)	Implement the organization's strategy	Deploy the organization's action plans	• Deploy action plans to the workforce and to key suppliers, partners, and collaborators, as appropriate, to ensure the organization achieves its key strategic objectives • Ensure that the organization can sustain the key outcomes of its action plans
2.2a(3)		Ensure that financial and other resources are available to support the achievement of action plans while the organization meets its current obligations	• Allocate financial and other resources to support action plans • Manage the risks associated with the plans to ensure the organization's financial viability
2.2a(4)		Describe the organization's key workforce plans to support its short- and longer-term strategic objectives and action plans	Address potential impacts on workforce members and any potential changes in workforce capability and capacity needs
2.2a(5)		Describe key performance measures or indicators used to track the achievement and effectiveness of action plans	Ensure the overall action plan measurement system reinforces organizational alignment
2.2a(6)		For key performance measures or indicators, list the performance projections for the short- and longer-term planning horizons	If there are gaps between the organization's projected performance and that of competitors or comparable organizations, ensure the gaps are addressed in action plans
2.2b		Recognize and respond when circumstances require a shift in plans and rapid execution of new plans	

2.2 Strategy Implementation

Basic Approach Element: *Implement the organization's strategy*

Overall Approach Elements:
- *List the organization's key short- and longer-term action plans [2.2a(1)]*
- *Deploy the organization's action plans [2.2a(2)]*
- *Ensure that financial and other resources are available to support achievement of action plans while meeting current obligations [2.2a(3)]*
- *Develop workforce plans to support short- and longer-term strategic objectives and action plans [2.2a(4)]*
- *Develop performance measures or indicators used to track the achievement and effectiveness of action plans [2.2a(5)]*
- *For these measures list the performance projections for the short- and longer-term planning horizons [2.2a(6)]*
- *Establish and implement modified action plans if circumstances require a shift in plans and rapid execution of new plans [2.2b]*

The following diagram describes key elements:

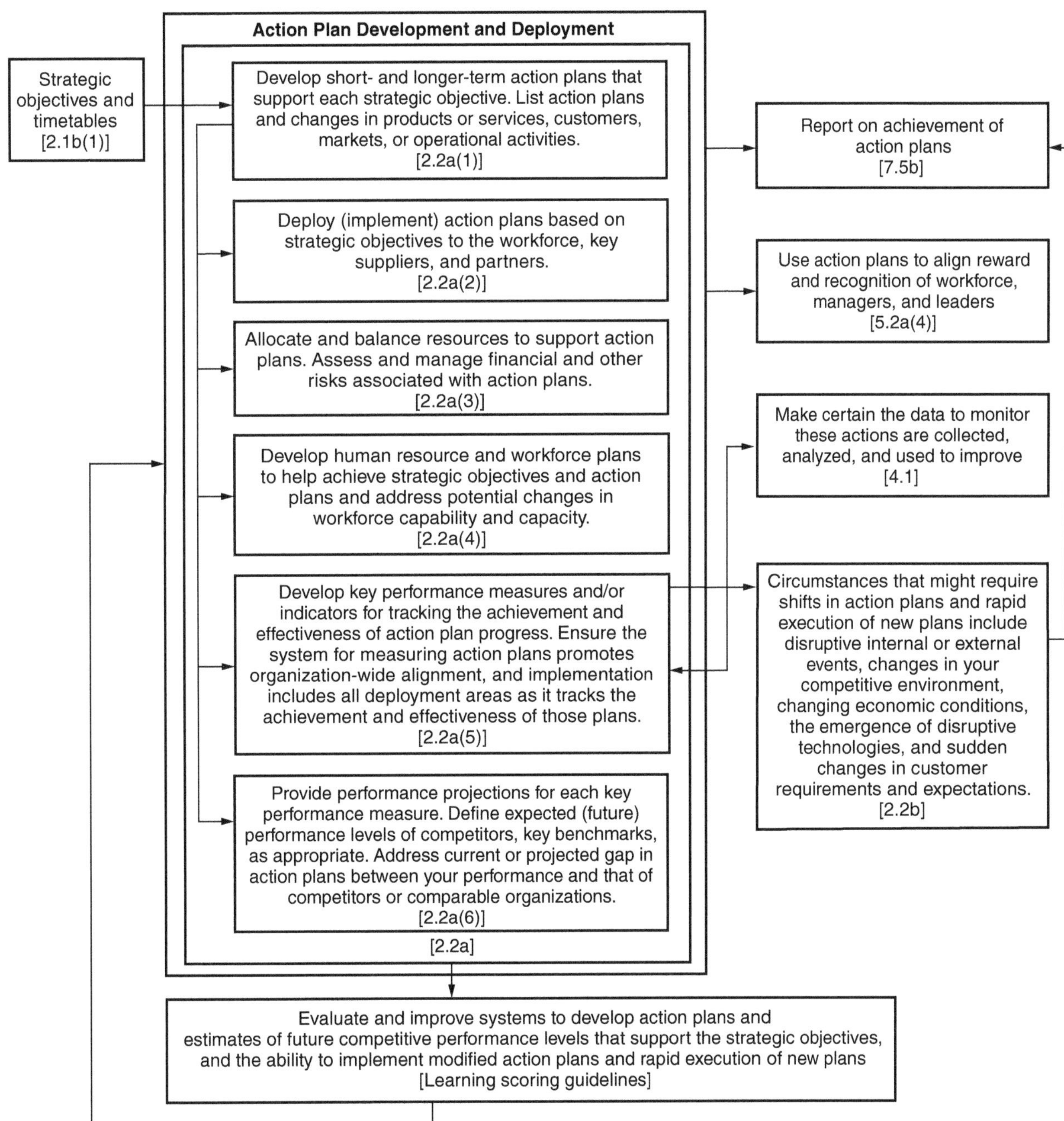

2.2 Key Strategy Implementation Item Linkages

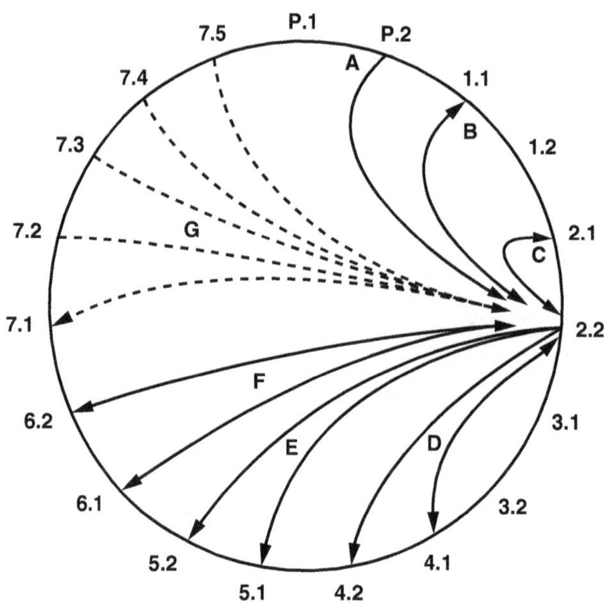

NATURE OF RELATIONSHIP	
A	The competitive environment defined in P.2a should help focus the projection of competitors' future performance in 2.2a(6).
B	To ensure vision is accomplished, the leadership team [1.1a] ensures that action plans are aligned throughout the organization with strategic objectives and implemented [2.2a(2)], and that resources are allocated to ensure the actions are accomplished [2.2a(3)]. Action plans [2.2a(1)] are aligned with leader performance reviews [1.2a(2)].
C	The planning process [2.1a] develops the strategic objectives [2.1b(1)] that are used to develop action plans to support these objectives [2.2a(1)]. Gaps between the organization's projected performance and that of competitors [2.2a(6)] may cause the planning process to change [2.1a(1, 2)], which may change strategic objectives [2.1b(1)].
D	The action plans [2.2a(1)] and related performance measures [2.2a(5)] define part of the data that need to be collected [4.1a], analyzed to support decision-making [4.1b], used to define improvement [4.1c], and help define requirements for data availability [4.2]. Comparative data [4.1a(2)] and performance projection data [4.1c(1)] are used to help project future performance of competitors and comparable organizations [2.2a(6)].
E	Action plans, workforce plans, and performance measures [2.2a(1, 2, 4, 5] are deployed and used to align and develop workforce-focused processes [5.1, 5.2]. It is particularly important that action plans, workforce plans, and performance measures [2.2a(1, 2, 4, 5)] are aligned with and supported by recognition and reward processes [5.2c(1)].
F	Measures and action plans [2.2a(1, 2, 4, 5)] are used to drive and align work processes to achieve improved performance [6.1, 6.2]. Feedback from work and operations processes [6.1, 6.2] helps reinforce alignment with action plans and measures [2.2a(5)] and may trigger the need to change action plans [2.2a(6)].
G	Results data [Category 7] are used to help develop performance projections to determine projected performance gaps [2.2a(6)]. In addition, 7.5b reflects progress on achieving strategy and action plans. *To avoid clutter and make the diagrams more readable, these relationships will not be repeated on all of the Category 7 linkage diagrams.*

IF YOU DON'T DO WHAT THE CRITERIA REQUIRE . . .	
Item Reference	**Possible Adverse Consequences**
2.2a(1)	**Action Plans** – The inability to articulate and communicate key short- and longer-term action plans usually means those plans do not exist, or are expressed as vague generalities. Without clear action plans, employees at all levels of the organization will find it difficult to understand what work they must do to help the organization achieve its strategy. Without clear direction from the top (action plans), employees will still work hard, but their work may be unfocused as they follow their own ideas for appropriate action—everyone will not be pulling in the same direction.
2.2a(2)	**Action Plan Implementation** – As with the failure to develop clear action plans, the failure to implement action plans to carry out strategic objectives and employ them at all levels of the organization usually means that work may not be aligned to achieve the strategy. Instead, there is a tendency for managers and other employees to focus their work on things they believe are important. This can result in excessive resources being spent on activities that do not contribute to the objectives the organization's leaders have determined are critical for its future success.
2.2a(3)	**Resource Allocation** – The failure to allocate appropriate resources or balance resources to accomplish action plans frequently means that some plans are not accomplished due to insufficient resources, while other plans are accomplished inefficiently because of too many resources. In both cases, the value to the customer and the organization is suboptimized. Failure to assess financial risks accurately may cause leaders to overestimate available resources and overcommit operationally. This, too, may lead to poor performance.
2.2a(4)	**Workforce Plans** – By definition, *plans* describe activities or actions that have not yet taken place. Many times, in order to execute plans, workers must possess skills, knowledge, or abilities they do not currently possess. Without appropriate plans to develop, acquire, or motivate the workforce to carry out desired actions, the organization may not be able to achieve its strategic objectives or related action plans.
2.2a(5)	**Performance Measures** – Without appropriate measures or indicators it is difficult for leaders, managers, and employees throughout the organization to determine if they are making appropriate progress. It is also more difficult for leaders to communicate expectations accurately. Unclear expectations increase the likelihood that employees will not understand what they are required to do to achieve strategic objectives. Consider the adage, "What gets measured gets done." Without appropriate measures it is difficult to focus everyone on doing the right things.
2.2a(6)	**Performance Projections** – In the best-performing organizations, strategic objectives and related action plans are designed to enable the organization to win in competitive situations. If an organization desires to achieve a leadership position, it must understand where the competition is likely to be in the future before it sets its goals. Unless the organization's leaders understand the likely future performance levels of key competitors (in the same planning horizon), they may set aggressive goals and action plans, achieve them, and still lose—finding themselves behind the competition.
2.2b	**Action Plan Modification** – In a fast-paced, highly competitive market, the failure to adjust plans quickly and implement new plans rapidly places the organization at a competitive disadvantage. It may cause significant market erosion from which recovery is difficult. For example, in the late 1990s Motorola was slow to change plans and deliver digital cellular phones to the market. They lost their position as market leader.

2.2 STRATEGY IMPLEMENTATION EFFECTIVE PRACTICES

a. Action Plan Development and Deployment

- Actions have been defined in measurable terms that align with strategic objectives and enable the organization to sustain leadership positions for major products and services for key customers or markets.
- Actions to achieve key organizational results (such as operational performance requirements) are defined and tracked at all levels of the organization.
- Expected performance and productivity levels are defined in measurable terms for all action plans.
- Planned actions are challenging, realistic, achievable, and understood by employees throughout the organization. Strategic action plans are rolled out with easy-to-understand communications and clear measures. Tests to evaluate whether communications are understood, such as *brief backs,* are used.
- Resources are available and committed to achieve the plans (minimize unfunded mandates). Capital projects are funded according to strategic plans and priorities.
- Plans are absolutely used to guide operational performance improvements. Plans drive budget and action, not the other way around.
- Incremental (short-term) tactics to achieve long-term plans are defined in measurable terms and timelines are in place to help monitor progress.
- Strategic plans, short- and long-term desired outcomes, and performance measures are understood and used to drive actions throughout the organization.
- All individuals in the organization, at every level, understand how their work contributes to achieving organizational (or their unit) goals and plans. Personal performance appraisals are based, in part, on relevant action plans.
- Plans are followed to ensure that resources are deployed and redeployed as needed to support goals.
- Workforce plans support strategic plans and goals. Plans show how the workforce will be developed to ensure capacity and capability exist to enable the organization to achieve its strategic objectives and actions.
- Key issues of training and development, hiring, retention, workforce engagement, diversity, equity and inclusion, involvement, empowerment, and recognition and reward are addressed as a part of the workforce plan, in the context of achieving strategy. Appropriate measures and targets for each are defined.
- Innovative workforce plans involve one or more of the following:
  - Action plans and associated performance measures provide the basis for individual worker performance management, reward, recognition, and compensation [links with processes in 5.2c(1)].
  - Redesigning work to increase worker responsibility and engagement.
  - Improving labor-management relations. (That is, prior to contract negotiations, train both sides in effective negotiation skills so those involved focus on the merits of issues, not on positions. One process goal, for example, is to improve relations and shorten negotiation time by 50%.)
  - Developing gain-sharing or equity-building compensation systems for all workers to increase motivation and productivity.
  - Broadening worker responsibilities; creating self-directed or high-performance work teams.
- Key performance measures (for example, workforce engagement or work-climate surveys) have been identified to gather data to manage progress. (Note: Improvement results associated with these measures are reported in 7.3.)

- The effectiveness of workforce planning and its alignment with strategic plans is evaluated systematically and refined based on the evaluation findings.
- The process to develop action plans to support strategic objectives is systematically evaluated and subsequently improved.
- Projections of two- to five-year (or longer) changes in performance levels are developed.
- Data from competitors, key benchmarks, and/or past performance form a valid basis for comparison and future projections. The organization has valid strategies and goals in place to meet or exceed the planned levels of performance for these competitors and benchmarks.
- Expected future levels of competitor or comparison performance are used to set and validate the organization's own plans and goals to achieve or sustain leadership positions.
- Future plans and performance projections consider new acquisitions, optimum but secure growth, cost reductions through operational-excellence processes, and anticipated research and development of innovations internally or among competitors. The accuracy of these projections is mapped and analyzed. Techniques to improve accuracy are developed to improve future planning cycles.

b. Action Plan Modification

- In highly volatile environments, which may be greatly affected by rapidly changing economic conditions, regulatory changes, customer requirements, or new technology, to name a few, strategic planners create alternate scenarios, such as plan A, B, and C. In the event that the expected future and plan A is threatened by these conditions, the organization moves to execute plan B quickly.
- Ongoing environmental scans are conducted to provide an early warning of emerging problems, which shortens the organization's reaction time to rapidly execute new plans.

Ineffective Practices

- The following ineffective practices make it difficult to align workers so they work together and provide cohesive support for the organization:
  - Action plans do not align with strategy or are confusing.
  - Action plans do not align with the organization's individual performance planning and appraisal process.
  - Action plans are not communicated to the workforce, leaving subordinates to guess at what is required of them.
  - Action plans are communicated to the workforce but not enforced or used to direct performance plans and unit assignments.
- Action plans are not funded adequately. Workers are told by leaders that the plans are important, but without resources are never implemented. Workers lose trust in leaders.
- Metrics to monitor progress are either not developed or are not relevant, causing workers to believe the plans are not that important. Accountability is weak or nonexistent.

3 Customers—85 Points

*The **Customers** Category asks how your organization engages its customers for ongoing marketplace success, including how your organization listens to the voice of the customer, serves and exceeds customers' expectations, and builds long-term customer relationships.*

This Category addresses how the organization engages its customers to exceed their expectations, build relationships, and develop a loyal brand and product following and create customers who are strong advocates for the organization and its products. Listening to the customer provides important insight and useful information not only on customers' views but also on their marketplace behaviors and how these views and behaviors may contribute to long-term organizational success. Engagement is an important outcome of an effective customer-focused culture and performance excellence strategy. Customer satisfaction and dissatisfaction results provide vital information to help understand customers and the marketplace.

This Category contains two interconnected Items. The first primarily focuses on listening to customers to better understand their expectations and determining products and services to meet their needs. The second focuses on engaging customers to strengthen relationships and loyalty.

Customer Expectations

- Listen carefully to the voice of the customer to obtain actionable information.
- Use various types of information and data from potential and former customers for planning process improvements and business development.
- Determine product and service offerings that will meet customer requirements and exceed expectations.
- Recognize the various stages of a customer life-cycle, as well as the various customer groups and segments that may impact decision-making.

Customer Engagement

- Build customer relationships and loyalty—ensure retention and enhance brand image.
- Use customer information and data to build a more customer-focused culture.
- Establish effective mechanisms to support customers' use of products.
- Handle complaints effectively and responsively.
- Ensure complaint data are used to eliminate causes of complaints, recover customer confidence, and avoid similar complaints in the future.
- Ensure fair treatment for different customers, customer groups, and market segments.
- Systematically measure customer satisfaction, dissatisfaction, and engagement to help exceed their satisfaction and secure long-term engagement.
- Build a customer-focused culture using the voice of the customer.
- Support operational decision-making using customer data and information.

3.1 CUSTOMER EXPECTATIONS: How do you listen to your customers and determine products and services to meet their needs? (40 Pts.) **PROCESS**

a. Customer Listening

(1) **Current Customers How do you listen to, interact with, and observe customers to obtain actionable information?** How do your listening methods vary for different customers, customer groups, or market segments? How do your listening methods vary across the customer life cycle? How do you seek immediate and actionable feedback from customers on the quality of products, customer support, and transactions?

(2) **Potential Customers How do you listen to potential customers to obtain actionable information?** How do you listen to former customers, competitors' customers, and other potential customers to obtain actionable information on your products, customer support, and transactions, as appropriate?

b. Customer Segmentation and Product Offerings

(1) **Customer Segmentation – How do you determine your customer groups and market segments?** How do you

- use information on customers, markets, and product offerings to identify current and anticipate future customer groups and market segments; and
- determine which customers, customer groups, and market segments to emphasize and pursue for business growth?

(2) **Product Offerings How do you determine product offerings?** How do you

- determine customer and market needs and requirements for product offerings and services;
- identify and adapt product offerings to meet the requirements and exceed the expectations of your customer groups and market segments; and
- identify and adapt product offerings to enter new markets, to attract new customers, and to create opportunities to expand relationships with current customers, as appropriate?

Notes:

3.1. Your results on performance relative to key product features should be reported in Item 7.1.

3.1. *For additional considerations on the products and business of nonprofit (including government) organizations, see the notes to P.1a(1) and P.2b.*

3.1a(1). Your customer listening methods might include monitoring comments on social media outlets.

3.1a(1). The customer life cycle begins in the product concept or pre-sale period and continues through all stages of your involvement with the customer. These stages might include relationship building, the active business relationship, and an exit strategy, as appropriate.

3.1b(2). In identifying product offerings, you should consider all the important characteristics of products and services and their performance throughout their full life cycle and the full consumption chain. The focus should be on features that affect customers' preference for and loyalty to you and your brand—for example, unique or innovative features that differentiate your products, or features that differentiate them from competing or other organizations' offerings. Those latter features might include price, reliability, value, delivery, timeliness, product customization, technology, ease of use, environmental or social stewardship, customer or technical support, the sales relationship, ease of transactions, a virtual customer experience, and the privacy and security of customer data.

Comparison with the Health Care and Education Criteria

Item 3.1a(1) in the Business Criteria asks, "How do your listening methods vary across the *customer life cycle?*" In both the Education and Health Care Criteria, this question has the same meaning but is phrased, "How do your listening methods vary across the stages of students'/patients' and other customers' *relationships with you?*"

Item 3.1 looks at the organization's processes for listening to customers [3.1a] and determining product offerings, determining their satisfaction, dissatisfaction, and engagement; and analyzing and using customer data to improve marketing and build a more customer-focused culture.

In Area to Address 3.1a, the customer listening processes help an organization gain knowledge about its current and future customers and markets in order to offer relevant products and services and understand emerging customer requirements, needs, and expectations. Customer listening processes required by Item 3.1 enable the organization to gather accurate intelligence about its customers and competition. This information is intended to support marketing, business development, planning, and customer engagement.

Information sought should be sensitive to specific product and service requirements and their relative importance or value to the different customer groups. Customer listening data should be cross-checked or verified with other types of information and data, such as complaints and gains and losses of customers.

In a rapidly changing technological, competitive, economic, and social environment, many factors may affect customer preference and loyalty, making it necessary to listen and learn on a continuous basis using multiple techniques to ensure accuracy and completeness. To be effective, such listening and learning techniques need to have a close connection with the organization's overall business strategy. For example, if the organization desires to customize its products, the listening and learning process needs to identify unique and common requirements to permit accurate predictions about their value. Social media and web-based technologies can provide rapid access to customer feedback.

Techniques for understanding customer preferences may include asking customers to rank their requirements in order of performance or group requirements into three categories (most important, important, least important). Another technique for determining priorities involves paired-choice or forced-choice analyses where customers are asked to state a preference of requirement A or B, A or C, A or D, B or C, B or D, and so on. Regardless of the techniques used, the organization should be able to prioritize key customer requirements and drivers of purchase decisions, which may be different for different customer groups and market segments.

It is important to obtain actionable information from customers that can be tied to key product offerings and business processes. This information is used to support decisions, such as determining cost and revenue implications to help set improvement goals and priorities for change and innovation.

Complete and accurate knowledge of customers, customer groups, market segments, competitors' customers, former customers, and potential customers using information and data from both 3.1 and 3.2 processes allows the organization to tailor its listening strategies and its product offerings and marketing approaches, to develop a more customer-focused culture, to develop new business, and to ensure organizational sustainability. (Note: A potential customer is a customer the organization wants but is currently being served by another organization or not being served at all.)

Because of the differences among customers, organizations are increasingly using multiple modes to gather actionable information. Some examples of effective listening and learning strategies include:

- Customer listening techniques that help ensure customer requirements, needs, and preferences are understood fully and accurately. Capturing the customer's actual words, rather than relying on summaries, may reduce errors due to faulty interpretations of customer requirements.

- Field trials of products and services to better link research and development and design to the market.
- Accurate identification and close tracking of technological, competitive, and other factors that may bear upon customer requirements, expectations, preferences, or alternatives.
- Defining the customers' value chains and how they are likely to change throughout the entire product life cycle.
- Focus groups or private interviews with influential or leading-edge customers.
- Use of critical incidents, such as complaints [3.2a(3)], to understand key product and service attributes from the point of view of customers and customer support employees.
- Interviewing lost and potential customers to determine the factors they use in their relationship or purchase decisions.
- Win/loss analysis relative to competitors and comparable organizations.

The organization should systematically follow up with customers regarding products, services, and recent transactions to receive feedback that is prompt and actionable and to verify accuracy [3.1a(1)]. Prompt feedback enables problems to be identified quickly to help prevent them from recurring. This helps reduce future customer dissatisfaction.

The organization should determine the satisfaction levels of the customers of competitors [3.2b(2)] in order to identify threats and opportunities to be derived from the organization's own comparative studies or from independent studies

Managing customer complaints [3.2a(3)] is essential to recover customer confidence and build and manage relationships [Item 3.2a(1)], which is why complaint management is part of the customer relationships and support section (Item 3.2a). Complaint data also provides useful and timely intelligence about products.

Customers are more likely to complain right after they experience a problem. They do not tend to hold their complaint until the organization finds it convenient to ask them. Data from the complaint processes in Item 3.2a(3) are provided at the customer's convenience. However, data collected by survey or similar means, as required by Item 3.2b, produce information at the convenience of the organization.

Although the complaint-type customer feedback is timely, it is often difficult to develop reliable trend data since relatively few customers who have a problem actually complain about it to the organization.

The survey and focus group processes in Item 3.2b make it easier to obtain accurate and reliable satisfaction, dissatisfaction, and engagement data over time. Both techniques are required to fully understand customer-satisfaction dynamics that build loyalty, retention, positive referral, and advocacy. To be effective, both techniques should be used to drive improvement actions, marketing, product and service selection, and innovation.

Before the organization determines its product offerings [3.1b(2)], it should have an effective method for listening to its current and potential customers and gathering complete, accurate information [3.1a(1, 2)]. This is a prerequisite to understanding their requirements.

To demonstrate maturity, the Scoring Guidelines require that the organization has a system in place to improve and innovate its customer-listening and learning strategies. A high-performing organization evaluates and improves its customer-listening and learning strategies more often than annually. The high-performing organization should demonstrate that it has made meaningful, value-added improvements in its techniques for understanding customer requirements and priorities.

2021–2022 Criteria Elements Listed Individually Without Duplication See page 279 for explanation of this table			
	Basic Approach Elements [A-B] for Scoring Between 10% and 45%	**Additional Approach Elements at the Overall Level [A-O] for Scoring Between 50% and 65%**	**Additional Approach Elements at the Multiple Level [A-M] for Scoring Between 70% and 100%**
3.1 Customer Expectations			
3.1a(1)	Listen to customers	Listen to, interact with, and observe customers to obtain actionable information	• Use various appropriate listening methods for different customers, customer groups, or market segments • Vary the listening methods across the customer life cycle • Seek immediate and actionable feedback from customers on the quality of products, customer support, and transactions
3.1a(2)		Listen to potential customers to obtain actionable information	Listen to former customers and competitors' customers to obtain actionable information as appropriate on— • Products • Customer support • Transactions
3.1b(1)		Determine customer groups and market segments	• Use information on customers, markets, and product offering to identify current and anticipate future customer groups and market segments • Determine which customers, customer groups, and market segments to emphasize and pursue for business growth
3.1b(2)	Determine products and services to meet customer needs	Determine product offerings	• Determine customer and market needs and requirements for product and service offerings • Identify and adapt product offerings to meet the requirements and exceed the expectations of the organization's customer groups and market segments • Identify and adapt product offerings to— – Enter new markets – Attract new customers – Create opportunities to expand relationships with current customers

3.1 Customer Expectations

Basic Approach Element: *Listen to customers and determine products and services to meet their needs*

Overall Approach Elements:
- *Listen to, interact with, and observe customers to obtain actionable information [3.1a(1)]*
- *Listen to potential customers to obtain actionable information [3.1a(2)]*
- *Determine customer and market groups and segments [3.1b(1)]*
- *Determine product offerings [3.1b(2)]*

The following diagram describes key approach elements:

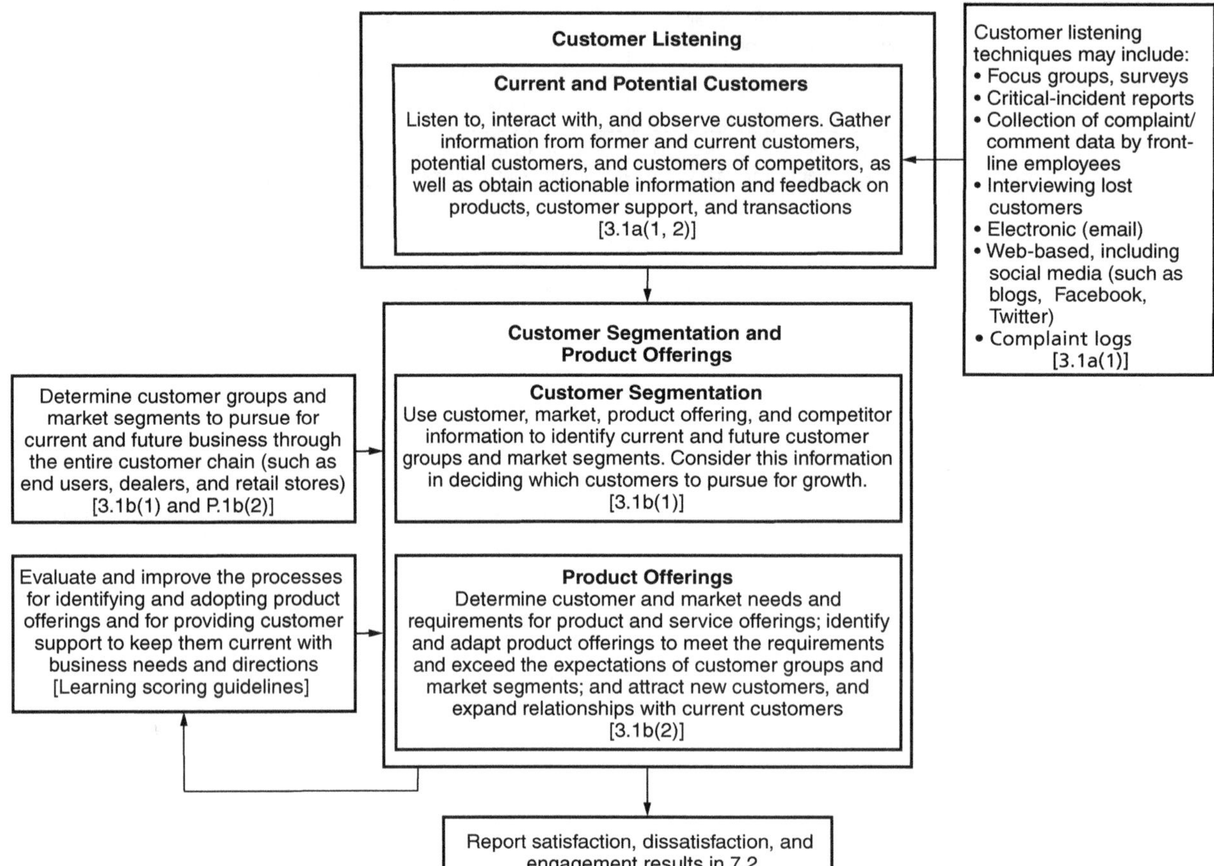

Customer Listening
Current and Potential Customers
Listen to, interact with, and observe customers. Gather information from former and current customers, potential customers, and customers of competitors, as well as obtain actionable information and feedback on products, customer support, and transactions [3.1a(1, 2)]
Customer listening techniques may include:
• Focus groups, surveys
• Critical-incident reports
• Collection of complaint/ comment data by front-line employees
• Interviewing lost customers
• Electronic (email)
• Web-based, including social media (such as blogs, Facebook, Twitter)
• Complaint logs [3.1a(1)]
Customer Segmentation and Product Offerings
Determine customer groups and market segments to pursue for current and future business through the entire customer chain (such as end users, dealers, and retail stores) [3.1b(1) and P.1b(2)]
Customer Segmentation
Use customer, market, product offering, and competitor information to identify current and future customer groups and market segments. Consider this information in deciding which customers to pursue for growth. [3.1b(1)]
Evaluate and improve the processes for identifying and adopting product offerings and for providing customer support to keep them current with business needs and directions [Learning scoring guidelines]
Product Offerings
Determine customer and market needs and requirements for product and service offerings; identify and adapt product offerings to meet the requirements and exceed the expectations of customer groups and market segments; and attract new customers, and expand relationships with current customers [3.1b(2)]
Report satisfaction, dissatisfaction, and engagement results in 7.2

3.1 Key Customer Expectations Item Linkages

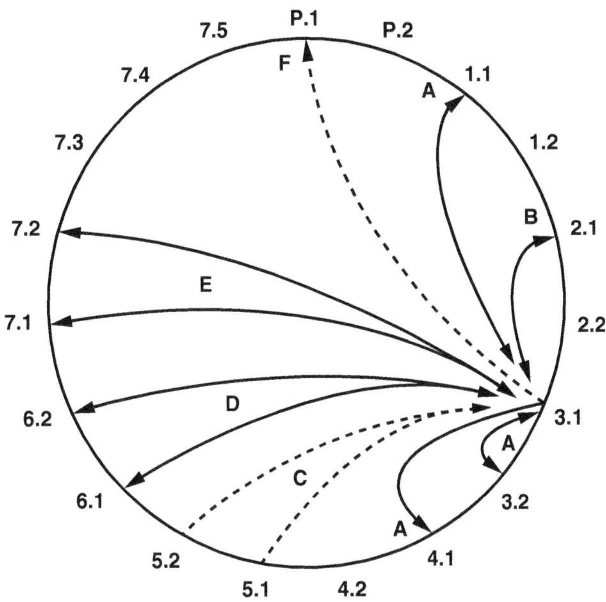

	NATURE OF RELATIONSHIP
A	Senior leaders [1.1] receive actionable information from customers and competitors' customers [3.1a] to improve management decision-making and communication with customers. Customer satisfaction, dissatisfaction, and engagement data [3.2b(1)] are also used by leaders to improve communication and engage customers, review performance [4.1b], and set priorities for improvement and innovation [4.1c(2)].
B	Information gained from listening to current and potential customers [3.1a(1)] is used in the planning process. In addition, strategic objectives [2.1b(1)] influence customer satisfaction and dissatisfaction determination processes [3.2b(1)] by identifying key focus areas.
C	Workers who interact with customers need to possess the capability [5.1a] to listen to customers [3.1a], and satisfy customers through effective and prompt complaint resolution [3.2a(3)]. Workforce, manager, and leader development [5.2c(2, 4)] and reward and recognition [5.2c(1)] are affected by customer satisfaction, dissatisfaction, and engagement [3.2b].
D	Information collected from customers [3.1 and 3.2)] is used to identify requirements for key work and operations processes [6.1 and 6.2].
E	Data/results from customer satisfaction, dissatisfaction, and engagement [7.2], and product and process results [7.1] can help design and adapt product offerings [3.1b(2)].
F	Processes in Item 3.1a produce actionable information about customers and competitors' customers, which helps to prioritize customer requirements and preferences [P.1b(2)].

IF YOU DON'T DO WHAT THE CRITERIA REQUIRE . . .	
Item Reference	**Possible Adverse Consequences**
3.1a(1)	**Listening to Current Customers** – The failure to have effective processes to listen to, interact with, and observe customers to obtain actionable information and feedback on products and services forces leaders and workers to substitute their own biases for the opinions of the customer. This is easily noticed by customers, who consider the practice to be arrogant, even hostile. Failure to listen makes it difficult to consistently focus on the areas most important to customers and wastes resources designing and delivering products that do not meet requirements.
3.1a(1)	**Listening to Current Customers** – Listening methods that are not customized for different customers, customer groups, or market segments may not produce accurate, complete, or valid data to support sound decision-making. Decision errors based on faulty information typically waste resources and contribute to delay and rework. Different techniques may be needed to understand the requirements of different groups of customers. The failure to listen and learn about the key customer requirements for products and services, especially those features that are most important to customer purchasing decisions may make it difficult to design and develop those products and services that are most likely to delight (or even satisfy) customers, and increase market share or ensure organizational sustainability.
3.1a(1)	**Listening to Current Customers** – If listening methods do not vary across the customer life cycle it may be difficult to capture information critical to sustaining excellence and customer support. Different methods are typically needed depending on the life cycle of the product or the nature of the customer relationship. For example, a car manufacturer might collect information about car quality based on the number and frequency of dealer service calls. That technique might not produce accurate information after the warranty period expires because the car owner may go to a local repair shop instead. It would be incorrect for the manufacturer to conclude, based on dealer-supplied repair records, that the car has fewer problems needing correction as it ages.
3.1a(1)	**Listening to Current Customers** – A natural opportunity to gather immediate and actionable customer feedback on the quality of products, customer support, and transactions occurs when customers interact with the organization. These interactions may involve placing an order, requesting support, or seeking information, to name a few. The failure to take advantage of these opportunities to acquire timely information may cause the organization to overlook a small problem and not correct it early. The longer it takes to identify a problem, the more costly it is to fix.
3.1a(2)	**Listening to Potential Customers** – The failure to listen to former customers, potential customers, and customers of competitors to obtain feedback on products, customer support, and transactions may cause the organization to receive unbalanced and incomplete information. This may contribute to costly decision errors. It is said that, "If you only listen to the customers that are foolish enough to do business with you, then you will have foolish data." In addition to gathering feedback directly from former customers, the organization should collect and analyze complaint and lost customer data to gain additional insights into unmet requirements and opportunities for future work. If an organization does not know why it lost or gained customers, it is more difficult to deliver the right products and services, maintain customer engagement, and grow or sustain the business.

Continued

IF YOU DON'T DO WHAT THE CRITERIA REQUIRE . . . *Continued*	
Item Reference	**Possible Adverse Consequences**
3.1a(2)	**Listening to Potential Customers** – Lost customers and potential customers can be defined as customers the organization desires, but they go elsewhere (or forego the product). By not considering the reasons why desired customers are not actual customers, the organization fails to acquire potentially valuable insight that could be used to change its products and support to be more attractive and build the business.
3.1b(1)	**Customer Segmentation** – Organizations segment or group customers and markets to help plan, design, develop, and manage the array of products and support to satisfy the bulk of customers efficiently. The failure to classify or group customers or markets into meaningful segments may make it difficult to identify and differentiate key requirements that may be critical to one group but not another. For example, frequent or high-volume customers may have different expectations than infrequent or low-volume customers. Dealers may have different requirements than end users. Unless these differences are understood, it may be difficult for the organization to customize information collection techniques as well as programs, products, and services according to the needs and expectations of different groups of customers.
3.1b(1)	**Customer Segmentation** – Organizations that do not have an effective process to determine which customers, customer groups, and market segments to pursue frequently misjudge (over-estimate) or improperly focus products and services and fail to reach their objectives.
3.1b(2)	**Product Offerings** – The failure to correctly identify product offerings to meet the requirements and exceed the expectations of customer groups and market segments will increase the likelihood that customers will not be satisfied, and cause the organization to engage in excessive rework. This, in turn, increases costs, adds delay, and reduces value to customers.
3.1b(2)	**Product Offerings** – The failure to adapt product offerings, to attract new customers, and to provide opportunities for expanding relationships with existing customers will eventually cause the customer base to erode. This is especially dangerous in a difficult economic climate where competitors are going to extraordinary lengths to attract a larger share of a smaller group of customers willing to purchase.
3.1b(2)	**Product Offerings** – The failure to anticipate key customer requirements (including products and product features) and changing expectations and their relative importance to customers' purchasing or relationship decisions across the customer life cycle causes the organization to lose agility, which is usually not a serious problem if all other providers are similarly stagnant. However, if some competitors accurately and systematically anticipate emerging customer requirements, then they are more likely to win the battle for the customer.

3.1 CUSTOMER EXPECTATIONS—SAMPLE EFFECTIVE PRACTICES

a. Customer Listening

- Closely monitor technological, competitive, societal, environmental, economic, and demographic factors that may bear on customer requirements, expectations, preferences, or alternatives.
- Conduct focus groups with leading-edge or demanding customers, not just *cream puff* customers. This is where the most valuable, honest feedback will probably originate.
- Train front-line (customer-facing) employees in customer listening and use these employees to collect feedback.
- Identify and analyze critical incidents in product or support performance or quality to understand key problems from the point of view of customers and front-line employees.
- Systematically interview lost customers to determine why they left.
- Conduct win/loss analysis relative to competitors.
- Analyze major factors affecting key customers.
- Use tools such as forced- or paired-choice analysis (where customers select between options A and B, A and C, B and C, and so on). Using this technique, organizations quickly prioritize requirements and focus on delivering those that make the greatest impact on satisfaction and engagement (repeat business and loyalty).
- Use various systematic methods to gather data and identify current requirements and expectations of customers (for example, surveys, focus groups, and the use of social media and web-based systems, such as blogs, Facebook, and Twitter).
- Evaluate and improve methods to listen and learn from customers and improve through several cycles. Examples of factors that are evaluated include:
  - The adequacy and timeliness of customer-related information
  - Survey design and questions
  - Approaches for getting reliable and timely information—surveys, focus groups, customer-contact personnel
- Collect requirements and satisfaction data from former customers for each customer or market segment. Use this information to identify blind spots that current customers might not reveal.
- Training and development plans and replacement procedures exist for customer support employees. These processes have been measured and refined.
- Identify requirements of customers of competitors and put processes in place to gather expectation data from potential customers. Track new-customer acquisition.
- Identify measurable customer support requirements (service standards) from customer expectations (for example, timeliness, courtesy, efficiency, thoroughness, and completeness).
- Identify requirements for building relationships that may include factors such as product knowledge, employee responsiveness, and various customer support methods.
- Use customer listening methods as part of Quality Function Deployment (QFD) to ensure customer needs and requirements are fully incorporated into the design and delivery of products and services.

b. Customer Segmentation and Product Offerings

- Customer data, such as complaints and gains or losses of customers are used to support the identification or validation of key customer requirements.
- Key product offerings are defined in order of importance to customers. Product offerings include all important characteristics that cus-

tomers want throughout the entire customer-product life cycle. Product features that bear on customer preference and loyalty—for example, features that enhance or differentiate products and services from competing offerings—are defined in measurable terms.

- Tools such as forced- or paired-choice analysis are used (where customers select between options A and B, A and C, B and C, and so on). Using this technique, the organization quickly prioritizes requirements and focuses on delivering those that make the greatest impact on satisfaction, repeat business, and loyalty.
- Customer requirements are identified or grouped to make it easier for the organization to plan, design, and deliver maximum value to each segment. This information is consistently used for planning, data analysis, product and service design, production and delivery processes, and for reporting and monitoring progress.
- Fact-based, systematic methods are used to identify the future requirements and expectations of customers. These are tested for accuracy, and estimation techniques are improved.
- Measurable customer support requirements (service standards) have been derived from customer expectations (for example, timeliness, courtesy, efficiency, thoroughness, and completeness).

Ineffective Practices

- Customer contacts are not coordinated and customers receive multiple, bothersome calls requesting similar feedback.
- When an organization loses customers, it contacts them repeatedly to get them to return. Of course, these customers wonder why the company never made contact to understand their needs before they left.
- The organization pays customers to take surveys and participate in focus groups, but does not use the data to improve in ways that are important to customers.
- The organization coaches customers to answer surveys a certain way, such as, "If you don't give me a perfect score, I get punished." Data collected this way are inaccurate or invalid, and customers question the organization's integrity.
- A hotel put a sign in their lobby asking departing guests to complete a survey, for which they would be entered into a drawing for a free night for every "10" (highest score) that guests entered on the survey. Customer should never be coached by the organization to provide high scores.
- The organization motto is "we try our best to please our customers." Nobody in the company knows what this motto means, nor do they really care what it takes to please customers.

3.2 CUSTOMER ENGAGEMENT: How do you build relationships with customers and determine satisfaction and engagement? (45 Pts.) PROCESS

a. Customer Experience

(1) **Relationship Management How do you build and manage customer relationships?** How do you

- acquire customers and build market share;
- manage and enhance your brand image;
- retain customers, meet their requirements, and exceed their expectations in each stage of the customer life cycle?

(2) **Customer Access and Support How do you enable customers to seek information and support?** How do you enable them to conduct business with you? What are your key means of customer support and communication? How do they vary for different customers, customer groups, or market segments, as appropriate? How do you

- determine your customers' key support requirements, and
- deploy these requirements to all people and processes involved in customer support?

(3) **Complaint Management How do you manage customer complaints?** How do you resolve complaints promptly and effectively? How does your management of complaints enable you to recover your customers' confidence, enhance their satisfaction and engagement, and avoid similar complaints in the future?

(4) **Fair Treatment How do your customer experience processes ensure fair treatment for different customers, customer groups, and market segments?**

b. Determination of Customer Satisfaction and Engagement

(1) **Satisfaction, Dissatisfaction, and Engagement – How do you determine customer satisfaction, dissatisfaction, and engagement?** How do your determination methods differ among your customer groups and market segments, as appropriate? How do your measurements capture actionable information?

(2) **Satisfaction Relative to Other Organizations – How do you obtain information on customers' satisfaction with your organization relative to other organizations?** How do you obtain information on your customers' satisfaction

- relative to their satisfaction with your competitors; and
- relative to the satisfaction of customers of other organizations that provide similar products or to industry benchmarks, as appropriate?

c. Use of Voice of the Customer and Market Data

How do you use voice-of-the-customer and market data and information? How do you use voice-of-the-customer and market data and information to build a more customer-focused culture and support operational decision-making?

Notes:

3.2. Results for customer perceptions and actions (outcomes) should be reported in Item 7.2.

3.2a(4). You should ensure that your approaches for managing customer relationships, enabling customers to seek information and support, and managing complaints promote equity and inclusion, and that they do not inadvertently discriminate unfairly or inappropriately against specific customers or customer groups.

Continued

Continued

3.2b(1). Determining customer dissatisfaction should be seen as more than reviewing low customer satisfaction scores. It should be independently determined to identify root causes and enable a systematic remedy to avoid future dissatisfaction.

3.2b(2). Information on relative satisfaction may include comparisons with competitors, comparisons with other organizations that deliver similar products in a noncompetitive marketplace, or comparisons obtained through trade or other organizations. Such information may also include information on why customers choose your competitors over you.

3.2c. Customer data and information should be used to support the overall performance reviews addressed in 4.1b. Voice-of-the-customer and market data and information to use might include aggregated data on complaints and, as appropriate, data and information from social media and other web-based or digital sources.

Comparison with the Health Care and Education Criteria

Item 3.2a(1), third bullet in the Business Criteria asks about exceeding expectations "in each stage of the customer life cycle?" In both the Education and Health Care Criteria, this question asks about exceeding expectations "in each stage of their relationship with you."

Item 3.2 looks at the organization's processes for positive customer experiences [3.2a], determining customer satisfaction, dissatisfaction, and engagement [3.2b], and use of voice-of-the-customer data [3.2c].

A customer orientation that drives engagement does not develop without a systematic, integrated effort. As a start, top leaders need to ensure the organization's values include a commitment to customer engagement and service [1.1a(1)]. When setting organizational performance expectations, top leaders need to ensure there is a focus on creating and balancing value for customers and other stakeholders [1.1c(2)]. These priorities should be considered as strategic planning takes place [2.1a] and should be a part of the organization's strategic objectives [2.1b(1)] and action plans [2.2a(1)]. Plans, however, are not enough. To ensure workers, managers, and leaders possess the desired traits and skills to support customers, the organization may need to hire, develop, and train its leaders, managers, and workers through the systems identified in Item 5.2c(2) (Performance Development). To ensure workforce alignment with this customer focus, specific performance requirements should be included in the performance planning and appraisals of workers and leaders [5.2c(1)], including executive compensation [1.2a(2)] and other incentives for workers [5.2c(1)].

Since business development and product or service improvement increasingly depend on maintaining close positive experiences with customers, for long-term success, organizations should build strong relationships with customers. Organizations should keep approaches to all aspects of customer relationships current with changing business needs and directions, since approaches to and bases for relationships may change quickly.

Different approaches to building customer relationships may be needed to ensure fair treatment for different customers, customer groups, and market segments, since one approach will not be fully effective for all. Moreover, these relationship-building approaches may need to be different during the various stages of the customer life cycle or their relationship with the organization.

If done correctly, customer experience processes [3.2a] should help produce such a high degree of loyalty that the customer will advocate for the organization's brand and product offerings. These engaged customers tend to remain loyal even if the organization makes mistakes—as all do, sooner or later.

It is important to provide easy access for customers and potential customers to seek information or assistance and to comment and complain. This access makes it easier to get timely information from customers about issues that are of real concern to them. Timely information, in turn, is transmitted to the appropriate place in the organization to drive improvements or new levels of product and service satisfaction. The organization should describe its key communication mechanisms for customers to seek information, conduct business, and make complaints.

Customer access and support requirements essentially refer to customer expectations for service after the sale. Customer access and support requirements should be set in measurable terms to permit effective monitoring and performance review.

- A good example of a measurable customer support requirement might be the customer expectation that a malfunctioning computer would be back online within 24 hours of the request for service. Another example might be the customer requirement that a knowledgeable and polite human being is available within 10 minutes to resolve a problem with software. In both cases, clear requirements and measurable performance standards are defined.
- A bad example of a customer support standard might be "we get back to the customer as soon as we can." With this example, no standard of performance is defined. Some customer support representatives might get back to a customer within a matter of minutes. Others might take hours or days. The failure to define the access requirement makes it difficult to allocate appropriate resources to meet that support requirement consistently.

These customer access and support requirements must be deployed to all employees who are in contact with customers. Such deployment needs to take into account all key points in the response chain—all units or individuals in the organization that make effective interactions possible. These standards then become another source of information to evaluate the organization's performance in meeting customer support requirements.

Different modes of access affect customer service expectations the customer might use to contact the organization. Customers expect a response within minutes of calling, the next day when emailing, and many days in response to a letter.

Complaint aggregation, analysis, and root cause determination can help focus action on the elimination of the causes of complaints and help set priorities for process and product improvements.

Effective complaint management [3.2a(3)] requires the prompt and courteous resolution of complaints. This leads to recovery of customer confidence. Customer loyalty and confidence are enhanced when problems are resolved with courtesy by the first person the customer contacts. Even if the organization ultimately resolves a problem, the likelihood of maintaining a loyal customer is reduced by approximately 10% each time that customer is referred to another place or person in the organization. In fact, prompt resolution of problems helps to produce higher levels of loyalty than if the customer never had a problem in the first place.

The organization should also have a mechanism for learning from complaints and ensuring that design, production, and delivery process owners [Category 6] receive the information they need to improve their work processes and eliminate the causes of complaints. Effective elimination of those causes involves aggregating and analyzing complaint information from all sources and determining the root causes of the complaints. That information is then used to set priorities for specific process, product, and service improvements that will result in overall organizational improvement in both design [6.1a] and work process management [6.1b] stages.

In Area to Address 3.2b(1), the organization must have effective, systematic processes in place to determine customer satisfaction, dissatisfaction, and engagement. These processes provide another source of excellent information about the behavior and support of customers, as well as information about the customer's perception of their overall experience.

An important aspect of customer satisfaction and dissatisfaction data is that the data permit comparative analyses with competitors, competing or alternative offerings, and organizations providing similar products. Such information might be derived from in-house comparative studies or from independent third-party studies. These comparison data allow leaders to understand better the factors that lead to customer preference and loyalty—critical to building lasting relationships [3.2a]. Understanding the factors that drive markets and affect competitiveness is essential for current and long-term organizational success.

When trying to learn about and understand customer satisfaction, dissatisfaction, or engagement, one size does not fit all. A relationship or listening strategy may work well with some customers, but not with others. For example, focus groups are well-established and effective in the United States, but in other countries, public focus groups might not generate a level of trust high enough to produce accurate information. In these cases, anonymity using survey tools might be critical to ensure accuracy.

The organization should determine the satisfaction levels of the customers of competitors [3.2b(2)] in order to identify threats and opportunities to improve future performance. Such information might be derived from the organization's own comparative studies or from independent studies.

Customer and market data should be utilized to help build a customer-focused culture. A fact-based customer-focused culture, supported by data, helps ensure a customer service orientation among all workers, managers, and leaders. This customer and market data should also be used to support operational decision-making.

To demonstrate maturity, the Scoring Guidelines require that the organization has a system in place to improve and innovate its customer-engagement processes. Typically, a high-performing organization evaluates and improves its customer-engagement processes more often than annually. It also should demonstrate that it has made meaningful, value-added improvements in its techniques for understanding the drivers of customer engagement and techniques for strengthening relationships and recovering customer confidence.

2021–2022 Criteria Elements Listed Individually Without Duplication See page 279 for explanation of this table			
	Basic Approach Elements [A-B] for Scoring Between 10% and 45%	**Additional Approach Elements at the Overall Level [A-O] for Scoring Between 50% and 65%**	**Additional Approach Elements at the Multiple Level [A-M] for Scoring Between 70% and 100%**
3.2 Customer Engagement			
3.2a(1)	Build relationships with customers	Build and manage customer relationships	• Acquire customers and build market share • Manage and enhance brand image • Retain customers, meet their requirements, and exceed their expectations in each stage of the customer life cycles
3.2a(2)		Enable customers to seek information and support	• Enable customers to conduct business with the organization • Define the key means of customer support and communication • Use various means to support different customers, customer groups, or market segments • Determine the customers' key support requirements • Deploy these requirements to all people and processes involved in customer support
3.2a(3)		Manage customer complaints	• Resolve customer complaints promptly and effectively • Through effective customer complaint management— – Recover customer confidence – Enhance customer satisfaction and engagement – Avoid similar complaints in the future
3.2a(4)		Ensure customer experience processes provide fair treatment for different customers, customer groups, and market segments	
3.2b(1)	Determine customer satisfaction and engagement	Determine customer dissatisfaction	• Use different satisfaction, dissatisfaction, and engagement determination methods among customer groups and market segments, as appropriate • Ensure customer satisfaction, dissatisfaction, and engagement measurements capture actionable information
3.2b(2)		Obtain information on customers' satisfaction relative to other organizations	Obtain customers' satisfaction information as appropriate— • Relative to their satisfaction with competitors • Relative to the satisfaction of customers of other organizations that provide similar products or to industry benchmark
3.2c		Use voice-of-the-customer and market data and information	Use voice-of-the-customer and market data and information to— • Build a more customer-focused culture • Support operational decision-making

3.2 Customer Engagement

Basic Approach Element: ***Build relationships with customers and determine satisfaction and engagement***

Overall Approach Elements:

- ***Build and manage customer relationships [3.2a(1)]***
- ***Enable customers to seek information and support [3.2a(2)]***
- ***Manage customer complaints [3.2a(3)]***
- ***Customer experience processes ensure fair treatment for different customers, customer groups, and market segments [3.2a(4)]***
- ***Determine customer satisfaction, dissatisfaction, and engagement [3.2b(1)]***
- ***Obtain information on customers' satisfaction with your organization relative to other organizations [3.2b(2)]***
- ***Use voice-of-the-customer and market data and information [3.2c]***

The following diagram describes key approach elements:

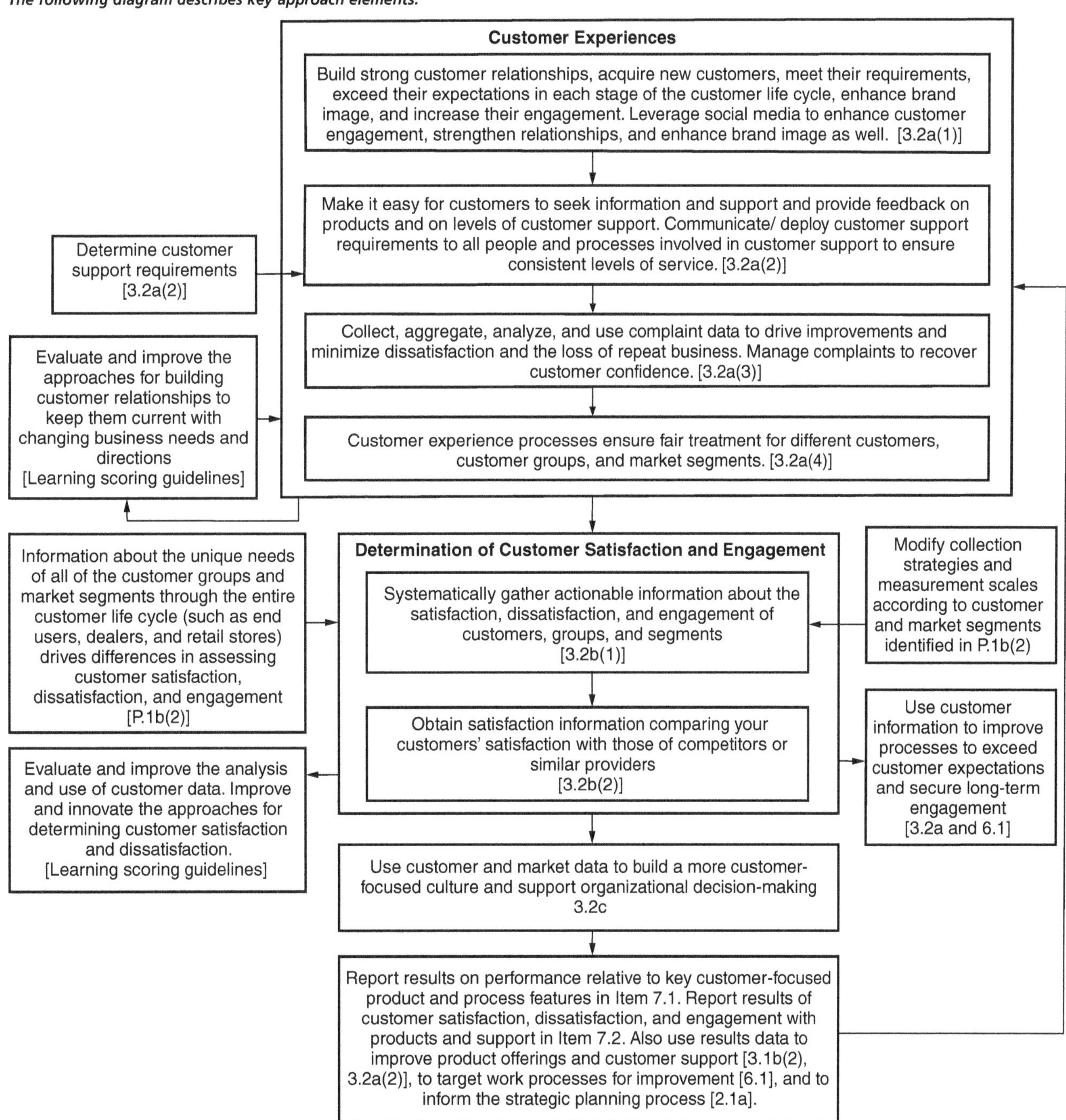

3.2 Key Customer Engagement Item Linkages

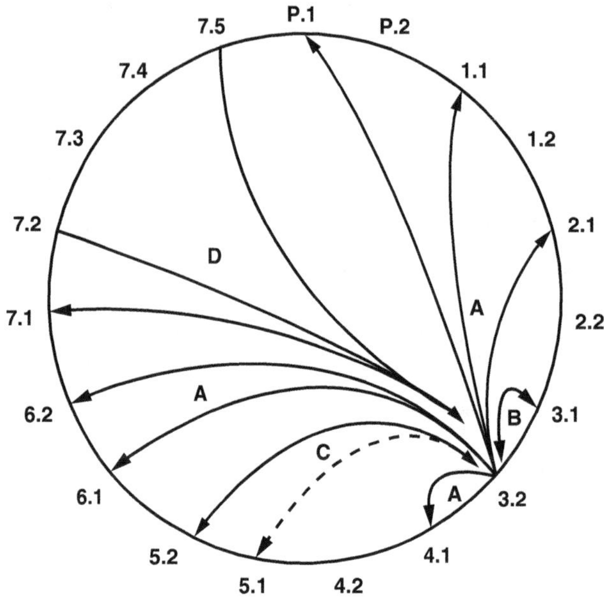

	NATURE OF RELATIONSHIP
A	Leaders create a workforce culture that promotes positive customer experiences and engagement [1.1c(1)] essential for building customer relationships [3.2a]. Customer input and related information about engaging customers to serve their needs and build relationships [3.2a(1)] are used to help determine and capitalize on core competencies [P.1a(2), 2.1a(4), 2.1b(2)], to determine work process requirements and design and manage work processes [6.1], and to help leaders set vision and directions for the organization [1.1a(1)]. Processes to identify and innovate product offerings to meet the requirements and exceed the expectations of customer groups and market segments [3.1b(2)] are central to organizational success. In addition, a clear definition of the product and service offerings is essential to guide the design of work processes [6.1a(3)], the identification of key work process requirements [6.1a(1)], and effective process management [6.1b]. Information concerning customer requirements, expectations, and preferences [3.1a(1)], benchmark data [4.1a(2)], and customer data [3.2c] are used to help identify customer support requirements (service standards) [3.2a(2)]. Customer complaint data [3.2a(3)] are analyzed [4.1b] and used [3.2c] to help leaders build a more fair customer-focused culture and help ensure conclusions and decisions to modify and improve are valid.
B	Customer complaints [3.2a(3)], customer satisfaction, dissatisfaction, and engagement data [3.2b(1)], and customer listening methods (3.1a) are used to help validate processes to ensure product and service offerings [3.1b(2)], customer support, and the customer culture are properly designed and managed to build strong customer relationships, and build market share, increase retention, and increase engagement.
C	The workforce performance management system [5.2c(1)], the workforce, manager, and leader development systems [5.2c], and the workforce capability and capacity methods [5.1a] are aligned to support and reinforce customer engagement [3.2].
D	Customer satisfaction [7.2a(1)], engagement [7.2a(2)], product and process results [7.1], and financial, market, and strategy results [7.5a] are used to help validate customer expectations and refine requirements for customer support [3.2a(2)], and help acquire new customers, increase engagement, strengthen brand perception, and expand relationships with existing customers [3.2a(1)].

IF YOU DON'T DO WHAT THE CRITERIA REQUIRE . . .	
Item Reference	**Possible Adverse Consequences**
3.2a(1)	**Relationship Management** – Building strong, positive customer relations is essential to promote and sustain customer engagement (loyalty, retention, enhance brand, and willingness to recommend and advocate for the organization and its products). Consistency requires broad commitment from the entire workforce; commitment and desire from a few are not enough. Certain attitudes and skills must be developed, and training is essential. Without such training and development [see 5.2c(3)], and reinforcement through the system of rewards, incentives, and compensation [see 5.2c(1)], the desired behaviors in support of a customer culture may be difficult to sustain. Failing to create an environment that provides a positive customer experience will cause customers to go elsewhere for products and support.
3.2a(1)	**Relationship Management** – The failure to build and manage lasting relationships and loyalty with customers makes it easier for customers to switch when problems arise. Loyal customers are twice as likely to use an organization's products and services as those who are simply satisfied. The TARP Studies have found that the cost to win a new customer versus retain a current customer varies from 2:1 to 20:1.* If the organization lacks a disciplined approach for building relationships and cultivating loyalty, it is difficult to achieve market leadership. For example, in many manufacturing companies today, service or support is a key differentiator. Products that were once considered specialty items, such as personal computers, are now commodities. In these cases, service has become the factor that differentiates companies and cultivates loyal customers. Furthermore, since it is more costly to acquire a new customer than to keep an existing customer, organizations can avoid unnecessary expenses by building relationships and strengthening the loyalty of current customers. Loyal customers are far more likely to provide positive referrals than a dissatisfied or even minimally satisfied customer. *From John Goodman. "Basic Facts on Customer Complaint Behavior and the Impact of Service on the Bottom Line." *Competitive Advantage* (June 1999): 1–5.
3.2a(2)	**Customer Access and Support** – Customer support requirements (sometimes called customer contact requirements or service standards) help define customers' expectations for support after the initial sale. For example, a large, direct-order computer company surveyed its customers and determined that they expected to have a technician helping to solve their problem within 10 minutes of making the initial contact. By knowing the customer support requirements and the hour-to-hour call volume, the organization was able to put enough technicians in place to ensure the average response time for technical support was nine minutes or less. The failure of any worker to understand and meet customer support requirements contributes to customer dissatisfaction and makes it more difficult to build relationships and customer engagement.
3.2a(2)	**Customer Access and Support** – Different techniques may be needed to understand the requirements of different groups of customers. The failure to listen and learn about the key customer requirements for product features and support services, especially those features that are most important to customer purchasing decisions, may make it difficult to design, develop, and adapt those products that are most likely to delight (or even satisfy) customers and increase market share.
3.2a(3)	**Complaint Management** – Once the organization learns about a customer problem, the speed and efficiency with which it resolves that problem contributes greatly to customer

Continued

IF YOU DON'T DO WHAT THE CRITERIA REQUIRE . . . *Continued*	
	loyalty, brand support, and willingness to make positive referrals (advocate). The failure to resolve a problem to the customer's satisfaction at the first point of contact significantly reduces the likelihood of maintaining a loyal customer. In addition, the failure to collect, aggregate, analyze, and use complaint data to drive improvements throughout the organization (and, as appropriate, to key suppliers or partners) increases the likelihood that the problem will recur.
3.2a(3)	**Complaint Management** – Resolving a customer complaint and recovering customer confidence are only part of an effective complaint management system. Unless complaint data are aggregated and analyzed and root causes of problems are eliminated, the problem will recur. Customers that face repeat problems are much less likely to forgive, and engagement and loyalty will be seriously threatened, causing the customer to look elsewhere.
3.2a(4)	**Fair Treatment** – Organizations that do not provide for equity and inclusion in their products, programs, and services risk adverse publicity, loss of customers, and erosion of markets.
3.2b(1)	**Satisfaction, Dissatisfaction, and Engagement** – The failure to accurately determine customer satisfaction, dissatisfaction, and engagement may make it difficult for the organization to make timely adjustments to the products and services it offers. Furthermore, if the data-collection processes do not help the organization understand what drives customer behavior, the organization may not know until it is too late (the customer goes elsewhere) that they have a serious problem. The failure to predict customer behavior and the likelihood for positive referral also make it difficult to forecast demand, which may create supply-network difficulties, such as excessive inventories or delays in restocking that hurt on-time delivery.
3.2b(1)	**Satisfaction, Dissatisfaction, and Engagement** – The failure to take into account differences in customer or market segments and adjust the techniques for collecting customer satisfaction and engagement data appropriately may cause the organization to collect inaccurate or unreliable information, which threatens the accuracy of the organization's decision-making and planning. Decision error wastes resources and adversely affects long-term customer engagement.
3.2b(1)	**Satisfaction, Dissatisfaction, and Engagement** – Meeting a defined set of customer expectations may be considered adequate, until another provider consistently exceeds expectations. Then, engagement and loyalty wane and *adequate* is no longer acceptable. Unless the organization can find ways to exceed expectations and produce more value than other providers, it may have difficulty sustaining its operations and loyal customer base. Sustainability requires continuous improvement and innovation in a competitive market.
3.2b(2) Scoring Guidelines	**Satisfaction Relative to Other Organizations** – By failing to obtain information on the satisfaction of competitors' customers, the organization may not learn what it must do differently to satisfy and acquire (win over) the customers of its competitors or other organizations providing similar products.
3.2b	Organizations that do not evaluate and improve the effectiveness of their techniques to determine customer satisfaction, dissatisfaction, and engagement run the risk of making bad decisions based on misleading or even useless information. It does little good to gather customer satisfaction data unless the organization asks the right questions. Failing to ask the right questions rarely produces accurate, actionable information to support effective decision-making. Moreover, the failure to evaluate and improve the effectiveness of the approaches used to assess customer satisfaction may make it difficult to keep up with changing customer

Continued

IF YOU DON'T DO WHAT THE CRITERIA REQUIRE . . . *Continued*	
Item Reference	**Possible Adverse Consequences**
	and market needs and gather critical information necessary for strategic planning, as well as the development of new or improved products and services.
3.2c	**Use of Voice-of-the-Customer and Market Data** – Customer satisfaction and engagement is every organization's ultimate competitive advantage—too important to be left to guesswork. Without gathering customer data, decisions about customers are left to the intuition of leaders and workers. Organizations that do not gather voice-of-the-customer data usually have poor relationships with their customers and do not want to hear more bad news. Customer data are critical for organizations that operate in a competitive environment in which customer loyalty may be fleeting. Failing to learn quickly about what satisfies and dissatisfies customers, including aggregate complaints, makes it difficult to focus resources on improvements that matter to customers and to organizational success.
Learning Scoring Guidelines	The failure to consistently improve approaches for engaging customers and building customer relationships increases the probability that the organization may overlook important areas for change and provide an opening for competitors to exploit. The failure to systematically evaluate and improve the processes used to build relationships, resolve complaints, and prevent them from recurring may make it difficult to correctly identify specific areas needing change. Making it easy for customers to complain but not resolving those complaints effectively and promptly may create even higher levels of frustration and dissatisfaction. Ignorance about the effectiveness of customer access and complaint resolution processes may blind the organization to a problem of its own creation, especially in a highly competitive arena where customer and market requirements can change quickly.

3.2 CUSTOMER ENGAGEMENT—SAMPLE EFFECTIVE PRACTICES

a. Customer Experience

- Requirements for building relationships are identified and may include factors such as product knowledge, employee responsiveness, and various customer support methods.
- A systematic approach is in place to evaluate and improve customer-focused decision-making and customer relationships. Several process improvements have been made as a result.
- A system exists to ensure that customer complaints are resolved promptly and effectively by the first point of contact. Customer support employees have been trained and given the authority for resolving a broad range of problems.
- Customer data, such as complaints and gains or losses of customers are used to support the identification or validation of key customer requirements. Fact-based, systematic methods are used to identify the future requirements and expectations of customers. These are tested for accuracy, and estimation techniques are improved.
- Complaint data are tracked, analyzed, and used to initiate prompt corrective action as well as to improve the processes that caused the complaint to prevent complaints from recurring.

b. Determination of Customer Satisfaction and Engagement

- Customer satisfaction, dissatisfaction, and engagement measurements include both a numerical rating scale and descriptors assigned to each unit in the scale. An effective (actionable) customer satisfaction and dissatisfaction measurement system provides the organization with reliable information about customer ratings of specific product and service features and the relationship between these ratings and the customers' likely market behavior (willingness to purchase again and recommend to others).

- Customer dissatisfaction indicators include complaints, claims, refunds, recalls, returns, repeat services, litigation, replacements, performance-rating downgrades, repairs, warranty work, warranty costs, misshipments, and incomplete orders.
- Competitors' customer satisfaction is determined using external or internal studies. This information is used to refine services and product features.
- Several customer-satisfaction indicators are used (for example, repeat-business measures, the volume and content of unsolicited praise letters, direct measures using survey questions and interviews, Twitter, Facebook, blogs, consumer websites and other social media tools).
- Comprehensive satisfaction, dissatisfaction, and engagement data are collected and segmented or grouped to enable the organization to predict customer behavior (likelihood of remaining a customer).

c. Use of Voice-of-the-Customer and Market Data

- Top leaders have made supporting the customer the single most important priority. It is a core value of the organization and a part of every performance appraisal. The failure to meet customer support requirements is so serious that the offender is not eligible for promotion or pay increase until the problem is resolved.
- The customer-focused culture is supported by ongoing workforce and leader training. Special training and development plans and replacement procedures exist for customer-support employees to maintain consistency.

Ineffective Practices

- Robo calls.
- More robo calls.
- The organization's customer policies make it clear that customers are not considered to be important to the organization.
- Customers with a complaint are shuffled to multiple workers to get relief since the first point of contact with the complaining customer lacks the training or authority to act.
- Social media sites are checked infrequently, leading to customer frustration and potential humiliation through public comments visible to all.
- Public protests such as Black Lives Matter and #MeToo result from discriminatory treatment of customers, employees, and other stakeholders.
- Complaint data are not viewed as important unless they are sent by an important person to a major executive. Complaints are not collected or analyzed otherwise.
- Satisfaction and dissatisfaction information is gathered from customers and stakeholders and ignored (or those customers and stakeholders are not shown how that information is used). Engagement data are generally not collected or considered to be relevant or important in the organization.
- Company values relationships with funders and policy makers and builds relationships with these groups. End-user customers are not viewed as important.

4 Measurement, Analysis, and Knowledge Management—90 Points

*The **Measurement, Analysis, and Knowledge Management** Category asks how your organization selects, gathers, analyzes, manages, and improves its data, information, and knowledge assets; how it uses review findings to improve its performance; and how it learns.*

The Measurement, Analysis, and Knowledge Management Category is the main point within the Criteria for all key information about effectively measuring, analyzing, and reviewing performance and managing organizational knowledge to drive improvement and organizational competitiveness. Simply speaking, Category 4 is the *brain center* for the alignment of the organization's operations consistent with its strategic objectives. Such use of data and information depends on their quality and availability. Moreover, since information, analysis, and knowledge management by themselves might be sources of competitive advantage and productivity growth, the Category also may have strategic value and its capabilities may be considered a challenge or advantage as part of the strategic planning process.

Measurement, Analysis, and Knowledge Management evaluates the selection, management, and effectiveness of use of information and data to support processes, action plans, and the performance management system. Systems to analyze, review, capture, store, retrieve, and distribute data to support decision-making are also evaluated.

Measurement, Analysis, and Improvement of Organizational Performance

- This Item looks at the processes associated with data collection, information, and measures (including comparative data) for planning, decision-making, improving performance, and supporting action plans and operations.
- The Item also looks at the analytical processes used to make sense out of the data to ensure decision makers draw valid conclusions. In addition, it looks at how these analyses are deployed throughout the organization and used to support organization-level review, decision-making, planning, and process improvement.
- In addition to using performance reviews to respond rapidly to changing organizational needs and challenges in the operating environment, the review may also help the applicant determine if there is any need for change in organizational structure and work systems.

Information and Knowledge Management

- This Item looks at how the organization verifies and ensures the quality and availability of its digital and other data and information. The data system must provide for and ensure data accuracy and validity (correctness), integrity (completeness) and reliability (consistency), and currency (timeliness).
- This Item examines how the organization ensures that data and information are available and accessible to workers, suppliers and partners, collaborators, and customers as needed to support decision-making. This Item also seeks to ensure that information technology systems (hardware and software) are reliable and available in a user-friendly format and timely manner. In many organizations, people with minimal

computer skills must be able to access and use data to support decision-making.

- This Item also looks at processes to build and manage organizational knowledge for use in innovation and strategic planning processes. It also focuses on the need to transfer workforce knowledge; blend and assimilate large data sets from diverse sources in order to build new knowledge, referred to by some as "big data"; share and implement best practices across the organization; and embed learning in the way the organization operates.

4.1 MEASUREMENT, ANALYSIS, AND IMPROVEMENT OF ORGANIZATIONAL PROCESS PERFORMANCE: How do you measure, analyze, and then improve organizational performance? (45 Pts.)

a. Performance Measurement

(1) **Performance Measures How do you track data and information on daily operations and overall organizational performance?** How do you

- select, collect, align, and integrate data and information to use in tracking daily operations and overall organizational performance; and
- track progress on achieving strategic objectives and action plans?

What are your key organizational performance measures, including key short- and longer-term financial measures?

(2) **Comparative Data How do you select comparative data and information to support fact-based decision-making?**

(3) **Measurement Agility How do you ensure that your performance measurement system can respond to rapid or unexpected organizational or external changes and provide timely data?**

b. Performance Analysis and Review

How do you review your organization's performance and capabilities? How do you use your key organizational performance measures, as well as comparative data, in these reviews? What analyses do you perform to support these reviews and ensure that conclusions are valid? How do your organization and its senior leaders use these reviews to

- assess organizational success, competitive performance, financial health, and progress on achieving your strategic objectives and action plans; and
- respond rapidly to changing organizational needs and challenges in your operating environment?

How does your governance board review the organization's performance and its progress on strategic objectives and action plans, if appropriate?

c. Performance Improvement

(1) **Future Performance How do you project your organization's future performance?** How do you use findings from performance reviews and key comparative and competitive data in your projections?

Continued

Continued

(2) **Continuous Improvement and Innovation How do you use findings from performance reviews to develop priorities for continuous improvement and opportunities for innovation?** How do you deploy these priorities and opportunities

- to work group and functional-level operations; and
- when appropriate, to your suppliers, partners, and collaborators to ensure organizational alignment?

Notes:

4.1. The questions in this Item are closely linked to each other and to other Criteria Items. The following are examples of key linkages:

- Your organizational performance measurement (4.1a)—including the comparative data and information you select, and the performance measures you report in your Criteria Item responses—should inform your organizational performance reviews (4.1b).
- Organizational performance reviews (4.1b) should reflect your strategic objectives and action plans (Category 2), and the results of organizational performance analysis and review should inform your strategy development and implementation, priorities for improvement, and opportunities for innovation (4.1c).
- Your performance projections for your key action plans should be reported in 2.2a(6).
- Your organizational performance results should be reported in Items 7.1–7.5.

4.1a. Data and information from performance measurement should be used to support fact-based decisions that set and align organizational directions and resource use at the work unit, key process, department, and organization levels.

4.1a(2). The comparative data and information you select should be used to support operational and strategic decision-making. Comparative data and information are obtained by benchmarking and by seeking competitive comparisons. Benchmarking is identifying processes and results that represent best practices and performance for similar activities, inside or outside your industry. Competitive comparisons relate your performance to that of competitors and other organizations providing similar products and services.

4.1a(3). Agility in your measurement system might be necessary in response to regulatory changes, other changes in the political or societal environment, disasters and emergencies, innovations in organizational processes or business models, new competitor offerings, or productivity enhancements. Responses to such changes might involve, for example, adopting different performance measures or adjusting the intervals between measurements.

4.1b. Performance analysis includes examining performance trends; organizational, industry, and technology projections; and comparisons, cause-effect relationships, and correlations. This analysis should support your performance reviews, help determine root causes, and help set priorities for resource use. Accordingly, such analysis draws on all types of data: product performance, customer-related, financial and market, operational, and competitive. The analysis should also draw on publicly mandated measures, when appropriate, and might also be informed by internal or external Baldrige assessments. Analysis may involve digital data analytics and data science techniques that detect patterns in large volumes of data ("big data") and interpret their meaning.

4.1b. Rapid response to changing organizational needs and challenges may include responding to the need for change in your organizational structure and work systems.

Comparison with the Health Care and Education Criteria

Item 4.1c(2), second bullet in both the Business and Health Care Criteria, asks how priorities for improvement and opportunities for innovation are deployed to your suppliers, partners, and collaborators to ensure organizational alignment. The Education Criteria adds feeder or receiving schools to this list.

Item 4.1, Measurement, Analysis, and Review of Organizational Performance, looks at the selection, collection, alignment, integration, analysis, and use of data and information in support of organizational decision-making, planning, and performance improvement. The processes and systems required by this Item provide a solid foundation for consistently good decision-making. These processes serve as a central collection and analysis point in an integrated performance measurement. These processes also enhance the organization's ability to anticipate and respond to rapid or unexpected organizational or external changes.

The first part of this Item, Performance Measurement [4.1a], requires the organization to select, collect, align, and integrate data and information to track daily operations and overall organizational performance; and track progress on achieving strategic objectives and action plans.

The frequency by which data are collected should be aligned with information needs to support decision-making. For example, the need to track progress on achieving strategic objectives and action plans should relate to timelines for accomplishing strategic milestones identified in Item 2.1b(1). Monthly strategic and operational progress reviews require at least monthly data collection and analysis.

Data alignment and integration are key concepts for successful implementation of the performance measurement system. Measures should be aligned to link key processes throughout the organization, integrated to yield organization-wide measures, and deployed by senior leaders to track workgroup and process-level performance on key measures of organization-wide success.

The organization should show how competitive comparisons and benchmarking data are selected and used to help drive performance improvement. The major reasons for using competitive and comparative information are (1) the organization needs to know where it stands relative to competitors and comparable organizations and best practices, especially as it works to achieve top levels of performance (which may be defined by a competitor or other provider); (2) comparative and benchmarking information often provides a focus for significant (breakthrough or innovative) improvement or change; (3) preparation for comparing performance information frequently leads to a better understanding of the organization's own processes and related performance; and (4) comparative performance projections and competitors' performance may reveal organizational challenges as well as the need for innovation. Benchmarking information also may support organization analyses and decisions relating to core competencies, and the potential need for forming partnership, collaboration, alliances, and outsourcing.

Effective selection of competitive comparisons and benchmarking information requires (1) determination of needs and priorities; and (2) criteria for seeking appropriate sources for comparisons—from within and outside the organization's industry and markets. Benchmarking or comparison data and information should be used to: (1) set stretch targets and to promote major or breakthrough improvements in areas most critical to the organization's competitive strategy; and (2) demonstrate the strengths or soundness of the organization's desired or actual performance outcomes.

The second part of this Item, Performance Analysis and Review [4.1b], looks at how the organization analyzes data to support decision-making, how leaders review performance and set priorities, and how performance results are used to drive the systematic evaluation and improvement of key processes throughout the organization.

Effective decision-making usually requires leaders to understand cause-effect relationships among and between processes and performance results. Process actions and their success or failure may have many resource implications.

High-performing organizations find it necessary to have systems in place that provide an effective analytical basis for decisions because resources for improvement are limited and cause-effect relationships are often unclear. Therefore, organizations must perform effective analyses to support senior leaders' assessments of all areas of performance and strategic planning. This includes assessment of current performance in addition to determining how well the organization is moving toward its desired future. Review findings should provide a reliable means to guide both improvement and opportunities for innovation that are tied to the organization's key objectives, success factors, and measures. The results of organizational-level analysis must be effectively communicated by leaders to support decision-making throughout the organization and to appropriate suppliers, partners, and key customers, and ensure those decisions are aligned with desired organizational results, strategic objectives, and action plans.

Effective analyses can help decision makers understand likely future consequences of a current action or process and may alert the leaders to the need for broad-based change in the organization structure, culture, and work systems.

Systematic processes must be in place for analyzing all types of data and to determine overall organizational health, including key organizational results, action plans, and strategic objectives. In addition, organizations must evaluate the effectiveness of their analytical processes and make improvements based on the evaluation.

Facts, rather than intuition, should be used to support most decision-making at all levels based on the analyses conducted to make sense out of the data collected. Organizations must provide an effective analytical basis for decisions because resources for improvement are limited and causality is often unclear. Analyses that organizations typically conduct to gain an understanding of performance and needed actions vary widely depending on the type of organization, size, competitive environment, and other factors. These analyses should be designed to help the organization's leaders understand the following types of issues as appropriate:

- The extent to which program, product, and service improvement drives customer satisfaction, customer engagement, customer retention, and market share
- The impact of customer-related problems and effective problem resolution on cost/revenue growth, repeat business, willingness to recommend, loyalty, and lost customers
- Market share changes related to customer gains and losses and changes in customer satisfaction, dissatisfaction, and engagement levels
- The impact of improvements in key operational performance areas such as productivity, cycle time, waste reduction, new-product introduction, rework, waste, and defect levels
- Relationships between personal and organizational learning (improvement processes) and cost reductions and value added per worker
- Financial benefits derived from improvements in workforce safety, absenteeism, and turnover
- Benefits and costs associated with education and training of all types, including e-learning and other distance learning methods
- Benefits and costs associated with improved organizational knowledge management and sharing of best practices
- The extent to which identifying and meeting workforce capability and capacity needs correlate with retention, motivation, and productivity
- Cost/revenue implications of workforce-related problems and effective problem resolution
- Individual or aggregate measures of productivity cost trends and quality relative to the performance of competitors or other providers
- Relationships among program/product/service quality, operational-performance indicators, and overall financial-performance trends as reflected in indicators such as operating costs, revenues, asset utilization, reserve fund balance, or value added per worker
- The impact of allocating resources among alternative improvement projects based on cost/benefit analyses and the pursuit of intelligent risk
- Determination of root causes of program, process, service, or product failure
- Net earnings (or cost-benefit ratios derived from quality, operational, and workforce performance improvements)
- The effect of improvement activities on cash flow, budget, available capital or fund reserves, and shareholder/stakeholder value
- Profit or revenue impacts of customer retention and loss
- Cost/revenue implications of entering or expanding into new markets

- Return on investment based on taking intelligent risks
- Market share versus profits/revenue
- Trends in economic, market, and shareholder indicators of value and the impact of these trends on organizational sustainability
- Comparisons among organizational units showing how quality and operational performance improvement affect financial performance

The availability of large amounts of data and information of many kinds (for example, financial, operational, customer-related, accreditation and regulatory), in many forms (such as printed, video, web-based, social media, and blogs) and from many sources (for example, internal, third party, and public sources, the internet, and behavioral tracking software) requires extensive analysis and correlations to extract useful information to support good decision-making. Effectively using and prioritizing such "big data" are important to the success—now and in the future—of top-performing organizations.

Senior leaders should use fact-based analysis and review findings to project the organization's future performance, identify potential performance shortfalls compared with future competitor performance, and drive improvement and innovation [4.1c]. This organizational review should cover all areas of performance, and provide a complete and accurate picture of the state of health of the organization. This includes not only how well the organization is currently performing but also how well it is changing to sustain or achieve future success.

- Key performance measures should focus on and reflect the key drivers of success such as those that relate to strategic objectives and action plans.
- Leaders should use these reviews to set priorities for focusing on improvement and change activities needed to achieve the organization's key objectives, success factors, and measures.
- Leaders should translate performance review findings into an action agenda, sufficiently specific for deployment throughout the organization and to suppliers and partners—the people who need to take action to improve.
- Effective performance review should help organizations identify best practices and lessons learned to share with units across the organization [see 4.2b(2)]. Information critical for improvement that is not known by others cannot be put to best use, making it difficult to embed learning in the way the organization operates and drive continuous improvement [see 4.2b(3)]. Improvement should be consistent and purposeful, not accidental.
- An analysis of historical performance, combined with assumptions about future internal and external changes and the performance of other organizations, allows the development of useful performance projections that are essential to effective strategic planning.

Organizational performance reviews will reveal excellent, adequate, and unacceptable levels of performance. These findings help leaders identify where additional evaluation and improvement of key work processes are most needed. This analysis should help leaders identify priorities and drive improvement in critical areas throughout the organization.

To demonstrate maturity, the Scoring Guidelines require that the organization has a system in place to improve and innovate the methods it uses to measure and analyze organizational performance and use this information to set and implement improvement priorities throughout the organization. The organization should evaluate these processes on a regular basis and demonstrate that it has made meaningful, value-added improvements in its techniques for measuring, analyzing, reviewing, sharing best practices, and improving organizational performance.

2021–2022 Criteria Elements Listed Individually Without Duplication See page 279 for explanation of this table			
	Basic Approach Elements [A-B] for Scoring Between 10% and 45%	**Additional Approach Elements at the Overall [A-O] Level for Scoring Between 50% and 65%**	**Additional Approach Elements at the Multiple Level [A-M] for Scoring Between 70% and 100%**
4.1 Measurement, Analysis, and Improvement of Organizational Performance			
4.1a(1)	Measure organizational performance	Use data and information to track daily operations and overall organizational performance	• Have an effective process to select, collect, align, and integrate data and information (which is also used to track daily operations and overall organizational performance) • Track progress on achieving strategic objectives and action plans • Describe the key organizational performance measures, including key short- and long-term financial measures
4.1a(2)		Select comparative data and information to support fact-based decision-making	
4.1a(3)		Ensure that the performance measurement system can respond to rapid or unexpected organizational or external changes and provide timely data	
4.1b	Analyze organizational performance	• Review the organization's performance • Review the organization's capabilities	• Use key organizational performance measures, as well as comparative data, in these reviews • Perform analyses to support these reviews • Ensure that conclusions of these reviews are valid • The organization and its senior leaders use these reviews to— – Assess organizational success, competitive performance, financial health, and progress on achieving the organization's strategic objectives and action plans – Respond rapidly to changing organizational needs and challenges in the operating environment • The governance board reviews the organization's performance and its progress on strategic objectives and action plans, if appropriate
4.1c(1)		Project the organization's future performance	Use findings from performance reviews and key comparative and competitive data in projecting future performance
4.1c(2)	Improve organizational performance	Use findings from performance reviews (addressed in 4.1b) to develop priorities for continuous improvement and opportunities for innovation	• Deploy the priorities for continuous improvement and opportunities for innovation— – To work group and functional-level operations – When appropriate, to suppliers, partners, and collaborators to ensure organizational alignment

4.1 Measurement, Analysis, and Improvement of Organizational Performance

Basic Approach Element: *Measure, analyze, and then improve organizational performance*

Overall Approach Elements:
- *Use data and information to track daily operations and overall organizational performance [4.1a(1)]*
- *Select and use comparative data and information [4.1a(2)]*
- *Ensure that performance measurement systems can respond to rapid or unexpected organizational changes [4.1a(3)]*
- *Review organizational performance and capabilities [4.1b]*
- *Project the organization's future performance [4.1c(1)]*
- *Use findings from performance reviews to develop priorities for continuous improvement and opportunities for innovation [4.1c(2)]*

The following diagram describes key approach elements:

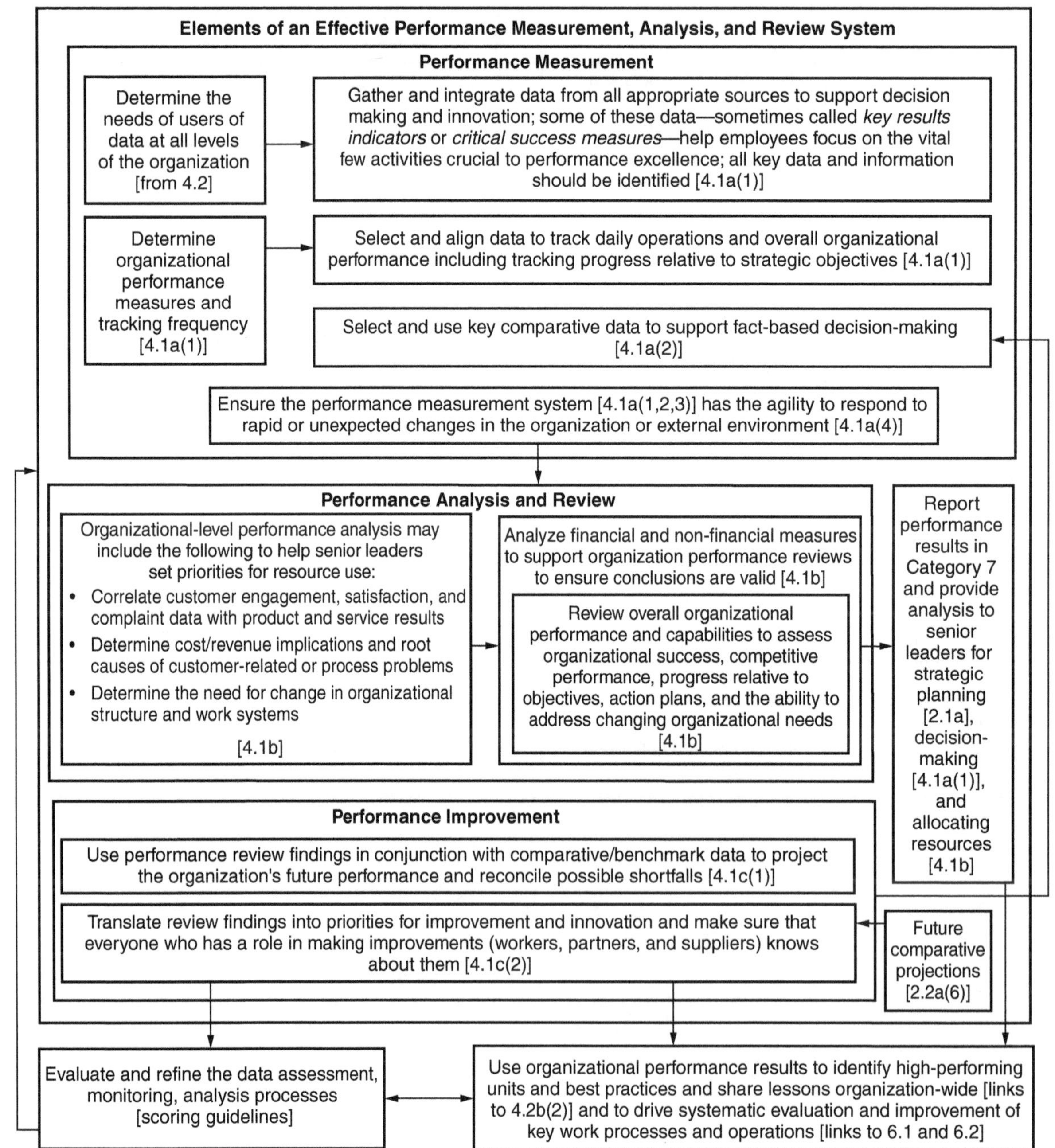

4.1 Key Measurement, Analysis, and Improvement of Organizational Performance Item Linkages

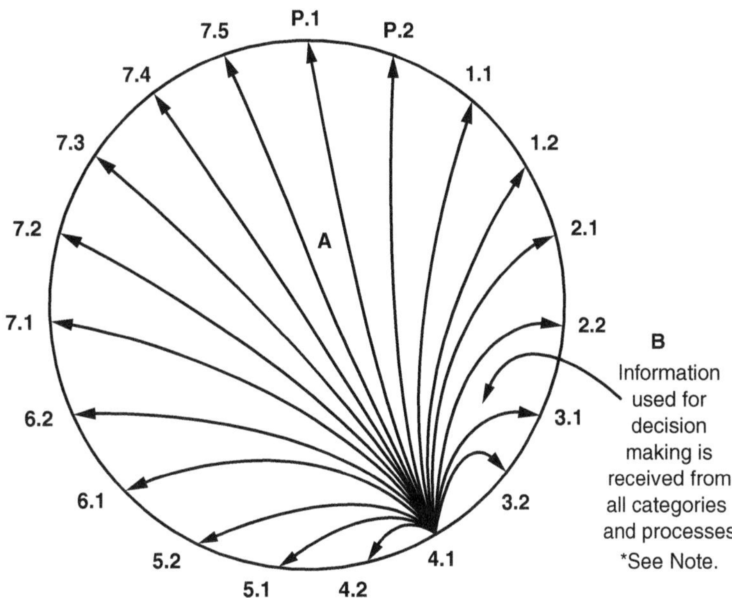

<table>
<tr><th colspan="2">NATURE OF RELATIONSHIP</th></tr>
<tr><td>A</td><td>Data and information are collected and analyzed [4.1] and made available [4.2] for developing the Organizational Profile [P.1 and P.2]; planning [2.1a]; setting strategic objectives [2.1b(1)]; day-to-day leadership and governance decisions [1.1 and 1.2]; setting and monitoring societal contributions standards (regulatory, legal, ethical) and for supporting community involvement [1.2b and 1.2c]; reporting performance results [7.1, 7.2, 7.3, 7.4, and 7.5]; designing, managing, and improving key work and operational processes [6.1 and 6.2]; assessing and managing workforce capacity and capability; workforce engagement and development [5.1 and 5.2]; listening to customers [3.1a]; determining customer experience and satisfaction, dissatisfaction, and engagement [3.2b]; and managing customer complaints and building customer relations [3.2a].</td></tr>
<tr><td>B</td><td>Data and information used to support analysis, decision-making, and continuous improvement [4.1] are received from all categories and processes. Customer satisfaction, dissatisfaction, and engagement data [7.2] are analyzed [4.1b] and used to help determine ways to assess customer requirements [3.2b(2)], to determine appropriate standards or required levels of customer support [3.2a(2)], and to design instruments to assess customer satisfaction, dissatisfaction, and engagement [3.2b(1, 2)]. Data and information are received from the following areas and analyzed to support decisions on capacity, capability, climate and workforce engagement and development, and equity and inclusion [5.1 and 5.2]. Data are aggregated and analyzed [4.1] to improve the design of work processes [6.1] and operational efficiency and improvement of key work processes [6.2] that will reduce cycle time, waste, and defect levels. Performance data from all parts of the organization are reviewed and analyzed [4.1b] to assess and help improve performance [4.1c(2)] in key areas such as product and process results [7.1], customer results [7.2], workforce results [7.3], leadership and governance results [7.4], and financial, market, and strategy results [7.5] relative to competitors or similar providers in all areas. Leaders at all levels use data to track daily operations, progress of strategic objectives and action plans [4.1a(1)], review organizational performance [4.1b], and understand relationships among performance, workforce engagement and satisfaction, customers, markets, and financial success. Leaders also use this information to support decision-making at all levels, to set priorities</td></tr>
</table>

Continued

NATURE OF RELATIONSHIP	*Continued*
	for action, project future performance, and identify opportunities for innovation [4.1c(2)]. Data are also used to focus improvements in key work processes and operations [6.1 and 6.2].

*Note: Because the information collected and used for decision-making links with all other Items, all of the linkage arrows will not be repeated on the other Item maps. Only the most relevant will be repeated.

IF YOU DON'T DO WHAT THE CRITERIA REQUIRE . . .

Item Reference	Possible Adverse Consequences
4.1a(1)	**Performance Measures** – The failure to select, gather, and align or integrate appropriate data and information from throughout the organization to track daily operations, support organizational decision-making, and track progress in achieving strategic objectives and action plans can create an environment where decisions are typically based on intuition or guesswork. Decisions based on intuition or guesswork tend to be highly variable and prone to error. Furthermore, in an environment where decisions are based on intuition it is usually the boss's intuition that drives the decision, which can lead to disengagement of the workers in the organization. Decisions made in this manner erode the organization's efforts to promote workforce initiative, innovation, and organizational agility [Item 1.1c(1)]. Finally, the failure to integrate data and information may make it difficult to monitor overall organizational performance. Disjointed, nonintegrated data are difficult to consolidate and report in a manageable, easy-to-understand dashboard to support effective decision-making.
4.1a(1)	**Performance Measures** – Data and information provide a basis for decision-making at all levels of the organization. Top leaders use the data to make decisions about the direction of the organization, and workers use data to make decisions about daily operational matters. Unless measures are selected and aligned to provide the right information, at the right time, and in the right format, the decisions of leaders and workers are likely to be sub-optimized. Moreover, although the failure to gather appropriate data tends to reduce decision-making quality, spending resources to gather data and information that do not support decision-making throughout the organization (useless data) adds unnecessary cost. It is difficult to collect the right data and information if the organization has failed to determine what data are needed to support decision-making at all levels. In addition, the failure to collect appropriate data and information makes it more difficult to monitor performance accurately [Item 4.1b], effectively communicate expectations throughout the organization [Item 1.1], and understand and implement actions needed to carry out strategy [Item 2.2a].
4.1a(2)	**Comparative Data** – The failure to collect and effectively use the right comparative data makes it difficult for the organization to learn from the best and take appropriate action to improve. Learning from the best helps provoke an understanding of what systems and processes may be required to make quantum leaps in performance as well as the levels that must be reached to achieve the leadership position projected during the planning process [Item 2.2a(6)]. For example, comparisons showing that the organization's projected performance outpaces the industrial average will have little meaning if the best competitor's rate of improvement is greater. Furthermore, if an organization collects comparative data from

Continued

IF YOU DON'T DO WHAT THE CRITERIA REQUIRE . . . *Continued*	
Item Reference	**Possible Adverse Consequences**
	world-class benchmarks [4.1a(2)], but does not effectively use those data to plan [Item 2.1a], to identify areas needing breakthrough performance, or to set priorities for innovation [Item 4.1c(2)], then it is simply wasting resources. If an organization does not collect comparative performance outcome data, it is not able to determine if its own rate of progress is sufficient to keep it ahead of the competition or evaluate the strength of its own performance results [required by Category 7].
4.1a(3)	**Measurement Agility** – Cumbersome data systems that do not keep pace with changes in the organization or in the external environment, may not provide the right information at the right time. The performance measurement system must be updated just as work processes, planning processes, leadership processes, and other key processes must keep pace with changes affecting organizational success.
4.1b	**Performance Analysis and Review** – Strategy identifies the outcomes that an organization must achieve to be successful in the future. Many actions must be taken in an organization to ensure strategic objectives are achieved. Performance analysis and review helps leaders and workers understand critical relationships between actions and outcomes to effectively achieve desired results. The failure to examine and understand the relationship between performance outcomes, action plans, and strategic objectives may cause senior leaders to make inappropriate decisions about the allocation of limited resources. This means that the organization may not realize the maximum benefit from the expenditure of those resources. For example, failing to understand the correlation between product and service quality improvement and improved customer satisfaction and retention may cause the leader to divert resources to less-important activities.
4.1b	**Performance Analysis and Review** – The lack of a system to analyze and make sense out of raw data may make it difficult for senior leaders to understand cause-and-effect relationships, root causes of problems, the impact of various processes on performance outcomes, and the need for change in organizational structure and work systems. This may make it more difficult for leaders to identify specific areas within the organization where improvement is required. It may send a message throughout the organization that performance outcomes are really not that important. If results are not important to top leaders, they may not be considered important at lower levels within the organization and workers at all levels may not contribute optimum effort to achieve these (unimportant) results. It also becomes more difficult for leaders to effectively set priorities. Consider the following examples: (1) without a cost–benefit analysis it is more difficult to determine whether project A or project B should receive support, because it is difficult to know which project is likely to be of greater benefit to the organization; (2) calculating C_{pk} (the capability of a process) helps leaders understand the extent to which their key processes are in control or need adjustment (the raw run data cannot support this kind of decision-making); and (3) failing to understand root causes makes it more difficult to prevent problems from recurring, which adds cost. The failure to understand the need for change in organizational culture, structure, or work systems may cause the leader to overlook key barriers to change and, therefore, not take all of the actions necessary to achieve desired outcomes.

Continued

IF YOU DON'T DO WHAT THE CRITERIA REQUIRE . . . *Continued*	
Item Reference	**Possible Adverse Consequences**
4.1c(1)	**Future Performance** – Accurately projecting the organization's future performance—combined with measurements of competitive future performance—is essential to determining if current performance is sufficient to sustain the organization, or if changes are needed. Without accurate projections of likely future performance, organizations may not have enough time to implement critical changes to become (and remain) successful.
4.1c(2)	**Continuous Improvement and Innovation** – Even if senior leaders have an effective process to review organizational performance, but do not effectively use these review findings to identify priorities for improvement and targets of innovation, they may not be providing appropriate focus and alignment throughout the organization and to affected suppliers and partners. This may make it difficult for workers, managers, partners, and suppliers to make the changes needed to correct problems or comply with the new priorities for improvement, contributing to wasted resources and performance failures. The longstanding failure to identify priorities for improvement or targets of innovation may contribute to the perception that the status quo is acceptable and continuous improvement is not important. This may further contribute to organizational stagnation and may make it difficult to keep pace with competitors and increasing customer requirements.
4.1c(2)	**Continuous Improvement and Innovation** – It is not enough to review performance results without taking steps to improve key processes that are underperforming. A key purpose of data and analysis is to support fact-based improvement to reduce guesswork and increase value and organization success.
Learning Scoring Guidelines	Organizations that fail to improve the speed and accuracy of decision-making typically do not perform well in a competitive environment. Without a process to evaluate the information system and how well it responds to organizational needs, leaders and members of the workforce may not know they are collecting insufficient or incorrect data and information. In addition, organizations may not know if the data effectively support daily operations and organizational decision-making. They may not know if the resources spent to collect benchmarking and comparison data produce appropriate benefits.

4.1 MEASUREMENT, ANALYSIS, AND IMPROVEMENT OF ORGANIZATIONAL PERFORMANCE—SAMPLE EFFECTIVE PRACTICES

a. Performance Measurement

- Above all, data and information are favored as a decision-making support tool, rather than a quick and easy reliance on intuition or gut feel.
- Data collected at the individual worker level are consistent across the organization to permit consolidation and organization-wide performance monitoring.
- The cost of (poor) quality (including rework, delay, waste, scrap, errors) and other financial concerns is measured for internal operations and processes and used to identify areas for improvement.
- Data are maintained on employee-related issues of engagement, empowerment, motivation, satisfaction, morale, safety, education and training, use of teams, and recognition and reward and used to identify areas for improvement.
- New sources of data, such as website queries and social media (Twitter, Facebook, blogs), support senior leader decision-making.
- A systematic process exists for data review and improvement, and standardization to support good decision-making. Training on the use of data systems is provided as needed.
- A systematic process is in place for identifying and prioritizing comparative information and benchmark targets. (Robert Camp and Greg Watson authored excellent books on best practices in benchmarking.)
- Research has been conducted to identify benchmark and best-in-class organization that may be competitors, similar providers, or non-competitors. Critical work and support processes are the subject of benchmarking. Activities that support the organization's goals and objectives, action plans, and opportunities for improvement and innovation, are the subject of benchmarking. Benchmarking also is applied to key products, services, customer satisfiers, suppliers, employees, and support operations.
- The organization reaches beyond its own business sector to conduct comparative studies on similar processes used by high-performing organizations in other sectors.
- Benchmark or comparison data are used to improve the understanding of work processes and to discover the best levels of performance that have been achieved. Based on this knowledge, the organization sets goals or targets to stretch performance as well as drive innovations.
- A systematic process is in place to improve the use of benchmark or comparison data in the understanding of all work processes.
- Performance management, and the data that support it, are treated as a major, value-added process to help maintain a marketplace advantage. It is a centerpiece of high performance, not an afterthought.

b. Performance Analysis and Review

- Systematic processes are in place for analyzing all types of data and to determine overall organizational health, including key organizational results, action plans, and strategic objectives. The organization continuously evaluates the effectiveness of the analysis process and improves upon it to make it more accurate and less costly.
- Fact-based analysis, rather than intuition, are used to support most decision-making at all levels based on the analyses conducted to make sense out of the data collected.
- The analysis process itself is analyzed to make the results more timely and useful for decision-making for quality improvement at all levels.
- Analysis processes and tools, and the value of analyses to decision-making, are systematically evaluated and improved.

- Analysis is linked to work groups to facilitate decision-making (sometimes daily) throughout the organization.
- Analysis techniques enable meaningful interpretation of the cost and performance impact of organization processes. This analysis helps workers at all levels of the organization make necessary trade-offs, set priorities, and reallocate resources to take intelligent risk and enhance overall organization performance.
- Reviews against measurable performance standards are held frequently to detect emerging problems early before they become serious.
- Senior leaders base their decisions on reliable data and facts pertaining to customers, operational processes, and worker performance and satisfaction.
- Senior leaders hold regular meetings to review performance results against strategy and action plans, and use this information to set priorities to resolve problems and evaluate and improve work processes.
- Senior leaders conduct monthly reviews of organizational performance. This review is supported by subordinates who conduct biweekly reviews, and workers and work teams that provide daily performance updates. Corrective actions are developed to improve performance that deviates from planned performance.

c. Performance Improvement

- Reviewing historical performance trajectories helps predict likely future performance outcomes. If projections show inadequate levels of future performance, the organization adjusts action plans, strategies, and resources.
- Customer, performance, and financial data drive priorities for organizational improvement and innovation when weaknesses are identified.
- Many processes throughout the organization have been improved or even innovated based on the analyses of the performance data. Tools such as Lean and Six Sigma are widely used.

Ineffective Practices

- Leaders' experience and intuition guide decision-making. They do not rely on facts and may even be threatened by or uncomfortable with the use of data and supporting analyses. Workers who use data to question the wisdom of decisions are not valued.
- Leaders persist in the belief that their organizations are unique (*"we are great"*) and find it a waste of time to seek best practices from other organizations.
- Intuition and opinions of the highest-ranking person in the room, not facts, guide decision-making at all levels.
- When performance declines, senior leaders meet to determine which subordinate to blame (a bad process is rarely seen as the root cause of a problem). No effective, fact-based analysis is conducted to uncover the true nature of the problem.
- Blind adherence to the status quo is demanded. Innovation is shunned.
- Blind adherence to leader dictates is demanded. No better method is possible.
- Meetings are filled with sentences beginning with, "I think … ," indicating a lack of data-based decision-making.

4.2 INFORMATION AND KNOWLEDGE MANAGEMENT: How do you manage your information and your organizational knowledge assets? (45 Pts.) PROCESS

a. Data and Information

(1) **Quality How do you verify and ensure the quality of organizational data and information?** How do you manage digital and other data and information to ensure their accuracy and validity, integrity and reliability, and currency?

(2) **Availability How do you ensure the availability of organizational data and information?** How do you make needed data and information available in a user-friendly format and timely manner to your workforce, suppliers, partners, collaborators, and customers, as appropriate? How do you ensure that your information technology systems are reliable and user-friendly?

b. Organizational Knowledge

(1) **Knowledge Management How do you build and manage organizational knowledge?** How do you

- collect and transfer workforce knowledge;
- blend and correlate data from different sources to build new knowledge;
- transfer relevant knowledge from and to customers, suppliers, partners, and collaborators; and
- assemble and transfer relevant knowledge for use in your innovation and strategic planning processes?

(2) **Best Practices How do you share best practices in your organization?** How do you identify internal and external organizational units or operations that are high performing? How do you identify best practices for sharing and implement them across your organization, as appropriate?

(3) **Organizational Learning How do you use your knowledge and resources to embed learning in the way your organization operates?**

Notes:

4.2a(2). Information technology systems include, for example, physical devices and systems; software platforms and applications; and externally based or shared information systems, such as those stored in the cloud or outside your organization's control.

4.2a(2). The security and cybersecurity of your information technology systems are addressed as part of your overall security and cybersecurity system in Item 6.2. That system involves managing and reducing risks to operational systems as well as to data and information.

4.2b(1). Building and managing organizational knowledge from different sources may involve handling big data sets and disparate types of structured and unstructured data and information, such as data tables, video, audio, photos, and text. Blending and correlating data may involve using artificial intelligence, digital data analytics, and data science techniques that detect patterns in large volumes of data and interpret their meaning. Using these techniques to make decisions with human consequences requires deploying technology and leveraging data in a way that protects information about organizations and individuals.

4.2b(3). Embedding learning in the way your organization operates means that learning (1) is a part of everyday work; (2) results in solving problems at their source; (3) is focused on building and sharing knowledge throughout your organization; and (4) is driven by opportunities to bring about significant, meaningful change and to innovate.

Item 4.2 examines how the organization ensures the availability of high-quality, timely data and information for all the workforce, suppliers, partners, collaborators, and customers. It also examines how the organization builds and manages its knowledge assets in a user-friendly format, especially as the sources of data and information grow. Top-performing organizations make data and information available and accessible when needed to all appropriate users. The organization's knowledge management systems must be reliable, facilitating full access, and encouraging routine use. The intent of building and managing knowledge assets is to improve organizational efficiency and effectiveness and to stimulate innovation.

As the sources of data and information and the number of users who need information within the organization grow, systems to manage information often require significant change and more resources. Top-performing organizations consider knowledge management as a strategic imperative. If the system cannot integrate data from many sources in a user-friendly manner, it will not be adequately used—intuition will prevail and a potential competitive advantage may be lost.

The organization's knowledge management system should provide for sharing workforce and organizational knowledge to avoid information isolation and maximize learning benefits. Leaders should determine what knowledge is critical for operations and then implement systematic processes for sharing this information.

The organization must provide the knowledge and information that people need to do their work; improve programs, processes, products, and services; keep current with changing needs and directions; and develop innovative solutions that add value for the customer and the organization. This Item addresses the properties necessary for data and information to meet user needs, including integrity (completeness—tells the whole story), reliability (consistency), accuracy (correctness), currency (available when needed), and appropriate levels of security and confidentiality (free from tampering and inappropriate access and release).

As with the other Items required for performance excellence, the organization must systematically evaluate and improve data-availability mechanisms, software, and hardware to keep them current with changing organizational needs and directions.

To demonstrate maturity, the Scoring Guidelines require that the organization has a system in place to improve and innovate the methods it uses to ensure data quality, security, and availability. The organization should evaluate these processes on a regular basis and demonstrate that is has made meaningful, value-added improvements in its techniques for managing knowledge and ensuring data quality, security, user friendliness, and availability.

2021–2022 Criteria Elements Listed Individually Without Duplication

See page 279 for explanation of this table

	Basic Approach Elements [A-B] for Scoring Between 10% and 45%	Additional Approach Elements at the Overall [A-O] Level for Scoring Between 50% and 65%	Additional Approach Elements at the Multiple Level [A-M] for Scoring Between 70% and 100%
4.2 Information and Knowledge Management			
4.2a(1)	Manage information	Verify and ensure the quality of organizational data and information	• Manage digital and other data and information to ensure its— – Accuracy – Validity – Integrity – Reliability – Currency
4.2a(2)		Ensure the availability of organizational data and information	• Make needed data and information available in a user-friendly format and timely manner to the workforce, suppliers, partners, collaborators, and customers, as appropriate • Ensure information technology systems are reliable and user-friendly
4.2b(1)	Manage organizational knowledge assets	Build ("manage" required at the Basic level) organizational knowledge	• Collect and transfer workforce knowledge • Blend and correlate data from different sources to build new knowledge • Transfer relevant knowledge from and to customers, suppliers, partners, and collaborators • Assemble and transfer relevant knowledge for use in innovation and strategic planning processes
4.2b(2)		Share best practices in the organization	• Identify high-performing internal and external organizational units or operations • Identify their best practices for sharing and implement them across the organization, as appropriate
4.2b(3)		Use knowledge and resources to embed learning in the way the organization operates	

4.2 Information and Knowledge Management

Basic Approach Element: *Manage information and organizational knowledge assets*

Overall Approach Elements:
- *Verify and ensure the quality of organizational data and information [4.2a(1)]*
- *Ensure the availability of organizational data and information [4.2a(2)]*
- *Build and manage organizational knowledge [4.2b(1)]*
- *Share best practices organization-wide [4.2b(2)]*
- *Use knowledge and resources to embed learning in the way the organization operates [4.2b(3)]*

The following diagram describes key approach elements:

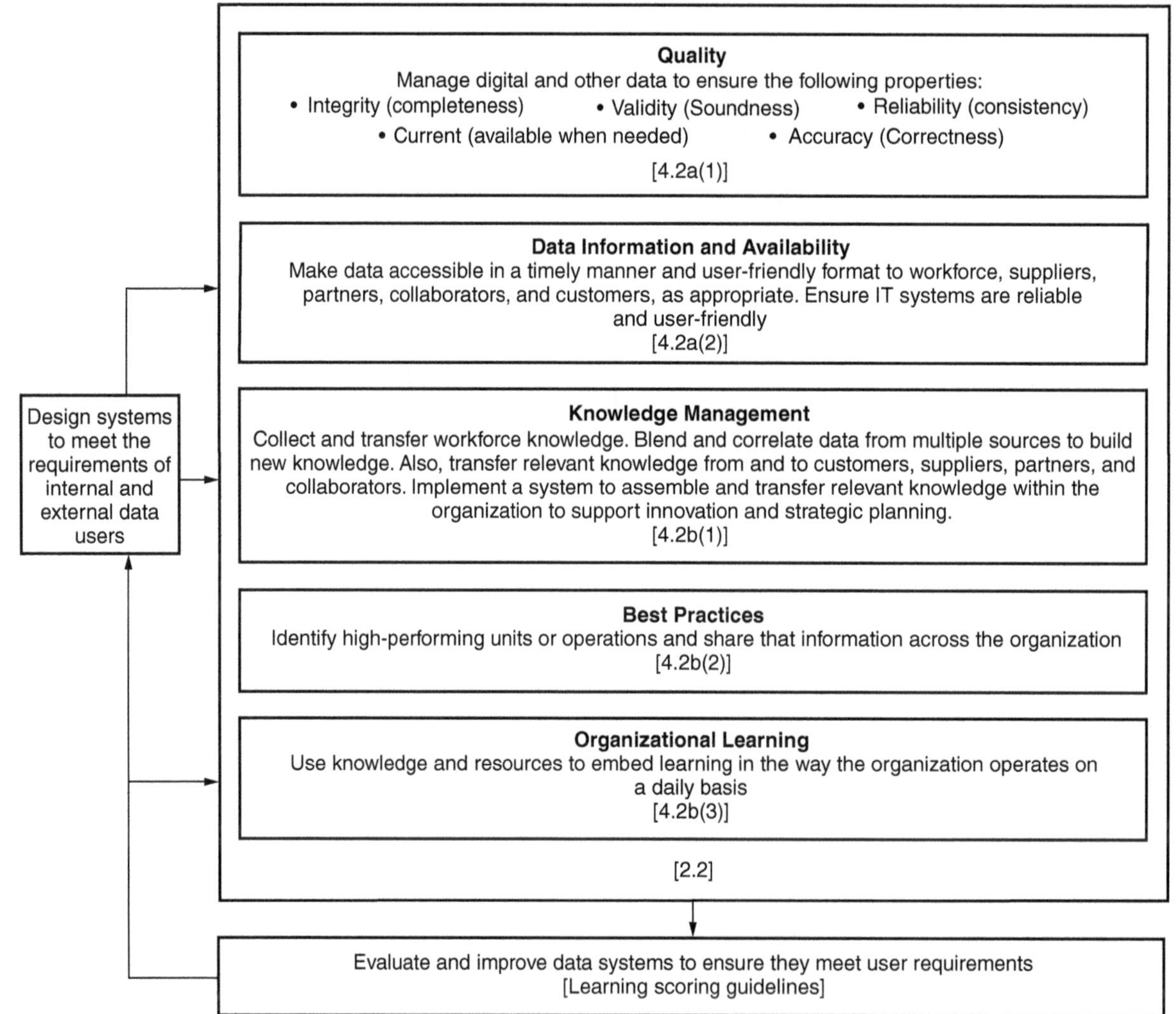

4.2 Key Information and Knowledge Management Item Linkages

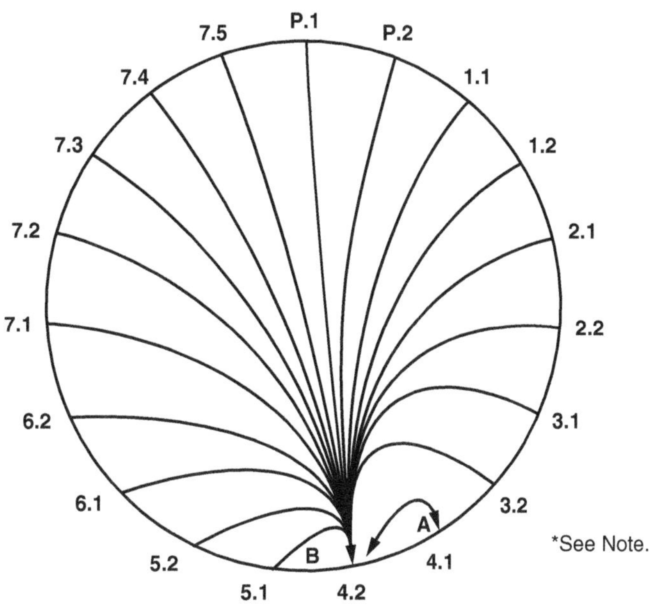

	NATURE OF RELATIONSHIP
A	Knowledge Management and Information [4.2] promotes proper data flow to internal and external users and indirectly interacts with all other Items (similar to the relationships identified and reported in the Item 4.1 diagram). These relationships tie this Item [4.2] with the Measurement, Analysis, and Improvement of Organizational Performance Item [4.1].
B	To ensure that data and information are accurate, valid, reliable, current, user-friendly, and demonstrate integrity [4.2], information from the following types of system users is gathered: leaders [Category 1]; planners [Category 2]; customer relationships and support staff [Category 3]; information specialists [Category 4]; human resource personnel, managers, and workers [Category 5]; operations workers, managers, suppliers, and partners [Category 6]; and people who monitor and interpret results [Category 7] for use in decision-making. The processes to ensure data security and cybersecurity in 6.2 are used to protect the information system [4.2].

*Note: Because the information collected and used for decision-making links with all other Items, all of the linkage arrows will not be repeated on the other Item maps. Only the most relevant will be repeated.

IF YOU DON'T DO WHAT THE CRITERIA REQUIRE . . .	
Item Reference	**Possible Adverse Consequences**
4.2a(1)	**Quality** – Decisions that are based on data and information may be compromised if the data are inaccurate or unreliable. For example, when a data-entry error is made and goes unnoticed ("garbage in"), it could drive decisions to deliver the wrong product at the wrong time to the wrong customer ("garbage out"). At the very least this may cause the product to be returned and restocked, adding cost but not value. The lack of current, timely information may cause decisions to be delayed. Consider, for example, an organization that conducts an employee (or customer) satisfaction survey but does not analyze or make the data available for many months. This not only sends a message to the organization that employee (or customer) concerns are unimportant, it also makes it difficult to identify real problems that may be contributing to customer dissatisfaction, low worker morale, and poor productivity.
4.2a(2)	**Availability** – Getting the right information to the right people at the right time and in the right format is essential to support effective decision-making. Just as different types of workers in an organization need different data to support decision-making, they may need to access information in different ways. Similarly, customers and suppliers may need access to information to facilitate ordering and delivery of required products and services. The failure to provide appropriate access to data may make it more difficult for workers to make timely decisions about their work; for customers to comment, complain, seek information, or obtain products and services; or for suppliers to ensure the smooth flow of materials to support the organization's product and service delivery. Providing inappropriate access for individuals inside or outside the organization may compromise data confidentiality and security or even violate certain privacy laws.
4.2b(1)	**Knowledge Management** – Knowledge is of little or no use unless the people who need it, have it. Knowledge sequestered in one corner of an organization cannot benefit the entire organization unless it is transferred to other employees in other units. The same is true for knowledge held by key customers, suppliers, and partners and collaborators. Knowledge withheld is knowledge (and resources) wasted. The failure to capture and transfer knowledge from long-standing employees who depart or retire is especially troublesome because they typically possess vast amounts of institutional memory.
4.2b(2)	**Best Practices** – Workers and managers at all levels of the organization need to see examples of good performance to serve as examples for their own improvement. The failure to ensure that people at every level share information on best practices—as well as what practices to avoid—makes it more difficult for them to identify and understand what they need to do to perform at certain agreed levels and why change may need to occur. Without this information, workers and managers throughout the organization must rely on intuition or incomplete data to support decision-making—typically reducing the accuracy of those decisions and, in some cases, sub-optimizing the overall performance of the organization.
4.2b(3)	**Organizational Learning** – Fact-based evaluation and subsequent meaningful improvement (learning) constitute the cornerstone of high performance, success, and long-term sustainability. The requirement is embedded in the scoring guidelines for all Process Items in Categories 1–6. Category 4, as the brain center for the Integrated Management System, provides the locus of control for fact-based evaluation, decision-making, improvement, and innovation. The failure to embed learning in the way the organization operates adversely

Continued

IF YOU DON'T DO WHAT THE CRITERIA REQUIRE . . . *Continued*	
Item Reference	**Possible Adverse Consequences**
	affects the likelihood the organization can keep pace with rapidly changing requirements and achieve a leadership position, let alone sustain it. The lack of ongoing fact-based evaluation and improvement will prevent the organization from optimizing its performance.
Learning Scoring Guidelines	In a rapidly changing world, access to information and the use of that information to provide insight and help decision-making can provide a strategic advantage. Rapid data availability is becoming more and more critical for organizational success, especially in e-commerce situations. In some industries such as banking, a few seconds can make the difference between capitalizing on currency rate fluctuations or being hurt by them. As product and delivery cycle times grow shorter, the need for rapid access to information grows greater. Without evaluating the quality and availability of data and information, and making refinements based on this evaluation, the organization leaves itself open to falling behind and not being able to respond rapidly to changing business needs and directions. Meaningful improvements and innovation should help support emerging business needs and customer expectations—as a means to an end, not the end itself.

4.2 INFORMATION AND KNOWLEDGE MANAGEMENT—SAMPLE EFFECTIVE PRACTICES

a. Data and Information

- A data reliability (consistency) team periodically and randomly checks data. Systems are in place to minimize or prevent human error in data entry and analysis.
- Users of data help determine what data systems are developed and how data are accessed.
- Every person has access to the data they need to make decisions about their work, from top leaders to individual workers or teams of workers.
- Procedures required to interface with the hardware and software are designed to meet the needs and capabilities of all computer users, to ensure that no one is excluded.
- Disciplined and automatic file backup occurs. Backup data are stored in secure, external facilities.

b. Organizational Knowledge

- A data and knowledge exchange is in place to receive useful knowledge and information from customers, suppliers, partners and key collaborators. The system is automated for easy update and access. Face-to-face and digital meetings (such as Zoom) are held regularly to share information.
- All key work processes are documented and stored in a searchable and accessible database and used to share best-practice improvements and avoid rework associated with reinventing effective processes.
- A *sunset* review is conducted to determine what data no longer need to be collected and can be eliminated.
- Data systems are benchmarked against best-in-class systems and continually refined.
- The performance measurement system is systematically evaluated and refined. Improvements are made to reduce cycle time for data collection and to increase data access, reliability, and ease of use.

- Formal processes are in place to solicit and reward the identification and sharing of best practices. The use of a formal data bank in which all key processes are mapped and shared through key word searches is widespread.
- Formal programs exist to recognize and reward best practices using independent judges and evaluators. All potential best-practice nominations receive on-site verification to ensure the practice performs as expected and is likely to benefit others who adopt it.

Ineffective Practices

- Access to relevant data and information is restricted by leaders and supervisors to enhance their own perceived worth and limit contributions that subordinates might make.
- Workers do not have the information or authority they need to complete their work. It takes too long to get the approvals for data access no matter how urgent or recurrent the need.
- Large amounts of useless data are required to be collected, without determining their purpose or how the data support decision-making.
- Once data are collected, it is difficult to stop collecting. No process exists to determine if the data are still useful or to terminate the collection of data deemed useless. Resources are wasted on collecting, reviewing, analyzing, and reporting useless data.
- Data systems are outdated and hard to use. Those who need to use the data systems are rarely, if ever, asked how the system could meet their needs better.
- New data systems are put in place before they are tested, debugged, validated, or understood by users. An especially ineffective practice is to convert data and information to a new system and have no other way to access them.
- Incomplete, inaccurate, and unreliable data are used because decision makers like the answers that these data produce.
- The information technology (IT) group makes software and hardware decisions without regard for user requirements or preferences.

5 Workforce—85 Points

*The **Workforce** Category asks how your organization assesses workforce capability and capacity needs and builds a workforce environment that is conducive to high performance. The Category also asks how your organization engages, manages, and develops your workforce to utilize its full potential in alignment with your organization's overall business needs.*

Workforce addresses key workforce practices—those directed toward creating and maintaining a high-performance work environment and toward engaging the workforce to enable it and the organization to adapt to change and to succeed. This Category covers the organization's capability and capacity needs and the workforce support climate. This Category also looks at workforce engagement, development, and management, which should be aligned with the organization's strategic objectives and action plans, particularly the workforce plans set forth in Item 2.2a(4).

Workforce Environment

- Assess workforce capacity and capability to accomplish the work of the organization.
- Recruit, hire, and onboard new employees to meet the organization's capability and capacity needs and ensure the fit of new workforce members with the organization's culture.
- Prepare the workforce for changing capability and capacity needs, including changes in organizational structure, workplaces, work systems, and technology. Prepare for periods of workforce growth and minimize the impact of necessary reductions.
- Organize and manage the workforce to accomplish the organization's work and exceed performance expectations to capitalize on core competencies and reinforce organizational resilience, agility, and a customer and business focus.
- Ensure workplace health, security, and accessibility.
- Support the workforce through services, benefits, and policies that are tailored to the needs of a diverse workforce.

Workforce Engagement

- Determine the key drivers that promote workforce engagement—helping workers contribute their utmost to the success of the organization and its customers.
- Assess workforce engagement and identify and implement improvements that promote higher levels of workforce performance and better organizational results.
- Foster a culture that supports open communication, high-performance work, and an engaged workforce. Empower the workforce. Promote workforce equity and inclusion.
- Provide a performance management system that supports high performance and that considers workforce compensation, reward, recognition, and incentives.
- Develop the workforce, managers, and leaders.

5.1 WORKFORCE ENVIRONMENT: How do you build an effective and supportive workforce environment? (40 Pts.) PROCESS

a. Workforce Capability and Capacity

(1) **Capability and Capacity Needs How do you assess your workforce capability and capacity needs?** How do you assess the skills, competencies, certifications, and staffing levels you need in the short and long term?

(2) **New Workforce Members How do you recruit, hire, and onboard new workforce members?** How do you ensure that your workforce represents the diversity of ideas, cultures, and thinking in your hiring and customer communities? How do you ensure the fit of new workforce members with your organizational culture?

(3) **Workforce Change How do you prepare your workforce for changing capability and capacity needs?** How do you

- balance the needs of your workforce and your organization to ensure continuity, prevent workforce reductions, and minimize the impact of any necessary reductions;
- prepare for and manage any periods of workforce growth; and
- prepare your workforce for changes in organizational structure, workplaces, work systems, and technology when needed?

(4) **Work Accomplishment How do you organize and manage your workforce?** How do you organize and manage your workforce to:

- capitalize on your organization's core competencies,
- reinforce organizational resilience, agility, and a customer and business focus; and
- exceed performance expectations?

b. Workplace Climate

(1) **Workplace Environment How do you ensure workplace health, security, and accessibility for the workforce?** What are your performance measures and improvement goals for your workplace environmental factors?

(2) **Workforce Benefits and Policies How do you support your workforce via services, benefits, and policies?** How do you tailor these to the needs of a diverse workforce and different workforce groups and segments?

Notes:

5. Results related to workforce environment and engagement should be reported in Item 7.3. People supervised by a contractor should be addressed in Categories 2 and 6 as part of your larger work system strategy and your internal work processes. For organizations that also rely on volunteers, workforce includes these volunteers. Workforce approaches should include these volunteers as appropriate to the functions they fulfill for the organization.

5.1a. Your assessment of workforce capability and capacity needs should consider not only current needs, but also future requirements based on the strategic objectives and action plans you identify in Category 2 and the future performance you discuss in 4.1c(1).

5.1a(3). Preparing your workforce for change might include preparing for alternate workplaces or telework, or for changes in customer or product requirements that lead to the use of new technology or redesigned work systems. Such preparation might include training, education, frequent communication, consideration of workforce employment and employability, career counseling, and outplacement and other services.

5.1a(3) 5.1a(4). The way you organize and manage your workforce may be influenced by changes in your internal or external environment, culture, or strategic objectives.

Continued

Continued

5.1b(1). Workplace accessibility maximizes productivity by eliminating barriers that can prevent people with disabilities from working to their potential. A fully inclusive workplace is physically, technologically, and attitudinally accessible without bias.

5.1b(1). If workplace environmental factors and their performance measures or targets differ significantly for your different workplace environments, you should include these differences in your response. You should address workplace safety in Item 6.2 as part of your overall safety system, which also ensures the safety of all other people who may be in your workplace.

Item 5.1 looks at the organization's workforce environment, the workforce capacity and capability needs, and how those needs are met so that the work of the organization is accomplished. This Item also looks at systems the organization has in place to provide the workforce with a healthy, secure, and accessible work climate. The goal is an effective environment that supports the workforce and is conducive to accomplishing the organization's work in the short and long term. The workforce includes permanent, temporary, part-time, and full-time personnel in all positions, volunteers, paid or unpaid interns, and contract personnel supervised by people internal to the organization.

Organizations must recruit, hire, and onboard new workers with the skills needed to perform the organization's work and ensure they fit with the organizational culture.

As the pool of skilled talent continues to shrink, it becomes more important than ever for organizations to define specifically the capabilities and skills needed by potential employees and create a work environment to attract them. Accordingly, it is critical to take into account characteristics and needs of diverse populations to make sure appropriate support systems exist that make it possible to attract skilled workers.

The workforce should not only reflect the diversity of the hiring community but also the customer community. By failing to reflect the customer community, the workforce may find it more difficult to develop and support strong customer relationships and customer engagement.

Especially in times of change, the organization should prepare its workforce to ensure continuity, prevent workforce reductions, and minimize the impact of these reductions should they become necessary. Similarly, the organization should prepare for periods of workforce growth and needed changes in organizational structure and work systems [links to 2.1a(4)].

The organization should organize and manage its workforce to enable it to exceed performance expectations. Hierarchical command-and-control management styles work against agility and high-performance capability. Agility and resilience reflect the speed with which employees and the organization do their work, including rapid response to changing needs and requirements. Organizations that are bogged down with bureaucratic inefficiencies, such as micromanaging leaders, cannot be agile. Unnecessary layers of management approval add delay and cost but not value.

All organizations are required to meet minimum regulatory standards for workplace health, security, and accessibility; however, high-performing organizations have processes in place to ensure they not only meet these minimum standards but also go beyond simple compliance. This includes designing proactive processes, with workplace health, security, and accessibility factors identified by people directly involved in the work. These organizations identify appropriate measures and goals for key workplace factors to ensure compliance and track progress toward these goals. The organization should show how it includes such factors in its planning and improvement activities. Organizations should also recognize that diverse workers and work groups might experience very different environments and need different services to ensure these workplace conditions are met.

The organization must provide appropriate services, benefits, and policies to enhance worker well-being, satisfaction, and motivation. The best organizations develop a holistic view of the workforce as key stakeholders. Most organizations have many opportunities to support their workforce. The best-performing organizations use a variety of approaches to satisfy a diverse workforce with differing needs and expectations in order to reduce attrition and increase motivation and engagement.

Ensuring workplace accessibility helps optimize productivity by eliminating barriers that inhibit workers from achieving their full potential. A fully accessible workplace addresses physical, technological, and attitudinal barriers.

Examples of services, benefits, and policies to support the workforce include: personal and career counseling; career development and employability services; recreational or cultural activities; formal and informal recognition; non-work-related education; day care; special leave for family responsibilities or for community service; home safety training; flexible work hours and benefits packages; outplacement services; and retiree benefits, including extended health care and ongoing access to services. Also, these services might include career-enhancement activities such as skills assessments, helping individuals develop learning objectives and plans, and conducting employability assessments.

As the workforce becomes more diverse (including workers who may work in other countries for multinational companies), it becomes more important to consider and support those with different needs.

To demonstrate maturity, the Scoring Guidelines require that the organization has a system in place to improve and innovate its workforce environment processes. The organization needs to evaluate and improve these processes more often than annually. The organization should demonstrate that it has made meaningful, value-added improvements in its techniques for providing a beneficial workforce environment.

2021–2022 Criteria Elements Listed Individually Without Duplication

See page 279 for explanation of this table

	Basic Approach Elements [A-B] for Scoring Between 10% and 45%	Additional Approach Elements at the Overall [A-O] Level for Scoring Between 50% and 65%	Additional Approach Elements at the Multiple Level [A-M] for Scoring Between 70% and 100%
5.1 Workforce Environment			
5.1a(1)		Assess workforce capability and capacity needs	Assess the skills, competencies, certifications, and staffing levels needed by the organization in the short and long term
5.1a(2)		Recruit, hire, and onboard new workforce members	• Ensure the workforce represents the diversity of ideas, cultures, and thinking of the organization's hiring and customer communities • Ensure the fit of new workforce members with the organizational culture
5.1a(3)		Prepare the workforce for changing capability and capacity needs	• Balance the workforce and its needs with the organization's needs to ensure continuity, prevent workforce reductions, and minimize the impact of any necessary reductions • Prepare for and manage any periods of workforce growth • Prepare the workforce for changes in organizational structure, workplaces, and work systems, and technology when needed
5.1a(4)		Organize and manage the workforce	Specifically, organize and manage the workforce to— • Capitalize on the organization's core competencies, • Reinforce organizational resilience, agility, and a customer and business focus, and • Exceed performance expectations
5.1b(1)	Build an effective workforce environment	Ensure workplace health, security, and accessibility for the workforce	Describe performance measures and improvement goals for workplace environmental factors
5.1b(2)	Build a supportive workforce environment	Support the workforce via services, benefits, and policies	Tailor these to the needs of a diverse workforce and different workforce groups and segments

5.1 Workforce Environment

Basic Approach Element: Build an effective and supportive workforce environment.

Overall Approach Elements:
- *Assess workforce capability and capacity needs [5.1a(1)]*
- *Recruit, hire, and onboard new workforce members [5.1a(2)]*
- *Prepare the workforce for changing capability and capacity needs [5.1a(3)]*
- *Organize and manage the workforce [5.1a(4)]*
- *Ensure workplace health, security, and accessibility for the workforce [5.1b(1)]*
- *Support the workforce via services, benefits, and policies [5.1b(2)]*

The following diagram describes key approach elements:

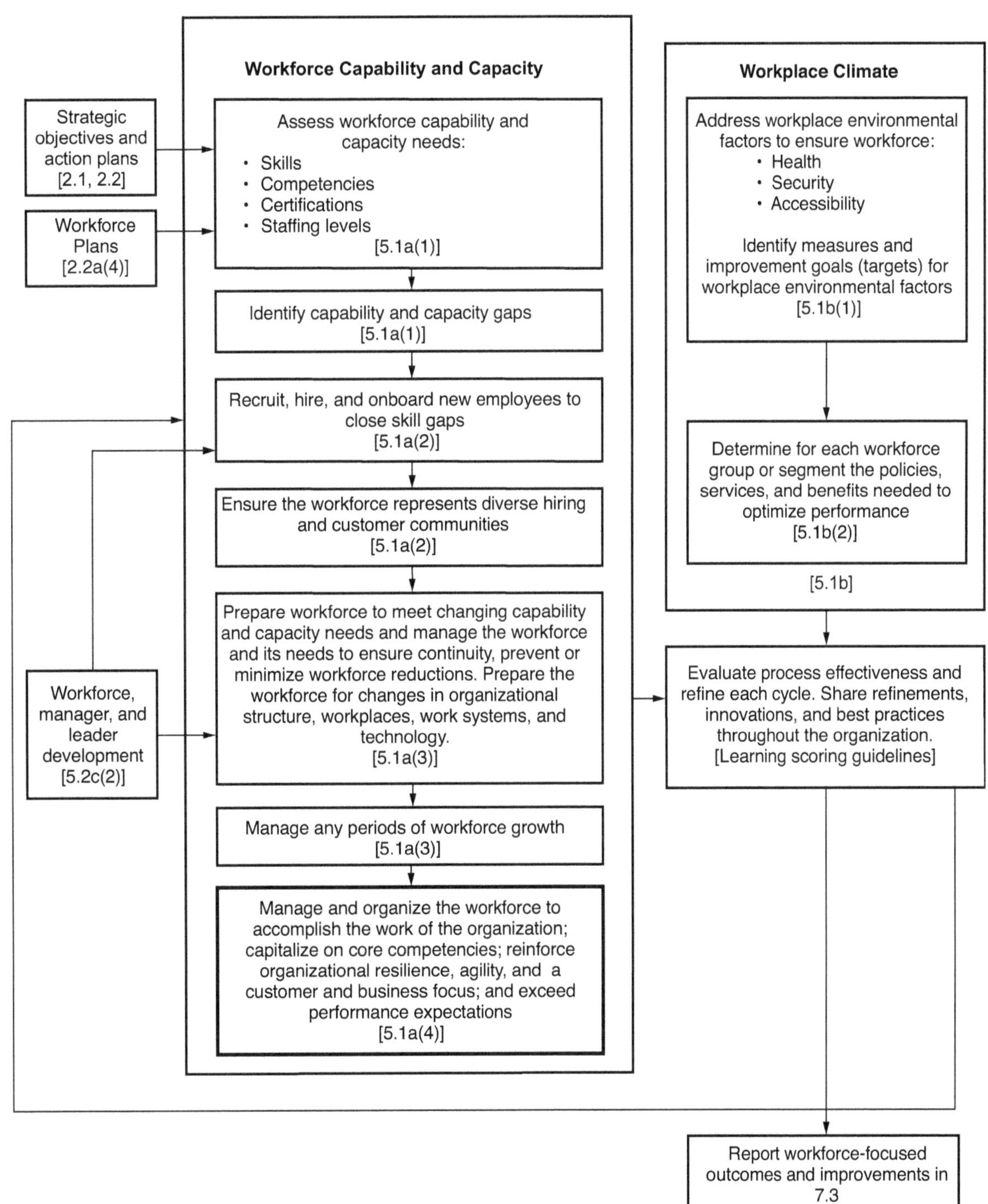

5.1 Key Workforce Environment Item Linkages

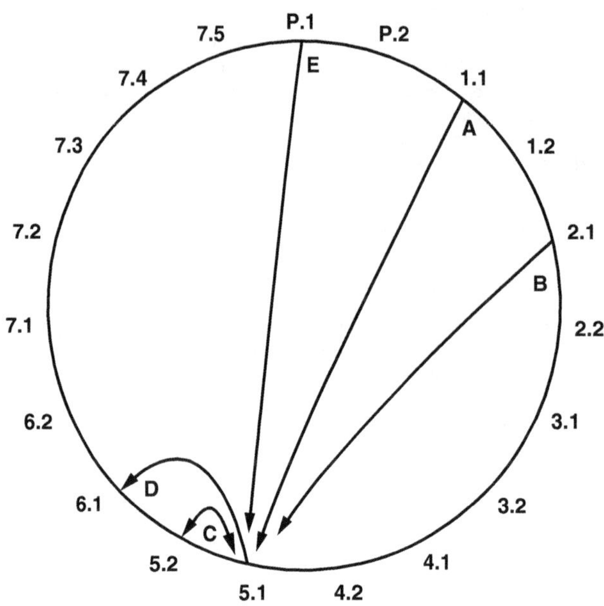

NATURE OF RELATIONSHIP	
A	Leaders [1.1c(1)] are responsible for creating a successful organization now and into the future, which requires a workforce with sufficient capability and capacity [5.1a], and effective systems to enhance workforce health, security, and accessibility [5.1b(1)]. Leaders [1.1b] must also communicate key decisions to motivate the workforce to reinforce organizational resilience, agility, high performance, and customer and business focus.
B	Workforce development plans [2.2a(4)] typically address or set the context for a healthy and secure work environment [5.1b(1)], future capacity and capability requirements [5.1a(1)], hiring targets [5.1a(2)], and preventing workforce reductions, managing periods of workforce growth, minimizing the impact of workforce reductions and preparing for changes in organizational structure and work systems as needed [5.1a(3)].
C	A strong work climate with excellent policies and benefits [5.1b(2)] can enhance employee engagement, initiative (self-direction), and innovation [5.2]; and strong workforce engagement enhances the work climate.
D	A secure, healthful, and accessible work environment [5.1b(1)] contributes to better process management and higher performance and productivity with fewer errors and rework [6.1 and 6.2]. Workers who possess the right skills (capabilities) in sufficient numbers (capacity) [5.1a] accomplish the work of the organization [6.1 and 6.2] more optimally.
E	Workforce characteristics such as changes in workforce composition or workforce needs, educational requirements of different workforce groups, workforce and job diversity, and other special requirements [P.1a(3)] help set the context for determining appropriate needs by workforce segment [5.1b(1)]. Employee characteristics such as educational requirements, workforce and job diversity, the existence of bargaining units, the use of contract employees, and other special requirements [P.1a(3)] may help set the context for tailoring benefits and services for the workforce according to its diverse types and categories [5.1b(2)].

IF YOU DON'T DO WHAT THE CRITERIA REQUIRE . . .	
Item Reference	**Possible Adverse Consequences**
5.1a(1)	**Capability and Capacity Needs** – Skill mapping is a process that many high-performing organizations use to compare the skills it needs to achieve strategic objectives with the skills its workforce currently possesses (capacity/capability). When a skill gap is identified, organizations are able to more effectively make better decisions as to whether they need to recruit, hire, reorganize, or train appropriate employees. The failure to identify the needed workforce capability and capacity levels, including skills, competencies, certifications, and staffing levels, increases the likelihood of not having appropriate staff in the right places when needed. When critical personnel shortages exist within an organization, it is frequently unable to achieve key objectives.
5.1a(2)	**New Workforce Members** – In a competitive labor market, slowness in recruiting and inefficiencies in hiring and onboarding workers in jobs may introduce delays that allow competitors to hire the best talent before the organization can act. Inefficient recruitment and bureaucratic bungling in the hiring process also provide a glimpse of the true management system and can scare off the best prospective employees. In addition, the hiring process represents a terrific opportunity to attract and hire workers with diverse ideas and cultures that fit within the organizational culture, without which it will be difficult to capitalize on diverse ideas, cultures, and thinking. This in turn may limit the ability of the organization's workforce to be engaged, innovative, resilient, agile, and empowered. Productivity suffers, as does the organization's ability to meet the challenges of today's highly competitive environment.
5.1a(2)	**New Workforce Members** – The failure to ensure the workforce reflects the customer communities makes it more difficult to build strong relationships with customers and promote solid customer engagement. This may erode customer confidence and loyalty.
5.1a(3)	**Workforce Change** – An organization that fails to prepare workers for changing capability and capacity needs, including potential changes in staffing levels, may threaten the sustainability of the organization and waste significant resources. This waste can be classified into two categories: (1) the failure to develop existing potential and take advantage of it; and (2) the failure to use skills and abilities that already exist. Workers usually recognize when their skills are underused and their productivity suffers further erosion, or they seek job opportunities outside the organization where they can develop and advance more fully, or both. Training workers in multiple jobs, rotational assignments, and job sharing provide more flexibility among workers to meet organizational needs and maintain job security when cutbacks are unavoidable. Also, preparing workers to meet future needs enhances their agility and engagement.
5.1a(4)	**Work Accomplishment** – The alignment of strategic objectives and the work to accomplish them is vital to the success and optimal performance of the organization. Once strategic objectives, timelines [2.1b(1)], and related actions [2.2a(1, 2, 4)] have been developed and implemented at all levels of the organization, leaders and managers can more effectively organize the workforce to perform the necessary work. In addition, appropriate responsibilities, authorities, and other tasks should be defined to ensure the actions are aligned (consistent) at all levels and effectively carried out. If the organization and management of the workforce are not aligned to support core competencies, strategic objectives, and related actions, the organization may waste resources by failing to optimize the work that is done and may fail to meet business needs.

Continued

IF YOU DON'T DO WHAT THE CRITERIA REQUIRE . . . *Continued*	
Item Reference	**Possible Adverse Consequences**
5.1b(1)	**Workplace Environment** – The failure to provide a healthy and secure workplace may increase accidents and illness, reduce employee effectiveness, and negatively impact morale and motivation. Poor working conditions, including poor accessibility, distract the workforce, reduce productivity, and increase errors, rework, cycle time, and waste, to name a few. If significant variation exists in the work environment for different employee groups or work units, employees may face different workplace issues. For example, carpal tunnel syndrome may be a problem for those who do substantial keyboarding but not for workers on the shop floor. Those workers may be more concerned about injury from lifting heavy objects. Accordingly, the failure to define performance measures and establish targets for each key environmental factor and each diverse employee group increases the likelihood the problems will go unnoticed and those employees will be distracted from their work, suboptimizing performance.
5.1b(2)	**Workforce Benefits and Policies** – Just as different workforce groups may have different needs for safety, different groups of workers may need different support services and benefits to keep them from being distracted in their work. When an organization fails to identify and tailor benefits, policies, and services to the needs of its diverse workforce, it may reduce optimum workforce participation and performance. Suboptimum workforce performance hurts productivity, customer satisfaction, and profitability.

5.1 WORKFORCE ENVIRONMENT—SAMPLE EFFECTIVE PRACTICES

a. Workforce Capability and Capacity

- Managers and workers conduct systematic needs analyses to ensure that skills required to perform work are routinely assessed, monitored, and maintained.
- Managers use cross-functional work teams to break down barriers, improve effectiveness, and meet goals.
- Although lower-performing organizations use teams for special improvement projects (while the regular work is performed using traditional approaches), higher-performing organizations use teams and self-directed workers as the way regular work is done. Self-directed or self-managed work teams are used throughout the organization. They have authority over matters such as budget, hiring, and team membership and roles.
- Worker skill mapping is in place to define current skills compared to an analysis of skills that are needed now and in the future. The resulting skill gap drives decisions to retrain, reorganize, or recruit.
- New employees are hired using tactics to identify people who will be supportive of the organization's mission.
- Senior leaders build a work climate that addresses the needs of a diverse workforce. Recruitment and training are tools to enhance the work climate.
- Workers are cross-trained to prepare for changing capability and capacity needs. Cross-training, job sharing, and rotational assignments promote a more engaged worker and make that worker more valuable to the organization.

b. Workplace Climate

- Issues and concerns relating to worker health, security, and accessibility are used to design the work environment. Plans exist and processes are in place to optimize the work environment and eliminate adverse conditions. The workplace is compliant with or exceeds the requirements of applicable state and federal laws such as the Americans with Disabilities Act of 1990 and the Accessibility Guidelines of implementing regulations.
- Root causes for health, security, and accessibility problems are systematically identified and eliminated. Corrective actions are communicated (shared) widely to help prevent the problem in other parts of the organization.
- Targets or goals are set and reviewed for all key factors affecting the work environment. Workers are directly involved in setting these targets or goals.
- Special activities and services are available for workers. These are varied according to their diverse needs. Examples include:
  - Flexible benefits plan including: age-appropriate health care options; on-site day care; dental care; portable retirement; education (both work and non-work-related); and maternity, paternity, and family-illness leave
  - Facilities for worker meetings to discuss their concerns
  - Group-purchasing-power program where the number of participating merchants is increasing steadily

Ineffective Practices

- Workers are not allowed to communicate and work with others in their organization who are outside of their immediate chain of command. Organizational silos support the prerogatives of leaders rather than the needs of the organization as a whole, its customers, or the workforce.
- Organizations recruit and hire employees whose background, culture, and thinking are all the same. Creative thinking is discouraged. Leaders communicate the expectation that, "When I want your ideas I will ask for them."
- Leaders seek to grow headcount to build their empire without regard to the capability and capacity needs of the organization to achieve strategic objectives and action plans.
- The organization takes shortcuts with security and a healthful work environment, believing it is cheaper to risk the occasional accident rather than make the workplace better for all.
- Benefits programs are *one size fits all,* typically meeting the needs identified by senior leaders or human resources professionals. *Lowest cost* is the primary benefit selection method. Employee input into desired benefits is not solicited.

5.2 WORKFORCE ENGAGEMENT: How do you engage your workforce for retention and high performance? (45 Pts.) **PROCESS**

a. Assessment of Workforce Engagement

(1) **Drivers of Engagement How do you determine the key drivers of workforce engagement?** How do you determine these drivers for different workforce groups and segments?

(2) **Assessment of Engagement How do you assess workforce engagement?** What formal and informal assessment methods and measures do you use to determine workforce satisfaction and workforce engagement? How do these methods and measures differ across workforce groups and segments? How do you also use other indicators to assess and improve workforce engagement?

b. Organizational Culture – How do you foster an organizational culture that is characterized by open communication, high performance, and an engaged workforce? How do you reinforce your organizational culture? How do you ensure that your organizational culture supports your vision and values; promotes equity and inclusion; and benefits from the diversity of ideas, cultures, and thinking of your workforce? How do you empower your workforce?

c. Performance Management and Development

(1) **Performance Management How does your workforce performance management system support high performance?** How does it consider workforce compensation, reward, recognition, and incentive practices? How does it reinforce intelligent risk taking, a customer and business focus, and achievement of your action plans?

(2) **Performance Development How does your learning and development system support the personal development of workforce members and your organization's needs?** How does it consider the learning and development desires of workforce members, support organizational performance improvement and intelligent risk taking, and support ethics and ethical business practices?

(3) **Learning and Development Effectiveness How do you evaluate the effectiveness of your learning and development system?** How do you

- correlate learning and development outcomes with findings from your assessment of workforce engagement and with key business results, and
- use these correlations to identify opportunities for improvement both in workforce engagement and in learning and development offerings?

(4) **Career Development – How do you manage career development for your workforce and your future leaders?** How do you carry out succession planning for management, leadership, and other key positions?

(5) **Equity and Inclusion – How do you ensure that your performance management, performance development, and career development processes promote equity and inclusion for a diverse workforce and different workforce groups and segments?**

Notes:

5.2a(1). Drivers of workforce engagement (identified in P.1a[3]) refer to the drivers of workforce members' commitment, both emotional and intellectual, to accomplishing the organization's work, mission, and vision.

5.2a(2). Other indicators to use in assessing and improving workforce engagement might include workforce retention, absenteeism, grievances, safety, and productivity.

5.2c(1). *In some government organizations, compensation systems are set by law or regulation; therefore, reward and recognition systems must use other options.*

Continued

Continued

5.2c(2). Your response should include how you address any considerations for workforce development, learning, and career progression that are unique to your organization. These might include development opportunities that address your organization's core competencies, strategic challenges, and action plans; organizational change and innovation; improvements in delivering a positive customer experience; and the reinforcement of new knowledge and skills on the job. Your response should also consider the breadth of development opportunities you might offer, including education, training, coaching, mentoring, and work-related experiences.

Item 5.2 looks at the organization's systems for engaging, developing, and assessing the engagement and satisfaction of the workforce, in order to enable and encourage all members of the workforce to contribute effectively and to the best of their abilities. Workforce engagement systems are intended to promote high performance, achieve action plans, enhance individual and organizational learning, and enable innovation and adaptation to change, thereby ensuring organizational sustainability.

High levels of workforce engagement have a significant, positive impact on organizational performance. Research has indicated that engagement is enhanced by performing meaningful work; having clear organizational direction, performance accountability, and an efficient work environment; having a safe, trusting, and cooperative environment; and developing work skills and establishing a clear career progression. Workers (including volunteers) in many organizations are drawn to and derive meaning from their work, because the work is aligned with their personal values.

Although satisfaction with pay and promotion potential is important, research indicates it is not the most important driver of engagement. The most critical factors that drive workforce engagement are (1) feeling valued by supervisors, and (2) being involved in decisions about their work. Contributors to engagement include the extent of involvement in decision-making, the extent to which workers voice their ideas (and managers listen), the extent to which workers develop their knowledge, skills, abilities, and career potential, and the extent to which the organization is concerned for and supports worker health, safety, and well-being.

Research on the drivers of workforce engagement by Tom Becker (reported in *Quality Progress* magazine, published by the American Society for Quality, January 2011, pp. 18–22) reinforces much of the existing literature on the topic. In particular, Becker found that effective career development programs [consistent with the requirements of Item 5.2c(2, 4)] can significantly improve employee engagement. Specifically, Becker found the following:

- Organizations that provide career development opportunities are six times more likely to engage their employees than organizations that do not.
- Organizations that provide career development opportunities are four times less likely to lose talent in the next year than organizations that do not.
- Organizations that provide career development opportunities are almost 2.5 times more productive than organizations that do not.
- Organizations judged to be the best performers are almost three times more likely to provide career development than those judged to be below-average performers.

Leader behavior helps or hinders employee engagement. To provide the environment where employees can be successful, leaders must:

- Be personally engaged, and demonstrate high energy in both their core job and supportive roles.
- Understand how each role helps support the business strategy and plan.
- Create an environment where achieving more than basic job requirements (tasks) is valued. Great leaders require workers to improve their knowledge, skills, and abilities; improve and innovate work processes; and work for the general betterment of co-workers and the organization as a whole. Senior leaders should get

their direct reports to do the same, and so forth down the chain.

Many factors adversely affect worker engagement. Factors that drain energy from leaders and workers and inhibit engagement include:

- Confusion (vague strategy, poor communication, unclear signals, conflicting or changing priorities/everything is a priority, much intuition-based decision-making)
- Distraction (nonrecognition of effort, punishment for trying to improve, crisis management, initiatives such as freezes or budget reductions)
- Overwork (too many projects, too few resources, lack of closure/completion, uneven distribution of workload, lots of rework)

Although these factors adversely affect leader effectiveness, the impact on workers is almost certainly worse. Unfortunately, too many senior leaders are not prepared to behave in a manner that promotes employee equity, inclusion, and engagement. Senior leaders who are promoted because of good technical skills may cause the organization great harm until they develop the leadership and management skills essential to promote workforce engagement or until they are removed. Leaders must take action to correct poor engagement and may need training and development opportunities [5.2c(2)] or changes in compensation [1.2a(2)] or both to facilitate their transformation.

- If a worker lacks clarity about his or her role or is confused about what the manager and the organization needs, make sure he or she has clearly defined priorities and has the right materials, equipment, and information/data to move toward and achieve those outcomes.
- Refocus the poor-performing worker. Reduce distractions. Consider alternative working structures, such as teams.
- Examine the knowledge, skills, and abilities (KSAs) required to contribute fully. Develop KSAs as needed.
- Recognize the worker for moving in the desired direction. Recognition should be aligned to reinforce priorities—strategic objectives, action plans, and organization values. Recognition reinforces worker behaviors that reflect those priorities, personal development, and co-worker and organizational benefits.

Key drivers of engagement are reflected in the survey statements in Table 4 on the next page, which could be used to assess engagement as required by Item 5.2a(2). Regarding worker satisfaction, high-performing organizations usually consider a variety of factors such as effective problem and grievance resolution; preparation for changes in technology; work environment; workplace safety and security; workload; effective communication, cooperation, and teamwork; job security; appreciation of the differing needs of diverse employee groups; and organizational support for serving customers.

A top-performing workforce is managed in such a way as to encourage workers to exercise optimum discretion, take intelligent risks, and make fact-based decisions. These behaviors typically produce higher engagement and better performance. *To exercise effective decision-making, workers need access to appropriate data and analyses concerning their work and must possess the knowledge and skills to interpret the data to make good decisions.* (This links to the information and knowledge management systems required in Category 4 as well as training in this Item [5.2c(2)].) Unless workers have access to data to support effective decision-making and understand how to analyze and interpret data, their decisions, by default, revert to intuition—which is highly variable. Managers are not likely to permit workers to substitute their intuition for that of managers. Without access to data to support decisions and the skill to interpret the data, worker decision-making will be limited, even if managers were inclined to release decisions to subordinates. Accordingly, systems to promote workforce engagement, empowerment, and agility should ensure workers have the authority and skill to make decisions about their work, as well as data and analysis systems to support effective and consistently good decisions.

The best organizations put in place a workforce performance management system that provides measurable feedback to workers, and ties reward, recognition, compensation, or other incentives to the achievement of high-performance objectives and a

Table 4 Sample workforce engagement themes.

	24 Workforce Engagement Statements/Themes	1 Never	2 Rarely	3 Sometimes	4 Often	5 Always
	Personal Contribution					
1	I try to exceed my manager's expectations.					
2	Nearly all of my co-workers try to exceed their managers' expectations.					
3	My work gives me a feeling of achievement.					
4	My work contributes to the success of the organization.					
	Personal Capabilities					
5	My job allows me to make full use of my knowledge, skills, and abilities.					
6	In the workplace, I have adequate opportunities to improve my skills.					
7	I have good opportunities for career and professional growth.					
8	I understand what is expected of me at work.					
	Reward, Recognition, Compensation					
9	My organization evaluates and promotes employees honestly and fairly.					
10	Recognition and rewards are fair and well understood.					
11	My performance is properly recognized.					
	Manager Attributes					
12	In the workplace, I get adequate support from my manager to succeed.					
13	My manager provides timely and accurate feedback that helps me to improve my performance (at least two to three times each year).					
14	My manager respects my thoughts, feelings, and ideas.					
15	Delivering customer value is a top priority for my manager.					
	Improvement, Initiative, Innovation					
16	Decisions in my organization are made at the appropriate levels.					
17	I am encouraged to make improvements in how work is done.					
18	As a part of my job, I am required to make improvements in how my work is done.					
19	During the past year, I have made or helped to make improvements in how work is done.					
	Workplace Climate					
20	This is a great place to work.					
21	I look forward to coming to work every day.					
22	I am excited about the future of my organization and I see great potential for growth here.					
23	My work contributes to meeting the needs of our customers.					
24	What questions are we not asking that are important to your workplace success? Which of the statements or themes above are not important?					

customer and business focus. Compensation and recognition systems are matched to support the work necessary for organizational success. Consistent with this, compensation and recognition might be tied to demonstrated skills and peer evaluations. Compensation and recognition approaches also might include profit sharing, rewarding exemplary team or unit performance, and "thank you" notes. Their approaches should clearly link to customer-satisfaction and loyalty measures, achievement of organizational strategic objectives, or other essential organizational objectives, such as intelligent risk taking to achieve improvements and innovation to reinforce a customer and business focus.

Once the organization determines its key strategic objectives and action plans, it should review compensation, reward, and recognition systems to ensure they support those objectives. *The failure to do this creates an environment where workers are focused on one set of activities (based on their compensation plan), while the organization has determined that another set of activities (the action plans to achieve the strategic objectives) is necessary for success.*

All workforce and leader development and learning systems should be evaluated to determine their effectiveness and to find ways to improve them [5.2c(3)]. Leaders should identify specific measures of effectiveness prior to conducting an evaluation of training. Such measures might examine individual, unit, and organizational performance against customer-related objectives and business objectives.

Organizations should ensure that workforce and leader development contribute to high performance. This may require organizations to provide training in the use of performance-excellence tools. Training may focus on the use of performance measures, skill standards, quality-control methods, benchmarking, problem-solving processes, and performance-improvement techniques, such as PDCA, Six Sigma, lean enterprise, After Action Reviews, and the use of Balanced Scorecards, to name a few.

High-performing organizations provide mechanisms for sharing the knowledge of workers and the organization [4.2b] to ensure that high-performance work is maintained through personnel and organizational transitions. Accordingly, systematic processes should be designed and implemented to share information critical to the organization's operations. This is particularly important for knowledge that is stored only in the memory banks of workers.

If an objective of the organization is to enhance customer satisfaction and loyalty, it may be critical to identify job requirements for customer-contact workers and then provide them with appropriate training. Such training is increasingly important and common among high-performing organizations that seek to differentiate themselves from competitors. It frequently includes acquiring critical knowledge and skills with respect to products, services, and customers; learning how to listen to customers; practicing recovery from problems or failures; and learning how to manage and exceed customer expectations effectively.

Workforce, manager, and leader development should also address high-priority needs, such as technological change, ethical business practices, management and leadership development, orientation of new employees, overall career development, safety, diversity, and performance measurement and improvement since many of these themes contribute to worker engagement and higher performance.

Unless knowledge and skills acquired in training are reinforced on the job, they are quickly and easily forgotten—even after a few days. Accordingly, leaders, managers, and supervisors throughout the organization must ensure that they and other workers actually use the skills acquired through recent training. In fact, one of the measures of leadership effectiveness [required by Item 1.2a(2)] should consider the extent to which leaders reinforce these skills throughout the leadership system and among their employees.

Developing and sustaining work processes that produce high-performance results require ongoing education and training [5.2c(2)], and information systems [4.2] that ensure adequate information availability. To help workers realize their full potential, many organizations use individual development plans prepared with the input of each worker and designed to address their career and learning objectives [5.2c(2, 4)].

Workforce development requirements [see P.1a(3)] might vary greatly depending on the nature of the organization's work, workforce responsibility, and stage of organizational and personal development. These requirements might include knowledge-sharing skills, communications, teamwork, problem solving, interpreting and using data, meeting customer requirements, process analysis and simplification, waste and cycle-time reduction, and priority setting based on strategic alignment or cost/benefit analysis. Education needs might include advanced skills in new technologies as well as basic skills, such as reading, writing, language, arithmetic, and computer use.

Organizations should consider job and organizational performance in education and training design and evaluation. Education and training should tie to action plans, and balance short- and long-term individual and organizational objectives. Workers and their supervisors or managers should help determine training needs and contribute to the design and evaluation of education and training, because these individuals frequently are best able to identify critical needs and evaluate success.

Education and training could be delivered by staff from inside or outside the organization and could involve on-the-job, classroom, computer-based, distance learning (including web-based instruction), or any combination of these. Apprenticeship, internship, and mentoring have proven to be effective techniques to deliver training and reinforce skills. Developmental assignments within or outside the organization have also proven to be effective.

Work and job factors important to consider include simplification of job classifications (less specialization and work isolation and more multiskilled workers), which can be addressed by cross-training, job rotation, use of teams (including self-directed teams), and changes in work layout and location. Other important methods to combat worker isolation involve fostering communication across functions and work units, maintaining a focus on customer requirements, creating an environment of knowledge sharing and respect, and engaging all workers in making improvements to their work processes.

The organization should perform effective succession planning for senior leaders, managers, and other workers at all levels of the organization [5.2c(4)]. The rate of new-knowledge acquisition is increasing throughout the world. Significantly more new knowledge is causing change to occur faster than ever before in history. To manage effectively in this climate of rapid change, the best organizations anticipate future workforce needs and prepare their future leaders, managers, and workers to take over. The best leaders do not wait for vacancies to occur before they take action to develop the knowledge and skills needed by successors. Succession and career planning enable organizations to identify future skill needs against current skill gaps, giving them the time needed to recruit and develop the necessary human resources. Workforce hiring and career-progression planning should consider all top candidates, both internal and external, with a focus on the future sustainability and growth of the organization.

To help people realize their full potential, some organizations prepare individual development plans with all workers to address their career and learning objectives. To achieve optimum worker productivity, the organization must understand and address the factors promoting engagement (such as career development opportunities) and inhibiting engagement (such as micromanaging and failing to value workers). A better understanding of these factors could be developed through exit interviews with departing workers, as well as through feedback from anonymous surveys of the current workforce. All processes associated with education, training, and developing the full potential of workers should be systematically evaluated and ongoing refinements should be made.

High-performing organizations also use both formal and informal assessment methods and measures to determine workforce engagement and satisfaction. These methods and measures are tailored to assess the differing needs of a diverse workforce. In addition, indicators other than formal or informal workforce surveys (for example, turnover, grievances, complaints, strikes, and absenteeism) are used to support the assessment. Taken together, these methods and measures ensure that assessment findings are relevant and relate to key organizational results in order to identify key priorities for improvement.

Information and data on engagement and satisfaction are used in identifying improvement priorities. Priority setting might draw upon workforce-focused results reported in Item 7.3 and might involve addressing workforce problems based on the actual or potential impact on organizational performance. Factors inhibiting engagement need to be prioritized and addressed. The failure to address these factors is likely to result in even greater problems, which may not only impact workforce results [7.3], but also adversely affect product and process results [7.1], customer satisfaction [7.2], leadership areas such as ethics [7.4], and financial performance and achieving strategy [7.5].

To demonstrate maturity, the Scoring Guidelines require that the organization has a system in place to improve and innovate its processes for workforce engagement including methods for strengthening the organizational culture, assessing engagement, managing performance, and developing the workforce and its leaders. The organization needs to evaluate these workforce engagement processes more often than annually and demonstrate that it has made meaningful, value-added, or innovative improvements.

2021–2022 Criteria Elements Listed Individually Without Duplication
See page 279 for explanation of this table

	Basic Approach Elements [A-B] for Scoring Between 10% and 45%	Additional Approach Elements at the Overall [A-O] Level for Scoring Between 50% and 65%	Additional Approach Elements at the Multiple Level [A-M] for Scoring Between 70% and 100%
5.2 Workforce Engagement			
5.2a(1)	Engage the workforce for retention and high performance	Determine the key drivers of workforce engagement	Determine the drivers of engagement for different workforce groups and segments
5.2a(2)		Assess workforce engagement	• Use formal and informal assessment methods and measures to determine workforce satisfaction and engagement • Use different methods and measures, as appropriate, to assess different workforce groups and segments • Also use other indicators to assess and improve workforce engagement
5.2b		Foster an organizational culture that is characterized by open communication, high performance, and an engaged workforce	• Reinforce the organizational culture • Ensure culture supports vision and values • Promote equity and inclusion • Ensure that the organizational culture benefits from the diversity of ideas, cultures, and thinking of the workforce • Empower the workforce
5.2c(1)		Ensure the workforce performance management system supports high performance	The performance management system considers workforce compensation, reward, recognition, and incentive practices. The performance management system also reinforces the following— • Intelligent risk taking • A customer and business focus • Achievement of the organization's action plans
5.2c(2)		Ensure the learning and development system supports personal development of workforce members and the organization's needs	The learning and development system also— • Considers the learning and development desires of workforce members • Supports organizational performance improvement and intelligent risk taking • Supports ethics and ethical business practices
5.2c(3)		Evaluate the effectiveness and efficiency of the learning and development system	The organization also: • Correlates learning and development outcomes with findings from the assessment of workforce engagement and with key business results • Uses these correlations to identify opportunities for improvement in both workforce engagement and learning and development offerings
5.2c(4)		Manage career progression for the workforce and future leaders	The organization also: • Manages career development for the workforce • Carries out succession planning for management, leadership, and other key positions

5.2 Workforce Engagement

Basic Approach Element: *Engage the workforce (get workers to contribute their utmost) for retention and high performance.*

Overall Approach Elements:

- *Determine the key drivers of workforce engagement [5.2a(1)]*
- *Assess workforce engagement [5.2a(2)]*
- *Foster an organizational culture that is characterized by open communication, high performance, and an engaged workforce [5.2b]*
- *Ensure the workforce performance management system supports high performance and workforce engagement [5.2c(1)]*
- *Ensure the learning and development system supports the personal development of workforce members and the organization's needs [5.2c(2)]*
- *Evaluate the effectiveness and efficiency of the learning and development system [5.2c(3)]*
- *Manage career progression for the workforce and future leaders [5.2c(4)]*

The following diagram describes key approach elements:

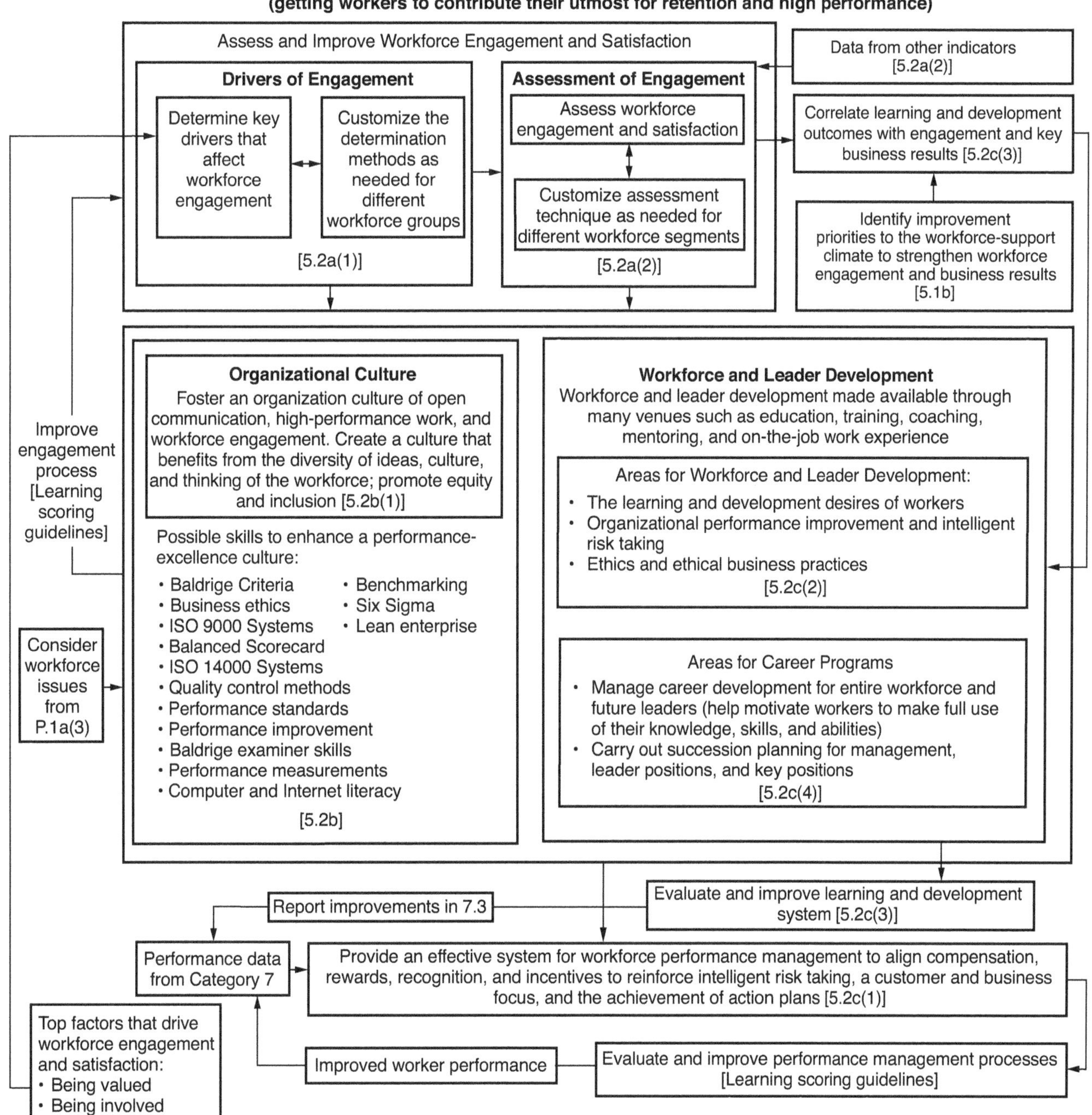

5.2 Key Workforce Engagement Item Linkages

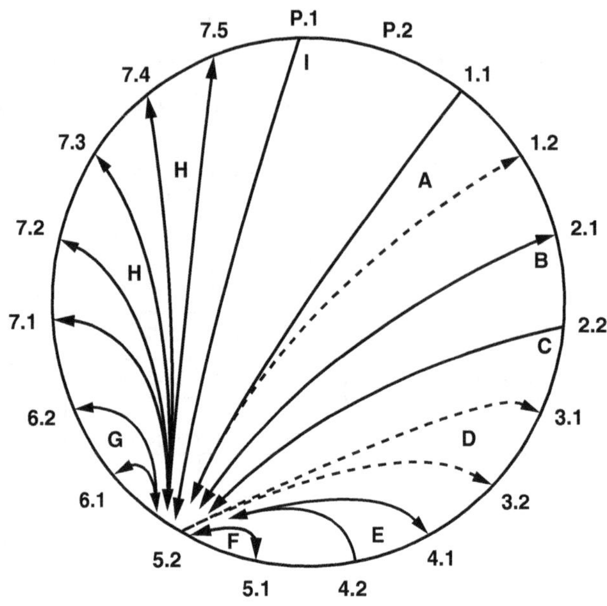

	NATURE OF RELATIONSHIP
A	Senior leaders [1.1] create a culture of open communication, high performance, and workforce engagement; set related policies; and actively role model appropriate behaviors essential to optimize worker engagement, performance, and productivity [5.2b]. Senior leaders must communicate effectively with the workforce (which is essential for building positive relations, equity and inclusion, trust, and setting clear directions) [1.1b]. In addition, part of evaluating the performance of the leadership system [1.2a(2)] should involve determining the extent to which leaders at all levels helped improve employee engagement [5.2c(1)]. Leaders [1.1b] are responsible for motivating the workforce, which may require training and development systems and reinforcing learning on the job, succession, and career development [5.2c(2, 4)]. In addition, specific training may be required to ensure employees understand governance, ethical, and regulatory requirements [1.2a, b].
B	Workforce diversity, engagement, and related skills [5.2] are factors that should be considered in the planning process [2.1a]. Also, clear, measurable, outcome-oriented strategic objectives are defined [2.1b(1)], which are essential for setting and clearly communicating performance expectations and establishing accountability through the performance management system [5.2c(1)].
C	Workforce plans [2.2a(4)] are used to help align training [5.2c(2)] to ensure workers, managers, and leaders possess appropriate knowledge, skills, and abilities. Workforce plans and goals [2.2a(4)] are used to help develop leaders and the workforce [5.2c(2)], and align reward and recognition [5.2c(1)] to reinforce intelligent risk-taking, a customer and business focus, and achievement of action plans. In addition, strategic objectives that have been converted into action plans are deployed to the workforce for implementation throughout the organization (which is essential to ensure full understanding of achievement expectations) [2.2a(1, 2)]. Key performance measures or indicators for tracking progress on action plans must be developed [2.2a(5)] (which are essential to ensure all workers are aligned, able to monitor their personal progress, and make adjustments as needed).

Continued

	NATURE OF RELATIONSHIP *Continued*
D	A culture of workforce engagement, open communication, and high-performance work [5.2b] is essential to customer engagement and building customer relations [3.2]. Training [5.2c(2)] can also enhance capabilities of customer-contact employees and strengthen customer engagement and relationship building [3.2].
E	Key comparative data [4.1a(2)] are used to design processes to enhance employee engagement and satisfaction. Comparative data [4.1a(2)] are used to improve training [5.2c(3)]. Information regarding training effectiveness [5.2c(3)] is used to support operational decision-making [4.1a], and make needed data and information available and accessible to the workforce (without timely access to correct data and information, decisions default to intuition, which introduces more variability in the decision-making process, contributing to incorrect decisions and more decisions raised to higher levels of management) [4.2].
F	A healthy, secure, accessible work climate [5.1b] helps prevent employee distractions and helps enhance employee engagement, motivation, participation, self-direction, and initiative [5.2b], and vice versa. Effective performance management and development [5.2c] is critical to maintaining and improving a secure, healthful work environment [5.1b(1)]. Supporting the workforce via policies, services, and benefits tailored to the needs of diverse workers [5.1b(2)] helps keep them from worrying about those that can be distracting to them and erode engagement [5.2].
G	Engaged, skilled, motivated workers [5.2] are essential to designing, managing, improving, and efficiently operating work processes [6.1 and 6.2] to increase customer value, organization productivity, and related business processes. Effective performance management (feedback, compensation, and recognition) [5.2c(1)] can help to improve work process design and management [6.1] and operational efficiency [6.2]. Effective training [5.2c(2, 3)] is essential to managing change and improving work process design, management effectiveness, and innovation [6.1 and 6.2]. In addition, training requirements [5.2c(2, 3)] are defined in part by key product and process requirements [6.1a(1)].
H	Compensation, incentives, recognition and rewards [5.2c(1)], and executive compensation [1.2a(2)] are based in part on performance results [Category 7]. Improvements in workforce engagement and communication [5.2] can result in improved performance outcomes [Category 7]. Systems that enhance workforce engagement can boost financial, market, and strategy performance [7.5], product and process effectiveness [7.1], customer satisfaction [7.2], and leadership outcomes [7.4]. Specific results of workforce-focused outcomes are reported in 7.3. Results of improved training and development [5.2c(3)] are reported in 7.3. In addition, results pertaining to product and process performance [7.1], customer satisfaction, engagement, and dissatisfaction [7.2], leadership and governance [7.4], and financial, market, and strategy performance [7.5], reflect, in part, and are monitored to assess, training effectiveness [5.2c(3)].
I	Workforce characteristics such as educational requirements, workforce and job diversity, the existence of bargaining units, the use of contract employees, and other special requirements [P.1a(3)] help set the context for determining the requirements for knowledge and skills needed of employees [5.2c(2)].

IF YOU DON'T DO WHAT THE CRITERIA REQUIRE . . .	
Item Reference	**Possible Adverse Consequences**
5.2a(1)	**Drivers of Engagement** – Although research indicates the key drivers of engagement include being valued and involved, other factors that affect workforce engagement and satisfaction can vary significantly from organization to organization or within an organization from site to site, or among different groups of employees in the same organization at the same work site. The failure to determine the key drivers of workforce engagement and satisfaction for each employee segment may make it difficult to identify key performance problems and take appropriate corrective action. The inability to identify and correct these problems can reduce employee morale and motivation which, in turn, hurts productivity and ultimately customer satisfaction. Failure to engage the workforce means they are not adequately motivated or empowered to contribute their utmost to the success of the organization or its customers.
5.2a(2)	**Assessment of Engagement** – Because the factors that affect workforce engagement and satisfaction can vary significantly among the diverse groups of employees, an organization that fails to differentiate assessment methods and measures may not be able to determine accurately the existence of problems and take timely and appropriate corrective action. The failure to identify and correct a problem that adversely affects workforce engagement or satisfaction can contribute to operational inefficiency, waste resources, and reduce product and service quality and customer satisfaction. Failing to consider data that relate to workforce engagement and satisfaction, such as absenteeism, grievances, and undesired workforce attrition, may also prevent a problem from being identified and corrected. Finally, the one-size-fits-all method of assessing workforce engagement and satisfaction (such as the annual climate survey) may fail to take into account parts of the organization that may be undergoing change and facing more turmoil than other parts of the organization. For organizations that are relatively stable, an annual survey may be appropriate. However, for organizations (or parts of organizations) that face a more volatile, unstable environment, more frequent assessments may be required. Failure to ask the right questions, at the right time, and in the right manner may prevent the organization from learning about and correcting serious problems that may adversely affect performance and productivity.
5.2b	**Organizational Culture** – The lack of workforce engagement creates an environment where workers wait for approval, do not take risks, and do not seek opportunities for innovation. This makes organizational agility nearly impossible and adversely affects productivity and motivation.
5.2b	**Organizational Culture** – The failure to capitalize on diversity of ideas, cultures, and thinking and promote equity and inclusion may limit the organization's ability to create an innovative and empowered workforce. This in turn may reduce productivity and limit the organization's ability to meet the challenges of today's highly competitive environment.
5.2b	**Organizational Culture** – The failure to promote open communication often contributes to redundancy and working at cross-purposes. The failure to promote knowledge and skill sharing often forces the organization to duplicate efforts in the search for more effective and efficient processes. The failure to communicate also contributes to isolationism within an organization and prevents pockets of excellence and best practices from spreading. Frequently, employees working in a hierarchical, command-and-control environment find individual initiative, empowerment, and innovation stifled, reducing engagement and morale and further eroding productivity and responsiveness.

Continued

IF YOU DON'T DO WHAT THE CRITERIA REQUIRE . . . *Continued*	
Item Reference	**Possible Adverse Consequences**
5.2b	**Organizational Culture** – Failure to promote open communication among workers and supervisors inhibits trust and openness. Problems that a subordinate would raise in an open, trusting environment are hidden from view or not raised for discussion. These problems may have serious consequences for customers where fear of retaliation prevents them from expressing concerns.
5.2c(1)	**Performance Management** – To optimize performance, work throughout the organization must be fully aligned to support strategic objectives, timelines [2.1b(1)], and related action plans [2.2a(1)]. The action plans should be deployed fully throughout the organization and implemented [2.2a(2)] at all levels with appropriate quantitative measures developed to monitor progress [2.2a(5)]. The work of individual employees, when taken together, should enable the organization to achieve its action plans and related strategic objectives and promote meaningful improvement and innovation. Two questions are fundamental to the work endeavors that performance management systems should address: (1) are the right things being done (the vital few); and (2) are they being done right (correctly). The failure to manage workforce performance, including providing timely feedback, may make it more difficult for workers to determine if they are doing the right thing in support of organization strategy or if they are doing things in the right way (process discipline). It forces workers to decide for themselves if they are doing a good job. The alignment of what is expected and what is rewarded sends strong messages throughout the organization about what is really important. Failing to align appropriate compensation, recognition, rewards, and incentives (including compensation [1.2a(2)]) with the strategic objectives also contributes to a lack of focus within the workforce, forcing employees to substitute their own ideas instead of being driven or guided by management. Many employees equate compensation with the important activities the organization wants to achieve. For example, if achieving profitability is critical for organization success, the organization typically rewards people for achieving financial goals. In this situation, everyone clearly understands the importance of profit or budget allocations because their own compensation and rewards are ultimately tied to them. Similarly, the failure to provide rewards, recognition, or compensation that support intelligent risk taking to achieve innovation, reinforce a customer focus, and reinforce the achievement of action plans may cause employees to remain risk averse, fail to innovate or achieve key action plans, or behave as if customers are unimportant. Rewards (or the absence of them) drive behavior and motivate people to respond in certain ways.
5.2c(2)	**Performance Development** – The failure to deliver education and training using appropriate methods, consistent with the learning styles and needs of the workers, usually suboptimizes the effectiveness of training. If participants do not acquire relevant knowledge, skills, or abilities from education and training, the organization has wasted resources. If workers do learn new skills and acquire new abilities and those new skills and abilities are not used on the job, the organization has also wasted resources. If the workers use the new skills and abilities on the job and it makes no difference to organizational performance or career progression, the organization has again wasted resources.
5.2c(2)	**Performance Development** – Creating a culture to focus on customers (and ensure a consistently positive customer experience) requires that all workers understand the importance of customers to organizational success and sustainability. Without this knowledge

Continued

IF YOU DON'T DO WHAT THE CRITERIA REQUIRE . . . *Continued*	
Item Reference	**Possible Adverse Consequences**
	and corresponding skills to engage customers, leaders and workers become internally focused (on their own priorities) rather than focusing on customer priorities.
5.2c(2)	**Performance Development** – The lack of intelligent risk taking that leads to innovation among leaders, managers, and workers makes it difficult for organizations to keep pace with increasing customer requirements and competition. This makes it difficult, if not impossible to achieve and sustain a competitive leadership position. Innovation processes can be taught—and improved with practice.
5.2c(2)	**Performance Development** – If it is worth training a worker to acquire new skills and abilities, it is also important to reinforce the use of those new skills when the worker returns to the job. The failure to reinforce the use of recently acquired knowledge and skills on the job may cause those new skills and abilities to become atrophied and quickly forgotten. Accordingly, the cost of training and the cost of lost productivity while the worker is receiving the training represent wasted resources. Most importantly, when the newly acquired skills are not utilized, the value of those skills and potential productivity gains are lost. Losses of this nature can materially impact an organization's rate of growth and its ability to achieve strategic objectives. A similar problem occurs when valuable organizational knowledge is lost because of employee retirement or attrition.
5.2c(2)	**Performance Development** – People who are most knowledgeable about the skills they need to be successful are typically the workers themselves. Organizations that do not take into account the learning and development desires of its workers may miss an important opportunity to engage them better in contributing their utmost for the success of the organization and its customers.
5.2c(2)	**Performance Development** – If leaders, managers, and workers lack the necessary skills to carry out required work, organizational performance is weakened and sustainability is threatened. Education and training that do not contribute to closing a skill gap that is essential to the achievement of required work, waste resources.
5.2c(3)	**Learning and Development Effectiveness** – When deciding what actions to take to improve workforce engagement (based on the results of appropriate surveys and related data), organizations risk wasting resources if they fail to understand the likely impact on business results of the improvement priorities they set in response to workforce engagement and satisfaction assessment findings.
5.2c(3)	**Learning and Development Effectiveness** – The failure to evaluate and improve the effectiveness of training makes it difficult to ensure training effectiveness or optimal performance. Ineffective or inefficient training and education waste resources directly (cost of training) and indirectly (cost of lost opportunity and productivity while employee is receiving training).
5.2c(4)	**Career Development** – Managers and leaders have a responsibility to help the workforce attain job- and career-progression development objectives. If workforce members and leaders fail to take advantage of appropriate education and training, they run the risk of weakening morale and motivation as well as contributing to skill obsolescence. This adversely impacts job security and employability and undermines the organization's ability to maintain a viable workforce to compete effectively. Career progression and worker development programs provide evidence

Continued

IF YOU DON'T DO WHAT THE CRITERIA REQUIRE . . . *Continued*	
Item Reference	**Possible Adverse Consequences**
	to workers that they are valued by the organization and its leaders. This, in turn, enhances employee engagement, which enhances productivity. In the face of worldwide shortages of highly skilled workers, an organization's failure to conduct effective succession planning for senior leaders (and for key positions throughout the organization) could threaten long-term sustainability and create performance problems in the short term. If succession planning does not look ahead at least as far as it might take to acquire or train replacement personnel, the organization may lack the talent it needs to fulfill its promises to customers or other key stakeholders.

5.2 WORKFORCE ENGAGEMENT—SAMPLE EFFECTIVE PRACTICES

a. Assessment of Workforce Engagement

- The performance management system provides feedback to workers that supports their ability to contribute to a high-performing organization.
- Leaders are able to describe the organization's mission-focused culture and how that culture is matured by leadership.
- Compensation, recognition, rewards, and incentives are provided for generating improvement ideas. In addition, a system exists to encourage and provide rapid reinforcement for submitting improvement ideas.
- Compensation, recognition, rewards, and incentives are provided for improving key performance results, such as reducing cycle time and exceeding target schedules with error-free products or services at less-than-projected cost.
- Workers, as well as managers, participate in creating the compensation, recognition, rewards, and incentives practices and help monitor their implementation and systematic improvement.
- The organization evaluates its approaches to workforce performance and compensation, recognition, and rewards, and training and development to determine the extent to which workers are satisfied with them, the extent of worker participation, and the impact of the system on improved performance, the results of which are reported in Item 7.3.
- Performance measures exist for workforce involvement, self-direction, and initiative. Goals for these measures are expressed in measurable terms. These measurable goals form a part of the basis for performance feedback and recognition.
- Recognition, rewards, incentives, and compensation are influenced by customer satisfaction ratings as well as other strategic, high-performance measures, such as implementing process improvements and achieving strategic action plans.
- The need for diverse ideas and cultures among workers is specifically considered during the skill-mapping and recruitment process. This helps to ensure workers possess the diversity of ideas needed to inspire creativity and innovation.
- A systematic process is used to evaluate and improve the effectiveness and extent of workforce engagement.
- Key workforce engagement and satisfaction opinion indicators are gathered periodically based on the stability or volatility of the organization. Highly stable organizations or subunits conduct

such assessments annually. Where volatility is high, subunit assessments are conducted more frequently, such as quarterly or monthly.

- Supervisors, managers, and leaders take consistent and prompt action to improve adverse conditions identified through workforce engagement and satisfaction surveys.
- On-demand electronic surveys are available for quick response and tabulations any time managers need workforce engagement or satisfaction feedback. Whenever the survey is completed, managers always follow up promptly to make improvements identified by the survey that relate to key business results.
- Engagement and satisfaction data are derived from worker focus groups, confidential surveys, turnover, absenteeism, and exit interviews.
- Managers and leaders use the results of these surveys to focus improvements in work systems and enhance workforce engagement and satisfaction. Actions to improve satisfaction are clearly tied to assessments so employees understand the value of the assessment, and the improvement initiatives do not appear random or capricious.
- Workforce engagement and satisfaction indicators are correlated with measures of business success to help identify where resources should be placed to provide maximum business benefit.
- Methods to improve assessment of workforce engagement and satisfaction are systematically evaluated and improved. Techniques to actually improve engagement and satisfaction are themselves evaluated and refined consistently.

b. Organizational Culture

- Leaders and managers at all levels require employees to use effective approaches to analyze their work, and take intelligent risks to make meaningful, value-added improvements and innovations to work processes as a basic part of job responsibility.
- Fully developing and using the talents of all workers are basic organizational values.
- Teams and individuals are trained and have access to data and are authorized to make decisions about their work (not just make recommendations).
- Worker opinion is sought (and obtained) regarding work design and work process management and improvement.
- Prompt and regular feedback is provided to teams and individuals regarding their performance. Feedback covers both results and processes.

c. Performance Management and Development

- Clear linkages exist between strategic objectives and education and training. Skills are developed based on work demands and workforce needs and preferences.
- Training plans are developed based on worker priorities and manager input.
- Career and personal-development options, including development for leadership, diversity, and safety, are enhanced through formal education and training. Some development uses on-the-job training, including rotational assignments or job exchange programs.
- The organization uses various methods to deliver training to ensure that it is suitable for differing workforce knowledge and skill levels.
- The organization uses various methods to deliver training to ensure that it is suitable for workforce knowledge and skill levels.
- To minimize travel costs, all training is examined to determine if electronic or distance-delivery options are viable alternatives to face-to-face training.
- Training is linked to work requirements, which managers reinforce on the job. Just-in-time training (rather than just-in-case training) is

used to help ensure that the skills will be reinforced immediately after training.

- Worker feedback on the appropriateness of the training is collected and used to improve course delivery and content.
- The organization systematically evaluates training effectiveness on the job. Performance data are collected on individuals and groups at all levels to assess the impact of training.
- Workforce satisfaction with courses is tracked and used to improve training content, training delivery, instructional effectiveness, and the effectiveness of supervisory support for the use of training on the job.
- Training design and delivery are systematically refined and improved based on regular evaluations.
- Formal career plans are in place for each employee. Progress against these plans is evaluated and adjustments are made to ensure they remain relevant.
- Workers receive incentives, such as bonuses or other rewards, for developing additional career-enhancing skills.
- A formal system is in place to develop future leaders. This includes providing training and practice in high-performance leadership techniques. Leaders receive specific training and practice using Baldrige Criteria and performance-improvement systems.
- Demonstrated proficiency in the use of the Baldrige Criteria is a prerequisite to promotion to a leadership position.
- Future leaders serve as examiners in the Baldrige process, state quality award process, or internal award process as a part of career progression and succession planning.

Ineffective Practices

- Improvements are the purview and responsibility of management and a small cadre of engineers or Six Sigma specialists (because lower-level workers are not considered capable of making valuable improvements).
- Organizations do not encourage employees to improve processes they are assigned because they are not trusted.
- Managers seldom seek or care about the opinions of workers and are known to tell workers to keep their opinions to themselves until asked.
- Managers are expected to think for workers and tell them what to do.
- Managers are more valuable to the organization than workers.
- A company sign, posted above the time clock at the workers' entrance, that announces "Leave your brains at the door—they will not be required inside."
- Suggestions from workers for improvement or innovation are either ignored or stolen by managers and presented as their own ideas.
- The organization cares about task completion, not customer or worker satisfaction, and makes no connection between the work environment, worker engagement, productivity, customer satisfaction, and organization success.
- Workers are required to complete numerous surveys about their concerns and problems at work. The results of the surveys are ignored by supervisors or become the workers' problems to solve.
- Workforce satisfaction and engagement is not related to business success. Organizations pay workers to produce, not to be happy. Worker satisfaction or fulfillment are considered to be irrelevant.
- Employee engagement surveys are only offered to professional employees. Front-line worker engagement is not assessed, demonstrating that the organization does not value those front-line workers.
- Training and development are provided if excess funds exist. Training is not seen as critical to organization success. Training is expendable. Training is considered a luxury and a waste of

limited resources. It is one of the first things cut when the budget is tight.

- No training or development plans are in place for employees other than those required by state and industry for safety or certification.
- The organization offers mandatory orientation and industry-required training to employees. Other than that, no training or development is provided.
- Workers are expected to come to work with the required skills necessary to do their work. Training is not seen as an organizational responsibility.
- Succession plans are not developed. When a leader leaves, the replacement process starts, frequently relying on filling the position from outside the organization.
- Promotions to management are based on a worker's technical competence, such as exceeding sales quotas or being a "good" worker, technician, engineer, or scientist. Leadership and management skills are not considered relevant or important to these promotion decisions.
- Diversity of the workforce is not acknowledged. Leaders say, "We treat everyone the same," but promotions and development opportunities go to employees who are similar to leaders.

6 Operations—85 Points

*The **Operations** Category asks how your organization designs, manages, improves, and innovates its products and work processes and improves operational effectiveness to deliver customer value and achieve ongoing organizational success.*

The Operations Category highlights the importance of efficient and effective work process management: effective design; a prevention orientation; a focus on value creation for all stakeholders; supply-network integration; operational and financial performance; cycle time; emergency readiness; and evaluation, continuous improvement, managing innovation, and organizational learning.

All the work that is required to produce programs, products, and related services to create value for customers and achieve organization success is defined as *work systems.* These work systems include work that may be carried out by the organization using its own workforce and other internal resources or work that is outsourced—performed by outside contractors (suppliers, partners, or collaborators). See Figure 33.

Decisions about defining the work systems and determining whether required work will be internal or external are made as a part of strategy development [see Item 2.1a(4)]. These strategic decisions take into account several factors, such as:

- The organization's core competencies and those of potential suppliers and partners
- Strategic challenges, advantages, and opportunities
- Competition
- Customer requirements
- Workforce capability and capacity

Work Systems
All work needed to produce products and related services to create value for customers and achieve organization success. During the Strategy Development process [Item 2.1], this work is classified into one of two categories: some work is external (outsourced) and the rest is internal.

Internal Work
Work carried out by the workforce under the supervision of the organization. This work typically aligns with the organization's core competencies and involves the majority of the workforce and may be considered a key work process. *Key work processes are always carried out by internal workers.*

External Work
Work carried out by outside contractors (suppliers, partners, collaborators). This work is typically outsourced when the organization had determined that outside contractors can deliver more value than if the work was done in house. Usually, this work does not involve the organization's core competencies.

Internal Work Categories
- Key work processes are critical to value creation and might include product design and delivery, customer support, and other business processes.
- Support processes provide *support* to the workforce engaged in product design and delivery, customer interactions, and business and enterprise management. These may include research and development, call center operations, human resources, information technology, procurement, accounting, maintenance, and supply-network management, to name a few.
  - Supply-network management is a subset of support processes, responsible for supplier-related activities such as soliciting, selecting, contracting, measuring, evaluating, providing feedback to, and improving suppliers; or dealing with poor-performing suppliers

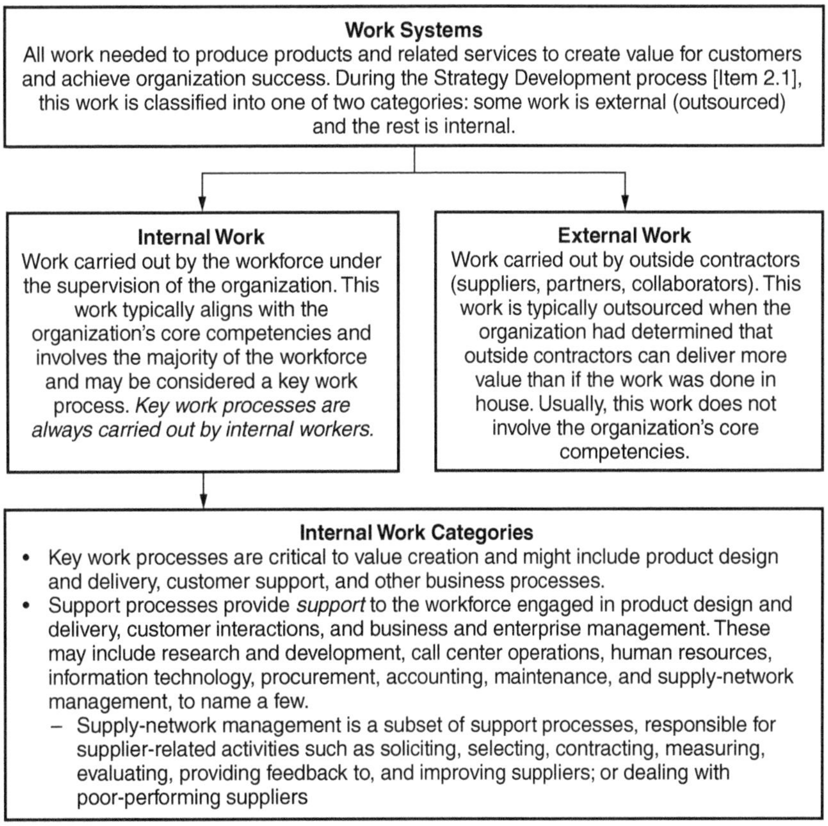

Figure 33 Work process management.

Well-designed and managed internal work processes help the organization to achieve operational success and long-term sustainability. Key work processes:

- Represent the organization's most important internal value-creation processes
- Are always carried out using internal workers and typically involve the majority of the workforce
- Produce customer, stakeholder, and stockholder value

Key work processes may be organized into broad categories such as product, educational program and service, or health care service; design and delivery; customer, student, or patient support; and business support, one of which may be supply-network management.

Key work processes are typically aligned with and supported by organizational core competencies. The lack of a critical core competency needed to support a key work process may threaten organizational success and sustainability. For example, in today's manufacturing environment, the inability to customize quickly limits the options of an organization—and may cause its customers to look elsewhere. On a trip to BMW's automobile manufacturing plant in Munich, Germany, it was obvious throughout the organization that Baldrige-required processes were evident, but no more so than in Category 6. The carmaker had achieved a high degree of agility in its manufacturing processes in order to expand options for its customers. In a sparkling clean facility, BMW managed to optimize virtually every aspect of twenty-first-century manufacturing techniques. Its operations processes include computer-assisted manufacturing with intelligent robots that allow very rapid changeover, enabling car-by-car customization on the fly. The Munich plant can produce 1000 luxury cars per day, and almost never are two identical vehicles consecutive on the assembly line.

For high-performing organizations, agility also means rapid changeover from one product to another and rapid response to changing demands, which strengthens its ability to produce a wide range of customized services. Agility also involves the elimination of unnecessary levels of review and approval prior to a decision; the increased engagement, equity, inclusion, and empowerment of highly skilled workers to make more decisions about their work; and eliminating bureaucratic barriers to efficiency. Increasingly, the need for greater agility and resilience affects outsourcing decisions, defining preferred suppliers, and establishing creative partnering arrangements. Flexibility might demand special strategies, such as implementing modular designs, sharing components, sharing manufacturing lines, and providing specialized training to promote multiple skill sets among workers.

Building on a core competency of agility, BMW enables its customers to change features on the car of their dreams online, up to six days before production starts. BMW's agility helps it produce for its customers their "ultimate driving machine."

Operations [Category 6] contains two Items that look at the design, management, and improvement of product and service processes (including key business processes and support processes). Operations is the focal point for key work processes internal to the organization that are required to produce products, programs, and services for customers. Strategy Development [Item 2.1] is the focal point within the Criteria for defining work systems after considering core competencies, strategic challenges, and strategic advantages. See the chapter on Clarifying Confusing Terms on page 347 for a more extensive explanation of differences between *work systems* and *work processes.*

6.1 WORK PROCESSES: How do you design, manage, and improve your key products and work processes? (45 pts.) **PROCESS**

a. Product and Process Design

(1) **Determination of Product and Process Requirements How do you determine key product and work process requirements?**

(2) **Key Work Processes What are your organization's key work processes?** What are the key requirements for these work processes?

(3) **Design Concepts How do you design your products and work processes to meet requirements?** How do you incorporate new technology, organizational knowledge, product excellence, customer value, consideration of risk, and the potential need for agility into these products and processes?

Continued

Continued

b. Process Management and Improvement

(1) **Process Implementation How does your day-to-day operation of work processes ensure that they meet key process requirements?** What key performance measures or indicators and in-process measures do you use to control and improve your work processes? How do these measures relate to end-product quality and performance measures?

(2) **Support Processes How do you determine your key support processes?** What are your key support processes? How does your day-to-day operation of these processes ensure that they meet key business requirements?

(3) **Product and Process Improvement How do you improve your work processes and support processes to improve products and performance, enhance your core competencies, and reduce variability?**

c. Supply-Network Management

How do you manage your supply network? How do you select suppliers that are qualified and positioned to meet your operational needs, enhance your performance, support your strategic objectives, and enhance your customers' satisfaction? How do you

- promote alignment and collaboration within your supply network;
- ensure supply-network agility and resilience in responding to changes in customer, market, and organizational requirements; and
- communicate performance expectations, measure and evaluate suppliers' performance, provide feedback to help them improve, and deal with poorly performing suppliers?

d. Management of Opportunities for Innovation

How do you pursue your identified opportunities for innovation? How do you pursue the strategic opportunities that you have determined are intelligent risks? How do you make financial and other resources available to pursue these opportunities? How do you decide to discontinue pursuing them at the appropriate time?

Notes:

6.1. The results of improvements in product and process performance should be reported in Item 7.1.

6.1a(3). Process design also includes the need to extensively redesign a process due to changes in requirements or technology, or the need to incorporate digital technology, such as enhanced automation, the Internet of Things, artificial intelligence, and cloud operations. Agility may be needed when work processes need to change as a result of overall work system changes, such as bringing a supply-network product or process in-house to avoid disruptions in supply due to unpredictable external events, or outsourcing a product or process formerly carried out in-house.

6.1b(2). Your key support processes should support your value-creation processes. They might include processes that support leaders and other workforce members engaged in, for example, product design and delivery, customer interactions, and business and enterprise management. Examples might include accounting and purchasing.

6.1b(3). Your approaches to improve process performance and reduce variability should be part of the performance improvement system you describe in P.2c in the Organizational Profile.

6.1c. To ensure that suppliers are positioned to meet operational needs and enhance your performance and your customers' satisfaction, you might partner with suppliers or form alliances among multiple organizations within the supply network for mutual benefit. Communication of expectations and feedback to suppliers should be two-way, allowing suppliers to express what they need from you and other organizations within the supply network. For many organizations, these mechanisms may change as marketplace, customer, or stakeholder requirements change.

Continued

Continued

6.1d. Your process for pursuing opportunities for innovation should capitalize on strategic opportunities identified as intelligent risks in 2.1a(2). It should also include other intelligent risks, such as those arising from your performance reviews (4.1c[2]), your knowledge management approaches (4.2b), and other sources of potential innovations.

Comparison with the Health Care Criteria

The Health Care Criteria have a requirement that neither Business nor Education Criteria contain: "6.1b(2) Patient Expectations and Preferences – How do you address and consider each patient's expectations? How do you explain health care service delivery processes and likely outcomes to set realistic patient expectations? How do you factor patient decision-making and patient preferences into the delivery of health care services. This additional requirement in 6.1b(2) has been in the Health Care Criteria since 2011.

Item 6.1 looks at key work processes with the intent of maximizing customer value and achieving optimum organizational success and sustainability. These processes can help create a competitive advantage and improve market and operational performance—necessary ingredients for current and future success.

Once the organization determines which work will be carried out in-house and which will be outsourced to external vendors as a part of the strategy development process [Item 2.1a(4)], members of the workforce and their managers and leaders do the following:

- Define or determine work process requirements.
- Define or determine the organizations key work processes.
- Design products and work processes to meet all key requirements, incorporating new technology, organizational knowledge, product excellence, customer value, the consideration of risk, and the potential need for agility.
- Manage and control key work processes to meet customer requirements in support of optimum value creation.
- Use in-process measures to control and improve the performance of these processes to achieve better end-product quality and performance.
- Define key support processes and ensure the day-to-day operations of these processes meet key business requirements.
- Improve key work processes to enhance core competencies, reduce variability, and obtain better product and service performance. To do this, organizations typically use approaches such as a Lean enterprise system, Six Sigma methodology, ISO quality system standards, Plan Do-Check-Act methodology, decision sciences, or After Action Reviews. These approaches could be described as part of the performance improvement system contained in P.2c in the Organizational Profile.
- Effectively manage the supply network by promoting alignment and collaboration within the network and ensuring network agility and resilience. Ensure suppliers are qualified and positioned to meet operational needs and enhance the organization's performance and customer satisfaction. Measure and evaluate supplier performance, communicate performance, provide feedback to help them improve, and deal with poorly performing suppliers.
- Make financial and other resources available to pursue opportunities for innovation that are determined to be intelligent risks, and be ready to discontinue pursuing weaker opportunities in favor of those with higher priority.

Top-performing organizations accurately and completely define key production and delivery processes, their key performance requirements, and key performance measures. These requirements and measures provide the basis for monitoring, maintaining, and improving products, services, and production and delivery processes.

Consider incorporating new technology, including e-technology, into the design of work processes. The use of e-technology might include new ways of electronically sharing information with suppliers, partners, and collaborators; communicating with customers using social networks, digital, and web-based systems; and giving them continuous (24/7) access to automated information.

Accurately determining work process requirements frequently requires organizations to capture information from customer-complaint data using the processes described in 3.2c. Immediate access to customer-complaint data allows the organization to make design or production changes quickly to prevent problems from recurring.

Top-performing organizations consider the needs and capabilities of suppliers, partners, and collaborators early in the design stage. This minimizes the chances that important requirements are not achieved because of supplier or partner limitations. For the same reasons, it is important to take into account the requirements of all stakeholders in the value chain.

Once requirements are fully understood, organizations enter the design stage. Here they must design work systems that include all of the work that needs to be done to deliver optimum value to customers.

Methods to design key work processes may differ significantly depending on the nature of the organization's product offerings—whether the products are entirely new, are variants, or involve major or minor changes. The customers' key requirements and expectations for the products drive the design process. Typical factors to consider in work process design may include safety, long-term performance, environmental impact, green manufacturing, measurement capability, process capability, manufacturability, maintainability, variability in customer expectations requiring multiple product or service options, supplier capability, requirements of relevant regulatory agencies [from P.1a(5)], and documentation, to name a few. Effective design also considers the cycle time and productivity requirements of production and delivery processes. This aspect of design might require detailed mapping of manufacturing or service processes and the redesign (reengineering) of existing processes or suppliers to achieve better efficiency and meet ever-changing customer requirements.

To enhance design-process efficiency, all related design and production activities should be well-coordinated within the organization. Coordination of design, production, and delivery processes involves all work units and individuals who take part in production and delivery, and whose performance materially affects overall process outcomes. If many design projects are carried out in parallel, or if the organization's products require parts, equipment, and facilities that are used for other products, coordination of resources can provide a way to reduce unit costs and time to market significantly.

Key work processes typically relate to the organization's core competencies, strategic objectives, and critical success factors. These key work processes typically include both product- and service-related processes including non-product-related business processes that are important to organizational success. Key business processes might include technology acquisition, knowledge management, mergers and acquisitions, expansion, project management, contract management, and sales and marketing. For non-profit organizations, business processes might include fundraising and media relations.

When managing key work processes to ensure they consistently deliver desired outcomes, in-process measures help the organization identify critical points in processes that enable the organization to predict whether the outcome will be desirable or not. In-process measures should occur as frequently as possible to minimize problems and costs that may result from unacceptable deviation from desired performance. By detecting a problem early, the cost to correct is minimized. This is not a new concept. One of our founding fathers, Benjamin Franklin, observed that "a stitch in time saves nine." The principle is still valid today.

To determine if an organization is making acceptable progress in its performance, it is often necessary to establish and monitor in-process performance levels. These in-process performance expectations, if not met, help decision makers determine whether or not corrective action is needed.

Top-performing organizations have systems in place to evaluate, improve, and innovate work processes to achieve better products and services. Better performance means not only better quality from the customers' perspective but also better financial and operational performance—such as productivity. A variety of process-improvement approaches are commonly used. These approaches include:

- Using organizational performance review results
- Sharing proven best practices or successful techniques across the organization to improve learning and innovation
- Conducting process analysis and research (for example, process mapping, value stream analysis, error proofing, and optimization experiments)
- Performing technical and business research and development
- Benchmarking
- Using alternative technology
- Using information from customers of the processes—within and outside of the organization

New process improvement approaches might also involve the use of cost data to evaluate alternatives and set improvement priorities. Taken together, these approaches offer a wide range of possibilities, including complete redesign of key processes to achieve new levels of operational excellence.

Creativity and innovation from all employees should be specifically required, measured, and recognized. Suggestion boxes are not enough. The number of innovative ideas or improvements actually implemented per person is a better indicator of innovation and idea quality than the number of ideas proposed.

In an organization that has a supportive environment for innovation, there are likely to be many more ideas than the organization has resources to pursue. The need to prioritize the good ideas calls for two critical decision points in the innovation management cycle:

1. Identifying priority targets for innovation that present the greatest likelihood of a solid return on investment and creating more value for customers and other stakeholders
2. Discontinuing less successful innovation projects and reallocating the resources to reinforce more successful projects or launch new projects

The innovation management process should capitalize on strategic opportunities identified in 2.1a(2).

For organizations that increasingly rely on outsourcing to provide key products and services, supply-network management has become a major factor in achieving productivity and profitability goals and overall organizational success. As organizations focus more on optimization, they tend to outsource when suppliers demonstrate they can perform better.

Supply-network management processes should help improve the performance of key suppliers and partners and help them provide better support to the outsourcing organization's overall operations. Feedback to suppliers regarding their performance should involve two-way communication, which allows suppliers to communicate their needs to the contracting organization.

Supply-network management might include processes for increasing preferred supplier and partner agreements to attract the highest-performing suppliers and reduce reliance on mediocre suppliers. The organization also needs to have effective processes in place to deal with poor-performing suppliers.

To demonstrate maturity, the Scoring Guidelines require that the organization has a system in place to improve and innovate its methods for determining requirements for its key work processes, designing work processes, measuring and managing work, support and business processes, and for managing innovation. The organization needs to systematically evaluate and make value-added improvements and share these innovative processes on a regular basis. In mature organizations, continuous improvement leading to innovation and sharing of best practices is a routine part of daily activities.

2021–2022 Criteria Elements Listed Individually Without Duplication See page 279 for explanation of this table			
	Basic Approach Elements [A-B] for Scoring Between 10% and 45%	**Additional Approach Elements at the Overall [A-O] Level for Scoring Between 50% and 65%**	**Additional Approach Elements at the Multiple Level [A-M] for Scoring Between 70% and 100%**
6.1 Work Processes			
6.1a(1)		Determine key product and work process requirements	
6.1a(2)		List the organization's key work processes	List the key requirements for organization's key work processes
6.1a(3)	Design key products and work processes	Design products and work processes to meet requirements	Incorporate the following into the organization's products and processes • New technology, • Organizational knowledge, • Product excellence, • Customer value, • The consideration of risk, and • The potential need for agility
6.1b(1)	Manage key products and work processes	Ensure the day-to-day operation of work processes meets key process requirements	• Use key performance measures or indicators and in-process measures to control and improve work processes • Describe these measures and show they relate to end-product quality and performance
6.1b(2)		Determine key support processes	• List the key support processes • Ensure the day-to-day operation of these processes meets key business requirements
6.1b(3)	Improve key products and work processes	Improve work processes and support processes to— • Improve products • Improve process performance • Enhance core competencies • Reduce variability	
6.1c		Manage the supply network	• Select suppliers and ensure that they are qualified and positioned to meet operational needs, support strategic objectives, and enhance the organization's performance and customer satisfaction • Promote alignment and collaboration in the supply network • Ensure supply-network agility and resilience in responding to customer, market, and organizational requirements • Communicate performance expectations to the supply network • Measure and evaluate supplier performance • Provide feedback to suppliers to help them improve
6.1d		Pursue identified opportunities for innovation	• Pursue the strategic opportunities the organization determines are intelligent risks • Make financial and other resources available to pursue these opportunities • Discontinue pursuing opportunities at the appropriate time

6.1 Work Processes

Basic Approach Element: *Design, manage, and improve key products and work processes*

Overall Approach Elements:
- *Determine key product and work process requirements [6.1a(1)]*
- *List the organization's key work processes [6.1a(2)]*
- *Design products and work processes to meet requirements [6.1a(3)]*
- *Ensure the day-to-day operation of work processes meets key process requirements [6.1b(1)]*
- *Determine the organization's key support processes [6.1b(2)]*
- *Improve work processes and support processes to improve products and performance, enhance core competencies, and reduce variability [6.1b(3)]*
- *Manage the supply network [6.1c]*
- *Pursue identified opportunities for innovation [6.1d]*

The following diagram describes key approach elements:

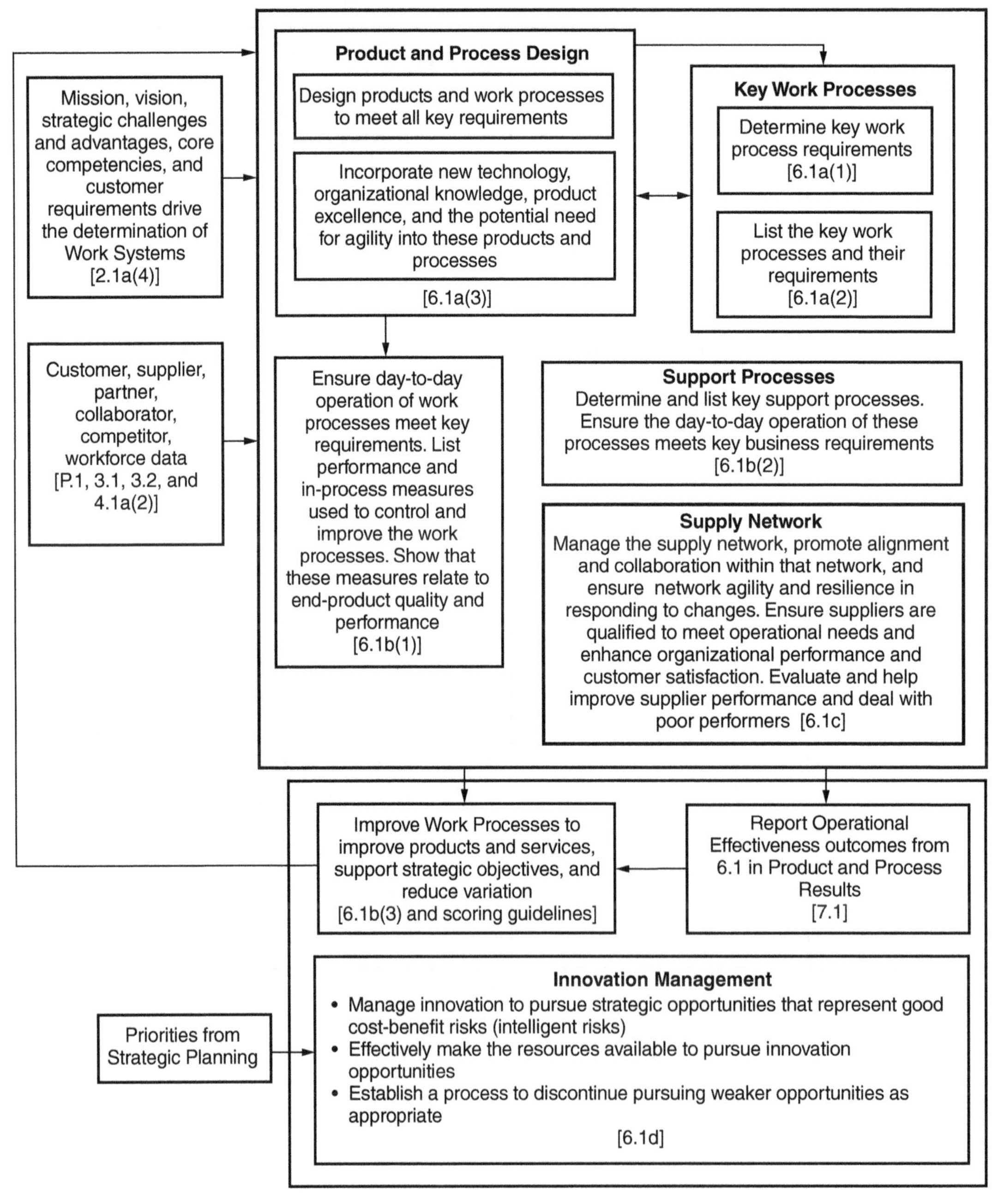

6.1 Key Work Processes Item Linkages

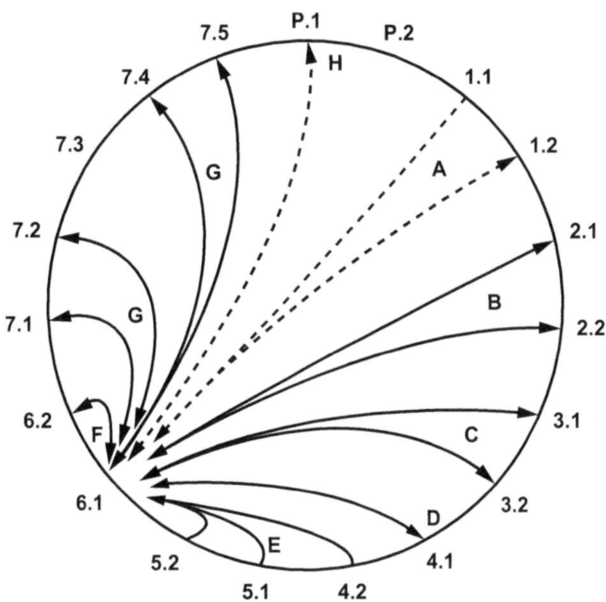

NATURE OF RELATIONSHIP	
A	Senior leaders [1.1] and the governance system [1.2a] have a responsibility for ensuring that work processes critical for growth and success are designed to meet all requirements [6.1] consistent with the organization's vision and values [1.1a(1)], ensuring legal, regulatory, and ethical requirements are met [1.2b], as well as those relating to societal contributions and good corporate citizenship [1.2c].
B	Core competencies and the components of work systems are considered during the planning process [2.1a(4)] and used to determine key work processes, which drive their design and management [6.1].
C	Product offerings to meet or exceed customer requirements [3.1b(2)] and mechanisms to support the use of products [3.2a(2)] must be considered in the design of work processes [6.1a(3)] and the identification of product and support and supply network requirements to deliver customer value [6.1a(1, 2), 6.1b(2), and 6.1c]. Factors of work processes that contribute to delivering customer value [6.1a(3)] help in the design of processes to listen to, interact with, and observe the customers [3.1a] and assess satisfaction, dissatisfaction, and engagement [3.2b(1)].
D	Key performance and in-process measures [6.1b(1)] help define data collection [4.1a(1)] and support analysis and operational decision-making [4.1b]. Performance improvement priorities [4.1c(2)] align with the selection and management of innovation priorities [6.1d].
E	A culture that promotes an engaged workforce and high-performance work [5.2b], effective recognition [5.2c(1)], workforce and leader development [5.2c(2)], a secure, healthful work climate [5.1b(1)], and ready access to knowledge and information to support decision-making [4.2] are essential to design, deliver, and improve work and support processes [6.1].
F	Process management [6.1b] considers cost control [6.2a] and other effectiveness and efficiency factors to improve work processes.

Continued

NATURE OF RELATIONSHIP	*Continued*
G	Data about product and process performance [7.1] and customer results [7.2] are used to target improvement efforts to help ensure work processes meet end-product quality and performance requirements [6.1b(3)]. Improved product and process design [6.1a(3)] can produce better customer satisfaction [7.2], product and process performance [7.1], financial results [7.5], and societal contributions [7.4a(5)] and regulatory compliance [7.4a(3)].
H	Information in P.1a(1) about main product offerings (see P.1, Note P and P.1a(1).) should align with product and process design requirements [6.1] and help set the context for examiner review of these processes.

IF YOU DON'T DO WHAT THE CRITERIA REQUIRE . . .

Item Reference	**Possible Adverse Consequences**
6.1a(1)	**Determination of Product and Process Requirements** – Failure to define work process requirements accurately and completely will produce undesired results and nonconforming products and services. This, in turn, requires even more rework or more people-intensive services, which can add significant delay and cost, and prevent the organization from achieving its objectives. When these processes fail to meet requirements, resources are wasted and the success of the organization may be jeopardized.
6.1a(2)	**Determination of Product and Process Requirements** – Failure to determine key product and work process requirements makes it difficult to measure and monitor the extent to which these requirements are being met. This causes delay in uncovering problems and increases the cost to correct them, eroding customer value. In turn this makes it difficult to sustain the organization or enable it to thrive.
6.1a(2)	**Key Work Processes** – The key work processes and their requirements can vary significantly within an organization depending on the nature of the products and services required by customers. Design processes may also vary based on whether the products and services are new or only involve minor variations to current product and service offerings. In any event, a design process that fails to consider the key requirements for products and services, and other factors such as environmental impact, process capability, measurement capability, customer service expectations, supplier capability, and customer documentation requirements (such as found in ISO 9001), may make it difficult or impossible for the organization to achieve desired results (satisfy customers) in an efficient and cost-effective (profitable) manner.
6.1a(3)	**Design Concepts** – Organizations that fail to consider all work system, customer, supplier, stakeholder, and key operational performance requirements when designing key work processes typically find that the system they designed is not optimum. Design flaws produce undesired results, such as nonconforming products and services. These, in turn, require even more rework to correct. The failure to identify and address all of the requirements may increase the likelihood of downstream problems with the design, production, and delivery of core products and services. Design processes that are not capable of incorporating changing customer or market requirements in a timely fashion are not sufficiently agile and may make it difficult to remain competitive. An organization that receives customer change requirements at a faster pace than it can implement the changes can be virtually paralyzed. Unwieldy design systems often lead to frustrated workers, excessive delay, and ultimately dissatisfied

Continued

IF YOU DON'T DO WHAT THE CRITERIA REQUIRE . . . *Continued*	
Item Reference	**Possible Adverse Consequences**
	customers and lost business. When faced with rapidly changing technology, customer requirements, or market demands, inflexible or cumbersome design processes can render a once-good design obsolete before it ever gets to production.
6.1a(3)	**Design Concepts** – As work processes are designed, the organization must ensure they meet all key requirements, especially those that might be considered *game changers* such as new technology and new standards of product excellence and agility. Failure to consider these factors in the design of work processes can cause key work processes to fail to meet requirements consistently, add cost, and erode customer value.
6.1a(3)	**Design Concepts** – In today's highly competitive global economy, flexibility and agility are important factors that distinguish the best-performing organizations from the rest. The best-performing organizations provide their customers with more value at a faster pace (agility), and across a wider range of areas (flexibility) than their competition. The advantages offered by new technologies typically enhance value. If applied properly, the leaders are able to distinguish their organizations in chosen markets, keeping their current customers and acquiring new ones. Even possessing the latest technologies does not guarantee an advantage if they are not properly used. For example, an organization may possess the latest computers, but those computers may not be used effectively to improve work processes in ways that are important to customers. One Fortune 500 company, learning that its customers placed a premium on accurate bills being delivered on time, acquired and implemented new technology to dramatically speed up its billing cycle. Unfortunately, the billing process itself was not capable of rendering an accurate invoice. Customers received their inaccurate invoices faster than ever (and were expected to pay sooner). Using technology to accelerate a bad process simply produces unsatisfactory results faster. The failure to incorporate the technology appropriately can have significant adverse effects on an organization's ability to add value for its customers and to operate in an efficient and effective manner.
6.1a(3)	**Design Concepts** – Eliminating unnecessary steps in any work process tends to reduce variation (increasing quality), reduce cycle time, and reduce cost. In addition, sharing knowledge and learning from the successes and mistakes of others help prevent workers from repeating the same problems (which add rework, waste, and delay). When designing new products and services and related production and delivery systems, the failure to consider factors such as risk, cost control, new technology, variability, and ways to enhance productivity and efficiency typically adds unnecessary cost, delay, and rework, making it more difficult to balance increasing demands from customers and the marketplace.
6.1b(1)	**Process Implementation** – The best-performing organizations consistently deliver programs, products, and services that meet key performance requirements. They do this by identifying key processes, monitoring them regularly, and improving then continuously. The failure to ensure consistent day-to-day operation of production and delivery processes increases the likelihood of defects, which contribute to rework, waste, delay, excessive costs, and customer dissatisfaction. Organizations can always tell if a work process is producing desired results by checking to see if the end product or service meets customer and operational requirements. Unfortunately, waiting for the end of the process to learn that it has not produced desired results is time-consuming and expensive, since most costs may have already been expended. The earlier an

Continued

IF YOU DON'T DO WHAT THE CRITERIA REQUIRE . . . *Continued*	
Item Reference	**Possible Adverse Consequences**
	organization determines if a process is not likely to produce desired results, the earlier it can take corrective action to minimize rework, scrap, delay, and avoid unnecessary cost. Top-performing organizations collect in-process data to identify problems early. The failure to collect and analyze in-process data makes it more difficult for workers to know when to adjust a process to make it work better. Inappropriate or unnecessary adjustments can actually increase variation and decrease productivity and quality. Customers are in an excellent position to determine if the products and services they receive meet (or exceed) their requirements. They can provide near-real-time feedback [3.2] that engaged workers use to make prompt adjustments to resolve complaints and meet customer requirements. The failure to gather and use this information makes it more difficult for organizations to make timely changes to reduce rework costs and increase customer satisfaction.
6.1b(2)	**Support Processes** – The failure to determine key support processes and ensure the effective day-to-day operation of these processes consistently meets key business requirements may undermine the ability of key work process functions to meet their customer requirements. For example, inefficient procurement or human resource support processes may cause critical and costly delays in obtaining supplies and filling key positions respectively. Ineffective maintenance may cause key equipment to fail, which could stop or delay production.
6.1b(3)	**Product and Process Improvement** – Organizations that fail to evaluate and improve key work processes systematically often lag behind the competition. Consider two comparable organizations, each using similar processes to develop and deliver similar products and services. Let's also assume that the organizations are equally competitive today. However, one organization has embedded into its work processes an ongoing evaluation and improvement of its design, production, and delivery systems; the other has not. As time passes, the first organization begins to see the impact of improved work processes. It is able to produce goods and services faster, better, and cheaper than its competitor. It has been able to pass a portion of its cost savings on to its customers (lowering prices), keeping the rest as increased profit, which helps expand R&D. As a result of better, timelier, and less-expensive products, it is acquiring greater market share—at the expense of its competitor—and making its stockholders exceedingly happy as its share price increases. In addition, the first organization has been able to accelerate performance by sharing improvements with other organizational units so they can get better as well. The organization that does not systematically improve continues to fall further and further behind in a highly competitive environment (or as the popular adage acclaims, "Today, if you're standing still, you're falling behind"). The failure to consistently improve and share these better practices with other organizational support units may cause them to waste time and other resources in redundant work—work that adds cost but not value.
6.1c	**Supply-Network Management** – If an organization's suppliers are unable to consistently meet requirements to provide required products and services, the organization and its customers will suffer. Defects and delays caused by suppliers create problems for the organization and adversely affect the satisfaction and engagement of its customers and workforce.
6.1d	**Management of Opportunities for Innovation** – For optimum effectiveness and value, innovation should be proactively managed rather than being driven by the random winds of fortune. The failure to pursue strategic opportunities that are determined to provide a good

Continued

IF YOU DON'T DO WHAT THE CRITERIA REQUIRE . . . *Continued*	
Item Reference	**Possible Adverse Consequences**
	benefit for the risk involved (referred to as *intelligent risk*), can contribute to a risk-averse culture that does not keep pace with its competition. Alternatively, taking foolish chances where the potential benefit is low and the risk is high contributes to needless losses. This approach will not enable the organization to surpass a competitor that practices intelligent risk taking. Spending the resources to identify intelligent opportunities for innovation and then failing to make resources available to pursue these opportunities also wastes resources and prevents advancement. The failure to stop investing in an opportunity for innovation that has proven marginal and shift resources to new, higher priority and more beneficial opportunity also wastes resources and limits advancement.

6.1 WORK PROCESSES—SAMPLE EFFECTIVE PRACTICES

a. Product and Process Design

- Product and key work process requirements are systematically translated into process specifications, with measurement plans to monitor process consistency.
- The work of all key functions is coordinated to bring the product or service through the design-to-delivery phases efficiently. Bureaucratic barriers between units have been eliminated.
- Concurrent engineering is used to determine key product and work process requirements and design several key work and support processes (for example, product and service planning; R&D; manufacturing; marketing; procurement; workforce management; and supplier certification) in parallel, rather than in sequence. All activities are closely coordinated through effective communication and teamwork.
- A multifunctional team of professional and support staff, customers, suppliers, and senior leaders reviews the requirements of each major work process to ensure it fully meets all requirements. Reviews are documented and shared to ensure consistency among teams. At the end of each requirement review cycle, the review process is evaluated and refinements are documented and shared throughout the organization.
- Highly agile production processes are put in place to enable greater customization and choice for individual customers and the marketplace.
- Steps are taken (such as product and service design testing or prototyping) to ensure that the production and delivery process will work as designed, and will consistently meet customer requirements.
- Performance and customer requirements are determined using facts and data.
- Internal process capacity and supplier capability, using measures such as C_{pk}, are reviewed and considered before work process and designs or plans are implemented.
- A systematic, iterative process (such as quality function deployment) is used to maintain a focus on voice-of-the-customer information and use customer requirements to guide design, production, and delivery.

b. Process Management and Improvement

- Product-design requirements are systematically translated into process specifications, with measurement plans to monitor process consistency.

- Processes are monitored using accurate in-process measures to uncover design or implementation errors and subsequent corrections are monitored and verified. Problem alerts and improvement notices are shared throughout the organization.
- Systems are in place to ensure process performance is maintained and customer requirements are met. In-process measures are defined and monitored constantly to ensure early alert of problems.
- Work processes are monitored using statistical or other process-control techniques.
- Work processes that produce errors or rework are systematically evaluated using tools (such as lean enterprise, Six Sigma, PDCA, or After Action Reviews) to reduce non-value steps. Improvements are documented and shared within the organization. Root causes of problems are systematically identified and corrected for processes that produce defects.
- Design processes are evaluated and improved so that future designs are developed faster (shorter cycle time), at lower cost, and with higher quality relative to key product or service characteristics that predict customer satisfaction.
- Work-process simplification and performance-improvement tools are applied to support processes with measurable sustained results.
- Measurable goals and related actions are used to drive higher levels of work-process performance.
- Key work processes are tracked using both quantitative and qualitative measures. These measures assess the extent to which customer requirements are met.
- For processes that produce defects (out-of-control processes), root causes are quickly and systematically identified and corrective action is taken to prevent their recurrence.
- Tools—such as flowcharting, work redesign, and reengineering—are used throughout the organization to review and improve work processes.
- Information about customer requirements, complaints, concerns, and reactions to products and services are captured near-real time and used directly by line workers to improve their work processes.
- Benchmarking, competitive comparison data, or information from customers of the process (in or out of the organization) are used to gain insight to improve processes.
- Results data that demonstrate better process performance, reduced unacceptable variability, and higher quality (improved) products are reported in Item 7.1. The impact of these improvements on customer satisfaction, engagement, and dissatisfaction are reported in Item 7.2.

c. *Supply-Network Management*

- Key suppliers participate in structured improvement processes using the Integrated Management System of the Baldrige Framework and the CPE. They participate in annual or biannual reviews, share feedback reports with the chief supply-network officer, and take corrective actions based on the opportunities for improvement identified by examiners. Suppliers are willing to align and collaborate within the supply network to help meet changing requirements.
- The organization's procurement process contains three major steps when deciding which supplier's proposal to accept:
  - Step 1: A Baldrige-based review of each prospective supplier's management system is conducted based on a written assessment. If the Baldrige score shows effective processes are in place, the proposal moves to step 2.
  - Step 2: An analysis and rating of the supplier's technical proposal (which describes the supplier's plan to deliver the required products and services) is conducted based on published selection factors. Top-scoring suppliers move to step 3.
  - Step 3: The supplier's cost proposal is reviewed and a cost-benefit analysis is performed. This analysis also covers projected

future cost reductions the supplier expects to pass on to the client due to improved efficiencies from using the Baldrige performance excellence processes.

d. Management of Opportunities for Innovation

- The organization requires its employees to allocate time each week to innovate processes consistent with business priorities.
- A formal innovation protocol is used to identify high-priority innovation targets to ensure they are consistent with mission, vision, and strategy. Cost-benefit analyses are conducted. Baseline operational measures capture performance measures before and after the innovation. Changed processes are tested through limited implementation, monitored, and measured to determine the impact of the innovation. One of two paths is typically taken: (a) If the change is positive and worth the investment, the innovation is approved for wider deployment and locked into place as a new protocol or standard procedure; or (b) If the change did not produce desired results the process is either modified further or dropped to permit resources to be dedicated to innovations that appear to be more worthy. If successful, the new process is subject to ongoing monitoring and subsequent refinement using the same formal innovation approach or continuous improvements techniques such as Lean, Rapid Improvement Exercises, PDCA, After Action Reviews, and Problem Solving Processes.
- Innovation funds are budgeted as part of the strategic planning and action planning processes. Innovation is considered a business imperative and not something to do only if leftover resources become available.

Ineffective Practices

- Work systems, such as manufacturing and supply network are not updated. Management sees investment in redesign as too expensive.
- Sharing and cross-functional teaming among work units is not encouraged and in some organizations is prohibited. Thus, leaders limit open communication and make nearly all decisions for workers.
- The organization does not change its designs unless required by regulations or statute. Facts and data related to customers do not affect design. The sentiment communicated to customers is, “Our engineers know how to make best use of our technology.”
- To drive higher levels of performance, the organization cuts the workforce to scare those left behind into working harder.
- Process improvement is the responsibility of the Continuous Process Improvement Team. Other units are required to follow standard operating procedures and leave the improvement and innovation to the experts.
- Waste is a problem for the organization but no improvements have been developed because “no one is any better than us, so why worry.”
- We have a monopoly. We do not need to worry about improving or innovating. Customers will have to use our services even if they do not like us.
- There is no effective process in place, such as root cause analysis and decision science, to analyze problems and systematically uncover and mitigate the causes of process or product failure. Politics and intuition drive decisions more than data and reason.
- The organization makes suppliers compete among themselves to squeeze every penny out of the bid and always award to the low-cost vendor. Supplier loyalty and partnering are considered to be overrated.
- Innovation happens only when senior leaders have ideas. Innovations are implemented with no assessment of intelligent risk.

6.2 OPERATIONAL EFFECTIVENESS: How do you ensure effective management of your operations? (40 Pts.) PROCESS

a. Process Efficiency and Effectiveness

How do you manage the cost, efficiency, and effectiveness of your operations? How do you

- incorporate cycle time, productivity, and other efficiency and effectiveness factors into your work processes;
- prevent defects, service errors, and rework;
- minimize warranty costs or customers' productivity losses, as appropriate;
- minimize the costs of inspections, tests, and process or performance audits, as appropriate; and
- balance the need for cost control and efficiency with the needs of your customers?

b. Security and Cybersecurity

How do you ensure the security and cybersecurity of sensitive or privileged data and information and of key assets? How do you manage physical and digital data, information, and key operational systems to ensure confidentiality and only appropriate physical and digital access? How do you

- maintain your awareness of emerging security and cybersecurity threats;
- ensure that your workforce, customers, partners, and suppliers understand and fulfill their security and cybersecurity roles and responsibilities;
- identify and prioritize key information technology and operational systems to secure; and
- protect these systems from potential cybersecurity events, detect cybersecurity events, and respond to and recover from cybersecurity incidents?

c. Safety, Business Continuity, and Resilience

(1) **Safety How do you provide a safe operating environment for your workforce and other people in your workplace?** How does your safety system address accident prevention, inspection, root-cause analysis of failures, and recovery?

(2) **Business Continuity and Resilience How do you ensure that your organization can anticipate, prepare for, and recover from disasters, emergencies, and other disruptions?** How do you consider risk, prevention, protection, continuity of operations, and recovery in the event of disruptions? How do you take into account customer and business needs and your reliance on your workforce, supply network, partners, and information technology systems?

Notes:

6.2b. For examples of what your information technology systems might include, see the Note to 4.2a(2).

6.2b. Managing cybersecurity includes protecting against the loss of sensitive information about employees, customers, and organizations; protecting assets, including intellectual property; and protecting against the financial, legal, and reputational aspects of breaches. There are many sources for general and industry-specific cybersecurity standards and practices. Many are referenced in the *Framework for Improving Critical Infrastructure Cybersecurity* (https://www.nist.gov/cyberframework). The *Baldrige Cybersecurity Excellence Builder* (https://www.nist.gov/baldrige/products-services) is a self-assessment tool incorporating the concepts of the Cybersecurity Framework and the Baldrige systems perspective.

6.2c(2). Some organizations are involved in communitywide efforts to ensure resilience. NIST's Community Resilience Planning Guide (https://www.nist.gov/topics/community-resilience/planning-guide) is a resource for communitywide efforts.

6.2c(2). Disasters and emergencies might be short- or longer-term and might be related to weather, climate, utilities, security, or a local or national health or other emergency. The extent to which you prepare for such events will depend on your organization's environment and its sensitivity to short- or longer-term disruptions of operations. Acceptable levels of risk will vary depending on the nature of your products, services, supply network, and stakeholder needs and expectations.

Comparison with the Education and Health Care Criteria

In Item 6.2c, Safety, Business Continuity, and Resilience, the Business, Health Care, and Education Criteria request slightly different information:

- The Business Criteria asks how the organization prevents defects, service errors, and rework and minimizes warranty costs or customers' productivity losses, as appropriate
- The Health Care Criteria asks about preventing rework and errors, but includes new part 6.2c(2), which addresses Patient Safety and asks how the applicant reduces patient harm, and medical errors and how the patient safety system (similar to the Business and Education Criteria) addresses accident prevention, root cause analysis of failures, and recovery.
- The Education Criteria asks how the safety system address accident prevention, inspection, root-cause analysis of failures, and recovery preventing errors and rework.

Item 6.2 examines processes to ensure operational efficiency and effectiveness through cost control, security and cybersecurity of data and information, a safe operating environment, and continuity of operations in an emergency.

The best way to minimize the need for tests, inspections, and audits is to consistently, without fail, produce desired outcomes. To help minimize unacceptable variation (errors), organizations use key measurements, observations, or interactions at the earliest points possible in processes. When deviations occur, corrective action is taken to restore the performance of the process to its design specifications.

Providing optimal value for customers and other stakeholders requires the most efficient and effective operational processes. Reducing error, waste, cost, and non-value-adding work is essential.

Top organizations prevent unacceptable variation in work processes to minimize the need for inspections, tests, and audits to avoid rework and warranty costs. Sometimes these processes involve error proofing, which makes it impossible to do the wrong thing the wrong way (for example, electrical cords with two-prong plugs on today's appliances have one plug blade wider than the other to prevent the plug from being inserted incorrectly into a wall outlet).

Lean process management techniques are widely used to eliminate unnecessary process steps, and in so doing, reduce non-value-adding work, cost, and cycle time. Six Sigma techniques are commonly used to reduce unacceptable variation, error, and defects, which help increase productivity and product yield and reduce cost.

The Item also examines efforts to prevent poor quality, such as rework, defective products, scrap, and waste, rather than incur costs to identify defects and errors through unnecessary testing and inspections or mitigate poor quality through warranty claims.

Efficient corrective action involves changes at the source (root cause) of the deviation. Effective corrective action minimizes the likelihood of this type of deviation occurring again or anywhere else in the organization.

Organizations must ensure data and information reliability since reliability is critical to good decision-making, successful monitoring of operations, and successful data integration for assessing overall performance. However, data reliability or consistency alone is not sufficient. To be useful, data must also be accurate [see 4.2a(1)]. Consistently incorrect data do not help leaders make consistently good decisions.

Processes should be in place to protect against data and information system failure that may damage or destroy critical data, including cybersecurity threats. This may require redundant systems as well as effective backup and storage of data at remote locations. Processes should be in place to protect against external security threats, including attacks from hackers, viral infections, power surges, and weather-related damage. The plans that support organizational continuity and ensure workplace preparedness for disasters and emergencies should be presented as a part of managing Security and Cybersecurity [6.2b(2)] and Safety, Business Continuity, and Resilience [6.2b].

Information management systems should facilitate the use of data and information and should recognize the need for rapid data validation, reliability assurance, and security—considering the frequency and magnitude of electronic data transfer and the challenges presented by cybersecurity threats.

Managing cybersecurity includes protecting against the loss of sensitive information about employees, customers, and organizations; protecting intellectual property; and protecting against the financial, legal, and reputational aspects of breaches. There are many sources for general and industry-specific cybersecurity standards and practices. Many are referenced in the *Framework for Improving Critical Infrastructure Cybersecurity* (http://www.nist.gov/cyberframework). The *Baldrige Cybersecurity Excellence Builder* is a self-assessment tool incorporating the Cybersecurity Framework and the Baldrige systems approach.

Organizations are required to meet statutory and regulatory standards for workplace and workforce safety. However, high-performing organizations not only meet these minimum standards but exceed them in recognition of the fact that accidents and injuries waste resources and hurt productivity. The best organizations put in place effective systems to prevent accidents, including regular safety inspections to identify potential problems before they occur. With input from people directly involved in the work, these organizations ensure a safe working environment.

Disasters and emergencies—whether man-made or natural—can significantly disrupt operations, add costs, and adversely impact customer and worker satisfaction and engagement. Efforts to ensure continuity of operations in an emergency to minimize these disruptions should consider all facets of the organization's operations that are needed to provide products and services to customers.

Disasters and emergencies might be related to infections spread such as pandemic, weather, utilities disruption, security breaches, or a local or national emergency. The extent to which an organization must prepare for disasters or emergencies typically depend on the organization's environment and its sensitivity to disruptions of operations. Acceptable levels of risk will vary depending on the nature or criticality of the organization's products, services, supply network, and stakeholder needs and expectations. The impact of climate change could impose greater disruptions on some organizations than on others.

The specific level of operations that will need to be sustained depends on the criticality of the product or service to customer needs. For example, a public utility that provides water or electricity is likely to have a more critical demand for services in an emergency than an organization that provides a nonessential product or service. Organizations such as the Red Cross and the Federal Emergency Management Agency (FEMA) will have a great need for service readiness and the ability to sustain operations and recover quickly if their operations are disrupted. These organizations develop contingency plans, test the processes through simulations and emergency drills, and consistently make improvements. In addition, these organizations ensure that the processes used to support business continuity are coordinated and aligned with processes to ensure the availability of data and information.

Emergency preparedness to help ensure business continuity for organizations that employ or serve weakened or impaired people should also consider their special needs for life-support and evacuation. This is especially true of health care organizations.

To demonstrate maturity, the Scoring Guidelines require that the organization has a system in place to improve and innovate and share the processes it uses to provide operational effectiveness. The organization needs to evaluate, improve, and innovate its operational effectiveness strategies more often than annually. The organization should demonstrate that it has made meaningful, value-added improvements in its techniques for cost control, workplace safety, business continuity, security and cybersecurity, the reliability of information systems and emergency preparedness.

2021–2022 Criteria Elements Listed Individually Without Duplication See page 279 for explanation of this table			
	Basic Approach Elements [A-B] for Scoring Between 10% and 45%	**Additional Approach Elements at the Overall [A-O] Level for Scoring Between 50% and 65%**	**Additional Approach Elements at the Multiple Level [A-M] for Scoring Between 70% and 100%**
6.2 Operational Effectiveness			
6.2a	Ensure effective management of operations	Manage the cost, efficiency, and effectiveness of operations	• Incorporate cycle time, productivity, and other efficiency and effectiveness factors into the organization's work processes • Prevent defects, service errors, and rework • Minimize warranty costs or customers' productivity losses, as appropriate • Minimize the costs of inspections, tests, and process or performance audits, as appropriate • Balance the need for cost control with the needs of customers
6.2b		Ensure the security and cybersecurity of • Sensitive or privileged data and information, and • Key assets	• Manage digital and physical data and information and key operational systems to ensure confidentiality and only appropriate physical and digital access • Be aware of emerging security and cybersecurity threat • Ensure that the workforce, customers, partners, and suppliers understand and fulfill security and cybersecurity responsibilities • Identify and prioritize information technology and operational systems to secure • Protect these systems from potential cybersecurity attacks and detect, respond to, and recover from cybersecurity incidents
6.2c(1)		Provide a safe operating environment for your workforce and other people in the workplace	Ensure the safety system addresses accident prevention, inspection, root-cause analysis of failures, and recovery
6.2c(2)		Ensure that the organization can anticipate, prepare for, and recover from disasters, emergencies, and other disruptions	The disaster and emergency preparedness system • Considers risk prevention, protection, continuity of operations, and recovery • Takes into account the organization's customer and business needs and its reliance on the workforce, supply network, partners, and information technology systems continue to be secure and available to serve customers and meet business needs

6.2 Operational Effectiveness

Basic Approach Element: ***Ensure effective management of operations on an ongoing basis and for the future***

Overall Approach Elements:
- ***Manage the cost, efficiency, and effectiveness of operations [6.2a]***
- ***Ensure the security and cybersecurity of sensitive or privileged data and of key assets [6.2b]***
- ***Provide a safe operating environment for your workforce and other people in your workplace [6.2c(1)]***
- ***Ensure the organization can anticipate, prepare for, and recover from disasters, emergencies and other disruptions [6.2c(2)]***

The following diagram describes key approach elements:

Ensure Operational Effectiveness

Process Efficiency and Effectiveness
Manage the cost, efficiency, and effectiveness of operations, incorporating cycle time, productivity, and other effectiveness and efficiency factors to prevent defects and errors and minimize warranty cost and customers' productivity losses while balancing customer needs. Minimize costs of tests and inspections. Balance cost controls with the needs of customers.
[6.2a]

Security and Cybersecurity
Ensure the security and cybersecurity of sensitive or privileged data and information. Manage electronic and physical data and information to ensure confidentiality and only appropriate access. Maintain awareness of emerging security and cybersecurity threats; ensure that the workforce, customers, partners, and suppliers understand and fulfill their security and cybersecurity roles and responsibilities; identify and prioritize key information technology and operational systems to secure; and protect these systems from potential cybersecurity events, detect cybersecurity events, and respond to and recover from cybersecurity incidents
[6.2b]

Safety and Emergency Preparedness

Safety
Provide a safe operating environment that addresses accident prevention, inspection, root-cause analysis of failures, and recovery
[6.2c(1)]

Business Continuity
Prepare for disasters and emergencies, taking into account prevention, continuity of operations, recovery, and reliance on supply networks and partners
[6.2c(2)]

[6.2c]

Improve priority areas of the Integrated Management System including operational effectiveness processes
[Learning scoring guidelines]

6.2 Key Operational Effectiveness Item Linkages

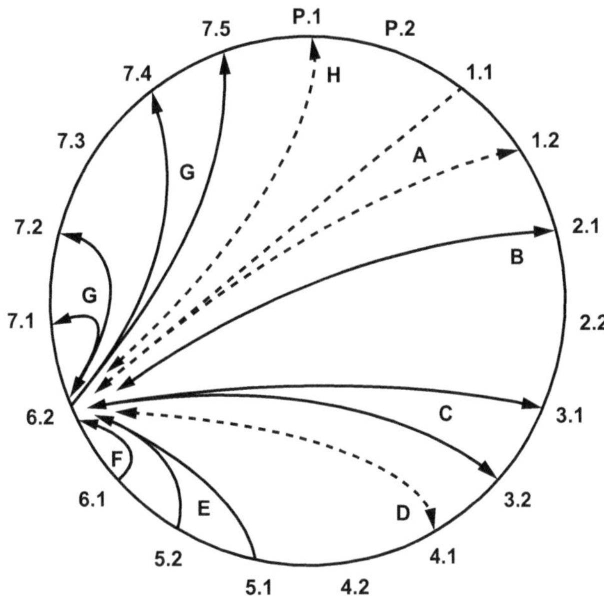

NATURE OF RELATIONSHIP	
A	Senior leaders are responsible for creating an environment for success, customer and workforce engagement, equity, and inclusion [1.1c(1)]; creating a focus on action [1.1c(2)]; and ensuring that operations are managed [6.2a] in an efficient and cost-effective manner consistent with the organization's vision and values, including those relating to ethical principles, societal contributions, and good corporate citizenship [1.2].
B	Operational effectiveness priorities [6.2] are consistent with strategic opportunities and priorities for innovation and intelligent risk taking [2.1a(2)].
C	The management of operational effectiveness on an ongoing basis [6.2] helps deliver customer value consistent with the customer-listening processes [3.1a] and mechanisms to support the use of products [3.2a(2)]. Factors that contribute to customer value help in the design of voice-of-the-customer processes [3.1a] and to assess satisfaction, dissatisfaction, and engagement [3.2b].
D	Operations cost, efficiency and effectiveness, safety, and emergency data [6.2] are used to help review performance [4.1b], identify benchmarking targets [4.1a(2)], and set priorities for improvement [4.1c(2)].
E	Effective reward and recognition [5.2c(1)], processes that promote equity and inclusion for a diverse workforce [5.2c(5)], leader, manager, and workforce development [5.2c(2, 4)], and a healthy, secure workplace environment [5.1b(1)], are essential to managing and improving operational effectiveness [6.2].
F	The work processes designed in Item 6.1a(3) must be managed [6.1b(1)] to ensure operational effectiveness [6.2] and include considerations related to cost control [6.2a], safety [6.2c(1)], and business continuity and resilience [6.2c(2)].
G	Information about product and process performance [7.1] and customer results [7.2] can be used to target improvement efforts in process effectiveness, efficiency, and cost control [6.2a], , and safety [6.2c(1)]. More effective operations [6.2] help produce better customer engagement and satisfaction

Continued

NATURE OF RELATIONSHIP *Continued*	
	[7.2], product and process quality [7.1], financial, market, and strategy results [7.5], societal well-being and support of key communities [7.4a(5)], and regulatory compliance [7.4a(3)].
H	Information in P.1a(1) about main product offerings [see P.1a(1) Note] and key suppliers and partners [P.1b(3)], should align with operational effectiveness priorities in 6.2 and help set the context for examiner review of these processes.

IF YOU DON'T DO WHAT THE CRITERIA REQUIRE . . .	
Item Reference	**Possible Adverse Consequences**
6.2a(1)	**Process Efficiency and Effectiveness** – An organization that fails to manage cost, efficiency, and effectiveness of operations and prevent defects and service errors, wastes resources. High-performing organizations do not rely on excessive inspection and testing to determine if process requirements are met or not. Instead, these organizations design process controls that let them know how well the process is performing during each of its critical steps. They develop processes that prevent problems using tools and techniques such as error proofing and statistical process control. The best that testing or inspection can hope to accomplish is to uncover and correct a problem before the customer is disrupted. Although this is better than causing problems for customers, it is still more costly to fix the problem than to prevent it from happening in the first place.
6.2b	**Security and Cybersecurity** – Information management systems that fail to protect and secure sensitive data, privileged information, and assets expose the organization and its workforce, suppliers, and customers to numerous security and cybersecurity threats. These threats appear to be growing exponentially and organizations of all sizes, including government security agencies, have fallen victim to debilitating cybersecurity attacks.
6.2c(1)	**Safety** – The failure to provide a safe operating environment that addresses accident prevention, inspection, root-cause analysis of failures, and recovery contributes to accidents and injuries that waste resources and hurt productivity. The best organizations put effective systems in place to prevent accidents, including regular inspections to identify potential problems before they occur.
6.2c(2)	**Business Continuity and Resilience** – Emergencies and disasters—whether natural or man made—are difficult to predict, but anticipating and preparing for them is essential. The stress and confusion created by a disaster, emergency, or other disruption can cause a normally efficient operation to become dysfunctional and fail. It is difficult to change processes during a disaster, which makes recovery nearly impossible until the emergency passes. Although the timing of disasters is difficult to predict, the possibility of one occurring is great enough to cause the best-performing organizations to make preparations, in advance, to minimize the potential adverse impact. Failure to prepare (in advance) increases the possibility of catastrophic failure, which many organizations may not survive.

6.2 OPERATIONAL EFFECTIVENESS—SAMPLE EFFECTIVE PRACTICES

a. Process Efficiency and Effectiveness

- Key operations are systematically reviewed to improve productivity, reduce cycle time and waste, and increase quality. These process improvements are shared throughout the organization.
- Cost-benefit analysis is performed for each major option step in the key operation to analyze the merits of alternate approaches.
- Benchmarking studies, consistent with the procedures in 4.1a(2) are conducted on critical, high-cost, high-value, or high-impact operations.
- Checklists are used to ensure all process steps are completed, minimizing rework and service errors.

b. Security and Cybersecurity

- A data reliability (consistency) team periodically and randomly checks data. Systems are in place to minimize or prevent human error in data entry and analysis.
- Data are protected against inappropriate access and misuse from external and internal sources through encryption and randomly changing user passwords. Extensive protections against the release of personal data, such as that required by the Health Insurance Portability and Accountability Act of 1996 (HIPAA), help ensure confidentiality and only appropriate access.
- Security concerns and threats are taken seriously as potential electronic terrorism, scamming, and viruses/worms all threaten the security and availability of data systems, hardware, and software.
- Depending on the importance of data and information, organizations employ specialists in security and cybersecurity who continuously test and inspect information systems and data for vulnerabilities.

c. Safety, Business Continuity, and Resilience

- A formal process exists to conduct emergency and disaster-scenario analysis, planning, and testing.
- Disaster and emergency plans are recorded and coordinated with relevant public and private organizations, such as the Red Cross, local law enforcement, National Guard, Coast Guard, hospitals, utility companies, schools, and other agencies.
- Partnering agreements are in place to run many operations remotely, such as redundant information systems located geographically apart to minimize the adverse impact of a disaster.
- A documented and tested emergency-recovery plan is in place and all employees are trained and understand the processes they will follow to minimize disruptions to business continuity.
- Simulations and tests (drills) are conducted to stress the emergency response system and identify weaknesses. Corrective actions help minimize risks to the workforce and customers in the event of a real crisis.
- Recovery procedures are developed based on benchmarking other organizations that successfully faced crises to ensure ethical and operational concerns are fully addressed (consider responsiveness of Tylenol versus Exxon from an ethical and public responsibility perspective).
- Information technology systems have been protected against external threats from hackers, viral threats, water, and electrical damage. Protection systems are updated as appropriate (for example, viral updates are made several times daily).

Ineffective Practices

- Safety goals identify an acceptable level of injuries with no practices in place to improve the safety of the workforce.
- Safety incidents are reported and measured, but no analysis is done to identify how to reduce or eliminate future incidents.
- "Emergency plans are in place because the accrediting agency required us to do so. We copied the plan of another provider. We are certainly not going to waste more time and energy checking the plan in a simulated disaster. We trust the plan will work in the unlikely event it is needed."
- "Emergencies have not occurred in this industry or area in many years. Preparing for something that will not happen is a waste of resources."
- "We are not in a high-risk industry and do not want to cause public or employee alarm by planning for the 'sky to fall.' "

7 Results—450 Points

*The **Results** Category asks about your organization's performance and improvement in all key areas—product and process results, customer results, workforce results, leadership and governance results, and financial, market, and strategy results.*

The Results Category seeks data and information outcomes that reflect the organization's product, service, and program offerings, the results of all key processes and process improvement activities, and leadership system results, including legal and ethical behavior as a part of practicing good citizenship and meeting societal responsibilities, workforce results, and overall financial and market performance.

The Results Category presents a balanced scorecard of organizational performance.

Category 7 reflects timely measures of progress for evaluation and improvement of processes, products, and services, aligned with organizational strategy.

Historically, businesses have been far too preoccupied with budgetary and financial performance. For many, performance reviews focused almost exclusively on achieving (or failing to achieve) expected levels of financial performance. As such, these reviews were considered *unbalanced.*

In an absolute sense, all measures lag behind the event they reflect; all measures are historical. However, some measures lag behind others (lagging indicators); and some predict or influence others (leading indicators).

- Financial and marketplace performance results are considered *lagging* indicators of business success. Financial and marketplace results are the net of all the good processes, bad processes, satisfied customers, dissatisfied customers, engaged workers, disgruntled workers, effective suppliers, and sloppy suppliers, to name a few. By the time these financial indicators become available, dissatisfaction with bad products or services have already driven customers to buy elsewhere.
- Customer satisfaction is a lagging indicator as well. Customers must experience the product or service before they are in a position to comment on their satisfaction with that product or service. As with financial results, customer satisfaction is affected by many variables including process performance, workforce engagement, and supplier performance.
- Leading indicators help organizations predict subsequent customer satisfaction and financial performance. Leading indicators include operational effectiveness and workforce engagement and satisfaction. Supplier network and partner performance, because it affects an organization's own operating performance, is also a leading indicator of customer satisfaction and financial performance.

Taken together, these measures represent a balance of leading and lagging indicators and enable decision makers to identify problems early and take prompt corrective action, as depicted in Figure 34.

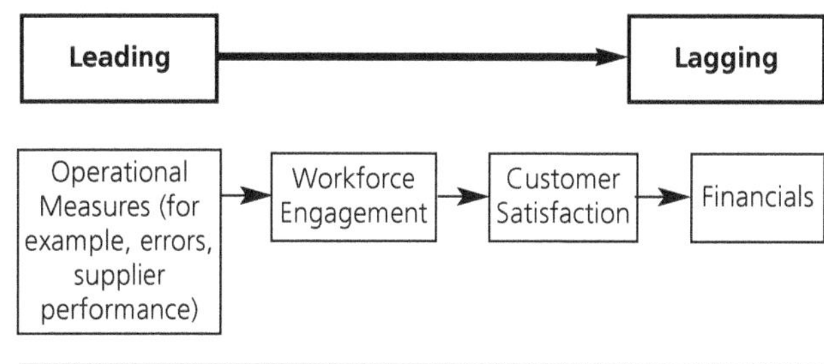

Figure 34 Balancing leading and lagging indicators.

Category 7 of the Integrated Management System provides near "real-time" measures of progress for evaluating, improving, and innovating processes and products, consistent with overall organizational strategy. Results that are reported in Category 7 should relate to areas of importance to the organization and provide answers to two questions: Is the organization getting better? Is the organization any good?

Category 7 asks organizations to report key measures and indicators for the following:

7.1 Product, program, and service performance important to customers, including indicators of service important to support customers; process effectiveness outcomes reflecting key work processes including other processes such as cycle time, errors, rework, time to market; Six Sigma and Lean results; productivity; supply network, partner and collaborator performance; safety; emergency preparedness; security and cybersecurity; and innovation rates

7.2 Customer satisfaction, dissatisfaction, and engagement results, such as retention, customer gains and losses, and customer-perceived value broken out by appropriate customer groups and market segments

7.3 Workforce-focused performance results, including workforce capability and capacity, workforce climate including health and security, workforce learning and development, and workforce engagement and satisfaction

7.4 Leadership results including results related to leadership communication effectiveness, engagement with the workforce, partners, and customers and cultivating innovation and intelligent risk taking; governance and fiscal accountability, regulatory and legal compliance; ethical behavior and stakeholder trust; and contributions to societal well-being and support of key communities

7.5 Financial, marketplace, and strategy performance, such as revenue, cash flow, business growth, earnings, new products, new markets entered, percentage of revenue from new products or services, and achievement of strategy and action plans

According to the scoring guidelines, organizations should include appropriate, relevant comparative data to enable examiners to determine what good means. Otherwise, even though performance may be improving, it is difficult to determine whether the levels of performance are poor, good, very good, or excellent.

If possible, mature organizations (those likely to score above 90% based on the Results Scoring Guidelines) should provide projections of future performance for key results in all Category 7 Items.

7.1 PRODUCT AND PROCESS RESULTS: What are your product performance and process effectiveness results? (120 Pts.) **RESULTS**

a. Customer-Focused Product and Service Results

What are your results for your products and your customer service processes? What are your results for key measures or indicators of the performance of products and services that are important to and directly serve your customers? How do these results differ by product offerings, customer groups, and market segments, as appropriate?

b. Work Process Effectiveness Results

(1) **Process Effectiveness and Efficiency What are your process effectiveness and efficiency results?** What are your results for key measures or indicators of the operational performance of your key work and support processes, including productivity, cycle time, and other appropriate measures

Continued

Continued

of process effectiveness, efficiency, security and cybersecurity, and innovation? How do these results differ by process types, as appropriate?

(2) **Safety and Emergency Preparedness What are your safety and emergency preparedness results?** What are your results for key measures or indicators of the effectiveness of your organization's safety system and its preparedness for disasters, emergencies and other disruptions? How do these results differ by location or process type, as appropriate?

c. Supply-Network Management Results

What are your supply-network management results? What are your results for key measures or indicators of the performance of your supply network, including its contribution to enhancing your performance?

Notes:

7. There is not a one-to-one correspondence between results Items and Criteria Categories 1–6. Results should be considered systemically, with contributions to individual results Items frequently stemming from processes in more than one Criteria Category.

The Baldrige scoring system asks for current, trended, comparative, and segmented data, as appropriate, to provide key information for analyzing and reviewing your organizational performance (Item 4.1), to demonstrate use of organizational knowledge (Item 4.2), and to provide the operational basis for customer-focused results (Item 7.2) and financial, market, and strategy results (Item 7.5).

In a few areas, your results may be qualitative or not amenable to trending over time. Some examples are results for governance accountability, training hours for suppliers on new products or processes, and results for limited or one-time projects or processes.

Comparative data and information are obtained by benchmarking (inside and outside your industry, as appropriate) and by seeking competitive comparisons. In a few cases, such as results for projects or processes that are unique to your organization, comparative data may not be available or appropriate.

7.1a. Results for your products and customer service processes should relate to the key customer requirements and expectations you identify in P.1b(2), which are based on information gathered through processes you describe in Category 3. The measures or indicators should address factors that affect customer preference, such as those listed in the notes to P.1b(2) and 3.1b.

7.1a. *For some nonprofit (including government) organizations, funding sources might mandate product or service performance measures. These measures should be identified and reported here.*

7.1b. Results should address the key operational requirements you identify in the Organizational Profile and in Category 6.

7.1b. Appropriate measures and indicators of work process effectiveness might include defect rates; rates and results of product, service, and work system innovation; results for simplification of internal jobs and job classifications; waste reduction; work layout improvements; changes in supervisory ratios; Occupational Safety and Health Administration (OSHA)-reportable incidents; measures or indicators of the success of emergency drills or simulations, such as cycle time, containment, and meeting of standards; and results for work relocation or contingency exercises.

7.1c Appropriate measures and indicators of supply-network performance might include supplier and partner audits; just-in-time delivery; and acceptance results for externally provided products, services, and processes. Measures and indicators of contributions to enhancing your performance might include those for improvements in subassembly performance and in supplier services to customers.

Comparison with the Health Care Criteria

Note 7.1 in the Health Care Criteria contains guidance that the Business Criteria do not provide: "Results should include those for representative key measures that are publicly reported and/or mandated by regulators, accreditors, or payors, such as the Healthcare Effectiveness Data and Information Set (HEDIS); Centers for Medicare and Medicaid Services (CMS) measures, including outpatient measures; and Agency for Healthcare Research and Quality (AHRQ) measures as appropriate." Similarly, the Education Criteria ask for results that include "those for representative key measures that are publicly reported and/or mandated by accreditors and regulators. These might include results for educational outcomes and for student retention, persistence, and completion."

Item 7.1 looks at the organization's key product and process outcomes to demonstrate how well the organization has been delivering product and service quality and value that lead to customer satisfaction, engagement, and positive referral.

Organizations should provide data to demonstrate key measures and/or indicators of product (and service) and process performance relating to key drivers of customers' satisfaction and engagement, as well as indicators of customers' views and decisions relative to future purchases and relationships. These measures of product performance are derived, in part, from customer-related information gathered in Items 3.1 and 3.2.

Product and service performance and customer indicators help leaders, managers, planners, and front-line workers:

- Define and focus on key quality and customer requirements
- Identify product and service differentiators in the marketplace
- Determine relationships between the organization's product and process attributes that lead to customer satisfaction, loyalty, and engagement, as well as positive referrals

Product and service performance results appropriate for reporting in this Item might be based upon one or more of the following:

- Internal (organizational) quality measurements
- Field performance of products, defect levels, service errors, and response time
- Data collected from customers on attributes that cannot be accurately assessed through direct measurement (for example, ease of use) or when variability in customer expectations makes the customer's perception a meaningful indicator (for example, courtesy and attitude)

Measures and indicators of process effectiveness and efficiency might include work system performance that demonstrates improved cost savings or higher productivity; reduced emission levels, carbon footprint, or energy consumption, waste reductions, and recycling; improved cycle times, set-up times, and time to market; and improved performance in terms of cost, time, or error of administrative and other support functions. *Process effectiveness and efficiency results should be related to a specific process, not to a lagging outcome.* Results related to cybersecurity effectiveness should also be included. Measures and indicators also might include business-specific indicators, such as innovation rates and increased product and process yields, lean enterprise and Six Sigma initiative results, and acceptable product performance at the time of delivery; supply-network indicators, such as reductions in inventory and incoming inspections, increases in quality and productivity, improvements in electronic data exchange, effectiveness of organizational safety systems, preparedness for disasters and emergencies, and reductions in supply-network management costs; and third-party assessment results, such as ISO 9001 or ISO14000 audits.

The organization may need to develop and report unique and innovative measures to track key processes and operational improvement. Unique measures should consider cause-effect relationships between operational performance and product quality or performance, which are considered predictors of product quality and customer satisfaction. All key areas of organizational and operational performance, including the organization's readiness for emergencies, should be evaluated by measures that are relevant and important to the organization.

Item 7.1 is the catch basin for reporting the organization's other key process results not reported in Items 7.2–7.5, which have the aim of demonstrating product performance, work process effectiveness and efficiency, emergency preparedness, and supply-network performance.

2021–2022 Criteria Elements Listed Individually Without Duplication

See page 279 for explanation of this table

	Basic Results Elements for Scoring Between 10% and 45%	Additional Results Elements at the Overall Level for Scoring Between 50% and 65%	Additional Results Elements at the Multiple Level for Scoring Between 70% and 100%
7.1 Product and Process Results			
7.1a	Report product performance results	Report results for products and[1] customer service processes	• Results for key measures or indicators of the performance of products and services that are important to and directly serve customers • Results are differentiated (segmented) by product offerings, customer groups, and market segments, as appropriate
7.1b(1)	Report process effectiveness results	Report results for process effectiveness and[1] efficiency	• Results for key measures or indicators of the operational performance of key work and support processes, including productivity, cycle time, and other appropriate measures of process effectiveness, efficiency, security and cybersecurity, and innovation • Results are differentiated (segmented) by process types, as appropriate
7.1b(2)		• Report results for safety • Report results for emergency preparedness	• Report results for key measures or indicators of the effectiveness of the organization's safety system and preparedness for disasters, emergencies, and other disruptions • Results are differentiated (segmented) by location or process type, as appropriate
7.1c		Report results for supply-network management	Results for key measures or indicators of the performance of the supply network including its contribution to enhancing the organization's performance

[1] Basic Element duplicated at Overall level.

7.1 Product and Process Results

Basic Elements: ***Provide product performance and process effectiveness results***

Overall Elements:
- ***Provide results for products and customer service processes [7.1a]***
- ***Provide results for process effectiveness and efficiency [7.1b(1)]***
- ***Provide results for safety and emergency preparedness [7.1b(2)]***
- ***Provide results for supply-network management [7.1c]***

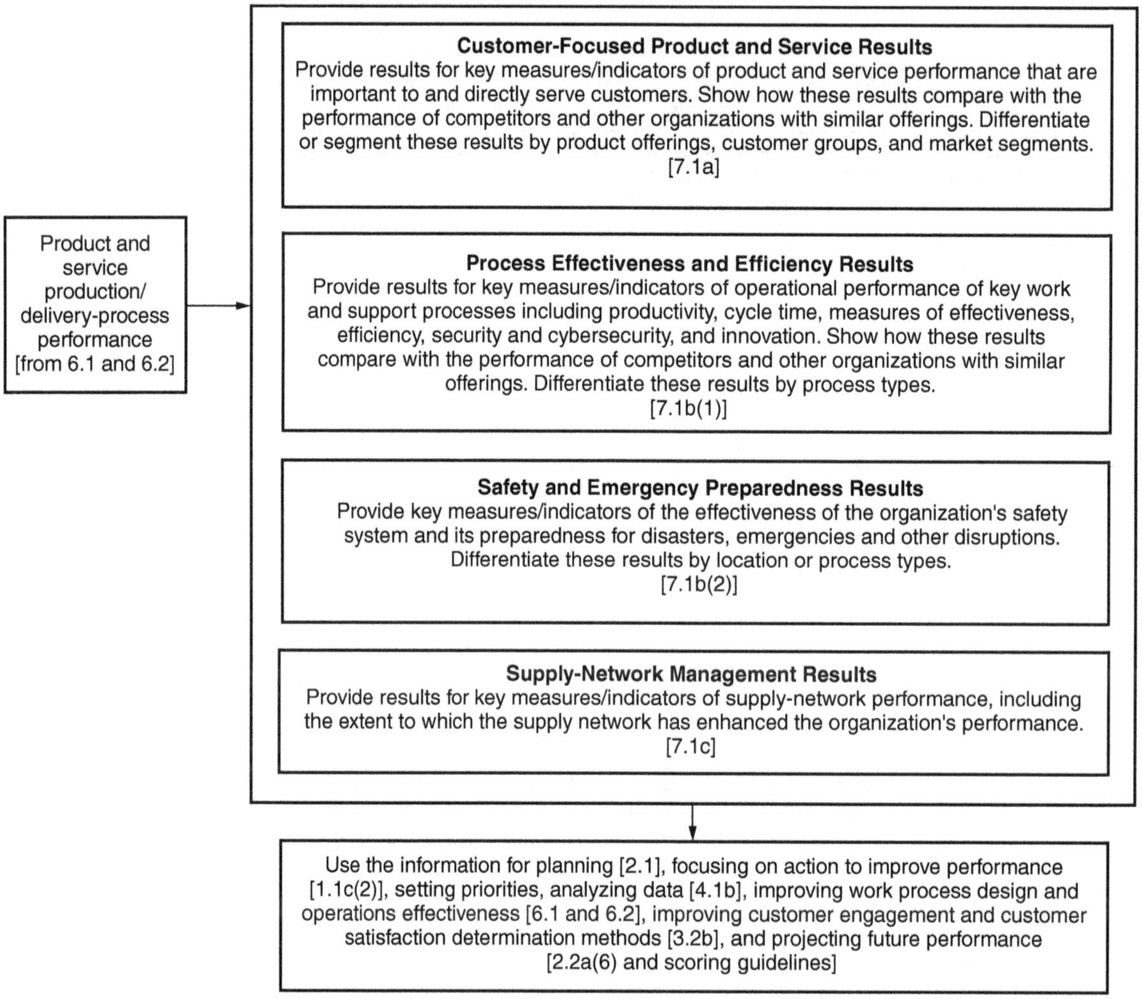

Product and service production/ delivery-process performance [from 6.1 and 6.2] →

Customer-Focused Product and Service Results
Provide results for key measures/indicators of product and service performance that are important to and directly serve customers. Show how these results compare with the performance of competitors and other organizations with similar offerings. Differentiate or segment these results by product offerings, customer groups, and market segments. [7.1a]

Process Effectiveness and Efficiency Results
Provide results for key measures/indicators of operational performance of key work and support processes including productivity, cycle time, measures of effectiveness, efficiency, security and cybersecurity, and innovation. Show how these results compare with the performance of competitors and other organizations with similar offerings. Differentiate these results by process types. [7.1b(1)]

Safety and Emergency Preparedness Results
Provide key measures/indicators of the effectiveness of the organization's safety system and its preparedness for disasters, emergencies and other disruptions. Differentiate these results by location or process types. [7.1b(2)]

Supply-Network Management Results
Provide results for key measures/indicators of supply-network performance, including the extent to which the supply network has enhanced the organization's performance. [7.1c]

↓

Use the information for planning [2.1], focusing on action to improve performance [1.1c(2)], setting priorities, analyzing data [4.1b], improving work process design and operations effectiveness [6.1 and 6.2], improving customer engagement and customer satisfaction determination methods [3.2b], and projecting future performance [2.2a(6) and scoring guidelines]

7.1 Key Product and Process Results Item Linkages

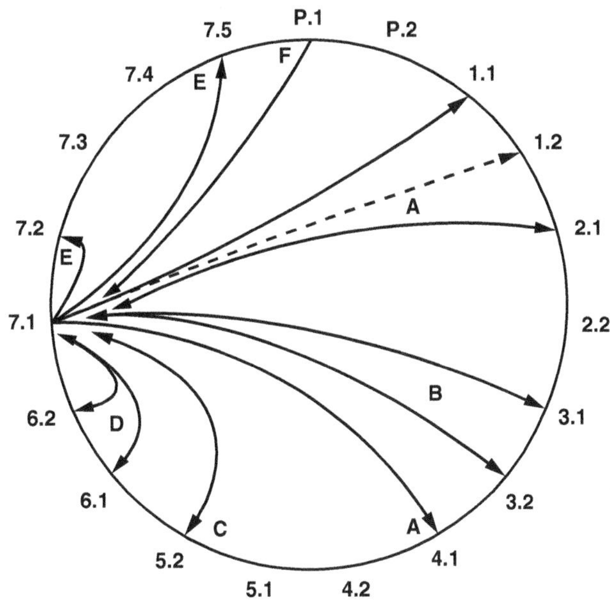

NATURE OF RELATIONSHIP	
A	Data on product and process effectiveness results [7.1] are monitored [4.1b] and are used for strategic planning [2.1], to set priorities for improvement and innovation [4.1b], and as a partial basis for compensation [1.2a(2)]. Strategic objectives and goals [2.1b] are used to help project future levels of performance in key result areas [7.1].
B	Customer-listening processes [3.1a] used to gather intelligence about customer requirements and preferences, strengthen customer relationships [3.2b], and determine customer satisfaction, dissatisfaction, and engagement [3.2b(1)], are used to define and produce product outcomes data [7.1]. In addition, product and process outcomes [7.1] are used to better understand customer requirements and preferences for products [3.2] and support processes [3.2a(2)].
C	Recognition and rewards [5.2c(1)] should be based, in part, on product and process outcomes [7.1]. Innovation, empowerment, and initiative developed by effective workforce enrichment systems [5.2b] can foster better product and service quality [7.1]. Product and process effectiveness data [7.1] are monitored, in part, to assess development and training effectiveness [5.2c(3)]. In addition, results pertaining to product and process effectiveness [7.1] can be improved with effective workforce and leader development [5.2c(2)]. Systems to enhance workforce engagement and performance [5.2] can produce better product and process results [7.1]. Improved product and process results can affect the rewards and recognition of workers [5.2c(1)].
D	Data on product and process effectiveness [7.1] may help define requirements, design, and manage [6.1] key work processes. Work process [6.1] and operational effectiveness [6.2] can have a direct impact on product and process effectiveness, safety, security, emergency response, and supply-network performance [7.1].
E	Better product and process effectiveness results [7.1] can enhance customer satisfaction and engagement results [7.2] and can improve financial, market, and strategy performance [7.5].
F	The information in P.1a(1), P.1b(2) and the Notes to P.1b(2) helps examiners identify the kind of products and performance requirements, broken out by customer and market segment, which should be reported in Item 7.1.

IF YOU DON'T DO WHAT THE CRITERIA REQUIRE . . .	
Item Reference	**Possible Adverse Consequences**
7.1	Failing to provide results data for at least most areas of importance to the organization makes it difficult to determine if performance is acceptable and getting better in key areas. Failing to provide comparison data makes it difficult for leaders (or Baldrige examiners) to determine if the level of performance achieved is good or not. Finally, the failure to provide this information as part of a Baldrige Award assessment is likely to reduce the score and may even prevent an organization from receiving a site visit (during which time additional results data are usually obtained).

7.1 PRODUCT AND PROCESS RESULTS—SAMPLE EFFECTIVE RESULTS

a. Customer-Focused Product and Service Results

- Data are presented for the most relevant product or service-quality indicators collected through the processes described in Items 3.1 and 3.2 or referenced in the Organizational Profile.
- Data are presented that correlate with, and help predict, customer satisfaction but are not direct measures of customer satisfaction (which belong in Item 7.2). These data show consistently improving trends and levels that compare favorably with competitors and lead the industry.
- All indicators show steady improvement. (Indicators may include data collected in Items 6.1 and 6.2 as a part of managing key work processes, which are important to customer satisfaction and engagement).
- Data are not missing. (For example, do not show a steady trend from 2016 to 2020, but leave out 2018.)
- Projections of expected levels of future performance are provided for key results. These projections correlate with planned improvements or initiatives and relate to strategic objectives and goals needed to ensure long-term organizational success.
- Graphs and information are accurate and easy to understand.

b. Work Process Effectiveness Results

- Indices and trend data are provided as graphs or charts for all operational performance measures identified in 4.1, 6.1, and 6.2, and the key factors identified in the Organizational Profile and not reported elsewhere in Category 7. Multiyear data are reported.

  Operational performance measures might address:

  - Productivity, efficiency, and effectiveness, such as productivity indices, and product or service design-improvement measures
  - Cycle-time reductions
  - Results of operational performance, key work and support processes demonstrate effective security and cybersecurity performance
  - Responsiveness to safety systems and emergency drills, evacuation times, recovery times, continuity of service
- Comparative data include industry best, best competitor, industry average, and appropriate benchmarks. Data are also derived from independent surveys, studies, laboratory testing, or other sources.
- Data are not missing. (For example, do not show a steady trend from 2015 to 2019, but leave out 2017.)

- Data are not aggregated, since aggregation tends to hide poor performance by blending it with good performance. Charts and graphs break out and report trends and current levels separately.
- Projections of expected levels of future performance are provided for key results. These projections correlate with planned improvements or initiatives and may relate to strategic objectives and goals needed to ensure long-term organizational success.

c. Supply-Network Management Results

- Graphs and information are accurate and easy to understand.
- Data reported in 7.1c reflect measures of supplier performance, such as innovative processes and products and improved reliability (mean time between failure), error rates, defects, pieces defective, on-time delivery, and cost reductions.
- Data are not missing. (For example, data would be considered missing if they show a steady trend from 2016 to 2020, but leave out 2018.)
- Projections of expected levels of future performance are provided for key results. These projections correlate with planned improvements or initiatives and relate to strategic objectives and goals needed to ensure long-term organizational success.

7.2 CUSTOMER RESULTS: What are your customer-focused performance results? (80 Pts.) **RESULTS**

a. Customer-Focused Results

(1) **Customer Satisfaction What are your customer satisfaction and dissatisfaction results?** What are your results for key measures or indicators of customer satisfaction and dissatisfaction? How do these results differ by product offerings, customer groups, and market segments, as appropriate?

(2) **Customer Engagement What are your customer engagement results?** What are your results for key measures or indicators of customer engagement, including those for building customer relationships? How do these results compare over the course of your customer life cycle, as appropriate? How do these results differ by product offerings, customer groups, and market segments, as appropriate?

Note:

7.2. Results for customer satisfaction, dissatisfaction, and engagement should relate to the customer groups and market segments you identify in P.1b(2) and the listening and determination methods you report in Category 3.

Comparison with the Health Care and Education Criteria

Item 7.2a(2) in the Business Criteria asks, "How do these (customer engagement) results compare over the course of your customer life cycle … ?" In the Health Care Criteria, gathering engagement data over the customer's "life cycle" may not be appropriate. In Health Care and Education Criteria the question is worded, "How do these results compare over the course of your patients' (or students') and other customers' relationship with you … ?"

Item 7.2 looks at the organization's customer-focused results to demonstrate how well the organization has been satisfying its customers and delivering products and services that lead to satisfaction, loyalty, repeat business, and positive referral (engagement).

Top-performing organizations use relevant data to determine and help predict the organization's performance as viewed by customers. Relevant data and information include:

- Customer satisfaction, dissatisfaction, and engagement
- Retention, gains, and losses of customers and customer accounts
- Customer complaints, complaint management, rapid complaint resolution, and warranty claims
- Customer-perceived value based on quality, price, convenience, and service
- Customer assessment of access and ease of use (including courtesy, professionalism, and knowledge when receiving services)
- Awards, ratings, and recognition from customers and independent rating organizations (however, the standards or criteria on which the recognition and awards were based should be clearly stated)
- Customer advocacy for product offerings, such as willingness to recommend (or actually recommending) the organization and its programs, products, and services to friends and family

This Item seeks customer-focused results that go beyond satisfaction measures because engagement measures, such as loyalty, repeat business, willingness to recommend, brand support, and longer-term customer relationships are strong indicators of current and future organizational success in the marketplace.

Organizations should provide appropriate external comparisons for key measures and/or indicators to permit the assessment of the strength or *goodness* of the organization's performance.

Mature, high-performing organizations should also provide projections of future performance for key results. These projections generally align with strategic objectives, goals, and organizational success measures.

2021–2022 Criteria Elements Listed Individually Without Duplication

See page 279 for explanation of this table

	Basic Results Elements for Scoring Between 10% and 45%	Additional Results Elements at the Overall Level for Scoring Between 50% and 65%	Additional Results Elements at the Multiple Level for Scoring Between 70% and 100%
7.2 Customer Results			
7.2a(1)	Report customer-focused performance results	Report results for customer satisfaction and dissatisfaction	• Report results for key measures or indicators of customer satisfaction and dissatisfaction • Differentiate (segment) results by product offerings, customer groups, and market segments, as appropriate
7.2a(2)		Report results for customer engagement	• Report results for key measures or indicators of customer engagement, including those for building customer relationships • Compare results over the course of the customer life cycle, as appropriate • Differentiate (segment) results by product offerings, customer groups, and market segments, as appropriate

7.2 Customer Results

Basic Elements: *Report customer-focused performance results*

Overall Elements
- ***Report customer satisfaction and dissatisfaction results [7.2a(1)]***
- ***Report customer engagement results [7.2a(2)]***

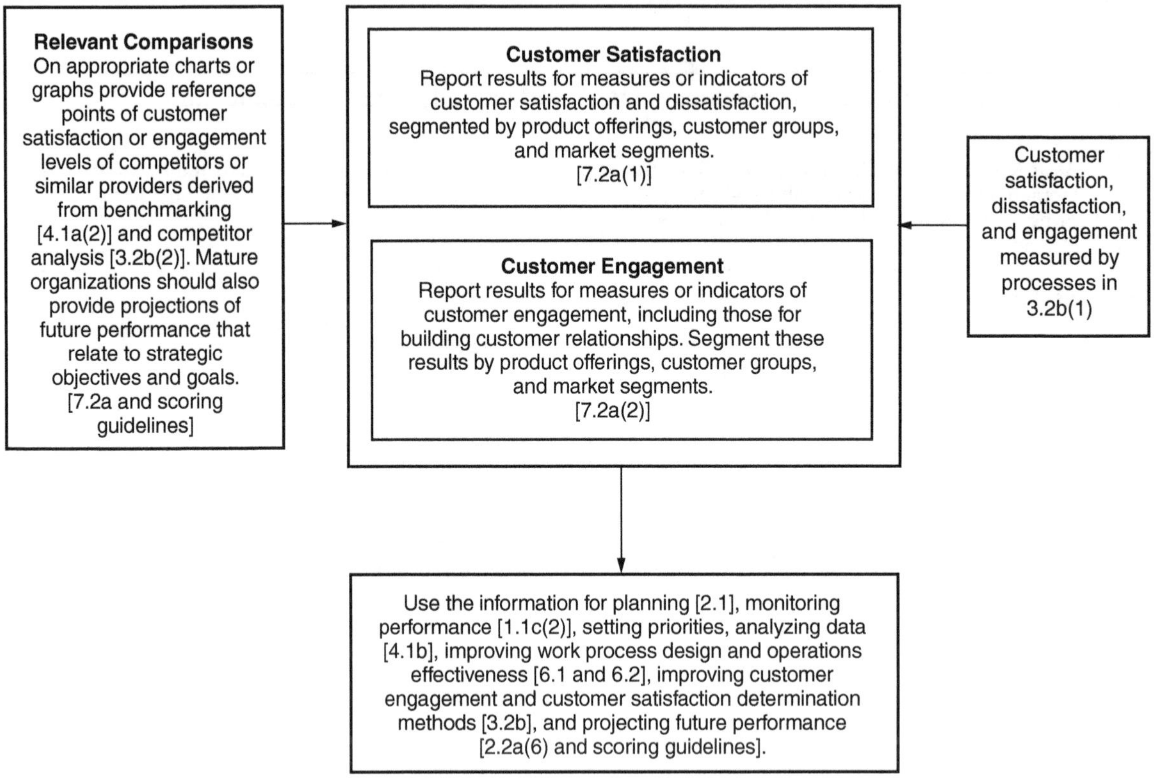

Relevant Comparisons
On appropriate charts or graphs provide reference points of customer satisfaction or engagement levels of competitors or similar providers derived from benchmarking [4.1a(2)] and competitor analysis [3.2b(2)]. Mature organizations should also provide projections of future performance that relate to strategic objectives and goals. [7.2a and scoring guidelines]

Customer Satisfaction
Report results for measures or indicators of customer satisfaction and dissatisfaction, segmented by product offerings, customer groups, and market segments. [7.2a(1)]

Customer Engagement
Report results for measures or indicators of customer engagement, including those for building customer relationships. Segment these results by product offerings, customer groups, and market segments. [7.2a(2)]

Customer satisfaction, dissatisfaction, and engagement measured by processes in 3.2b(1)

Use the information for planning [2.1], monitoring performance [1.1c(2)], setting priorities, analyzing data [4.1b], improving work process design and operations effectiveness [6.1 and 6.2], improving customer engagement and customer satisfaction determination methods [3.2b], and projecting future performance [2.2a(6) and scoring guidelines].

7.2 Key Customer Results Item Linkages

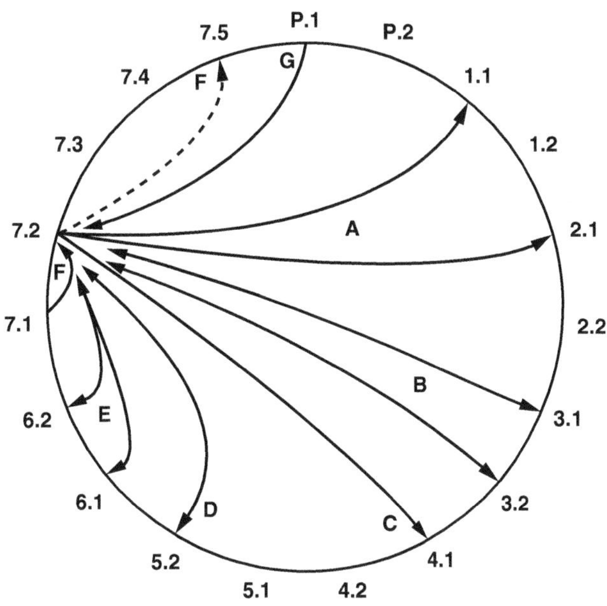

	NATURE OF RELATIONSHIP
A	Data on customer satisfaction and engagement [7.2a(1, 2)] are used for strategic planning [2.1a] and are monitored by senior leaders to ensure the appropriate balance of value for customers and stakeholders [1.1c(2)].
B	Processes used to gather intelligence about current customer requirements for product offerings [3.1b(2)] and support requirements [3.2a(2)], strength of customer relations [3.2a(1)], and to determine customer satisfaction, dissatisfaction, and engagement [3.2b] produce customer satisfaction results data [7.2a(1)]. In addition, customer-focused results [7.2] are used to help identify customer support requirements (service standards) [3.2a(2)] and better understand customer requirements and preferences [3.2a(2)].
C	Data on levels of satisfaction, dissatisfaction, and engagement of customers [7.2] are monitored and analyzed [4.1b] to identify priorities for improvement [4.1c(2)].
D	Recognition and rewards [5.2c(1)] should be based, in part, on customer-focused results [7.2]. Customer satisfaction, dissatisfaction, and engagement data [7.2] are used, in part, to provide performance feedback to leaders and workers [5.2c(1)]. In addition, customer-focused results [7.2] can be improved with effective workforce and leader development [5.2c(2)]. Systems to manage high-performance work [5.2c(1)] can produce higher levels of customer satisfaction [7.2]. Workforce innovation and initiative [5.2b] can foster better customer satisfaction and engagement [7.2].
E	Data on customer satisfaction, dissatisfaction, and engagement [7.2a(1, 2)] are used to help determine requirements and design work processes [6.1a(1, 2, 3)], improve work process implementation [6.1b] and supply-network management [6.1c], and to set priorities for managing innovation [6.1d] and improving operational effectiveness [6.2]. These processes [6.1 and 6.2] have a direct effect on customer satisfaction, dissatisfaction, and engagement [7.2a].
F	Better product and process-effectiveness outcomes [7.1a] can enhance customer-focused results [7.2]. Better customer-focused results [7.2] can improve financial, market, and strategy performance [7.5].
G	The information in P.1b(2) and the Notes related to P.1b(2) helps examiners identify the kind of results, broken out by customer and market segment, which should be reported in Item 7.2.

IF YOU DON'T DO WHAT THE CRITERIA REQUIRE . . .	
Item Reference	**Possible Adverse Consequences**
7.2	Failing to provide results data for at least most areas of importance to the organization makes it difficult to determine if performance is acceptable in key areas. Failing to provide comparison data makes it difficult for leaders (or Baldrige examiners) to determine if the level of performance achieved is good. Finally, the failure to provide this information as part of a Baldrige Award assessment is likely to reduce the score and may even prevent an organization from receiving a site visit (during which time additional results data are usually obtained).

7.2 CUSTOMER RESULTS—SAMPLE EFFECTIVE RESULTS

a. Customer-Focused Results

- Trends and indicators of customer satisfaction, dissatisfaction (including complaint data), and engagement—segmented by customer groups—are provided in graph and chart form for all key measures. Multiyear data are provided.
- All indicators compare favorably to competitors or similar providers.
- Graphs and information are accurate and easy to understand.
- All indicators show steady improvement. (Indicators include data collected in Area 3.2b, such as customer assessments of products and services, customer awards, and customer engagement and complaint data [3.2a(3)].)
- Data are not missing. (For example, data would be considered missing if they show a steady trend from 2016 to 2020, but leave out 2018.)
- Projections of expected levels of future performance are provided for key results. These projections are supported by enhanced processes [6.1 and 6.2] and are consistent with strategic objectives [2.1b(1)] and action plans [2.2a].

7.3 WORKFORCE RESULTS: What are your workforce-focused performance results? (80 Pts.) **RESULTS**

a. Workforce-Focused Results

(1) **Workforce Capability and Capacity What are your workforce capability and capacity results?** What are your results for key measures of workforce capability and capacity, including appropriate skills and staffing levels? How do these results differ by the diversity of your workforce and by your workforce groups and segments, as appropriate?

(2) **Workforce Climate What your workforce climate results?** What are your results for key measures or indicators of your workplace climate, including those for workforce health, security, accessibility, and services and benefits, as appropriate? How do these results differ by the diversity of your workforce and by your workforce groups and segments, as appropriate?

(3) **Workforce Engagement What are your workforce engagement results?** What are your results for key measures or indicators of workforce satisfaction and workforce engagement? How do these results differ by the diversity of your workforce and by your workforce groups and segments, as appropriate?

Continued

Continued

(4) **Workforce Development What are your workforce and leader development results?** What are your results for key measures or indicators of workforce and leader development? How do these results differ by the diversity of your workforce and by your workforce groups and segments, as appropriate?

Note:

7.3. Results reported in this Item should relate to the processes, measures, and indicators you report in Category 5. Your results should also respond to the key work process needs you report in Category 6 and to the action plans and workforce plans you report in Item 2.2. Organizations that rely on volunteers or interns should report results for them, as appropriate.

Item 7.3 looks at the organization's workforce-focused outcomes to determine how well the organization has created, maintained, and enhanced a productive, engaging, learning, and caring work environment.

Organizations should provide data demonstrating current levels and trends for key measures and indicators of workforce engagement, satisfaction, and development. Indicators of workforce capacity and capability should be reported, and might include organizational unit staffing levels, skill certification requirements and achievements, and organizational restructuring and job rotations designed to meet strategic directions or customer requirements.

Results reported for indicators of workforce engagement and satisfaction might include: improvement in local decision-making (both decision quality and increased decision-making authority), organizational culture changes (which may be related to transformational change initiatives), and workforce or leader development and knowledge sharing.

Organization-specific factors might be those that are assessed and reported for workforce engagement and climate, and may include extent of training, retraining, or cross-training to meet capability and capacity requirements, the extent and success of self-direction, the extent of union-management partnering, and the extent of volunteer involvement in process and program activities. Results reported might include input data, such as extent of training, but the emphasis should be on data that show effectiveness and improvement of outcomes, not inputs. For example, relevant measures might include productivity enhancements or cost savings realized from the redesign of work processes by work teams, new skills acquired, pre-training/post-training knowledge acquisition, and increased use of new skills on the job. Another example of an outcome measure might be increased workforce retention resulting from establishing a peer recognition program or the number of promotions that have resulted from the organization's leadership and workforce development program.

Additional results reported for workforce engagement and satisfaction might include generic factors such as: accessibility, absenteeism, turnover, satisfaction ratings of work climate, equity and inclusion, and complaints (grievances). (Note: Local or regional comparisons may be appropriate for measures such as absenteeism and turnover, but a rationale supporting the comparison should be provided in the narrative next to the data to help ensure that examiners consider the comparison data to be relevant and appropriate.)

Other factors important to the workforce, such as data on wage-scale comparisons with industry standards, or perceived job security, may be important to report.

If possible, because of the scoring guidelines, organizations should provide appropriate comparisons for key measures and indicators of workforce results to permit the assessment of the strength or goodness of the organization's performance. Organizations should also provide projections of future performance for all key results. These projections correlate with and relate to strategic objectives, goals, and organizational sustainability.

2021–2022 Criteria Elements Listed Individually Without Duplication See page 279 for explanation of this table			
	Basic Results Elements for Scoring Between 10% and 45%	**Additional Results Elements at the Overall Level for Scoring Between 50% and 65%**	**Additional Results Elements at the Multiple Level for Scoring Between 70% and 100%**
7.3 Workforce Results			
7.3a(1)	Report workforce-focused performance results	Report results for workforce capability and capacity	• Report results for key measures of workforce capability and capacity, including appropriate skills and staffing levels • Differentiate (segment) results by the diversity of the workforce and by workforce groups and segments, as appropriate
7.3a(2)		Report results for workplace climate	• Report results for key measures or indicators of workplace climate, including those for workforce health, security, accessibility, and services and benefits, as appropriate • Differentiate (segment) results by the diversity of the workforce and by workforce groups and segments, as appropriate
7.3a(3)		Report results for workforce engagement	• Report results for trends in key measures or indicators of workforce satisfaction and workforce engagement • Differentiate (segment) results by the diversity of the workforce and by workforce groups and segments, as appropriate
7.3a(4)		Report results for workforce and leader development	• Report results for key measures or indicators of workforce and leader development • Differentiate (segment) results by the diversity of the workforce and by workforce groups and segments, as appropriate

7.3 Workforce Results

Basic Element: *Report workforce-focused performance results*

Overall Elements:
- *Report workforce capability and capacity results [7.3a(1)]*
- *Report workforce climate results [7.3a(2)]*
- *Report workplace engagement results [7.3a(3)]*
- *Report workforce and leader development results [7.3a(4)]*

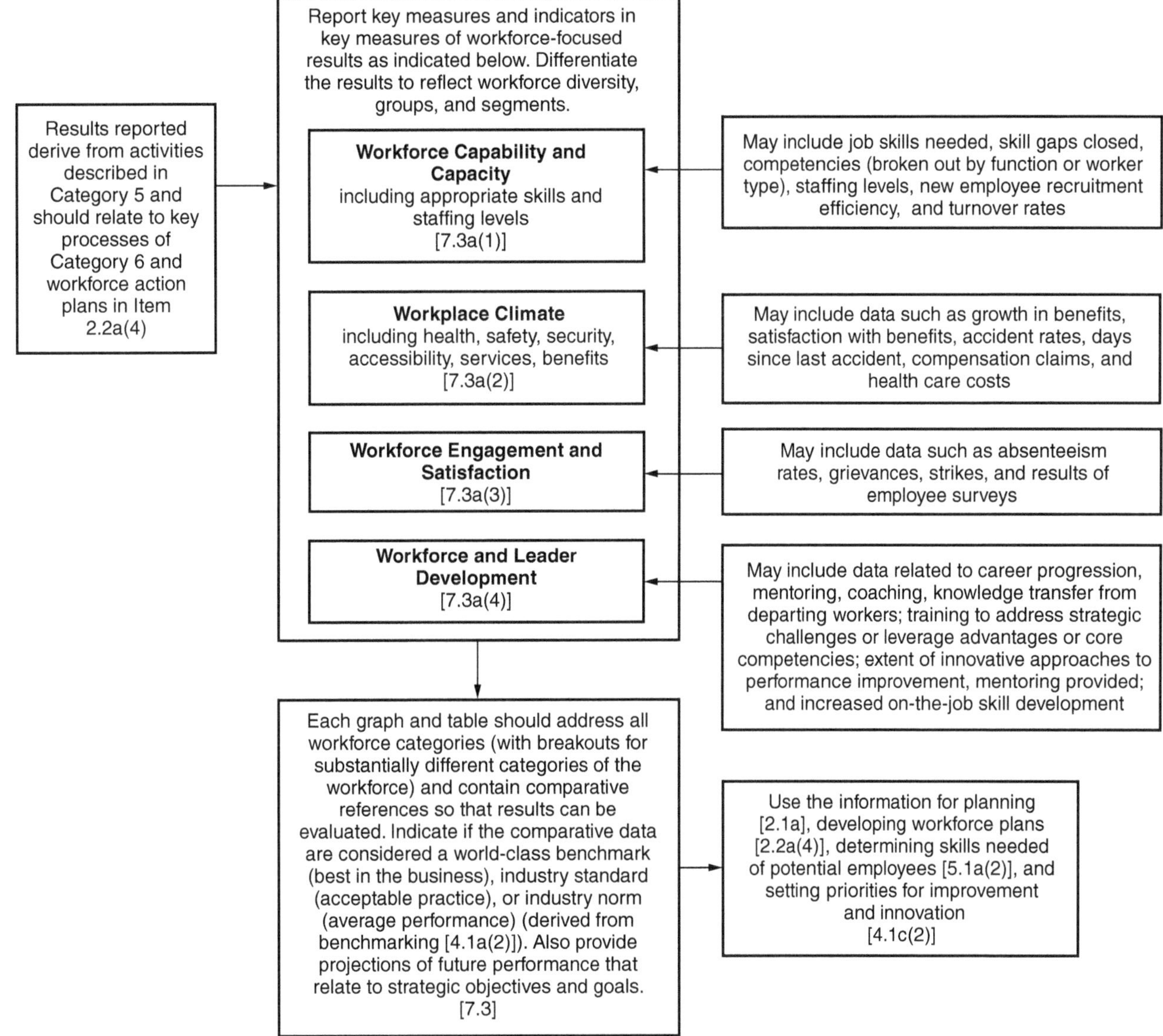

7.3 Key Workforce Results Item Linkages

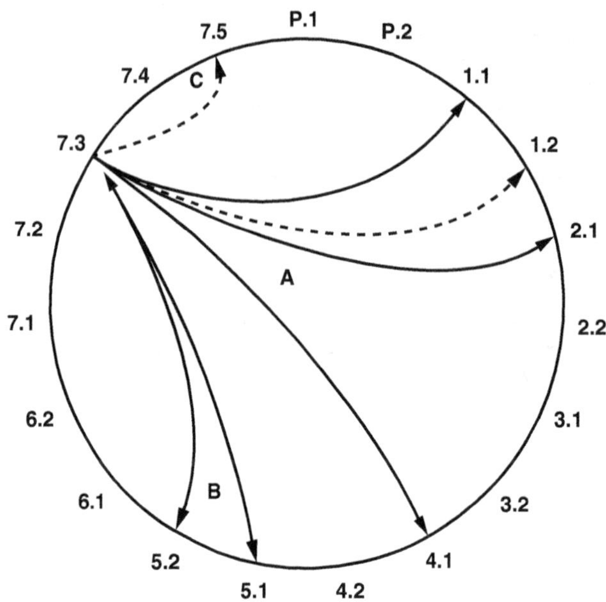

NATURE OF RELATIONSHIP	
A	Workforce-focused results [7.3] are reported and used for planning [2.1a], for monitoring organizational performance to focus on action and value production [1.1c(2)], and for analysis [4.1b] and setting priorities for improvement [4.1c(2)]. These results [7.3] may also affect leader compensation [1.2a(2)].
B	Workforce-focused outcomes derive from and are enhanced by stronger workforce satisfaction, engagement [5.2], and capacity and capability, by strengthening worker recognition systems [5.2c(1)], and more effective and relevant training and development [5.2c(2)]. In addition, human resource results data [7.3] are monitored, in part, to assess training effectiveness [5.2c(3)].
C	Better financial performance [7.5a(1)], market performance [7.5a(2)], and strategy implementation results (all lagging indicators) can be enhanced by better workforce engagement and satisfaction results [7.3].

IF YOU DON'T DO WHAT THE CRITERIA REQUIRE . . .	
Item Reference	**Possible Adverse Consequences**
7.3	Failing to provide results data for at least most areas of importance to the organization makes it difficult to determine if performance is appropriate in key areas. Failing to provide comparison data makes it difficult for leaders (or Baldrige examiners) to determine if the level of performance reported is good. Finally, the failure to provide this information as part of a Baldrige Award assessment is likely to reduce the score and may even prevent an organization from receiving a site visit (during which time additional results data are usually obtained).

7.3 WORKFORCE RESULTS—SAMPLE EFFECTIVE RESULTS

a. Workforce-Focused Results

- The results reported in Item 7.3 are primarily aligned with activities described in Category 5 and the human resource plans from Item 2.2a(4).
- Multiyear data are provided to show sustained performance.
- All results show steady improvement.
- Data are not missing. (For example, data would be considered missing if they show a steady trend from 2016 to 2020, but leave out 2018.) If human resource results are declared important, relevant and related data are reported.
- Data reported are segmented for the workforce categories or segments.
- Comparison data for benchmark or competitor organizations are reported, and the organization compares favorably.
- Trend data are reported for employee satisfaction with working conditions, accessibility, retirement packages, and other services and benefits. Satisfaction with management is also reported.
- Trends for declining absenteeism, grievances, worker turnover, strikes, and worker compensation claims are reported.
- Being recognized as one of the top organizations in America to work for provides some evidence of excellent human resource results.
- Projections of expected levels of future performance are provided for key results. These projections correlate with planned improvements or initiatives and relate to strategic objectives and goals and organizational stability.

7.4 LEADERSHIP AND GOVERNANCE RESULTS: What are your senior leadership and governance results? (80 Pts.) RESULTS

a. Leadership, Governance, and Societal Contribution Results

(1) **Leadership What are your results for senior leaders' communication and engagement with the workforce, partners, and customers?** What are your results for key measures or indicators of senior leaders' communication and engagement with the workforce, partners, and customers to deploy your vision and values, encourage two-way communication, cultivate innovation and intelligent risk taking, and create a focus on action? How do these results differ by organizational units and customer groups, as appropriate?

(2) **Governance What are your results for governance accountability?** What are your results for key measures or indicators of governance and internal and external fiscal accountability, as appropriate?

(3) **Law and Regulation What are your legal and regulatory results?** What are your results for key measures or indicators of meeting and surpassing regulatory and legal requirements? How do these results differ by organizational units, as appropriate?

(4) **Ethics What are your results for ethical behavior?** What are your results for key measures or indicators of ethical behavior, breaches of ethical behavior, and stakeholder trust in your senior leaders and governance? How do these results differ by organizational units, as appropriate?

(5) **Society What your results for societal well-being and support of your key communities?** What are your results for key measures or indicators of your societal contributions and support of your key communities?

Notes:

7.4. Responses should relate to the communication processes you identify in Item 1.1 and the governance, legal and regulatory, ethics, and societal contribution processes and measures you report in Item 1.2. Workforce-related occupational safety and health results (for example, OSHA-reportable incidents) should be reported in 7.1b(2) and 7.3a(2).

7.4a(2). Responses might include financial statement issues and risks, important internal and external auditor recommendations, and management's responses to these matters. *Some nonprofit organizations might also report results of IRS 990 audits.*

7.4a(4). For examples of measures of ethical behavior and stakeholder trust, see the Note to 1.2b(2).

7.4a(5). Measures of contributions to societal well-being might include those for reduced energy consumption, the use of renewable energy resources and recycled water, reduction of your carbon footprint, waste reduction and utilization, alternative approaches to conserving resources (for example, increased virtual meetings), and the global use of enlightened labor practices.

Comparison with the Education and Health Care Criteria

Item 7.4a(3) in the Business Criteria contains the subtitle "Law and Regulation." In the Education and Health Care Criteria, that subtitle is "Law, Regulation, and Accreditation," and this part expects results reported for accreditation, in addition to regulatory and legal requirements.

To the Business Criteria's Item 7.4a(5), the Health Care Criteria adds "and its contributions to community health" in addition to fulfilling its societal responsibilities and support of its key communities.

Item 7.4 looks at the leadership and governance results that reflect the behavior of a fiscally sound and ethical organization that is a good citizen in and supports its communities. Organizations should provide data and information on key measures or indicators of organizational accountability, stakeholder trust, and ethical behavior as well as regulatory and legal compliance and citizenship.

There is an increased focus nationally on issues of governance and fiscal accountability, ethics, and board and leadership accountability. The best-performing organizations monitor and practice high standards of overall conduct. The failure to do so may threaten an organization's public trust, which may in turn threaten its long-term success, if not its survival. Boards and senior leaders should track performance measures that relate to governance and societal contributions on a regular basis and emphasize high-performance expectations in stakeholder communications.

Measures reported in 7.4 should include legal, environmental, and regulatory compliance and highlight noteworthy achievements in these areas, as appropriate. Oversight audits from government or funding agencies should be reported. Other results worth reporting might include reduced emission levels, waste-stream reductions, by-product use, and recycling.

Summarize and report any sanctions or adverse findings (including independent audit findings) under law, regulation, or contract the organization has received during the past five years, including the nature of the incidents and their current status.

Results also should include contributions to societal well-being and indicators of support for key communities and other public purposes. These might include data showing increased levels of time that leaders and workers commit to volunteer activities, increased levels of support to community-based service organizations, and increased support for community health care, education, and the arts, for example.

To the extent possible, because of the scoring guidelines, organizations should provide appropriate comparisons for key measures and indicators to permit the assessment of the strength or goodness of the organization's performance.

Mature, high-performing organizations should provide projections of future performance for all key results. These projections typically correlate with and relate to strategic objectives, goals, and organizational sustainability and long-term success.

2021–2022 Criteria Elements Listed Individually Without Duplication See page 279 for explanation of this table			
	Basic Results Elements for Scoring Between 10% and 45%	**Additional Results Elements at the Overall Level for Scoring Between 50% and 65%**	**Additional Results Elements at the Multiple Level for Scoring Between 70% and 100%**
7.4 Leadership and Governance Results			
7.4a(1)	Report leadership results	Report results for senior leaders' communication and engagement with the workforce, partners, and customers	• Report results for key measures or indicators of senior leaders' communication and engagement with the workforce, partners, and customers to— – Deploy the organization's vision and values – Encourage two-way communication – Cultivate innovation and intelligent risk taking – Create a focus on action • Differentiate (segment) results by organizational units and customer groups, as appropriate
7.4a(2)	Report governance results	Report results for governance accountability	• Report results for key measures or indicators of internal and external fiscal accountability, as appropriate • (No segmentation required)
7.4a(3)		Report legal and regulatory results	• Report results for key measures or indicators of meeting and surpassing regulatory and legal requirements • Differentiate (segment) results by organizational units, as appropriate
7.4a(4)		Report results for ethical behavior	• Results for key measures or indicators of— – Breaches of ethical behavior – Stakeholder trust in senior leaders and governance • Differentiate (segment) results by organizational units, as appropriate
7.4a(5)		Report results for societal well-being and support of key communities	• Results for key measures or indicators of societal contributions and support of key communities • (No segmentation required)

7.4 Leadership and Governance Results

Basic Element: *Provide results for senior leadership and governance*

Overall Elements:
- *Report results for senior leader communication and engagement with the workforce, partners, and customers [7.4a(1)]*
- *Report results for governance accountability [7.4a(2)]*
- *Report legal and regulatory results [7.4a(3)]*
- *Report results for ethical behavior [7.4a(4)]*
- *Report results for societal well-being and support of key communities [7.4a(5)]*

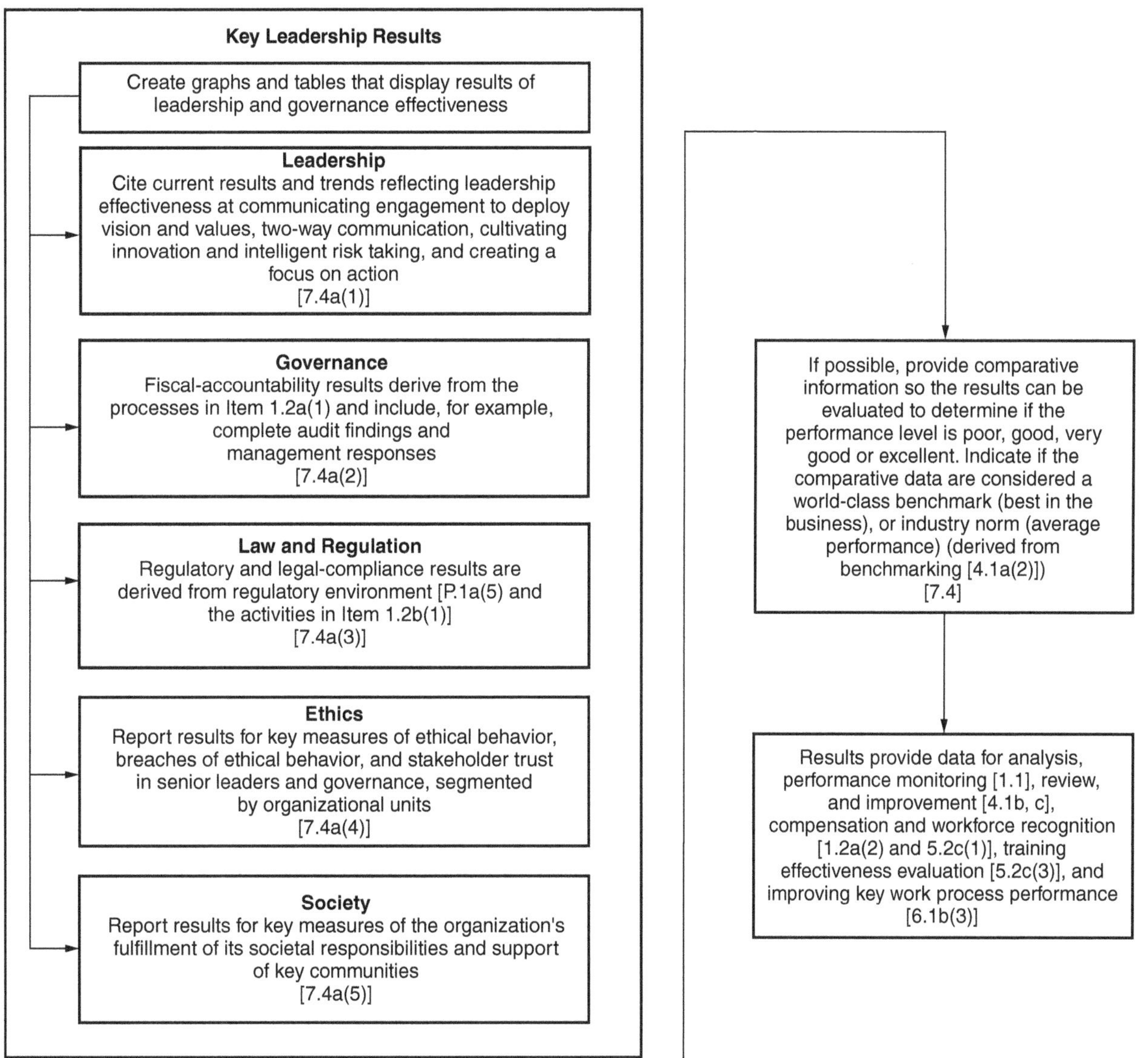

7.4 Key Leadership and Governance Results Item Linkages

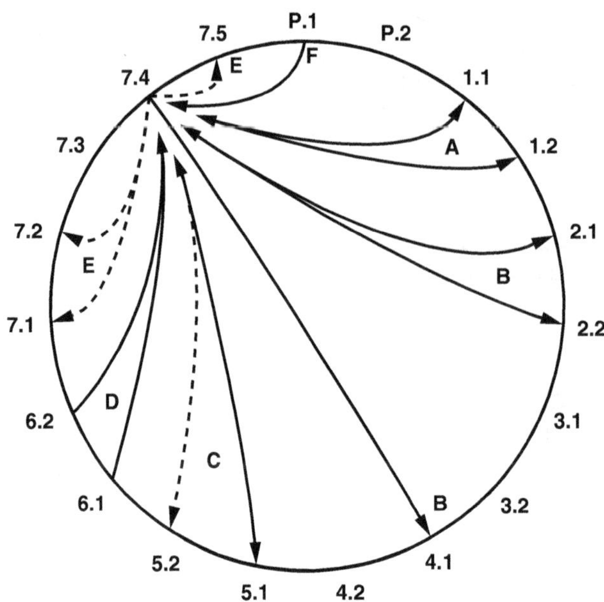

NATURE OF RELATIONSHIP	
A	Results for regulatory and legal compliance, related to the activities in Item 1.2, should be reported in 7.4a(3). These results are monitored by senior leaders [1.1c] and the governing body [1.2a(1)] to determine if process changes are needed. In addition, compliance with societal responsibilities may affect compensation [1.2a(2)]. Results that reflect leader effectiveness at communicating, cultivating innovation and intelligent risk taking, deploying vision and values, balancing value, and maintaining a customer focus are reported in 7.4a(1) and used by leaders and governing boards to check their effectiveness [1.1c(2) and 1.2a(2)].
B	Leadership results that relate to fiscal accountability, regulatory compliance, and ethical behavior [7.4a(2, 3, 4)] are used for planning [2.1a], management improvement, performance monitoring, and priority setting [4.1b] and improvement [4.1c(2)].
C	Workforce engagement and satisfaction [5.2a(1, 2)] and reward/recognition/compensation [5.2c(1)] affect societal contributions results and may affect ethical behavior and regulatory compliance [7.4a(3, 4)]. In addition, results pertaining to these key areas [7.4] should be monitored to identify needs for benefits and policies [5.1b(2)] and help identify workforce, manager, and leader development needs [5.2c(2)].
D	Work process [6.1] and operational effectiveness [6.2] affect regulatory compliance and possible ethical behavior [7.4a(3, 4)] and the achievement of strategic objectives [7.5b].
E	Leadership and governance results [7.4a(1, 2)] may affect financial, market, and strategy results [7.5a(1, 2)], product and process performance [7.1a and 7.1b(1)], and customer-focused results [7.2].
F	The regulatory elements described in P.1a(5) define the related performance results that should be reported in 7.4a(3).

IF YOU DON'T DO WHAT THE CRITERIA REQUIRE . . .	
Item Reference	**Possible Adverse Consequences**
7.4	Failing to provide results data for at least most areas of importance to the organization makes it difficult to determine if performance is adequate in key areas. Failing to provide comparison data makes it difficult for leaders (or Baldrige examiners) to determine if the level of performance reported is good. Finally, the failure to provide this information as part of a Baldrige Award assessment is likely to reduce the score and may even prevent an organization from receiving a site visit (during which time additional results data are usually obtained).

7.4 LEADERSHIP AND GOVERNANCE RESULTS—SAMPLE EFFECTIVE RESULTS

a. Leadership, Governance, and Societal Contribution Results

- Leaders have measured and reported their effectiveness at communicating with workers to deploy values, vision, and expectations and cultivating innovation and intelligent risk taking. These and other measures are reported in 7.4 and used to identify areas to improve. These results may also be used [1.2a(2)] to help evaluate senior leadership performance and determine compensation.
- Indices and trend data are provided in graph and chart form for all regulatory and legal compliance elements identified in 1.2b(1), P.1a(5), and relevant strategic objectives [2.1b].
- Results address public responsibilities, such as environmental improvements and the increased use of technologies, materials, and work processes that are environmentally friendly.
- A large percentage of board members are independent; that is, not part of the organization's operational structure or influence zone. Independent audits demonstrate full compliance with ethics rules established by the organization.
- Areas of community support demonstrate increasing success in strengthening local community services, education, health care, the environment, and related trade and business associations (including sponsoring more employees to be Baldrige examiners).
- Data indicate many-to-most measures of regulatory compliance exceed requirements. Performance is leading the industry. No sanctions or violations have been reported.
- Data show steady, substantial improvements in waste reduction and energy efficiency.
- Resources allocated to support key communities, consistent with business strategy, demonstrate positive desired results, increasing in effectiveness over time.
- Comparative data, when available and appropriate, include industry best, best competitor, industry average, and appropriate benchmarks. Data are also derived from independent surveys, studies, laboratory testing, or other sources.
- Data are not missing. (For example, data would be considered missing if they show a steady trend from 2016 to 2020, but leave out 2018.)
- Data are not aggregated, since aggregation tends to hide poor performance by blending it with good performance. Charts and graphs break out and report trends separately.
- Projections of expected levels of future performance are provided for key leadership and governance results.

7.5 FINANCIAL, MARKET, AND STRATEGY RESULTS: What are your results for financial viability and strategy implementation? (90 Pts.) **RESULTS**

a. Financial and Market Results

(1) **Financial Performance What are your financial performance results?** What are your results for key measures or indicators of financial performance, including aggregate measures of financial return, financial viability, and budgetary performance, as appropriate? How do these results differ by market segments and customer groups, as appropriate?

(2) **Marketplace Performance What are your marketplace performance results?** What are your results for key measures or indicators of marketplace performance, including market share or position, market and market share growth, and new markets entered, as appropriate? How do these results differ by market segments and customer groups, as appropriate?

b. Strategy Implementation Results

(1) **What are your results for the achievement of your organizational strategy and action plans?** What are your results for key measures or indicators of achievement of your organizational strategy and action plans? What are your results for taking intelligent risks?

Notes:

7.5a. Results should relate to the financial measures you report in 4.1a(1) and the financial management approaches you report in Item 2.2.

7.5a(1). Aggregate measures of financial return might include those for return on investment (ROI), operating margins, profitability, or profitability by market segment or customer group. Measures of financial viability might include those for liquidity, debt-to-equity ratio, days cash on hand, asset utilization, and cash flow. *For nonprofit (including government) organizations, measures of performance to budget might include additions to or subtractions from reserve funds; cost avoidance or savings; responses to budget decreases; lowering of costs to customers or return of funds as a result of increased efficiency; administrative expenditures as a percentage of budget; and the cost of fundraising versus funds raised.*

7.5a(2). *For nonprofit organizations, responses might include measures of charitable donations or grants and the number of new programs or services offered.*

7.5b. Measures or indicators of strategy and action plan achievement should relate to the strategic objectives and goals you report in 2.1b(1), the elements of risk you report in 2.1a(3), and the action plan performance measures and projected performance you report in 2.2a(5) and 2.2a(6), respectively.

Comparison with the Education and Health Care Criteria

The title of Item 7.5 in the Business and Health Care Criteria is "Financial, Market, and Strategy Results." In the Education Criteria, the same Item is titled "Budgetary, Financial, Market, and Strategy Results." The same difference is also noted in the subtitles of 7.5a and 7.5a(1).

Item 7.5a(2) in the Education Criteria refers to "Market Performance," while the Business and Health Care Criteria use the term "Marketplace Performance."

Item 7.5 looks at the organization's key financial, market, and strategy to provide a complete picture of financial sustainability, marketplace success and challenges, and progress in achieving strategy and action plans. Organizations should provide data showing levels, trends, and appropriate comparisons for key financial, market, and business indicators. Measures reported in 7.5 are regularly tracked by senior leaders to assess organization-level financial performance and viability.

- Appropriate financial measures and indicators might include:
  - Revenues (income)
  - Budgets (planned versus actual expenditures)
  - Profits or losses (reserves)
  - Cash position (cash flow)
  - Net assets
  - Order-to-cash cycle time
  - Cost per person served
  - Debt leverage
  - Earnings per share
  - Financial returns
  - Financial operations efficiency (collections, billing, receivables)
- Market performance measures might include:
  - Market share
  - Measures of business growth
  - New products, programs, or services and markets entered (including e-markets and exports)
  - Percent of sales from new products, programs, or services
  - Charitable donations or grants received
- Data showing progress toward achieving outcome oriented strategic objectives and action plans should be reported, as well as reporting on the effectiveness of taking intelligent risks. Many organizations use a Green-Amber-Red scale to indicate the extent to which objectives, goals, and action plans are on track, moderately behind schedule, or in danger of failing respectively.

Because of the scoring guidelines, organizations should provide appropriate comparisons for key measures and/or indicators to permit the assessment of the strength or *goodness* of the organization's performance.

2021–2022 Criteria Elements Listed Individually Without Duplication See page 279 for explanation of this table			
	Basic Results Elements for Scoring Between 10% and 45%	**Additional Results Elements at the Overall Level for Scoring Between 50% and 65%**	**Additional Results Elements at the Multiple Level for Scoring Between 70% and 100%**
7.5 Financial, Market, and Strategy Results			
7.5a(1)	Report financial viability results	Report financial performance results	• Report measures and indicators for – Aggregate measures of financial return – ~~Financial viability~~ (already listed as a basic performance requirement) – Budgetary performance, as appropriate • Differentiate (segment) results by market segments and customer groups, as appropriate
7.5a(2)		Report marketplace performance results	• Report key measures and indicators for – Market share or position – Market and market share growth – New markets entered, as appropriate • Differentiate (segment) results by market segments and customer groups, as appropriate
7.5b	Report strategy implementation results	Report achievement of organizational strategy and action plans results	• Report key measures and indicators for – Achievement of organizational strategy – Achievement of action plans – Taking intelligent risks

7.5 Financial, Market, and Strategy Results

Basic Element: ***Report results for financial viability and strategy implementation***
Overall Elements:
- ***Report results for financial performance [7.5a(1)]***
- ***Report results for marketplace performance [7.5a(2)***
- ***Report results for achievement of organizational strategy and action plans [7.5b]***

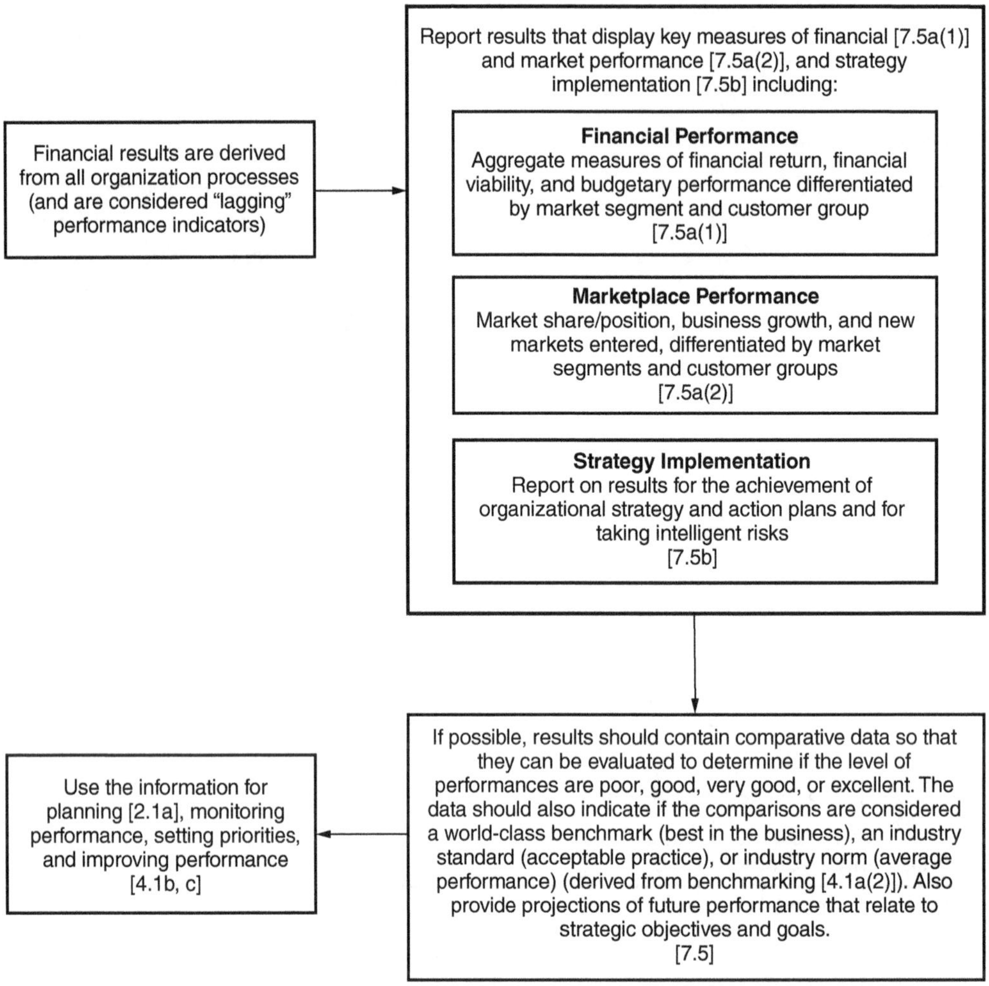

Financial results are derived from all organization processes (and are considered "lagging" performance indicators)

→

Report results that display key measures of financial [7.5a(1)] and market performance [7.5a(2)], and strategy implementation [7.5b] including:

Financial Performance
Aggregate measures of financial return, financial viability, and budgetary performance differentiated by market segment and customer group
[7.5a(1)]

Marketplace Performance
Market share/position, business growth, and new markets entered, differentiated by market segments and customer groups
[7.5a(2)]

Strategy Implementation
Report on results for the achievement of organizational strategy and action plans and for taking intelligent risks
[7.5b]

↓

If possible, results should contain comparative data so that they can be evaluated to determine if the level of performances are poor, good, very good, or excellent. The data should also indicate if the comparisons are considered a world-class benchmark (best in the business), an industry standard (acceptable practice), or industry norm (average performance) (derived from benchmarking [4.1a(2)]). Also provide projections of future performance that relate to strategic objectives and goals.
[7.5]

←

Use the information for planning [2.1a], monitoring performance, setting priorities, and improving performance
[4.1b, c]

7.5 Key Financial, Market, and Strategy Results Item Linkages

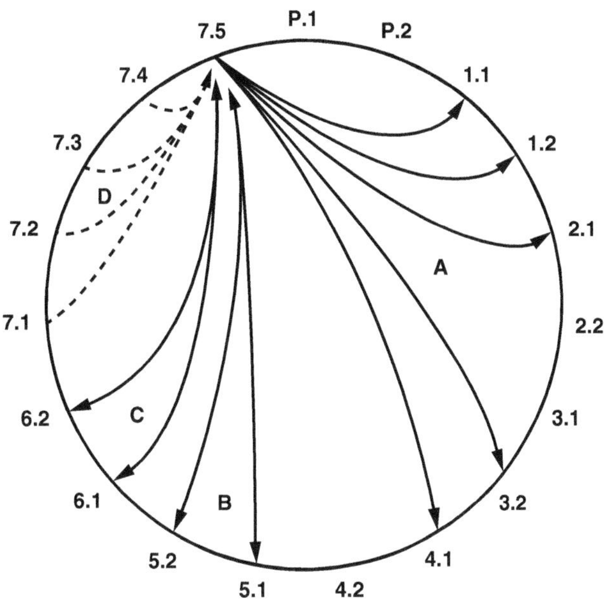

	NATURE OF RELATIONSHIP
A	Financial [7.5a(1)], market [7.5a(2)], and strategy implementation [7.5b] results are monitored by senior leaders [1.1c(2)] to ensure a focus on actions to accomplish organizational objectives [2.1b], and are used for strategic planning [2.1a]; understanding market requirements and customer preferences [3.1]; and monitoring, priority setting, and analysis [4.1b]. Financial and market performance [7.5] may also affect compensation [1.2a(2)].
B	Financial results [7.5a(1)], market results [7.5a(2)], and strategy implementation [7.5b] are monitored, in part, to assess training effectiveness [5.2c(3)] and could be used as a partial basis for workforce compensation, recognition, and reward [5.2c(1)]. Workforce engagement and satisfaction [5.2a] affect financial and market performance results [7.5a], and vice versa. Workplace climate and workforce capacity and capability [5.1] are affected by financial performance [7.5].
C	Financial [7.5a(1)], market [7.5a(2)], and strategy implementation [7.5b] results are enhanced by improvements in work processes [6.1] and operational processes [6.2]. Those processes may be modified or improved based on financial, market, and strategy performance.
D	Better financial [7.5a(1)], market [7.5a(2)], and strategy implementation [7.5b] results (all lagging indicators) can be driven by better customer satisfaction [7.2], product quality and process efficiency and effectiveness [7.1], workforce engagement [7.3], and compliance with laws and regulations, good ethical behavior, and societal contributions [7.4].

IF YOU DON'T DO WHAT THE CRITERIA REQUIRE . . .	
Item Reference	**Possible Adverse Consequences**
7.5	Failing to provide results data for at least most areas of importance to the organization makes it difficult to determine if performance is acceptable in key areas. Failing to provide comparison data makes it difficult for leaders (or Baldrige examiners) to determine if the level of performance reported is good. Finally, the failure to provide this information as part of a Baldrige Award assessment is likely to reduce the score and may even prevent an organization from receiving a site visit (during which time additional results data are usually obtained).

7.5 FINANCIAL, MARKET, AND STRATEGY RESULTS—SAMPLE EFFECTIVE RESULTS

a. Financial and Market Results

- Key measures and indicators of organization market and financial performance address the following areas:
  - Effective use of materials, energy, capital, and assets
  - Asset utilization
  - Market share, business growth, new markets entered, and market shifting
  - Return on equity
  - Operating margins (income minus expenses)
  - Pre-tax profit (surplus)
  - Earnings per share
  - Generating enough revenue to cover expenses (nonprofit sector)
  - Operating within budget
- Measures and indicators show steady improvement.
- All key financial and market data are presented.
- Comparative data include industry-best, best-competitor, and other appropriate benchmarks.
- Data are not missing. (For example, data would be considered missing if they show a steady trend from 2016 to 2020, but leave out 2018.)
- Projections of expected levels of future performance are provided for key results. These projections correlate with planned improvements or initiatives and relate to strategic objectives and goals and long-term organizational success.
- Marketplace results provide data to indicate performance against relative competitors. Outcomes such as census in health care organizations provide competitive organizations data used to assess relative performance.

b. Strategy Implementation Results

- Measures reported in 7.5b reflect actual progress on each measurable, outcome-based strategic objective, which should be listed in 2.1b(1) and action plans, which would be listed in 2.2a(1). Results show the extent to which planned or expected outcomes have been actually achieved, including results for managing risk, taking intelligent risks, and building and strengthening core competencies. Top-performing organizations usually perform at or above expected strategic outcomes. This is the only part of Category 7 in which goodness is determined by comparing current with desired (target) results. In all other Category 7 Items, goodness is determined by an external comparison or standard.

Tips on Preparing a Baldrige Award Application

Applications are put together by every conceivable combination of teams, committees, and individual efforts, including consultants. There is no *right* or *best* way to do it. There are, however, lessons that have been learned and are worth considering because they contribute to people and organizations growing and improving.

The thoughts that follow are intended to generate conversation and learning. They are not intended to present a comprehensive treatment of the subject.

Start Writing Early

We have never worked with an applicant that complained they started too early. However, everyone seems to wish they had more time. The task of writing, editing, and publishing the application takes the least amount of time. Deciding what to write and reviewing and improving processes take much more time. Allow four to six months of part-time effort.

Getting the Fingerprints of the Organization on the Application

How do we put together a *good* application? To be *good* from a technical perspective, it must both be accurate and respond fully to the *multiple* questions of the Criteria and address the relevant maturity levels of the Scoring Guidelines. It must convey to examiners a succinct description of the organization's integrated management system. It must be clear and internally consistent.

To be effective, the application must be more than technically accurate. The organization should reflect a sense of commitment and ownership for the application. Ownership requires a role for the workforce throughout the organization as well as top leadership. The actual *putting of words on paper* can be accomplished in a variety of ways. However, ignoring this larger question of ownership exposes the organization to developing a sterile, disjointed, or unrecognizable document that diminishes its value as a vehicle for excellence.

The Spirit and Values in an Application

Like it or not, many in the organization will be closely watching those responsible for developing an application. The people coordinating the development of the application need to be perceived as *walking the talk.* They need to be seen as believers and role models for what is being written. The application should reflect the following:

- ***Continuous improvement must be fully embedded into all management and work processes.*** *Do not make the common mistake of only describing how the processes work today. Make sure that the methods used to evaluate each key process are described. Then list the techniques that were used to improve the process based on the evaluation.* Be sure to describe innovative approaches you have developed and explain why they are perceived as innovative. (Note: Basic innovation means making meaningful change to improve products, processes, or organizational effectiveness and create new value for stakeholders. More advanced or "classic" innovation involves the creation or adoption of an idea, process, or technology that is unique, or new to its proposed use.)
- The application describes the system used to run the organization. This includes not just a description of the pieces, but also the linkages among the activities that make the organization function effectively. Briefly describe how widely each process is used so examiners can

assess *deployment.* Instead of writing that "senior leaders communicate expectations ..." it would be better to say "*all* senior leaders across all functions communicate expectations ..."

- *Put your best foot forward, but do not exaggerate.*

Core Values and Recurring Themes

In a document as complex and fact-filled as a Baldrige Award application, make sure key messages are clearly communicated. There are eleven interrelated Core Values and the application should address and reflect all of them. The organization needs to decide at the onset what key messages reflect the drivers of its success. These key messages should be reflected in each Category and tie together the entire application. This is one of the reasons it is so important to design and write the Organizational Profile early and well. Too many applicants do not understand the importance of the Organizational Profile as a tool for ensuring alignment and integration within the application. An effective Organizational Profile clearly identifies the key elements that are important to the organization, its customers and stakeholders; factors that contribute to current and future success. These key elements should guide the development of the application. We are often asked, "How many of these key elements should an organization include?" The answer depends on how many the organization actually uses. Try starting with five.

It is important to remember that the information presented in the Organizational Profile causes examiners to expect certain information to be provided in the application. For example, if the organization states it has three customer groups, examiners expect to see processes the organization uses to listen to and understand the requirements of all three [3.1a(1)]; assess the satisfaction, dissatisfaction, and engagement [3.2b(1)] of all three; and report product and process outcomes [7.1] and satisfaction, dissatisfaction, and engagement [7.2] of all three groups.

Interim Review and Feedback

During the development of an application, conduct *tests* periodically with two groups of people: the senior executive team and subordinate workforce members.

Every Baldrige application effort should use the occasion of self-assessment to drive significant process improvements throughout the organization as weaknesses are uncovered. The development of an application offers an opportunity to review and improve these areas. Each fact-based improvement of an existing process is a candidate for inclusion in the application to demonstrate learning.

At the front-line worker level, conduct a reality check. Determine whether the application as written reflects the way the organization is actually run. When people are given the opportunity to review an application during the developmental stages, several things happen:

- It demonstrates that leaders value the involvement of workers, an element of engagement.
- It provides the writer(s) an opportunity to calibrate the written words with reality.
- It allows workers to see a top-level perspective—which can be a learning experience in itself.
- It forces the writers to walk in the shoes of workforce members—again, learning.
- It provides a *sanity check* to ensure the narrative can be understood by *cold* readers—those with limited knowledge of what the words are supposed to say.
- The tests of understandability by outsiders is a test that every application ultimately has to pass.

Test the Application

As an application comes together, a question asked by everyone—particularly the leadership team—is, "How well are we doing; what's the score?" Although the real value of an application is identifying opportunities for improvement, the competitive nature of people typically comes to the forefront. After all, that spirit helps drive people to higher levels of excellence. Nurture that spirit.

The best means of getting an objective review is to have people who are expert in the Baldrige process, but unbiased with respect to the organization and its processes, examine the application. It is surprising how differently outsiders view the workings of the organization. The important aspect of this review is obviously the skill of the reviewers or examiners. For the organization, an early assessment sets expectations and reduces surprises, and also provides opportunities for an early start on improvement initiatives.

Take Time to Celebrate and Continuously Improve

Developing an application is demanding work. At the end of the day, the application represents: (1) a document highlighting the accomplishments and aspirations of the organization; (2) a plan for getting there; and (3) an operations manual explaining how the organization is run. A recommendation is to adopt a best practice of the EFQM and begin calling the application a "management document." This helps the workforce and other stakeholders realize that this is not just an award application, but a valuable document that describes how the organization works.

At key milestones in the development of an application, it is important to take time to celebrate the accomplishments just achieved. The celebration should be immediate, inclusive, and visible. Such a celebration raises questions within the organization, and it raises expectations—all of which are critical when trying to engage in change and improve the overall culture and performance of the organization. It also presents an ideal opportunity to promote improvement initiatives.

In the words of David Kearns, former CEO of Xerox and one of the world's greatest leaders of performance excellence, "Quality is a journey without an end." Every organization today is faced with the struggle over change—and the pace quickens each year. The Baldrige application is a mechanism that can help focus the energy for change in a most productive manner. Used properly, it can help companies break out of restrictive paradigms and continue the journey to top levels of performance excellence.

2021–2022 CRITERIA RESPONSE GUIDELINES

The guidelines given in this section are intended to assist Baldrige Criteria users in responding most effectively to the elements of the 17 Criteria Items. Writing an application for the Baldrige Award involves responding to these elements in 50 or fewer pages.

The guidelines from the Baldrige Performance Excellence Program are presented in three parts:

1. General guidelines regarding the Criteria booklet, including how the Items are formatted
2. Guidelines for responding to Process Items
3. Guidelines for responding to Results Items

General Guidelines

Read the Entire Criteria Booklet

To obtain a complete copy of the *2021–2022 Criteria for Performance Excellence* visit the website of the Baldrige Performance Excellence Program *(https://www.nist.gov/baldrige/publications/baldrige-excellence-framework).*

The main sections of the booklet provide an overall orientation to the Criteria, including how responses are to be evaluated for self-assessment or by award examiners. Become thoroughly familiar with the following Criteria booklet sections:

- Criteria for Performance Excellence (also see the Notes following each Item). Also check in this book the table accompanying each Item that displays a list of the *basic*, *overall*, and *multiple* elements of the Item listed individually without duplication.
- Scoring System (also see the Scoring Calibration Guide in the online resources).
- Criteria Commentary provided on the Baldrige website that provides additional detail on the Criteria.
- Glossary of Key Terms (also see the explanation of confusing terms on page 345 of this book).
- Category and Item Descriptions (also see the flow charts and linkage diagrams and sample effective practices in this book).

Recognize that the three parts of the application and the alignment among them tell a "story" of your application:

- Organizational Profile asks, "Who are we and what's important?"

- Process Categories ask, "What do we do, how do we do it, and how do we improve?"
- Results Category asks, "Were we successful?"

Review the Item Format and Understand How to Respond to the Item Requirements

The Item format shows the different parts of Items, the role of each part, and where each part is placed. It is especially important to understand the *multiple* elements in the Areas to Address. Item Notes are there to help users understand the Areas.

Each Item is classified as either Process (Categories 1 through 6) or Results (Category 7), depending on the type of information required. Item elements are generally presented in question format. Areas to Address include multiple questions. Responses to an Item should answer all questions (however, each question need not be answered separately). Responses to multiple questions within a single Area to Address should be grouped, as appropriate to the organization. These multiple questions serve as a guide in understanding the full meaning of the information being requested.

Carefully read the information describing the linkages, sample effective practices, and process-flow diagrams presented in this book. In particular, be certain to understand how the various elements of the CPE are integrated into a comprehensive management system.

Look at applications from previous Baldrige recipients. All recent Baldrige recipients publish at least a sanitized copy of their applications. Some publish the entire application. Visit the Baldrige Award website (*http://www.nist.gov/baldrige/award-recipients*) and use the links to recipient organizations. These applications were all written well enough to earn a site visit from the Baldrige Performance Excellence Program.

Start by Preparing the Organizational Profile

The Organizational Profile is the most appropriate starting point. The five-page Organizational Profile is intended to help everyone—including organizations using the Criteria for self-assessment, application writers, and Baldrige examiners—understand the basic description of the organization and what is most relevant and important to the organization's business and mission and to its performance requirements.

GUIDELINES FOR RESPONDING TO PROCESS ITEMS

The answers to the Process Item questions, when combined with the Scoring Guidelines, permit the diagnosis of the organization's most important processes—those that impact organizational performance improvement and contribute to key outcomes or performance results. Accurate diagnosis and meaningful feedback depend heavily on the completeness of Item responses. Applicants that embellish their responses to the Criteria questions or exaggerate the maturity of key processes are not likely to receive useful feedback.

Understand the Meaning of "How"

Process Items include questions that begin with the word *how*. Responses should outline key process steps that address *approach, deployment, learning,* and *integration.* Responses lacking such process detail, or merely providing an example, are referred to in the Scoring Guidelines as *anecdotal* information, and will score very low. Describe the steps in required processes. Show process detail. *It is very helpful to present a flow diagram of the main process steps. Note that if a process flow diagram is presented, be sure to show where processes are evaluated and improved.*

Show That Processes Are Systematic

Ensure that the response describes a systematic approach, not merely an anecdotal example. Systematic approaches are disciplined, consistent, repeatable, and predictable. At the higher scoring levels it is expected that systematic approaches involve the use of data and information that permit evaluation, subsequent improvement, innovations, and sharing across the organization (see *Learning* on the following page and the Glossary). *Be sure to provide detail that conveys consistency.* For example, indicating that "senior leaders must *regularly* review business performance" appears random and nonsystematic. Explaining that "senior leaders meet every Friday at 2:00 p.m. to review progress against strategic objectives" conveys a much more consistent, predictable, and systematic approach.

Understand the Meaning of "What"

Two types of questions in Process Items begin with the word *what*. Answers to these questions provide examiners with background information to help set a context for the assessment they are about to perform. One type of question requests basic information on the elements or components of key processes. Although it may be helpful to include *who* performs the work, merely stating *who* does not permit effective diagnosis or feedback. Another type of question may also request information on key findings, plans, objectives, goals, or measures. This type of question sets the context for examining alignment and integration in the performance management system. For example, when key strategic objectives, action plans, workforce development plans, and key performance measures are identified in Categories 1 through 6, examiners will expect to find related results reported. If these *expected* results are not presented, examiners may assume they are missing and reduce the score accordingly.

The linkage (circle) diagrams in this book will help identify the systems and processes that interrelate and should be clearly aligned in the management system and explained in the application.

Show Deployment

Ensure that the response gives clear and sufficient information on deployment in different parts of the organization. Examiners must be able to determine from a response whether the approach described is used in one, some, most, or all parts of the organization. If the process is widely used in the organization, be sure to state where it is deployed.

Deployment can be shown compactly by using summary tables that outline what is done in different parts of the organization. *This is a particularly effective supplement when the systematic approach is described in a narrative.*

Show Evidence of Learning

The Scoring Guidelines require evaluation and improvement in order to score above the 50% level, even if the Criteria Item does not ask for an explanation of the processes used to support learning. Therefore, it is critical to show that processes include fact-based evaluation and improvement cycles that are based on the evaluation, as well as breakthrough change (innovation). Show the process by which improvements are shared with other appropriate units of the organization to enable organizational learning. Each key process described in the application should include a brief explanation of how fact-based evaluations occur, what is covered, a list of refinements that have been made based on the evaluations, and how those refinements have been implemented throughout the organization, as appropriate. It is important to describe innovative approaches that have been put in place; that is, show how the improvements have resulted in meaningful change in products, processes, or organizational effectiveness that created new value for stakeholders. Failure to do this may result in a significantly lower score, as a reflection of immature processes.

The Scoring Guidelines currently require, at the 50 to 65% level, that applicants show fact-based, systematic evaluation and improvement, including some examples of use of best practices, instances of innovation, or sharing of refinements for improving the efficiency and effectiveness of key processes. Accordingly, in addition to describing fact-based systems to evaluate and improve, applicants should explain clearly the nature of the improvement and the extent to which the improvement was shared throughout the organization, could be considered a best practice or innovation, and added value to the organization, the workforce, or customers and other stakeholders.

Show Integration

Integration involves alignment and harmonization between processes, plans, measures, actions, and results. This integration enhances organizational effectiveness and efficiency and helps demonstrate a *systems perspective*. For example, strategic objectives listed in 2.1b(1) must address challenges and advantages listed in 2.1b(2), and timetables for implementation [2.1b(1)] must be consistent with the measures of organizational performance [4.1a(1)] and the frequency of performance reviews [4.1b]. For example, if senior leaders review progress toward a specific customer-satisfaction strategic objective each quarter, then customer-satisfaction data should be collected at least quarterly, and the timetables in 2.1b(1) should indicate the desired progress expected each quarter. Otherwise, leaders will have no factual basis for determining whether the organization is on track or not when they review progress each quarter. This lack of alignment between senior leader review frequency and projected timelines is a failure of integration.

The following four factors provide examples of internal alignment, focus, and consistency:

1. The Organizational Profile should describe the organization and what is important.
2. Strategic objectives and action plans, core competencies, and work systems should highlight areas of greatest focus and describe how strategy and action plans are implemented.
3. The organizational-level analysis and review [Item 4.1b] should show how the organization uses performance information to set priorities for improvement consistent with mission, vision, and strategy.
4. Strategic planning [Item 2.1a(4)] and Operations [Category 6] should highlight the work systems and key work processes that are essential to overall performance and show how they are used to achieve strategic objectives and goals.

Showing focus and consistency in the Process Items and tracking corresponding measures in the Results Items should help align (and possibly improve) organizational performance.

Respond Fully to Item Requirements

Ensure that the response fully addresses all important parts of each Item (such as 1.1 or 3.2) and each Area to Address (such as 1.1a(1) and 6.2b). Missing or incomplete information will be interpreted by examiners as a system deficiency—a gap and potential opportunity for improvement. *All Areas to Address should be included in the application.* Individual components of an Area to Address (subparts) may be addressed individually or together. Organizations should focus on identifying where gaps exist because no one has an answer for the question and may then begin closing gaps even before the examiners conduct their analysis and prepare the feedback report.

Cross-Reference When Appropriate

Since space in the application is limited, avoid repeating information. Cross reference where some responses to different Items might be mutually reinforcing and demonstrate integration. *For example, leaders may use parts of the strategy development process to set and deploy vision [1.1a(1)]. It is best to refer to the other responses as a cross-reference, rather than to repeat information.* While some criteria questions sound similar, if you find that you are providing the same response, review the questions as each question should have a unique response.

Use a Compact Format

Applicants should make the best use of the 50 application pages permitted. Complete sentences are not required when lists convey the information just as well. Use flowcharts, tables, and bulletized text to present information concisely. A typical application would have a five-page Organizational Profile (not counted in the total 50-page limit), about 33 to 34 pages of Process category responses, and 16 to 17 pages of Results responses. This is general guidance only. *Use color to focus attention; for example, when describing an improved or innovative process, use blue-colored text.*

Refer to the Scoring Calibration Guidelines

The evaluation of Process Item responses is accomplished by consideration of the Criteria Item elements and the maturity of the organization's approaches, breadth of deployment, extent of learning, and integration of other elements of the performance management system, as described in the Scoring Guidelines and clarified in the Scoring Calibration Guide contained in the online resources accompanying this book. Therefore, applicants should consider both the Criteria and the Scoring Guidelines in preparing responses. ***Many organizations fail to score in the upper part of***

the 50%–65% range or higher because they do not describe their fact-based evaluation process and corresponding improvements, including sharing refinements and innovation (meaningful improvements) for the key processes.

Remember, the Scoring Guidelines make the *Learning* requirement applicable to all Items in Categories 1 through 6, even if the Criteria questions do not specifically ask for a description of systematic, fact-based evaluation, improvement, sharing refinements, and innovation (Learning). Before examiners can give an organization full credit for mature processes, an explanation must be provided to show how the processes are systematically evaluated, subsequently refined, and meaningfully improved (innovated). List the process improvements and innovations that have been made during the last three to four years and use a colored font to focus attention.

Avoid "Red Flag" Words and Phrases

Certain words and phrases should be avoided when writing an application because they alert examiners to attempts to mislead or exaggerate. For example, when an applicant indicates that, "Senior leaders *regularly* communicate with the workforce," examiners typically conclude that the communication is not consistent or systematic. To convey the existence of a consistent, predictable, and systematic process, the applicant could have provided adequate process detail; for example, "Senior leaders communicate to workers using weekly all-hands review meetings that occur each Friday afternoon."

Many other vague or misleading terms are used in applications to obscure the organization's lack of effective, systematic processes that meet Criteria elements. The following list provides examples of *red flag* words and phrases with a summary of the suspicions that examiners typically develop:

- ***Encourage***. "Senior leaders encourage ..." Yes, but do senior leaders actually make it happen?
- ***Strive***. "Workers strive to understand customer requirements ..." Yes, but do they have a system in place to make sure they understand those requirements consistently, for all customer groups? One can *strive* and actually accomplish nothing.
- ***Oxymorons***. "We respond proactively to societal concerns ..." Reacting quickly to put out fires is not the same as anticipating and preventing them.
- ***A committee was formed to ...*** A committee may operate in a reactive, ad hoc manner. The existence of a *committee* does not ensure it uses disciplined, consistent, systematic, fact-based processes or that it is effective.
- ***A committee (or person) is responsible for ...*** Someone may be *responsible* and still not follow systematic processes or be effective in meeting Criteria elements.
- ***"We are able to ..." "We are authorized to ..."*** Being *able* is not the same as actually *doing* the right thing (see *strive*).
- ***Repeating Criteria questions as statements***. For example, Item 1.1a(2) asks, "How do senior leaders promote an environment that fosters and requires legal and ethical behavior?"

  An inappropriate response that should receive no credit would be, "Senior leaders follow the values of the organization and adhere to the required legal and ethical principles." Such a response provides no process details.

  A more appropriate response would identify the process for communicating, monitoring, and dealing with violations. A description of the training senior leaders *personally* provide to support desired behavior and other programs that involve mechanisms to ensure proper behavior should be discussed. *The role of an Inspector General or other audit function could be part of the environment that senior leaders build.*
- ***We believe***. Applicant should describe what it does, not what it believes. Offering statements of *beliefs* or providing mini lectures such as, "We believe customer satisfaction is critical to our success," or "Our leaders must communicate effectively in order to motivate workers," do not establish the existence of systematic, fact-based processes, which the criteria require. Instead, look for processes that are in place; for example, "First we grouped our customers into three segments based on purchasing power. Then we conducted focus groups within each segment to

determine the priorities and preferences of each group for services and cost. Then we ..."

- ***We plan to ...*** Intentions (except as a part of the Strategy Category response) are worth nothing. Examiners should look for actions and accomplishments, not the applicant's desires. Except as part of goals, objectives, and action plans in Category 1, phrases such as "we plan to ..." should be ignored.

GUIDELINES FOR RESPONDING TO RESULTS ITEMS

The Baldrige Criteria place great emphasis (and 45% of the total score) on achieving and reporting results. Category 7 Items call for results related to all key requirements, stakeholders, and goals. Examiners are likely to prepare a list of results they expect to find in Category 7 based on information provided in the application that the organization considered important, such as key factors in the Organizational Profile and process details contained in Categories 1 through 6. Examiners will compare their list of expected results with the data in Category 7 to determine what is missing. (See pages 330–331.)

Focus on Reporting the Most Critical Organizational Results

Results reported should cover the most important requirements for success highlighted in the following areas: Organizational Profile and the Leadership; Strategy; Customer; Measurement, Analysis, and Knowledge Management; Workforce; and Operations Categories.

Key requirements for effective reporting of results data should answer the following questions: ***For results that are important to organization success and required by the Criteria, (1) is performance improving? and (2) is performance good or not?***

- *Important results are reported.* Integration, including breadth and importance, shows that important results are included and appropriately segmented or differentiated (that is, by important customer, workforce, process, and product-line groups, to name a few).
- *Trends that show improving performance.* Results are moving in a desired direction with good rates of change, together with an indicator of the extent of deployment.
- *Levels and comparisons that show the relative strength or goodness.* Results that show current levels of performance on a meaningful measurement scale with data to show how results compare with those of other relevant organizations.

Complete Data

Be sure that results data are displayed for all relevant customer, process, financial, market, workforce, and supplier-performance characteristics. If you identify relevant performance measures and goals in the Organization Profile or Categories 1 through 6, be sure to include the results of these performance characteristics in Category 7. If an important result is not reported because it is unfavorable, an experienced Examiner team will identify the missing result as an opportunity for improvement. Better to receive an OFI for an unfavorable result than not provide it, giving the opportunity to evaluate and improve the process that drives the result.

As each relevant performance measure is identified in the assessment process, create a blank chart and label the axes. Define all units of measure, especially if they are industry-specific or unique to the applicant. As data are collected, populate the charts. If expected data are not provided in the application, examiners may assume that the trends or levels are not good. Missing data drive the score down in the same way that poor trends do.

After you complete all of the data in Category 7, review the Organizational Profile and the processes described in Categories 1 through 6. Make a list of all of the results that an examiner would expect to find in Category 7. Then, cross-check this list with the data provided in Category 7. If any *expected* data are missing, be sure to add the appropriate charts or graphs.

We recommend that examiners and applicants complete Tables of Expected Results, two samples of which are presented here. Table 5 simply contains a list of results that would be *expected* based on the text of the application and Organizational Profile, plus one additional column that is used to identify whether the

Table 5 Table of expected results containing results expected based on the application and Organizational Profile.

Sample Table of Expected Results

Title of the Expected Result	Source Reference	Category 7 Reference	Figure #
Describe the expected result including key segments expected	List where the applicant indicated this was important to report in Cat 7	List where in Cat 7 the result belongs	Identify the page or figure that contains the results
Wait time (Reservation or not)	Fig. 2.1-4	7.1a	7.1-1
Customer Satisfaction (E, T, or C)*	P.1b(2)	7.2a(1)	7.2-1
Profit (E, T, or C)*	P.1a(1)	7.5a(1)	7.5-1
Market share	P.1a(1), P.2a(2)	7.5a(2)	Missing
Worker turnover	P.1a(3)	7.3a(2)	7.3-3

* E = eat in; T = takeout; C = catering

expected result is present or missing. Table 6 shows an example typically completed by examiners after evaluating the actual results the applicant reported. The additional columns summarize the scope and magnitude of trends, comparison data, and levels to help with both comment writing and scoring.

Actual Time Periods for Tracking Trends

No minimum period of time is required for trend data; however, a minimum of three historical data points are needed to determine a trend. Reporting-time intervals between data points should be meaningful for the specific measures reported. Trends might be much shorter for some of the organization's more recent results and span several years for others. Because of the importance of showing deployment and focus, new data should be included even if long-term trends and comparisons are not yet well established. It is better to report four quarterly measures covering a one-year period than two measures for the beginning and end of the year. The four measures may help to demonstrate a sustained trend (if one exists), but two data points are not considered a trend. In addition, when reporting results, if only two data points are provided and no relevant comparative data are provided, the result cannot be given any credit because it does not enable examiners to determine if performance is (1) improving, or (2) good or not.

Project Future Performance

The Scoring Guidelines at the 90%–100% scoring band expect the applicant to project future performance (and be able to validate the projection). When performance projections are provided they should be consistent with the organization's goals and objectives in Item 2.1b(1) and projections in 2.2a(6). For each projection, explain briefly the supporting rationale.

Compact Presentation

Results should be reported compactly using graphs and tables. Graphs and tables should be labeled for easy interpretation. Results over time or compared with others should be *normalized*—presented in a way (such as with the use of ratios) that takes into account various size factors. For example, reporting

Table 6 Table of expected results typically completed by examiners using actual results.

Prototype Expanded Table of Expected Results

Name of Expected Result	Source Reference	Cat 7 Reference	Results Found in Figure #	Time Frame	Segmentation	Level/ Trend	Direction of Trend	Comparison	Performance Against Comparison	Process Item Linkages	Gaps
Describe the expected result including key segments expected	List where the applicant indicated this was important to report in Cat 7	List where in Cat 7 the result belongs	Identify the page or figure that contains the results	Identify the time covered by the data	Identify whether data are segmented and list the segment names	Describe trend/rate of improvement [decline] or the level of performance	Use: + favorable trend = flat, ^ uneven, U unfavorable	Type of comparison data: None, Industry, Key competitor, Best in class, Baldrige Recipient	Comparative position: Leading, Top quartile, Above average, Below average, bottom quartile/Poor	Linkages [if any] to objectives, values, priorities, or goals	Describe gaps in results presented or missing results
Wait time (Reservation or not)	Fig. 2.1-4	7.1a	7.1-1	2015 to 2018	By reservation	45 to 20 minutes	+	K	L	Goal 1.1 – improve wait time	
Customer satisfaction Eat-In, Take-Out, Catering (E, T. or C)	P.1b(2)	7.2a(1)	7.2-1	2015 to 2018	E, T, C	Eat-in – 82%–93%; Take-out – 85%–94%	^	K	L	3 types of customers	No data for catering customers
Sales (E, T, or C)	P.1a(1)	7.5a(1)	7.5-1	2015 to 2018	Eat-in, Take-out, Catering	E: $156 to $123M; T: $98 to $73M; C: $56 to $29M	U	K	L	3 types of services	
Market share	P.1a(1) P.2a(2)	7.5a(2)	Missing	None	None	12%		N		3 services—market share key to success	Missing

safety trends in terms of lost workdays per 100,000 worker-hours worked would be more meaningful than total lost workdays, if the number of workers has varied over the reporting period or if comparison organizations are different in terms of size, volume, and other key factors. When reporting cost data over many years, it may be appropriate to show constant (for example, 2020) dollars.

Integrate Results with Text

Narrative descriptions of results and the corresponding charts, tables, or graphs should be in close proximity in the application. Trends that show a significant positive or negative change should be explained. Use figure numbers that correspond to Items. For example, the third figure for Item 7.1 should be 7.1-3 (see Figure 35).

Figure 35 illustrates data an applicant might present as part of a response to Item 7.1, Product and Process Results. In the Organizational Profile, in Item 2.1b(1), and in Item 3.1, the applicant has indicated on-time delivery as a key customer requirement.

Using the graph, the following characteristics of clear and effective data presentation are illustrated:

- A figure number is provided for reference to the graph in the text.
- Both axes and units of measure are clearly labeled.

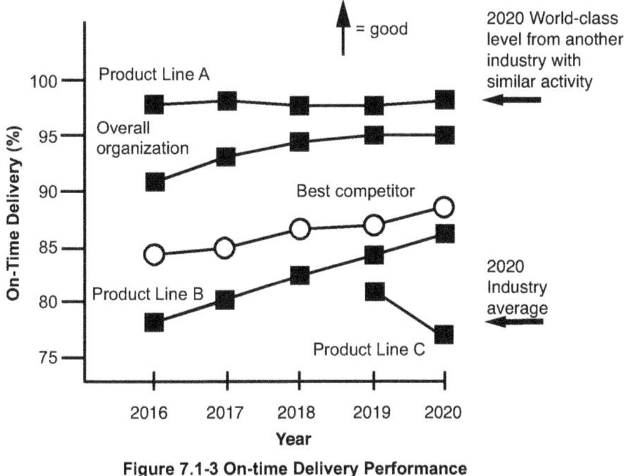

Figure 35 Linking results with text.

- Trend lines report data for an important customer requirement—on-time delivery.
- Results are presented for several years.
- Appropriate comparisons are clearly shown.
- The organization shows, using a single, compact graph, the segmented results for its three divisions.
- If different segments or components exist, show each as a separate measure. Avoid aggregating data when the segments are meaningful.
- An upward-pointing arrow appears on the graph, indicating that increasing values are *good.* (A downward-pointing arrow indicates that decreasing values are *desired.*) The *desired direction* arrows may seem obvious to the authors of the application, but some desired directions are not obvious to examiners who are not familiar with certain data displays or specific organization results.

To help interpret the Scoring Guidelines, the following comments on the graphed results in the previous sample would be appropriate.

- The current overall organization performance level is very good. This conclusion is supported by the comparison with competitors and with a *world-class* level.
- The organization exhibits good improvement trends for product lines A and B sustained over time.
- Product Line A is the current performance leader—showing sustained high performance at approximately 97%. Product Line B shows rapid improvement. Its current performance is near that of the best industry competitor but trails the world-class level.
- Product Line C—a new product—is having early problems with on-time delivery. (The applicant should analyze and explain the early problems in the application text.) Its current performance is not yet at the level of the best industry competitor and is declining. This represents a potential opportunity for improvement.

Break Out Data

This point, mentioned earlier, bears repeating: avoid aggregating the data. Where appropriate, break data into meaningful segments. If several different customer groups are served, display performance and satisfaction data for each group. As Figure 36 demonstrates, only one of the three trends is positive, although the average is positive. To support high scores above 70%, examiners will seek component data when aggregate data are reported. Presenting aggregate data instead of meaningful component data may keep the score in the 50%–65% range or lower.

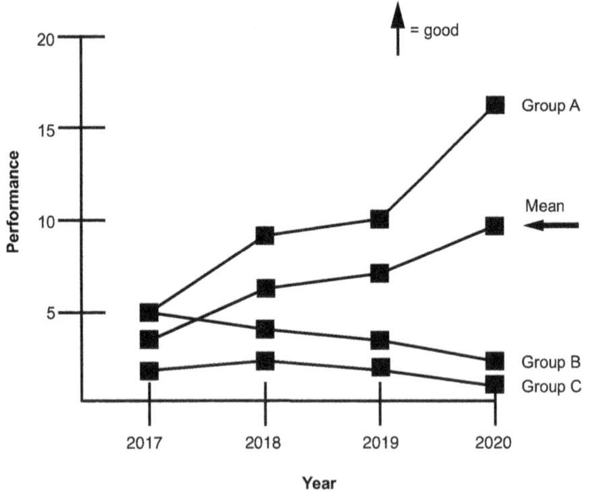

Figure 36 Break out group data.

Data and Measures

Comparison data are needed to score Items in Category 7. With few exceptions, comparison data are needed to demonstrate how well the organization is performing. In Figure 37, performance is represented by the line connecting the squares. Clearly the organization is improving, but how *good* is its performance? Without comparison data, answering that question is difficult.

Now consider the chart with comparison data added (Figure 38). Note the position of three hypothetical comparisons, represented by the letters A, B, and C. Consider the following two scenarios:

1. If A represents the industry average and both B and C represent competitors, then examiners would conclude that your organization's performance was substandard or poor, even though it is improving.
2. If A represents a best-in-class (benchmark) organization and B represents the industry average, then examiners would conclude that your organizational performance is very good.

In both scenarios, the organizational performance remained the same, but the examiner's perception of it changed based on changes in comparison data.

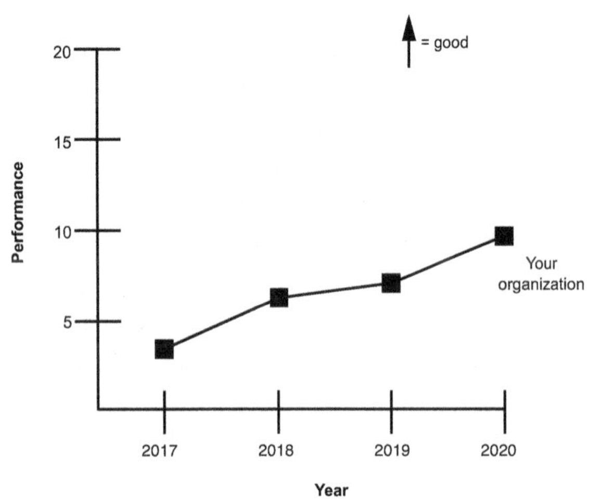

Figure 37 Getting better.

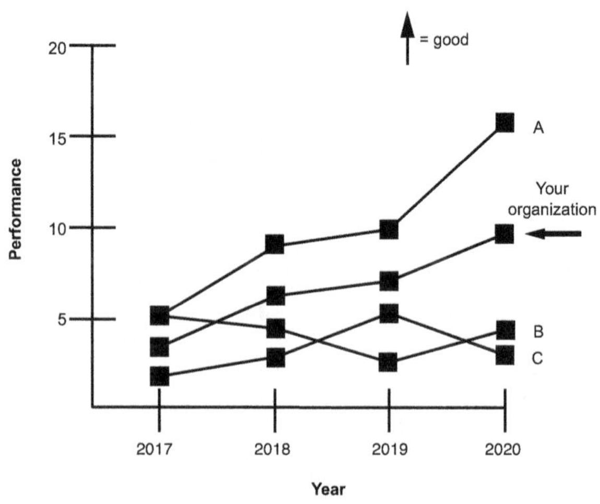

Figure 38 Comparison data.

Measures

Agreeing on relevant measures is difficult for organizations. The task is easier if the following guidelines are considered:

- *Clearly define customer requirements.* Clear customer requirements are easier to measure. Clearly defined customer requirements require probing and suggesting. For example, customers of new computers want the equipment to be reliable. After probing to find what *reliable* means, we discover that: (1) the customer expects it to work all of the time; (2) prompt appearance by a repair technician at the site if it stops working; (3) immediate access to parts; and (4) the ability to fix it right the first time.
- *For each of the four requirements defined, identify a measure.* Mean time between failures is one indicator of reliability, but it does not account for all of the variation in customer satisfaction. Since the customer is concerned with response time, we must assess how long it took the repair technician to arrive at the site, diagnose the problem, and fix it. Measures include time in hours, days, weeks between failures, time in minutes between the service call and the computer regaining capability (time to fix), time in minutes waiting for parts, and the associated costs in terms of cash and worker effort.
- *Collect and report data.* Several charts might be required to display these factors, or one chart with several lines.

Refer to the Scoring Guidelines

Considerations in the evaluation of Results Item responses include the Criteria Item elements and the significance of the results trends, actual performance levels evaluated against relevant comparative data, alignment with important elements of the performance management system, and the strength of the improvement process relative to the Scoring Guidelines. Therefore, consider both the Criteria and the Scoring Guidelines. The Scoring Calibration Guidelines in this book's companion online resources (examples are on pages 286–293) combine both the Criteria elements and the Scoring Guidelines and help examiners produce consistently accurate scores with much less variability than the scores produced using only the Baldrige Scoring Guidelines.

Scoring System

Introduction

The Baldrige Criteria for Performance Excellence, together with the Scoring Guidelines, provide a diagnostic tool to help examiners identify the strengths and vital few areas needing improvement to help leaders focus their resources on the steps needed to get to the next developmental level. Unfortunately, for several years, national and state examiners tended to nitpick applicants by citing minute, inconsequential opportunities for improvement—even when basic or fundamental processes were not in place. Because of the tendency to select trivial issues as opportunities for improvement, scores were inappropriately low and comments were not properly focused.

To help mitigate this problem, the Baldrige Performance Excellence Program redefined the Scoring Guidelines to focus attention on a hierarchy of developmental scoring ranges moving from 0%–100%. The purpose of this hierarchy was to keep examiners focused on the most important factors each applicant needed to put in place to get to the next higher developmental level and not turn the examination process into a compliance-oriented checklist.

The *strengths* comments were intended to describe the processes and systems an applicant had in place that supported or justified the score assigned. The *opportunities for improvement* comments were intended to identify the *vital few* processes or systems that were not in place that kept the organization from moving to higher levels. By focusing on insignificant issues (nits) in the feedback report, an applicant might spend resources fixing a relatively low-impact problem, and overlook a key area essential for growth and improvement.

We believe that the Baldrige Performance Excellence Program was correct in identifying the need to keep examiners focused on the vital few issues. To achieve this objective, *it is essential that all examiners reviewing applications for national, state, regional, or "in-house" Baldrige-based recognition programs interpret the Criteria and Scoring Guidelines consistently.* Unfortunately, many process descriptions and definitions presented in the 2003 to 2021–2022 Criteria and Scoring Guidelines do not help many examiners achieve this objective consistently.

From our experience in training tens of thousands of examiners on the use of the Baldrige Criteria, we have found that perhaps the greatest source of unacceptable variation is caused by examiners who each believe different aspects of the Criteria are most important or basic. The lack of clarity in defining precisely what systems and processes are required for each scoring range in five-percent increments forces examiners to decide for themselves which elements of each Item they deem more critical than others. With examiners holding many different opinions as to what constitutes basic and overall processes, their comments and scores have not been consistent, either from team to team or examiner to examiner. For example, in several examiner training classes, Mark Blazey asked the participants to list the factors they would look for as a suitable response for the basic question of Senior Leadership (Item 1.1). Each class generated a list of processes or actions they would expect senior leaders to use similar to the following:

The organization's senior leaders should personally carry out actions to:

- Set vision and values
- Deploy vision and values
- Communicate with the workforce
- Communicate with customers
- Encourage the effective use of social media like Twitter, blogs, and websites
- Require legal and ethical behavior

- Promote workforce learning
- Encourage two-way communication throughout the organization
- Make sure their actions match their values
- Ensure steady performance improvement and innovation throughout the organization
- Create an environment for a consistently positive customer experience that fosters customer engagement
- Create an environment for intelligent risk taking
- Participate in succession planning
- Reinforce high performance and a customer and business focus
- Focus on improving performance
- Balance value for customers and stakeholders

The list of so called basic elements for Item 1.1 that the individual examiners produced (required for a score of 10%–45%), more accurately addresses many of the overall- and multiple-level questions (needed for a score of 50%–65% and 70%–100%). With this kind of variation in defining the processes needed to address basic questions of Item 1.1—a relatively straightforward Item—imagine the differences a team of six to 10 examiners will have interpreting the processes needed to address the questions contained in all of the 12 Process Items in Categories 1 through 6 and the five Results Items in Category 7. It is difficult to conduct a consistently accurate assessment when each examiner's interpretation of the basic and many of the overall questions is so varied.

During the past 15 years, many Baldrige-based award programs tested and subsequently implemented an approach to scoring that produces more accurate scores—based on the *Baldrige Scoring Calibration Guidelines* in this book—consistent with the scores that the most senior Baldrige examiners produced using the official Baldrige scoring guidelines.

Having been provided clearer definitions of Criteria questions for the *Approaches* at the *basic* and *overall* levels with examples of Deployment, Learning, and Integration embedded in the scoring range, examiners are able to accurately and consistently assess, score, and provide meaningful feedback to award applicants.

Scoring Definitions

Criteria Questions (Formerly Requirements)

The basic-, overall-, and multiple-level questions in the Criteria Items ask about processes, practices, and results found in high-performing organizations. As in the past, these questions vary in their importance to different organizations depending on the factors that enable and ensure that organization's success and sustainability. Especially at the multiple level, these questions should not be considered a checklist that all organizations must meet.

To help convey this concept, the Baldrige Award Office changed the terminology and now refers to these Criteria "requirements" as "questions."

Baldrige Award applicants are still expected to respond to these questions, but if they believe that some are not important to their current or future success, they should explain why.

As subject-matter experts, Baldrige examiners should consider the applicant's explanation but also use their industry and Criteria knowledge to make their own judgment about the importance of the questions to the applicant. Merely declaring that "a Criteria question does not apply to our organization" is not likely to convince examiners that the Criteria question should be ignored (see " 'Importance' as a Scoring Consideration,")

Accordingly, examiners may identify opportunities for improvement in an application—which may affect scoring—if (a) an applicant does not provide a reasonable or valid rationale for failing to respond to one or more Criteria questions, or (b) the response provided does not demonstrate that the process or result in question meets the relevant scoring range in the Baldrige Scoring Guidelines (such as the existence of an effective, systematic approach, responsive to important basic-, overall-, or multiple-level Criteria questions in the Item).

Basic Questions:

The term "basic question" refers to the most central concept of a Baldrige Criteria Item, as presented in the Item title question.

Only addressing or meeting the basic question of the Item could result in a score at the 10%–45% levels, depending on the level of development and alignment of the basic systems and the extent of deployment of those systems.

Accordingly, for Item 1.1, an applicant can meet the basic question by ensuring that its senior leaders effectively lead the organization (the Item title question of Item 1.1). For Item 2.1, the organization must have a process to "develop your strategy" (also undefined). What do these terms mean? What does "develop strategy" include at the basic-question level? Different examiners have different opinions. There is simply not enough information presented by these terms alone to ensure a consistent review, appropriate feedback, and a reliable, accurate score.

Overall Questions:

The term "overall questions" refers to the most important features of a Baldrige Criteria Item, as elaborated in the first question (the leading question in boldface) under each lettered/numbered Area to Address.

Meeting the overall-level questions of the Item could result in a score at the 50%, 55%, 60%, or 65% level depending on the maturity of the overall systems, the extent of deployment of those systems, the extent of systematic evaluation, refinement, and innovation and integration of those systems.

Much more detail is provided in the overall-level approach questions than is provided for the basic-level approach questions. However, many of the overall-level questions are still too limited to enable examiners to provide a consistent review, appropriate feedback, and an accurate score.

For example, the overall level of Item 1.1 requires that senior leaders set the organization's vision and values; personally demonstrate their commitment to legal and ethical behavior; communicate with and engage the entire workforce, key partners, and key customers; create an environment for success now and in the future; and create a focus on action that will achieve the organization's mission. Ask any five trained examiners what systems and processes might be appropriate to meet these elements and five different answers are likely. However, it is implicit that more systems are expected at the overall level than the basic level, where senior leaders simply lead.

Multiple Elements

The terms "multiple elements" or "multiple questions" refer to the details of a Baldrige Criteria Item, *as expressed in the individual questions under each lettered/numbered Area to Address.*

The Baldrige award office goes on to state that the first element expressed in a set of multiple-level questions describes the most important element in that group. The elements that follow expand on or supplement that first, most important element. Unfortunately, defining the same question/element as both *overall* and *multiple* causes confusion, even among experienced, well-trained examiners.

The 50%–65% scoring range requires, in part, that "an effective, systematic approach, responsive to the overall questions of the Item, is evident." The 70% to 85% scoring range requires, in part, that "an effective, systematic approach, responsive to the multiple questions of the Item, is evident."

Scoring consistency requires an answer to the following question: "What would an applicant be able to score by meeting the Approach expectations set forth in boldface questions?" Let's break down the answer as follows:

- To score in the 50% to 65% range, an applicant shows that it has an effective, systematic approach in place that meets at least some of the overall (boldface) elements (plus some of the Deployment, Learning, and Integration standards in the 50% to 65% range). To score at the top of the range (65%), it must meet all of the overall (boldface) elements plus the Deployment, Learning, and Integration standards in the 50%–65% range).
- To score 70% or higher, an applicant must meet the expectations for scoring 65% and meet additional multiple-level Approach elements—plus some of the Deployment, Learning, and Integration standards in the 70%–85% range.

To summarize, meeting the overall and some-to-all of the multiple-level questions/elements of an Item could result in a score at the 70%–100% levels, depending also on the maturity of the multiple-level systems including the extent of deployment, systematic evaluation, refinement, innovation, and alignment or integration of those systems throughout the organization.

Scoring System

The scoring of responses to Criteria Items (Items) and Award applicant feedback are based on two evaluation/scoring dimensions: Processes and Results.

Process

Process refers to the methods the organization uses and improves to address the Item elements in Categories 1 through 6. The four factors used to evaluate process are Approach, Deployment, Learning, and Integration (ADLI).

Approach refers to the methods used to accomplish the process; the appropriateness of the methods to the Item elements and the organization's operating environment, the effectiveness of the methods used, and the degree to which the approach is repeatable and based on reliable data and information (for example, systematic).

Deployment refers to the *extent* to which the approach is applied in addressing Item elements that are relevant and important to the organization, the approach is applied consistently, and the approach is used (executed) by all appropriate work units.

Learning refers to refining the approach through cycles of evaluation and improvement, encouraging breakthrough change to the approach through innovation, and sharing of refinements and innovation with other relevant work units and processes in the organization.

A cycle of improvement requires the use of a fact-based, systematic approach to evaluation and improvement. Examples of such an approach include implementing a lean enterprise system; applying Six Sigma methodology; using PDCA or PDSA, or After Action Reviews; improving processes using standards from the International Organization for Standardization (ISO; for example, 9000 or 14000); decision science; or other improvement tools. One such improvement tool could be based on a state or national organizational assessment using the Baldrige Criteria, generating a feedback report, and then taking action to correct the opportunities for improvement identified in the report.

Conducting a fact-based, systematic evaluation without implementing an improvement based on that evaluation does not constitute a cycle of improvement. Broadly stated, a fact-based cycle of improvement involves repeatable steps such as:

- Identifying an issue/problem
- Gathering data to examine or analyze the characteristics of the issue/problem (which may include identifying potential causes)
- Developing potential solutions based on the examination or analysis of the data and causes
- Testing or examining alternative solutions
- Deciding which solution(s) to implement (considering relevant factors such as feasibility, cost, benefit)
- Implementing the solution
- Monitoring the implemented solution to determine its value-added impact and, if appropriate, locking it in place

Refining the improved process using steps such as these would constitute another cycle of improvement.

A relevant organizational outcome reported in Category 7 *might* be considered evidence of the cycle of improvement value or impact on performance. To ensure relevance, there should be a logical link between the specific cycle of improvement and performance metric reported. *However, outcome results reported in Category 7 are generally not required to prove a process has improved. A process can be improved significantly before a change in organizational performance is observed. For example, cycle time of an individual work process can be reduced well before lagging indicators such as cost, quality, customer satisfaction, or profitability demonstrate measurable changes in outcomes.*

Moreover, a meaningful process improvement may occur with no corresponding reduction in measurable outcomes. For example, costs saved through process simplification may be offset by increases in the cost of raw materials, transportation, or labor.

Two other points are important to understand when evaluating whether or not a fact-based cycle of improvement has occurred. First, benchmarking a work process used by top-performing organizations and then adopting or adapting the process internally may constitute a fact-based, systematic approach to meaningful change (learning). Second, random acts of improvement are not considered fact-based or systematic and should not be credited as a cycle of improvement for purposes of Baldrige scoring.

The last process scoring dimension, *Integration* refers to the extent to which the approach is aligned with the organizational needs identified in the Organizational Profile and other Process Items; measures, information, and improvement systems are complementary across processes and work units; and plans, processes, results, analysis, learning, and actions are harmonized across processes and work units to support organization-wide goals.

Results

Results refers to outputs and outcomes achieved by an organization in addressing the elements in Items 7.1 to 7.5 (Category 7). The factors used to evaluate results are Levels (Le), Trends (T), Comparisons (C), and Integration (often referred to as Importance) (I).

Levels and Comparisons. Levels refers to the organization's current level of performance on a meaningful measurement scale. *Comparisons* refers to performance relative to competitors or similar organizations and/or benchmarks or industry leaders.

In practice, unless the level of performance approaches the extremes of possibility (such as zero lost-time accidents or 99% customer satisfaction), *in order to evaluate goodness or strength of performance, relevant comparison data must be provided.* Accordingly, Levels (Le) and Comparisons (C) are usually analyzed together.

Trends refers to the rate of performance improvements or the sustainability of good performance (that is, the slope of trend data) and the breadth (that is, the extent of deployment) of performance results.

Integration refers to the extent to which results measures (often through segmentation) address *important* customer, product, market, process, and action plan performance requirements identified in the Organizational Profile and in Process Items. Unimportant or irrelevant results should not be given credit in results scoring.

To summarize, examiners look for key measures or indicators to answer the following: For results that are important to the organization (I), is its performance getting better (T), and is its performance any good? (Le/C)

"Importance" As a Scoring Consideration

The Process and Results evaluation dimensions described previously are critical to providing an organization with accurate, consistent feedback and scores. However, another key consideration in feedback and scoring is the importance of the reported processes and results to the organization's key business factors. The areas of greatest importance are typically identified in the Organizational Profile. Key customer requirements, workforce characteristics, the competitive environment, key strategic objectives and action plans, and other drivers necessary for current and future success are particularly important.

Assignment of Scores

The following guidelines should help improve consistency and accuracy in assigning scores to Item responses:

- To score in the higher levels, all Areas to Address should be included in an Item response. However, regardless of the assigned scoring level, in all cases, the applicant's narrative responses should reflect what is important to the organization.
- *In assigning a score to an Item, first look at the strengths that have been identified that show what the applicant is doing in response to the Criteria elements.* Based on those strengths, determine which scoring range (for example, 50% to 65%) is *most descriptive* of the organization's processes or achievement level. The most descriptive can include some gaps in one or more of the ADLI (process) factors or the LeTCI (results) factors for the chosen scoring range.
  - *For example, if the applicant does everything required in the 50%–65% scoring range and nothing in the higher ranges, then the score should be at the top of the 50%–65% range. If the applicant does everything required in a scoring range and meets Approach, Deployment, Learning, or Integration elements in any of the higher ranges, then the "best fit" score should be at least in the next higher scoring range.*

  - *Assigning the actual score (which is set in 5% increments) within the chosen range requires evaluating whether the Item response is closer to the statements in the next higher or next lower scoring range.*

- *Opportunities for Improvement* reflect elements about which the Criteria ask that the applicant does not appear to address in an effective manner. The key or vital few opportunities for improvement that should be reported to the applicant in a feedback report include those that should be done to move the applicant to the next higher scoring range (or, if at the bottom of a range to the top of the same range).

- A Process score of 50%–65% represents an approach that meets the elements in the 30%–45% range), effectively addresses at least some overall-level questions of the Item, is deployed consistently to most work units covered by the Item, has been through some cycles of improvement and learning, and addresses the key organizational needs. Higher scores reflect greater achievement, demonstrated by broader deployment, significant organizational learning and meaningful change (innovation), and increased integration

- A Results Score of 50%–65% represents a clear indication of improvement trends and/or good levels of performance with appropriate comparative data in the results areas covered in the Item and *important* to the organization and its mission. (Results that are meaningless or irrelevant to the success of the organization, its mission, vision, strategic objectives, action plans, or regulatory requirements count for nothing.) Higher scores are given based on better improvement rates and/or levels of importance, better comparative performance, and broader coverage and integration with business requirements.

Calibration Guidelines

Defining scoring terms may help reduce unnecessary variability. We have been frequently asked by examiners to define, in terms of percent, the meaning of *most*. Some define *most* as 51%. Others have a higher standard, even up to 90%. Defining *good* and *very good* is even more difficult. To reduce this variability, the following guidelines are suggested:

Few:	5%–15% (major gaps in deployment exist)
Some:	Greater than 15%–30% (deployed, although in the early stages)
Many:	Greater than 30%–50% (well-deployed, although deployment may vary in some areas)
Most:	Greater than 50%–80% (well-deployed, with no apparent gaps in most areas)
Nearly All:	Greater than 80%–to less than 100% (fully deployed, with no significant gaps in any areas or work units)
All:	100%
Good:	*Better than average for relevant competitors or similar providers; above industry average or median. (Note: performance equal to or better than a Baldrige recipient should be considered "good" unless the applicant provides information that the performance level of the Baldrige recipient is very good or excellent.)*
Very Good:	*In the top quartile of relevant competitors or similar providers*
Excellent:	*At or near the top of relevant competitors or similar providers; top 10%; best benchmark; better than best competitor*

Score	**Baldrige Scoring Guidelines** **For Use With Categories 1–6** **Process**
0% or 5%	• No systematic approach to Item questions is evident; information is anecdotal. (A) • Little or no deployment of any systematic approach is evident. (D) • An improvement orientation is not evident; improvement is achieved by reacting to problems. (L) • No organizational alignment is evident; individual areas or work units operate independently. (I)
10%, 15%, 20%, or 25%	• The beginning of a systematic approach to the basic question of the Item is evident. (A) • The approach is in the early stages of deployment in most areas or work units, inhibiting progress in achieving the basic question of the Item. (D) • Early stages of a transition from reacting to problems to a general improvement orientation are evident. (L) • The approach is aligned with other areas or work units largely through joint problem solving. (I)
30%, 35%, 40%, or 45%	• An effective, systematic approach, responsive to the basic question in the Item, is evident. (A) • The approach is deployed, although some areas or work units are in early stages of deployment. (D) • The beginning of a systematic approach to evaluation and improvement of key processes is evident. (L) • The approach is in the early stages of alignment with the basic organizational needs identified in response to the Organizational Profile and other process Items. (I)
50%, 55%, 60%, or 65%	• An effective, systematic approach, responsive to the overall questions in the Item, is evident. (A) • The approach is well deployed, although deployment may vary in some areas or work units. (D) • Fact-based, systematic evaluation and improvement process and some **examples of use of best practices, instances of innovation, or sharing of refinements** are in place for improving the efficiency and effectiveness of key processes. (L) • The approach is aligned with your overall organizational needs as identified in response to the Organizational Profile and other process Items. (I)
70%, 75%, 80%, or 85%	• An effective, systematic approach, responsive to multiple questions in the Item, is evident. (A) • The approach is well deployed, with no significant gaps. (D) • Fact-based, systematic evaluation and improvement, **adoption of best practices, managing for innovation, and sharing of refinements** are key tools **for improving organizational efficiency and effectiveness.** (L) • The approach is integrated with your current and future organizational needs as identified in response to the Organizational Profile and other process Items. (I)
90%, 95%, or 100%	• An effective, systematic approach, fully responsive to the multiple questions in the Item, is evident. (A) • The approach is fully deployed without significant weaknesses or gaps in any areas or work units. (D) • Fact-based, systematic evaluation and improvement, **development of best practices, achievement of innovation, and sharing of refinements** are key organization-wide tools **for improving organizational efficiency and effectiveness.** (L) • The approach is well integrated with your current and future organizational needs as identified in response to the Organizational Profile and other process Items. (I)

Note: Words highlighted in bold print are changes from the 2019–2020 Baldrige Framework

Score	**Baldrige Scoring Guidelines** **For Use With Category 7** **Results**
0% or 5%	• There are no organizational performance results, or the results reported are poor. (Le) • Trend data either are not reported or show mainly adverse trends. (T) • Comparative information is not reported. (C) • Results are not reported for any areas of importance to the accomplishment of your organization's mission. (I)
10%, 15%, 20%, or 25%	• A few organizational performance results are reported, responsive to the basic question in the Item, and early good performance levels are evident. (Le) • Some trend data are reported, with some adverse trends evident. (T) • Little or no comparative information is reported. (C) • Results are reported for a few areas of importance to the accomplishment of your organization's mission. (I)
30%, 35%, 40%, or 45%	• Good organizational performance levels are reported, responsive to the basic question in the Item. (Le) • Some trend data are reported, and most of the trends presented are beneficial. (T) • Early stages of obtaining comparative information are evident. (C) • Results are reported for many areas of importance to the accomplishment of your organization's mission. (I)
50%, 55%, 60%, or 65%	• Good organizational performance levels are reported, responsive to the overall questions in the Item. (Le) • Beneficial trends are evident in areas of importance to the accomplishment of your organization's mission. (T) • Some current performance levels have been evaluated against relevant comparisons and/or benchmarks and show areas of good relative performance. (C) • Organizational performance results are reported for most key customer, market, and process requirements. (I)
70%, 75%, 80%, or 85%	• Good-to-excellent organizational performance levels are reported, responsive to multiple questions in the Item. (Le) • Beneficial trends have been sustained over time in most areas of importance to the accomplishment of your organization's mission. (T) • Many to most trends and current performance levels have been evaluated against relevant comparisons and/or benchmarks and show areas of leadership and very good relative performance. (C) • Organizational performance results are reported for most key customer, market, process, and action plan requirements. (I)
90%, 95%, or 100%	• Excellent organizational performance levels are reported that are fully responsive to the multiple questions in the Item. (Le) • Beneficial trends have been sustained over time in all areas of importance to the accomplishment of your organization's mission. (T) • Industry and benchmark leadership is demonstrated in many areas. (C) • Organizational performance results and projections are reported for most key customer, market, process, and action plan requirements. (I)

Explaining Similar Baldrige Performance Excellence Criteria Questions that Appear More than Once in an Item

Introduction

The Baldrige Criteria for Performance Excellence Scoring Guidelines help to define levels of organizational maturity in implementing the CPE. To assess the maturity of and score an applicant's approach to performance excellence and related results, and for scoring purposes, Criteria questions are segmented into three groups or levels:

- *Basic*, for scores in the 10%–45% range
- *Overall*, for scores in the 50%–65% range and
- *Multiple*, for scores in the 70%–100% range

> ***To promote scoring consistency among examiners, if an element is listed more than once in an Item, the initial placement of the element establishes its level for scoring purposes.***

Since repeating questions at more than one level causes confusion, we have prepared an analysis that lists each question only once, placing it where it first appears. A sample table appears in Figure 39. Because the table in Figure 39 does not restate questions that have been listed in the Criteria more than once, readers must combine the questions from the different columns.

> ***In this book, tables similar to Figure 39, showing Criteria elements listed individually without duplication, accompany the descriptions and analyses for each Item in Categories 1 through 7.***

A guiding principle for reading the table is that to understand the questions at one level, you must add the questions listed at that level to all of the questions in the same row to the left.

- Multiple = Multiple + Overall + Basic
- Overall = Overall + Basic
- Basic = Basic

Figure 39 presents the questions of 1.1c(1) but lists similar questions only once, where they appear first:

- At the *basic* level, there is not a question that relates directly to creating a successful organization so the cell is empty.
- At the *overall* level senior leaders must ensure they create an environment for success now and in the future.
- At the *multiple* level senior leaders are expected to create an organization that is successful now and in the future (from the Overall column) and (from the Multiple column) create an environment for the achievement of mission; create and reinforce an organizational culture and a culture that fosters customer and workforce engagement; cultivate organizational agility, account-

2021–2022 Criteria Elements Listed Individually Without Duplication			
	Basic Approach Elements [A-B] for Scoring Between 10% and 45%	**Additional Approach Elements at the Overall Level [A-O] for Scoring Between 50% and 65%**	**Additional Approach Elements at the Multiple Level [A-M] for Scoring Between 70% and 100%**
1.1 Senior Leadership			
1.1c(1)		Senior leaders create an environment for success now and in the future	Senior leaders: • Create an environment for the achievement of mission • Create and reinforce an organizational culture that fosters customer and workforce engagement, equity, and inclusion • Cultivate organizational agility and resilience, accountability, organizational and individual learning, innovation, and intelligent risk taking • Participate in succession planning and the development of future organizational leaders

Figure 39 Partial table of elements listed individually without duplication.

ability, organizational and individual learning, innovation, and intelligent risk taking; and participate in succession planning and the development of future organizational leaders.

IMPORTANT PROCESS SCORING TERMS

Anecdotal

If the application narrative describes a process or procedure that is random, ad hoc, or anecdotal and does not address the Criteria in a predictable, disciplined manner, it is worth very little (zero to five points). The following is a typical anecdotal narrative:

> *Senior Leaders meet regularly to review performance and set directions. We support a strong value of customer-focused excellence.*

The main problem with this narrative is that it provides no details of the process, no information about the steps taken, no description of specific actions—nothing from which to determine if the process is consistent, systematic, predictable, and effective.

Complete

Each Item contains one or more Areas to Address. Many Areas to Address contain several subparts. Failure to completely address the Areas and subparts can push the score lower. *If an Area to Address or part of an Area does not apply to an organization, it is important to explain why.* Otherwise, examiners may conclude that the applicant's management system is incomplete.

Continuous Improvement

Continuous improvement is a bedrock theme for top-performing organizations. It is the method that helps organizations establish and keep a competitive edge. Continuous improvement involves the fact-based evaluation and improvement of processes crucial to organizational success. Evaluation and improvement, including meaningful improvements and the creation of innovative, new, and unique processes, completes the high-performance management cycle. Fact-based evaluations can be complex statistical processes, or as simple as focus groups discussing and recording what went right, what went wrong, and how it could be done better (such as After Action Reviews of the U.S. Army). The key to optimum performance lies in the pervasive evaluation of all processes. If the organization practices systematic, pervasive, continuous improvement, time becomes its ally. Consistent, fact-based evaluation and refinement practices with correspondingly good deployment and innovative approaches can drive the score to 60% or higher. Without the beginning of a systematic approach to evaluation and refinement a score above 40% is unlikely.

Cycle(s) of Improvement

A fact-based, systematic approach to evaluation and improvement might include implementing a lean enterprise system, applying Six Sigma methodology, using PDCA methodology, improving processes using standards from the International Organization for Standardization (ISO; for example, 9000 or 14000), using decision science, or employing other improvement tools. Even addressing an Opportunity for Improvement that was derived from a previous Baldrige-based evaluation conducted by trained examiners may be considered a meaningful, value-added cycle of improvement.

Broadly stated, a cycle of improvement involves repeatable steps such as:

- Identifying an issue or problem; gathering data to examine or analyze the characteristics of the issue or problem (which may include identifying potential causes);
- Developing potential solutions based on the examination or analysis of the data and causes, benchmarking, and testing alternative solutions;
- Deciding which solution(s) to implement (considering relevant factors such as feasibility, cost, benefit), monitoring the selected action to determine its impact; and
- Implementing the solution.

It is not appropriate to demand outcome results to prove a process has improved. A process can be improved significantly before a measurable improvement in organizational performance is observed. For example, cycle time of an individual work process can be reduced well before lagging indicators such as cost, quality, customer satisfaction, or profitability. Moreover, a meaningful process improvement may occur with no apparent reduction in measurable outcomes. For example, costs saved through process simplification may be offset by higher-priced raw materials.

Random acts of improvement are not considered fact-based or systematic and should not be seen as a cycle of improvement for purposes of Baldrige scoring.

Benchmarking better work processes used by top-performing organizations and then adopting or adapting the processes internally may constitute a fact-based, systematic approach to meaningful change. In addition, conducting a Baldrige-based analysis and then implementing improvements based on the opportunities identified in the feedback report may constitute a cycle of improvement.

Deployment

The extent to which processes are widely used by appropriate organization units affects scoring. For example, a systematic approach that is well-integrated, evaluated consistently, and refined routinely with evidence of an innovative approach may be worth 70%–85% or more. However, if that process is not in place in appropriate key parts of the organization, the score may be reduced—perhaps significantly—depending on the nature and extent of the deployment gap.

Major gaps are expected to exist at the 5%–25% level. At the 30%–45% levels, no major gaps exist, although some units may still be at the early stages of development. At the 70%–85% level, no major gaps exist and the approach is well-integrated with organizational needs identified in other parts of the Criteria.

Integrated

Show the extent to which the system is integrated or interconnected with other elements of the overall management system. Show the linkages across Categories for key themes such as those displayed earlier for each Item. Consider the extent to which the work of senior leaders is integrated. For example:

1. Senior executives [1.1a(1)] are responsible for shaping and deploying the organization's values and performance expectations through the leadership system to the workforce, key suppliers and partners, and customers and other stakeholders.
2. They communicate with key customers [1.1b] and develop relationships with and satisfy customers [3.2] and report customer engagement, satisfaction, and dissatisfaction [7.2], and related product outcomes and operational performance [7.1].
3. Leaders (and others in the organization) convert goals and strategic objectives into measurable milestones and timetables [2.1b(1)] to serve as a basis for monitoring [4.1a(1)] and reviewing [4.1b] performance and setting improvement priorities [4.1c(2)]. Also, to be considered integrated, timetables [2.1b(1)] should be set to coincide with the review cycle [4.1b]. If leaders review progress quarterly, then quarterly timetables or expected milestones should be set.)
4. This information, when properly collected and analyzed [4.1], helps leaders focus on actions needed to achieve mission and vision [1.1c(2)] and make more informed decisions to optimize customer satisfaction and operational and financial performance.

Similar relationships (linkages) exist between other Items. In the application, highlight these linkages using cross-references to demonstrate integration. In this book, key linkages among each of the Items are presented in the *circle diagrams* with that Item.

Prevention-Based

Prevention-based systems are characterized by actions to minimize or prevent the existence or recurrence of problems. In an ideal world, all systems would produce perfect products and flawless service. Since that rarely happens, high-performing organizations are able to act quickly to recover from a problem (fight the fire) and then take action to identify the root cause of the problem and prevent it from occurring again. The nature of the problem, its root cause, and appropriate corrective action are communicated to all relevant workers, suppliers, partners, and customers so that they can implement the corrective action in their area before the problem arises again.

Tools, such as cause-effect analysis, PDCA, After Action Reviews, and lean enterprise, to name a few, are used to correct problems and prevent them from recurring.

Systematic

Provide evidence of a system—repeatable, predictable processes that use data and information to promote improvement and learning and fulfills the Item questions. The application should briefly summarize the overall system, explain the steps in the process, how it works, how it is evaluated, and what refinements have been made as a result. The application must communicate the nature of the system to people who may not be familiar with it. Many times it helps to use a flow diagram to convey the steps in the process.

Scoring Summary

For each Item, examiners are asked to assign a score in 5% increments that best fits or reflects the maturity of the applicant's management processes. To help identify the best scoring fit, the following summary will be helpful:

Approach and Learning Factors

- Anecdotal: 0%–5%
- Beginnings of a systematic approach to meet *basic*-level Item questions (perhaps recently piloted or implemented processes): 10%–25%
- Effective, systematic approaches in place to meet some *basic*-level Item questions: 30%–35%
- Effective, systematic approaches in place to meet most *basic*-level Item questions, and/or the beginnings (planned or piloted) of a process to evaluate and improve these basic processes: 40%
- Effective, systematic approaches in place to meet all *basic*-level Item questions, with the beginnings (planned or piloted) of a process to evaluate and improve these basic processes with no additional *overall* or higher-level questions met: 45%
- Effective, systematic approaches in place to meet some *overall*-level Item questions, with fact-based evaluation process in place: 50%–55%
- Effective, systematic approach in place to meet most *overall*-level Item questions, with fact-based evaluation process in place and a subsequent cycle of refinement with some innovation or meaningful change: 60%
- Effective, systematic approach in place to meet all *overall*-level Item questions, with fact-based evaluation process in place and a subsequent cycle of refinement with some innovation or meaningful change with no additional *multiple*-level questions met: 65%
- Effective, systematic approach in place to meet many to most *multiple*-level Item questions, with fact-based evaluation process in place and multiple cycles of refinement, innovation, and integration based on the evaluation: 80%–85%

Deployment and Integration Factors:

- Aligned: 60%–65%, demonstrating linkages (alignment) among most of the *overall*-level approach questions
- Integrated: 70%–100% demonstrating numerous tight linkages (integration) among many *multiple*-level approach questions
- Refined and innovative: 60%–100%
- Widely used, with no significant gaps in deployment: 70% or greater

Systematic, integrated, prevention-based, and continuously improved systems that are widely used are generally easier to describe than undeveloped systems. Moreover, describing activities or anecdotes does not convince examiners that an integrated, systematic process is in place. In fact, simply describing activities and anecdotes suggests that an integrated system does not exist. However, by tracing critical success threads through the relevant Items in the Criteria, the organization demonstrates that its system is integrated and fully deployed.

To demonstrate system integration, pick several critical success factors and show how they work together. For example, to demonstrate alignment or integration with leadership activities:

- Identify performance-related data that are collected [4.1a] to indicate progress against goals and strategic objectives [2.1b(1)] and action plan measures [2.2a(5)].
- Show how senior leaders analyze and review performance data [4.1b], and use them to set priorities for continuous improvement and innovation [4.1c(2)]. (Be sure to highlight in the application the meaningful, value-added process improvements that have been made based on these evaluations.)
- Show how performance effectiveness and innovation are stimulated in the planning process [2.1a(2)] and how work at all levels is aligned to implement action plans [2.2a(2)] and how the action plans compare with the performance of competitors [2.2a(6)].
- Demonstrate the impact of workforce engagement [5.2a] and development [5.2b] on performance and show how both tie to the strategy and workforce plans [2.2a(4)].
- Show how work process design [6.1] and operations effectiveness [6.2] are enhanced to improve results. Demonstrate innovative (meaningful, value added or new and unique) approaches to work process design and management.
- Report the results of improved performance outcomes [7.1, 7.2, 7.3, 7.4, and 7.5] and be sure key results are reported with relevant comparative or benchmark data included to demonstrate good-to-excellent levels of performance.
- Show that improved product and process performance [7.1] affects customer engagement and satisfaction/dissatisfaction levels [7.2].
- Show how customer requirements and preferences [P.1b(2)] are used to drive the selection of key measures [4.1a(1)] and impact work system selection [2.1a(4)] and key work process design [6.1] and operational effectiveness [6.2].

Note that the application is limited to 50 pages, not including the five-page Organizational Profile. This may not be sufficient to describe in great detail the process, results, integration, and refinement of all systematic critical success factors, goals, or processes. Thus, it is better to pick the most important few, identify them as such, and then thoroughly describe the threads and linkages throughout the application. *Distribute the important examples of integration throughout all 12 process Items in Categories 1 to 6.*

Clarifying the Baldrige Scoring Requirements

Clarifications for Scoring

The descriptions on the following pages are intended to help improve consistency of scoring interpretation and are offered as calibration guidelines only. Presented here are examples from the Scoring Calibration Guide: the first is for Item 1.1, representing a Process Item, and the second is for Item 7.1, representing a Results Item.

Prior to using these clarifying statements, the staff, judges, and senior examiners of the award program should reach consensus that the *basic, overall,* and *multiple* elements listed on the following pages appropriately capture the levels and meaning of the Criteria.

Remember that the Notes at the end of each Item in the Baldrige Criteria provide additional clarification about information that is expected as part of the review. These Notes do not create additional requirements but explain the things an organization can do to meet Item elements. Read the Notes carefully and be aware of where the words *should* and *might/may* are used.

The full version of the Scoring Calibration Guide, which is in the online materials included with this book, includes cross-referenced Notes for each Criteria Item.

- The word *should* creates an expectation that the process is in place. For example, Note 1.1a(1) for Item 1.1 indicates that, "Your organization's vision *should* set the context for the strategic objectives and action plans you describe in Items 2.1 and 2.2." This means that examiners expect to find these linkages.
- The word *might* or *may* is meant to suggest alternatives or examples, but not establish the expectation that a process requires specific elements. For example, Note 1.1b below Item 1.1 indicates that the "use of social media *may* include delivering periodic messages through internal and external websites, tweets, blogging, and customer and workforce digital forums, as well as monitoring external social media outlets and responding, when appropriate."

To make the following clarifying tables more complete, for the process Items in Categories 1 through 6 the Best Fit Scoring Guidelines are presented in the first column as a reminder of the key points in the scoring for each level. For results Items in Category 7, the *basic, overall,* and *multiple* elements of each Item are presented, along with the scoring calibration statements and corresponding actual scoring guidelines that apply to all the Category 7 Items.

The Scoring Calibration Guidelines helps ensure *comment score alignment* within a feedback report and *consistency of scoring* among multiple applicant organizations.

The full version of the Scoring Calibration Guide is located in the online materials that accompany this book.

The following analysis is presented only as a guideline that national, state, and other Baldrige-based recognition programs may want to consider to help their examiners provide more consistent and meaningful scoring and feedback to applicants.

1.1 Senior Leadership *(70 points)*	
Best Fit Scoring Guidelines	**Expected Findings or Observations**
0–5% If examiners observe the applicant is not responsive to the questions of an Item or provides no relevant information, no Strength comments would be reported and the score should be zero (0%). If the applicant provides some anecdotal information addressing Item questions (even though no systematic approach has begun), the score should be 5%.	***0–5% Scoring Range: No Systems to Meet Basic Criteria Levels*** ***1.1 Senior Leadership.*** Senior leaders have no effective processes to lead the organization. *(A).* *The guidance that senior leaders provide has not been deployed (D). Reacting to problems is the normal way of approaching work and no improvement orientation is evident (for example, no consistent effort is made to prevent problems) (L). There is no effective alignment in the organization related to mission and direction; workers and/or units seem to operate independently (I).*
10–25% If examiners observe the applicant is barely doing some of the things required in the 10–25% scoring range, the score should be in the lower part of this range. If they observe the applicant is doing everything required in the 10–25% range, but nothing in the higher ranges, the score should be 25%.	***10–25% Scoring Range: Beginning to Meet Basic Criteria Levels*** ***1.1 Senior Leadership.*** Senior leaders are *beginning* to use systematic processes to lead the organization (which ***may***, for example, include beginning to set clear values [1.1a(1)] or effectively communicating to workers [1.1b]) *(A-B).* *The leadership that senior leaders provide is not widely deployed or understood by the workforce (D). Senior leaders are starting to transition from reacting to problems to a general improvement orientation (e.g., reacting to problems is widespread and they are not focused on improvement of leadership processes) (L). Joint problem-solving activities are sometimes used to help promote alignment within the organization (I).*
30–45% If examiners observe the applicant is doing everything required in the 10–25% scoring range, and additional things in the higher ranges, the score should be in the lower part of the 30–45% range. If they observe the applicant is doing everything required in the 30–45% range, but nothing in the higher ranges, the score should be 45%.	***30–45% Scoring Range: Systematically Meeting Basic Criteria Levels*** ***1.1 Senior Leadership.*** Senior leaders have effective, systematic processes *in place* to lead the organization (which ***may***, for example, include setting or deploying clear vision and values [1.1a(1)] or effectively communicating to workers [1.1b]) (A-B). *The leadership that senior leaders provide is not widely deployed or understood by the workforce (D). Senior leaders are starting to transition from reacting to problems to a general improvement orientation (e.g., reacting to problems is widespread and they are not focused on improvement of leadership processes) (L). Joint problem-solving activities are sometimes used to help promote alignment within the organization (I).*
50–65% If examiners observe the applicant is doing everything required in the 30–45% scoring range, and additional things in the higher ranges, the score should be in the 50–65% range. If they observe the applicant is doing everything in the 50–65% range, but nothing non-bold required in the next higher 70–85% range, the score should be 65%.	***50–65% Scoring Range: Systematically Meeting Overall Criteria Levels*** *1.1* ***Senior Leadership.*** he applicant demonstrates that senior leaders, through their personal actions, use effective, systematic processes to do the following: (A-O): ***a. Establishing Vision and Values**** (1) Senior leaders set and deploy the organization's vision and values [1.1a(1)] (2) Senior leaders' personal actions demonstrate their commitment to legal and ethical behavior. [1.1a(2)] ***b. Communication*** Senior leaders communicate with and engage the entire workforce, key partners, and key customers. ***b. Mission and Organizational Performance*** (1) Senior leaders create an environment for success now and in the future. [1.1c(1)] (2) Senior leaders create a focus on action that will achieve the organization's mission. [1.1c(2)] ***Deployment:*** *Deployment of key Approach processes listed in Item 1.1 (a), (b), and (c) above may exhibit relatively minor gaps in some areas or work units of the organization (D).*

Continued

1.1 Senior Leadership *(70 points)*	*Continued*
Best Fit Scoring Guidelines	**Expected Findings or Observations**
	Learning: *Fact-based, systematic methods are in place for improving the efficiency and effectiveness of key Approach processes listed in Item 1.1 (a), (b), or (c) above –with some examples of the use of (a) best practices, (b) instances of innovation, or (c) sharing of refinements (L).* ***Integration:*** *The key senior leadership processes listed in Item 1.1 (a), (b), and (c) above are generally aligned with overall organizational needs set forth in the Organizational Profile (for example, mission, vision, values, customer requirements, and workforce characteristics and needs), and the overall-level questions of other Process Items (for example, evaluating the performance of senior leaders and the governance board [1.2a(2)], strategic objectives [2.1b(1)], action plan development [2.2a(1)], implementation [2.2a(2)], and their performance measures [2.2a(5)], and career development [5.2c(4)]) (I* **Note that the throughout this guidebook, bold titles for Areas to Address (for example, 1.1a Vision and Values above) simply identify the theme being assessed and do not establish additional requirements.*
70–85% If examiners observe the applicant is doing everything required in the 50–65% scoring range, and additional questions in the 70–100% scoring range, the score should be in the lower part of the scoring range (for example, 70%). If they observe the applicant is meeting many to most questions in the 70–100% scoring range, including some to many Deployment (D), Learning (L), and Integration (I) standards, the score should be 85% **90–100%** If examiners observe the applicant fully addressing the multiple Approach questions and most of the Deployment, Learning, and Integration standards described in the 70–100% scoring range, the score should be 90–95%. If examiners observe the applicant is meeting all of the standards in the 70–100% range, the score should be 100%. **Note**: A score of 100% is possible only if all questions are fully addressed and no Opportunities for Improvement can be identified. In addition, examiners must observe full deployment, extensive and ongoing evaluation, improvement, organizational learning, innovation, and knowledge sharing throughout the organization. Required approaches must be well integrated with organizational needs identified in response to most other Criteria Items.	***70–85% and 90–100% Scoring Ranges: Meeting Multiple Criteria Levels*** ***1.1 Senior Leadership.*** Senior leaders have effective, systematic processes in place to do the following *(Non-bold regular text below = A–M):* ***a. Establishing Vision and Values*** (1) **Setting Vision and Values. Senior leaders set the organization's vision and values.** Senior leaders deploy the vision and values through the leadership system, to the workforce, to key suppliers and partners, and to customers and other stakeholders, as appropriate. Senior leaders' personal actions reflect a commitment to those values. (2) **Promoting Legal and Ethical Behavior. Senior leaders' actions demonstrate their commitment to legal and ethical behavior.** They promote an organizational environment that requires legal and ethical behavior. ***b. Communication.*** **Senior leaders communicate with and engage the entire workforce, key partners, and key customers.** Senior leaders: • encourage frank, two-way communication; • communicate key decisions and needs for organizational change; and • take a direct role in motivating the workforce toward high performance and a customer and business focus ***c. Mission and Organizational Performance*** (1) **Creating an Environment for Success. Senior leaders create an environment for success now and in the future.** Senior leaders: • create an environment for the achievement of mission; • create and reinforce organizational culture, and a culture that fosters customer and workforce engagement, equity, and inclusion; • cultivate organizational agility and resilience, accountability, organizational and individual learning, innovation, and intelligent risk taking; and • participate in succession planning and the development of future organizational leaders. (2) **Creating a Focus on Action. Senior leaders create a focus on action that will achieve the organization's mission.** Senior leaders: • create a focus on action that will improve the organization's performance; • identify needed actions; • in setting expectations for organizational performance, include a focus on creating and balancing value for customers and other stakeholders; and

Continued

1.1 Senior Leadership *(70 points)*	*Continued*
Best Fit Scoring Guidelines	**Expected Findings or Observations**
	• demonstrate personal accountability for the organization's actions ***Deployment:*** *The approach to the Items mentioned above is well deployed with no significant gaps (D).* ***Learning:*** *For scores of 70% to 85%, fact-based, systematic evaluation and improvement are key tools used to improve the efficiency and effectiveness for many to most of the Approach elements listed above, with clear evidence of adoption of best practices, managing for innovation, and sharing of refinements of these Approaches. (L).* ***For scores of 90% to 100%,*** *fact-based, systematic evaluation and improvement are key Organization-wide tools used to improve the efficiency and effectiveness for most to nearly all of the Approach elements listed above, with clear evidence of development of best practices, achievement of innovation, and sharing of refinements. (L).* ***Integration:*** *The Approaches listed above are integrated with the organizational needs set forth in the Organizational Profile and other Process Items (for example, governance, improving the leadership system, and societal contributions [1.2], strategic objectives [2.1b(1)], action plan development [2.2a(1)], implementation [2.2a(2)], and their performance measures [2.2a(5)], customer engagement [3.2], career development [5.2c(4)]) (I).*

Notes:

1.1. Your organizational performance results should be reported in Items 7.1–7.5. Results related to the effectiveness of leadership and the leadership system should be reported in Item 7.4.

1.1a(1). Your organization's vision should set the context for the strategic objectives and action plans you describe in Items 2.1 and 2.2.

1.1b. Two-way communication may include use of social media, such as delivering periodic messages through internal and external websites, tweets, blogging, and customer and workforce digital forums, as well as monitoring external social media outlets and responding, when appropriate.

1.1b. Senior leaders' direct role in motivating the workforce may include participating in reward and recognition programs.

1.1b. Organizations that rely heavily on volunteers to accomplish their work should also discuss efforts to communicate with and engage the volunteer workforce.

1.1c(1). A successful organization is capable of addressing current business needs and, by addressing risk, agility, resilience, and strategic opportunities, of preparing for its future business, market, and operating environment. In creating an environment for success, leaders should consider both external and internal factors. Factors might include risk appetite and tolerance; the need for technological and organizational innovation, including risks and opportunities arising from emerging technology, data integration, and digitization; readiness for disruptions; organizational culture, work systems, the potential need for changes in structure and culture, workforce capability and capacity, resource availability; societal benefit and social equity; and core competencies.

1.1c(1). Promoting equity means ensuring that all customers, and workforce members are treated fairly and that all workforce members can reach their full potential. Inclusion refers to promoting the full participation of all workforce members and ensuring a sense of belonging for them.

1.1c(2). Senior leaders' focus on action considers your strategy, workforce, work systems, and assets. It includes taking intelligent risks, implementing innovations and ongoing improvements in performance and productivity, taking the actions needed to achieve your strategic objectives (see 2.2a[1]), and possibly establishing plans for managing organizational change or responding rapidly to significant new information.

Glossary Terms Not Described In the Notes:

Senior leaders refer to an organization's senior management group or team. This typically consists of the head of the organization and his or her direct reports.

Stakeholders refer to all groups that are or *might* be affected by the organization's actions and success. Key stakeholders *might* include customers, the workforce, partners, collaborators, governing boards, stockholders, donors, suppliers, taxpayers, regulatory bodies, policy makers, funders, and local and professional communities.

7.1 Product and Process Results *(120 points)*

7.1 ***Product and Process Results:*** At the **Basic** level, results are expected for product performance ***and*** process effectiveness.
At the **Overall** level, expected results are listed in **bold** type below.
At the **Multiple** Level, expected results are listed in regular black text.

a. ***Customer-Focused Product and Service Results.*** **At the Overall level, report results for products and customer service processes.**
Also, additional results at the *multiple* level are reported as follows:
- Results for key measures or indicators of the performance of products and services that are important to and directly serve customers
- Differentiate these results by product offerings, customer groups, and market segments, as appropriate

b. ***Work Process Effectiveness Results.***
1. **At the Overall level, report results for process effectiveness and efficiency.**
Also, additional results at the *multiple* level are reported as follows:
   - Results for key measures or indicators of the operational performance of key work and support processes, including productivity, cycle time, and other appropriate measures of process effectiveness, efficiency, security and cybersecurity, and innovation
   - Results are differentiated (segmented) by process types, as appropriate
2. **At the Overall level, report results for safety and emergency preparedness.**
Also, additional results at the *multiple* level are reported as follows:
   - Results for key measures or indicators of the effectiveness of the organization's safety system and its preparedness for disasters, emergencies, and other disruptions
   - Results are differentiated (segmented) by location or process type, as appropriate

c. ***Supply-Network Management Results.*** **At the Overall level, report results for supply-network management.**
Also, additional results at the *multiple* level are reported as follows:
- Key measures or indicators of the performance of the supply network, including its contribution to enhancing the organization's performance

Scoring Calibration Observation	Baldrige Scoring Guidelines
0 or 5% **Scoring Variables for the 0–5% Range**: a. No product performance and process effectiveness results important to the accomplishment of the organization's mission are reported (I) (0%). b. Mainly poor product performance and process effectiveness results are reported (5%). (Note: Comparative information is not expected at this level.).	• Results are ***not*** reported for any areas of importance to the accomplishment of your organization's mission (I). • Trend data either are not reported or show mainly adverse trends (T). • There are no organizational performance results or the results reported are poor (Le). Comparative information is not reported (C).
10–25% Basic **Scoring Variables for the 10–25% Range:** a. All of the requirements of the 0–5% scoring range have been met; and b. Taken together, of the results expected that are important to the accomplishment of the organization's mission the following are reported for a *few* areas: (1) Product performance results [7.1a] *and/or* (2) Process effectiveness results [7.1b(1)] (I) (10%); and, of those provided: c. *Some* positive trend data are reported but *some* may show adverse trends (T) (15%); or d. A *few* results show good levels of performance (although little or no comparative data may be reported) (Le/C) (20%).	• Results are reported for a ***few*** areas of importance to the accomplishment of the organization's mission. (I) • Some trend data are reported, with some adverse trends evident. (T) • A few organizational performance results are reported, responsive to the ***basic question*** in the Item, and early good performance levels are evident. (Le) Little or no comparative information is reported. (C).

Continued

7.1 Product and Process Results *(120 points possible)* *Continued*	
Scoring Calibration Observation	**Baldrige Scoring Guidelines**
Scoring Summary: The score should be 10% if the applicant meets only a and b in this scoring range; 15% with a, b, and c; 20% with a, b, and d, and 25% with a, b, c, and d, and paragraph b in the next higher range has not been met.	
30–45% Basic **Scoring Variables for the 30–45% Range:** a. All of the requirements for the 10–25% scoring range have been met; and b. Of the results expected that are important to the accomplishment of the organization's mission, the following are reported for *many* areas: (1) Product performance [7.1a] *and* (2) Process effectiveness [7.1b(1)] (I) (30%); and, of those provided: c. *Some* trend data are reported for product performance [7.1a] and process effectiveness [7.1b(1)] and most are favorable (T) (35%) d. *Some* levels of product [7.1a] and process performance [7.1b(1)], when compared to other providers, show good (average or better) levels of performance (Le/C) (40%). **Scoring Summary:** The score should be 30% if the applicant meets only a and b in this scoring range; 35% with a, b, and c; 40% with a, b, and d, and 45% with a, b, c, and d, and paragraph b in the next higher range has not been met.	• Results are reported for ***many*** areas of importance to the accomplishment of your organization's mission (I) • Some trend data are reported, and most of the trends presented are beneficial (T). • Good organizational performance levels are reported, responsive to the ***basic question*** of the Item (Le). Early stages of obtaining comparative information are evident
50–60% Overall **Scoring Variables for the 50–65% Range:** a. All of the requirements of the 30–45% scoring range have been met; and b. Taken together, *most* of the expected results that are important to the accomplishment of key customer, market, and process requirements are reported for the following areas: (1) products and customer service processes [7.1a] (2) process effectiveness and efficiency [7.1b(1)] (3) safety and emergency preparedness [7.1b(2)] (4) supply-network management [7.1c], and *(Note: See the notes at the end of Item 7.1 for clarifications of appropriate measures. The expected results relate to processes that directly serve customers and impact operations, safety and emergency preparedness, and supply-network management. These results are not required to be segmented at the Overall scoring level.) (I) (50%);* c. *Some* product and customer service processes, process effectiveness and efficiency, safety and emergency preparedness, and supply-network management [7.1a–c] trend data are reported. Most of the results reported show beneficial trends (T) (55%); or d. *Some* current levels of product performance and customer service processes, process effectiveness and efficiency, emergency preparedness, and supply-network management [7.1a–c], when evaluated against relevant comparisons and/or benchmarks, show good (average) levels of performance (Le/C) (60%).	• Organizational performance results are reported for ***most*** key customer, market, and process requirements. (I) • Beneficial trends are evident in areas of importance to the accomplishment of the organization's mission. (T) • Good organizational performance levels are reported, responsive to the ***overall questions*** in the Item. (Le) Some current performance levels have been evaluated against relevant comparisons and/or benchmarks and show areas of good relative performance. (C) (also Le).

Continued

7.1 Product and Process Results *(120 points possible)* *Continued*	
Scoring Calibration Observation	**Baldrige Scoring Guidelines**
Scoring Summary: The core should be 50% if the applicant meets only a and b in this scoring range; 55% with a, b, and c; 60% with a, b, and d; and 65% with a, b, c, and d and paragraph b in the next higher range has not been met. *Note: Before you give a score of 65%, the following analysis must be made to determine if the score should be reduced or sustained:* • Retain a score of 65% if results for all four subparts in paragraph b(1) to b(4) are reported • Reduce the score to 60% if results for only three of the four subparts in paragraph b(1) to b(4) are reported • Reduce the score to 55% if results for only two of the four subparts in paragraph b(1) to b(4) are reported • Reduce the score to 50% if results for only one of the four subparts in paragraph b(1) to b(4) are reported. For example, if most of the expected results required by paragraph b were reported but no results for subpart b(3) safety and emergency preparedness were reported, the score of 65% should be reduced to 60%.	
70–85% Multiple **Scoring Variables for the 70–85% Range:** a. All of the requirements of the 50–65% scoring range have been met; and b. Taken together, *most* of the expected product performance and process effectiveness/efficiency results that are important to the accomplishment of key customer, market, process, and action plan requirements, are reported for the following multiple requirements as indicated below: 1. Results reflecting the performance of products and processes that are important to directly serving customers, differentiated or segmented by product offerings, customer groups, and market segments, as appropriate [7.1a] 2. Results reflecting the process effectiveness and efficiency of key work and support processes, including productivity, cycle time, and other appropriate measures of process effectiveness, efficiency, security and cybersecurity, and innovation, differentiated or segmented by process types, as appropriate [7.1b(1)] 3. Results reflecting the preparedness for disasters, emergencies, and other disruptions differentiated or segmented by location or process type, as appropriate [7.1b(2)] 4. Results reflecting the performance of the supply network, including its contribution to enhancing the organization's performance [7.1c] (I) (70%) c. *Most* of the trend results reported show sustained performance over time (for example, three or more data cycles) (T) (75%); or d. *Many to most* trends and current levels of product performance and process effectiveness/efficiency, disaster and emergency preparedness, and supply-network management [7.1a–c] performance, when compared to other providers, show areas of leadership and very good (for example, top quartile) relative performance (T/Le/C) (80%). **Scoring Summary:** The score should be 70% if the applicant meets only a and b in this scoring range; 75% with a, b, and c; 80% with a, b, and d; and 85% with a, b, c, and d; and paragraph b in the next higher range has not been met.	• Organizational performance results are reported for ***most*** key customer, market, process, and action plan requirements. (I) • Beneficial trends have been sustained over time in most areas of importance to the accomplishment of the organization's mission. (T) (also I) • Good-to-excellent organizational performance levels are reported, responsive to the ***multiple questions*** in the Item. (Le) Many to most trends and current performance levels have been evaluated against relevant comparisons and/or benchmarks and show areas of leadership and very good relative performance. (C) (also T and Le).

Continued

<table>
<tr><th colspan="2">7.1 Product and Process Results *(120 points possible)* *Continued*</th></tr>
<tr><th>Scoring Calibration Observation</th><th>Baldrige Scoring Guidelines</th></tr>
<tr><td>Note: Before you give a score of 85%, the following analysis must be made to determine if the score of 85% should be reduced:
• Retain a score of 85% if results for all four subparts in paragraph b(1) to b(4) are reported
• Reduce the score to 80% if results for only three of the four subparts in paragraph b(1) to b(4) are reported
• Reduce the score to 75% if results for only two of the four subparts in paragraph b(1) to b() are reported
• Reduce the score to 70% if results for only one of the four subparts in paragraph b(1) to b(4) are reported.

For example, if most of the expected results required by paragraph b were reported but no results for subpart b(3) safety and emergency preparedness were reported, the score of 85% should be reduced to 80%.</td><td>• Organizational performance results *and projections* are reported for ***most*** key customer, market, process, and action plan requirements (I).
• Beneficial trends have been sustained over time in all areas of importance to the accomplishment of the organization's mission (T) (also I).
• Excellent organizational performance levels are reported that are fully responsive to the ***multiple questions*** of the Item (Le). Industry and benchmark leadership is demonstrated in many areas (C)</td></tr>
<tr><td>**90–100% Multiple**
Scoring Variables for the 90–100% Range:
a. ***All*** of the requirements of the 70–85% scoring range have been met; and
b. ***Most*** of the expected product performance and process effectiveness/efficiency results and *projections of performance* that are important to the accomplishment of key customer, market, process, and action plan requirements are reported for the following multiple requirements:
• Customer-Focused Product and Process Results reflecting the performance of products and processes that are important to directly serving customers, differentiated or segmented by product offerings, customer groups, and market segments, as appropriate [7.1a]
• Work Process Effectiveness Results
– Process Effectiveness and Efficiency of key work and support processes, including productivity, cycle time, and other appropriate measures of process effectiveness, efficiency, security and cybersecurity, and innovation, differentiated or segmented by process types, as appropriate [7.1b(1)]
– Preparedness for disasters, emergencies, and other disruptions differentiated or segmented by location or process type, as appropriate [7.1b(2)]
• Supply-Network Management Results reflecting the performance of the supply network, including its contribution to enhancing the organization's performance
c. *All* of the trend results reported show sustained performance over time (for example, three or more data cycles); or
d. *Many to most* trends and current levels of product performance and process effectiveness/efficiency, disaster and emergency preparedness, and supply-network management (7.1a–c] performance, when evaluated against relevant comparisons and/or benchmarks, show areas of industry leadership and excellent (for example, top decile or best in class) relative performance (T/Le/C) (95%).

Scoring Summary: The score should be 90% if the applicant meets only a and b in this scoring range; 95% with a, b, and c or d, and 100% with a, b, c, and d.</td><td></td></tr>
</table>

Notes:

7. There is not a one-to-one correspondence between Results Items and Criteria Categories 1–6. Results should be considered systemically, with contributions to individual Results Items frequently stemming from processes in more than one Criteria Category.

   The Baldrige scoring system asks for current, trended, comparative, and segmented data, as appropriate, to provide key information for analyzing and reviewing your organizational performance (Item 4.1), to demonstrate use of organizational knowledge (Item 4.2), and to provide the operational basis for customer-focused results (Item 7.2) and financial, market, and strategy results (Item 7.5).

   In a few areas, your results may be qualitative in or not amenable to trending over time. Some examples are results for governance accountability, training hours for suppliers on new products or processes, and results for limited or one-time projects or processes.

   Comparative data and information are obtained by benchmarking (inside and outside your industry, as appropriate) and by seeking competitive comparisons. In a few cases, such as results for projects or processes that are unique to your organization, comparative data may not be available or appropriate.

7.1a. Results for your products and customer service processes should relate to the key customer requirements and expectations you identify in P.1b(2), which are based on information gathered through processes you describe in Category 3. The measures or indicators should address factors that affect customer preference, such as those listed in the notes to P.1b(2) and 3.1b.

7.1a. For some nonprofit (including government) organizations, funding sources might mandate product or service performance measures. These measures should be identified and reported here.

7.1b. Results should address the key operational requirements you identify in the Organizational Profile and in Category 6.

7.1b. Appropriate measures and indicators of work process effectiveness might include defect rates; rates and results of product, service, and work system innovation; results for simplification of internal jobs and job classifications; waste reduction; work layout improvements; changes in supervisory ratios; Occupational Safety and Health Administration (OSHA)-reportable incidents; measures or indicators of the success of emergency drills or simulations, such as cycle time, containment, and meeting of standards; and results for work relocation or contingency exercises.

7.1c. Appropriate measures and indicators of supply-network performance might include supplier and partner audits; just-in-time delivery; and acceptance results for externally provided products, services, and processes. Measures and indicators of contributions to enhancing your performance might include those for improvements in sub-assembly performance and in supplier services to customers.

From a Culture of Compliance to a Culture of Excellence—Worldwide

Helping Leadership Make a Commitment to Performance Excellence

Leaders are often challenged in seeing the value of embarking on a *performance excellence journey.* "The way things have always been …" has helped them move to their current position. They ask themselves the following questions:

- Why change things when things have worked well in the past, and isn't it risky to try something new?
- What will the Board of Directors think?
- Do I have the staff needed to move to higher levels of performance excellence?
- How do I even describe what I mean by performance excellence?

Global performance excellence models like the Baldrige Framework, the China Association for Quality (CAQ) Criteria for Performance Excellence, and other global models allow an organization to define performance excellence and learn from best practices proven to drive performance excellence.

The Baldrige, CAQ, and other models can best be defined as *outcome-focused, evidence-based management models that represent the leading edge of validated leadership and performance practice.* Key phrases in these definitions include:

- **Outcome-focused**. These performance excellence models don't focus only on describing processes. They identify processes that meet or exceed requirements and drive toward constantly improving results. Processes that don't improve outcomes probably allow your performance to fall behind your competitors.
- **Evidence-based**. These performance excellence models are not just ideas of what might work to improve outcomes. The Criteria are based on what has been proven in the past to drive improved outcomes.
- **Validated leadership and performance practices**. Performance excellence model programs have driven change as best practices in leadership and management practices are identified. These models evolved over their existence from manufacturing-focused quality models to enterprise-level performance excellence models that are relevant to any industry.

When considering the use of a performance excellence model, an initial self-assessment is essential. It helps leaders determine where to start. Consider, for example, whether the organization is more focused on compliance or excellence. Many organizations emphasize compliance in their daily activities with any focus on excellence usually delegated to a particular person or department. *A key role of leaders should be to move their organizations from a culture focused on compliance to a culture focused on performance excellence* (Figure 40).

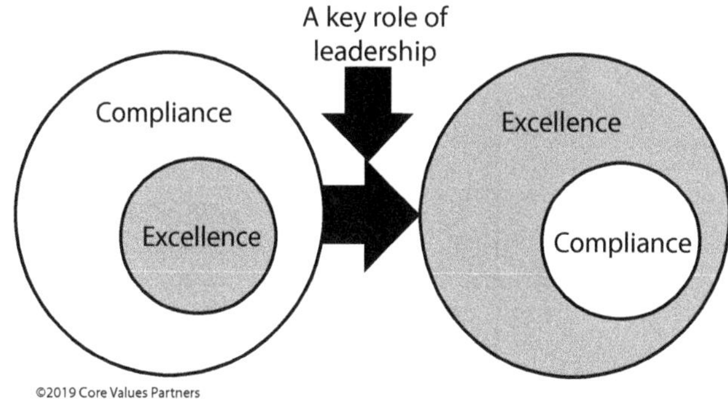

Figure 40 Moving from a culture of compliance to a culture of excellence.

This does not minimize the importance of compliance. It merely emphasizes that compliance should be the minimum standard and excellence should be the aspiration of the organization. Compliance should be viewed as the threshold requirement for performance—typically meeting regulatory requirements. Meeting compliance requirements usually is a *yes/no* test—"Do you meet compliance requirements or not?" The challenge for any organization meeting only compliance requirements is that every competitor has to meet those same requirements, so compliance only provides no competitive advantage.

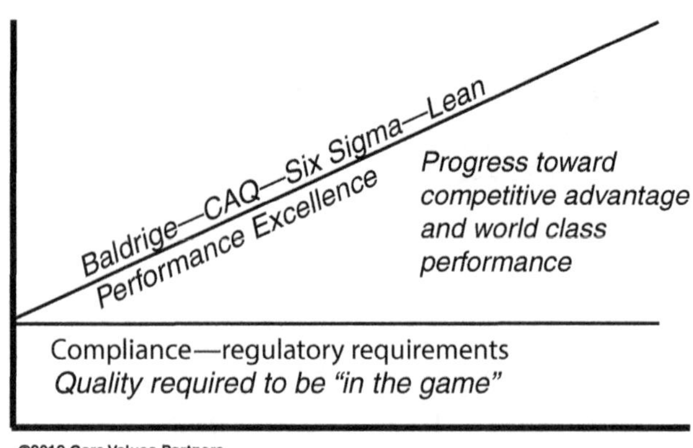

Figure 41 Value of compliance versus excellence.

Compliance versus Excellence

To gain a competitive advantage in the market, an organization must move beyond mere compliance, and focus on what can set it apart in the eyes of the customer. Performance excellence strategies are not explained by *yes/no* responses—they are indicators of continuous progress. No organization is perfect, but the aspiration to continuously advance on the performance excellence journey helps the organization move toward competitive advantage and world-class performance (Figure 41).

Leaders should ask themselves "Is our organization satisfied with maintaining the status quo or should it aspire to excellence *in the eyes of our customers?*" If so, how do we describe excellence? The principles set forth in the various performance excellence models help provide an answer to this question. Baldrige calls these principles *Core Values and Concepts*; in the China Association for Quality they are the *Basic Ideas.* All excellence models define similar key concepts that are common among high-performing organizations (Table 7).

When reviewing performance excellence model characteristics, leaders find it useful to understand where their organization is on the path from compliance to excellence (Figure 42 and Figure 43). Comparing compliance characteristics to excellence characteristics helps identify areas of strength and opportunities for improvement from a high-level

Table 7 Comparison of Baldrige and CAQ characteristics of excellence.

Baldrige Core Values	China Quality Award Basic Ideas
1. Systems Perspective	1. Leadership with Foresight and Sagacity
2. Visionary Leadership	2. Strategic Orientation
3. Customer-Focused Excellence	3. Customer-Driven
4. Valuing People	4. Social Responsibility
5. Agility and Resilience	5. Workforce Focus
6. Organizational Learning	6. Win-Win Cooperation
7. Focus on Success and Innovation	7. Process Focus and Results Focus
8. Management by Fact	8. Learning, Improvement, and Innovation
9. Societal Contributions	9. System Management
10. Ethics and Transparency	
11. Delivering Value and Results	

Compliance	Excellence
1. *Silo* mentality	1. Systems Perspective
2. Management of people	2. Visionary Leadership
3. Meet customer requirements	3. Customer-Focused Excellence
4. Employees as a commodity	4. Valuing People
5. Process constrained	5. Agility and Resilience
6. Status quo	6. Organizational Learning
7. Short-term perspective	7. Focus on Success and Innovation
8. Management by opinion	8. Management by Fact
9. Inward focus	9. Societal Contributions
10. Poor ethics and minimal communication	10. Ethics and Transparency
11. Requirements focus	11. Focus on Results and Creating Value

Figure 42 Baldrige comparison of compliance to characteristics of excellence.

Compliance	Excellence
1. Management of people	1. Leadership with Foresight and Sagacity
2. Quarterly perspective	2. Strategic Orientation
3. Meet basic requirements	3. Customer Driven
4. Inward focus	4. Social Responsibility
5. Employees as a commodity	5. Workforce Focus
6. Self-centered perspective	6. Win-Win Cooperation
7. Requirements focus	7. Process Focus and Results Focus
8. Status quo	8. Learning, Improvement, and Innovation
9. Silo mentality	9. Systems Management

Figure 43 CAQ comparison of compliance to basic ideas.

perspective. *See the Baldrige Core Values Assessment and the China Association for Quality Assessments.*

Practical Self-Assessment Exercise

To assess your organization's *current state,* conduct the following exercise with your organization's leaders:

1. Require leaders to read the Baldrige Core Values and Concepts, the China Association for Quality Basic Ideas, or relevant excellence models, values, and concepts in advance of meeting.
2. With that information in mind, complete the appropriate Performance Excellence Assessment on each of the characteristics of excellence. *(See separate Performance Excellence Assessments at the end of this chapter.)*
3. After compiling the results of this individual self-assessment, as a *leadership group* identify the three most important strengths and three opportunities for improvement for these characteristics of excellence.

Table 8 demonstrates the alignment of Baldrige Criteria to Core Values and Concepts. Table 9 refers to alignment of CAQ Criteria and Basic Ideas.

Recognizing strengths and opportunities for improvement only identifies the *need* for improvement. Using the Baldrige, EFQM, CAQ, or other relevant criteria lets an organization identify *where* to focus their efforts. The alignment of Baldrige Core Values and Concepts to the Baldrige Criteria or the CAQ Basic Ideas to the CAQ Criteria helps identify where to focus the *What do you do … ?* and *How do you … ?* tactics to make progress on performance improvement.

If an organization makes a commitment to become an organization represented by Baldrige Core Values and Concepts or other similar concepts, then the Baldrige, EFQM, or CAQ Criteria are the road map to help them get there.

Committing to Excellence

Once the organization recognizes that is has strengths on which to build and opportunities for improvement that need to be addressed, the difficult work begins.

Leaders must be convinced that there is value in following the Baldrige, EFQM, or CAQ processes—above and beyond applying for an award.

Senior leaders and board members look for additional value, especially considering the investment of time involved in developing a 50-page application. A best practice from the EFQM process is a simple change of language. Call the document you are completing your *management document* rather than an application—and help people understand that the purpose of the management document is to put on paper how your business operates.

The following seven *Added Values* of the performance excellence model processes demonstrate the benefits of developing a management document—even if that document is never submitted to an award process:

1. **Accountability Tool**. The structure of the performance excellence model processes forces accountability. When senior leaders take responsibility for a particular category, they *own* the linkage among the three components of the application:
   - Baldrige Organizational Profile or EFQM Key Information. *What is important to the organization?*
   - Baldrige and CAQ Process or EFQM Direction and Execution categories. *Based on what is important, what do we do, and how do we do it?*
   - Baldrige, EFQM, or CAQ Results Category. *Now that we've done it, were we successful?*
2. **Sustainability Tool**. The performance excellence model processes help document how business is done at the organization. The departure of a senior leader doesn't have to mean starting all over again. The application describes how the organization operates, and a new senior leader is able to *hit the ground running* because processes are already in place to ensure sustainability over time.
3. **Improvement Tool**. While the application is being written, opportunities for improvement (OFIs) are already being identified, prioritized, and addressed. This set of cross-cutting OFIs ensures a cross-functional approach to improvement.
4. **Alignment Tool**. The performance excellence model processes help move the organization past the *silo* mentality that sub-optimizes performance. Senior leaders can no longer view success in their functional area as sufficient. The Baldrige, EFQM, and CAQ processes require a *systems view* of success. CEOs, boards of directors, and other stakeholders should view this as a key value of the process because their responsibility requires a systems perspective.
5. **Recruitment Tool.** The application/management document is a valuable tool for recruiting board members, senior leaders, and other key staff and stakeholders. Sharing the application (or just the Organizational Profile or Key Information) with the request that they review the document helps them determine if this is an organization and improvement culture to which they want to belong.

Table 8 Baldrige criteria alignment to Baldrige core values and concepts.

	1. Leadership						2. Strategy				3. Customer				4. Measurement, Analysis, and Knowledge Management					5. Workforce				6. Operations						
	Senior Leadership			Governance and Social Responsibility			Strategy Development		Strategy Implementation		Customer Expectations		Customer Engagement		Management, Analysis, and Improvement of Organizational Performance			Information and Knowledge Management		Workforce Environment		Workforce Engagement		Work Processes				Operational Effectiveness		
Baldrige Core Values	1.1	1.1	1.1	1.2	1.2	1.2	2.1	2.1	2.2	2.2	3.1	3.1	3.2	3.2	4.1	4.1	4.1	4.2	4.2	5.1	5.1	5.2	5.2	6.1	6.1	6.1	6.1	6.2	6.2	6.2
	a	b	c	a	b	c	a	b	a	b	a	b	a	b	a	b	c	a	b	a	b	a	b	a	b	c	d	a	b	c
Systems Perspective	■			■		■	■						■		■		■					■	■	■	■	■	■			
Visionary Leadership	■	■	■	■	■	■	■									■						■	■			■	■			
Customer-Focused Excellence	■		■					■			■	■	■	■									■					■		
Valuing People	■	■	■						■								■			■	■	■	■							■
Agility and Resilience	■		■						■	■					■			■	■	■			■							
Organizational Learning	■						■	■									■						■							
Focus on Success and Innovation	■						■								■		■	■				■	■							
Management by Fact							■		■	■	■	■			■	■			■				■	■	■	■	■	■	■	
Societal Contributions					■	■														■										■
Ethics and Transparency	■	■	■	■	■							■										■	■							
Delivering Value and Results	■		■					■						■		■							■					■		

6. **Reward and Recognition Tool**. The performance excellence model processes have an award component to them. Whether through internal assessment or assessment at various levels within the Baldrige, EFQM, and CAQ systems, recognition of progress is an effective method of encouraging leaders and staff to continue to progress on the performance excellence journey.

7. **Language Tool**. The Baldrige, EFQM, and CAQ criteria allow an organization to have a *common language of high-performance.* This consistent language allows all employees to view the organization through the same *lens.*

The Baldrige, EFQM, and CAQ processes allow leaders to view the organization as a synergistic whole. Getting started on assessment is the first step, and demonstrating the value of the Baldrige, EFQM, or CAQ processes is key to helping leaders understand why they should take that first important step.

Table 9 CAQ criteria alignment to CAQ basic ideas.

	Leadership			Strategy		Customer and Market		Resource						Process Management		Measure, Analysis, and Improvement	
CAQ Basic Ideas	Senior Leadership	Organizational Governance	Social Responsibility	Strategy Development	Strategy Deployment	Customer and Market Knowledge	Customer Relationships and Satisfaction	Human Resources	Financial Resources	Information and Knowledge Resources	Technical Resources	Infrastructure	Relevant Stakeholder Relationships	Process Identification and Design	Process Implementation and Improvement	Measurement, Analysis, and Review	Improvement and Innovation
Leadership with Foresight and Sagacity	■	■	■	■	■			■	■							■	
Strategic Orientation	■			■	■				■			■	■			■	■
Customer-Driven				■		■	■							■			
Social Responsibility	■		■														
Workforce Focus	■		■		■			■		■							
Win-Win Cooperation	■		■			■							■	■			
Process Focus and Results Focus	■								■		■	■		■	■		
Learning, Improvement, and Innovation	■	■		■			■	■	■					■	■	■	■
Systems Management	■			■	■			■	■	■	■	■	■	■	■	■	■

Performance Excellence Assessment – Baldrige Core Values and Concepts

Consider each of these characteristics of excellence and rate your organization's performance from 1 to 10:

1. **Do we manage in our functional silos, or do we recognize and manage based on how our organization's systems work together?**

   1 2 3 4 5 6 7 8 9 10

   Silo mentality — Systems Perspective

2. **Do we micromanage our staff, or do we provide effective direction to them, allowing them to learn and develop?**

   1 2 3 4 5 6 7 8 9 10

   Management of people — Visionary Leadership

3. **Do we focus on meeting basic customer requirements or do we want to provide products and services that engage our customers?**

   1 2 3 4 5 6 7 8 9 10

   Meet customer requirements — Customer-Focused Excellence

4. **Do we treat our employees as easily replaceable resources, or do we value them as key contributors to our success?**

   1 2 3 4 5 6 7 8 9 10

   Employees as a commodity — Valuing People

5. **Do we view ourselves as limited by how we've always done things, or do we constantly look for opportunities for improvement?**

   1 2 3 4 5 6 7 8 9 10

   Process constrained — Agility and Resilience

6. **Are we primarily concerned with meeting short-term objectives, or do we balance short-term outlook with a focus on long-term sustainability?**

   1 2 3 4 5 6 7 8 9 10

   Quarterly perspective — Organizational Learning

7. **Do we tend to be satisfied with doing things the way we've always done them, or are we looking for opportunities for innovation?**

   1 2 3 4 5 6 7 8 9 10

   Status quo — Focus on Success and Innovation

8. **Do we base decisions on individual or group opinion, or do we ensure we have facts to ensure effective decision-making?**

   1 2 3 4 5 6 7 8 9 10

   Management by opinion — Management by Fact

9. **Do we focus only on our internal operations, or do we recognize and address opportunities to address relevant societal and community needs?**

   1 2 3 4 5 6 7 8 9 10

   Inward focus — Societal Contributions

10. **Do we ignore ethical guidelines and communication needs or do we have methods to ensure ethical behavior and transparency with stakeholders?**

    1 2 3 4 5 6 7 8 9 10

    Poor ethics and minimal communication — Ethics and Transparency

11. **Are we meeting only compliance requirements, or do we have systematic methods to ensure progress toward results and creating value in the eyes of our customers and stakeholder?**

    1 2 3 4 5 6 7 8 9 10

    Requirements focus — Focus on Results and Creating Value

Performance Excellence Assessment – China Association for Quality Basic Ideas

Consider each of these characteristics of excellence and rate your organization's performance from 1 to 10:

1. **Do we micromanage our staff, or do we provide effective direction to them, allowing them to learn and develop?**

   1 2 3 4 5 6 7 8 9 10

   Management of people — Leadership with Foresight and Sagacity

2. **Are we primarily concerned with meeting short-term objectives, or do we balance short-term outlook with a focus on long-term sustainability?**

   1 2 3 4 5 6 7 8 9 10

   Quarterly perspective — Strategic Orientation

3. **Do we focus on meeting basic customer requirements or do we want to provide products and services that engage our customers?**

   1 2 3 4 5 6 7 8 9 10

   Meet basic requirements — Customer-Driven

4. **Do we focus only on our internal operations, or do we recognize and address opportunities to address relevant social needs?**

   1 2 3 4 5 6 7 8 9 10

   Inward focus — Social Responsibility

5. **Do we treat our employees as easily replaceable resources, or do we value them as key contributors to our success?**

   1 2 3 4 5 6 7 8 9 10

   Employees as a commodity — Workforce Focus

6. **Do we have adversarial relationships with others, or do we look for opportunities to partner with others for mutual success?**

   1 2 3 4 5 6 7 8 9 10

   Self-centered perspective — Win-Win Cooperation

7. **Are we meeting only compliance requirements, or do we have systematic processes that drive toward improving results?**

   1 2 3 4 5 6 7 8 9 10

   Requirements focus — Process Focus and Results Focus

8. **Do we tend to be satisfied with doing things the way we've always done them, or are we looking for opportunities for learning, improvement, and innovation?**

   1 2 3 4 5 6 7 8 9 10

   Status quo — Learning, Improvement, and Innovation

9. **Do we manage in our functional silos, or do we recognize and manage based on how our organization's systems work together?**

   1 2 3 4 5 6 7 8 9 10

   Silo mentality — Systems Management

Baldrige-Based Self-Assessments of Organizations and Management Systems

Baldrige-based self-assessments of organization performance and management systems take several forms, ranging from rigorous and time-intensive to simple and superficial. The various approaches to organizational self-assessment each have pros and cons. Curt Reimann, the first director of the Baldrige Performance Excellence Program, spoke of the need to streamline assessments to get a better sense of strengths, opportunities for improvement, and the vital few areas on which to focus leadership and drive organizational change. The online materials available with this book contain a full discussion of three distinct types of self-assessment: the written narrative to include full-length and short versions; the Likert-scale survey; and the behaviorally anchored survey.

The discussion of self-assessments or organizations and management systems includes sections on:

- Full-length written narrative
- Short written narrative
- The Baldrige Excellence Builder
- The simple survey approach, to include Likert-style surveys

The full version of the Self-Assessment of Organizations and Management Guide may be downloaded using the Online Resources URL found in the Table of Contents on page viii.

The Site Visit

INTRODUCTION

Many examiners and organizations have asked about how to prepare for site visits. This section is intended to help answer those questions and prepare the organization for an on-site examination. It includes rules of the game for examiners and what they are taught to look for. The best preparation for this type of examination is to see things through the eyes of the trained examiner.

Before an organization can be recommended to receive the Malcolm Baldrige National Quality Award, or top state award, it must receive a visit from a team of organizational assessment experts from the Board of Examiners. Although the number varies from year to year, approximately 25–30% of organizations applying for the Baldrige Award in recent years have received these site visits. Although the panel of judges does not have a predetermined scoring minimum for site-visit candidates, generally a score of 550 points or more is needed.

The site-visit team usually includes two to five senior examiners—one of whom is designated as team leader—and three to eight other examiners. In addition, the team is usually accompanied by a monitor from the Baldrige or affiliated program.

The site-visit team usually gathers at a hotel near the organization's headquarters on the day immediately preceding the site-visit launch. During the day, the team makes final preparations and plans for the visit.

Each examiner is assigned responsibility for leading the discussion and analysis for one or more Categories of the Award Criteria. Each examiner is usually teamed with one other examiner for most interviews during the site visit. These examiners usually conduct the visit in pairs to ensure the accurate understanding and recording of information.

Site visits usually begin on a Monday morning and last one week. By Wednesday afternoon or Thursday morning, most site-visit teams will have completed their on-site review, although geographically dispersed organizations may require more time. The examiners usually gather at a nearby hotel to confer and write their reports. By the end of the site visit, the team must reach consensus on the findings and score and prepare a final report for the panel of judges. This report also becomes the basis of the final report to the applicant identifying strengths and opportunities for improvement. Every applicant receives such a report.

Purpose of Site Visits

Site visits help clarify uncertain points and verify self-assessment (that is, application) accuracy. During the site visit, examiners investigate areas most difficult to understand from self-assessments, such as the following:

- Deployment: How widely a process is used throughout the organization.
- Integration: Whether processes fit together to support performance excellence.
- Process ownership: Whether processes are broadly owned, simply directed, or micromanaged.
- Workforce member involvement: The extent to which workers' participation in managing processes of all types is optimized.
- Continuous improvement maturity (learning): The number and extent of fact-based improvement cycles and resulting refinements in all areas of the organization and at all levels.

Characteristics of Site-Visit Issues

Examiners look at issues that are essential components of scoring and role-model determination. They use the site visit to:

- Clarify information that is missing or vague and verify significant strengths identified from the self-assessment.
- Verify deployment of the practices described in the self-assessment.

Examiners will:

- Concentrate on cross-cutting issues.
- Examine data, reports, and documents.
- Interview individuals and teams.
- Receive presentations from the applicant organization.

Examiners may not conduct their own focus groups or surveys with customers, suppliers, or dealers. Conducting these focus groups or surveys would violate confidentiality agreements as well as be statistically unsound. During health care site visits, examiners may not interview patients or be present during treatment, which could constitute a violation of federal privacy protections.

Discussions with the Applicant Prior to the Site Visit

Prior to the official Baldrige Award site visit, all communication between the applicant organization and its team must be routed through their respective single points of contact. Only the team leader may contact the applicant on behalf of the site-visit team prior to the site visit. This helps ensure consistency of message and communication for both parties. It prevents confusion and misunderstandings. The team leader should provide the applicant organization with basic information about the process. This includes schedules, arrival times, and equipment and meeting room needs.

Applicant organizations usually provide the following information prior to the site-visit team's final planning meeting at the hotel on the day before the site visit starts:

TYPICALLY IMPORTANT SITE-VISIT ISSUES

- Role of senior management in leading and serving as a positive role model
- Independence and effectiveness of governance system to protect stakeholder interests, provide fiscal accountability, and evaluate and improve senior leader performance
- Degree of involvement and self-direction of members of the workforce below upper management
- Comprehensiveness, accessibility, and ease of use of the information system
- Extent that facts and data are used in decision-making at all levels
- Degree of emphasis on customer engagement and consistently positive experiences; effective use of voice of the customer to understand customer expectations and prompt complaint resolution
- Extent of systematic approaches to designing and improving work processes
- Workforce and leadership development effectiveness
- Strategic identification of work systems and use of core competencies as a decision factor in determining which work remains internal and which is outsourced to suppliers and partners
- Focus on innovation and intelligent risk taking to identify good opportunities for innovation
- Extent that strategic plans align organizational work
- Extent of the use of measurable goals at all levels in the organization
- Evidence of evaluation and improvement cycles in all work processes and in system effectiveness
- Improvements in cycle times and other operating processes
- Extent of integration of all work processes including operational, support, and supply-network management
- Extent and use of benchmarking

- List of key contacts
- Organization chart
- Facility layout
- Performance data requested by examiners

The team leader, on behalf of team members, will ask for supplementary documentation to be compiled (such as results data brought up to date) to avoid placing an undue burden on the organization at the time of the site visit. The team will select sites that allow them to examine key issues and check deployment in key areas. This information may or may not be discussed with the applicant prior to the site visit. Examiners will need access to all areas of the organization.

Considerable effort is made to ensure no applicant has an advantage over any other. As a result, virtually no substantive information is exchanged prior to the site visit between the applicant and the team. Most state quality awards, however, do not impose a limit on the number of applicants that may receive recognition. These quality award programs provide recognition to any applicant that is qualified to receive it. In addition, a key mission of most state quality awards includes developing performance excellence within organizations, not simply recognizing it. As a result, many states permit much more information to change hands prior to a site visit. Some states even permit representatives of the organization to assist in planning the site visit.

Conduct of Site-Visit Team Members (Examiners)

Baldrige examiners, and most state quality award examiners, are not allowed to discuss findings with anyone but team members. Examiners may not disclose the following to the applicant:

- Personal or team observations and findings
- Conclusions and decisions
- Observations about the applicant's performance systems, whether complimentary or critical

Examiners may not discuss the following with anyone:

- Observations about any applicants
- Names of other award program applicants

Examiners may not accept trinkets, gifts, or gratuities of any kind, so applicant organizations should not offer them. (However, normal things that go in the stomach, such as coffee, cookies, rolls, breakfast, and lunch, are okay.) At the conclusion of the site visit, examiners are not permitted to leave with any of the applicant's materials including logo items or catalogs—not even items usually given to visitors. Examiners will dress in appropriate business attire unless instructed otherwise by the applicant organization.

Opening Meeting

An opening meeting will be scheduled to introduce all parties and set the structure for the site visit. The meeting is usually attended by senior executives and the self-assessment/application writing team. The opening meeting usually is scheduled first on the initial day of the site visit (8:30 a.m. or 9:00 a.m.). The team leader generally opens the site visit by starting the meeting, introducing the team, and reviewing the rules of conduct. When multiple site visits are conducted, it is usually a good idea for an award program to prepare a set of talking points or a script for the team leader to use so a common message is communicated by all teams.

After the team leader opens the site-visit meeting, the applicant organization usually has one hour to present any information it believes important for the examiners to know. This includes time for a tour, if necessary.

Immediately after the meeting, examiners usually meet with senior leaders and those responsible for preparing sections of application, since those people are likely to be at the opening meeting.

Conducting the Site Visit

The team will follow the site-visit plan, subject to periodic adjustments according to its findings. The site-visit team will need a private room, on-site, to conduct frequent caucuses. Applicant representatives are not present at these caucuses. The team will also conduct evening meetings at the hotel to review the findings of the day, reach consensus, write comments, and revise the site-visit report and modify the site-visit agenda for the following day.

If, during the course of the site visit, someone from the applicant organization believes the team or any of its members are missing the point, the designated point of contact should inform the team leader. Also, anyone from the organization who believes an examiner behaved inappropriately should inform the designated point of contact, who will inform the team leader. A good practice is for the organization key point of contact, the site visit team leader, and the Baldrige or other program representative to have a short check-in meeting at the end of each day of the site visit.

Members of the workforce should be instructed to mark every document given to examiners with the name and work location of the person providing the document. This will ensure that it is returned to the proper person. Records should be made of all material given to team members. Organization personnel may not ask examiners for opinions and advice. Examiners are not permitted to provide any information of this type during the site visit.

GENERIC SITE-VISIT QUESTIONS

Examiners must verify or clarify the information contained in an application, whether they have determined a process to be a strength or an opportunity for improvement. Examiners must verify the existence of strengths as well as clarify the nature of each of the vital opportunities for improvement in the final feedback report.

Before and during the site-visit review process, examiners formulate a series of questions based on the Baldrige Criteria. This chapter identifies the types of questions that examiners are likely to ask during the site-visit process. During a site visit, actual questions will be tailored to the specific key factors of the organization deemed to be most relevant. The questions in the following section are presented to help prepare applicants and examiners for the site-visit process.

Leaders and workforce members are usually focused on the process they have in place today. They often fail to describe how they systematically refined the process and show how it became the process of today. Therefore, after learning how the process works, all examiners should ask the following questions: *"Have you always done it this way? How did you do it before? Why did you change? Do you have additional improvements in the works?"* If examiners do not ask these questions, each member of the workforce should offer the answer as if they were asked.

Category 1—Leadership

1.1 Senior Leadership

1. **Vision and Value (Establishing and Understanding Values).** (To top leaders) Please share with us the values of your organization. Pick one at random and ask, how did you determine this value was important to guide the organization? [1.1a(1)] How do you make sure other leaders or workers understand this value? How do you make sure suppliers, customers, and other stakeholders understand this value?

2. **Vision and Values (Embracing Values).** (To leaders) What actions do you take to convince your workforce, customers, suppliers, and other stakeholders that you fully embrace the values you mentioned? [1.1a(1)]

   - (To the workforce) What are the values and priorities of the organization? What does your leader do to show you that he or she actually believes these values are important and adheres to them?

3. **Vision and Values (Vision Priorities).** (To top leaders) Please describe your vision for the organization. What are your top priorities to achieve vision?

   - How do you ensure that your entire workforce understands the organization's vision and the priorities and the work they need to do to achieve it? How do you make sure other leaders and workers understand these values? How do you make sure suppliers, customers, and other stakeholders understand these values?

   - How do you know how effective you and your subordinates are at instilling the vision and values in the workforce, and communicating them to customers, partners, and suppliers?

   - How do you know your messages to the workforce, customers, partners, and suppliers are understood as you intended?

4. **Promoting Legal and Ethical Behavior.** What do you (the leader) do to demonstrate through your actions a commitment to legal and ethical behavior? Describe your actions. What do you do to make sure everyone in the organization behaves in a legal and ethical manner? What are ethical rules that must not be violated (zero tolerance)?
   - What happens when someone—even a senior manager—breaks these rules? Ask members of the workforce the same question. [1.1a(2)]
   - What processes have you put in place to achieve the desired ethical behavior? How well do these processes work? How do you know?
   - What has been done to improve them? [Scoring Guidelines]
5. **Communication (Two-Way).** What does two-way communication mean to you (the leader)? What do you do to promote two-way communication at all levels in the organization? How widely is the process actually used? How do you determine if the two-way communication is effective? [1.1b]
   - To check deployment, ask members of the workforce about how this two-way communication works and whether they have used it
6. **Communication (Workers and Suppliers).** What are the ways you communicate critical information, including key decisions, throughout the organization to the entire workforce (including members of the volunteer workforce if relevant) and to key partners and suppliers? What kind of information do you communicate? To what extent do you use social media and other web-based techniques to communicate? When do you do this? [1.1b]
   - How do you know your communications are understood as you intended? What kinds of communication or feedback do you receive from members of the workforce and partners or suppliers? What do you do with this information? How well do these processes work? How do you know? What has been done to improve them?
7. **Communication (Customers).** What are the ways you communicate critical information, including key decisions, to customers? What kind of information do you communicate? [1.1b]
   - What do you do to engage customers?
   - How do you know your communications are understood as you intended? What kinds of communication or feedback do you receive from customers? What do you do with this information? How well do these processes work? How do you know? What has been done to improve them?
8. **Communication (Encouraging High Performance).** What is your role in supporting performance excellence (high performance)? [1.1b]
   - How do you encourage continuous improvement, innovation, and workforce engagement and motivation? Please provide some examples of improved engagement or motivation throughout the organization as a result of your efforts. In what way do you participate in reward and recognition programs? How does your personal involvement reinforce high performance and a customer and business focus? (Follow up on these examples with other members of the workforce.)
   - How do you ensure that middle managers and other leaders promote workforce engagement and motivation throughout the organization?
9. **Creating an Environment for Success (Understanding Organizational Sustainability).** What does it mean to you (senior leader) to create a successful organization, now and in the future? How do you make sure that your organization will continue to excel even after you leave? (Note: "I do not plan to leave" is not an acceptable answer. Follow this answer with what might happen if you were hit by a bus or otherwise incapacitated?) What do you do to support succession planning and the development of future leaders? [1.1c(1)]
10. **Creating an Environment for Success (Learning).** What do you do to increase learning (continuous improvement) throughout the

organization, with all units and the entire workforce? What are some examples of new knowledge they have acquired? [1.1c(1)]

11. **Creating an Environment for Success (Sustaining High Achievement).** What techniques have you put in place to ensure the organization achieves its mission and winning levels of performance leadership in your industry or sector? [1.1c(1)]

12. **Creating an Environment for Success (Environment for Improvement).** The Criteria ask how you "create an environment or cultivate" several things such as the improvement of organizational performance, performance leadership, accountability, and organizational and personal learning. What do you do to make certain that this environment or culture is in place throughout the organization? [1.1c(1)]

13. **Creating an Environment for Success (Engagement, Innovation, Agility, and Resilience).** What does innovation mean to you? For your workforce? For your organization? What process have you put in place to encourage innovation, agility, and resilience? What innovative approaches have you personally implemented? What innovations have come from your workers? [1.1c(1)]

    - What does customer and workforce engagement mean to you? What do you do to create a culture that enhances customer and workforce engagement and promotes equity and inclusion?
    - What does organizational agility and resilience mean to you? What barriers to agility and resilience have you identified in the organization? Pick some barriers and for each ask, what have you done to overcome this barrier?
    - What processes have you put in place to ensure that innovations, best practices, and other knowledge are effectively shared throughout the organization to appropriate managers and members of the workforce? How well do these processes work? How do you know? What innovations have been shared?
    - How do you determine whether pursuing an innovation or new idea is worth the risk? To what extent do you consider opportunities arising from emerging technology, data integration, digitization, readiness for disruptions, the potential need for changes in organizational structure and culture, workforce capability and capacity, societal benefit and social equity, and your organization's core competencies?

14. **Creating an Environment for Success (Leader Succession).** Please describe the methods you use to prepare people for leadership roles. What is your role in this effort? If they have a program to prepare future leaders, ask who is currently involved in the effort to develop future leaders? (If anyone is currently involved, randomly pick one or two to interview and validate the effectiveness of the process.) [1.1c(1)]

    - How do you know this process is working? What improvements, best practices, or innovations have you made in it? [Scoring Guidelines]

15. **Focus on Action (Improve Performance).** What steps have you (senior leader) taken to focus the organization on actions to achieve your objectives, mission, and vision? What actions have you taken to improve performance? How do you as senior leaders demonstrate personal accountability for the organization's actions? (Note that some leaders may use techniques such as PDCA, Six Sigma, and Lean to make ongoing improvements in productivity.)

    - What have you done to promote innovation and analyze risk?
    - What performance data [links to 4.1] do you use to determine whether the benefits of the proposed innovation or improvement are worth the risk (intelligent risk taking), are likely to be successful, or whether other actions are needed? [1.1c(2)]

16. **Focus on Action (Balancing Customer Value).** Do your various customer segments have differ-

ent priorities or value different things? If yes, ask for examples. Pick some differences and ask, how do you make sure that your organization balances these different requirements and delivers what the customers want most? [1.1c(2)]

17. **Vision and Values, Focus on Action.** What are your key customer or stakeholder segments? [1.1a(1), 1.1c(2)] [links to P.1b(2) and 3.1b(1)]
    - Pick one and ask, what does this customer or stakeholder group require?
    - Are the requirements expected of this customer group different from any other group? If so, what are the differences, and how have you ensured that your organization is addressing the different or competing interests of these groups?

1.2 Governance and Societal Responsibilities

1. **Governance System.** How independent is your board of directors? [1.2a(1)]
    - What percentage of the board is not affiliated with your organization in any way (other than being a board member)?
    - How do you ensure the audit function is effective and independent?
    - Have problems existed in the past where stakeholder interests were threatened? If so, what was done to prevent the possibility of those problems recurring?
    - How does the board make sure senior leaders behave properly and are accountable for their actions in the organization, including accountability for achieving the strategic plan?
    - What policies are in place to ensure the board remains alert and becomes aware of management problems in the organization?
    - What type of fiscal oversight does the board provide? What problems or issues have the board identified in the past three to five years? Pick some and ask, what was the board's reaction to this issue? How was it resolved? What steps were taken to prevent the problem from happening again?
    - For public nonprofit organizations: Explain your process for serving as a trusted steward of public funds. What is done to emphasize the importance of this stewardship?
    - What processes have been put in place to ensure the board effectively protects shareholder value? How well do these processes work? How do you know? What has been done to evaluate and improve them?
2. **Performance Evaluation (Leadership System).** To senior leaders: How do you check or evaluate the effectiveness of the leadership system? How is the effectiveness of your own personal leadership checked? [1.2a(2)]
    - Please provide specific examples where you and the leadership system have improved as a result of these evaluations. How do managers evaluate and improve their personal leadership effectiveness?
3. **Performance Evaluation (Senior Leaders).** What are the criteria for promoting and rewarding leaders within the organization? [1.2a(2), links to 5.2c(1)]
    - How are you making leaders and top managers accountable for performance improvement, workforce involvement, and customer-satisfaction objectives? (Look at randomly chosen samples of leaders' evaluations and check to see if they reflect refinements based on organizational performance review findings and worker feedback. If the applicant is reluctant to share personally identifiable information such as performance appraisals, tell the point of contact that personally identifiable information may be redacted prior to your review.)
    - Describe the system you have in place to use senior leader performance evaluations to help determine executive compensation. How has your compensation been affected?
    - Please provide examples where performance evaluations were used to help leaders develop

skills and improve their own effectiveness as leaders. Share some recent improvements that have been made in the effectiveness of leaders throughout the organization.

- How have you improved the process of evaluating senior leaders and managers over the years?
- What processes have been put in place to evaluate and improve the effectiveness of the board of directors as a whole and as individual board members? How well do these processes work? How do you know? What has been done to improve these processes?

4. **Legal and Regulatory Compliance (Public Risks).** How do you anticipate legal, regulatory, and community concerns over the possible impact of your organization? How do you determine what risks the public faces because of your current or future products, services, and operations? [1.2b(1)]
   - What are some examples of risks you have identified in general, and in regard to conservation of natural resources and effective supply-network management? Pick some risks at random and ask, what have you done to reduce the risk or threat to the public? How do you know you are successful in these areas? How do you measure progress?
   - What measures and goals have been developed to identify and reduce risks to the public?
   - How do you know that your processes are effective for protecting the public from risks associated with your products, services, and programs? How have you improved these processes?
5. **Legal and Regulatory Compliance (Compliance).** What processes are in place to conserve natural resources? How did you determine what areas of conservation were important? How effective are these conservation processes? How do you know? [1.2b(1)]
   - Tell me the most critical legal or regulatory compliance requirements your organization faces (for example, EPA, FDA, CMS). Pick one and ask, how do you make sure you meet or exceed requirements in this area?
6. **Ethical Behavior.** What are some ways your organization ensures that members of the workforce and key partners act in an ethical manner in all business and stakeholder transactions? How is this measured and monitored to ensure ethical behavior is maintained? (Note that measures may include, for example, instances of ethical conduct or compliance breaches and responses to them, survey results showing workforce perceptions of organizational ethics, ethics hotline use, and results of ethics reviews and audits.) [1.2b(2)]
   - What breaches or violations of ethical behavior have occurred? Pick one and ask, what happened as a result of this violation? Have you done anything to prevent these breaches from occurring again?
7. **Societal Contributions.** How do you incorporate societal well-being and benefit into strategy and daily operations? What are the biggest environmental issues your organization faces? As a corporate citizen, what is your process for contributing to and improving the environment? For improving social systems, economic systems, or society? [1.2c(1)]
   - For gathering information on improving economic systems ask, how has your organization contributed to the economy of the local region (or state, nation, world depending on the mission and reach of the organization)? Areas for consideration here may include use of *green* technology; resource-conserving activities; reduction of carbon footprint; improvements in social impacts, such as the global use of enlightened labor practices; reduction in waste; and contributing to support local community services, such as schools, hospitals, or clinics, and professional associations.
8. **Community Support.** What support does your organization provide to local communities?
   - Why do you provide this support? How does this support align with organizational priorities and strategy? [1.2c(2)] What do your (senior

leaders) do personally to contribute to improving local community organizations?

- What has the organization done to support workers to strengthen or contribute to local community organizations? (Note that some charitable organizations may contribute to society and support their key communities totally through mission-related activities. In such cases, it is appropriate to determine the extent to which they make an *extra effort* to provide support.)
- How do you know that the processes you have in place for identifying and supporting key communities are appropriate?
- How do you know the resources allocated for these purposes are appropriately used?
- What have you (senior leader) done to improve your personal and organizational efforts to support these communities?

Category 2—Strategy

2.1 Strategy Development

1. **Strategic Planning Process (Participants and Planning Horizon).** When was the strategic plan last updated? Were you involved in the strategic planning process? What was your role? Who else was involved and what did each person do? [2.1a(1)]
    - How far out does your strategic planning look? Why? Why not shorter or longer?
    - How does the overall process for developing strategy work? (Ask the people who were involved in the planning process to explain how the process works without referring to written documentation. Examiners must determine whether a consistent planning process is in place that meets the requirements of the Criteria—and should receive similar explanations from the people doing the planning. Examiners are not testing the ability of the planners to read a written document.)
2. **Strategic Planning Process (Change).** What does change mean to you? To what extent does your strategic planning process consider the need for change, prioritization of change initiatives, and organizational agility and resilience? Please give me an example of a strategy that required the organization to change culture, prioritize change initiatives, or strengthen organizational agility and resilience in order to implement the strategy. [2.1a(1)]
3. **Innovation (Strategic Opportunities and Intelligent Risks).** How do you use the planning process to help stimulate and incorporate innovation? Please give an example of a specific innovation that resulted from the strategy development process.
    - Tell me about the strategic opportunities that were identified in the planning process? Pick one and ask, explain the process (analysis method and data) used to decide that this strategic opportunity represented an intelligent risk—a risk worth pursuing. [2.1a(2)]
4. **Strategy Considerations (Challenges and Advantages).** What challenges does the organization face that might hurt future success? What advantages do you have that might help your competitive position and enhance your future?
    - Pick a challenge at random from the Organizational Profile [P.2a] and ask, how has this [insert name of challenge] influenced your strategic planning? Show me how your plan is designed to overcome or mitigate the challenge, risk, or disruptions the organization faces.
    - Pick a strategic advantage from the list in the Organizational Profile [P.2a] and ask, how has this [insert name of advantage] influenced your strategic planning? Show me how your plan is designed to build on or leverage the advantage (which may include technological changes and innovations affecting your products, services, and operations). (Ask this type of question about other challenges and advantages until you are satisfied you understand their approach.) [2.1a(3)]
5. **Strategy Considerations (Risks to the Organization's Future Success [formerly sustainability]).** Please give some examples of how

your planning process analyzes factors that constitute the competitive environment now and in the future; changes that might affect the value to customers of the organization's products and services; the climate of employee engagement and continuous improvements that leaders were able to instill (or not); resource needs; and financial, societal, ethical, regulatory, and security issues, to name a few.

6. **Strategy Considerations (Blind Spots).** Please give some examples of how your planning process has helped you to identify problems, trouble areas, challenges, or threats that you might not have known about otherwise (Note: Also referred to as blind spots). [2.1a(3)]
   - What have you done to check the accuracy of planning assumptions and projections you used in the past to develop your strategic plan? What flawed assumptions have been made in previous planning cycles? What have you done to eliminate flawed assumptions (Note: Also called blind spots)?
7. **Strategy Considerations (Ability to Execute the Strategy).** Please give some examples of how planners determine whether the organization can realistically execute the strategic plan. For example, (pick a goal or strategic objective), why do you think your organization can accomplish this? What data or other factors did you consider in making this determination? [2.1a(3)]
8. **Strategy Considerations [General Factors from Note 2.1a(3)].**
   - What is your organization doing to handle data that are coming at increasingly higher rates, greater volume, and speeds? How are you capitalizing on data including large data sets from multiple venues such as numeric, social media, video, surveys, and research studies?
   - Does your organization depend on key suppliers or partners to be successful? If the answer is yes, ask which ones? Pick one or two from their list and ask, how did you consider the needs and capabilities of these suppliers or partners during the process of developing your strategic plan?
   - Does your organization have key competitors that affect your ability to be successful? If the answer is yes, ask which ones? Pick one or two from their list and ask, what abilities does this competitor possess that may create a problem for your organization? How did you consider the threats posed by this key competitor during the process of developing your strategic plan?
   - What new technologies such as enhanced automation, the adoption of cloud operations, the use of data analytics, the Internet of Things, artificial intelligence, large data set-enabled businesses, and process modeling affect your organization? Pick one or two from their list and ask, how did you consider these new technologies during the process of developing your strategic plan?
   - What future regulatory, legal, financial, economic, or ethical risks does your organization face? Pick some and ask, how did you determine this was a risk? How did your planning process consider the potential problems presented by this risk when developing your plan?
9. **Work Systems and Core Competencies.** (Note that work systems encompass all of the work that an organization must accomplish, using both internal and external resources, to achieve its mission. Accordingly, work systems involve the organization's internal workforce and its external key suppliers and partners, contractors, collaborators, and other components of the supply network.) Explain the methods you used and the factors you considered to decide (a) what work needed to be done, and (b) which work would be carried out internally or externally. [2.1a(4)]
   - What are your work systems?
   - What are your organization's core competencies? (You may have to ask, what are the things you do well that provide you with an advantage in the marketplace or among other providers? What sets you above the rest?) From the list, pick one and ask, how did you determine that this was a core competency?
   - When you decided to outsource key work, what core competencies did those suppliers

(or contractors, partners, or collaborators) possess that made them better than your organization and set them apart from other outside organizations?

10. **Planning Improvement.** What have you done to improve the accuracy and effectiveness of your planning process? What refinements have you made during the past few years? [Scoring Guidelines]

11. **Key Strategic Objectives.** How often do you review progress of your key strategic objectives? Please show me the timelines or projections for achieving each objective. How did you develop the projected or expected levels of future performance for each strategic objective (also called goals)? [2.1b(1)]

12. **Strategic Objective Considerations.** Review the list of strategic challenges and advantages the organization provided in P.2b. Pick one, then ask, please show me how you check your objectives to be sure this strategic challenge or advantage was addressed. Then repeat the question for another challenge or advantage. [2.1b(2)]
    - Based on this information, where do you expect to be on each objective when you next review performance? Next quarter? Next year? In two years? (Note: The frequency of review should be consistent with the review processes described in Item 4.1b. For example, if the senior leadership team reviews progress toward achieving the customer satisfaction objectives quarterly, then for proper alignment or integration, quarterly timelines or milestones should be defined to permit effective review. In addition, the timelines reported under 2.1b(1) should identify the measurable, outcome-based levels of performance that are expected during these reviews, not just a list of activities.)
    - How did you determine the appropriate frequency or period to review progress for these objectives?
    - Give some examples of strategic objectives that were designed to balance competing organizational needs such as the desire for cost control and better service to customers (only an example).

2.2 Strategy Implementation

1. **Action Plans (Developing Actions—Planned Changes).** Pick at random a strategic objective then ask, would you describe your long- and short-term action plans for this strategic objective? What changes are planned in your products or services, your customers or markets, or your operations to achieve your strategic objectives? [2.2a(1)]
2. **Action Plan Implementation (Deployment).** What is the process you use to deploy the actions that need to be taken throughout the organization in order to implement your strategy to meet your goals or achieve strategic objectives? [2.2a(2)]
3. **Action Plan Implementation (Communicate).** How do you communicate at all levels of the organization? How do you ensure that goals, objectives, and action plans are understood and used throughout the organization to drive and align work and implement the strategy? [2.2a(2)]
4. **Action Plan Implementation (Work Alignment to Plan).** How do you make sure that every member of the workforce knows what work he or she must do to implement his or her part of the plan? [2.2a(2)]
5. **Action Plan Implementation (Sustainability).** Ask to see a previous plan. Pick an action that drove improvement. Determine the extent to which the changes that were put in place have been sustained. If the change was not sustained, determine what process changes were made to ensure that future changes can be sustained. (In other words, determine what they learned from the previous failure and what they did with that knowledge.) [2.2a(2) and Scoring Guidelines]
    - How do you ensure that organizational, work unit, and individual actions and resources are aligned at all levels to ensure effective implementation?

6. **Resource Allocation.** What are some examples of resource allocations that you made that allowed you to accomplish your action plans and, at the same time, meet your other obligations? [2.2a(2), 2.2a(3), and Scoring Guidelines]
   - From the list of actions, pick one or two and ask the leader to explain specifically how resources were allocated to ensure these plans could be accomplished.
   - Then, ask how the leader checks to determine if appropriate resources were allocated and whether they were sufficient. If they were not sufficient, what happened next?
   - Ask if any improvements have been made in resource allocation processes over the past few years. Repeat this line of questioning at different levels in the organization to check alignment. [Scoring Guidelines]
7. **Workforce Plans (People and Skills Needed).** How do you determine what people and skills you will need to carry out your strategic objectives and related action plans? What changes have been made in your workforce plan during the past few years to help you achieve your strategic objectives and related action plans? How effective and accurate have your workforce plans been? [2.2a(4)]
8. **Workforce Plans (Changes Made to Help Strategy Succeed).** Summarize the organization's workforce plans needed to carry out the strategic objectives and related action plans. Pick an action plan at random and ask, how do you ensure the workforce has sufficient skills and staffing to achieve action plan requirements? [2.2a(4)]
   - What are examples of changes to the workforce plans based on inputs from the strategic planning areas important to business success, such as recruitment, training, compensation, rewards, incentives, benefits, and other programs, as appropriate?
9. **Performance Measures.** Please show me a list of the measures you use to determine if your strategic objectives and actions are being accomplished as planned. [2.2a(5)]
   - Pick an action at random and say, please show me how this particular action is measured. Who has responsibility for doing the work to achieve the objective or action? Then ask that person the same question.
10. **Performance Projections (Goal Setting Information).** How did you determine the goals or objectives you set were appropriate? How do you know that achieving this goal will make you a leader in the industry or sector? [2.2a(6)]
11. **Performance Projections (Identify Performance Gaps).** Who do you consider your top competitors? [Links with P.2a(1)] How did you determine your top competitors? How do your planned future performance levels (goals) compare to those of your top competitors? [2.2a(6), Scoring Guidelines]
    - At what level do you expect your key competitors or other similar providers to perform during the same period that your plan covers? How did you figure this out?
    - How accurate have your past estimates been of your competitor's future performance? What have you done to make these projections more accurate?
    - What gaps in your performance have you identified where the competitor is ahead or likely to be ahead? How are you adjusting your action plans to close the gaps?
12. **Action Plan Modification (Changes Driven by Circumstance).** In what way have changing circumstances (such as disruptive internal or external events, changes in the competitive environment, changing economic conditions, disruptive technologies, and sudden changes in customer requirements and expectations) caused your organization to change action plans? How did you make sure that everyone involved understood and took appropriate action promptly to make the change to plans? [2.2b]
13. **Action Plan Modification (Changes Driven by Products, Customers, Markets, or Operations).** Have any changes been made in key products, customers, markets, or operations since the Baldrige application was submitted? If

no, go to the next issue. If yes, ask, how were actions required by these changes identified and deployed to appropriate units and people to implement? Follow the action trail to determine if those who need to take action know about the changes, how they learned about them, when, and what action they are taking. [2.2b]

14. **Action Planning Improvement.** Summarize your process for evaluation and improvement of the strategic planning and plan deployment processes, including workforce planning. [Scoring Guidelines]
    - What are examples of improvements, best practices, or innovations made as a result of these evaluation processes? Where and when did they occur?
    - Why did you decide to focus on these improvements?
    - What facts or data helped you decide to improve the planning process?

Category 3—Customers

3.1 Customer Expectations

1. **Current Customers (Interact, Observe).** Describe your process for listening to customers to get information from them to help you take appropriate action as an organization. How do you typically interact with or observe them?
    - For your different customer groups, how do your listening methods differ? (Listening methods might include monitoring comments on social media outlets.)
    - Do the methods vary based on the position in the customer life cycle with your organization? If so how? (Note: The customer life cycle may begin in the product concept or pre-sale period and continue through all stages of the organization's involvement with the customer. These stages might include relationship building, the active business relationship involving service after the sale, upgrades, and an exit strategy.) [3.1a(1)]
2. **Current Customers (Taking Action).** What do you do with the feedback you solicit from customers regarding products, support services, and transactions? Is the information actionable? If so, what actions have been taken based on the customer information? [3.1a(1)]
3. **Current Customers (Follow up).** Describe your process for following-up with customers after they have contacted the organization or used its products and services. [3.1a(1)]
4. **Potential Customers.** What customer-satisfaction information do you have about your competitors or benchmarks? What do you do with this information? [3.1a(2)]
    - What former customers, potential customers, or customers of competitors would you like to attract and make your customers? Pick one and ask, how do you get information from this (former, potential, or competitor) customer that relates to your products, customer support, or transactions? In this example, what actions have you taken based on this information?
5. **Customer Segmentation (Future Growth Targets).** Which customers, groups, and market segments do you want to attract for future business? How did you make this determination? What data or decision process did you use? Have you always done it this way? Why or why not? [3.1b(1) and Scoring Guidelines]
    - What is most important to the different customer groups you serve or want to serve? What features of products and services are most important to getting them and keeping them happy? How did you determine this? How do you separate the most important customer requirements from less important requirements? [3.1b(1)]
6. **Evaluation and Improvement.** What processes do you use to evaluate and improve your methods for innovating product offerings and customer support? What meaningful improvements, best practices, or innovations have been made as a result? [Scoring Guidelines]

7. **Product Offerings (Requirements of Different Customer Groups).** How did you figure out what your different customers groups and segments expect of your organization? [3.1b(2)]
   - Do you use the same techniques to understand requirements for all customer groups? Why or why not? Please give us examples of different techniques (if applicable) and explain why they were used.
8. **Product Offerings (Adapt to Meet Requirements).** How do you figure out what your customers require of your products and services? How do you identify and adapt product features to meet these requirements and exceed their expectations? [3.1b(2)]
   - Provide an example of the product or service customers want most.
   - Provide another example of an innovation or adaptation you made in your product offerings that helped to attract new customers or enter a new market. Overall, how successful were these innovations or adaptations in strengthening the relationships you have with existing customers to engage them better?
   - How do you evaluate and improve processes for determining customer requirements? Provide some examples of improvements, best practices, or innovations that you have made in the past few years.

3.2 Customer Engagement

1. **Relationship Management (Acquire Customers).** What steps does your organization take to build relationships to acquire and retain more customers? To increase market share? [3.2a(1)]
2. **Relationship Management (Brand Image).** What steps have you taken to enhance your customers' perceptions with and value of your organization's brand image (including leveraging social media to enhance your brand image and customer engagement? What are the key brand images you are trying to enhance? How do you know your efforts in this area are effective? [3.2a(1)]
3. **Relationship Management (Retain Customers).** For one of your key customer groups or market segments, what do you do to keep those customers throughout the major stages in the customer life cycle? (Note: The customer life cycle covers all interactions from initial inquiries, to purchase, delivery, service, repair and use, and discard or replacement. Each of these stages may pose differing challenges for the customer and the organization and require different customer support options and processes.) [3.2a(1)]
4. **Relationship Management (Increase Engagement).** What steps does your organization take to increase customer engagement? How long has this process been in place? [3.2a(1)]
5. **Relationship Management (Evaluation and Improvement).** What have you done to evaluate the effectiveness and take steps to improve the way you strengthen customer relationships and engagement? What are some improvements, best practices, or innovations that you have made? How did you decide what changes were important to make, and when they should have been made? [Scoring Guidelines]
6. **Customer Access and Support (Easy Access).** How do you make it easy for your customers to contact you, get information and assistance, conduct business, or provide feedback about products or support services? What process did you use to figure this out? What improvements, best practices, or innovations have you made in providing support and access and why? [3.2a(2) and Scoring Guidelines]
   - What do you learn from customer questions, comments, and feedback? Please provide examples and changes you made as a result.
7. **Customer Access and Support (Varying Support and Service).** What are the customer-support requirements or service standards you identified? To what extent do they vary for different customer groups or segments? Please give examples. [3.2a(2)]

- Are customer-support requirements the same for customer inquiries made by phone, email, and postal services? Why or why not? How did you determine the differences in support requirements?

8. **Customer Access and Support (Deploying Requirements).** How do you make sure that every member of the workforce involved with customer support understands and works to meet or exceed these customer support requirements? [3.2a(2)]

9. **Complaint Management (Receiving and Processing Complaints).** What processes are in place to encourage customers and make it easy for them to complain? How do you handle customer complaints? What occurs between receiving the complaint and resolving the complaint? (Ask to see some sample complaints and follow the data trail. Determine how the data are analyzed and used to drive improvements in the work process that produced the error.) [3.2a(3)]

10. **Complaint Management (Prompt Resolution).** What does prompt and effective resolution of a complaint mean to your organization? What do you do to resolve complaints promptly? What causes delay in complaint resolution? What have you done to correct this situation? [3.2a(3)]

    - What processes do you have in place to ensure complaints are resolved by the first person in your organization to receive the complaint? [3.2a(3)]

    - What skills and authority do your customer-support workers need to resolve complaints promptly and effectively? To what extent do they possess these skills? How do you know?

11. **Fair Treatment.** How do your customer experience processes, which include relationship management, customer access and support, and complete management, ensure fair treatment for different customers, customer groups, and market segments? Provide some specific examples of changes you made to ensure fair treatment of customers.

12. **Satisfaction, Dissatisfaction, and Engagement (Measures).** What are your key measures for customer satisfaction? For customer dissatisfaction? For customer engagement? (Note: When asking questions about customer satisfaction, dissatisfaction, or engagement, do not ask for an explanation of all three at once because different approaches may be required for each. Ask about satisfaction, then dissatisfaction or engagement separately.) [3.2b(1) and Scoring Guidelines]

    - How do you know you are asking customers the right questions when trying to determine satisfaction, dissatisfaction, and engagement and produce actionable information?

    - How do you know you are asking customers the right questions when trying to determine satisfaction, dissatisfaction, and engagement to get at the most important issues?

13. **Satisfaction, Dissatisfaction, and Engagement (Vary Methods by Group).** Do you measure satisfaction, dissatisfaction, and engagement for all key customer groups and segments? Do important differences exist among the various customer groups you serve? If yes, do your methods vary according to customer group? If yes, please tell me how they are different and why. What do you do with the information? [3.2b(1)]

14. **Dissatisfaction.** How do you determine customer dissatisfaction? What are the key dissatisfiers for each key customer group or segment listed in P.1b(2)? Pick one at random and ask, how did you use this information to make changes to meet or exceed their requirements? [3.2b(1)]

    - Please provide some examples of how this information has helped you identify areas needing improvement, and the nature of the improvement you subsequently made.

15. **Satisfaction Relative to Competitors.** How do you learn about your customers' satisfaction relative to their satisfaction with your competitors or other organizations providing similar products? Why did customers choose your competitors over you, or vice versa? How do you use this information? [3.2b(2)]

16. **Customer Data.** Describe how you collect and use voice-of-the-customer data, aggregated complaint data, and data from social media to support your daily operational decision-making and innovation. Please provide an example of how each of the three types of information is used to make improvements. [3.2c]

17. **Complaint Management (Evaluating and Improving).** How do you check to determine if your complaint-resolution processes are effective or not? What improvements have you made in these processes over the past few years? What has been the impact of these improvements on customer satisfaction? [Scoring Guidelines]

18. **Evaluating and Improving.** How do you go about checking and improving the way you determine customer satisfaction, engagement, and dissatisfaction? Please provide some examples of how you have improved these techniques over the past several years. Please identify any processes you believe are exemplary (best practices) or innovative. [Scoring Guidelines]

Category 4—Measurement, Analysis, and Knowledge Management

4.1 Measurement, Analysis, and Improvement of Organizational Performance

1. **Performance Measures (Decisions Supported).** What kind of decisions do you have to make in your job? Show me the data that are collected to help you make these decisions. [4.1a(1)]
   - What are the major performance indicators critical to decision-making in your job?

2. **Performance Measures (Selecting Data).** How do you determine whether the information you collect and use for decision-making, continuous improvement, and innovation is appropriate? How do you use this information for tracking your daily work and (to leaders) the performance of the entire organization? [4.1a(1) and Scoring Guidelines]
   - What criteria do you use for data selection? How do you ensure that all data collected meet these criteria?

3. **Performance Measures (Tracking Strategic Plans and Objectives).** What is the process you use to select and collect the information used to track progress related to strategic planning objectives and action plans? [4.1a(1)]

4. **Comparative Data.** Please describe how needs and priorities for selecting comparisons and benchmarking are determined. [4.1a(2)]
   - Show us samples of comparative studies and how the resulting information was used to support innovation throughout the organization. Picking some at random, ask:
     - Why was the area selected for benchmarking?
     - How did you use competitive or comparative performance data?
     - How are the results of your benchmarking efforts used to set appropriate goals, make better decisions about work, and set priorities for improvement or innovation?
     - How are the results of your benchmarking efforts used to improve work processes?
     - How do you evaluate and improve your benchmarking processes to make them more efficient and useful?

5. **Measurement Agility.** Explain how your data system is capable of rapid adjustments in response to new data needs caused by unexpected changes in the organization or external environment that may be due to political or societal changes, disasters and emergencies, innovations in organizational processes or business models, new competitor offerings, or productivity enhancements. Provide an example of recent adjustments that were made. [4.1a(3)]

6. **Performance Analysis and Review (Analysis Tools).** Please share with us an example of analysis important to help you understand organizational performance and capabilities. [4.1b]

- How are data analyzed to determine relationships between customer information and financial performance, operational data and financial performance, or operational data and workforce requirements and/or performance? Identify the specific analytical methods used. Show how the following types of analyses are used to support decision-making and innovation or improvements [4.1b]:
  - Technology projections
  - Cause–effect relationships
  - Root-cause analyses
  - Descriptive analyses, such as statistical process control, central tendencies, Pareto analysis, and histograms
  - Other statistical tools, such as correlation analysis, regression and factor analyses, and tests of significance (t-tests, f-tests)
- What analyses do you use to check if adequate progress is being made in achieving strategic objectives?

7. **Performance Analysis and Review (Analysis for Planning and Improvement).** What data and analyses do you use to understand your people, your customers, your competitors, and your market to help with strategic planning? [4.1b]
   - What are you doing to improve the analysis process and make it more useful for organizational and operational decision-making?
   - How are your performance reviews helping the organization to respond to changing needs and challenges including the need for changes in culture, organizational structure, and work systems (transformational change)? Please provide examples.
8. **Performance Analysis and Review (Performance Monitoring).** What is the process used to monitor the performance of your organization? How does it relate to the organization's strategic business plan? [4.1b]
   - What measurable goals exist? How are they monitored? How does the governance board review progress toward achieving these goals, objectives, and action plans? How often? How well do these monitoring processes work? How do you know? Have you always done it this way? What has been done to improve them?
   - What are the key success factors (or key result areas, critical success factors, key business drivers) for your organization, and how do you use them to drive performance excellence?
   - What percentage of your time is spent on performance review and improvement activities? How do you review performance to assess the organization's health, competitive performance, and progress against key objectives? What key performance measures do you and other senior leaders, and the governing board regularly review?
9. **Future Performance.** Please provide some examples of using performance review findings and external comparative data to project your likely future performance and develop key action plans. [4.1c(1)] (Note: If they do not understand the question, use the example of an Olympic sprinter comparing his current performance with the improving historical trend line of best competitors to predict the time required to win a gold medal in the future.)
10. **Continuous Improvement and Innovation.** Please show us how you use organizational review findings to identify priorities for innovation. Have you set or changed priorities for innovation and resource allocation? Please give examples of how this is done. [4.1c(2)]
    - How do you ensure that these priorities and opportunities for innovation are understood and used throughout the organization to align work?
    - After you identify a top priority for innovation, ask the leaders to provide specific examples of how they ensure these priorities are implemented throughout the organization, as appropriate.
    - To what extent do these priorities and innovation opportunities involve support from key suppliers, collaborators, and partners? (Pick

one example of a priority and ask the leader to help you understand how the organization works with affected suppliers or partners to drive improvement and innovations.)

4.2 Information and Knowledge Management

1. **Data and Information Quality (Accuracy, Validity, Integrity, Reliability, and Currency).** How do you manage digital and other data to ensure data quality? Have you experienced a situation in which you might have made a different decision if you had access to more complete and accurate data? What do you do to make sure the data that support decision-making are complete and tell the whole story (data integrity)? What kind of reliability problems have you experienced with your electronic or other data? How have you resolved them? What have you done to prevent these types of problems from happening again? What does data currency mean to you? How do you decide how current the data need to be to be useful? [4.2a(1)]
2. **Data and Information Availability (Timeliness).** How do you make sure that data, information, and analysis needed to support decision-making at all levels of the organization are available when needed (timely)? Check the availability of physical systems, software, platforms, externally based or shared information systems, such as those stored in the cloud or outside your organization's immediate control. [4.2a(2)]
3. **Data and Information Availability (User-Friendly).** How do you make sure relevant data and information are appropriately shared throughout the organization and with suppliers, partners, and customers in a user-friendly format? With whom are your data shared? How do you determine the requirements of those who use your data? [4.2a(2)]
4. **Knowledge Management (Transfer Workforce Knowledge).** What are some examples of workforce knowledge the organization lost due to planned or unplanned departures, such as retirements, force reductions, or terminations? What processes have been put in place to prevent the loss of worker knowledge? [4.2b(1)]
5. **Knowledge Management (Build New Knowledge).** Given the volume of data the organization has to manage, how do you blend (merge) and correlate data from different sources to extract new knowledge? This may involve the use of artificial intelligence, digital data analytics, and data science techniques to detect patterns in large volumes of data and interpret their meaning. Provide an example of multiple sets of data and analytics that have come together to produce new knowledge. [4.2b(1)]
6. **Knowledge Management (Supporting Innovation).** What relevant knowledge do you capture and make available to support innovation and strategic planning? Provide a recent example of this knowledge and how it was assembled and transferred within the organization. [4.2b(1)]
7. **Best Practices (Sharing Best Practices).** How do you identify organizational units or operations that are considered high performing? Provide one or two examples of high-performing units and the factors that you use to identify them? How are worthy processes and work practices of high-performing exemplary units shared and implemented among all appropriate members of the workforce quickly and effectively? (These processes and practices are also known as best practices, exemplary practices, role-model practices, or innovative practices.) [4.2b(2)]
8. **Organizational Learning.** What processes and resources have been put in place to ensure learning is a part of the culture and daily work of everyone in the organization? Please provide some examples of leaders and workers at all levels using relevant personal and organizational knowledge to make learning a routine part of organizational operations. [4.2b(3)]

Category 5—Workforce

5.1 Workforce Environment

1. **Capability and Capacity (Capability).** How do you determine what workforce knowledge, skills, abilities, and certifications your organization needs now to support operations for the short and long term? ...and in the future to support its strategy and action plans? [5.1a(1)]
   - What areas of shortfall skills (or surplus skills) have you identified? What actions did you take to address the issue?
2. **Capability and Capacity (Capacity).** How do you figure out the number of workers (staffing levels) that are needed by your organization now to support operations ... and in the future to support its strategy and action plans? [5.1a(1)]
   - What areas of staffing shortfall skills (or surplus or outdated skills) have you identified? What actions did you take to address the issue?
3. **New Workforce Members.** How do you attract and hire new workers with the diverse skills and traits your organization needs to be successful? [5.1a(2)]
   - How do you make sure that the workforce represents the diversity of the general community from which you hire and the customers you serve? What diverse workers do you recruit and why? How does this recruitment help you get the right mix of diverse ideas, culture, and thinking? How do you ensure that new workforce members will fit within your organizational culture?
4. **Workforce Change Management.** What system is in place to prepare your workforce for changing capability and capacity needs? How does it work? (Note: Such systems might include cross-training, job sharing, shadowing, training, education, career counseling and development, and outplacement services.) [5.1a(3)]
   - What processes have been put in place to manage the workforce to ensure continuity of operations and prevent or minimize the impact of workforce reductions? (Note: Such systems might also include cross-training, job sharing, training, formal education, career counseling, and outplacement services.)
   - What systems or processes are in place to prepare for and manage workforce growth? How do you prepare your workforce for changes in organizational structure, workplaces, work systems, and technology as needed?
5. **Work Accomplishment.** How do you organize your workforce to do the following [5.1a(4)]:
   - Carry out the work and achieve mission (for example, using self-directed work teams or cross-functional teams).
   - Take advantage of core competencies (sustain the advantages that core competencies offer).
   - Reinforce organizational resilience, agility, and a customer and business focus (customer-centric culture).
   - Exceed performance expectations and meet strategic challenges and action plans (for example, through the use of process improvement tools, such as ISO 9000, Baldrige Criteria, lean enterprise, Six Sigma, PDCA, and After Action Reviews).
6. **Workplace Environment (Standards and Targets).** What are your standards, performance measures, and improvement goals for workplace health, security, and accessibility? [5.1b(1)]
   - What main differences exist in your workplace environments that affect workplace health, security, and accessibility (for example office areas where repetitive stress injuries may pose a threat versus areas where heavy lifting or exposure to disease may pose a threat)? Tell us your performance measures and improvement goals for each of these workforce factors in turn (health, security, and workplace accessibility). [Links with P.1a(3) and 7.3 (which should contain data showing the organization is improving and meets or exceeds performance targets).]

- Pick some members of a workforce group or segment and ask, what is the organization doing to make sure your health, security, and accessibility needs are met?
- To what extent does your organization comply with or exceed requirements of the Americans with Disabilities Act (ADA) pertaining to workplace accessibility? Please provide examples of actions taken to ensure accessibility.

7. **Workplace Environment (Evaluating and Improving).** How do you determine that you have a safe and healthy work environment? [5.1b(1) and Scoring Guidelines]
   - What are your procedures for systematic evaluation of workplace health, security, and accessibility?
   - What have you done to improve workplace health, security, and accessibility, and develop best practices and innovations?
8. **Workforce Benefits and Policies.** What benefits and services do you provide your workforce (those people supervised by your organization) to enhance motivation and satisfaction? [5.1b(2)]
   - To what extent are these customized for different workforce types or groups? How did you determine what changes in the benefits and services should be offered to the different groups? Ask for specific examples for different groups. (Note: The workforce includes paid personnel, volunteers, and contract personnel under the supervision of the organization but not people supervised by a contractor.)

5.2 Workforce Engagement

1. **Drivers of Engagement.** What does workforce engagement mean to you? What are the most important things you do to enhance workforce engagement in your organization? [5.2a(1)]
   - How did you determine these were the most important drivers of workforce engagement? Are they the same for all groups or segments of the workforce? How do you know?
   - Please show us how your workforce assessment tools (for example, surveys) reflect the key elements you identified that affect workforce engagement. [links with 5.2a(2)]
2. **Assessment of Engagement (Assessing).** How do you assess workforce engagement and satisfaction? [5.2a(2) and Scoring Guidelines]
   - If a survey is used, ask how they know they are asking the right questions on the survey. Unless they have already told you, ask for some specific examples about how they use other information, such as worker retention, absenteeism, grievances, safety, and productivity data, to assess and improve worker engagement and satisfaction.
3. **Assessment of Engagement (Using Assessment Data).** What do you do with the workforce engagement and satisfaction assessment information (such as surveys, focus group information, and exit interviews)? Provide examples. How are indicators, such as workforce retention, absenteeism, grievances, safety, and productivity used to assess and improve workforce engagement? Provide several examples. [5.2a(2)]
   - When was the last assessment?
   - How quickly was this information made available after the assessment was complete?
   - How quickly did you communicate the results to the workforce?
   - How did you use this information to drive improvements?
4. **Organizational Culture (Benefitting from Diversity).** How do you make sure the different skills, diverse ideas, and cultures of your workforce are used to maximum advantage within your organization? [5.2b]
5. **Organizational Culture (High Performing and Engaged).** What does workforce empowerment mean to you? What authority do workforce members have to direct their own actions and make decisions about their work to promote worker engagement and high-performance work? [5.2b]

- (To members of the workforce) What authority do you have to make decisions about your work, such as resolving problems and improving work processes? What have managers done to demonstrate they value the contribution of workers?
- (To managers) How do you engage the workforce? What do you do to encourage initiative and self-directed responsibility among members of the workforce in their regular work and jobs? What have you done to increase engagement in areas such as worker innovation, where members of the workforce actually make improvements, not just suggestions? Show examples of actions taken and improvements, best practices, and innovations you made. When were they made?

6. **Organizational Culture (Diverse Ideas and Thinking).** What have you done to promote equity and inclusion and draw out and use the diversity of ideas and thinking of your workforce? What have you done to empower your workforce? [5.2b, links with 5.1a(2)]
7. **Organizational Culture (Lateral Communication).** What do you do to ensure open, effective communication among members of the workforce and work units (unit-to-unit, not top-down communication)? [5.2b and Scoring Guidelines]
   - How do you break down barriers to effective sharing and communication? Show me some examples.
   - How do you know the communication among members of the workforce and work units is understood correctly? What have you done to check understanding and improve communication?
   - (To members of the workforce) What does your organization do to ensure open communication among the diverse workforce?
8. **Performance Management.** Describe your approach to workforce reward, incentives, recognition, and compensation. [5.2c(1)]
   - What specific reward and recognition programs are in place? Is the reward and recognition the same for all members of the workforce? Why are they the same (or different)?
   - How does the organization link recognition, reward, and compensation to achieve high-performance objectives (which are usually stated as strategic objectives or goals)?
   - How do compensation, recognition, and related reward and incentive systems reinforce, strengthen, or support intelligent risk taking to achieve innovation? How do they support a customer and business focus (for example, customer satisfaction and customer engagement objectives)?
   - (To members of the workforce) What do you get rewarded for around here? What recognition is offered and why? Are the reward and recognition systems consistent? Fair? Can you show me how your reward and recognition supports strategic objectives or action plans? What does intelligent risk taking to achieve innovation mean in this organization? Ask for a copy of a performance appraisal document to check alignment with strategy, intelligent risk taking, customer focus, and so on.
9. **Evaluation and Improvement.** What improvements, best practices, and innovations have you made in the processes of assessing and improving workforce engagement and satisfaction? [Scoring Guidelines]
10. **Learning and Development System (Training Needed).** What training is provided for your leaders, managers, and members of the workforce? What are the needs that your training and development system are designed to meet? [5.2c(2)]
11. **Learning and Development System (Training Provided).** After you determine the key groups or segments of the organization's workforce, ask, what training and development do you provide to ensure that you meet the education and training needs of all categories of the workforce, including workforce members, managers, and leaders? [5.2c(2)]

- From the action plans identified in 2.2, pick some and ask what training and development is provided to workers, managers, and leaders to support the achievement of the selected action plans. How was it determined that these training and development opportunities were needed? How did you consider the desires for learning and development of workforce members?
- Pick one of the organization's core competencies and ask what training is provided to support it.
- Pick one of the organization's core strategic challenges that relates to workforce capability or capacity and ask what training is provided to support it.
- Ask what training is provided to support ethics and ethical business practices. Who receives this training? Who provides it?
- Ask what training is provided to improve customer focus, customer engagement, and customer responsiveness.
- Ask what training and development is provided to help ensure the transfer of knowledge from departing or retiring workers.

12. **Learning and Development System (On-the-Job Reinforcement).** How do you make sure that the knowledge and skills acquired during training are actually used and reinforced on the job? Provide some examples (then select from this list and follow up with workforce members and their supervisors to determine how skills are reinforced on the job). [5.2c(2)]

13. **Learning and Development Effectiveness (Performance Improvement).** How does your training program affect operational-performance goals? How do you know your training improves your business results? What evaluation of training effectiveness has been done? How often? What improvements in performance were made as a result? What improvements in innovation were made as a result? Show examples. [5.2c(2)]

14. **Learning and Development Effectiveness.** What is your system for evaluating effectiveness of training and development provided by the organization? Please give us some examples of improvements that were made to the training and development process and when they were made. [5.2c(3)]

15. **Learning and Development Effectiveness (Correlation with Business Results).** Describe the process you use to analyze workforce-engagement and satisfaction data and other indicators (from Category 7) to determine what problems exist that may disrupt or hurt organization performance outcomes? [5.2c(3)]
    - What factors do you consider?

16. **Learning and Development Effectiveness (Determining Improvement Priorities).** How do you use the correlational analysis of business results to identify priorities for improving workforce engagement and satisfaction? [5.2c(3)]
    - What are the top three or four improvement priorities? (Pick one and ask the leader.)
    - What specific finding from the workforce engagement or satisfaction assessment tool did the organization use to identify this priority action? How is this priority for improving the work environment likely to affect key business results? How did you determine the potential impact on business results?

17. **Career Development (For the Workforce).** To what extent is training provided to enhance career development and progression of the workforce? What do you (senior leaders, managers, and supervisors) do to develop the full potential of members of the workforce? Give specific examples. [5.2c(4)]

18. **Career Development (For Management and Future Leaders).** What development or replacement strategy or process do you have in place for key leaders and managers throughout the organization? (For example, if the organization knows key senior leaders or a key manager is scheduled to retire, determine what it is doing to fill the resulting gap.) [5.2c(4)]

19. **Equity and Inclusion.** How do you ensure your performance management, performance development, and career development processes promote equity and inclusion for your entire workforce?

Category 6—Operations

6.1 Work Processes

1. **Determining Product and Process Requirements.** Ask for a list of key work processes. Pick one and ask, what are the requirements that this work process must meet? How did you determine these requirements? If the answer is not clear, pick another work process and ask the question again. Also, from a list of key products, pick one and ask them to explain the process they used to determine the key product requirements; in other words, how did you determine the customer requirements for this particular product? [6.1a(1, 2)]
2. **Design Concepts (Product and Process Design).** How do you design internal work processes for a new program, product, or service? Pick one process and ask, how did you design this process and incorporate or leverage new technology, knowledge of the organization, product excellence, customer value, and the need for agility? If they have trouble answering this question pick one of the design characteristics such as customer value and ask, please show me how the need to ensure customer value was considered in the design of this product or service. Repeat the question with another design characteristic or another product or service. [6.1a(3)]
   - What products have you designed over the years? Pick the most recent product and ask, how did you design this new product to build in or incorporate new technology? Knowledge of the organization? Product excellence? The need for agility?
3. **Process Implementation (Meeting Key Process Requirements).** Pick another work process and ask, how do you operate this work process day-to-day and ensure it meets all key process requirements? (Then, pick another work process and ask the question again.) [6.1b(1)]
   - What in-process measures do you use to control and ensure process consistency?
   - Show how these in-process measures are used to predict the performance consistency of the organization's work processes.
4. **Process Implementation (Meeting Product and Quality Requirements).** Pick another work process and ask, how do you operate this work process day-to-day and ensure it meets all key product requirements, including those for in-product quality and performance? (Then, pick another work process and ask the question again.) [6.1b(1)]
   - What (in-process) measures do you use on a day-to-day basis to help ensure the end product meets all customer requirements?
   - Show how these day-to-day (in-process) measures effectively predict end-product quality.
   - Once you determine that a key work process is not meeting goals or performing according to expectations, what techniques do you use to determine why this is happening? What method do you use to get to the underlying causes (root causes) and make appropriate changes (process improvements) to correct the problem and provide better end-product quality?
5. **Support Processes.** How do you decide which key support processes are needed by your organization? Ask, how do you operate this support process day-to-day and ensure it meets all key business-support process requirements, Please give me a sample list of these key support processes. [6.1b(2)]
6. **Product and Process Improvement.** How do you evaluate and improve work processes to improve products and performance, reduce unacceptable variability, and make meaningful and innovative improvements? Please provide some examples of improvements, best practices, or innovations and when they were put in place. [6.1b(3) and Scoring Guidelines]
   - (To workers) To what extent are you expected to make improvements to your work process?

- What is done to ensure that lessons learned in one part of the organization (or from past improvement efforts) are transferred to others in the organization to save time and prevent rework?
- Please give an example of how a customer request or complaint resulted in an improvement of an existing work process or contributed to the creation of a best practice or innovative, new process. How has a work process been refined and shared throughout the organization, as appropriate to respond more quickly to customer requirements, especially when those requirements change frequently? [Links with 3.2b(3), customer complaint management]
- What steps have you taken to improve the effectiveness and efficiency of work processes by addressing factors such as improved productivity, and reduced error rate, cycle time, and variability?

7. **Supply-Network Management.** What process is in place for managing your supplier network? Who are your most important [key] suppliers? How do you establish and communicate to your key suppliers their requirements to meet your needs? What are the key performance requirements? [6.1c]
   - Please explain how you measure your suppliers' performance and provide feedback to help them improve. To help them excel? (Note: Some organizations provide training to help their suppliers improve performance, productivity, and quality—which ultimately benefits the organization.)
   - Please tell me about a poor-performing supplier and how you handled it.
8. **Management of Opportunities for Innovation.** What innovations have been made to improve operational effectiveness? Have any of these innovations been designed to pursue a strategic opportunity that has been determined to be an intelligent risk (a risk where the potential benefit is perceived to be better than the potential risk)? [6.1d]
   - By what process do you make financial resources available to pursue these strategic opportunities that have been deemed intelligent risks? Please provide a specific example of how this process has been used.
   - What method do you use to decide to discontinue pursuing a strategic opportunity in order to provide support for higher priorities? Provide examples where this has occurred.

6.2 Operational Effectiveness

1. **Cost, Process Efficiency, and Effectiveness.** Pick one of the organization's key operations at random and ask, what techniques do you use to control the costs of this operation? [6.2a]
   - What do you do to prevent added costs due to errors, defects, rework, warranty costs, or productivity losses?
   - What kinds of tests, audits, or inspections do you routinely conduct to ensure products and services are defect-free and require no rework? Provide specific examples of reducing the need for these tests, audits, or inspections. (Note: The question here deals with reducing the need for tests and audits, not eliminating them simply to save money. We are trying to figure out if the organization is making its work processes so accurate and consistent that they do not produce significant error, such as achieving a Six Sigma level of performance, which has eliminated the need for inspections, audits, and tests.)
   - What steps do you take to balance your need for controlling costs with the needs of customers for product quality? Provide some concrete examples of how this works.
2. **Security and Cybersecurity.** What processes are in place to ensure your physical and digital data and information are free from attack (secure) and free from inappropriate release (confidential)? What do you do to keep your electronic data free from hacking or other cybersecurity threats? What problems have you had in this area? Pick a problem and ask, how did you address this issue? What improvements

have been made in the area of information and data security? What are the data-security requirements you believe are critical to your system? (For example, certain statutes and regulations, such as National Security statutes or the Family and Education Rights and Privacy Act, may require certain levels of security and data protection.) [6.2b and Scoring Guidelines].

3. **Safety.** What processes are in place to provide a safe operating environment for your workforce and other people in your workplace?
   - What kind of safety issues, such as accidents or injuries, has your organization experienced? What processes do you have in place now to avoid these safety issues and provide a safer operating environment? [6.2c(1)]
   - How does your safety system address accident prevention using tools such as inspection and root cause or other analyses of safety failures? What do you do to ensure prompt recovery from conditions that cause accidents?
4. **Business Continuity and Resilience (Emergency Preparedness).** What emergencies or disasters have occurred that affect the organization? What was the impact on the workplace, your workforce, and your customers? [6.2c(2)]
   - What are you doing to ensure these types of events do not disrupt your operations (and ensure continuity of operations and organizational resilience)? Is your organization involved in any communitywide efforts to ensure resilience?
   - What are you doing to ensure that customer needs continue to be met in the event of a disaster or disruption of work processes
   - What are you doing to prepare for and ensure rapid recovery in the event of a disaster or emergency?
   - How do you know these systems work as intended? What kinds of drills or tests have you conducted to determine these emergency preparedness systems are effective?
   - Please walk me through the process you use to make sure data and information systems (hardware and software) will continue to be available during an emergency to serve both customers and the organization's operational needs. How is this process tested and improved? [6.2c(2) and Scoring Guidelines]
   - When was the last emergency that disrupted hardware, software, or data availability? What changes were made to prevent a recurrence of the disruption? [Scoring Guidelines]

Category 7—Results

Normally, applicants are eager to display good results but sometimes neglect to report results that are not as good. The scoring guidelines penalize applicants for failing to provide results that are important to the organization's key business requirements. To arrive at accurate scores, examiners must be able to determine what results should be reported in the application that are important to the organization's success and required by the CPE. In the early 1990s, Mark Blazey developed the Table of Expected Results (TOER) based on the Criteria questions and what the applicant indicated was important to achieve.

To use the TOER properly, examiners first develop a list of the results that they *expect* to see in Category 7 based on what the organization reported was important to its success. Then, by comparing the list of expected results to the results actually provided in the application, examiners can determine what important results are missing.

Usually, clues to important results can be found in many places in the application, such as the Organizational Profile, legal, regulatory, and ethical requirements [1.2], strategic goals and objectives [2.1b], the list of actions and measures required to achieve strategic objectives [2.2a(1, 5)], measures of customer satisfaction, dissatisfaction, and engagement [3.2b(1)], the priority customer requirements [3.1b(2)], customer complaints [3.2a(3)], or other places in the application.

Table 10 represents the type of information that might be presented by an applicant in the Organizational Profile [P.1b(2)], listing Customer Segments and Requirements. Note that three customer segments were identified, each with several requirements.

Table 10 Example of applicant customer segments and corresponding key requirements provided in the Organizational Profile.

Customer Segments (As Reported by the Applicant)	Key Customer Requirements (As Reported by the Applicant)
Individual End Users	Reliability, prompt repair, friendly service, value
Dealers	Reliable vehicles, order accuracy, parts availability, billing accuracy
Commercial/Fleet Users	Speedy access to service, reliability, value, loaner vehicles

Table of Expected Results (TOER)

This information serves as a basis for deciding which results should be reported related to the satisfaction of these customers. Accordingly, note that in Table 11, the first column describes the name of the expected result. The second column lists the source reference for the requirement as found in the Organizational Profile. The third column identifies where in Category 7 the examiner expects the results to be reported. The fourth column indicates where the results were actually reported and where they can be found (figure reference number). The remaining columns provide additional details to help examiners readily see trends, comparisons, and gaps in the data provided by the organization. In this way, examiners can easily determine if few, some, many, or most important results were reported. Applicants should prepare a similar table to ensure the actual results are aligned with the important results.

After finishing the TOER, you can work on completing the feedback comments for the Results Items. Shown below are the starts of both strength and OFI comments (referred to as "stems"). For example, "the applicant reported results for few/many/most/all areas of importance related to Health Care and Process Results (I). Few/Some/Many/Most/All of the results reported showed good performance levels and beneficial trends (T, Le, C), including but not limited to: XXX." Construct a feedback comment by selecting the appropriate "stem" and selecting one of the Few/Some/Many/Most/All phrases, followed by details of the comment. A feedback comment does not have to be written for each "stem," just those relevant to the application.

For example, in this health care example:

Of the important Health Care and Process results reported, some showed favorable trends and good performance levels (T, Le, C):

- Reducing readmissions (Figure 7.1-12)
- Reducing antipsychotic use (Figure 7.1-15)

When evaluating results, remember that for Results (Category 7) comments, examiners will ensure that the order of comments follows the template provided (that is, the six buckets) as detailed below:

First, answer the question about the number of results that were expected (denominator), compared with the number of relevant results that were actually reported (numerator).

For example, if 35 results were expected and 19 were reported, the following comment would be appropriate for the working draft feedback reports: "The applicant provided most results (19/35 = 54%) the applicant indicated were important for success." (Note: The fraction information in parentheses does not go to the applicant but is used by the examiner team to validate each examiner's conclusion.)

Then write comments about specific Strengths and OFIs grouped (assigned to buckets) as follows:

1. Results showing favorable trends.
2. Results showing good levels based on relevant comparative data.
3. Results showing unfavorable trends.
4. Results showing poor levels or no relevant comparative data to show a level.
5. Results showing incomplete or flat trend data. (This is where the applicant did not provide sufficient data to demonstrate trends, minimum

Table 11 Sample table of expected results (TOER).

Title of Expected Result	Source Reference (pg in app where you found it)	Cat 7 Reference (where in Cat 7 it belongs)	Figure # (Where found in Cat 7)	Segmentation (Names of Segments)	Trend & Time (From x to y level in a to b timeframe)	Perf vs Comp (Position and type of comparison)	Bucket Assignments
Defects per Delivered Unit	4	7.1a	7.1-6	None	2018 .02 2019 .108 2020 .015	National competitor 2020 .018	1, 2
Time to Delivery	3	7.1b(1)	71.-6	None	2018 45 days 2019 42 days 2020 29 days	Local competitor 2020 38 days	1, 2
Supplier On-time Delivery of Key Parts	25	7.1c	7.1-24	None	2018 98% 2019 97% 2020 97%	National competitor 2020 96%	3, 2
Workforce Safety DART rate	2	7.1b(2)	7.1-20	None	2018 1.5/100 2019 1.5/100 2020 1.5/100	None	5, 4

of three data points, or results do not demonstrate either a favorable or unfavorable trend.)

6. Missing results (important and expected—but not provided).

If no results are reported to populate one or more of the groupings/buckets listed above, the associated comment is left out. For example, if no results are reported that show both declining trends and poor levels, no comment is written.

1. If no process effectiveness result is reported in the application, you cannot score Item 7.1 higher than the 10%–25% range. Similarly, if the applicant does not provide at least one result for each of the basic results elements in 7.4 and 7.5, the score cannot be higher than the 10–25% range.
2. Segmentation may be reported—but is not required until the higher scoring ranges—in response to Category 7. If important segmented results are provided, then each segmented result is included in both the expected (denominator) and provided (numerator) counts.
3. Examiners will complete the TOER as part of their Independent Review phase. This step assists the team in reaching consensus on placing comments in one or more of the appropriate "six buckets."
4. The required results should be evaluated the same way that any of the other results in the application are. No special weight is provided to the required results.

Definitions for Results:

Few—5% to 15%
Some—more than 15% to 30%
Many—more than 30% to 50%
Most—more than 50%
All – 100%

Note that when importance is assessed in the results categories, only few (5–30%), many (31–50%), most (more than 50%), and all (100%) are utilized. This is due to the structure of the Baldrige scoring guidelines.

The following information should be provided for Category 7:

7.1 Product and Process Results

1. **Customer-Focused Product and Service Results.** Provide current levels and trends in key measures or indicators of the performance

of products and services that are important to and directly serve customers. [Links to P.1, Items 2.1b(1), 2.2, 3.1 and 3.2, and Items 4.1, 4.2, 6.1, 6.2, and 7.2] [7.1a]

- Show how these results compare with the performance of competitors and other organizations with similar offerings.
- Break out (differentiate) the results reported by product offering or service lines, customer group or segment, and market segments.

Note: Applicants in the education sector should provide **Student Learning and Process Results.** Applicants in the health care sector should provide **Health Care and Process Results.**

2. **Process Effectiveness and Efficiency Results.** Provide current levels and trends in key measures or indicators of the operational performance of key work and support processes, including productivity, cycle time, and other appropriate measures of process effectiveness, efficiency, security and cybersecurity, and innovation. [7.1b(1)]
   - Show how these results compare with the performance of competitors and other organizations with similar offerings.
   - Break out (differentiate) the results reported by process types as appropriate.
3. **Safety and Emergency Preparedness Results.** Provide current levels and trends in key measures or indicators of workplace and workforce safety and preparedness for disasters or emergencies and other disruptions. [7.1b(2)]
4. **Supply-Network Management Results.** Provide results for key measures or indicators of supply network performance, including its contribution to enhancing organizational performance. [7.1c]

7.2 Customer Results

1. **Customer Satisfaction.** Provide the customer satisfaction and dissatisfaction trends and levels. [Links to P.1b(2) and the elements in Items 3.1 and 3.2] [7.2a(1)]
   - Differentiate or break out results by customer group or segment.
   - Bring your customer satisfaction, dissatisfaction, and related results up to date and close any information gaps that may have been noted in the award application.
   - Show how these trends and levels compare with those of competitors or similar providers.
2. **Customer Engagement.** Provide the customer-engagement and relationship-building trends and levels. Show how these results compare over the customer life cycle (or the period of the customers' relationship with your organization). [Links to P.1b(2) and the elements in Items 3.1 and 3.2] [7.2a(2)]
   - Differentiate or break out results by customer group or segment.
   - Provide current levels and trends for customer engagement, such as loyalty, positive referral, customer-perceived value, and relationship building.
   - Bring your customer-engagement and relationship-building results up to date and close any information gaps that may have been noted in your application.
   - Show how these trends and levels compare with those of competitors or similar providers.

7.3 Workforce Results

1. **Workforce Capability and Capacity.** Provide data showing current levels and trends of workforce capability (skills) and capacity (staffing levels). Differentiate these results according to the diversity of the workforce, and by appropriate workforce groups and segments. [Links to processes in Category 5] [7.3a(1)]
2. **Workforce Climate.** Provide data showing current levels and trends of workplace climate, security, accessibility, and services/benefits

provided including workforce health. Differentiate these results according to the diversity of the workforce, and by appropriate workforce groups and segments. [7.3a(2)]

3. **Workforce Engagement.** Provide data showing current levels and trends of workforce engagement and satisfaction (including data such as absenteeism, undesired attrition, grievances, and litigation as well as engagement and satisfaction survey data). Differentiate these results according to the diversity of the workforce, and by appropriate workforce groups and segments. [7.3a(3)]
4. **Workforce Development.** Provide data showing current levels and trends of workforce development. Differentiate these results according to the diversity of the workforce, and by appropriate workforce groups and segments. [7.3a(4)]
   - Bring your workforce results up to date and close any information gaps that may have been noted in your application.
   - Show how performance on these key indicators compares with competitors, other providers, or benchmarks. [from Scoring Guidelines]

7.4 Leadership and Governance Results

1. **Leadership.** Provide key measures or indicators of leadership communication and engagement with the workforce and customers to deploy vision and values, encourage two-way communication, cultivate innovation and intelligent risk taking, and create a focus on action. Differentiate these results by appropriate organizational units and customer groups. [7.4a(1)]
2. **Governance.** Provide performance data showing current findings and trends in key measures of governance and internal and external fiscal accountability. [7.4a(2)]
3. **Law and Regulation.** Provide results for key measures or indicators of meeting and surpassing legal and regulatory requirements. Differentiate these results by organizational units, as appropriate. [7.4a(3)]
4. **Ethics.** Provide results for key measures or indicators of ethical behavior, breaches of ethical behavior, and of stakeholder trust in the senior leaders and governance of your organization. Differentiate these results by organizational units as appropriate. [7.4a(4)]
5. **Society.** Provide results reflecting the organization's fulfillment of its societal responsibilities and support of its key communities. [7.4a(5)]

7.5 Financial, Market, and Strategy Results

1. **Financial Performance.** Provide data showing key measures and indicators of key financial measures, such as return on investment, operating profits (or budget reductions as appropriate), or economic value added.
2. **Marketplace Performance.** Provide appropriate data showing key measures and indicators of market share or business growth. Identify new markets entered and the level of performance in those markets.
   - Break out data by customer and market group or segment.
   - Update financial and marketplace performance results and close any information gaps that may have been noted in your application.
3. **Strategy Implementation Results.** Provide key measures or indicators of the achievement of organizational strategy and action plans, including taking intelligent risks and building and strengthening core competencies. [7.5b]
   - Bring your Senior Leadership and Governance Results up to date and close any information gaps that may have been noted in the award application.

General Cross-Cutting Questions to Ask Members of the Workforce

- What are the organization's mission, vision, and values? (Note: Ask one at a time, not all three at once.) [Links to P.1a(2), 1.1a(1), and 1.1b]
- What is the strategic plan for the organization? What are the organization's goals you help to achieve? What do you do to help achieve these goals? How did you learn these

were part of your responsibilities? [Links to 2.1b(1) and 2.2a]

- What kind of training have you received? Was it useful? What kind of on-the-job support did you get for using the new skills you learned during training? Was the training effective? Helpful? [Links to 5.2c]
- What kinds of decisions do you usually make about your work and the work of the organization? What data or information do you use to help make these decisions? Is this information readily available to help make decisions easier? [Links to 4.1a, 4.1b, 4.2a, 5.2a]
- What activities or work are recognized and rewarded? Is achieving customer satisfaction a critical part of your job? Are your rewards and recognition determined in part on achieving certain customer-satisfaction levels? If so, explain how this works. [Links to 5.2c(1)]
- What does your organization do best? What sets it above other organizations that do similar work? [Links to P.1a(2), Core Competencies]
- *Remember to ask each worker you encounter how processes are improved and innovated. Are improvements and innovations based on factual evaluations or are they random? Be sure to ask if the process you are examining has been improved, represents a best practice, and has been shared, as appropriate, in the organization. Ask how the improvement was identified. Ask what steps are being taken to continue to evaluate and improve the process. [Links to Scoring Guidelines]*

Site Visit Summary—Ensure the Site Visit does not Become an Audit

The following suggestions (©2019 by Core Values Partners and used with permission from Paul Grizzell) may help keep the site visit productive and positive—and avoid an audit environment.

- As site visit leaders, ensure a collaborative environment as you start to work with the applicant's site visit contact. Explore previous site visit experiences and ask about what worked in the past, what did not work so well, and what concerns the organization may have about the upcoming site visit. Business, health care, and education sectors may have different expectations. Be sure to use the Considerations for Reviewing Small Organizations or Considerations for Health Care Organizations at Site Visit from Baldrige Examiner Resources when appropriate.
- Do not let the applicant control the site visit or its preparation, but get their feedback and engagement.
- Get to know the applicant's culture before the site visit so that people can select appropriate dress and *lighten up* or *tighten up* in approach and demeanor as the need arises. Basically, the risk is that a team might get sidetracked by being so tuned in to a laid-back culture that the work doesn't get done. This is the balance that senior examiners and team leaders have to define for the team.
- Focus on site visit issues. Ensure that the examiner team knows not to ask verbatim questions from the CPE. Alignment of site visit issues with Key Factors ensures that the applicant knows that examiners are focusing on their issues, and not doing a "criteria audit." Use CPE themes to set context for your inquiry, then drill down to ask specific questions.
- Although examiners are not allowed to provide feedback to the applicant during the site visit, examiners should, nevertheless, present a friendly, personable, and professional demeanor, but not appear "chummy." An unfriendly, badgering, or poker face approach with applicant leaders and employees may make them feel like they have been through an unpleasant compliance audit.
- An audit is a checklist. An assessment frames inquiries differently. Audits most often generate a *yes/no* response. Assessments require more information about process and deployment,

measurement, and learning systems. This can be addressed ahead of time as the team leader and category partners review each other's questions since it provides a good opportunity to discuss some best practices for conducting good site visits, especially with new examiners.

- Daily check-ins with the key contact by the team leader can help facilitate modifications in approach as necessary. Make it clear to the applicant's point of contact that examiners do not want the site visit to be an intimidating process. Regularly ask the key contact to give feedback about the site visit as well as report information received from employees. Be sure to plan time in the site visit schedule to check in with the key contact at the end of each day, if not more frequently. Take the feedback to the team and plan corrective action or other improvements as appropriate.

Global Performance Excellence Models: Making a Difference Around the World

Performance excellence programs around the world have helped organizations move from a focus on compliance to performance excellence—a leadership-driven focus on providing products and services that go beyond basic customer requirements. These high levels of product and service performance generate competitive advantage-based role model processes and performance outcomes—a key reason for leaders to commit to move their organizations beyond mere compliance.

Our work in helping organizations focus, align, and accelerate their performance excellence efforts has given us the opportunity to work with organizations around the world—as well as with the quality award programs that support those countries. The impact that quality award programs have had in advancing performance excellence concepts around the world is inspirational.

The Global Excellence Model (GEM) Council was founded to provide a forum for sharing knowledge and good practices among member organizations. GEM Council is positioned as "the guardians of premier excellence models and award processes in their specific geographical area or trading bloc." Members are nonprofit organizations that represent the leading performance excellence organizations around the world.

Current members of the GEM Council are:

- *Australian Organisational Excellence Foundation (Australia) http://aoef.org.au
- *Baldrige Performance Excellence Program (USA) http://www.baldrige.nist.gov
- China Association for Quality (China) http://www.caq.org.cn
- Confederation of Indian Industry - Institute of Quality (India) http://www.cii-iq.in
- Dubai Government Excellence Program (United Arab Emirates) https://dgep.gov.ae/en
- *European Foundation for Quality Management (Europe) http://www.efqm.org
- Ibero-American Model of Excellence in Management (Iberian Peninsula and Latin America) http://www.fundibeq.org
- Institute for Total Quality Promotion (Mexico) http://competitividad.org.mx
- *Japan Quality Award Council (Japan) http://www.jqac.com
- Malaysia Productivity Corporation (Malaysia) (associate member) http://www.mpc.gov.my
- National Quality Foundation (Brazil) http://www.fnq.org.br
- *Enterprise Singapore (Singapore) http://www.enterprise.gov.sg
- Africa Excellence Forum (Africa) http://www.aefx.africa

*Founding members of GEM Council

How are these programs similar and what can they learn from others? The global excellence models tend to share three key components (Figure 44):

1. They provide a set of foundational characteristics of high-performing organizations that answer the question *"Why would I want to embark on a performance excellence initiative? To become an organization represented by the characteristics of high-performing organizations."*

Figure 44 Basic characteristics of global performance excellence models.

2. They provide a set of criteria for performance excellence that identifies practices of high-performing organizations that answer the question *"What do I need to do to become a high-performing organization?"* Compare your organization's systems and processes to these evidence-based characteristics of high-performing organizations, then develop action plans to make improvement progress.
3. They provide an evaluation and improvement and scoring system that helps answer the question *"How do I know I have improved my performance?"* The scoring system and related evaluation and improvement model help identify strengths and opportunities for improvement based on a scoring maturity model.

These similar excellence model characteristics ensure that the quality award programs continue to help drive improved processes and outcomes for those organizations that are willing to commit to becoming high performers—a willingness to do the hard work of moving beyond mediocrity to performance excellence.

Foundational Characteristics

Most global excellence models are based on a set of descriptors that explain the foundational characteristics of high-performing organizations (Table 12). Experience has shown that the key predictor of success in implementing a performance excellence initiative is senior leader commitment. These foundational characteristics—the Baldrige Core Values and Concepts, the Australian Business Excellence Framework (ABEF) Nine Principles of Business Excellence, or the China Association for Quality (CAQ) Basic Ideas—represent what senior leaders *should desire* as descriptors of their organization. Performance excellence award programs from widely varied economies around the globe demonstrate similar foundational characteristics.

Table 12 The foundational characteristics of Baldrige, ABEF, and CAQ programs.

Baldrige Performance Excellence Program (USA)	Australian Business Excellence Framework (ABEF)	China Quality Award (CAQ)
Core Values	**Nine principles of business excellence**	**Basic Ideas**
Systems perspective	Clear direction and plans...	Leadership with foresight and sagacity
Visionary leadership	Understand customer and stakeholder value...	Strategic orientation
Customer-focused excellence	All people work in a system...	Customer-driven
Valuing people	Engaging people improves organizational performance	Social responsibility
Agility and resilience	Innovation and learning influence agility and responsiveness...	Workforce focus
Organizational learning	Effective use of facts, data, and knowledge leads to improved decisions	Win-win cooperation
Focus on success and innovation	Variation impacts predictability, profitability and performance	Process focus and results focus
Managing by fact	Sustainable performance is determined by an organization's ability to deliver value for all stakeholders in an ethically, socially and environmentally responsible manner	Learning, improvement, and innovation
Societal contributions	Leaders determine the culture and value system of the organization through their decisions and behavior	System management
Ethics and transparency		
Delivering value and results		

Criteria for Performance Excellence

Effective organizations around the world engage senior leaders in a performance excellence program to gain their commitment to foundational elements of excellence. Once that commitment is made, the need to develop processes to help answer the key question "How do you know… ?" becomes evident.

For example:

- How do you know that leaders provide "clarity of purpose and alignment of direction?" *ABEF Category 1 Leadership*
- How do you know that you have effective processes to "build and manage customer relationships?" *Baldrige Category 3 Customers*
- How do you know that you have processes to "determine the key factors influencing workforce satisfaction and enthusiasm and the effects of these factors on different work groups?" *CAQ Category 4.4.2 Human Resources*

The Baldrige *Process,* ABEF *Enabler,* or CAQ *Key Processes* criteria (Table 13) ask what an organization does, how it does it, and how it evaluates and improves processes. The *Results* criteria for each performance excellence model describes outcomes or achievements focused on what is important to organizational success. High-performing organizations demonstrate alignment between the enablers or process categories and the results categories.

Baldrige, ABEF, and CAQ all demonstrate very similar enablers/process and results criteria. All are non-prescriptive; not telling an organization what it has to do, but asking how it addresses the criteria in the context of what is important to the organization. *If an organization aspires to be represented by the foundational characteristics of performance excellence, then the criteria of each of the quality award programs is the road map to help them get there.*

The Baldrige, ABEF, and CAQ programs all demonstrate alignment of their foundational characteristics and their performance excellence criteria.

Table 13 Performance excellence criteria of Baldrige, ABEF, and CAQ award programs.

Baldrige Core Values and Concepts (USA)	ABEF Nine Principles of Business Excellence (Australia)	CAQ Basic Ideas (China)
Process	**Enablers**	**Key Processes**
Leadership	Leadership	Leadership
Strategy	Strategy & planning	Strategy
Customer	Information and knowledge	Customer and Market
Measurement, Analysis, and Knowledge Management	People	Resource
Workforce	Customers and other stakeholders	Process Management
Operations	Process management improvement and innovation	Measurement, Analysis, and Improvement
Results	**Results**	**Results**
Product and process outcomes	Measuring and communicating organizational results	Product and service outcomes
Customer results	Achieving sustainable results	Customer and service outcomes
Workforce results	Society results	Financial outcomes
Leadership and governance results	Business results	Resource outcomes
Financial, market. and strategy results		Process effectiveness outcomes
		Leadership outcomes

EFQM Model

Integrated management models around the globe are updated on varying schedules. The Baldrige Framework is updated every two years. The biannual updates are sometimes significant and sometimes less significant. The EFQM Model (www.efqm.org) is updated on an "as needed" basis. The EFQM Model was updated in 2020 with a very significant update from the previous 2013 Model. A rigorous process of gathering stakeholder input (described in the new Best Practices section) was used to review the 2013 Model and provide input into the most recent Model.

The most recent EFQM Model (Figure 45) restructured the Model to focus on three areas: Direction, Execution, and Results compared to the 2013 Model with Enablers and Results. Direction, Execution, and Results are still assessed using the RADAR assessment method, described below. The RADAR Model is integrated into the borders of the EFQM Model diagram.

The new EFQM Model has a significant change in moving from a set of Fundamental Concepts of Excellence, similar to the Baldrige Core Values and Concepts, to a set of underlying principles:

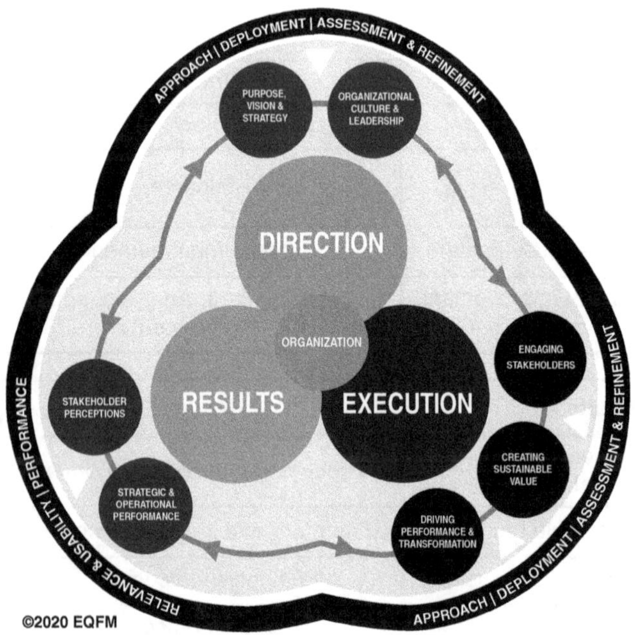

Figure 45 Alignment of components of the EFQM model.

- The primacy of the customer
- The need to take a long-term, stakeholder-centric view
- Understanding the cause and effect linkages between why an organization does something, how it does it, and what it achieves as a consequence of its actions

In addition, the EFQM Model states "There is an assumption and expectation that any organization using the EFQM Model will respect and act upon the essence of the messages contained in the European Values and United Nations Global Compact Ten Principles (www.unglobalcompact.org) and 17 Sustainable Development Goals (www.unglobalcompact.org/sdgs/17-global-goals)] regardless of whether it is legally obliged to do so or not." The EFQM Model is aligned to the 17 UN Sustainable Development Goals:

The Ten Principles of the United Nations Global Compact are:

Human Rights

Principle 1: Businesses should support and respect the protection of internationally proclaimed human rights; and

Principle 2: make sure that they are not complicit in human rights abuses.

Labor

Principle 3: Businesses should uphold the freedom of association and the effective recognition of the right to collective bargaining;

Principle 4: the elimination of all forms of forced and compulsory labor;

Principle 5: the effective abolition of child labor; and

Principle 6: the elimination of discrimination in respect of employment and occupation.

Environment

Principle 7: Businesses should support a precautionary approach to environmental challenges;

Principle 8: undertake initiatives to promote greater environmental responsibility; and

Principle 9: encourage the development and diffusion of environmentally friendly technologies.

Anti-Corruption

Principle 10: Businesses should work against corruption in all its forms, including extortion and bribery.

UN 17 Sustainable Development Goals:

1. No Poverty
2. Zero Hunger
3. Good Health and Well-Being
4. Quality Education
5. Gender Equality
6. Clean Water and Sanitation
7. Affordable and Clean Energy
8. Decent Work and Economic Growth
9. Industry, Innovation and Infrastructure
10. Reduced Inequalities
11. Sustainable Cities and Communities
12. Responsible Consumption and Production
13. Climate Action
14. Life Below Water
15. Life on Land
16. Peace and Justice Strong Institutions
17. Partnerships for the Goal

In addition to an organization's assessment of its processes and results, the emphasis on the European Values and the UN Global Compact demonstrates EFQM Model encouragement of the organization's societal contributions.

EFQM Evaluation and Improvement System

Each quality award organization has an evaluation and scoring system that is the basis for quality award recognition. This evaluation may be an external evaluation that is the basis of the quality award recognition level. It may also be an internal assessment or an external assessment by independent assessors or examiners for the review of the organization's performance excellence systems.

More than just systems that assess an organization for an award level, these evaluation systems are a measure of the performance excellence maturity of an organization. EFQM's RADAR logic (Results—Approach—Deployment—Assess—Refine) is a role model performance assessment method. EFQM has integrated the RADAR logic into the EFQM Model in a manner that makes it an effective tool for evaluating an organization's Direction, Execution, and Results.

In addition, the RADAR logic is an effective tool to evaluate and improve processes on a high level—similar to PDCA improvement. The integrated Results review in the RADAR logic provides the basis for identification of improvement targets, with the rest of the model forming a systematic improvement framework. RADAR encompasses the following:

Analysis of Direction:

Approaches
- Sound
- Aligned (Not applied to Direction)

Deployment
- Implemented
- Flexible (Not applied to Direction)

Assessment and Refinement
- Evaluated and Understood
- Learn and Improve

Analysis of Execution:

Approaches
- Sound
- Aligned

Deployment
- Implemented
- Flexible

Assessment and Refinement
- Evaluated and Understood
- Learn and Improve

Analysis of Results

Relevance and Usability
- Scope and Relevance
- Usable Data

Performance
- Trends
- Targets
- Comparisons
- Future Focus

Baldrige Evaluation and Improvement System

The Baldrige Performance Excellence Program uses a similar model to assess an organization's performance excellence. A set of Process and Results Scoring Guidelines are based on the following parameters:

- **Approach**. Are the organization's approaches responsive to the Criteria requirements?
- **Deployment**. Are the organization's approaches effectively deployed?
- **Learning**. Does the organization have fact-based evaluation and improvement methods? Does the organization innovate?
- **Integration**. Are the approaches aligned and integrated to organizational needs?

Results scoring guidelines include:

- **Levels**. Do the results demonstrate current performance on a meaningful measurement scale?
- **Trends**. Do the results measure performance over time?
- **Comparisons**. Do the results measure performance relative to appropriate competitors or similar organizations?
- **Integration**. Do the measures of performance address important performance requirements?

For a more thorough explanation of Baldrige scoring guidelines, see the Scoring System chapter that starts on page 271.

Summary

Global performance excellence models have advanced significantly since their origin in the late 1980s with the introduction of the Baldrige Criteria. These models have moved from being primarily manufacturing quality award programs to organizational performance excellence models that are relevant to any organization of any size. These models demonstrate assessment and refinement—systematic evaluation and improvement of the performance excellence models based on learnings about practices of high-performing organizations. Each model has been evaluated and improved many times over the life of the model.

The performance excellence models have evolved to become systems, incorporating the three areas of focus described above. These systems identify the why, the what, and the how of organizational performance excellence (Figure 46). Leaders of organizations that are committed to achieving and sustaining performance excellence—in the eyes of their customers—would do well to adopt the performance excellence model of the country or region in which their headquarters is located. For multinational organizations, it is best to choose one model for the organization to ensure they use a common language (model) that will drive performance excellence across the entire enterprise.

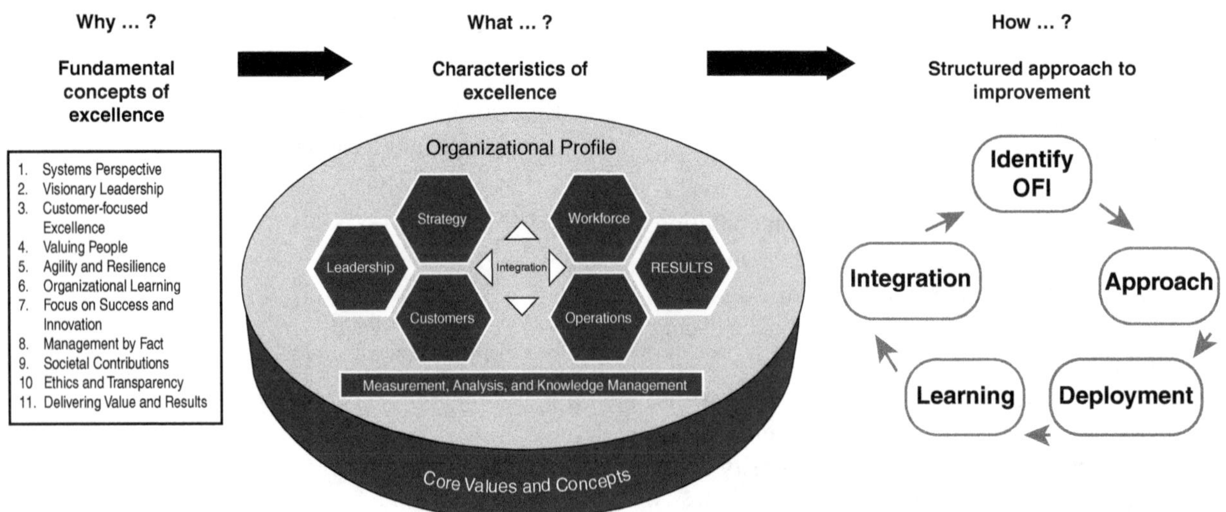

Figure 46 Alignment of components of the Baldrige Criteria.

Performance Excellence Program Best Practices

Global performance excellence programs, including programs internal to an organization, demonstrate various practices that drive success in providing valuable products and services for their members and other users of their performance excellence models. Several best practices are summarized here; more extensive descriptions are provided in this book's online resources.

We welcome your suggestions of additional best practices that you would be willing to share—or that you would be interested in learning from global performance excellence practitioners. Please contact co-author Paul Grizzell at *paul.grizzell@corevaluespartners.com* with suggestions. We are able to provide best practices in our online resources between editions of *Insights to Performance Excellence.*

Adding Member Value Using a Baldrige-Based Award Program in a Membership-Based Organization

The American Health Care Association and National Center for Assisted Living (AHCA/NCAL) has implemented a Baldrige-based quality award program that has grown to over 1,500 applications at various levels in 2020. Key to the success of this program is being able to demonstrate that Silver and Gold Award recipients have superior performance compared to the national average in key quality measures, regulatory measures, and business measures.

— *David Gifford, Chief Medical Officer, Senior Vice President of Quality and Regulatory Affairs*

Urvi Patel, Senior Director, Quality Improvement AHCA/NCAL

Achieving Financial Sustainability: How The Partnership for Excellence Became Fiscally Sound

Sustainability of a quality award program is important in driving performance excellence in states and regions in support of the national Baldrige program. A key to the success of The Partnership for Excellence (TPE) is the accountability of the executive director to a set of outcome-focused strategic objectives. The Partnership for Excellence demonstrates high performance in accomplishing their operational objectives, resulting in a strong financial performance, including significant financial reserves.

— *Margot Hoffman, President and CEO The Partnership for Excellence*

Engaging Stakeholders in the Refinement of the EFQM Model

EFQM recognized the need to refine their model in 2018, leading to the development of the recently updated EFQM Model. The refinement of the model was guided by the EFQM Core Team, 17 volunteers from various EFQM stakeholder groups: practitioners, consultants, academia, and EFQM Partners (national award programs). Input from an extensive survey, C-Suite interviews of EFQM members and non-members, and co-development testing by 24 volunteer organizations led to the next-generation EFQM Model. The new EFQM Model is described on pages 339–341.

— *info@efqm.org EFQM*

Board Engagement at Tennessee Center for Performance Excellence

The role of members of the Board of Directors (BOD) of a performance excellence program is frequently non-systematic and does not add value to the program. Tennessee Center for Performance Excellence (TNCPE) recognizes the important role of the BOD by establishing board accountability and leveraging BOD member contacts for business development.

— *Tamera Fields, President and CEO*
Tennessee Center for Performance Excellence

Incorporating Cultural Characteristics into the Excellence Model

The African Excellence Forum developed their quality award criteria based on review of both Baldrige and EFQM and other quality award criteria; however, it was recognized that the original criteria was not suitable to developing country requirements. Through various iterations, the incorporation of cultural aspects of the African continent resulted in the UBUNTU Excellence Framework (UEF). This framework provides a deliberate focus on People and Humanity. The concept of "Humanity" includes trust, respect, and mutual benefit guided by indigenous African philosophy.

— *Ed van den Heever, Founder, CEO*
Africa Excellence Forum

Senior Leaders Ensure Sustainability of Performance Excellence Program in a Large Organization

While the name Tata Group may not be familiar, the names of subsidiary companies like Jaguar, Land Rover, and Tetley Tea may be more familiar. Tata Group in India has used Tata Business Excellence Model (TBEM), based on the Baldrige criteria, as their management model since 1994. Tata's senior leadership demonstrates commitment to the use of the TBEM. Tata has been able to demonstrate the correlation between high TBEM scores and company performance. The focus is on the use of the TBEM to manage Tata businesses as opposed to an award program.

— *Devraj Chattaraj, Deputy General Manager*
Tata Business Excellence Group

Building a Baldrige Users Group to Refresh a Performance Excellence Program

Reenergizing a performance excellence program is a challenge, and unsuccessful efforts can lead to declining results. Rocky Mountain Performance Excellence, a regional performance excellence program serving Colorado, Wyoming, Montana, and Nebraska, is using the Baldrige Criteria as a model to determine steps to engage members, including a revised Mission, Vision, and Values, as well as establishing Communities of Practice.

— *Michael Gratz, Executive Director*
Rocky Mountain Performance Excellence

Clarifying Confusing Terms

Comparative Information versus Benchmarking

Comparative information includes benchmarking and competitive comparisons. Benchmarking refers to collecting information and data about processes and performance results that represent the best practices and performance for similar activities inside or outside the organization's business or industry. Competitive comparisons refer to collecting information and data on performance relative to direct competitors or similar providers.

For example, a personal computer manufacturer, ABC Micro (a fictitious company), must store, retrieve, pack, and ship computers and replacement parts. ABC Micro is concerned about shipping response time, errors in shipping, and damage during shipping. To determine the level of performance of its competitors in these areas, and to set reasonable improvement goals, ABC Micro would gather competitive comparison data from similar providers (competitors). However, the industry of which ABC Micro is a part may not have an organization within its ranks that demonstrates best practices for storage, retrieval, packaging, and shipping.

Effective benchmarking would require ABC Micro to find organizations that execute these processes better than any other organization, such as the catalog company L.L. Bean or Amazon.com, and examine both their processes and performance levels.

Benchmarking seeks best-practices information. Competitive comparisons look at competitors, whether or not they are the best.

Customer-Contact Workers

Customer-contact workers are any members of the workforce who are in direct contact with customers. They may be direct-service providers or answer complaint calls. They may be volunteers, paid or unpaid interns, or contract workers. Whenever a customer makes contact with an organization, either in person or by phone or other electronic means, that customer forms an opinion about the organization and its workforce. Members of the workforce who come in contact with customers are in a critical position to influence customers for the good of the organization or to its detriment.

Customer Engagement versus Customer Satisfaction

Customer engagement refers to the level that customers are vested in an organization's brand and product offerings. Factors that contribute to customer engagement typically include loyalty, retention, willingness to make an effort to do business and increase business, and the willingness to actively advocate for and recommend the organization's product offerings. Similar to engaged workers, engaged customers put forth an extra effort to support the organization. Customers that are merely satisfied may not exert this special level of support—and would not be considered engaged.

Customer Satisfaction versus Customer Dissatisfaction

One is not the inverse of the other. The lack of complaints does not indicate satisfaction, although the presence of complaints can be a partial indicator of dissatisfaction. Measures of customer dissatisfaction can include direct measures through surveys as well as complaints, product returns, and warranty claims.

Customer satisfaction and dissatisfaction are complex areas to assess. Customers are rarely *thoroughly* dissatisfied, although they may dislike a feature of a product or an aspect of service. There are usually degrees of satisfaction and dissatisfaction.

Data versus Information

Information can be qualitative and quantitative. Data lend themselves to quantification and statistical analysis. For example, an incoming inspection might produce a count of the number of units accepted, rejected, and total shipped. This count is considered data. These counts add to the base of information about supplier quality.

Measures and Indicators

The Award Criteria do not make a distinction between measures and indicators. However, some users of these terms prefer the term indicator: (1) when the measurement relates to performance but is not a direct or exclusive measure of such performance—for example, the number of complaints is an indicator of dissatisfaction, but not a direct or exclusive measure of it; and (2) when the measurement is a predictor (leading indicator) of some more significant performance—for example, an increase in product quality and on-time delivery might lead to a gain in customer satisfaction, which might be a leading indicator of market share gain.

Performance Requirements versus Performance Measures

Performance requirements are an expression of customer requirements, expectations, and preferences. Sometimes performance requirements are expressed as design requirements or engineering requirements. They are viewed as a basis for developing measures to enable the organization to determine whether the product or service meets design specifications and, in turn, whether the customer is likely to be satisfied.

Performance measures can also be used to assess work process efficiency, effectiveness, and productivity. Process-performance measures might include variance to standard, cycle time, error rate, or throughput.

Teams and Natural Work Units

Natural work units reflect the people who normally work together because they are a part of a formal work unit. For example, on an assembly line, three or four people may habitually work together to install a motor in a new car. Hotel employees who prepare food in the kitchen might constitute another natural work unit.

Teams may be formed of people within a natural work unit or may cross existing (natural) organization boundaries. To improve room service in a hotel, for example, certain members of several natural work units, such as the switchboard, kitchen workers, maintenance personnel, maids, and waiters, may form a special team. This team might be called a cross-functional work team because its members come from different functions within the organization.

Workforce Engagement, Empowerment, and Involvement

Engagement refers to a condition where workers contribute their utmost to the success of the organization and its customers. Empowerment generally refers to processes and procedures designed to provide individuals and teams with the tools, skills, and authority to make decisions that affect their work—decisions traditionally reserved for managers and supervisors. Empowerment is a tool used to enhance engagement. The most powerful drivers of engagement are feeling valued and involved.

Empowerment as a concept has been misused in many organizations. For example, managers may appear to extend decision-making authority under the guise of chartering teams and individuals to make recommendations about their work, while continuing to reserve decision-making authority for themselves.

This practice has given rise to another term—involvement—which describes the role of workers who are asked to become involved in decision-making, without necessarily making decisions. Involvement is a practice that many agree is better than not involving workers at all, but still is not sufficient to optimize their contribution to initiative, flexibility, and fast response.

Consider the metaphor of a clutch in an automobile. The clutch is considered *engaged* when it is fully in place and providing maximum pull or torque. During the process of becoming fully engaged, the clutch is gradually released, causing some slippage before it is locked in. This slippage is analogous to the act of partial involvement or empowerment.

Workforce Engagement versus Workforce Satisfaction

Workforce engagement involves getting the workers to contribute their utmost for the success of the organization and its customers. Workforce satisfaction refers to the degree to which the workforce feels positive about the organization, the workplace, supervisors, and coworkers. It is possible, even likely, that a worker can be highly satisfied with his or her work and be almost fully disengaged. Some workers can be fully satisfied collecting a paycheck and doing little for the organization—but they are not engaged.

Work Systems versus Work Processes

Work systems encompass all of the work that must be done for the organization to achieve its mission—regardless of who does the work. Work systems, therefore, typically involve the organization's workforce, its key suppliers and partners, contractors, collaborators, and other components of the supply network needed to produce and deliver products, educational programs and services, or health care services, and carry out related business and support processes. Work systems comprise both the internal work processes and external (outsourced) resources needed to develop and produce products and services, deliver them to customers (which may include students and patients), and succeed in the marketplace.

Decisions about work systems are strategic. These decisions may involve protecting and capitalizing on core competencies and deciding what should be procured or produced outside the organization in order to be efficient and sustainable. Generally, a process is considered for outsource contracting if the supplier can perform the process better, faster, and cheaper, and deliver the product or service more reliably and with fewer errors than the contracting organization.

Work processes consist of the work that the organization carries out internally. These internal work processes may be classified into three groups (for Baldrige review purposes) according to their importance in supporting the organization's creation of value:

- *Key work processes*, which constitute the bulk of the organization's workforce/resources and create the value needed to achieve mission
- *Key support processes*, which provide primary support to value creation
- *All other work processes*, including business processes, which provide services that the organization needs to conduct its business that are not considered by the organization to provide substantial value creation or primary support to value creation processes

Key work processes make up the organization's most important internal value-creation processes. It might be said that an organization exists to carry out its key work processes, and because of its key work processes, it exists. *Key work processes are carried out by the organization's workforce.*

Key work processes frequently relate to the organization's core competencies, the factors that determine success relative to competitors, and the factors senior leaders consider important for success and growth, now and in the future. Key work processes vary by individual organization, although they may be similar within sectors. For example, key work processes:

- In the business sector, might include product design, production, and delivery; research and development; and customer support
- In the health care sector, might include health care service design, patient care and treatment, and clinical diagnostics
- In the education sector, might include educational program and service design and delivery, student services, curriculum development, and instructional processes

Key support processes are also considered important to organizational success and sustainability and provide support to the internal value creation processes (also known as key work processes). Key support processes do not directly create value for customers. (If a key support process was actually creating value for customers in order to achieve the organization's mission, it might be reclassified as a key work process.)

Unlike key work processes, an organization does not exist to carry out a key support process or other (non-key) work processes. For example, one reason a hospital exists is to deliver health care services (a key work process). It does not exist to provide food and dietary services (a possible key support process), although those services help support its mission of patient care. Key support processes:

- In the business sector, might include maintenance, information technology, human resources or workforce management, public relations, legal services, billing and accounting, or marketing, to name a few
- In the health care sector, might include some of those listed for business, plus others such as admissions, food and dietary services, institutional development, public relations, diagnostic imaging, lab services, or medical records
- In the education sector, might include some processes already listed plus bussing and transportation services, guidance counseling, testing or other diagnostics, extracurricular activities, in-service education and training, and administration service

All other work processes make up the balance of the organization's work and workforce and are not a primary focus of a Baldrige Performance Excellence examination.

Taken together, key work processes and key support processes (which are all internal to the organization) involve the majority of the organization's workforce. It is also important to note that, depending on its importance to value creation for an individual organization, some of the processes listed here as key work processes may be deemed key support processes, and vice versa. For example, in Hospital A, diagnostic imaging may be essential for value creation and considered by the organization to be a key work process. In Hospital B, the same function may be defined as a key support process (because it supports value creation but is not perceived by the organization as a value-creation process itself). In Hospital C diagnostic imaging may be outsourced because it does not have the capacity or competency of its diagnostic imaging supplier.

Accordingly, if the organization decides to outsource any process, whether it is considered a value-creation or support process, it is no longer considered a work process, since work processes are internal to the organization. Work systems and work processes are intertwined, interconnected components of an integrated management system.

Figures 47, 48, and 49 provide examples of three different work systems, with their externally provided contracted processes and their internal key work process and key support process. The samples provided for business, health care, and education represent one set of decisions about the grouping of work systems and work processes. Any individual organization may make different decisions about these processes.

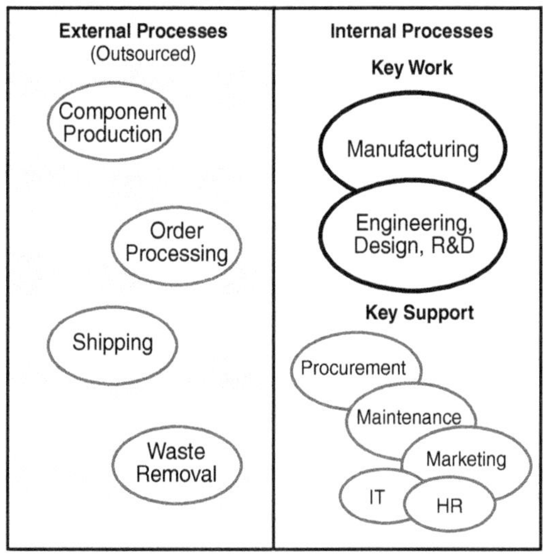

1. Key work processes considered by the organization to be important to create value for customers: R&D, engineering, and product manufacturing
2. Key support processes for the value creation processes: procurement (supply-network management), maintenance, marketing, IT (information technology), and HR (human resource management and recruiting)
3. Internal support processes that are not considered by the organization to be key to support value creation are not listed
4. External (outsourced) processes the organization decided were better performed by another organization: component parts supply, order processing, shipping, and waste removal

Figure 47 Business Sample: Manufacturing Organization Work Systems.

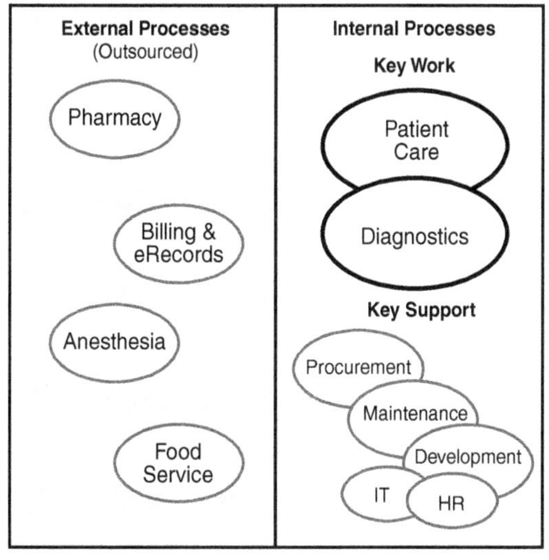

1. Key work processes considered by the organization to be important to create value for patients: patient care, diagnostics
2. Key support processes for the value creation processes: procurement (supply-network management), maintenance, institutional development (fund raising), IT (information technology), and HR (human resource management, including credentialing, volunteer coordination, and recruiting)
3. Internal support processes that are not considered by the organization to be key to support value creation are not listed
4. External (outsourced) processes the organization decided were better performed by another organization: pharmacy, billing and electronic medical records, food and dietary services

Figure 48 Health Care Sample: Health Care Work Systems.

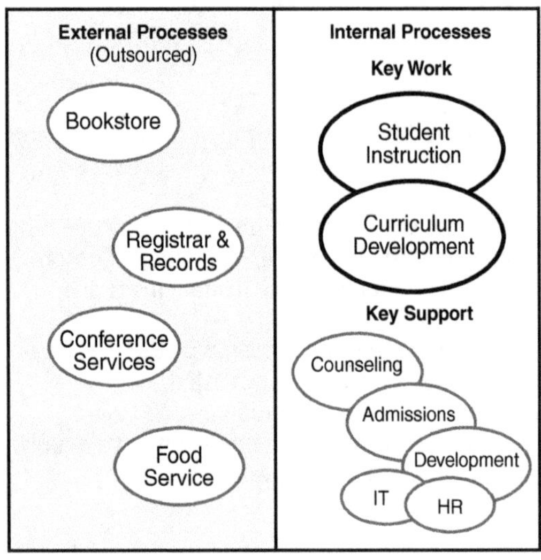

1. Key work processes considered by the organization to be important to create value for students: curriculum development and instruction
2. Key support processes for the value creation processes: counseling and placement, admissions, financial aid, institutional research and development (including fund raising), IT (information technology including computer services), and HR (human resource management including faculty and staff credentialing and recruiting)
3. Internal support processes that are not considered by the organization to be key to support value creation are not listed
4. External (outsourced) processes the organization decided were better performed by another organization: book store, registrar, billing and records, conference services and noncredit training, food services (cafeteria, dining halls, and on-campus restaurants)

Figure 49 Education Sample: Education Work Systems.

Glossary

This glossary defines and briefly describes key terms used throughout the Criteria that are important to performance management and assessment.

action plans—specific actions that respond to short- and longer-term strategic objectives. Action plans include details of resource commitments and time horizons for accomplishment. Action plan development represents the critical stage in planning when strategic objectives and goals are made specific so that effective, organization-wide understanding and deployment are possible. In the Criteria, deployment of action plans includes creating aligned measures for all departments and work units. Action plan deployment also might require specialized training for some members of the workforce or recruitment of new personnel.

An example of a strategic objective for an organization in a highly competitive industry might be to develop and maintain price leadership. Action plans to achieve the strategic objective could entail designing more efficient processes, creating an accounting system that tracks activity-level costs, and aligning work processes and accounting systems across the organization.

To deploy action plans, the organization might need to train work units and teams in setting priorities based on costs and benefits. Organizational-level analysis and review and related results might include productivity growth, cost control, and quality. Also see *strategic objectives.*

alignment—consistency of plans, processes, information, resource decisions, actions, results, and analysis to support key organization-wide goals. Effective alignment requires a common understanding of purposes and goals. It also requires the use of complementary measures and information for planning, tracking, analysis, and improvement at three levels: the organizational level, the key process level, and the work-unit level. See the definition of *integration.*

analysis—assessments performed by an organization, its work units, or external suppliers/partners to provide a basis for effective decisions. Every organization must analyze data to support effective decision-making. The types and amount of analysis depend on the complexity and decision needs of the organization, its leaders, and employees. Overall organizational analysis is necessary to assimilate increasingly large amounts of data and guide process management toward achieving key business results and strategic objectives.

Despite their importance, individual facts and raw data do not usually provide an effective basis for actions or setting priorities. Actions depend upon understanding cause-effect relationships. Understanding such relationships comes from analysis of facts and data. Examples of these analyses include, but are not limited to:

- Correlating product and service-quality improvement with key customer indicators, such as customer satisfaction, customer retention, and market share
- Cost/revenue implications of customer-related problems and problem-resolution effectiveness
- Interpretation of market-share changes in terms of customer gains and losses and changes in customer satisfaction
- Improvement trends in key operational performance indicators, such as productivity, cycle time, waste reduction, new-product introduction, and defect levels
- Relationships between workforce/organizational learning and value added per employee
- Financial benefits derived from improvements in workforce safety, absenteeism, and turnover
- Benefits and costs associated with education and training

- The need for change in organizational structure and work systems
- Benefits and costs associated with improved organizational-knowledge management and sharing
- Correlating the ability to identify and meet workforce requirements with workforce retention, motivation, and productivity
- Cost/revenue implications of workforce-related problems and effective problem resolution
- Determining whether a new program or initiative is an intelligent risk worth taking
- Individual or aggregate measures of productivity and quality relative to competitors
- Cost trends relative to competitors
- Relationships between product/service quality, operational-performance indicators, and overall financial-performance trends as reflected in indicators, such as operating costs, revenues, asset utilization, and value added per employee
- Allocation of resources among alternative improvement projects based on cost/revenue implications and improvement potential
- Net earnings derived from quality, operational, and workforce performance improvements
- Comparisons among business units showing how quality and operational-performance improvement affect financial performance
- Contributions of improvement activities to cash flow, working-capital use, and shareholder value
- Profit impacts of customer retention
- Cost/revenue implications of new-market entry, including global-market entry or expansion (part of an intelligent risk assessment)
- Cost/revenue, customer, and productivity implications of engaging in or expanding e-commerce
- Market share versus profits
- Trends in economic, market, and shareholder indicators of value

anecdotal—in a response to a Baldrige Criteria requirement, information that lacks specific methods; measures; deployment mechanisms; and evaluation, improvement, and learning factors. Anecdotal information frequently consists of examples and describes individual activities rather than systematic processes.

For example, an anecdotal response to how senior leaders deploy performance expectations, might describe a specific occasion when a senior leader visited the organization's facilities. On the other hand, a properly described, systematic process, might include the methods all senior leaders use to communicate performance expectations regularly (at defined intervals) to all locations and workforce members, the measures leaders use to assess the effectiveness of the methods, and the tools and techniques used to evaluate and improve the methods. Also see *systematic.*

analytical tools—tools for analyzing data may include brainstorming, Pareto charts, cause-and-effect diagrams, cost-benefit analyses, scatter diagrams, correlation and regression analysis, and histograms, to name a few.

approach—the methods used by an organization to address the Baldrige Criteria Item elements. Approach includes the appropriateness of the methods to the Item elements and the effectiveness of their use. Approach is one of the dimensions considered in evaluating Process Items and is subdivided into three developmental areas: *basic* elements, *overall* elements, and *multiple* elements.

basic question—the topic Criteria users address when responding to an Item's most central concept. *Basic* elements are the fundamental theme of Item. In the Criteria, the *basic* elements of each Item are presented as the Item title question. Refer to the *Scoring System* and *Clarifying the Baldrige Scoring Requirements* chapters in this book for a detailed explanation of *basic*, *overall*, and *multiple* elements.

benchmarks—processes and results that represent best practices and performance for similar activities, inside or outside an organization's industry. Organizations engage in benchmarking as an approach to understand the current dimensions of world-class performance and to achieve discontinuous (non-incremental) or breakthrough improvement.

Benchmarks are one form of comparative data. Others that organizations might use include industry data collected by a third party (frequently industry averages), data on competitors' performance, and comparisons with similar organizations in the same geographic area or that provide similar products and services in other geographic areas.

capability, workforce—see *workforce capability.*

capacity, workforce—see *workforce capacity.*

change—involves achieving changes in organizational vision, culture, values, attitudes, work structures, and individual skill sets so that the organization performs at a much higher level, maximizing its opportunities to achieve stakeholder objectives. Successful change requires persistence on the part of senior leaders as they drive workforce involvement and engagement with a new or modified culture, vision, strategy, and actions (expected behaviors). Tools leaders often use to promote change include effective two-way communication, organizational and personal learning, meaningful reward and recognition, and stimulating continuous improvement and innovation

collaborators—those organizations or individuals that cooperate with the organization to support a particular activity or event or that cooperate intermittently when their short-term goals are aligned or similar. Typically, collaborations do not involve formal agreements or long-term arrangements. Also see *partners.*

comparisons—the term *comparisons* as it applies to Results scoring, refers to evaluating the organization's performance relative to appropriate (that is, relevant) competitors or similar organizations, as well as benchmarks or industry leaders. In most cases, appropriate comparison data are needed to determine the *goodness*, strength, or maturity of the organization's performance results.

continuous improvement—the ongoing improvement of products, programs, services, or processes by small increments or major breakthroughs, including innovation and reengineering.

core competencies—the organization's areas of greatest expertise. The organization's core competencies are those strategically important capabilities that provide an advantage in the marketplace or service environment. Core competencies frequently are challenging for competitors or suppliers and partners to imitate, and they may provide a sustainable competitive advantage. The absence of a needed core competency may result in a significant strategic challenge or disadvantage for the organization in the marketplace. Core competencies may involve technology expertise, unique service offerings, a marketplace niche, or business acumen in a particular area (for example, business acquisitions).

cross-purposes—actions taken by different people or units in an organization that are not integrated or aligned, and do not support the overall mission and objectives of the organization. For example, to improve customer support and satisfaction, the information technology unit installs a new phone system but neglects to work with the training unit to ensure everyone understands and can use the system. Customers become angry when their calls go unanswered, resulting in lower customer satisfaction and loyalty than with the old system.

customer—actual and potential users of the organization's products, programs, or services (referred to as *products* in the Criteria). Customers include the end users of the organization's products, as well as others who might be the immediate purchasers or users of its products, such as wholesale distributors, agents, or organizations that further process the product as a component of their product. The Baldrige Framework and Performance Excellence Criteria address customers broadly, referencing current and future customers, as well as customers of competitors. In health care, customers include patients. In education, customers include students. See the definition of *stakeholders* for the relationship between customers and others who might be affected by the organization's products.

customer-focused excellence—a Baldrige core value embedded in the beliefs and behaviors of high-performing organizations.

customer-interaction process—the process by which an organization approaches, responds to, and follows up with customers. It helps strengthen customer relationships and provides greater insight into customer needs and expectations. The process of interacting with customers can be carried out by many methods including phone, fax, e-mail, social media, blogs and other internet postings, and face-to-face meetings. Attending to these interactions is important because customers frequently make decisions about the organization based on one interaction.

customer engagement—the customers' investment in or commitment to the organization's brand and product offerings. It is influenced by the organization's ongoing ability to serve their needs and build relationships so customers continue using the organization's products. Characteristics of customer engagement include customer retention and loyalty, customers' willingness to make an effort to do business with the organization, and customers' willingness to actively advocate for and recommend the organization's brand and product, program, and service offerings.

customer focus—relates to an outcome of performance excellence in which customer requirements and preferences impact and integrate with the organization's strategic directions, work systems and work processes, and business results.

customer value chain—usually several entities that are involved as customers at different stages of the life of a program, product, or service. In the example of the automobiles (see definition of *end user*), the original equipment manufacturer (car maker) sells to dealers, the first segment of the customer chain. When the dealer resells the car to a cab company, that company becomes the next customer in the chain as car owner. Finally, the ultimate users of the car, the cab driver and passengers, become the users. Customer chains typically can be considered to extend through the life cycle of the product. In the case of automobiles, the secondary market of used cars begins and used-car dealers and their customers may extend the customer chain. Each customer in the chain may have different requirements that must be met.

cycle of improvement—one of the evaluation factors in the Scoring Calibration Guidelines, requiring the use of a fact-based, systematic approach to evaluation and improvement. Examples of such an approach include implementing a lean enterprise system, applying Six Sigma methodology, using PDCA or PDSA, After Action Reviews, improving processes using standards from the International Organization for Standardization (ISO; for example, 9000 or 14000), decision science, or other improvement tools.

Conducting a fact-based, systematic evaluation without implementing an improvement based on that evaluation constitutes the beginning of a cycle of improvement but does not constitute the completion of a cycle of improvement. Broadly stated, a cycle of improvement involves repeatable steps such as:

- Identifying an issue or problem
- Gathering data to examine or analyze the characteristics of the issue or problem (which may include identifying potential causes)
- Developing potential solutions based on the examination or analysis of the data and causes
- Testing or examining alternative solutions
- Deciding which solution(s) to implement (considering relevant factors such as feasibility, cost, benefit)
- Implementing the solution
- Monitoring the implemented solution to determine its value-added impact and, if appropriate, locking it in place.

Refining the organization's fact-based, systematic approach to evaluation and improvement process using steps such as those above would constitute another cycle of improvement.

A relevant organizational outcome reported in Category 7 might be considered evidence of the cycle of improvement value or impact on performance. To ensure relevance, there should be a logical link between the specific cycle of improvement and performance metric reported. However, outcome results may not be required to prove a process has improved. A process can be improved significantly before a change in organizational performance is observed. For example, cycle time of an individual work process can be reduced well before lagging indicators such as cost, quality, customer satisfaction, or profitability are measured. Moreover, a meaningful process improvement may occur with no apparent reduction in measurable outcomes. For example, costs saved through process simplification may be offset by increases in the cost of labor or raw materials.

Benchmarking a work process used by top-performing organizations and then adopting or adapting the process internally may constitute a fact-based, systematic approach to meaningful change (learning).

Random acts of improvement are not considered fact-based or systematic and should be disregarded as a cycle of improvement for purposes of Baldrige scoring.

cycle time—the amount of time required to complete a defined process from end to end. For example, the time required from the beginning of design to the delivery of product can be measured as the *design-to-delivery cycle time*. Additionally, each component of this cycle can be also measured. The design phase can have one cycle time, the production phase can have another, and the delivery phase a third. Organizations are responsible for defining work cycles in meaningful terms. These defined cycles should make sense to the organization and help its workers measure and monitor the processes in the cycles in order to drive improvements. Time measurements play a major role in the assessment because of the great importance of time performance to improving competitiveness and overall performance. Time-related terms in common use are setup time, customer response time, lead time, changeover time, delivery time, order-fulfillment time, time to market, changeover time, and other key process times.

data validity and utility—data are numerical information. They are used as a basis for reasoning, discussion, determining status, decision-making, and analysis. Data proven to measure a particular construct or characteristic are *valid data*. Data *utility* (usefulness) is determined by the customers of the data—the people who must use them.

deployment—the extent to which an organization's approach is applied to the elements of a Baldrige Criteria Item. Deployment is evaluated on the basis of the breadth and depth of application of the approach to relevant work units throughout the organization. Deployment is one of the dimensions considered in evaluating Process Items.

diversity—personal differences among workforce members that enrich the work environment and are representative of the organization's hiring and customer communities. These differences address many variables, such as race, religion, color, gender, national origin, disability, sexual orientation, age and generation, education, geographic origin, and skill characteristics, as well as ideas, thinking, academic disciplines, and perspectives.

The Baldrige Criteria refer to valuing and benefiting from the diversity of the organization's workforce hiring and customer communities. Capitalizing on both in building the organization's workforce increases opportunities for high performance; customer, workforce, and community satisfaction; and customer and workforce engagement.

effective—how well a process or a measure addresses its intended purpose. Determining effectiveness requires (1) evaluating how well the process is aligned with the organization's needs and how well it is deployed, or (2) evaluating the outcome of the measure. When evaluating the *effectiveness* of a process described in an application, examiners determine whether the process is likely to do what the Criteria require.

empowerment—giving people the authority and responsibility to make decisions and take actions. Empowerment results in decisions being made closest to the front line, where most work-related decisions should be made.

Empowering members of the workforce enables them to satisfy customers on first contact, improve processes and increase productivity, and improve the organization's performance results. An empowered workforce requires information to make appropriate decisions based on data and sound analysis.

end user—the ultimate user of the programs, products, or services an organization produces and delivers. For example, a manufacturer of automobiles sells to a network of dealers. However, except for the cars the dealer actually puts into service and uses, it is not considered an end user. The end user is the person at the end of the customer chain actually using the car (see definition of *customer chain*). A dealer may resell the car to a taxi company. The taxi company (car owner) hires people to drive the car. The cab driver and passengers may be considered end users until the car is resold to a new end user.

engagement—see *workforce engagement* or *customer engagement,* as applicable.

ethical behavior—the actions an organization takes to ensure that all its decisions, actions, and stakeholder interactions conform to the organization's moral and professional principles. These principles should support all applicable laws and regulations. They are the foundation for the organization's culture and values and define right from wrong. The Baldrige Criteria do not prescribe a particular model of ethical behavior or set of principles.

Senior leaders act as role models for the principles of ethical behavior, which apply to everyone involved in the organization, from temporary, part-time workers, to suppliers, to members of the governing board. Senior leaders are responsible for aligning the organization's mission and vision with its ethical principles. The organization's desired principles of ethical behavior should be followed by all stakeholders, including the workforce, shareholders, customers, partners, suppliers, and the organization's local community.

While some organizations may view their ethical principles as boundary conditions restricting behavior, well-designed and clearly articulated ethical principles should empower people to make effective decisions with great confidence.

For additional insight, see the related Baldrige core value, Ethics and Transparency.

evaluation and improvement—evaluation and improvement is a component of *learning,* which refers to acquiring new knowledge or skills through evaluation, study, experience, and innovation. Evaluation is based on factual assessment, which is used to promote value-added improvement and innovation. Random acts of improvement consist of change that is accidental, unpredictable, and not based on factual evaluations.

excellence—see *performance excellence.*

fact-based—data and information are used to support knowledge-driven decision-making (as opposed to intuition, *gut feel,* or guesswork) for setting and aligning organizational directions and resource use at the work unit, key process, departmental, and organizational levels.

goals—a future condition or performance level that one intends to attain. Goals can be both short- and long-term. Goals are ends that guide actions. Quantitative goals, frequently referred to as *targets,* include a numerical point or range. Targets might be projections based on comparative data and/or competitive data. The term *stretch goals* refers to desired major, discontinuous (nonincremental), or breakthrough improvements, usually in areas most critical to the organization's future success.

Goals can serve many purposes, including clarifying strategic objectives and action plans to indicate how success will be measured, fostering teamwork by focusing on a common end, encouraging *out-of-the-box* thinking (innovation) to achieve a stretch goal, and providing a basis for measuring and accelerating progress. Also see *performance projections.*

governance—the system of management and controls exercised in the stewardship of the organization. It includes the responsibilities of the organization's owners or shareholders, board of directors, and senior leaders. Corporate or organizational charters, bylaws, and policies document the rights and responsibilities of each of the parties and describe how the organization will be directed and controlled to ensure accountability to owners, shareholders, and other stakeholders; transparency of operations; and fair treatment of all stakeholders. Governance processes may include approving strategic direction, ensuring accountability for achieving strategic plans, monitoring and evaluating CEO performance, succession planning, transparency in operations, financial auditing and accountability, establishing executive compensation and benefits, managing risk, disclosure, and reporting to shareholders. Ensuring effective governance is important to stakeholders' and the larger society's trust and to organizational effectiveness.

groupings and segments—ways in which the organization clusters or subdivides various people and organizations with which it interacts. Groupings are formed for the convenience of the organization and are defined by the organization. Sometimes the organization will group or segment customers with similar requests, such as high volume, low volume, high risk, or geographical regions. Workforce elements may be grouped as well for the convenience of the organization (for example, hourly, salary, manufacturing, technical, physicians, nurses, teachers, and so on).

high-performance work—work processes used to systematically pursue ever-higher levels of overall organizational and individual performance, including quality, productivity, innovation rate, and cycle-time performance. High-performance work results in improved service for customers and other stakeholders. Approaches to high-performance work vary in form, function, and incentive systems. High-performance work depends on workforce engagement. It frequently includes cooperation between management and the workforce, which may involve workforce bargaining units; cooperation among work units, often involving teams; the empowerment of people, including self-directed responsibility; employee input to planning; individual and organizational skill building and learning; learning from other organizations; flexibility in job design and work assignments; a flattened organizational structure, where decision-making is decentralized and decisions are made closest to the front line; and effective use of performance measures, including comparisons. Many high-performance work systems use monetary and nonmonetary incentives based upon factors such as organizational performance, team and/or individual contributions, and skill building. Also, high-performance work processes align the organization's structure, core competencies, work, jobs, workforce development, and incentives.

how—descriptions of the systems and processes that an organization uses to accomplish its mission requirements. In responding to *how* questions in the Process Item elements, descriptions should include information such as approach (methods and measures), deployment, learning, and integration factors (see *scoring guidelines*).

indicators and measures—see *measures and indicators.*

innovation—a component of the Baldrige scoring guideline. The Baldrige definition of innovation is two-tiered:

- At one level (50%–65% scoring range) "basic" innovation involves making "meaningful change" to improve services, processes, or organizational effectiveness and create new value for stakeholders
- At a higher level, (70%–100% scoring ranges) "classic" innovation involves adopting an idea, process, technology, service, or business model that is either new or new to its proposed application

Making meaningful change is typically an easier standard to achieve than creating something entirely new or new to its proposed application, which is why it is assigned to the 50%–65% scoring range. An outcome of higher-level, "classic" innovation is typically a discontinuous or breakthrough change in results, products, or processes.

Innovation at both levels benefits from a supportive environment, a process for identifying strategic opportunities, and a willingness to pursue intelligent risks. Successful organizational innovation is a multistep process of development and knowledge sharing, a decision to implement, implementation, evaluation, and learning. Although higher-level innovation is often associated with technological innovation, it is applicable to all key organizational processes that can benefit from change through innovation, whether breakthrough improvement or a change in approach or outputs. Innovation could include fundamental changes in an organization's structure or business model to accomplish work more effectively.

In a Baldrige-based review, applicants receive feedback that identifies—by definition—the most important, "vital few" opportunities for improvement that are keeping the organization from achieving higher levels of performance excellence. A Baldrige-based review conducted by trained examiners who adhere to national or state protocols is considered a fact-based evaluation. An applicant that uses this evaluation and feedback, addresses the opportunities for improvement, and produces positive change as a result should be considered to have made "meaningful change" to improve services, processes, organizational effectiveness and create new value for stakeholders.

inspection and testing—assessments of product or service suitability, checks to determine if requirements are met or whether defects exist. Counting the number of bubbles in a glass lens is an end-process inspection since it is conducted after the glass is made. The term testing refers to determining whether the product or service works as intended. The same lens might be tested by shining a light through it and measuring the refraction or distortion of the light. The components of a computer can be inspected to ensure they are all in place. The computer is tested by turning it on and performing calculations. In the education sector testing is used to assess levels of education progress, student achievement, or knowledge mastery.

integration—as the term applies to Process scoring, *integration* refers to the extent to which an organization's approach to meeting the Criteria elements is aligned with organizational needs identified in the Organizational Profile and other Process Items; measures, information, and improvement systems are complementary across processes and work units; and plans, processes, results, analyses, learning, and actions are harmonized or aligned across processes and work units to support organization-wide goals. Effective integration goes beyond alignment and is achieved when the individual components of a performance management system operate as a fully interconnected unit.

As the term applies to Results scoring, *integration* refers to the extent to which the organization's Results address *important* performance elements identified in the Organizational Profile and in Process Items. For further description, see the *Scoring System.* Also see *alignment.*

intelligent risks—defines opportunities for which the potential gain outweighs the potential harm or loss to the organization's sustainability if you do not explore them. Taking intelligent risks requires a tolerance for failure and an expectation that innovation is not achieved by initiating only successful endeavors. At the outset, organizations must invest in potential successes while realizing that some will fail.

The degree of risk that is intelligent to take will vary by the pace and level of threat and opportunity in the industry, market, or sector in which the organization operates. In a rapidly changing competitive environment with constant introductions of new products, processes, or business models, there is an obvious need to invest more resources in intelligent risks than in a stable industry. In the latter, organizations must monitor and explore growth potential and change but, most likely, with a less significant commitment of resources. Also see *strategic opportunities.*

key—the major or most important elements or factors, those that are critical to achieving the intended outcome. The Baldrige Criteria, for example, refer to key challenges, key plans, key work processes, key measures—those that are most important to the organization's success. They are the essential elements for pursuing or monitoring a desired outcome.

key communities—defined by the organization, key communities refer to elements of the public that may be affected by the presence of the organization, and factors such as its programs, products, services, operations, and facilities. Key communities may include schools, colleges, health care organizations, charitable organizations, or any group the organization believes key to its business objectives. A key community may also include individuals who are affected by the process, products, services, and processes of the organization. Residents in the vicinity of an industrial facility might be considered a key community since they may impact the organization and its ability to expand or conduct business. Key communities for a local public school may include organizations such as the local library, volunteer organizations, and education or professional associations. Key communities for a health care system may also include local residents who may benefit from free clinics, health care awareness programs, and other community health initiatives.

knowledge assets—the accumulated intellectual resources of the organization. It is the knowledge possessed by the organization and its workforce in the form of information, ideas, learning, understanding, memory, insights, cognitive and technical skills, and capabilities. The workforce, software, patents, databases, documents, guides, policies and procedures, and technical drawings are repositories of an organization's knowledge assets.

Knowledge assets are held not only by an organization but reside within its customers, suppliers, and partners as well. Knowledge assets are the know-how that the organization has available to use, to invest, and to grow. Building and managing its knowledge assets are key components of creating value for stakeholders and to acquiring or sustaining competitive advantage.

leadership system—the methods by which leadership is exercised, formally and informally, throughout the organization—the basis for and the way key decisions are made, communicated, and carried out. It includes structures and mechanisms for decision-making; two-way communications; selection and development of leaders and managers; and reinforcement of values, ethical behavior, directions, and performance expectations.

An effective leadership system respects the capabilities and requirements of the workforce and other stakeholders, and sets high expectations for performance and performance improvement. It builds loyalties and teamwork based on the organization's culture, vision, and values and the pursuit of shared goals. It encourages and supports initiative and appropriate risk taking. An effective leadership system focuses on substance over form, subordinating organization structure to purpose and function, and avoids long, rigid chains of command and cumbersome decision paths. An effective leadership system encourages leaders conduct self-examinations—such as provided by 360° evaluations—to receive actionable feedback from supervisors, peers, and subordinates and use that feedback to improve.

learning—new knowledge or skills acquired through evaluation, study, and analysis that leads to meaningful change and innovation. The Baldrige Criteria include two distinct kinds of learning: organizational and personal (which includes learning by the members of the workforce). *Organizational learning* is achieved through research and development, evaluation and improvement cycles, workforce and stakeholder ideas and input, best-practice sharing, and benchmarking. Learning tools may include the practices of lean enterprise, Six Sigma methods, Rapid Improvement Exercises, PDCA/PDSA, Design of Experiments, Value Stream Analysis, After Action Reviews and many other techniques. *Personal or workforce learning* is achieved through education, training, and developmental opportunities that promote the growth of the organization's workers, managers, and leaders.

To be effective, learning should be embedded in the way an organization operates. Learning contributes to a competitive advantage for the organization and its workforce. Learning is one of the dimensions considered in evaluating Process Items. For further description of organizational learning, see the related core value *Organizational Learning* on pages 25–26 of this book.

levels—numerical information that places or positions an organization's results and performance on a meaningful measurement scale. Performance levels, together with comparison data, enable the evaluation of the *goodness* or strength of the organization's performance (for example to determine if its performance is poor, good, very good, or excellent). Performance levels provided over time permit trend analysis to determine if performance is getting better or not. As the term applies to Results scoring, it refers to the organization's current level of performance. For further description, see the *Scoring System* chapter.

measures and indicators—numerical information that quantifies input, output, and performance dimensions of processes, products, programs, projects, services, and the overall organization (outcomes). Measures and indicators might be simple (derived from one measurement) or composite.

The Baldrige Criteria do not make a distinction between measures and indicators. However, some users of these terms prefer the term indicator: (1) when the measurement relates to performance but is not a direct measure of such performance (for example, the number of complaints is an indicator of dissatisfaction but not a direct measure of it), and

(2) when the measurement is a predictor (leading indicator) of some more significant performance (for example, increased customer satisfaction might be a leading indicator of market-share gain).

mission—the overall function of an organization; its reason for existing. The mission answers the question, "What is this organization attempting to accomplish?" As the mission statement defines the organization's reason for existing, it might also define its customers or markets served, distinctive or core competencies, or technologies used.

multiple questions—the details of an Item's elements, as expressed in the individual questions under each lettered/numbered Area to Address. The first question in a set of *multiple* elements expresses the most important question in that group. The questions that follow expand on or supplement that question. Examiners should refer to the *Scoring System* and *Clarifying Baldrige Scoring Requirements* chapters in this book for a detailed explanation of *basic*, *overall*, and *multiple* elements and their impact on scoring.

objective—usually considered to be a subset of goals. A goal may relate to financial success. Objectives needed to meet this goal may be a monthly or annual sales target. See *outcome-based strategic objectives*.

organization—a group of people with common goals and mission. The group may be any size, formal or informal, ad hoc or permanent. An organization may provide business products and services, health care services, or educational programs and services.

organization leaders and senior leaders—the executives in the organization being reviewed by the Baldrige process. At a bank, senior leaders could include the president, vice presidents, branch managers, and staff managers. For a company, senior leaders typically include the chief executive officer and his or her direct reports. For a hospital, senior leaders include top medical and administrative officers. If the unit under review is a division of a larger organization, the chief officer of the division and direct reports are considered senior leaders.

organizational agility—the ability of the organization to act quickly or change quickly. Speed of response of all aspects of organizational operations is increasingly important as organizations experience less tolerance from customers and stakeholders for slow, plodding service and bureaucratic inefficiency. Organizational agility, like the agility demonstrated by an Olympic gymnast, suggests the ability to move quickly and bend the organization to adapt to changing requirements and environmental constraints. For further description of agility, see the related Core Value and Concept *Agility and Resilience* on pages 24–25 of this book.

outcome-based strategic objectives—(also called *results-oriented* or *results-based* strategic objectives) define in measurable terms the outcomes or results that the organization must achieve to be successful in the future. To achieve *outcome-based strategic objectives* the organization must engage in activities, but it should be outcome achievement not activity completion that is used to measure success. Since it is possible to carry out the assigned activity and still fail to achieve the desired outcome, strategic objectives define the outcome required for success, not the activities to be carried out.

overall questions—the most important features of a Criteria Item, which are set forth in the first question (in boldface) in each lettered/numbered Area to Address. Examiners should refer to the *Scoring System* and *Clarifying Baldrige Scoring Requirements* chapters in this book for a detailed explanation of *basic*, *overall*, and *multiple* elements and their impact on scoring.

partners—those key organizations or individuals who are working in concert with the organization to achieve a common goal. Typically, partnerships are formal arrangements for a specific aim or purpose, such as to achieve a strategic objective or to deliver a specific product or service. Formal partnerships last for extended periods of time and involve a clear understanding of the individual and mutual roles and benefits for the partners. Also see *collaborators*.

patient—the person receiving health care, including preventative, promotional, acute, chronic, rehabilitative, skilled nursing, assisted-living, and other services in the continuum of care. Other terms used for patient include *member, consumer, client,* and *resident.*

performance—output results and their outcomes obtained from processes, products, and customers that permit evaluation and comparison relative to goals, standards, past results, and other organizations. Performance might be expressed in nonfinancial and financial terms. The Baldrige Criteria address four types of performance: (1) product, (2) customer-focused, (3) operational, and (4) financial and marketplace.

Product performance refers to performance relative to measures and indicators of product and service characteristics important to customers. Examples include product reliability, on-time delivery, customer-experienced defect levels, and service-response time. These are considered indirect measures of customer satisfaction since the organizations are using measures or indicators of product and service quality to predict what the customer is likely to think without actually asking the customer or waiting for customer feedback.

Examples of product performance in health care include hospital admission rates, mortality and morbidity rates, nosocomial infection rates, length of hospital stays, readmission rates, patient-experienced error levels, and patient compliance levels, to name a few. Health care performance might be measured at the organizational level and segmented, for example, by procedure, service, or patient characteristics.

Examples of product performance in education include the effectiveness of curriculum development and instruction, assessment of student learning, participation in professional development opportunities, and student placement following program completion (such as entry into the job market or college admission rates).

For nonprofit organizations, product performance examples might include program and project performance in areas of rapid response to emergencies, at-home services, or multilingual services. In the Criteria these results are reported in Item 7.1.

Customer-focused performance refers to performance relative to measures and indicators of customers' perceptions, reactions, and behaviors. Examples include customer retention, complaints, and customer-survey results. These are considered direct measures of customer satisfaction since customers are telling organizations directly about their levels of satisfaction, dissatisfaction, or engagement. In the Criteria these results are reported in Item 7.2.

Operational performance refers to workforce performance, leadership performance, and organizational performance (including ethical and legal compliance) relative to measures and indicators of effectiveness, efficiency, and accountability. Examples include cycle time, productivity, waste reduction, workforce turnover, workforce cross-training rates, safety and accident rates, measures of workforce capability and capacity, regulatory compliance, fiscal accountability, accreditation, community involvement and, in health care, contributions to community health. Operational performance outcomes might be measured at the work-unit, key work process, and organizational levels. In the Criteria these results are reported in Items 7.1, 7.3, and 7.4.

Financial, marketplace, and strategy performance includes measures of cost or cost containment, revenue, and market position, asset utilization, asset growth, market share, return on investments, return on assets, value added per employee, debt-to-equity ratio, operating margins, performance to budget, amount of reserve funds, cash-to-ash cycle time (which reports on the cash conversion cycle of receivables, payables, inventory costs), other profitability and liquidity measures, market gains, and strategy accomplishment. For the education sector, examples of budgetary, financial, and market performance, might include instructional and general administration expenditures per student as a percentage of budget, program expenditures as a percentage of budget, performance to budget, annual budget increases or decreases, income, expenses, reserves, endowments, grants and awards received, and the percentage of budget for research. In the Criteria these results are reported in Item 7.5.

performance excellence—a comprehensive, integrated approach to organizational-performance management that results in: (1) delivery of ever-improving value to customers and stakeholders, contributing to current and ongoing organizational success; (2) improvement of overall organizational effectiveness and capabilities; and (3) organizational and personal learning. The Baldrige CPE constitute an integrated management system that defines the factors that are both necessary and sufficient to achieve optimum performance over time. If any element of the integrated management system is not in place or not fully deployed the organization usually faces some adverse consequences.

performance projections—estimates of future performance. Projections may be inferred from past performance, may be based on competitors' or similar organizations' performance that must be met or exceeded, or may be predicted based on assumptions about changes in a dynamic environment, internal or external to the organization.

Performance projections state the organization's expected future performance outcomes. Goals state the organization's desired future performance outcomes. Projections integrate estimates of the organization's rate of improvement and change, and they may be used to indicate where breakthrough improvement or change is needed. In areas where the organization intends to achieve breakthrough performance or innovation, its performance objectives and goals may overlap. Performance projections serve as a key management-planning tool.

prevention-based intervention—determining the root cause of a problem and preventing its recurrence rather than just solving the problem and waiting for it to happen again (reactive posture).

process—linked activities with the purpose of producing a product or service for a customer (user, patient, student) within or outside the organization. Generally, processes involve combinations of people, machines, tools, techniques, materials, and improvements in a defined series of steps or actions. Processes rarely operate in isolation and must be considered in relation to other processes that impact them. In some situations, processes might require adherence to a specific sequence of steps, with documentation (sometimes formal) of procedures and requirements, including well-defined measurement and control steps.

In many service situations, particularly when customers are directly involved in the service, process is used in a more general way; that is, to spell out what delivering the service might entail or what must be done, possibly including a preferred or expected sequence. If a sequence is critical, the service needs to include information to help customers (students, patients) understand and follow the sequence. Service processes involving customers also require guidance to the providers of those services on handling contingencies related to customers' likely or possible actions or behaviors.

In knowledge work, such as teaching, strategic planning, research, development, and analysis, process does not necessarily imply formal sequences of steps. Rather, process implies general understandings regarding competent performance, such as timing, options to be included, evaluation, and reporting. Sequences might arise as part of these understandings.

In the Baldrige Scoring System, process maturity is assessed. This assessment is based on four factors: Approach, Deployment, Learning, and Integration. For further description, see the *Scoring System* chapter in this book.

productivity—measures of the efficiency of resource use. Although the term often is applied to single factors such as the workforce (labor productivity), machines, materials, energy, and capital, the productivity concept applies as well to the total resources used in producing outputs. The use of an aggregate measure of overall productivity allows a determination of whether the net effect of overall changes in a process—possibly involving resource trade-offs—is beneficial. Measures of productivity may be part of an analysis to determine if a new program or process is an intelligent risk worth taking

resilience—ability of an organization to anticipate, prepare for, and recover from disasters, emergencies, and other disruptions; and protect and enhance workforce and customer engagement, supply-network and financial performance, organizational productivity, and community well-being when disruptions occur. Organizational resilience requires organizational agility.

Not only does resilience require an organization to "bounce back" to a prior state when a disruption occurs, it also means having a plan to continue operating as needed during disruptions. To achieve resilience, leaders must cultivate the agility to respond quickly to both opportunities and threats, adapt strategy to changing circumstances, and have robust governance with a culture of trust. Organizations must adopt an ecosystem mindset, embrace data-rich thought processes, and equip their employees with ongoing learning of new skills.

results—outputs and outcomes achieved by an organization in addressing the elements of a Baldrige Criteria Item. Results are evaluated on the basis of the rate, breadth, and importance of performance improvements; current performance relative to appropriate comparisons; and performance changes over time. Results are one of the two dimensions evaluated in a Baldrige-based assessment. This evaluation is based on the following factors: levels and comparisons, trends, and integration (importance). For further description, see the chapters in this book on the *Scoring System* and *Clarifying the Baldrige Scoring Requirements.*

rework and defects—problems associated with not doing things right the first time. In all sectors—business, education, health care, and not-for-profit—rework (doing the job again) typically results when someone notices that a product has flaws (is defective or contains defects). This forces the organization to make the product or deliver the service again. Since the work must be done again, it is considered rework. Other examples of rework caused by defective processes might include remedial education, rewriting a sentence to correct typographical or grammatical errors, repealing faulty legislation and passing new or replacement legislation, or repairing an incisional hernia caused by faulty surgical procedures. The list of defects that cause work to be done again is virtually endless. Although rework may be needed to deliver the correct product or service, it is important to understand it never adds value since it always comes at an increased cost over doing the right thing in the first place.

root cause—the original or basic cause or reason for a condition. The root cause of a condition is that cause which, if eliminated, ensures that the condition will not recur.

segment—a part of an organization's overall customer (student, patient), market, product offering, or workforce base. Segments typically have common characteristics that can be logically grouped. In Results Items, the term refers to disaggregating results data in a way that allows for meaningful analysis of an organization's performance. Each organization must determine the relevant factors to segment its customers, markets, products, and workforce.

Relevant segmentation is critical to identifying the distinct needs and expectations of different customer, market, and workforce groups and to customizing product offerings to meet their different needs and expectations. For example, market segmentation might be based on geography, distribution channels, business volume, health care service or educational program offerings, key requirements, or technologies employed. Workforce segmentation might be based on geography, skills, educational needs, work assignments, or job classification.

senior leaders—an organization's executive or senior management group or team. This typically consists of the head of the organization and his or her direct reports, but may include any additional people designated as part of the senior leadership group or team.

societal risk—potential dangers to the community and society at large that might be created by an organization. For example, speculative investing by a bank or issuing unsecured loans to people or organizations with questionable ability to repay may pose a risk to the public as well as the customers of the bank. A leak on an oil drilling platform can affect investors, customers, employees, the environment, and in turn the public at large.

stakeholders—all groups that are or might be affected by an organization's actions and success. Examples of key stakeholders might include customers, students and their families, patients and their families, the workforce, partners, collaborators, governing boards, stockholders, donors, suppliers, taxpayers, regulatory bodies, policy makers, funders, and local and professional communities. Also see *customer*. A stakeholder is not automatically considered a customer unless it is an actual or potential user of the organization's products, programs, or services

strategic advantages—those benefits that exert a significant positive influence on an organization's likelihood of future success. These advantages frequently are sources of an organization's current and future competitive success relative to other providers of similar products. Strategic advantages generally arise from two sources: (1) core competencies or unique internal capabilities, and (2) strategically important external resources, which can be leveraged to the organization's benefit. See the definitions of *strategic challenges, strategic objectives*, and *strategic opportunities*.

strategic challenges—those pressures that exert a significant negative influence on an organization's likelihood of future success. These challenges frequently are driven by an organization's anticipated future competitive position relative to other providers of similar products, programs, or services. Strategic challenges are generally, but not exclusively, externally driven. However, in responding to externally driven strategic challenges, such as the need to provide more cost-effective health care, an organization may face internal strategic challenges and face the need to mitigate system weaknesses.

External strategic challenges may relate to customer (student, patient) or market needs or expectations; product demographics, regulatory changes, or technological changes; or financial, societal, and other risks or needs. Internal strategic challenges may relate to an organization's capabilities, process deficiencies in the face of new requirements, or workforce and other constraints.

strategic objectives—an organization's articulated aims or responses to address major change or improvement, competitiveness, social issues, or strategic advantages and opportunities. Strategic objectives generally are focused both externally and internally and relate to significant customer, market, product, service, or technological opportunities and challenges (strategic challenges). Broadly stated, strategic objectives define what an organization must achieve to be successful in the future—the organizational outcomes needed to remain or become competitive and ensure long-term success. Accordingly, strategic objectives set an organization's long-term directions and guide resource allocations and redistributions. See the definition of *action plans*.

strategic opportunities—prospects arising from outside-the-box thinking, brainstorming, capitalizing on serendipity, research and innovation processes, nonlinear extrapolation of current conditions, and other approaches to imagining a different future. The generation of ideas leading to strategic opportunities benefits from an environment that encourages nondirected, free thought. Choosing which strategic opportunities to pursue involves consideration of relative risk, financial and otherwise, and then making intelligent choices. Also see *intelligent risks*.

supplier and partner capability—the ability of suppliers and partners to provide products and services as required. If an organization fails to consider the capability and capacity of its key suppliers and partners when planning or designing new products or services, its ability to meet customer requirements, which were dependent on the deliverables of those key suppliers and partners, may be in jeopardy.

sustainability—an organization's ability to achieve current and long-term success. To do this in a dynamic, competitive environment, the organization must be able to meet current customer and operational needs as well as continuously improve to prepare successfully for future business, market, operating, and competitive demands. As the environment becomes more volatile and competitive demands increase, the need for continuous incremental and breakthrough improvement becomes more critical. Organizations that face serious threats from competitors that are continuously improving must find ways to improve faster than those competitors; they find that they must get better at getting better.

system versus process—a *system* is a set of disciplined, consistent, well-defined, and well-designed *processes* for meeting the organization's quality and performance requirements. For example, the leadership system refers to the many processes by which leadership is exercised throughout the organization and includes all people exercising leadership, from top executives to managers, supervisors, and team leaders. Everything done in an organization is a process but not all processes are part of a system and not all processes are systematic; that is, consistent, disciplined, and predictable.

systematic—approaches that are well-ordered and repeatable (consistent), and exhibit the use of data and information so learning is possible. Approaches that are well-ordered, consistent, and repeatable and include the opportunity for evaluation, improvement, and sharing, thereby enabling maturity gains are generally considered systematic.

timetable—a *timetable* for accomplishing strategic objectives sets forth the expected levels of achievement that leaders use to monitor progress periodically to achieve the outcome-based strategic objectives. To be aligned with strategic objectives, each objective should have a corresponding set of milestones to track progress. To be well-integrated, the timetable should be aligned and the intervals in the timetable should match the review cycle of the leaders. For example, if leaders review progress each quarter, then milestones (timetables) should be developed that identify the level of progress that is expected to be made each quarter. Without timetables that predict the desired level of achievement at each performance milestone, it is difficult for leaders to know if progress is on track or whether adjustments are needed.

trends—numerical information that shows the direction and rate of change for an organization's results. *Trends* provide a time sequence of organizational performance for data reported in Category 7.

To be given credit in Category 7, a trend generally requires a minimum of three historical (not projected) data points. Defining a statistically valid trend may require more data points. The cycle time of the process being measured determines the time between the data points for establishing a trend. To report a meaningful trend, shorter cycle times might require more frequent measurement, while longer cycle times might require less frequent measurement over longer periods.

Examples of trends called for by the Baldrige Criteria include data on product performance; results for customer and workforce satisfaction, engagement, and dissatisfaction; financial performance; marketplace performance; and operational performance, such as cycle time, defects, and productivity.

In the Education Criteria, trend data may also include results on student learning, student satisfaction and dissatisfaction, and the productivity of educational program and service delivery processes. In the Health Care Criteria trend data may also include results on health care outcomes and health care service performance for patients.

value—the perceived worth of a product, service, process, asset, or function relative to cost and possible alternatives. Organizations frequently consider *value* to determine the benefits of various options relative to their costs, such as the value of various product and service combinations to customers. Organizations need to understand what different stakeholders value and then deliver that value to each group. When different groups of stakeholders value or require different things, leaders may encounter problems ignoring one group in favor of another. For long-term success it is usually necessary to balance the value delivered to various customers and stakeholders.

values—the guiding principles and behaviors that embody how the organization and its people are expected to operate. *Values* reflect and reinforce the desired culture of the organization. Values support and guide the decision-making of every workforce member, helping the organization to accomplish its mission and attain its vision in an appropriate manner. Examples of values might include demonstrating integrity and fairness in all interactions, exceeding customer expectations, valuing individuals and diversity, protecting the environment, and demonstrating performance excellence every day.

vision—the desired future state of the organization. The *vision* describes where the organization is headed, what it intends to be, or how it wishes to be perceived in the future.

voice of the customer—the process for capturing customer-related information. Voice-of-the-customer processes are intended to be proactive and innovative to capture stated, unstated, and anticipated customer requirements, expectations, and desires. The goal is to use this information to build positive customer relationships and achieve customer engagement. Listening to the voice of the customer might include gathering and integrating various types of customer data that affect customers' purchasing and engagement decisions, such as survey data, focus-group findings, interviews, web-based information such as consumer rating sites, blogs, tweets and other social media, warranty data, and complaint data.

work processes—internal value creation processes. They might include product design, manufacture, delivery, customer support, supply-network management, business, and support processes. Key work processes involve the majority of the organization's workforce and produce customer, stakeholder, and stockholder value. Work processes are always carried out by internal workers under the organization's supervision. Key work processes are the organization's most important internal value-creation processes and frequently relate to core competencies, to the factors that determine success relative to competitors, and to the factors considered by senior leaders as important for organizational growth and current and ongoing success.

For a more detailed explanation of *work systems versus work processes,* see page 347.

work systems—encompass all of the work that must be accomplished, using both internal and external resources, for the organization to achieve its mission. Work systems involve the organization's workforce, its key suppliers and partners, contractors, collaborators, and other components of the supply network needed to produce and deliver products and carry out business and support processes. Work systems comprise both the internal work processes and external (outsourced) resources needed to develop and produce products, deliver them to customers, and succeed in the marketplace.

Decisions about work systems are strategic and occur as a part of the strategy development process in Item 2.1. These decisions involve protecting and capitalizing on the organization's internal core competencies and deciding what should be procured or produced outside the organization to be efficient and sustainable in the marketplace.

For a more detailed explanation of *work systems versus work processes,* see page 347.

workforce—all people supervised by the organization who contribute to the delivery of its products and services, including paid employees (such as permanent, part-time, temporary, and telecommuting employees), contract employees and interns supervised by the organization, and volunteer workers. The workforce includes team leaders, supervisors, and managers at all levels. Contract employees supervised by a contractor are covered by the requirements of supply-network management in Item 6.1c.

workforce capability—an organization's ability to accomplish its work processes through the knowledge, skills, abilities, and competencies of its people. Capability may include the ability to build and sustain relationships with customers; to innovate and transition to new technologies; to develop new products and work processes; and to meet changing business, market, and regulatory demands.

workforce capacity—an organization's ability to ensure sufficient staffing levels to accomplish its work processes and successfully deliver products, programs, and services to customers, including the ability to meet seasonal or varying demand levels.

workforce engagement—the extent of workforce commitment, both emotional and intellectual, to accomplishing the work, mission, and vision of an organization. Organizations with high levels of workforce engagement are often characterized by high-performing work environments in which people are motivated to do their utmost for the benefit of their customers and for the success of the organization. Research indicates that key drivers of engagement involve workforce members feeling valued by the organization and its supervisors and involved in decisions about work. Workforce members feel engaged when they find personal meaning and motivation in their work and when they receive positive interpersonal and workplace support. An engaged workforce benefits from trusting relationships, a secure and cooperative environment, good communication and information flow, empowerment, and performance accountability. Factors contributing to engagement include being valued by the organization and involved in decision-making, training and career development, fair and honest recognition and reward systems, equal opportunity and equitable treatment, and a family-friendly workplace.

workplace—the places in the organization where the workforce accomplishes its work.

References

Baldrige Performance Excellence Program. 2020. *2021–2022 Baldrige Excellence Framework: A Systems Approach to Improving Your Organization's Performance,* Gaithersburg, MD: U.S. Department of Commerce, National Institute of Standards and Technology. *http://www.nist.gov/baldrige*

EFQM. 2019. The EFQM Model, Brussels, Belgium: EFQM. *http://www.efqm.org*

The People's Republic of China National Standard. 2012. Criteria for Performance Excellence, Beijing City, China: China Standards Press. *http://www.spc.net.cn*

SAI Global. 2011. The Australian Business Excellence Framework 2011, Sydney, Australia: SAI Global. *http://www.saiglobal.com/improve*

Index

Note: Italicized page numbers indicate figures, tables, or illustrations.

A

B

C

D

E

F

G

N

O

P

Q

R

S

About the Authors

Mark L. Blazey, EdD

Mark Blazey has retired from more than 28 years as president of Quantum Performance Group, a management consulting and training firm specializing in organization assessment and high-performance systems development. Dr. Blazey has an extensive background in quality systems. For seven years he served as an examiner, senior examiner, and alumni examiner for the Malcolm Baldrige National Quality Award.

He also served as the lead judge for Baldrige-based awards for the U.S. Army Communities of Excellence Award, New York State, Vermont, Delaware, and Aruba, and as a judge for the Wisconsin Forward Award and the national quality award for the American Health Care Association/National Center for Assisted Living. Dr. Blazey has participated on and led numerous site-visit teams for national, state, and company quality awards and audits over the past 28 years.

Dr. Blazey has trained thousands of quality award examiners and judges for state and national quality programs, as well as managers and examiners for schools, health care organizations, major businesses, and government agencies. He has set up numerous Baldrige-based programs to enhance and assess performance excellence for all sectors and types of organizations, many of which have subsequently received state and Baldrige recognition.

Dr. Blazey has written many books and articles on quality, including the ASQ Quality Press bestseller *Insights to Performance Excellence*, *Baldrige Express*, and other Baldrige-based survey instruments. He also co-authored *Baldrige in Brief: A Guide to the Baldrige Performance Excellence Criteria.*

He is a senior member and a (retired) certified quality auditor of the American Society for Quality.

Dr. Blazey may be contacted via email at markblazey@gmail.com or by telephone at 585-721-4444. He encourages feedback, recommendations for improvement, and questions about this book.

Paul L. Grizzell

Paul Grizzell is president of Core Values Partners, a performance excellence consulting firm that helps organizations focus, align, and accelerate their improvement efforts through the use of the Baldrige Framework for Performance Excellence and the European Foundation for Quality Management (EFQM) Criteria. Paul brings experience in helping organizations use the Criteria to gain competitive advantage through the use of the Baldrige Framework and the EFQM Model.

Paul has served as an examiner, senior examiner, team leader, examiner trainer, and master examiner with the Malcolm Baldrige National Quality Award. He is also a Certified Advisor, Certified Trainer, and Assessor with EFQM. Paul is the only person to have these multiple qualifications, demonstrating his commitment to global performance excellence.

He has led multiple site visits and trained hundreds of Baldrige examiners during nineteen years of participation with the program. He has served as a Judge for the Performance Excellence Network, the Illinois Performance Excellence Award, the Virginia-based Senate Productivity and Quality Award, the American Health Care Association (AHCA) Quality Award, and the U.S. Army Communities of Excellence Award. He is a senior member of the American Society for Quality. He contributed to the development of both the 2021–2022 Baldrige Excellence Framework and the most recent EFQM Model.

Paul has worked with many organizations in multiple sectors to implement performance excellence methods that have led to state, regional, and Baldrige-level recognition. He has also worked with international organizations leading to EFQM recognition.

Paul is a frequent keynote presenter at performance excellence conferences. He serves as the Performance Excellence Partner with ASQ China and as the Foreign Evaluation Expert for the China Association for Quality, where he has provided guidance to site visit teams. Paul has also delivered performance excellence keynote addresses across the U.S. and in Saudi Arabia, India, and China.

Paul may be contacted via email at *paul.grizzell@corevaluespartners.com*, or by telephone at 651-792-5149. He welcomes feedback, recommendations for improvement, and questions about this book.

NOTES

NOTES

NOTES

NOTES

NOTES

Printed in the USA
CPSIA information can be obtained
at www.ICGtesting.com
LVHW081623071224
798595LV00007B/312
* 9 7 8 1 6 3 6 9 4 0 0 2 1 *